Nicholson's Guide to
Great Britain

D1553952

ROBERT NICHOLSON PUBLICATIONS
COMMUNICA-EUROPA

© Robert Nicholson Publications Limited
1978/79

ISBN: 905522 05 2

Special thanks are extended to the British
Tourist Authority, all the national and
regional tourist boards and the numerous
organisations and contributors who helped
with the preparation of this guide.

Drawings: Dick Reid

Pages 1-28
designed by Kinneir, Calvert, Tuhill

Cartography: Fairey Surveys Limited,
Maidenhead to © design by Robert
Nicholson Publications Limited.
Maps revised by Engineering Surveys
Reproduction Limited, Surrey.
Maps based upon the Ordnance Survey
with the sanction of Her
Majesty's Stationery Office. Crown
copyright reserved.

Printed in Scotland by Morrison and Gibb
Limited, Edinburgh.

Contents

13　Belfast

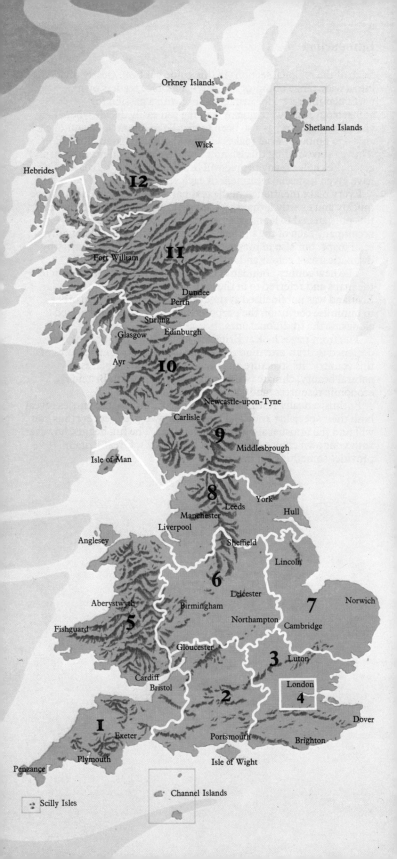

Introduction

Each of the regional sections in this guide has been clearly divided
into a wide range of topics which will embrace readers' own
particular interests: for instance those with a passion for
archaeology, bird watching or walking can easily decide where to
visit. Our concern has also been to distill the essential flavour of each
area – to pinpoint what makes Cornwall different from Norfolk.
The sea surrounding this island exercises a powerful magnetism and
given the choice many people will head straight for the coast, so we
have given it special treatment in each section.

Every place mentioned in the text has a map reference so it can be
quickly and exactly located on the grid system imposed on the maps;
this puts an end to laborious map reading. Individual maps
accompany each of the thirteen regions: these are useful not only as
road maps, but also in presenting a vivid picture of the country by
dramatic use of colour and hill shading.

The new county boundaries of England and Wales are shown in
the maps and referred to in the text. The re-organisation of
Scotland was not finalised at time of going to press, and in order
to minimise confusion the proposed new names have been used
alongside the traditional ones.

The front pages look at Britain as a whole, with a series of maps
designed to draw attention to some of the most striking features of
this country: its structure and scenery, outstanding places of
natural beauty, climate (where *is* the wettest place in Britain?),
economic resources, and other useful information.

Enthusiastically researched by a team of authors, the entries reveal
both their specialist knowledge and their own preferences: thus you
will find the unusual alongside the familiar. The fun begins, however,
with your own choice – for, as this book shows, Great Britain
provides something for everyone.

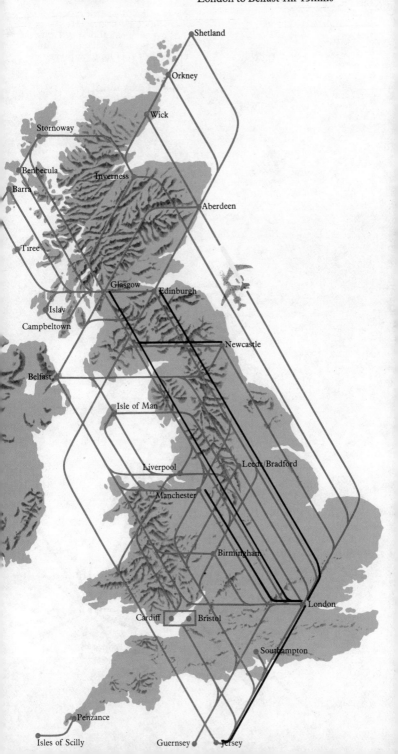

U.K. domestic air routes

British Airways

British Caledonian

Typical flight times:
London to Edinburgh 1hr 5mins
London to Birmingham 40mins
London to Belfast 1hr 15mins

Shetland

Orkney

Wick

Stornoway

Benbecula

Barra

Inverness

Tiree

Aberdeen

Glasgow

Edinburgh

Islay

Newcastle

Campbeltown

Belfast

Isle of Man

Liverpool

Leeds/Bradford

Manchester

Birmingham

London

Cardiff

Bristol

Southampton

Penzance

Isles of Scilly

Guernsey

Jersey

Main roads and motorways

Recorded reports on road conditions are available 24 hours a day by ringing the following centres:
Belfast (0232) 8021
Birmingham (021) 246 8021
Bristol (0272) 8021
Edinburgh (031) 246 8021
Glasgow (041) 246 8021

Leeds, Bradford, Sheffield and Doncaster (0532) 8021
London (01) 246 8021
Liverpool and Manchester (061) 246 8021
Newcastle and Teesside (0632) 8021
Southampton (0703) 8021
The overall maximum speed limit is 70 miles per hour (30 mph in built up areas). Other limits apply where indicated.

▬▬▬ Motorways
▬▬▬ Trunk roads

Main rail and sea routes

Britain still has a very extensive passenger railway network—around 19,000 route miles. And in this land of short distances and crowded roads, rail travel is often ideal in terms of speed, comfort and safety. There is an excellent sleeper service for long-distance overnight travel, while the summer Motorail service is well suited to motorists wanting to make a fast but completely relaxed start to their holiday. And, of course, all the principal ferry ports are linked to the railway network.

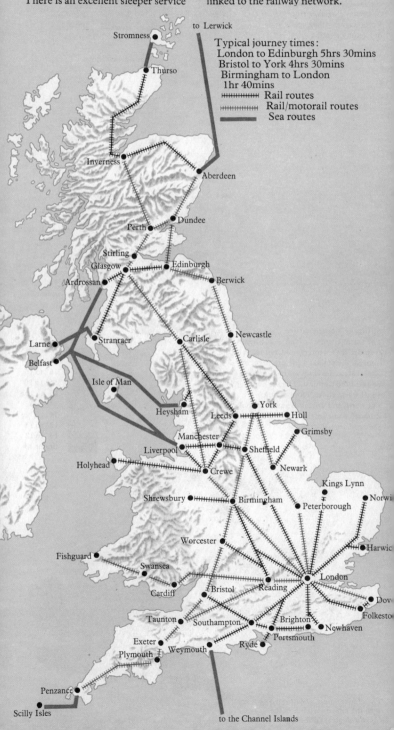

Typical journey times:
London to Edinburgh 5hrs 30mins
Bristol to York 4hrs 30mins
Birmingham to London
1hr 40mins

╫╫╫╫╫╫ Rail routes
╫╫╫╫╫╫ Rail/motorail routes
━━━━━ Sea routes

The climate

Summer Sunshine
The north and north west of
England often catch the cloud
formed by the cool Atlantic
airstream, and become overcast.
South and south eastern
England are often influenced
by cyclonic weather from
Europe, giving long spells of
dry, sunny weather.

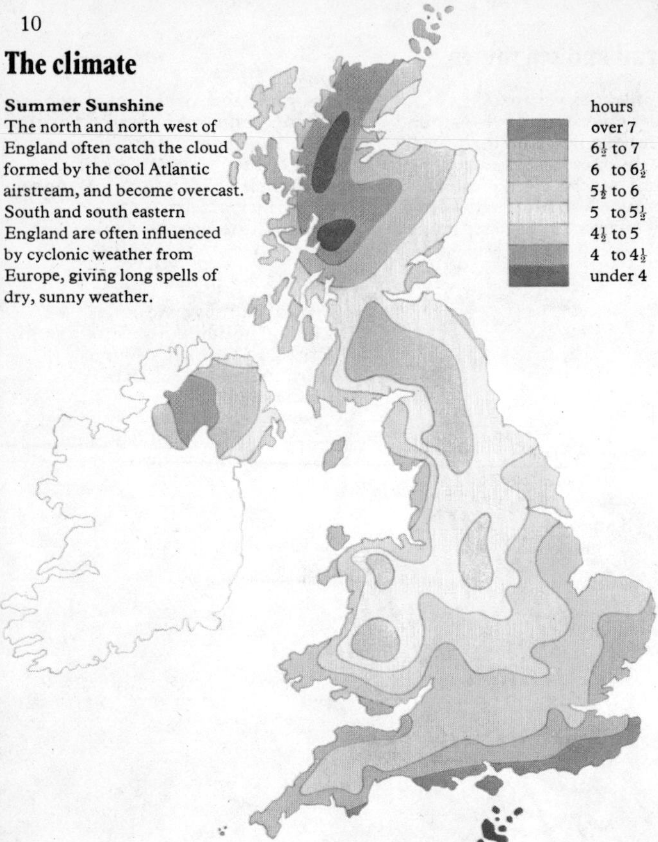

hours
over 7
6½ to 7
6 to 6½
5½ to 6
5 to 5½
4½ to 5
4 to 4½
under 4

Summer Temperature
The warm currents of the Gulf Stream
keep Britain's winters mild, although in
summer the sea has a cooling effect on
coastal areas, leaving central Southern
England the warmest. The sea here
is just warm enough for bathing.
The north and upland Britain are cool,
although some small parts of western
Scotland are sub-tropical.

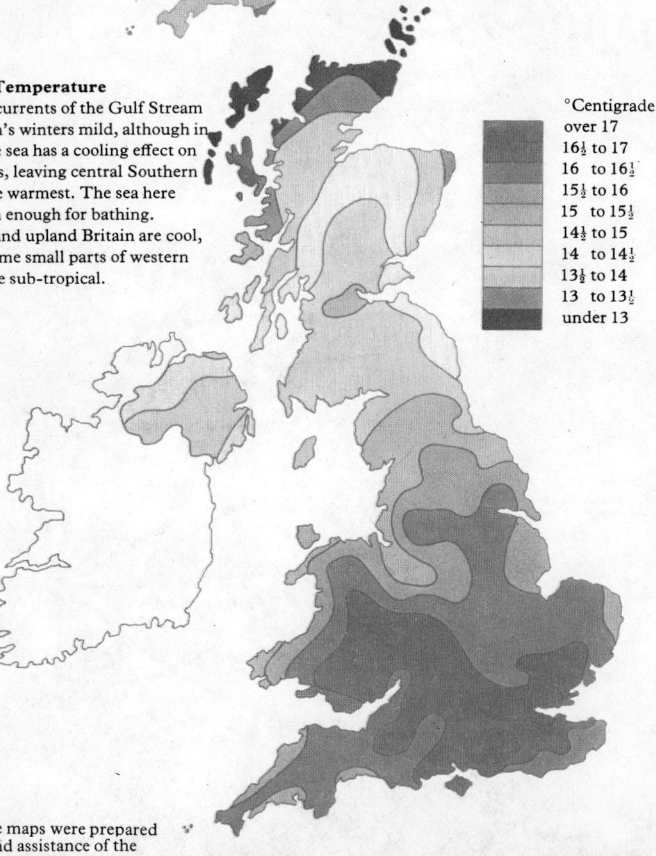

°Centigrade
over 17
16½ to 17
16 to 16½
15½ to 16
15 to 15½
14½ to 15
14 to 14½
13½ to 14
13 to 13½
under 13

The climate maps were prepared
with the kind assistance of the
Meteorological Office.

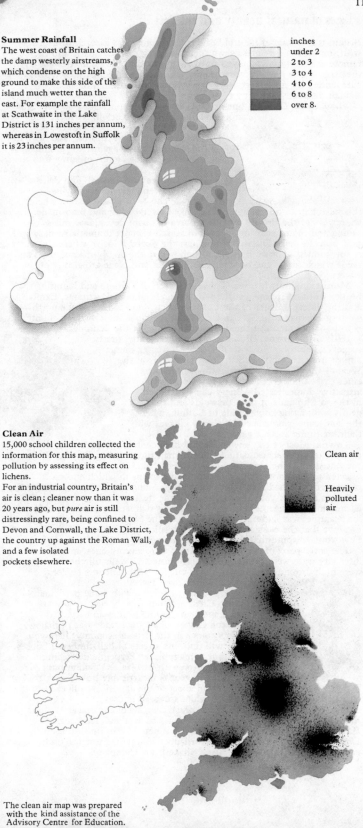

Summer Rainfall

The west coast of Britain catches the damp westerly airstreams, which condense on the high ground to make this side of the island much wetter than the east. For example the rainfall at Scathwaite in the Lake District is 131 inches per annum, whereas in Lowestoft in Suffolk it is 23 inches per annum.

inches
under 2
2 to 3
3 to 4
4 to 6
6 to 8
over 8.

Clean Air

15,000 school children collected the information for this map, measuring pollution by assessing its effect on lichens.

For an industrial country, Britain's air is clean; cleaner now than it was 20 years ago, but *pure* air is still distressingly rare, being confined to Devon and Cornwall, the Lake District, the country up against the Roman Wall, and a few isolated pockets elsewhere.

Clean air

Heavily polluted air

The clean air map was prepared with the kind assistance of the Advisory Centre for Education.

Places of natural beauty and interest

Britain is a mosaic of natural beauty: this beauty has a patchwork quality, with snippets of loveliness sewn together so that the dramatic and the remote are rarely far removed from the pretty and the domesticated. Even the areas which have become heavily populated and industrialised are surrounded by superb scenery, partly through the design of nature, though discreetly aided by government planning.

The Coast. The coastline exhibits a variety of contrasting scenery: for example, along the North Norfolk coast the salt marshes finger their way gently into the sea, while in Cornwall, Pembroke and Scotland the waves thunder against the granite rocks flinging clouds of spray into the air.

Rivers and Lakes. The British have a reputation for enjoying 'messing about in boats': there is a wide choice of inland waters where this pastime can be indulged. The linked rivers, lakes and man-made waterways of the Broads provide an area of about 200 square miles for sailing and motor cruising. People in search of more dramatic scenery will find it in the Lake District or amongst the Scottish lochs, where the water is surrounded by towering hills as opposed to the gently-massed trees and reeds which fringe the Broads. The Thames and Nene are also popular waterways for boating.

Mountains and Moors. Those in search of solitude and haunting beauty will find it amongst the windswept heights of Dartmoor, Exmoor and the deserted peaks of the Lake District, Snowdonia and the north-western Highlands of Scotland. Some of Britain's finest walking country is to be found amongst the desolate splendour of the Pennines.

Hills and Downs. Britain can also offer gentle, pretty scenery. The rolling downs of Kent and Sussex merge almost imperceptibly with the rich farmlands of the Weald—the 'Garden of England'—where narrow lanes twist amongst the orchards. Similarly attractive domesticated scenery can be enjoyed in the soft uplands of the Cotswolds and the gently undulating countryside of Suffolk, where the landscape is enhanced by sleepy villages with their charming cottage gardens.

Giant's Causeway

Antrim Mts

The Sperrin Mts

Fermanagh Lakes

Lough Neagh

The Lagan Valley

Armagh

Mountains of Mourne

Towns. Most of the towns selected here contain a superb mixture of architecture dating from Roman times through to the present day. Abingdon, Cambridge, Norwich and Rye could be selected as just four examples of the many towns in which endless pleasure can be had simply by wandering around the streets: each time you turn a corner your eye alights on some fresh gem. In some cases the harmonious arrangement of the buildings is deliberate; much of Bath for example, was laid out in the C18th by the brothers Wood who wished to prove that the classical system of town planning was worth copying. Few would dispute that they proved their point.

The early years of the nation's history were stormy ones, invasions and inter-city wars were commonplace and protective walls, ditches and gates were built around most towns. Look out for these defences at York, Lincoln, Chester and Berwick-on-Tweed.

Certain towns are especially associated with some particular period of history. Chester is remarkably rich in Roman remains. Lavenham had its heyday in the C15th, when the East Anglian wool trade was of major importance in the British economy; here you will find fine streets of half-timbered houses, and a magnificent Perpendicular church. Brighton with its bizarre Pavilion built to satisfy the whim of the Prince Regent is inextricably linked with the Regency era: the fashionable London set of the early C19th flocked to the resort and lined the streets with white-stuccoed houses.

Some of the towns selected have special sporting or cultural attractions: in recent years Aviemore, in the Spey Valley of Scotland, has become Britain's answer to St Moritz. Aldeburgh is noted for its musical festivals and Chichester for its theatre. At Stratford-upon-Avon the theatrical tradition is admirably maintained by the Royal Shakespeare Company.

Outstanding beaches

A day at the seaside is an institution as British as afternoon tea. Made popular by the Victorians, a trip to the coast is still considered to refresh and revitalise the most weary townsman; the sea air clearing the smoke from his lungs, the salt water washing the grime from his skin. It is only surprising that, with a coastline as rich and varied as Britain's, no one before the Victorians took much notice of it. Now every weekend sees thousands of trippers off to the coast to find a beach where they can sunbathe, swim or simply watch the waves.

Use the descriptions with the map to discover Britain's coast. Bear in mind the beaches indicated are not all sandy; some, like the magnificent shingle Chesil beach, are here simply because they are unusual and beautiful. Refer also to 'The coast' in the following main sections.

The West Country. Catching the full force of the Atlantic, but warmed by the Gulf Stream, the coast is broken and irregular, giving sheltered bays and fine, open sandy surf beaches. It becomes a series of long shingles weeps in Dorset, backed by cliffs brought to a halt by the superb 18 mile long Chesil beach. Strong currents prevail in most of these places, so swimmers should beware.

The South Coast. More popular for its lively resorts in close proximity to London than for its outstanding beaches which are mostly sand and shingle, sometimes backed by chalk cliffs. This is the retreat of the weekend sailor.

The Kent Coast. Its closeness to Europe has left this coast rich in history. Hastings, Winchelsea, Rye and Deal are all ancient seaside towns, while the most popular resorts are Ramsgate and Margate. The beaches shown are all sandy.

East Anglia. The long sandy beaches at Clacton and Great Yarmouth have made these resorts popular and sometimes crowded. But further north there are miles of unspoilt sand backed by dunes and the low-lying broads and fens.

The Wash to the Humber. Flat sandy beaches backed by low-lying land. Very often unspoilt and deserted.

The North East Coast. Long sandy beaches edging some of England's finest coastal scenery. Generally safe swimming along a breezy seashore. Stand well back when storms roll in off the North Sea.

The East Coast of Scotland. A rugged, craggy coastline of inaccessible bays and rock-strewn cliffs. Deserted away from the towns, the fine beaches indicated are clean and empty, and will reward those with the energy to explore. Where streams cut the cliffs, fishing villages nestle overlooked by the ever present highlands. Very strong currents prevail in the far north.

The West Coast of Scotland. Spectacular lochs and remote islands; a magnificent coast with some good sandy beaches in the south. Access is difficult and the firths that cut into the land make a coastal tour laborious.

The North West Coast. Morecambe, Fleetwood and Blackpool have flat sandy beaches, often exposed for miles at low tide. The resorts are all 'kiss-me-quick' and rock candy, but walkers can find solitude on some completely unspoilt sands.

North Wales. Backed often by mountains, ending in cliffs at the sea's edge, the coast is steep and often remote. There are some clean, sandy beaches, Prestatyn and Rhyl being the most well known. Porth Neigwl is a fine remote surf beach.

South Wales. The mountains generally recede here and many of the long, sandy beaches are backed by dunes. So firm and flat are Pendine Sands that they were used in the 1920's for attempts on the land speed record. The beaches are often deserted and the prevailing winds create good surfing conditions in many areas.

Northern Ireland. A rocky coast of cliffs and narrow beaches. From Portstewart to the unique Giant's Causeway the beaches are sandy and popular with the local holidaymakers.

Portstewart to Giant's Causeway

12°C

13°C

Melness
Dunnet Bay
Sinclair's Bay
Dornoch Sands
Burghead to Fort George

North Uist
Benbecula and
South Uist

Big Sand

Morar

Ganavan

Kilberry

Carradale

Rothesay to Innellan

Saltcoats to Lendalfoot

Sandhead

Southerness

Church Bay to Llanddwyn Bay

Aberdaron Bay and Porth Neigwl

Barmouth

13°C

14°C

Borth

Whitesand Bay

St Brides Bay
to Sandy Haven

Broadhaven to Pendine Sands

Rhossili Bay

Porteynon Bay

Morte Bay to Saunton Sands

andy Mouth to Northcot Mouth
Trebarwith Strand

Tregirls Beach
Newquay Beaches
Perranporth
Chapel Porth
St Ives Bay
therand
rsand
Bay

Whitesand Bay
Pendower Beach
Maen Porth

Kennack Sands

Mount's Bay

15°C

Peterhead to Fraserburgh

Cruden Bay
Balmedie

St Cyrus

Lunan Bay

Lower Largo

Drum Sands   White Sands

Amble to Berwick-upon-Tweed

Druridge Bay

Cresswell

Whitley Bay

Redcar

Duddon Sands
Morecambe Bay

Fleetwood to Blackpool

Prestatyn to Colwyn Bay
Red Wharf Bay

Horse Shoe Point (Cleethorpes)
Mablethorpe

14°C

Skegness

15°C

Hunstanton to Wells-next-the-sea

Winterton to Cromer

Great Yarmouth

Dunwich and Southwold

Clacton

Minnis Bay

Sandwich Bay

16°C

Camber Sands

Margam Sands to Nash Point

Branscombe Mouth
Dawlish
Tor Bay to Babbacombe Bay
Slapton Sands
Bigbury

Chesil Beach
Durdle Door
Studland Bay
Bournemouth

15°C

17C°

Rivers and canals

England is fortunate still to possess such an extensive network of delightful and under-used waterways. Our principal rivers—the Trent, the Thames, and above all the Severn—have been navigable in an uncontrolled tidal form for many hundreds of years. The canals, on the other hand, nearly all date from the late 18th century. But now the trading boats have nearly all gone from our canal and river network, and we are left with a 2,000-mile linear playground for everyone to enjoy. And there is indeed plenty to enjoy. Inland waterways offer endless opportunities: you can hire a boat from bases all over the network and simply go where you like for a week—or a month if you can afford it. These boats cost anything between £30 and £150 a week, depending on the time of year, the size of the boat, and the standard of fitting out. (A typical boat would work out at around £15 to £20 per person per week, including fuel—not an expensive holiday.) Or you can go on hotel boats, where you have all your meals cooked for you—and you don't even have to work the locks. This costs around £50 per week per person.

But the waterways are not just there for people on boats. Most of them have a good towpath which provides an excellent long-distance footpath from one side of the country to the other—and you need never step across a public road. Bird-watchers and lovers of wildlife find the rural canals and rivers like the Thames a haven of peace and a fruitful hunting ground for kingfishers, herons, water rats, ducks, etc—although, of course, the lesser-used waterways are the best for this.

Among the best of the navigable rivers are the Thames and the Nene. The latter is smaller and less well-known than the Thames and flows through some of the finest country in East Anglia. It also features a special kind of 'guillotine' lock gates. Other popular boating rivers are the Trent (good for sailing) and the Yorkshire Ouse, while over in Cheshire is the undiscovered and very delightful river Weaver.

As will be seen from the map, most of the canals radiate from the Midlands, binding the principal towns and centres of industry firmly together. The greatest concentration of waterways in this country is in the Black Country between Wolverhampton and Birmingham, although few inhabitants even know where the canals run. The Black Country canals have fallen on hard times nowadays, but they are fascinating for the insight they provide into the early stages of the Industrial Revolution.

The canals of Northamptonshire, Leicestershire and Warwickshire are the epitome of English rural canals at their most peaceful and pleasant. Further south are the architectural glories of the unnavigable Kennet & Avon Canal.

There are three canals in Wales, all of them traversing superb upland country, and one of them (the Llangollen Canal) sporting the most famous canal aqueduct in Britain. The West Country contains all manner of fascinating derelict canals, many of them with unique engineering features. Up in the north-east is a network of wide waterways which are far removed from the narrow canals further south. The Yorkshire waterways still carry a substantial volume of traffic and convey a type of barge not seen anywhere else in Britain.

So there is an enormous variety of canals in this country, each with a slightly different character from its neighbour and completely distinct from canals in other regions. But most of them are worth seeing, whether by boat, by foot or by car. Of course the best way to see any canal is by boat, but this way it takes a long time to cover the waterways (a 6-month trip would just about get round the navigable network) and it cannot include the derelict and forgotten waterways that are strewn about the country.

The sections in the Guide describe the waterways to be found in each area, although some areas naturally have more than their fair share of canal mileage—in which case a selection has been made of the waterways worth the most interesting things to see. We hope that with this book and perhaps the relevant one inch Ordnance Survey maps, you should be able to indulge in plenty of rewarding expeditions.

Rivers
Canals

Dee

Tyne

Ouse

Trent

Witham

Severn

Wye

Avon

Nene

Great Ouse

Avon

Thame

Lee

Wey

Geology

Sedimentary Rocks

These rocks represent deposits which gradually accumulated in horizontal layers on the seashore and at the bottom of rivers, lakes and oceans. Powerful movements of the earth thrust these beds upwards, contorting the layers and thus forming hills.

WEALDEN CLAYS AND SANDSTONES. An oval of land cradled within the downs of Kent and Surrey. The central wooded ridge is surrounded by lowland plains so fertile that they are known as the 'Garden of England'.

YOUNGER CLAYS AND SANDS. These produce excellent soil, hence the gently undulating farmlands found in parts of East Anglia and the London Basin. The rocks are easily eroded: the coastline of Suffolk, for example, is gradually being eaten away by the sea.

CHALK. The rolling hills clothed with springy turf of southern and eastern England are composed of chalk. Their gently rounded slopes contrast strongly with the sheer drop of the cliffs along the coast (e.g. Beachy Head).

JURASSIC LIMESTONE. Limestone gives a slightly bolder and more dramatic version of the scenery produced by chalk. A typical feature of this landscape is that the fields are separated not by hedges but by walls built, like many of the houses in the region, of local stone.

JURASSIC LIMESTONE SCARPLANDS. A broad belt of limestone ridges stretches from the coast of Dorset and Devon to Yorkshire. These ridges include the Cleveland Hills of Yorkshire, Lincoln Edge and the Northampton Uplands and the Cotswolds.

MARLS AND NEW RED SANDSTONE. These were formed between 160 and 190 million years ago when desert conditions existed in Britain. The salt beds of Cheshire almost certainly represent salt lakes which evaporated in the heat. The rocks are of varying resistance; the sandstone tends to stand out as ridges in what is otherwise fairly flat dairyland.

CARBONIFEROUS LIMESTONE AND MILLSTONE GRIT. This limestone owes its name to the fact that it contains measures of coal. It is even more resistant than Jurassic Limestone, thus the "backbone of England"— the Pennine Chain—is underlain by it.

Extensive platforms of almost pure limestone are found in the Central Pennines around Malham Tarn. The rock is so porous that despite the heavy rainfall there is no surface water as all the rain immediately soaks through to the subterranean caverns which riddle the area.

MARLS AND OLD RED SANDSTONE. These are rocks of varying resistance. On the coast, they produce steep cliffs separated by deep valleys running inland. These rocks feature mainly in Scotland, where their high iron content accounts for the red soil.

Metamorphic Rocks

These are composed of sedimentary rocks which have been hardened as the result of being subjected to great pressure and heat.

OLD GRITS AND SLATES. These metamorphosed rocks produce the austerely wild scenery which is found in much of Wales, the Lake District and southern Scotland. Intruded volcanic rocks increase the rugged aspect of the landscape.

ANCIENT GNEISS AND SCHISTS. Created up to 2,600 million years ago, these rocks are the oldest found in Great Britain. They form much of the Scottish Highlands and occur also in parts of Wales, Anglesey and the Lake District. The scenery, particularly along the coastline, has a majestic grandeur that becomes positively menacing in parts of the Outer Hebrides.

Igneous Rocks

These rocks are formed of molten material thrust up from the earth's core.

EXTENSIVE LAVA SHEETS. In Skye, Mull and Antrim lava welled out of great cracks in the earth, blanketing the surrounding countryside. In some instances as the rock cooled it produced extraordinary six-sided columns – hence the Giant's Causeway in Ireland.

GRANITE MASSES. The scenery of Dartmoor and Bodmin Moor is typical of the bleak landscape produced by granite. The land is unsuited to cultivation and consists of stretches of furze, heather and peat-bog rising to large bare peaks.

Alluvium

Sand, silt and mud deposited by the rivers and tides since the Ice Age. The largest areas of alluvium are the Fens and the Romney Marshes. Both exhibit the same flat, treeless landscape.

Archaeology

Prehistoric

PALAEOLITHIC (Old Stone Age) from 500,000 BC
Britain was barely habitable during this period, because of the southern
extension of the Polar ice-cap and its effect on the climate. Few traces of
early man survive.

MESOLITHIC (Middle Stone Age) from 20,000 to 4,000 BC
Until about 6,000 BC Britain was still joined to Europe by a land-bridge. No
permanent dwellings apparently survive, but seasonal camping sites are
frequently indicated by finds of small worked flints and tools.

NEOLITHIC (New Stone Age) from 4,000 to 1,500 BC
Immigration of peoples from Europe introduced agriculture and the
domestication of animals, and the first monuments that are visible today
were built during this period. *Causewayed camps* were probably used as
assembly or religious places. *Long barrows* were constructed for the burial of
the dead. *Long cairns*, barrows built of stone, were probably used as vaults for
a family or social group. *Henges*, the mysterious circular monuments,
sometimes set with stones, which are believed to have had some religious
significance. *Flint-mines*, essential for the manufacture of tools, were made by
digging through chalk and mining out the flint layers below.

BRONZE AGE from 1800 to 400 BC
The Bronze Age saw the first application of primitive metal technology. The
best known Bronze Age civilisation in Britain was the Wessex Culture,
centred on Wiltshire and Dorset. Some of the finest *henges*, including
Avebury and Stonehenge, belong to this period. *Stone circles, avenues, rows,*
and single *standing stones*, probably usually of religious significance, can
frequently be seen in remote areas. *Round barrows* and *round cairns* replaced
the long varieties of the Neolithic, some cairns having chambers and entrance
passages. *Settlements* of round stone huts with associated *enclosures* are typical
of the Bronze and later periods.

IRON AGE from 500 BC to 50 AD
The most impressive monuments of this period are the
hill forts, often having complex multiple defences and
elaborate entrances, occupying hilltops and similar
defensible sites. *Settlements of huts* within
enclosures, and their associated *field-systems*,
survive in places, and were often occupied well into
the Roman period. Some of the carved *hill-figures* cut
into the chalk downs are Iron Age in date. In Scotland, round
tower-like dwelling-places, known as *brochs*, can be seen.
Underground structures, called *fogous* in Cornwall and *souterrains* in Scotland
and Ireland, are found in those areas; their purpose is still unknown.

Tirnony

Budore

White Island
Lough Erne

Giant's
Grave

Annaghmare

Roman

43 AD to the early fifth century
Britain was conquered by the Romans under the emperor Claudius in 43 AD.
Military monuments include complex *frontier works*, of which Hadrian's
Wall is the best example; *fortresses* for a legion of 6,000 men, and *forts* for an
auxiliary unit of 500 or 1,000—both built to a standard pattern, with
headquarters, barracks, granaries, workshops, officers' quarters, and a
hospital; temporary *marching camps* built on campaign; *siege-works* and
camps built to drill the soldiers in constructing earthworks; and
signal-stations. In the civil zone can be seen the impressive remains of *town
walls* and *gates*, often incorporated in later structures; *villas*, usually with
fine mosaic pavements, architectural detail, and elaborate central heating;
roads, frequently followed by modern roads or surviving as country lanes;
canals; *theatres* and *amphitheatres*; and magnificent public *bath-houses*.
More humble monuments also survive: *workshops*, *potteries*, and the outline
of *field systems*.

Dark Ages

SAXON and CELTIC from the fifth to the eleventh century AD
Following the collapse of Roman control and the settlement of Saxon
colonists from the Continent, England and Wales evolved into Saxon and
Celtic areas, with the Saxons dominant in the east and north and the Celts
surviving in the west and south-west. Visible Saxon monuments include
massive *linear earthworks*, which probably marked frontiers rather than
served for defence. Defensive strongholds, known as *burhs*, were built by
Alfred and his son against the Danes. Burial *barrows*, and Christian *churches*
and *crosses*, were erected. Celtic monuments that survive are *defensive* and
monastic sites, and carved Christian *stones* and *crosses*. Iron Age *hillforts* were
sometimes reoccupied at this period, both by Celts and Saxons. In Scotland, the
activity of Celtic missionaries from Ireland is reflected in the remains of
monasteries and *crosses*, and the native Picts carved *stones* with symbols and
animal motifs. Invading Vikings reached many parts of Britain, and their
settlements and *forts* have survived in coastal Scotland and on the Isle of Man.

Prehistoric
Dark Age (Saxon & Celtic)
Roman

Skara Brae
Maes Howe
Jarlshov
Dun Telve
Dun Mor Vaul
Finavon
Inchtuthil
Rough Castle
Antonine Wall
Traprain Law
Ballochray
Edin's Hall
Yeavering Bell
Housesteads
Chesterholm
Hadrian's Wall
Chesters
Corbridge
Tynwald Hill
Thornborough Circles
Scarborough
Ribchester
Aldmondbury
York
Caer Gybi
Pen-y-Corddyn
Mam Tor
Bryn Celli Ddu
Chester
Arbor Low
Tre'r Ceiri
Caernarvon
Lincoln
Old Oswestry
Wroxeter
North Elmham
Offa's Dyke
Leicester
Burgh Castle
St. David's Head
Midsummer Hill
Grimes Graves
Nab Head
Chedworth
Devil's Dyke
Parc Cwm
Caerwent
Caerleon
Windmill Hill
St. Alban's
Bath
Avebury
West Kennet
Silbury
London
Old Sarum
Stonehenge
South Cadbury
Hod Hill
Lullingstone
Richborough
Tintagel
Bignor
Lydford
Portchester
Fishbourne
Pevensey
Dartmoor
Maiden Castle
Cissbury
Chysauster

Mineral resources and industry

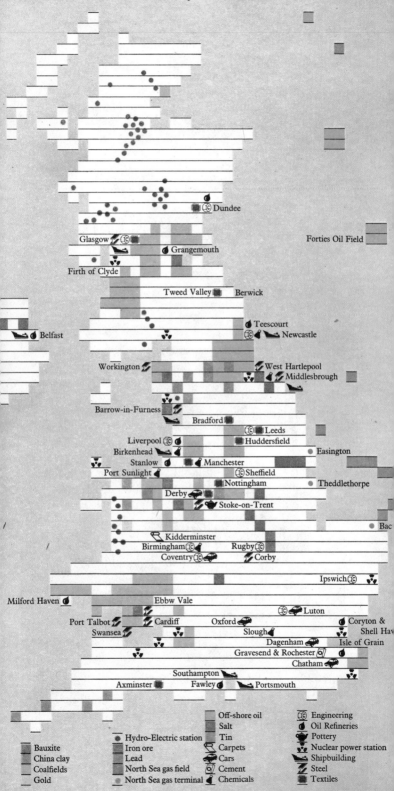

Dundee

Glasgow

Forties Oil Field

Grangemouth

Firth of Clyde

Tweed Valley   Berwick

Teescourt

Belfast

Newcastle

Workington   West Hartlepool

Middlesbrough

Barrow-in-Furness

Bradford

Leeds

Liverpool   Huddersfield

Birkenhead   Easington

Stanlow   Manchester

Port Sunlight   Sheffield

Derby   Nottingham   Theddlethorpe

Stoke-on-Trent

Bac

Kidderminster

Birmingham   Rugby

Coventry   Corby

Ipswich

Milford Haven   Ebbw Vale

Luton

Port Talbot   Cardiff   Oxford   Coryton &

Swansea   Slough   Shell Hav

Dagenham   Isle of Grain

Gravesend & Rochester

Chatham

Southampton

Axminster   Fawley   Portsmouth

	Off-shore oil		Engineering
	Salt		Oil Refineries
Bauxite	Hydro-Electric station	Tin	Pottery
China clay	Iron ore	Carpets	Nuclear power station
Coalfields	Lead	Cars	Shipbuilding
Gold	North Sea gas field	Cement	Steel
	North Sea gas terminal	Chemicals	Textiles

Land use and farming

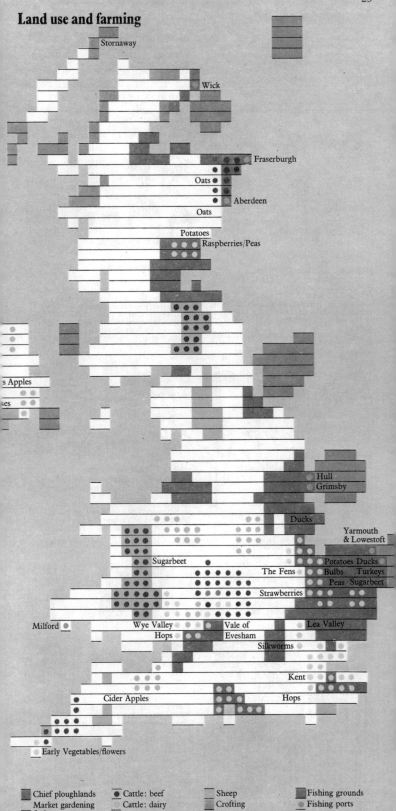

Stornaway

Wick

Fraserburgh

Oats

Aberdeen

Oats

Potatoes

Raspberries/Peas

s Apples

ses

Hull

Grimsby

Ducks

Yarmouth
& Lowestoft

Sugarbeet

The Fens

Potatoes   Ducks

Bulbs   Turkeys

Peas   Sugarbeet

Strawberries

Milford

Wye Valley

Vale of
Evesham

Lea Valley

Hops

Silkworms

Kent

Cider Apples

Hops

Early Vegetables/flowers

Chief ploughlands	● Cattle: beef
Market gardening fruit	Cattle: dairy

Sheep

Crofting

Fishing grounds

Fishing ports

Architectural styles

Anglo-Saxon (410-1066)
Buildings composed of fragments or of rough copies of Roman architectural details. Arches were semicircular, whilst windows had either round or triangular heads. Vaulting was plain and simple. Decoration limited. Wall angles in 'long and short' courses.
Typical examples – the churches at Greenstead, Earls Barton and Bradford-on-Avon.

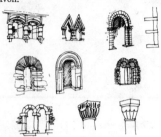

Norman (1066-1189)
Norman architecture is bold and massive with semicircular arches, ponderous cylindrical piers and flat buttresses. Windows are small and deeply splayed. Rib and panel vaulting introduced. Elaborately carved mouldings are important features of the style.
Typical examples – the keep and chapel of the Tower of London; the crypt of St Mary-le-Bow, Cheapside; Durham Cathedral; Barfreston Church, Kent.

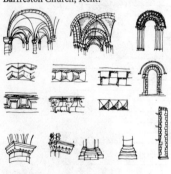

Early English Gothic (1189-1307)
Use is made of the pointed arch. Tall and narrow lancet windows give height to the buildings whilst projecting buttresses and pinnacles are developed. Massive Norman pillars are replaced by groups of slender shafts. Introduction of dog-tooth ornament. Typical examples – Salisbury Cathedral; the Galilee Porch, Ely; Stokesay Castle, Shropshire; Little Wenham Hall, Suffolk.

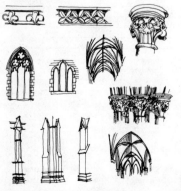

Decorated Gothic (1307-77)
Windows increased in size, and angle buttresses, set diagonally, were introduced. Window tracery consisted of geometric forms, later curvilinear or flowing lines were introduced. Battlemented parapets were used. An increased number of intermediate ribs were used in vaulting. Carving was generally more naturalistic.
Typical examples – the Angel Choir, Lincoln Cathedral; the Eleanor Crosses; Penshurst Place, Kent; Ightham Mote, Kent; Ludlow Castle, Shropshire.

Perpendicular Gothic (1377-1485)
Window tracery and panelling have vertical lines. Windows are enlarged whilst fan vaults, with their numerous ribs and panels, are typical. Hammer-beam roofs are numerous; piers more slender, whilst the Tudor rose, the portcullis and the fleur-de-lys are all characteristic ornaments. Typical examples – Westminster Hall, London; Haddon Hall, Derbyshire; Hever Castle, Kent.

Tudor (1485-1558)
Houses were usually timber-framed with lath and plaster panels. Brick became a fashionable material, whilst moats and elaborate gatehouses were retained as architectural features. Chimney stacks became very prominent. Typical examples – Compton Wynyates, Warwickshire; Bramhall Hall, Cheshire; Tattershall Castle, Lincs; Hampton Court Palace, London.

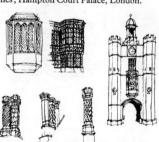

Early Renaissance (1558-1625)
Elizabethan Architecture (1558-1603)
The age of great mansions. It was a transition style with Gothic features and Renaissance details.

Jacobean Architecture (1603-1625)
The great houses were large, imposing and in the grand manner. Classic columns and entablatures replaced the quaint irregularity of Elizabethan architecture. Decoration, particularly carving, was lavish.
Typical examples – Little Moreton Hall, Cheshire; Hardwick Hall, Derbyshire;

Montacute House, Somerset; Keevil Manor House, Wiltshire; Hatfield House, Hertfordshire; Knole House, Sevenoaks, Kent.

Late Renaissance (1625-1837)
Stuart Architecture (1625-1702).

For the first time in England architecture was determined by individual architects. The two most influential architects were Inigo Jones and Wren. Inigo Jones (1573-1652) was an ardent disciple of Italian Renaissance architecture following prolonged studies in Italy. Sir Christopher Wren (1631-1723) was strongly influenced by the French Renaissance.

The verticality of the Elizabethan gable was replaced by the straight wall crowned by the strong horizontal line of the cornice. Roofs were hipped and sometimes hidden by parapets. The large built-up window was abandoned for small rectangular ones set in a large wall space. Under Wren, classic features such as domes and columns were used for architectural emphasis. Typical examples – Banqueting House, Whitehall, London; Queen's House, Greenwich; St Paul's Covent Garden, London; Sheldonian Theatre, Oxford; Pembroke College Chapel, Cambridge.

Victorian (1837-1901)

Tradition ceased to maintain its former power. Architects grouped themselves under the banners of the 'Greek Revival' and the 'Gothic Revival' and the battle of the styles' began in earnest. In the late Victorian period the characteristic elements were the use of iron and glass for railway stations, exhibition halls, warehouses and bridges. Typical examples – Birmingham Town Hall; Westminster Palace, London; St Georges' Hall, Liverpool; the Palm House, Kew.

Georgian Architecture (1702-1837)

The Baroque style strove for greater freedom in design and novelty of treatment whilst the influence of the work of Italian architects like Palladio was profound. The smaller Georgian houses were simple rectangles with handsome entrance doors. The last thirty years of the period saw the development of the Regency style with fine town planning schemes and the profusion of wrought iron work in canopied windows and balconies. Typical examples – Royal Crescent, Bath; Blenheim Palace, Oxfordshire; Chiswick House, London; Mereworth Castle, Kent; Portland Place and Regent's Park, London, Brighton Pavillion.

Twentieth Century

In the early part of this century the Classic and Renaissance Styles were reserved for civic architecture, the Gothic style for churches and educational buildings. Domestic architecture ran amuck amongst the Georgian, Tudor and Jacobean styles, and the suburban ideal proliferated. Steel-framed construction produced fresh alternatives. But with the profusion of new materials and the development of more sophisticated mechanical servicing almost anything could be done, and nearly everything was done. Look around you to see the result.

Typical examples – Liverpool Cathedral; Arnos Grove Underground Station, London; Boots Factory, Nottingham; Alton Housing Estate, Roehampton, London; Liberty's, London.

Rustic buildings

West

Cornish buildings often have slate roofs and granite walls, sometimes hung with tiles. In Devon and Dorset thatched cottages are typical with rubble walls, plastered and whitewashed or built of granite blocks. Some houses in Dorset have limestone roofs.
In Wiltshire numerous houses were built of porous chalk block, with a thatched roof, whilst in the Cotswolds you have fine limestone buildings.

East

Flint work has been the signature of East Anglia since Saxon times. Sometimes a complete wall was faced in pebbles, while doors and windows were squared off with brickwork.
Thatching, often used for roofs, is seen at its best in Norfolk. Here distinctive surface patterns are created by the laying and cutting of reeds. In Suffolk many half-timbered houses have ornamental plasterwork known as pargetting. First used in the Elizabethan age, it developed in the 17thC, but was out of fashion by the middle of the 18thC. Pantiled roofs are typical. Imported from Holland by the end of the 17thC, they are virtually unknown in the western half of the country. In Lincolnshire red brick houses were gabled in the Dutch style.

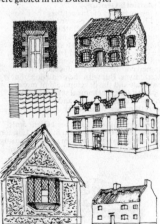

South

Sussex is rich in tile-hung houses. A feature of south-east England since the 17thC, tiles were hung on wood-and-plaster walls of houses to protect them from the weather. Weather-boarding, used for

farm building since the late 16thC, was adopted for cottages and smaller houses in south-east England by the end of the 18thC. It was usually oak or elm pegged to timber-framing. Mathematical tiles were introduced in the south-eastern counties in the middle of the 18thC and used well into the 19thC. They provided a cheap means of giving a fashionable appearance to timber-framed buildings while avoiding the brick taxes.

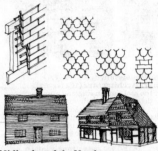

Midlands and the North

Box-framed houses with darkened timbers and white painted walls are typical of Cheshire. The houses of Derbyshire are of mellow stone with slate roofs, and simple ornamentation. In the Lake District slate roofs are common. Walls are usually rubble, set on a base of hewn stone, often plastered over and whitewashed. In Shropshire timber-framed houses were built on a base of local red sandstone. Slate instead of thatch was used for the roofs resulting in sturdy beams.

Wales
Buildings were usually constructed of slate
and stone.
In the 15thC timber-framed buildings were
sometimes built on cruck trusses, and roofed
in straw. There was no smoke hole in the
roof; the smoke escaped through the
windows and doors.
Some sturdy stone-built houses in
Pembrokeshire have massive side chimneys
which are rounded in the top stage. In
Montgomeryshire houses sometimes have a
rush thatch roof with a turf-ridge, whilst in
Cardiganshire thatched roofs are often laid
in decorative patterns.

Maltings
Mostly 19thC, these buildings lack the rural
charm of their country cousin, the oast.
They are used for preparing and storing
malt, barley or other grain which is steeped
in water until it germinates, and then dried
in a kiln for use in brewing or distilling.
These kilns have high pyramid roofs of slate
and louvered cupolas for ventilation.

Windmills
Windmills, like watermills, were in use from
the 12thC and not superseded until after
the advent of steam power in the 18thC.
They were mainly used for milling wheat
into flour.
Most windmills were either post mills or
smock mills. In the former the whole
chamber, built of a light timber-framed
construction and containing the gears and
millstones, could be rotated according to the
direction of the wind. In the latter only the
'cap' could be turned, whilst the machinery
was contained within a brick or weather-
boarded tower.

Scotland
Granite used extensively, whilst stepped
projections on the sloping sides of gables are
characteristic. On the stormy Atlantic some
houses have a thatch of heather held in place
by weighted ropes. In many Highland areas,
you find the Long House where shelter was
provided in a single building for family and
cattle.

Northern Ireland
Stone or rubble-built houses are typical.
Often whitewashed, with a slate, thatch or
turf roof. There are some examples of cruck-
frame built houses.

28

Map key

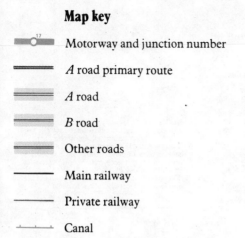

Motorway and junction number

A road primary route

A road

B road

Other roads

Main railway

Private railway

Canal

River

Height above sea level in feet

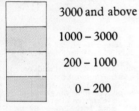

3000 and above

1000 – 3000

200 – 1000

0 – 200

·1334   Spot height

Built up area

County boundaries

Boundary of Nicholson's guide areas

Scottish Boundaries

In 1974 new regions of Scotland were
created, which absorbed all the existing
counties. Although the old counties have
ceased to exist for administrative purposes,
they are still recognised by the G.P.O. and
often used in postal addresses.

To avoid confusion, the name of the region
is included immediately after each place
name in the text and the county name is
shown in italics on the next line.

The West Country

I

Moors, tight coombes and the sea are the essential elements of Britain's most westerly counties. At the farthest western point are the Isles of Scilly – they are the tops of long submerged granite hills that were once linked to Cornwall as part of the long lost kingdom of Lyonesse. Cornwall has more sea coast than anywhere else in England, and all of it is spectacular. Don't ignore inland Cornwall, the wooded valleys of the Camel and the Fowey are remote and rich with fuchsias and veronica in high summer.

Devon is rich and varied. You can lose yourself in the steeply banked lanes full of ferns and foxgloves and the cosy cob and thatch villages aren't far removed from their counterparts on chocolate boxes. But tear yourself away from the Devonshire cream and rough cider to see craggy Dartmoor or the gorselands of Exmoor, and slip quietly down one evening to the peaceful ports still redolent with the memories of the great sailing days when Devon men scuttled the galleons of Spain.

Somerset and the new county of Avon has a quieter inland beauty with stone building that reaches its apotheosis in Bath – a masterpiece of town planning. Don't avoid busy Bristol, it is the hub of the region and a good cultural centre.

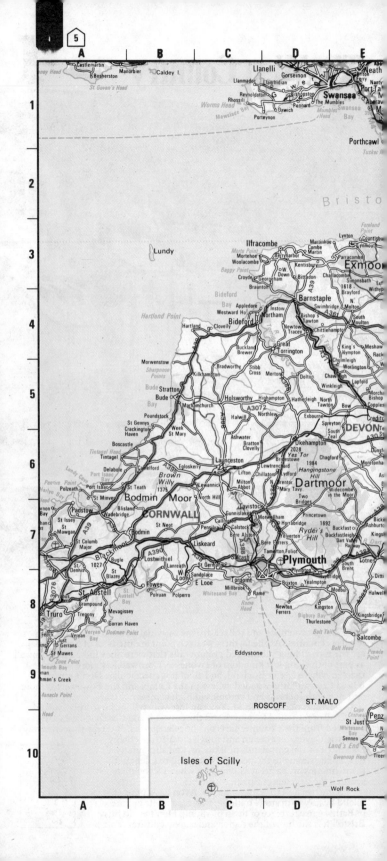

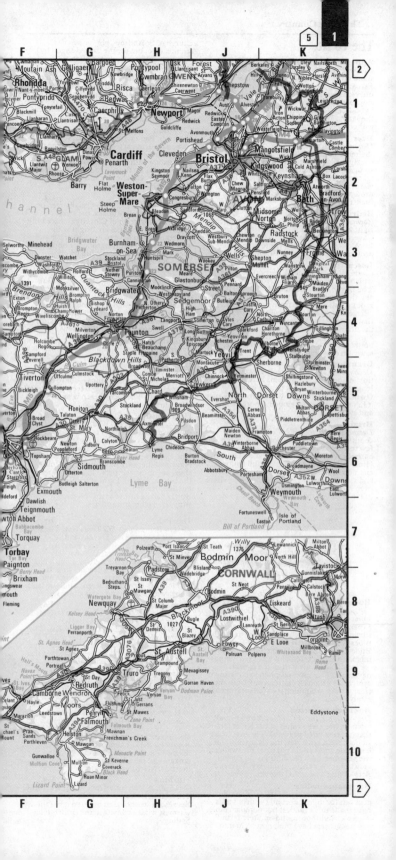

The coast

Appledore and Instow   **C4**
Devon. Pop 800. EC Wed. The two towns
stand on either side of the Torridge
Estuary. Appledore has an elegant strand of
quayside houses and the largest covered
shipyard in Britain. Instow is a good spot for
light dinghy sailing and children's games on
the sands. Winkle, cockle and scallop
gathering on the mud flats.

Beer 90c1   **G6**
Devon. Pop 1,500. EC Thur. Snug and
sheltered fishing village that lies below the
dazzling chalk cliffs. Lacemakers and
smugglers have made Beer famous, although
no one knows how it got its name. Always
warm and cosy – you can hear the heavy
droning of contented honey bees among the
fuchsias by the sea.

Bedruthan Steps   **A8**
Cornwall. Great rocks that are a magnificent
sight when the surf is rushing over them.
Caverns and tiny unapproachable beaches.
Look out for Queen Bess, a rock in the
profile likeness of Queen Elizabeth I.

Boscastle   **B6**
Cornwall. A landlocked, natural harbour
which has an incredibly narrow entrance.
The tiny village is surrounded by steep hills
and the Normans built their castle on rising
ground half a mile up from the harbour. The
village houses are small, pleasant cottages
that scramble up the hillside. Watch out for
the dramatic 'blowhole' when rough seas
blow spray right across the harbour about an
hour before low tide. Visit the macabre
museum of witchcraft.

Branscombe   **G6**
Devon. Pop 500. EC Thur. Branscombe is a
tiny inland village, but come here for the
long stretch of unspoilt pebble beach.
Owned and protected by the National Trust
it has never been developed. Shore fishing
and swimming.

Brixham   **F8**
Devon. Pop 10,700. EC Wed. Once the
county's leading fishing port, now only a
few trawlers work regularly. But the
harbour with its replica of Drake's Golden
Hind and lobster pots has the full nautical
air. You can take a cruise around Tor Bay
and visit Brixham Cavern, rumoured to have
been inhabited in the stone age. Pebble
beach at Shoalstone and swimming pool.

Brixham

Bude   **B5**
Cornwall. Pop 4,000. EC Thur. Cornwall's
quiet and modern resort is gradually
expanding and is now one of the best
surfing areas (Crooklets beach to the north
is best). Bude started as a seaport for the
Bude Canal (1819-26), which went 30 miles
inland to Launceston and was used mainly
for sand. Now only part of the canal is
navigable. The spacious plain looking town
centre has a modest castle. Away from the
river mouth swimming is excellent from firm,
sandy beaches.

Budleigh Salterton   **F6**
Devon. Pop 4,000. EC Thur. A quiet small
town, in the green valley of the River Otter,
that has remained peaceful. The beach has
smooth round pebbles, the clear sea water
has made snorkelling popular. The walk on
the 500-foot-high red cliffs gives amazing
views of the whole of Lyme Bay. Visit the
Arts Centre in a 15thC thatched house.

Burnham-on-Sea   **H3**
Somerset. Pop 12,300. EC Wed. The tide
goes out for miles here and the firm sands
have made this a modest but popular resort.
There's a lighthouse, and on Stert Island
oyster-catchers have their nests. Go into the

church of St Andrew, not for its
architecture, but for the carved angels by
Grinling Gibbons from the altar of
Whitehall Palace.

Cape Cornwall   **E10**
Cornwall. Stone-walled fields wander down
to the sea in this totally remote village.
Worth a visit to feel the essence of Cornwall
which is summed up here among the silent
cliffs and the rugged capes.

Clevedon   **H2**
Somerset. Pop 15,100. EC Wed. A
tree-shaded, attractive town with some good
early 19thC seafront houses. Now a mecca
for bowling enthusiasts, there are
tournaments on the placid greens throughout
the summer. Beaches are mostly pebbles.
Visit nearby Clevedon Court.

Clovelly   **C4**
Devon. Pop 400. EC Wed. Usually seen on
the lids of chocolate boxes, the steep
cobbled main street of Clovelly is incredibly
picturesque. Cottages are bright with
flowers and you have to leave your car and
walk down to the tiny harbour. The old or
tired can be driven up the hill by
Land-Rover. Don't miss the lovely drive
through the woods above the village.

Coverack   **G10**
Cornwall. EC Sat. Fishing village in a small
cove on the east side of the Lizard, which has
succumbed only slightly to the tourist
invasion. Clear sea waters reminiscent of
more southerly regions. Tiny and friendly
but swimming is slightly hazardous.

Crackington Haven   **B5**
Cornwall. For sheer dramatic beauty this is a
place not to be missed. Enormous black
cliffs rise up to more than 400 feet.
To the west are the Strangles, the rocky
resting place for many ships—above the
rocks High Cliff soars to 730 feet, the highest
in Cornwall. The rocky beach is sandy at low
tide. Surfing.

Dartmouth   **F8**
Devon. Pop 6,700. EC Wed. MD Fri. The
mouth of the River Dart is still guarded by
two romantic castles, and this small town
retains its naval and defence connections.
The College trains cadets for the Royal
Navy and there are moorings for training
ships and minesweepers. The long quay is
the boarding point for boat trips up the
peaceful River Dart. Don't miss The
Butterwalk, a row of 17thC houses
supported on granite pillars.

Dawlish   **F7**
Devon. Pop 10,000. EC Thur, Sat. The place
to come to for the red Devon sand; the
beach at Dawlish positively glows. An
attractive Victorian seaside town only
slightly marred by the railway going along
the sea front. Southern beaches provide
sheltered bathing. Between Dawlish and
Exmouth is Dawlish Warren, a mile of sand
dunes with chalets and caravan sites.

Exmouth   **F6**
Devon. Pop 26,800. EC Wed. The fashion
for sea bathing in the 18thC has left
Exmouth a legacy of fine marine villas. The
town overlooks the mouth of the wide Exe
River and there is plenty of sailing activity.
The town is busy and well equipped for the
holiday trade; good beaches at Sandy Bay.

Falmouth   **G10**
Cornwall. Pop 17,000. EC Wed. Harbour,
seaside resort and dockyard are the three
faces of Falmouth. It is superbly sited at the
estuary of seven rivers and guarded by two
of Henry VIII's forts. Take the scenic
journey along Castle Drive to Pendennis
Point where the views are magnificent. Note
also the amazing tropical gardens at
Kimberley Park. Falmouth Docks are still
flourishing, maintaining and repairing
tankers and salvage ships. Some bathing at
low tide. Maritime museum.

Flushing   **G9**
Cornwall. A long waterfront of elegant 18thC
houses that look across to Falmouth.
Because of its sheltered position it has the
warmest winter climate in the British Isles.
Sailing.

Fowey B8
Cornwall. Pop 2,300. EC Wed. A town for sailors and ship watchers, Fowey is full of marine activity with large ships turned by tugs in the deep harbour to load up with Cornish china clay. Take a boat trip to get the full flavour of the six miles of navigable tidal Fowey River. Safe, sandy beach at Readymoney Cove.

Frenchman's Creek G10
Cornwall. Scene of Daphne du Maurier's romantic pirate novel, it is still a beautiful tree-hung tidal waterway. Best seen from a boat if you drift lazily from the Helford River under the overhanging trees.

Hartland Point B4
Devon. Headland in north-west Devon where the coast turns abruptly from a north to an eastward direction. The 700-foot moors of Hartland's plateau, with its little market town, end abruptly here in storm-swept cliffs, breached by hidden combes. Clovelly, in a sheltered inlet, is a tiny fishing village whose main street is a succession of cobbled steps.

Hell's Mouth F9
Cornwall. Can seem a fearful place in rough weather; spectacular views of the sea and sea birds at any other time. Caves and tunnels lead for miles under the cliffs. Clifftops, many owned by the National Trust, are unspoilt and you can walk on the springy turf from Portreath to Godrevy Point.

Ilfracombe D3
Devon. Pop 9,800. EC Thur. North Devon's most popular resort that has dozens of beautiful beaches. You can walk or drive the short distance to Woolacombe where there are two miles of surfing beach below the sand hills. Look at St Nicholas Chapel, 1300, where a light still burns to guide sailors. Boats from Ilfracombe to Lundy Island. (see below).

Land's End E10
Cornwall. Beyond the little seaport of Penzance, surrounded by fields of broccoli and daffodils, a hammerhead of granite rock divides the Atlantic Ocean from the English Channel. This bare, treeless, stone-walled plateau, up to 800 feet high, culminates dramatically in the cliffs of Land's End, England's westernmost point. Here the tides and storm-pressed swells of the wide Atlantic surge ceaselessly round the Longships Lighthouse, marking a dangerous off-shore reef.
Wolf Rock Lighthouse is eight miles out to sea, and further out still is the infamous Seven Stones Reef where the giant oil tanker, Torrey Canyon, was wrecked in 1967.

Lizard Point G10
Cornwall. The main road south, A3083, from Helston to the Lizard crosses the wild Goonhilly Downs, common land ablaze with Cornish heaths in August. Lizard Point, the farthest south that England goes, has a lighthouse, hidden coves below steep cliffs, and a remarkable red-and-green veined igneous rock called serpentine. Craftsmen shape this into serviceable souvenir ashtrays.

Looe B8
Cornwall. Pop 4,100. EC Thur. The approaches to Looe are more beautiful than the town itself. Steep wooded valleys and abandoned wooden hulks on the mud flats lead you to expect a romantic village. But now Looe is a commercialised holiday town pretending to be a real Cornish village. Good walks at low tide across the narrow estuary. All the amusements are here, speed boats and slot machines. Looe Island is now a bird sanctuary.

Looe, Cornwall

Lundy Cove A6
Cornwall. Between Port Isaac and Polzeath, this sheltered sandy beach is an ideal spot for secluded picnics. Safe swimming in calm weather, and lovely walks along coastal paths with great views.

Lundy Island B3
Devon. A 23-mile sea trip from Ilfracombe to this tiny island in the Bristol Channel. Mostly inhabited by puffins, seals, and wild ponies, although there are about 40 people.

Marisco Tavern, Lundy.

Lynton and Lynmouth E3
Devon. Pop 2,000. EC Thur. Lynton stands 600 feet above Lynmouth but the two places are connected by road and a cliff railway. Shelley, Wordsworth and Southey were all entranced by the romantic beauty of this spot. Heavily wooded with rushing streams running through from Exmoor. In 1952 Lynmouth was terribly damaged by a great flood and over 30 people died. Walks behind Lynmouth to Watersmeet, Valley of the Rocks and beautiful Exmoor. Coastal walks to Lee Bay and Woody Bay.

Marazion F10
Cornwall. Pop 1,400. EC Wed. With one little twisting street, the town is the starting point for the ferries to St Michael's Mount. Best view of the Mount is from the west side of the town. Safe, shallow bathing.

Mevagissey A8
Cornwall. Pop 2,100. EC Thur. A steep, slate-hung fishing village that remains relatively unscathed by over-development. Now a shark fishing centre. Has a good 1842 Methodist chapel and a small inland church with a Norman font. It is a holiday town but still has a Cornish air.

mevagissey

Minehead F3
Somerset. Pop 8,100. EC Wed. Daniel Defoe called Minehead the best port and safest harbour in Somerset, and it still amazingly keeps a village air. The scene of the church, cottages and harbour belie the existence of the neighbouring holiday camps. At the other end of Blue Anchor Bay is the small village of Watchet, where Coleridge was inspired to write 'The Ancient Mariner' in 1797.
Sailing, swimming and water skiing in Blue Anchor Bay.

Morwenstow B5
Cornwall. Pop 600. An inn, a few cottages and a bosky combe of windswept trees make up this tiny village overlooking the Atlantic. Rising above the trees are the vicarage chimney stacks in the shape of miniature church towers. All part of the Gothic fantasy of the builder, the Celtic poet and Tractarian priest of the village from 1834-75, Rev. Robert Hawker.
The church of St Morwenna is full of dim, religious atmosphere, and it was the scene of the first Harvest Festival service. Look out

for the hut on the splendid cliff where Hawker went to meditate. See also Tonacombe to the south of the valley, a fine 16thC manor house.

Mousehole   F10
Cornwall. EC Wed. Pronounced 'Mowsal', once the centre of the pilchard fishing industry and now an attractive port filled with summer visitors. In the church is Dolly Pentreath's tomb – she was the last Cornish speaker and died in 1777.

Newquay   G8
Cornwall. Pop. 15,000. EC Wed. Cornwall's largest holiday resort, rightly famous for its beaches, rocks and magnificent surf. Here are some of the finest beaches in Britain, all sandy and safe. Great breakers roll into Fistral Bay where the surfing is excellent. Lusty Glaze and Tolcarne are the more sheltered family beaches. There are two miles of surf at Watergate Bay, a short car ride to the east. It's worth a walk to the Gannel Estuary and the unspoilt St Columb Minor, where you can get some idea of what the area was like before the developers moved in. The town is almost one large hotel, but it's always full in the season. Bring your Malibu board.

Newquay.

Padstow   A7
Cornwall. Pop 2,700. EC Wed. Began life as one of the largest mediaeval towns in Cornwall and still retains its unspoilt narrow streets and stone buildings. The old town is full of small cottagey houses with gardens overflowing with fuchsias. From Padstow there are lots of good walks – take the public path to Chapel Stile above Brabyn's Yard and on to St George's Cove. On May Day the town holds the Hobby Horse Dance Festival. Visit the life boat station.

Paignton   F7
Devon. Pop 30,300. EC Wed. Devon's family holiday resort, where the beach slopes so gradually that it's ideal for tiny children. There is a pier, a Festival Hall and masses of lovely public gardens. Don't miss the zoo, one of the largest in England.

Penzance   F10
Cornwall. Pop 19,400. EC Wed. MD Thur. A beautiful town wrapped around by Mounts Bay, it expanded in Regency times to become the Brighton of the west. Full of pleasing houses in luxuriant gardens, Penzance remains a fashionable town to stay in and enjoy the winter sunshine. Boats sail from the harbour to the Scilly Isles, and shark and mackerel fishing trips run all summer. Safe, sheltered beaches.

Perranporth   G9
Cornwall. EC Wed. The heart of surfing country, long stretches of golden sand and constantly thundering surf. The dunes and rough tufty grass are disturbed only by the craggy Gull Rocks. Just off the sandy tracks among the caravans are the few remaining walls of St Piran's, almost the earliest Christian building in England (6th or 7thC).

Plymouth   D8
Devon. Pop 250,000. EC Wed. MD Mon. It was to Plymouth's natural harbour that Sir Francis Drake returned after sailing round the world in 1580. On the Hoe is where he finished his game of bowls before tackling the Spanish Armada in 1588. In 1620 the Pilgrim Fathers set sail in the Mayflower for America from the point now called Mayflower Steps. The historic city was the target for German bombers during World War II and much of it was flattened. Now much of the central area is new, the planning is spacious but unsympathetic and anaemic. The naval dockyard at Devonport is still an important strategic base and the fleet can frequently be seen in Plymouth Sound. Things to see: The Hoe, the Citadel, the rebuilt Eddystone Lighthouse, the Barbican area, and to the west the two Tamar Bridges. Sailing but little bathing.

Plymouth

Polzeath   A6
Cornwall. EC Wed. Very popular seaside town with a superb setting; a long, sandy bay protected on the north by Pentire Point and the rocky island of Newland, to the south the distant view of Stepper Point. Rather too many shacks and bungalows have spoiled the landscape but put your head down in the surf and you needn't notice. Superb sandy beaches overlooked by low hills and cliffs; the surfing is good.

Porlock Weir   F3
Somerset. Tiny, hidden little quay which is surrounded by a group of attractive whitewashed cottages. Some sailing and a good starting point for walking through steep bluebell woods. Porlock village lies on the hillside where the A39 road climbs dramatically at a gradient of one in four.

Port Isaac   A6
Cornwall. Pop 1,000. EC Wed. Still an active fishing port – steep, sheltered and severe. It is full of little slate-hung houses with tiny gardens full of shells brought home from more exotic voyages. The harbour is full of lobster pots, and you can take a trip out to sea for some mackerel fishing.

Prah Sands   F10
Cornwall. Good beach, one mile of sands that are edged with holiday houses and camping sites. The western end is sheltered and the surf comes in in a beautiful calm sweep.

St Agnes Head   G9
Cornwall. Gorse and bracken cliff tops command a view from Land's End to Newquay. The character of the place comes from the gaunt remains of engine houses once used for the tin mines. The tiny cottages are fast being out-numbered by the tourist bungalows. Handsome Georgian Methodist chapel.

St Ives   F9
Cornwall. Pop 9,700. EC Thur. Artists were attracted to this town in the 19thC because of the quality of the light, and it remains a town full of sculptors, painters and potters. Granite, cobbles and silver blue slates catch the almost mediterranean light. Visit the Penwith Art Gallery, Bernard Leach potteries and the church for Barbara Hepworth's huge 'Mother and Child'. Surfing from Porthmeor Beach, sheltered swimming in the harbour, and from the sands of Porthminster Beach.

St. Mawes   A9
Cornwall. EC Thur. Serenely contemplating its incomparable marine views, St Mawes has the air of rich retirement. Sun-tanned mature sailors ease their expensive yachts into the Carrick Roads, and return for gin slings in the bars of the quietly opulent hotels. You can smell the lobsters and mayonnaise around supper time. The perfect Tudor castle remains glowering at France.

Seaton   G6
Devon. Pop 4,500. EC Thur. Small resort with pebble beach that shelves steeply. Close by, the tiny village of Axmouth remains unspoilt. The wide valley of the Axe River behind the town is often full of sea birds and cormorants.

Sidmouth   G6
Devon. Pop 12,000. EC Thur, Sat. Old fashioned seaside at its best. Queen Victoria stayed here as a young girl, and the place still has the hallmarks of gentility. Elegant Fortfield Terrace crowned by imperial eagles holds sway over the smooth cricket pitch. Peak Hill and Salcombe Hill guard

the town on each side, but the best spot for sea views is up Jacob's Ladder, a lookout tower in the Connaught Gardens. West beach, sandy and safe.

Slapton Sands · E8
Devon. An excellent three-mile stretch of beach, bordered on the landward side by low lying farmland and freshwater lakes. The lakes are now a nature reserve for wild fowl and rare marsh birds. Excellent bathing, ideal for children.

Tintagel · A6
Cornwall. Pop 1,300. EC Wed. Legend and landscape combine to produce an air of romance that is still strongly felt in King Arthur's birthplace. The castle, built around 1140, has been split by the sea's erosive action. The gateways and outer courts are on the mainland while the great hall and inner courts are isolated on an island.
The remains of a great Celtic monastery can be seen on the highest point of the island. Go on a stormy, wet day and the full force of the Atlantic greyness and powerful scenery will convince you that legendary knights and kings walked these incredible cliffs. On a more everyday level, the little town of Tintagel has teashops, an old post office, and a museum of sorcery.

Torquay · F7
Devon. Pop 54,000. EC Wed, Sat. Smart, warm and amusing – Torquay is Devon's nearest thing to Cannes. Its palm trees, illuminated promenades, modern theatres and superb harbour have made Torquay a beautiful and successful resort. Spend a few days here to enjoy exotic gardens, the marine drive and the good beaches all round the bay.
Sailing conditions in Torbay are almost always ideal. Torquay is that rare thing 'an ideal centre' in the middle of twenty miles of varied coastline with the hinterland of beautiful countryside. Best beaches in Torquay: Livermead Sands, Corbyn Sands, Beacon Cove.

Trevose Head · H7
Cornwall. Great spot for a real taste of Cornwall's rocky coast. Go up to the little grass hills along the shore and look towards Dinas Head. On the east side of the headland good, sandy swimming beaches.
Lighthouse open afternoons Mon-Sat.

Treyarnon Bay · H7
Cornwall. A beautiful sweep of a beach, quiet, relaxed and it has not been over-developed. Not safe to swim at low tide or near rocks on the south of the beach – there is a natural pool among the rocks on the north. Surfing.

Weston-super-Mare · H2
Somerset. Pop 50,800. EC Thur. Perfect for travel agents' brochures, because there really are acres of golden sands in Weston Bay. Donkey rides and pony carriages, and now the most popular new sport is sand yacht racing. There is everything you need here, even two indoor pools if it's too cold to bathe outside.

Westward Ho! · C4
Devon. Pop 2,200. EC Tue. Named by Victorian developers after Charles Kingsley's novel about sturdy Elizabethan sailors, the town has grown into a popular resort over the last 100 years. The beach is good for surfing and the 650-acre common is perfect for seaside family picnics.

Zennor · F9
Cornwall. Pop 300. Treeless heather-strewn tors slope down to the valley where the little granite village stands. Awe-inspiring granite cliffs sweep into a sea that constantly changes colour with the sun.

Scilly Isles · C10
An archipelago of some 150 islands and rocks that lie 36 miles to the south-west of Land's End, reached by sea or helicopter from Penzance. There are five main inhabited islands. The sea between is very shallow, at one time they were probably linked, and even now, in calm weather during exceptionally low tides, it is possible to wade between the islands.

The first sight of the islands from the sea can be disappointing: they are small, bare and close together, and lack the majestic cliffs of Cornwall. But they have a variety of their own, there are good sandy beaches which are seldom crowded. The islanders are friendly, and they have arranged things well; they pick flowers for export between November and April so they can take visitors during the whole summer.
Fairly accessible but seldom overwhelmed with visitors, they keep their distinctive local administration, and a sense of separate identity from the rest of Britain. In ancient times the islands were regarded as an ideal burial place for bronze age heroes who named the Scillies 'Isles of the Blest'. Their more recent history has been dominated by the local feudal landlords on Tresco, the Dorrien-Smiths. This family leased the islands 1835–72 and they introduced not just flower farming but compulsory education.

Hugh Town, St. Marys, Scilly Isles.

Bryher. The island has about 80 inhabitants. On the west the seas are seldom calm – Shipman's Head is the place for watching the breakers.
St Agnes is the most westerly, craggy and remote with about 70 inhabitants and a sturdy lighthouse. To the east lies the island called The Gugh, full of ancient tombs.
St Martin's. About 140 people. Once very insular with lots of inter-marriage. The south-west side is sheltered and cultivated, and the north-east is open downland that rolls down steep cliffs into the sea. There is one shop and five good beaches.
St Mary's is the largest island with the Scillies' only town, Hugh Town, on the harbour where the 'Scillonian' arrives every day from Penzance and the launches leave every morning for the off islands. Along the main street are good examples of the low built granite houses that suit these exposed places. The New Church was simply built in 1835 and it has above the door the large wooden lion, rescued from Sir Cloudesley Shovel's wrecked flagship in 1707. Go to see the Star Castle built in the shape of an eight-pointed star, 1593-94. The main bronze age tombs on St Mary's are at Porth Mellan, Bant's Carn and Innisidgen.
Tresco. The second largest island is still the home base of the Dorrien-Smith family, and their Victorian home surrounded by verdant sub-tropical gardens is open to the public. Look out for the Valhalla in the gardens, a collection of ships' figureheads. On the northern, bleaker end of Tresco are Cromwell's Castle and the church of St Edula. Beaches are sandy.
The other tiny islands are uninhabited and easy to visit by sea. There are special trips arranged to watch the sea birds on Annet and the black rabbits on Samson.

Inland towns & villages

Barnstaple · D4
Devon. Pop 17,300. EC Wed. MD Tue, Fri. An inland port on the River Taw, Barnstaple has two interesting museums, the Dodderidge Room, Old Guildhall, which displays plate and ancient seals, and St Anne's Chapel Museum, where John Gay, who wrote 'The Beggar's Opera', was a pupil when it was still the grammar school.

Bath K2
Avon. Pop 84,500. EC Mon, Thur. MD Wed.
This is one of the finest 18thC cities in
Europe. Planned for pleasure and spurred
on by the spa's health-giving qualities, the
city grew under the watchful eye of
Beau Nash. Visit the Pump Room for
coffee with a string orchestra; take the
waters (warm and rather nasty), and wander
through the steamy Roman baths.
Don't miss the Royal Crescent, the Circus,
Robert Adam's Pulteney Bridge, and in
the restored Assembly Rooms, the Museum
of Costume.

Bath, Royal Crescent

Bideford C4
Devon. Pop 12,600. EC Wed. MD Tue, Sat.
The Kingsley novel 'Westward Ho!' was set
in this famous seaport. There are many
mediaeval streets and the lovely 24-arch
bridge was built in the 15thC.

Blisland B7
Cornwall. Pop 500. On the moors around the
town are vestiges of pre-Christian stone
circles and monoliths. On the sloping valley
within is this little granite village, of
Georgian and earlier houses clustered
around the green lawn planted with tall elms.
Don't miss the marvellous church dedicated
to St Protus and St Hyacinth with its
colourful carved screen.

Bodmin B7
Cornwall. Pop 10,400. EC Wed. MD Sat.
Cornwall's county town with a long history
that goes back to the iron age, when the hills
around were thickly populated. In the
middle ages it was the centre of a cult
surrounding the relics of St Petroc, and the
town then had twelve churches and a
monastery. The only surviving church is
St Petroc, the largest church in Cornwall.
The misty Bodmin Moor surrounds the
town and still gives it an air of Celtic mystery
– once you leave the main road, that is.

Bristol J2
Avon. Pop 421,800. Of all Britain's major
provincial cities, Bristol has had a heavy
bashing from wartime bombs, and more
recently developers, but it remains the
business and communications centre of the
west. The port's business has moved down
to Avonmouth with the arrival of container
traffic, and the port where the Cabots set sail
for America in 1497 is now a quieter place.
Trade in sugar, tobacco, and rum made
Bristol rich and the great churches are
evidence of the town's mediaeval prosperity.
Be sure to visit St Mary Redcliffe church,
which dates from the 13thC, and is widely
regarded as the finest parish church in
England.
An evening can be spent at the Theatre
Royal, England's oldest theatre; recently
restored and linked to the Palladian Cooper's
Hall which now serves as the theatre's
entrance foyer.
The city has an excellent university and art
gallery, both heavily endowed by the Wills
family, whose fortune was made from
tobacco in Bristol. Go up to Clifton where
the Georgian squares and terraces are equal
to those in Bath. High above the Avon gorge
is Brunel's famous suspension bridge,

Clifton Suspension Bridge, Bristol

designed in 1830, that looks as though it was
just lightly thrown across the chasm.
Also of interest in Bristol, the cathedral,
Lord Mayor's Chapel and the Arnolfini
Gallery for modern paintings.

Dunster F3
Somerset. Pop 1,000. EC Wed. One of
Somerset's most beautiful towns with its
yarn market and romantically perched castle.
The castle has belonged to the Luttrell
family since 1376, and is open to the public.
Look out for the mainly 17thC Luttrell
Arms, and the round mediaeval dovecote in
the garden of the splendid St George's
Church.

Dunster

Exeter F6
Devon. Pop 95,600. EC Wed, Sat. MD Fri.
Devon's capital city is still dominated by
William the Conqueror's Rougemont Castle
and the great cathedral in its own quiet close
Large areas of the city were rebuilt after the
war and it has lost much of its character.
The university is worth visiting for its
amazing planting and fine site. Visit the
Guildhall and the unique Ship Museum.

Honiton G5
Devon. Pop 5,100. EC Thur. MD Tue. Once
famous for its wool, Honiton is now known
for its lace, potteries and by-pass.

Langport H4
Somerset. Pop 800. EC Wed. One of the
lesser known attractive inland towns in
Somerset, it is tightly built around a square
with a fine church and good early Georgian
houses. Look at the Ham stone, round-
arched Guildhall (1733), and All Saints
Church for its good glass.

Launceston C6
Cornwall. Pop 5,300. EC Thur. MD Tue.
The first town you come to in Cornwall if
you are travelling from Devon – once over
the Tamar and you are in the Duchy. It has
a good sky-line, the Norman castle on its
steep hill with the huddle of houses around.
The great church of St Mary Magdalene is
a triumph of 16thC Cornish craftsmanship.
Look out for beautifully carved granite,
particularly the Mary Magdalene
surrounded by minstrels. Visit also the
market square, the castle remains and the
elegant Georgian Castle Street.

Lostwithiel B7
Cornwall. Pop 1,900. EC Wed. Dominated
by the ruined Restormel Castle to the
north-west, this town has a lot to offer the
discriminating. Small and neatly planned,
the main street shows off the whole range of
English domestic architecture from the
mediaeval Duchy Palace to the Guildhall of
1740. The church of St Bartholomew has a
spire like those seen in Brittany, giving the
whole town a French air. Well worth
visiting.

Mells K3
Somerset. Pop 700. Feudal dignity is the
quality of this stone village. The great
church of St Andrew has a majestic tower
104 feet high, and it seems to rise out of the
trimmed yew hedges of the Manor House
gardens. The grave of Ronald Knox,
Roman Catholic priest and scholar, is a
place of pilgrimage near the east wall of
the graveyard.

Redruth G9
Cornwall. Pop 10,800. EC Thur. MD Fri.
Like so many of Cornwall's inland towns,
Redruth at first sight seems dull, but its
interest lies in its history. With Camborne,
it was at the heart of the Cornish tin and
copper mining district. The viaduct of the
West Cornwall Railway and the ruined mine
workings still dominate the town.
A house at the back of Druid's Hall was the

home of William Murdock, the inventor of gas lighting, who lit his own house by gas as early as 1792. Look at the unusual church, a strange combination of 1756 classicism with a 15thC granite tower.

St Just-in-Roseland   H9
Cornwall. Pop 3,600. EC Thur. Cornwall's own Forest Lawn, only this one is the real thing. The visitor comes here not for the charming village but for the country's most beautiful graveyard. At the lych gate you look down on the top of the church tower, and the tombs cascade down the richly planted hillside to the calm waters of the creek.

Selworthy   F3
Somerset. Pop 600. A superb approach to this Exmoor village from the west, as the road tunnels under overhanging trees. The white-washed cottages, church and tithe barn make a traditional English rural scene at this gateway to Exmoor. Good riding centre.

Somerton   J4
Somerset. Pop 3,200. A warm stone-built town that comes to life in the market place. Here the full quality of the grouping of the church, cross, market hall and 16th and 18thC houses becomes apparent. Look out for the elegant Red Lion Hotel.

Taunton   G4
Somerset. Pop 37,400. EC Thur. MD Sat.

For generations farmers from the surrounding Blackdown, Brendon and Quantock hills have brought their produce to Taunton market. It's still a thriving trading centre and worth a visit, not just for its fine churches and houses, but also for its importance as an historic centre of revolution. Look at the castle and its museum. St. Mary Magdalene Church and the Market Hall.

St Mary

Tavistock   D7
Devon. Pop 7,600. EC Wed. Birthplace of Sir Francis Drake, and site of a fine ruined Benedictine abbey. The area was once a thriving base for copper mining in the early 19thC. At its height the great Consols copper mine was one of the richest in the world. Visit Morwellham (3½ miles sw) once the thriving port of the mining trade – now a museum of industrial archaeology.

Totnes   E7
Devon. Pop 5,800. EC Thur. MD Tue. On the River Dart, steeply raked Fore Street with a rare survival, the East Gate. Totnes is still a centre for the livestock industry and now also for antiques and craft shops, especially in the Butterwalk. Visit the church of St Mary, a good 15thC example.

Truro   A8
Cornwall. Pop 15,700. EC Thur. MD Wed. Lying in a bowl of hills, Truro is a pleasant well kept town that has taken care of itself. It is unofficially the capital of Cornwall, and it does have the county's only cathedral. It's the cathedral you first notice sailing over the roof tops with its three graceful towers. From its mediaeval origins Truro has grown into a well planned city with some notable 18thC streets, particularly Lemon Street and Boscawen Street.
Look out for the elegant Walsingham Crescent, the Victorian park of semi-tropical plants, and the superb modern (1908) viaduct that carries the railway into Truro over 28 granite arches.

Wells   J3
Somerset. Pop 8,600. EC Wed. MD Wed, Sat. Dominated by the massive carved stone cliff of the cathedral's west front, Wells seems like a tiny town dedicated to serving the cathedral. The Vicar's Close is a range of early houses, some definitely of mediaeval origin. Look out for the Bishop's Palace (begun in 1206) and fine Cathedral School.

Widecombe-in-the-Moor   E6
Devon. Pop 600. A Dartmoor village associated with the folk song 'Widdicombe Fair'. There is the interesting 14thC church of St Pancras with a 120-foot-high tower, and the 15thC Church House. The fair is held on the second Tuesday in September.

Regional oddities

Celtic Crosses
The cross on a circle is an ancient relic of Celtic Christianity, often elaborately carved from granite. Good examples at St Buryan, Lanhewe, St Mawgan, St Michael's Mount, Chapel Amble, St Kew, Minions and St Cleer, all in Cornwall.

China Clay Tips
Like a moonscape the grey white cones of the china clay workings dominate parts of the Cornish scene. Often surrounded by milky greenish lakes, you'll see them north of Newquay and at Nanpean – spectacular ones at St Stephen in Branell, and St Austell.

Cornish Tin Mines
Throughout Cornwall you will see the tall chimneys of the disused tin mine workings. Vast pumping engines were built at the end of the 18thC, which pumped out the water fast enough for the tin to be streamed away. In the 1930s Cornish tin became too expensive compared with tin from Malaya, but there's plenty left and the industry may revive. Good workings to be seen at St Agnes, Cam Brea, Camborne and Morvah.

Morhah, deserted tin mine

East Pool Winding and Pumping Engine   G9
East Pool, Cornwall. Beside the A30 road between Redruth and Camborne is a reminder of Cornwall's once great industry, tin mining. Above the deserted mine at East Pool stands an old stone engine house and stack complete with preserved Victorian machinery. *Open Mon-Fri Mar-Oct.*

Lighthouses
On the hazardous coasts of Devon and Cornwall you see many stalwart lighthouses. The most southerly in Britain is eleven miles south of Helston, Cornwall, on the Lizard.
Good lighthouses to visit – *Cornwall:* St Agnes, St Anthony, Trevose, Pendeen, Scilly Isles; *Devon:* Bull Point, Hartland Point, Lynmouth, Plymouth, Start Point; *Open most afternoons except Sun by arrangement with the keeper.*

Famous people

King Arthur (died c538)   J4
Cadbury Castle, Cadbury, Somerset. Thought to be the site of Camelot and King Arthur's Court, where Lancelot, Guinevere, Sir Tristram, Kay, Bedevere, Merlin, Gawain and all gathered. It is said that on St John's Eve, midsummer, you can hear the horses' hoof beats as Arthur and his knights ride down from Camelot to drink at the spring near Sutton Morris church. Tintagel and Glastonbury also have strong associations with Arthur. Legend persists that the king was born in Tintagel Castle, Trevena, Cornwall. The ruins of that ancient stronghold still glower over the wild Cornish coast. At Glastonbury Abbey, King Arthur and Guinevere are said to be buried in front of the high altar. But there

are Arthurian relics everywhere: Winchester claims the Round Table, and Dover Castle Gawain's skull. *Tintagel Castle open daily. Castle: ramparts only accessible by footpath.*

S. T. Coleridge   G3
Coleridge Cottage, at w end of Nether Stowey, nr Bridgwater, Somerset. The poet lived in this small house 1797–1800 for the sum of £7 per year. During his stay 'The Ancient Mariner' was written (it was planned during a walk across the Quantocks in November 1797), and 'Kubla Khan' and 'Christabel'. *Open 11.00–17.00 Sun–Thur Mar–late Oct. By written application Nov–Apr.*

Lorna Doone   F5
Old Blundell's School, Station Rd, Tiverton, Devon. R. D. Blackmore's famous historical novel, 'Lorna Doone', haunts Exmoor, from Pinkery Pond to Minehead, to the Bristol Channel. Doone Valley itself is not nearly so dark and romantic as Blackmore's tantalising description, but close your eyes and you can hear that rowdy band of highwaymen and murderers returning to their lair in the valley. There are traces of the foundations of huts from the real Doones' settlement dating from the 17thC.
Blundell's is where Blackmore, like his hero, John Ridd, went to school in 1836 at the age of eleven. The north-east façade of the building has hardly changed since then. *Forecourt open any reasonable time.*

Sir Francis Drake (1542–96)   D7
Buckland Abbey, Yelverton, Devon. Drake bought this 13thC Cistercian monastery from the Grenville family in 1581.
There are reminders of Drake in many parts of Devon: he was born in Crowndale, near Tavistock (a tablet on a nearby farmhouse bears witness to the demolished house), and married in St Budeaux, Bossiney. The abbey is now a museum devoted to Drake. *Open 11.00–18.00 daily (Closed Sun morning) Mar–late Sep. 15.00–17.00 Wed, Sat & Sun Oct–Mar.*

Cathedrals, abbeys & churches

Bath Abbey   K2
Bath, Avon. The amazing west front carved with ascending and descending angels on Jacob's Ladder is only a foretaste of the delights inside the abbey. Simple fine fan vaulting extends throughout the chancel, aisles and nave. Look out for Prior Bird's Chantry, an elegant carved corner. The abbey is full of memorials, 614 tablets commemorate those who lived and died in Bath during its heyday as a spa. In 972 in a Saxon abbey on the site of the present building Edgar was crowned King of England.

Culbone Church

St. Clement, Cornwall   *St Mary, Taunton*

Buckfast Abbey   E7
Buckfast Abbey, Devon. This abbey church of the Benedictine monks is an amazing example of faith and skill; the monks themselves have built the abbey from 1907 to the present day. It is an impressive, rather than beautiful, building, tainted by the commercial nature of the busy monks' activities. You can buy Buckfast honey, pottery, images, pictures and, to revive you, Buckfast tonic wine.

Downside Abbey   J3
Downside, Somerset. A mainly Victorian range of monastic buildings, and now a school run by the Benedictine community. The church is a memorable mixture of Victorian and 20thC work. The tower is 166 feet high and the length of the church 328 feet, making the whole into a cathedral-sized building. A scene of great harmony – there is a spiritual atmosphere here.

Exeter Cathedral   F6
Exeter, Devon. If you visited Exeter Cathedral 600 years ago it would have appeared much as it does now, although its origins go back at least 900 years. On the west front an amazing array of 14thC sculpture survives, while the elaborate mouldings and vaults give the interior a unique richness. The two transept towers are the main Norman survivors. Look out for the clock in the North Tower and the minstrels' gallery over the north porch. There is a peal of thirteen bells, and the curfew is still rung each evening.

Holy Cross   E5
Crediton, Devon. More like a collegiate church than a parish one, it seems almost too splendid for the peaceful little town. Of red sandstone, it was begun as a cruciform church in the 12thC with a noble central tower. Worth a visit for its dignified splendour.

St Catherine   H4
Swell, Somerset. A rare survivor, this church is of 12thC origin, with some later additions. Tucked away off the Taunton–Langport road, it has to be reached through a farmyard. Inside it is small, white and simple, and somehow very moving.

St Mary   H5
Ilminster, Somerset. A great church with a soaring central tower that has dominated this little town since the 15thC. Clear glass lets in the sun on to the amazing monuments. Note especially those to the Wadham family, who are commemorated by exceptional brasses. Good 18thC brass chandelier.

St Mary   G6
Ottery St Mary, Devon. Largely built in the 1340s by Bishop Grandisson who modelled it on Exeter Cathedral. It does look like a rather squat version of Exeter from outside; within it is very grand with a fine fan-vaulted aisle. Full of interesting tombs; avoid the Victorian font.

St Michael   J4
North Cadbury, Somerset. Classic example of Somerset Perpendicular style, this church makes a good village group alongside the manor house. Glorious chancel that might have been built for a college to use. Note the rare 15thC painted glass in the west window.

SS Probus and Gren   A8
Probus, Cornwall. This early 16thC tower is the tallest in Cornwall. Carved granite and light loftiness are its two characteristics. Note the three great eastern windows.

SS Protus and Hyacinth   B7
Blisland, Cornwall. Solidly made of blocks of moorland granite, this church gazes over a steep, wooded valley. Inside slate floors, white walls and wagon roofs quietly accept the flamboyant carved screen that gives the rich chancel its air of festal mystery.

St Winwalloe   G10
Gunwalloe, Cornwall. Amazingly sited in total isolation by the sea, its tower stands alone built into the rock. The grey-green pillars of the arcade look as though they have been under water for years. Worth seeing for a taste of undeveloped Cornwall.

Truro Cathedral   A8
Truro, Cornwall. Built from 1880 to 1909 to designs by J. L. Pearson, the cathedral rises out of the town in the French manner. The style is a late Victorian interpretation of Early English and Normandy Gothic. Inside is a constantly changing series of vaults and vistas. The colouring is cool, the granite, Doulting and Bath stone are untouched, so that the glass and embroideries provide the colour. As an example of the Victorian Gothic revival Truro Cathedral is masterly.

Truro Cathedral

Wells Cathedral   **J3**
Wells, Somerset. It was in 909 that Wells became the see of a bishop, and the present cathedral dates from two main periods 1180-1240 and 1290-1340. On the west front is the most extensive array of mediaeval sculpture to survive in Britain – 12th and 13thC. The three towers were not built until the late 14thC. The most exciting features of the interior are the inverted arches that support the columns, that in turn support the massive weight of the central tower.
Things to look out for: the 14thC astronomical clock with knights that joust every hour; the glass in the Lady Chapel; the green and gold Jesse window in the choir; and the stair to the marvellously vaulted Chapter House.

Castles & ruins

Compton Castle   **F7**
Devon. 1 mile n of Marldon. One of the many fortified manor houses of the West Country, strengthened as a defence against the French. The castle lies low against a backdrop of Devonshire countryside. It is built around a courtyard and retains its chapel, great hall and kitchen.
Still the home of the Gilbert family whose ancestors include Sir Humphrey Gilbert, who colonised Newfoundland in 1583. A romantic and beautiful place. *Open 10.00-12.00, 14.00-17.00 Mon, Wed & Thur Apr-Oct.*

Dartmouth Castle   **F8**
Dartmouth, Devon. One of a pair of castles built for the defence of the entrance to the River Dart in the 15thC. Now cared for by the Department of the Environment, it remains in superb condition and should be visited as a lesson in coastal defence. *Open 9.30-17.30 daily Apr & 9.30-19.00 May-Sept (9.30-17.30 Mar & Oct & 9.30-16.00 Nov-Feb. Closed Sun morning).*

Dunster Castle   **F3**
Dunster, Somerset. Owned by the same family since 1376, this castle stands high on a hill overlooking the little market town. Parts of the structure go back to 1070, most of the form you see today was built between the 13th and 19thC. In the late 17thC the dining room was panelled, the gorgeous rich plaster ceiling installed, and the carved staircase added. In the banqueting hall are six magnificent coloured leather panels from Spain showing the story of Antony and Cleopatra. Dunster Castle has kept a very 'lived in' feel and is a warm, welcoming castle to visit. *Open 10.15-12.30, 14.15-16.30 Wed & Thur Jun. Tue-Thur Jul-Sep & B. Hols. 14.15-15.30 Wed Oct-May.*

Glastonbury Abbey   **J3**
Glastonbury, Somerset. The remains of a great abbey. The most substantial part left standing is the Lady Chapel with its sculptured doorways and late Norman decoration. The Abbot's kitchen, the main survivor of the monastic buildings, is one of the most complete and best preserved mediaeval kitchens in Europe, with fireplaces fitting into the four corners to create an octagon. It must have been a very warm place to cook in!
The monastery gatehouse with its two entrances, one for vehicles and one for pedestrians, survives. The abbey at Glastonbury was founded about the year 700, but legend persists that it was founded by Joseph of Arimathea who travelled to Britain with the Holy Grail and began evangelizing from an oratory on the marshes. It is King Arthur's legendary burial place, and now hippies camp around still hoping to find Nirvana among the ancient stones. *Open daily all year.*

Pendennis Castle   **G10**
Nr Falmouth, Cornwall. One of the chain of castles which Henry VIII erected from 1538 onwards in the face of a French invasion threat, Pendennis was started in 1544 and built quickly. Its final form is a circular keep in the centre of two rings of fortified walls. You might still have to storm the battlements as the complete portcullis and drawbridge are preserved. The main octagonal room in the castle has walls sixteen feet thick. It still seems to resound with the sound of muskets. *Open 9.30-17.30 daily Apr & 9.30-19.00 May-Sep (9.30-17.30 Mar & Oct 9.30-16.00 Nov-Feb. Closed Sun morning).*

Powderham Castle   **F6**
Kenton, Devon, 8 miles se of Exeter on A379. In the middle of a great park stocked with deer stands the ancestral home of the Earls of Devon. Built in 1390, damaged in Civil War skirmishes, and restored in the 18th and 19thC, it has the air of a powerful castle that has been domesticated. On every Tuesday when the castle is open displays of falconry are arranged – a rare chance to see this mediaeval sport. *Open daily 14.00-17.30 May-Sep.*

St Mawes Castle   **A9**
St Mawes, Cornwall. Henry VIII's great fortress, built to protect these tidal waters from the French. It was finished in 1540 and has the form of a clover leaf with its stalk marking the entrance. Rumour has it that the castle represented a Tudor rose in plan, as a compliment to Henry. The decorative carvings indicate the early flowering of the Renaissance in England. *Open daily.*

St Michael's Mount   **F10**
Penzance, Cornwall, ½ mile from shore at Marazion. A totally romantic pile of masonry that crowns the rock of St Michael off the coast of Penzance. Once the home of Celtic saints, it was visited by St Michael the archangel and became a shrine. Secularised after the Reformation in 1660, it was sold to the St Aubyn family who modified the monastic buildings. Now visited for its tropical gardens and the magnificent prospects of Land's End and the Lizard. At high tide it is an island, but a causeway from Marazion links the Mount to the mainland at low tide. *Open 10.30-15.45 Mon, Wed & Fri (10.30-16.45 Nov-Mar).*

St. Michael's Mount

Unusual buildings

A la Ronde   **F6**
Exmouth, Devon. A unique house built in 1798 by the two Misses Parminter. The rooms radiate from the central octagonal hall 45 feet high. Above this is the Shell Gallery where those indefatigable ladies gallantly stuck all the shells on in intricate patterns during long winter evenings. The design of the house was based upon that of San Vitale at Ravenna; the inspiration for the seaweed and feather pictures came from the devoted sisters themselves.

Glastonbury

The Kitchens, Glastonbury

Burton Pynsent Column   H4
Curry Rivel, Somerset. A lofty stone column erected as a memorial to Sir William Pynsent. A spiral staircase once led to the top for the extensive views. One day a cow decided to take a look for herself. Having mounted the stairs, she was so overcome with vertigo or fright that she plunged to her death. To prevent further tragedies the column has now been bricked up.

Eye Catcher   C8
Mount Edgcumbe Park, nr Plymouth, Cornwall. A broken down ruined chapel that was deliberately built that way to catch the eye in this lovely landscaped park. All erected in the late 18thC, it is an amazing sylvan scene.

Haldon Belvedere   E6
Doddiscombsleigh, Devon. Built by a one-time Governor of Madras to remind him of the delights of the Orient in this bleak setting on the moors near Exeter. The floor of the hall and the spiral staircase in the south-east tower are made of rare marble, the gift of the Nizam of Hyderabad. Now lived in by a farmer, it opens occasionally.

Knill Monument   F9
St Ives, Cornwall. Just south of St Ives, John Knill, mayor of the town in 1782, erected this stone pyramid. Showing a rare determination to ensure that his name lived forever, Knill provided in his will for a group of ten young virgins and two elderly ladies to dance around the pyramid on the 25th July each year singing Psalm 100. Clearly that is the only day in the year to visit this spot.

Saltash Bridges   K8
Saltash, Cornwall. Isambard Kingdom Brunel's Royal Albert Bridge was an engineering feat in 1859 – a mighty iron bridge that is a combined suspension and arched bridge on giant granite piers. It took the Great Western Railway into Cornwall from Devon. Now there is a new (1963) road bridge alongside, that is a simple steel and concrete suspension structure.

Wadebridge Bridge   H8
Wadebridge, Cornwall. A terrific mediaeval bridge, it has seventeen arches, is 320 feet long, and still stands although it was finished in 1468. The piers are said to have been sunk on a foundation of packs of wool.

Houses & gardens

Antony House   C7
Torpoint, Cornwall. 5 miles w of Plymouth via Torpoint car ferry. A disciplined stone centre block is joined to brick-built wings by colonnades – a perfect design that hasn't been altered since 1721. The same family have lived on the site since 1492, among them Sir Richard Carew, the Elizabethan author of 'The Survey of Cornwall', which gives an unforgettable picture of England at the time of the Armada. The present house is a rare example of classical perfection in Cornwall, crisp and severe in silver granite. Panelled rooms and portraits are some of the attractions for visitors today. Sweeping lawns, fine trees and clipped yew hedging form the basis of the garden, which runs down to the River Lynher. There is a certain amount of topiary including an enormous cone, some giant ilex trees planted in 1760, and a maidenhair tree. *Open 14.00-18.00 Tue-Thur & B. Hol Mon Apr-Sep.*

Clevedon Court   H2
Clevedon, Somerset. A well preserved mediaeval manor house dating from the early 14thC. Look at the upstairs chapel with its fine windows, and take a wander along the terraced gardens laid out in the 18thC. Thackeray stayed here and wrote part of 'Vanity Fair'; the house is renamed 'Castlewood' in his 'Henry Esmond'.

Cotehele House   C7
Cornwall. 2 miles w of Calstock. The least changed mediaeval house in Britain; to visit Cotehele is to sniff deeply the atmosphere of the past. Built 1485–1539, its two granite quadrangles give it the air of an Oxford college set down in a beautiful Cornish garden, and encircled by a large well wooded

park. The great hall has all the armour, banners and plain furniture of the time when the house was new. In the chapel is a clock that was there in 1489.
The informal part of the garden around the charming mediaeval dovecote retains a Cornish wildness. Set around the water garden with its ferns, primulas and irises are some lovely rhododendrons, azaleas and white wistarias, palms, bamboos and maples. *Open 11.00-18.00 Apr-Oct. Garden only daily mid Oct-Mar.*

East Lambrook Manor   H4
Somerset. 2 miles n of South Petherton. A sophisticated cottage garden, created by the late Margery Fish, author of many gardening books, where old favourites and rare species thrive together in gay but controlled abandon. The mellow stone walls of the 15thC house shelter eucalyptus, clematis, fuchsias and euphorbias. There is also a little silver garden, and a woodland ditch garden with hellebores, hardy geraniums, violets and primroses beneath the willows. *Open daily Feb-Nov. Closed Sun. (House open 14.00-17.00 Thur Mar-Oct.)*

Glendurgan   G10
Cornwall. 4 miles sw of Falmouth, 12 miles sw of Mawnan Smith. A wooded valley garden sloping gently down to the estuary and containing many exotic species. Near the house can be found a Mexican agave and in the walled garden many interesting climbing shrubs. There are also large groups of the South American evergreen *drimys winteri*, and down by the water garden Asiatic primulas and gunneras. *Open 10.30-16.30 Mon & Wed Apr-Sep (also Fri Apr & May).*

Knightshayes Court   F5
Devon. 2 miles n of Tiverton. A garden thoughtfully planned to embrace a wide variety of plants and moods. In a series of small individual areas enclosed by castellated hedges, groups of gentians and alpines can be found, and a circular unadorned pool. The woodland garden, at its best in spring, provides meandering walks. *Open 14.00-19.00 daily Apr-Oct. Closed Fri & Sat.*

Montacute House   J4
Montacute, Somerset. Perhaps the finest Elizabethan house in England, since few changes have been made since it was built. Tall, symmetrical, with large windows, it is undeniably handsome and the Ham stone glows in the sun. On the garden side the little walls and summer-houses present a picture of a complete Elizabethan garden. The interior has good panelled rooms with elaborate fireplaces, and the furnishings are enriched by the addition of a collection of Tudor and Jacobean portraits from the National Portrait Gallery. *Open 12.30-18.00 Wed-Sun & B. Hols Apr-Sep, or by appointment.*

Saltram House   D8
Plymouth, Devon. 2 miles w of Plympton. The plain, orderly entrance front gives no clue to the richness of the inside – for Saltram has some of the finest 18thC decoration in the country. The salon and dining room were decorated by Robert Adam down to the fittings and carpets. Note how he skilfully echoed the patterns of the ceilings in his carpets.
All the contents are of enormous interest, furniture, pictures, pottery and porcelain. Sir Joshua Reynolds' portrait of the two Parker children remains where it was first positioned, over the fireplace in the morning room. The park is well landscaped, alas now likely to be threatened by a major road. *Open 11.00-13.00 & 14.00-18.00 daily Apr-mid Oct. Nov-Mar garden only.*

Tintinhull House   J4
Somerset. 5 miles nw of Yeovil. A beautiful four-acre garden largely created by Mrs P. E. Reiss who gave the property to the National Trust in 1953. Symmetrical layout, immaculate lawns, flagstone paths, and neatly clipped cone-shaped box hedges provide good contrast to the loosely planted borders where red roses, regalia, day lilies, and blue agapanthus mingle happily together. *Open 14.00-18.00 Wed, Thur, Sat & B. Hols Apr-Sep.*

Trengwainton Gardens　　F10
Cornwall. 2 miles nw of Penzance on B3312.
Tender plants from all over the world,
especially New Zealand, Chile, Australia, the
Himalayas and Burma, are assembled here
in the shelter of the walled garden. The
collection was built up over 40 years by
Lt-Col Sir Edward Bolitho who presented
it to the National Trust in 1961. There are
many half-hardy shrubs as well as magnolias
and rhododendrons. *Open 11.00-18.00
Wed-Sat & B. Hols Mar-Sep. (Closed Fri.)*

Tresco Abbey　　C10
Tresco, Scilly Isles. A sub-tropical garden
created by Augustus Smith, Lord
Proprietor of the Scilly Isles in 1834, it is
well worth the travelling necessary to reach
it. Pink and white lampranthus are good
examples of the many mesembryanthemums;
ixias, sparaxis, hebes, acacias and
pelargoniums grow prolifically amongst
the yuccas and succulents of the rock
garden. There are many palms including
the New Zealand Cabbage Tree. Daffodils,
of course, are also here, particularly the
'Scilly White' and 'Soleil d'or' believed to
have first been planted by mediaeval monks.
Open 10.00-16.00 Mon-Fri.

Museum & galleries

American Museum in Britain　　K2
Claverton Manor, Avon. 3¼ miles se of Bath.
The New World re-created above the valley
of the Avon. Sixteen period rooms with
original furniture dating 1680-1860 depict
American life from the elegance of
Washington's Mount Vernon to the New
England country store with cracker barrel
and stove. *Open 14.00-17.00 Tue-Sun Apr-
late-Oct. Nov-Mar by application.*

Bath Museum of Costume　　K2
Assembly Rooms, Bath, Avon. The world's
largest collection of costumes from the
17thC to the present, including Byron's
Albanian dress. *Open daily (11.00-17.00
Sun). Tel 28411.*

Bath Roman Museum　　K2
Abbey Churchyard, Bath, Avon. Adjoining
the fabulous Roman baths, the museum
holds relics from the baths and other Roman
sites: altar stones, pewter, utensils, lead
plumbing and pottery. *Open 9.00-18.00
Mar-Oct, 9.00-17.00 Nov-Feb, Sun
11.00-17.00.*

Bristol City Art Gallery　　J2
Queen's Rd, Bristol, Avon. The gallery holds
the great altarpiece by Hogarth, works by
Constable, Gainsborough, Reynolds,
collections of Bristol glass, Chinese ceramics
and ivories. *Open daily. Closed Sun.*

Buckland Abbey　　D7
Devon. 2¼ miles w of Yelverton. Founded by
the Cistercians in 1278, and once the home
of Sir Francis Drake, it is now a museum
devoted to Drake, the Navy and the West
Country. *Open 11.00-18.00 mid-Apr-Sep.
Closed Sun morning (Open 15.00-17.00 Wed,
Sat & Sun afternoon Oct-Apr).*

The Cornish Museum　　B8
Lower St, East Looe, Cornwall. A folklore
and crafts museum with a special collection
of magic and witchcraft: charms, things
magical and grisly. *Open 10.00-21.00 daily
May-late Sep.*

Exeter Maritime Museum　　F6
The Quay, Exeter, Devon. In a group of
warehouses on the quay, and in the water,
is a unique collection of working craft,
including an Arab pearling dhow and a
320-ton Danish steam tug. Boating and
launch trips are also available. *Open daily.*

Fleet Air Arm Museum　　J4
*Royal Naval Air Station, Yeovilton,
Somerset.* A fine display of aircraft, model
aircraft and ships illustrating the
development of naval aviation from 1910 to
the present. *Open 10.00-17.30 daily. (Closed
Sun morning.)*

Gough's Cave Museum　　H3
Cheddar, Somerset. An almost complete
skeleton dating from the ice age was found in
Gough's Cave and can be seen in the

museum, together with flints, amber and
engraved stones. *Open 10.00-19.30 Apr-Oct.
Daily.*

**The Holburne of Menstrie
Museum**　　K2
Great Pulteney St, Bath, Avon. This elegant
Palladian building houses one of the finest
collections of silver in the country. Porcelain,
important paintings and miniatures,
including the work of Gainsborough,
Reynolds and Stubbs. *Open 11.00-17.00
daily. (Closed Sun morning.)*

**Honiton and Allhallows Public
Museum**　　G5
High St, Honiton, Devon. Fine displays of
Honiton lace, relics of the world wars, a
reconstructed Devon kitchen, and the bones
of a 100,000-year-old straight-tusked
elephant, hippo and ox, all unearthed from
the Honiton by-pass. *Open 10.00-17.00
daily May-Sep. Closed Sun.*

Morwellham Quay　　D7
Morwellham, nr Tavistock, Devon. The
museum in this historic river port on the
Tamar is devoted to industrial archaeology.
Open 10.00-18.00 daily.

Museum of Witchcraft and Black Magic
　　B6
Boscastle, Cornwall. 5 miles n of Camelford.
Claimed to be one of the most extensive and
least-known museums of witchcraft and
black magic in Europe, the collection
includes paintings by diabolist Aleister
Crowley, the skeleton of witch Ursula Kemp,
executed in 1589, and the thigh bone of a
Tibetan sorcerer-priest. There are also
samples of witches' flying ointment and
powder used for wasting-away magic. *Open
10.00-21.00 daily Apr-mid Oct.*

**Plymouth City Museum and
Art Gallery**　　D8
Tavistock Rd, Plymouth, Devon. Reynolds
family portraits, Joshua Reynolds's diaries,
the Cottonian Collection of paintings, a small
but superb collection of silver including the
Drake Cup and the Eddystone salt are all
here. *Open daily (10.00-20.00 Fri, 15.00-
17.00 Sun.)*

Shepton Mallet Museum　　J3
Market Place, Shepton Mallet, Somerset.
Tiny museum near the ancient market with
a jumble of relics and displays: birds and
insects, artefacts of early man, bronze age,
iron age, Roman and mediaeval collections.
Open Mon-Fri.

Valhalla Maritime Museum　　C10
Tresco Abbey, Tresco, Scilly Isles. Housed in
a 19thC building of rough sea-boulders and
timber from wrecked ships, the museum
offers a tantalising collection of wood-
carvings dating from the 17thC – many
figureheads and ships' ornaments. *Open
10.00-16.00 daily Mar-Sep. Closed Sun.*

Wookey Hole Cave Museum　　J3
Wookey Hole, Somerset. This is the earliest
known home of man in Britain. The
museum displays a fine selection of Celtic
and Roman relics, as well as the earlier
remains of animal and human bones, cooking
utensils and jewellery. Visit the Witch of
Wookey in the Great Cave – a massive
stalagmite said to be a petrified old woman.
*Open 10.00-18.00 daily Apr-Sep, 10.00-16.30
Oct-Mar.*

Botanical gardens

Bicton Gardens Arboretum　　F6
*Devon. 3½ miles n of Budleigh Salterton on
A376.* There are three quite distinct
gardens: the Italian, a classical sweep of
lawns and water dotted with statuary and
fountains; the American, with species from
that continent including the scarce
Montezuma pine; and the Pinetum, with an
outstanding collection of conifers. All can be
viewed from an eighteen-inch gauge railway.
*Open 14.00-18.00 daily Mar-May & early
Oct. Daily May-early Sep. 11.00-18.00 Sep.*

Killerton Park Arboretum　　F6
Devon. 5 miles ne of Exeter. Tender shrubs
and trees flourish here due to both the mild
climate and the acid volcanic soil. There are

some beautiful magnolias, eucalyptus, enormous tulip trees, the vibrant South American embothrium and some old cork oaks with their grey textured bark. *Open daily during daylight.*

Zoos, aquaria & aviaries

Bristol Zoo   **J2**
Clifton, Bristol, Avon. Many difficult and rare species have been bred here: okapi, white tigers, polar bears and black rhinoceros. Animal houses include the monkey temple and several avaries exhibiting tropical birds from all over the world, and there's the bust of Alfred, the zoo's famous gorilla. *Open 9.00-19.30 (10.00-19.30 Sun) Apr-Oct. 9.00-16.30 Nov-Mar.*

Cricket St Thomas Wildlife Park
                                                  H5
Somerset. 3 miles e of Chard on A30. In a beautiful unspoilt setting with ponds and a stream is this 80-acre park with paddocks of deer, zebra, llama and wallaby. Many birds live wild on the water. There are also smaller mammals in the old walled garden. *Open 10.00-18.00 daily.*

Murrayton Monkey Sanctuary   **C7**
Cornwall. Off the B3253 4 miles e of Looe. This is the special home of Humboldt's woolly monkeys. They live in a huge cage on the lawn, but can swing across from tree to tree with the help of handy ladders and ropes, or roam freely among the visitors. Don't touch – they bite. *Open daily Apr-late Sep.*

Paignton Zoological & Botanical Gardens   **F7**
Tweenaway Cross, Paignton, Devon. 100 acres of zoo and gardens in the beautiful Clennon Valley, with a reputation for breeding animals. Fine collection of monkeys and parrots. Don't miss the red-faced spider monkeys, pigmy hippo, kookaburras, electric eel and piranha. *Open 10.00-dusk daily,*

Pinevalley Wildlife Park   **D6**
Follygate, Okehampton, Devon. A small mixed collection of animals living in a natural environment with lots of space. Many birds and small mammals: heron, black ibis, pelicans, eagles, vultures, Himalayan bear, donkeys, sheep and goats. Opened in 1969 it is still expanding. *Open 10.00-dusk daily.*

Plymouth Aquarium   **D8**
The Hoe, Plymouth, Devon. One of the finest aquaria in Britain. *Open daily Oct-Apr & 10.00-20.00 May-Sep. Closed Sun.*

Plymouth Zoological Garden   **D8**
Central Park, Plymouth, Devon. A small mixed collection of animals. The emphasis is on African species: lions, giraffes, antelope. The quarantine station close by, where imported animals are held, is not open to the public, but during 'open' quarantine they are often exhibited before leaving for other zoos around the country. *Open 10.00-sunset daily.*

The Tropical Bird Gardens   **K3**
Rode, nr Bath, Avon. A small zoo set in the beautiful gardens of Rode Manor. The population includes macaws, flamingos, penguins, vultures and owls. *Open 11.00-19.00 daily Apr-Oct (11.00-sunset Nov-Mar).*

Wildlife Park   **J2**
Westbury-on-Trym, Bristol, Avon. Park devoted to British wildlife: foxes, badgers, deer, seals. Avaries house magpies, barn owls, eagles, herons, pochard and duck. *Open daily.*

Nature trails & reserves

Braunton Burrows National Nature Reserve Trail
Nr Braunton, Devon. Dunes and seashore. There are two trails – 1½ miles through the dunes (start at the American Road Car Park) and 1½ miles along the shore (start at the south end of American Road). Booklets from the Nature Conservancy Warden, Pounds Mead, Hills View, Braunton.

Bridgwater Bay National Nature Reserve
Somerset. Excellent for waders, winter wildfowl, including regular large numbers of white-fronted geese, and unique late summer/autumn moulting shelduck flock. Best observed from Start Point area, reached via A39 west from Bridgwater to Cannington, Combwich and Steart; or via A38 north from Bridgwater to West Huntspill, thence along Huntspill River and northwards.

Ebbor Gorge National Nature Reserve Trail
Nr Wells, Somerset. Mainly woodland birds in a superb scenic area. Start at the car park. Guide available at the nearby display centre at Ebbor Gorge National Nature Reserve, and further details from the Nature Conservancy Warden, East House, Wookey Hole, Wells.

Lundy Nature Reserve
Lundy, Devon. Boat from Ilfracombe. Breeding seabirds, raven, buzzard, and a wide variety of migrants. Field Station and Bird Observatory are in the Bristol Channel. Full details from The Agent, Lundy, Bristol Channel, via Ilfracombe, Devon.

Quantock Forest Trail
Quantock Forest, Somerset. Birds and other wildlife including buzzard and red deer of a commercially managed forest. 1-3 miles. Start at Seven Walls Bridge. Forestry Commission guide available at the site.

Slapton Ley Nature Reserve
Slapton, Devon. Open water and reedbed birds. Migrant waders, terns and passerines. Field Studies Centre and Bird Observatory. Full details from Field Studies Council, 9 Devereux Court, Strand, London WC2.

Slapton Ley Nature Trail
Slapton, Devon. Birds of open water, reed and lake margins. 1½ miles, starting at Slapton Bridge. Leaflets available.

Yarner Wood National Nature Reserve Trail
Nr Bovey Tracey, Devon. Woodland birds and woodland conservation. 3 miles. Free guide from the Nature Conservancy Warden, Yarrow Lodge, Yarner Wood, Bovey Tracey.

Bird watching

Chew Valley Reservoir
Avon. 8 miles of Bristol. This reservoir is among the most important wildfowl waters in the country, with a wide selection of duck in winter. Gadwall and the feral ruddy duck are among the breeding birds. In both spring and autumn the area is noted for its passage waders and black terns. Kingfishers are readily seen. There are good public viewpoints at the dam, Herriott's Bridge, Heron Green and Villice Bay, and permits to enter the area are available from the Fisheries Officer, Bristol Waterworks, Woodford Lodge, Chew Stoke, Bristol.

Dartmoor
Devon. A vast area, but much can be seen from the roads and there is ample scope for exploration on foot. Breeding birds include red grouse, buzzard, curlew, raven, dipper, wheatear, ring ouzel, whinchat, stonechat, redstart, wood warbler and grey wagtail. In addition, Burrator and Fenworthy reservoirs have small numbers of winter wildfowl. Recommended areas are: Black Tor – Yes Tor (upland birds); the moors and heaths of the central area; and the oak woodland from Dartmeet (A384) towards Buckfastleigh.

Exe Estuary
Devon. Between Exeter and Exmouth, best observed from Powderham, Starcross and Dawlish Warren on the west side, and Lympstone on the east. Excellent for waders at all seasons, with interesting greenshank, spotted redshank, godwits, purple sandpipers at Exmouth, and especially good for duck in winter, brent geese and both Slavonian and

black-necked grebes. Dawlish Warren adds seaward views and also has sanderling in winter.

Exmoor
Somerset. Moors, combes and deep-wooded valleys with many birds including red grouse, merlin, buzzard, dipper, pied flycatcher, nightjar, warblers.

Hayle Estuary
Cornwall. Best observed from A30. A good selection of winter and autumn waders occurs, the latter including spotted redshank, godwits, curlew, sandpiper and little stint. Winter wildfowl include wigeon and pintail, and Slavonian grebes are regulars.

Lye Rock
Nr Bossiney, Cornwall. N of Tintagel. A superb piece of coastal cliff. The largest puffin colony in Cornwall and a good breeding ground for auk. Also buzzard, razorbill and guillemot.

Scilly Isles
Seabirds and migration: Western Rocks and Gorregan for breeding auks and kittiwakes. Annet is outstanding with manx shearwaters, storm petrels, puffins and terns. St Mary's, Tresco and St Agnes are excellent for migration, and Horse Point, St Agnes for sea-watching. The islands are famous for rare migrants and vagrants. Regular sailing and, in summer, BEA helicopter service from Penzance.

Tamar Estuary
Devon. An estuary complex with good numbers and a variety of autumn and winter waders, and winter wildfowl including occasional white-fronted geese. Of particular interest are wintering avocets and black-tailed godwits. In the north of the area, Weirquay and Bere Ferrers offer good views of the Tamar and Tavy respectively, the former being good for seeing the avocets, while the Torpoint area is recommended at the southern end.

Brass rubbing

The following is a short list of churches that have brasses for rubbing. Permission is almost invariably required.
Cornwall. Callington, St Mellion, Fowey, Mawgan in Pyder, St Columb Major and St Michael Penkivel.
Devonshire. Dartmouth (St Saviour), Exeter Cathedral, Stoke Fleming, St Giles-in-the-Wood.
Somerset. Ilminster, South Petherton, Wells Cathedral, Yeovil.

Fossil hunting

Visit the local museum. Its fossil collection usually states where individual fossils have been found. When visiting quarries always seek permission to enter if they look privately owned or worked. Be careful of falls of rock.

Bath *Avon*
Plant remains can be found in the spoil heaps of the old coal mines in the Radstock, Camerton and Midsomer Norton areas.

Bleadon *Somerset*
Gravel pits in this area have yielded Pleistocene bones and antlers.

Bridgwater Bay *Somerset*
Search the lower Jurassic of the cliffs and foreshore west of Bridgwater, i.e. Watchet, Kilve and Hinkley Point.

Bude *Cornwall*
Look for arthropods and fish fossils in the cliffs.

Cheddar *Somerset*
Many exposures of fossils in the limestone of the Mendips around Cheddar, Burrington Combe, etc.

Crackington Haven *Cornwall*
The coastal parts of the culm yield lamellibranchs and goniatites.

East Somerset Quarries
Jurassic fossils in exposures in quarries at Chesterblade, Corton Denham, Dundry, Dunkerton, Keynsham, Maperton, Marston Magna, Midford, Shepton, Beauchamp and Welton.

Haldon Hills *Devon*
Look for fossil coral particularly in exposures of the limestone.

Quarries *Somerset*
Numerous quarries of carboniferous limestone give corals and brachiopods, notably, Backwell, Binegar, Burrington, Cleeve, Dulcote, Failand, Long Ashton, Portishead, Waterlip and Wrington.

Seaton *Devon*
Plentiful Cretaceous and Jurassic fossils along this coast at Seaton, Beer, Branscombe and east of Seaton in and below the cliffs.

Taw River *Devon*
Along the coast and in quarries in this area. Lower carboniferous plants, corals, brachiopods and fish remains are to be found near Bishops Tawton, Bideford, Fremington and Westleigh.

Winford *Somerset*
Quarries here yield milstone grit goniatites.

Moors

Bodmin Moor
Cornwall. Open moorland twelve miles wide, owned by the Royal Duchy of Cornwall and grazed by cattle and ponies belonging to the 'commoners' of neighbouring farms. Rocky outcrops of granite, reaching 1,375 feet on Brown Willy, give wide views. Great walking and riding country, easily reached from the small towns of Bodmin, Camelford, Launceston and Liskeard.

Dartmoor
Devon. In the heart of Devon this magnificent 200-square-mile expanse of granite moorland, now a National Park, rises steeply from surrounding farmlands to heights around 2,000 feet. Grazed since Saxon times by herds of half-wild ponies and hardy cattle, owned by local farmers. Grand riding and walking country, but caution is needed in the north where the highest point, High Willhays, 2,039 feet, lies on a military firing range.
Rocky outcrops called 'tors' make good landmarks and viewpoints, but beware of sudden mists. Picturesque reservoirs lie in the valleys, or combes, especially Burrator in the south. Wistman's Wood, one mile north of Two Bridges, is a nature reserve of fantastic oaks, dwarfed by exposure. Stately spruce woods at Bellever and Fernworthy. Enormous open-cast china clay workings north of Ivybridge. Grim prison at Princetown.
Charming unspoilt towns ring Dartmoor and offer homely accommodation, notably Okehampton, Chagford, Moretonhampstead, Buckfastleigh, Totnes, Yelverton and Tavistock.

Exmoor
Somerset and Devon. National Park on 100 square miles of high, breezy moorlands facing the Bristol Channel, with views north to the South Wales mountains. Source of the River Exe, home of hardy half-wild ponies, and scene of R. D. Blackmore's romantic historical novel 'Lorna Doone'. Reached from the coastal resorts of Ilfracombe, Lynmouth and Minehead by tortuous roads with fierce gradients. Finest scenery at Heddon's Mouth Valley, where oak woods run down to the cragbound shore. Highest point is 1,599 feet, near Pinkworthy Pond, Challacombe; often misty up there.

Sedgemoor
Somerset. Aptly named, this dead-flat plain, 25 miles across in each direction, was for long a wilderness of sedges, reeds and rushes. Here, on the Isle of Athelney, around 878, King Alfred burnt the cakes while planning campaigns against the invading Danes. Here too, in 1685, the rebel

Duke of Monmouth was defeated by King James II. Nowadays the moor is all well drained farmland, with fascinating basket willow beds around Langport.

Hills & combes

Blackdown Hills
This broken upland plateau between Honiton in Devon, and Taunton in Somerset, is a maze of valleys winding every way. Highest point, on the north face, is Staple Hill, 1,035 feet.

Brendon Hills
Somerset. Inland from Minehead, near Dunster with its castle and quaint market square, the Brendons form an eastern extension of Exmoor. More rugged and open, with huge woods of spruce and Douglas fir, they reach 1,390 feet on Lype Hill. Explore the scenic upper Exe along the A396, winding south towards Tiverton.

Combes and woods
Magnificent forests of Douglas fir, Corsican pine, and other tall conifers have been established locally by the Forestry Commission and private landowners, notably in the Glynn Valley east of Bodmin (Bodmin Forest) and over Haldon Hill, east of Exeter (Exeter Forest). The Cornish elm, a stately hedgerow tree with a slender crown, originates here and is now widely planted elsewhere in England.
Outstanding natural woods, owned by the National Trust, at Arlington Court, near Barnstaple, Holne Woods, ten miles west of Newton Abbot, Lydford Gorge near Tavistock, Lynmouth, and Goodmeavy near Yelverton. Fine arboreta, or collections of specimen trees, open to the public at Killerton, north-east of Exeter, and Bicton, near Budleigh Salterton.

Mendip Hills
Somerset. Ridge of limestone hills, 25 miles long, wending south-east from Weston-super-Mare on the coast south-west of Bristol to Shepton Mallet. The area is waterless except for Chew Valley Lake on the north, and there are many old lead mines, now exhausted. Precipitous winding gorges of white rocks run down to Cheddar on the south where huge underground caverns are open to the public. Elsewhere the short green pastures are bounded by stone walls. Wide views over Sedgemoor.

Quantock Hills
Somerset. Between Taunton and Minehead on the coast, this twelve-mile range affords real highland scenery, though nowhere over 1,260 feet. Tall woods of Douglas firs, introduced from Oregon, shelter a native herd of red deer which range across breezy commons that give expansive views over the Bristol Channel.

Rivers

Dart
Devon. The Dart begins as two moorland streams close to the highest point of Dartmoor. The East Dart runs through Postbridge and the West Dart through Two Bridges, to join at Dartmeet, an exceptionally beautiful spot where you will find an ancient stone 'clapper' bridge for packhorses, an old arch bridge for cars, and a restaurant. The Dart then cuts through a deep valley wooded all the way to Totnes, where it becomes navigable by small craft.

Exe
Devon. The Exe rises in Somerset on a high moorland ridge of Exmoor, within a few miles of the Bristol Channel. Flowing first east, then south, right across Devon, it follows a deep, winding and narrow valley fringed with oak woods, past Tiverton to the cathedral city of Exeter. Aided by a canal, coastal craft can ascend this far. Below Topsham the Exe flows through a broad sandy estuary to its narrow outlet, checked by sandbanks, at Exmouth.

Fowey and Fal Rivers
Cornwall. Typical Cornish rivers, these two streams rise on high hills, cut through very narrow and deep valleys, and end in harbours that once sheltered the sailing navies of merchant venturers in the Elizabethan age. Magnificent Douglas fir forests fringe the Fowey south of Bodmin. At Falmouth, south of Truro, the Fal ends in a great estuary, deep enough for the world's largest ocean-going ships to anchor safely.

Parret
Somerset. Central Somerset forms a broad, flat plain, broken by little hills and artificially drained low marshes, which is the basin of the big River Parret. This draws together the waters of lesser streams from encircling hills on the south, including the Yeo from Yeovil, and the Tone from Taunton. At aptly-named Bridgwater, the lowest road crossing, the Parret becomes tidal and navigable, flowing forth towards broad mud-flats at Burnham-on-Sea.

Tamar
Famous as the boundary between Saxon Devon and the ancient Celtic kingdom of Cornwall, the Tamar rises on the Morwenstow Hills, near Hartland, only four miles from the peninsula's north coast. Flowing due south past Launceston with its castle, it cuts a deep, well wooded valley between Tavistock in Devon and Callington in Cornwall. At Saltash, just west of Plymouth's port and naval base, it has become a broad tidal estuary, crossed by a high railway viaduct and a modern road bridge.

Taw and Torridge
Devon. These two North Devon rivers share a common estuary, close to the little seaport and shipbuilding town of Appledore, on what the geographers confusingly call Barnstaple or Bideford Bay. The Taw flows in north-westwards from mid-Devon, past the old port and bridgehead town of Barnstaple. The Torridge comes from the Cornish border, flowing north-east past Great Torrington, and the 'twin' seaport and bridgehead town of Bideford. Both harboured sea-dogs and men-of-war in Elizabethan days, and are thronged with holiday craft and fishermen today.

Canals

The Chard Canal
Somerset. Historically, this canal is remarkable for its very short life. A late starter, it opened for traffic in 1835 and was closed after a mere 25 years of profitless existence. However there is luckily quite a lot to see of the navigation, which contained three tunnels and four 'inclined planes'. The best things to see, but don't expect to find too much water, are the aqueduct and embankment across the Tone Valley outside Taunton, and the inclined plane and the entrance to the mile-long tunnel at the village of Wrantage (the old canal pub on the A378 road is still open). At Ilminster there is, again, a tunnel and an inclined plane close together. The boats used to travel down the inclined planes in water-filled tanks running on rails, and at Ilminster a change in height of over 80 feet is accounted for in this way. In Chard itself the final inclined plane can be traced, but little else remains.

The Exeter Ship Canal
Devon. This is one of the oldest canals in Britain, built in the 16thC well before our canal system as we know it today had even been thought of. The canal starts in Exeter and, fed by the River Exe, pursues its own course for just 5½ miles down to rejoin the Exe Estuary near Topsham. The canal is still occasionally used by small ships, which bring petrol to a wharf just outside Exeter. There are several locks, with circular balance beams, and all the bridges either lift or swing, in order to accommodate the considerable headroom of sea-going craft. The towpath provides an unusual circular walk along the canal from Exeter down to within a mile of the last lock into the estuary.

At this point there is a small ferry across to Topsham. Visit the remarkable Maritime Museum in the terminal basin at Exeter. (See 'Museums')

The Grand Western Canal.
Devon & Somerset. An intriguing little waterway, formerly envisaged as part of a canal connecting the Bristol Channel with the English Channel. Only the north end of the canal was built, and an eleven-mile branch to Tiverton. But there is a lot to see, although most of the canal is today without water.

Archaeology

Cadbury Castle   J4
South Cadbury, Somerset. For several centuries Cadbury Castle has been popularly regarded as the site of King Arthur's Camelot, and recent excavations have found evidence of fortifications and buildings of the Arthurian period. The basic rampart system is iron age, with phases of building dating from an earth bank of the 5thC BC through to a dry-stone wall destroyed by the Romans. During the Roman period the hilltop was apparently cultivated, and remains of a Romano-British temple have been found.
In the late 5th–6thC, the Arthurian period, the defences were refurbished and a hall built inside. Later structures on the site date mostly from the early 11thC, when Aethelred the Unready built a defensive hall against the Danes. There are also traces of mediaeval walling. *Ramparts only accessible by footpath.*

Charterhouse-on-Mendip   J2
Nr Blagdon, Somerset. Charterhouse was an important lead-mining centre during the Roman period, and traces of their workings can be seen on the surface as shallow depressions marking the pits and trenches cut to extract the ore. The settlement associated with the mines lay in Town Field, and an earthwork to the west of this may have been an amphitheatre. Lead pigs with imperial stamps are on display in Wells Museum. *Accessible any time.*

Chysauster Ancient Village   F9
Gulval, Cornwall. Chysauster is a classic example of a peculiarly Cornish type of iron age settlement. The number of huts suggests a village settlement, although there are no defences. The basic hut type is roughly circular, enclosed in massive walls, with rooms for living and storage opening on to a central unroofed courtyard. The site dates from the 1stC BC, and though there is evidence for its continuing into the Roman period, its character is native rather than Romano–British. *Open 9.30–17.30 daily Apr & 9.30–19.00 May-Sep. (Open 9.30–17.30 Mar & Oct & 9.30–16.00 Nov-Feb. Closed Sun morning.)*

Dartmoor   D6
Devon. Dartmoor has several groups of visible antiquities, probably dating from the early bronze age. Circular stone enclosures containing stone hut-circles, their walls supported by banks of earth, can be seen at Grimspound, and at Legis Tor. Stone avenues and rows survive at Merrivale and Trowlesworthy Warren, and other groups of similar monuments can be seen at Ditsworthy Warren, Erme Valley and Shovel Down.

Halligey   G10
Trelowarren, Cornwall. One of the best-preserved of the Cornish fogous, a type of subterranean structure which has parallels in Scotland, Ireland and Brittany. They were probably constructed during the 1stC BC, and were built by excavating a trench, lining and roofing it with stone, and replacing the soil on top. Their purpose is unknown: defensively they would be deathtraps, and they are rather oddly constructed for storage.

Lydford Castle   D6
Lydford, Devon. One of the most westerly of the fortified strongholds (*burhs*) established across southern England by Alfred and Edward the Elder as defences against the Danes in the late 9th and early 10thC. In the case of Lydford, an earthwork bank was constructed across the neck of a river promontory to create a defensible position. A Norman keep was built on the site during the 12thC. *Accessible any time.*

Roman Baths   K2
Bath, Avon. The small Roman town of Aquae Sulis grew up around its curative hot springs, and the baths built there form one of the best-preserved Roman monuments in western Europe; until recently they were still in use. The Great Bath was surrounded by a colonnade, of which the piers survive, and was probably open to the sky; the oblong Lucas Bath and small circular bath were contained in rectangular halls. Details of the Roman plumbing, the heavy lead linings to the baths, and fragments of mosaic floors are visible. The Roman Baths Museum displays finds from the site, including a bronze head of Minerva and, one of the finest pieces of Romano-British art, a carved Gorgon head from the façade of the Temple of Sulis Minerva, the presiding goddess of the springs. *Open 9.00–18.00 daily (11.00–17.00 Sun Nov-Mar).*

Stoney Littleton Long Barrow   K2
Stoney Littleton, Somerset. These characteristically neolithic tombs were probably designed as vaults for families or groups rather than as burials for one individual. Stoney Littleton barrow consists of a stone-built chamber and access passage, covered with a long earth-barrow – the finest English example of this is at West Kennet in Wiltshire. *Access from the farm.*

Tintagel   A6
Cornwall. The ruined monastery at Tintagel is without parallel in Celtic Britain for the sophistication of its rectangular buildings. The site occupies a dramatic headland, and may have been chosen initially for a solitary hermitage; the monastery was defined by a broad bank and ditch across the neck of the promontory. The buildings are arranged in groups, and include a library, guest-house, and cells for the monks. Despite legend, there is no evidence of any connection with King Arthur. A 12thC castle now dominates the promontory. *Open 9.30-17.30 Mar, Apr & Oct, 9.30-19.00 May-Sep, 9.30-16.00 Nov-Feb. Closed Sun morning Oct-Mar.*

Footpaths

South-West Peninsula Coast Path
When it is officially completed this will be the longest unbroken path in Britain, covering 515 miles from Minehead, Somerset, along the coast via Ilfracombe, Devon; Newquay, St Ives and Penzance, Cornwall; Plymouth, Torquay and Seaton, Devon to Studland in Dorset. There is still no right of way over some stretches of path, but these are relatively few and far between. In Somerset the path crosses the wild and desolate moorlands of Exmoor, with Dunkery Beacon rising over 1,700 feet above sea level. North-west of Lynton, Devon, the path leads through the magnificent Valley of Rocks, to Woody Bay, a tiny seaside resort surrounded by steep, wooded cliffs. From there the old coach road, now a green track, leads to Hunter's Inn.
There are 268 miles of pathway along the north and south coast of Cornwall, hugging the cliff tops with spectacular views of headlands, beaches, and quaint harbours and fishing villages.
From Newquay to Perranporth the path goes through sand-dune country. The inland way from Holywell, three miles from Newquay, to Penhale Sands, leads to the famous lost church of St Piran, once buried in the drifting sands.
Land's End is a shambles of straggling development along the A30, with petrol stations, car park, hotels, shops and endless tourist mementoes, but walking along the path from Sennen Cove, two and a half miles away, all the commercial paraphernalia of modern life is happily out of sight.

Between Polkerris and Fowey, four miles away, there are spectacular views of Gribbin Head looking seaward across the Fowey Estuary to the surrounding steep cliffs and wooded slopes. Fowey itself (pronounced 'Foy') is a picturesque Cornish town of labyrinthine cobbled streets.

Eastwards the path covers 93 miles of south Devon. The section across Bolberry Down from Bolt Tail to Bolt Head and The Warren are both protected by the National Trust and cross magnificent cliff tops, with wooded slopes descending to Salcombe with its waterside houses and ruined castle.

The 72 miles of Dorset path offers cliffs, downland, shingle and sand-dunes. Above Old Harry Rocks at Handfast Point the last stretch of the Peninsula Coast Path passes through Studland hamlet, along the shore of Studland Bay to the ferry at South Haven Point, with Sandbanks, Poole and Bournemouth within sight across the water.

Regional sports

Angling

Salmon can be taken on the Camel, Fowey, Plym and Tamar. The West Somerset 'fens' present a vast area of good coarse fishing possibilities. What makes West Somerset particularly good is the large number of rhynes, or drainage dykes, which provide nurseries for small fish. North and south Devon offer splendid game fishing on most rivers. Devon is particularly worried about the spread of the salmon disease UDN, and the authority handbook contain rules for reporting salmon catches and disinfecting fishing tackle.

Fishing licences and guides from the three River Authorities of Somerset, Devon and Cornwall.

The Exe Descent

River Exe, Devon. One of the most spectacular spectator sports ever. Over 100 canoeists race the eighteen miles down the turbulent River Exe to Exeter, with breathtaking descents down fifteen-foot weirs and rock-filled rapids.

Cowley 'Steps' where four skin divers fish out broken canoes and half-drowned canoeists who plunge down this turmoil of savage water. *Held once-yearly in mid Nov.*

Rugby

Rugby Union is played in Cornwall with the same fierce Celtish enthusiasm that keeps the game so alive in the Welsh valleys.

The two best teams are Camborne and Redruth. Such is the strength of Cornish Rugby that most international touring teams come down to play. For details of the major forthcoming matches in the south west, telephone the West Country Tourist Board, *Exeter 76351.*

Sailing

The deeply incised south coasts of Devon and Cornwall are a sailing paradise to rival the more crowded Solent. The area contains the two finest deep water harbours on the south coast, Falmouth, with the Carrick Roads, and Plymouth. The following sailing clubs, as do many others, offer temporary membership:

Salcombe Yacht Club. Salcombe, Devon. Estuary sailing. Classes of dinghy sailed Hornet, Solo, Salcombe Yawl, Mirror, and Handicap. Racing season Mar-Dec. Launching off beach and slipways all times except last hour of tide. Dinghy parking space available.

Mayflower Sailing Club. Plymouth, Devon. Plymouth Sound and open sea sailing. Classes of dinghy sailed unrestricted. Racing season Apr-Sep. Launching from slip at all states of the tide. Dinghy parking space – permit required from City of Plymouth Corporation.

For further details the Devon County Tourist Office, Trinity Court, Southernhay East, Exeter, Devon, publish an excellent booklet, or for the rest of the area contact the West Country Tourist Board, at the same address.

Shark fishing

Centred in Looe on the south Cornwall coast, where the holidaymaker as well as the serious fisherman can hire the tackle, book on a boat and cruise 20 miles offshore, fishing for blue shark, makos and porbeagles that can weigh well over 100 lbs! Late afternoon sees the day's catch being weighed on the quayside, and the size of the fish will amaze you.

All the sea angling is good around this coast, 'wreck' fishing yielding superb specimens. Virtually every harbour has boatmen operating trips.

Skittles

The traditional game for the dedicated indoor sportsman and drinker of southern Somerset, and not to be confused with its expensive modern American counterpart 'ten pin bowling'. One pub in two has its wooden skittle alley, and local competition is fierce. If you fancy a game try the Dolphin Hotel, Langport. Tel 200 – it is also a fishing pub.

Sub-aqua

The clear waters and rocky foreshore of the Scillies, south Cornwall and south Devon, warmed by the Gulf Stream, make for excellent diving conditions – and wrecks are more concentrated in this area than in any other part of the world.

The local boatmen will either hate you (divers have a bad reputation in some areas here) or hire out their boat and crew and take you to some superb sites like the Manacles and the Lizard. Diving centre at Fort Bovisand, Plymouth where courses are run.

Surfing

Twenty years ago this sport barely existed in Britain – now it is a way of life along the north Cornwall coast. When a good swell comes in, uninterrupted, off 3,000 miles of Atlantic it meets the gently sloping sandy beaches between Polzeath and Porthmeor. Then 'surfs up' and out come the malibu boards and their tanned and salt encrusted riders. Spectacular to watch, exhilarating to participate – if you dare! Newquay is the centre of activity (visit the Bilbo surfshop). Boards can be hired at various points along this coast. You can surf elsewhere in Britain, but this is where it 'happens'!

Festivals

For information and tickets for festivals go to the local information centre or ticket agent.

Bath Festival

Bath, Avon. This famous music festival was started by Yehudi Menuhin, who trained the festival orchestra and has played an active part from the first Bath Festival in 1959. Michael Tippett now directs the festival and modern British music is prominent. Performances are in the Assembly Rooms, Guildhall, the Abbey and Wells Cathedral. *10 days in June.*

Dawlish Arts Festival

Dawlish, Devon. Started as a local festival, it now attracts performers and enthusiasts from all over the country. Concerts are held in the parish church, and the repertory company puts on a new production. *Mid June.*

Minehead and Exmoor Festival

Minehead, Somerset. Begun as a small festival run almost entirely by the pupils of Minehead Grammar School, the festival has expanded to include neighbouring Dulverton, Taunton and Exeter, and events include music, folk dancing, drama, pottery exhibitions and painting. Every year the Festival Society commissions a special work. *2 weeks in July.*

Thornbury Arts Festival

Thornbury, Bristol, Avon. Now boasting a new Armstrong Hall, the festival has expanded to include performances by distinguished visiting companies such as the London Opera Group. But the tone of the Thornbury Festival is still set by the blend of amateur and professional talent. *1 week in early May.*

Fun things

Babbacombe Model Village F7
Torquay, Devon. An excellent model village, which features a model farm, churches and even an illuminated football match, in an attractive woodland setting. Fascinating for the children.

Bicton Gardens F6
Devon. W of A376, 3½ miles n of Budleigh Salterton. A mile-long narrow-gauge railway through plantations of mature pine and deciduous trees, and past a large ornamental lake. *Open daily Mar–May.*

The Brixham Cavern F8
107 Mount Pleasant Rd, Brixham, Devon. Accidentally discovered in 1858, the cave is 600 feet long. Prehistoric bones, stalactites and stalagmites. *Open 10.00–18.00 daily mid Apr–Sep. Closed Sat.*

Burgh Island Ferry E8
Off the Kingsbridge–Plymouth Rd (A379) at Aveton Gifford. Burgh Island can be reached at low water by a causeway, but when the sands are covered there is a most unusual ferry with a high platform on four stilts, and at the foot of each stilt is a motorised caterpillar track. The ferry literally walks across to its destination.

Butlin's Holiday Camp Amusement Park F3
Minehead, Somerset. For boating, swimming, miniature railway and monorail. The park is open to day visitors for a fee. Very good value as once you are in all the rides are free.

Dart Valley Railway
Buckfastleigh, Devon. (E7) Running seven miles along the River Dart from Buckfastleigh to Totnes-Riverside, the railway gives the traveller breathtaking and beautiful views of the River Dart which are denied to the motorist. All trains are hauled by steam engines of the Old Great Western Railway. *Open daily Apr–Oct.*
Kingswear, Devon. (F8) This line runs from Paignton to Kingswear, with unusual views of Tor Bay and the lower reaches of the *Dart. For enquiries telephone Buckfastleigh Station. Tel 2338.*

Donkey Rides H2
Weston-super-Mare, Somerset. Donkeys and Punch and Judy on the beach are part of the traditional, but disappearing, English beach scene. Weston has both. The donkey rides are still great favourites with the children and have been here since the mid 19thC. The animals are bred locally, take their first rider at the age of two and are retired after fourteen or fifteen years' work.

Forest Railway B7
Dobwalls, Cornwall. On the A38 road between Liskeard and Bodmin. On entering Dobwalls going westward, turn right on the road to St Cleer. Half a mile up the road you will come to the Forest Railway, a 7¼-inch gauge line. There is a car park, picnic area, swings and slides. The line, which is being extended, has an interesting selection of model steam locomotives, and a comprehensive signalling system. Very good value for an afternoon. *Open 10.00–18.00 May–Sep & Sun all year.*

Goonhilly Down Radio Station G10
Helston, Cornwall. Two gigantic reflectors for receiving radio signals from earth satellites. *Viewing area open daily.*

Gwennap Pit G9
Gwennap, Cornwall. On A393 between Falmouth and Redruth. Gwennap Pit, sometimes called the Methodist Cathedral, is a natural amphitheatre caused by the subsidence of a mine. John Wesley, when preaching at Gwennap in 1762, discovered the pit when he and his congregation were forced to find shelter from a wild gale. The pit was remodelled in 1806 with seating for 20,000 people, and now looks rather like a classical Greek theatre. Services are still held in it.

Kent's Cavern F7
Ipsham Rd, Wellswood, nr Torquay, Devon. Once occupied by prehistoric man. Stalactites and stalagmites. *Open daily.*

SS Great Britain J2
Bristol, Avon. An early steamship designed by that erratic genius, the great Isambard Kingdom Brunel. The Great Britain was large for her time (1843) at 3,618 tons, and the first ship of any size to rely solely on screw propulsion. In 1866 she was driven ashore in the Falkland Islands and used as a coaling hulk. In 1970 she was towed home to Bristol, and appropriately enough the tow was also a great feat of engineering and seamanship. Now in dry dock at Bristol, there are well signposted routes to reach her.

Hotels

The following indicate the price range of a single room per night:
£   inexpensive
££   medium priced
£££ expensive

Barnstaple Devon D4
Imperial Hotel, Taw Vale Parade. Tel 5861. Impressively Edwardian, carefully modernised. Overlooks the Taw Estuary. ££.

Bath Avon K2
Francis Hotel, Queen Square. Tel 24257. Elegant Georgian-fronted. Interior comfortable and richly coloured. ££.

Bridgwater Somerset H3
Bristol Hotel, High St. Tel. 8197. A comfortable centrally situated. All bedrooms have private baths. £.

Bristol Avon J2
Unicorn Hotel, Prince St. Tel 294811. Large ultra modern hotel, beautifully situated overlooking the harbour and with views of Clifton Hill. Good restaurant. ££.

Budock Vean Cornwall G10
Budock Vean Hotel, nr Mawnan Smith. Tel Mawnan Smith 288. Well situated with many amenities including golf, tennis and swimming. £££.

Chagford Devon E6
Mill End Hotel, Sandy Park. Tel 2282. This former water mill is in the Dartmoor National Park. Fine period furniture and open fires. Good for families. £. *Closed Nov–Feb.*

Dartmouth Devon F8
Royal Castle Hotel, 11 The Quay. Tel 2397. Bow-fronted and overlooking the quay. Queen Victoria was once a guest. Many nautical curios. ££.

Dunster Somerset F3
Luttrell Arms Hotel, 36 High Street. Tel 555. Has an ancient tradition of hospitality. It began life as a monastic guest house and has been an inn since the 15thC. The former Gothic hall is now the lounge and bar. £.

Exeter Devon F6
Royal Clarence Hotel, Cathedral Yard. Tel 58464. Pleasantly old-world and faces the cathedral. Bedrooms are named after famous West Countrymen. Good restaurant. ££.

Exmouth Devon F6
Devoncourt Hotel, Douglas Avenue. Tel 72277. Has 4 acres of magnificent sub-tropical gardens sloping to the sea-front, and access to the beach. Traditional comfort in the public rooms. £.

Falmouth Cornwall G10
Green Bank Hotel, Green Bank. Tel 312440. This old haunt of Packet skippers has a good traditional atmosphere. It overlooks the harbour and displays model ships, prints and posters in its public rooms. ££.

Hope Cove Devon E8
Cottage Hotel, nr Kingsbridge. Tel Galmpton 555. A cottage which has been extended into a pleasant hotel. Good views of Bigbury Bay. Good English cooking. £. *Closed June.*

Moretonhampstead Devon R6
Manor House Hotel. Tel 355. Set in 200 acres on the edge of Dartmoor; relaxing and spacious. Well cooked food. £££.

Newquay Cornwall　　　　　**G8**
Glendorgal Hotel, Lusty Glaze Rd. Tel 4937.
Situated on a headland above Porth Bay,
this comfortable hotel offers tennis and a
private beach. *££. Closed Oct–mid May.*

Newton Abbot Devon　　　　**F7**
Globe Hotel, Courtenay Street. Tel 4106.
A 'grand' hotel now modernised and well
situated for both business and touring. *£.*

Plymouth Devon　　　　　　**D8**
Duke of Cornwall Hotel, Millbay Rd.
Tel 266256. A Victorian Gothic building
with some views of Drake's Island. Cheerful
and comfortable public rooms. *££.*

St Mawes Cornwall　　　　　**A9**
Hotel Tresanton. Tel 544. Quiet and
sophisticated with flower-decked terraces.
Personal service. *£££. Closed Nov–Feb*
(except Christmas). No children under 12.

Taunton Somerset　　　　　**G4**
Castle Hotel, Castle Green. Tel 2671.
This was once part of the castle and the
Norman section is retained. Large public
rooms are furnished with antiques. Good
service and food. *£££.*

Torquay Devon　　　　　　　**F7**
Imperial Hotel, Park Hill Rd. Tel 24301.
Elegant and modern with numerous
amenities including a sub-tropical garden,
well appointed bedrooms, large public
rooms and excellent views of Torbay. *£££.*

Wells Somerset　　　　　　　**J3**
White Hart Hotel, Sadler St. Tel 72056.
An attractive half-timbered inn situated just
outside the cathedral precincts. Reputedly
the town's oldest inn. *£.*

Weston-super-Mare Somerset　**H2**
Grand Atlantic Hotel, Beach Rd. Tel 26543.
With its own swimming pool this is ideal for
children. Turrets and balconies add to the
character of the building. *££.*

Wilmington Devon　　　　　**G6**
Home Farm Hotel, nr Honiton. Tel 278.
A thatched 16thC farmhouse, which has
been tastfully modernised to enhance the
atmosphere. Restful with attractive
gardens. *£. Closed Jan and early Feb.*

Regional food & drink

Cider
From the Somerset and Devon apple
orchards, draught cider is made and is
available in most pubs. It is deceptively
alcoholic and more bitter than Kentish cider.
Known locally as 'scrumpy'. The making of
it can be seen at Sheppy's Farm, near
Wellington; also Lancaster's Farm at
Felldown Head, near Tavistock.

Clotted Cream
Cream teas are a speciality in Devon and
Cornwall served with scones and strawberry
jam but without butter. The cream (and
good butter) is produced from the South
Devon breed of cattle, rarely seen outside
the West Country. Clotted cream is at its
best bought loose by the pound, but most
shops and some farms provide a postal
service too. Devon cream is very slightly
whiter and runnier than Cornish, which is
very solid.

Cornish Pasty
Traditionally the tin-miners' portable
lunch, which was shaped like a torpedo to
fit in his pocket. It was a balanced meal but
tough enough to survive being dropped
down a mineshaft. Various meats are used,
but mutton is usually mixed with potatoes
and onions and always swedes enclosed in a
pastry which is pinched high along its entire
length. Known locally as 'tiddy-oggies'.
The best are home-made in pubs and shops.

Fish
Lobsters and crabs are available all along
the coast. Start Bay crabs are really superb.
Conger eels are also caught and often made
into pies. Oysters from the Helford River
beds are slightly smaller than the native, but
just as much appreciated.
There is also delicious shellfish like small
scallops called 'Queens'. Fresh mackerel and
pilchards are sold on stalls and barrows and
make excellent eating since they are so fresh.

Locally caught freshwater salmon and trout
at hotels on Dartmoor and Exmoor.

Sally Lunn
A sweet light cake of flour, eggs, yeast and
cream baked in a muffin hoop. Available in
and around Bath.

Stargazey Pie
Pilchards or herrings are the basis of this
local dish. The fish are arranged in a dish
with the tails to the centre and the eyes to
the edge like a cartwheel. The pastry cover
is then cut short so the eyes gaze out.
A Cornish speciality but not easily come by
because of the overfishing of pilchards.

Restaurants

The following indicates the price range for a
meal.
£　　inexpensive
££　　medium priced
£££　　expensive

Bath Avon　　　　　　　　　**K2**
Priory Hotel, Weston Rd. Tel 21887. Quiet,
family-run hotel. Well planned set meals.
English and French. *D. Closed Christmas Sun*
for a week. ££. Book.

Hole in the Wall, 16 George St. Tel 25242.
Serves excellent French cooking from the
converted coal cellar. Friendly service.
LD. Closed D Sun. ££. Book.

Bristol Avon　　　　　　　　**J2**
Harvey's Restaurant, 12 Denmark St.
Tel 27665. Smart cellar next to a wine shop.
Outstanding wines. Cooking mainly French.
LD. Closed L Sat & Sun. ££. Book.

Brixham Devon　　　　　　　**F8**
Randall's Restaurant Français, Harbour.
Tel. 3357. French cooking to high standards.
LD. Closed D Mon & L Mon–Sat. £££.
Book.

Chittlehamholt Devon 86W　**D4**
Highbullen Country House Hotel. Tel 248.
Informal country hotel with outstanding
restaurant. English and French. *LD. Closed*
L Mon–Sat. ££. Book.

Dartmouth Devon　　　　　　**F8**
Carved Angel, 2 South Embankment.
Tel 2465. Beautiful views over the Dart
estuary through the large picture windows.
European cooking. *LD. Closed Mon &*
D Sun. ££. Book.

Doddiscombleigh Devon 90Y　**F6**
Nr. Exeter. Tel Christow 52394. An old
rustic inn right on the edge of Dartmoor.
Mostly French cooking and very friendly
service. *D. Closed Sun & Mon. ££. Book.*

Gulworthy Devon　　　　　　**C7**
Horn of Plenty. Tel Gunnislake 832528.
Individual French cooking to extremely high
standards. Outstanding wines. *LD. Closed*
Thu & L Fri. £££. Book.

Polperro Cornwall　　　　　**B8**
House on Props, The Harbour. Tel 310.
Beautifully situated overlooking the small
fishing harbour. Cordon Bleu cooking and
served in this small 16thC building. *LD.*
Closed Jan & Feb, L Mon–Fri, & D Mon &
Tue Oct–Jan. ££. Book.

St Mawes Cornwall　　　　　**A9**
Rising Sun. Tel 233. Cheerful hotel on the
harbour. Varied set menus, mainly English.
Individual cooking. *LD. Closed mid-Nov–Dec*
££. Book.

Taunton Somerset　　　　　**G4**
Castle Hotel, Castle Green. Tel 2671.
Historic hotel. Sound British cooking. *LD.*
£L. ££D. Book.

Truro Cornwall　　　　　　　**A8**
Roundhouse, 37 St Austell St. Tel 2218.
Pleasant, comfortable restaurant, which
specialises in French and Italian cooking.
LD. Closed Sun. £. Book.

Yeovil Somerset　　　　　　**J5**
Plucknett Hotel Restaurant, 142 Preston St.
Tel 6566. A choice of two rooms, one small
and cosy, the other large and open. Simple
but well prepared food, mainly grills. *LD.*
Closed Sun & L Sat. £.

The Southern Counties 2 and Channel Isles

Six counties and the Isle of Wight and the Channel Islands, all part of the tightly woven historical fabric of southern England. Dorset, still haunted by the spirit of Thomas Hardy, must be one of the loveliest counties. It has a long intriguing coastline and the mysterious Isle of Purbeck, while inland it is rich in stone manor houses sitting serenely on their richly farmed acres.

Hampshire seems less lush especially around the pine and heather lands near Aldershot where the army trains the recruits. But the main part of Hampshire is chalky downland with swift flowing rivers full of trout, and the microcosm of England's countryside is to be found at Selbourne where Gilbert White examined nature in his inimitable way. Gloucestershire and Oxfordshire are all full of towns and villages that grew out of the local stone. Oxfordshire and Berkshire are thick with history – they have grown up around the royal Thames linking learning and majesty to the nations capital. The Channel Islands each have their own style but they are still little bits of England despite their French connections.

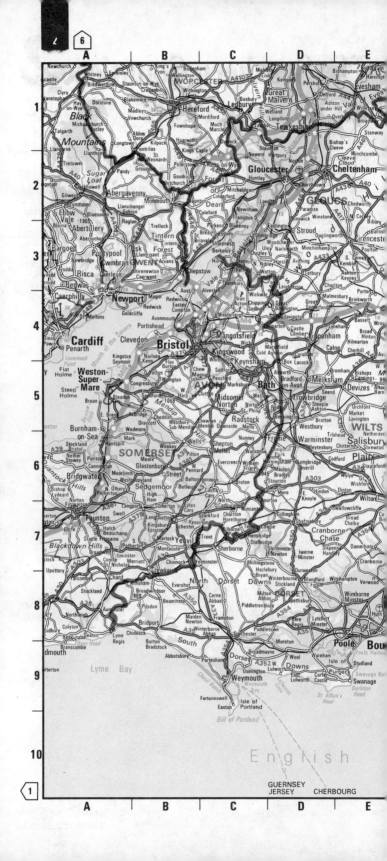

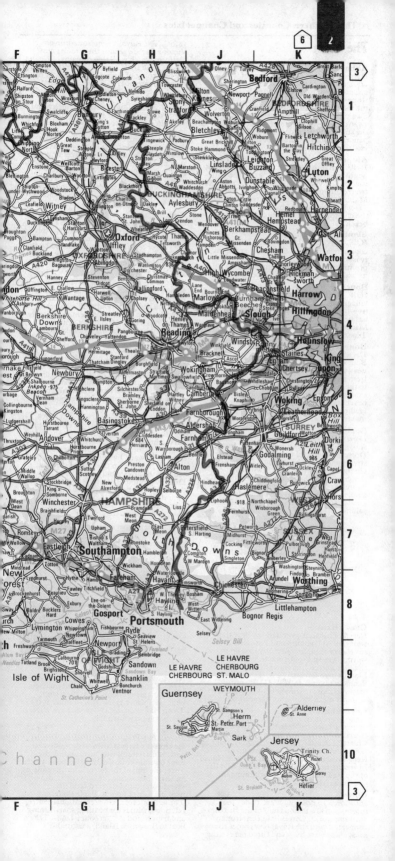

The coast

90F1

Abbotsbury   C9
Dorset. Pop 500. A large village of orange-stoned countenance, which inherited two fine Benedictine legacies: the stone-buttressed Great Tithe Barn built by the monks in the 15thC and the famous Swannery, today housing thousands of swans. Camellias and hydrangeas flourish in the sub-tropical gardens. Splendid panoramic view of the coast from White Hill.

Alum Bay   F9
IOW. From this bay comes one of the most popular souvenirs of a holiday on the island. The variegated sandstone cliffs offer twelve differently coloured sands. Here Marconi made his first radio transmission, a fact commemorated by a memorial stone on the cliff top. Good bathing from sandy beach.

Bembridge   H8
IOW. Pop 3,200. Unexploited by commercial tourism, Bembridge remains reasonably free from invasion. Its prominence as a sailing centre derives from its wide natural harbour. Good bathing.

Bonchurch   H9
IOW. Famous for its natural beauty this old village, with H. de Vere Stacpoole's tree-framed pond and tiny Norman church, has been host to Tennyson, Dickens, Macaulay and Anna Sewell (author of 'Black Beauty').

Bournemouth   E8
Dorset. Pop 147,000. EC Wed, Sat. Bournemouth started as a holiday resort nearly 200 years ago. Its character derives from its hilliness, the chines running down to the sea and the ubiquitous pine trees. The extensive pleasure gardens, superb sandy beaches and excellent entertainment facilities prove most attractive to the holiday maker. Very good bathing.

Bridport   B8
Dorset. Pop 6,400. EC Thur. MD Sat. This straggling brick town is one of the best in Dorset, a beautiful townscape with wide streets and broad pavements. It retains its Georgian ambience. The town hall, designed by William Tyler, and the 15thC church are particularly worth visiting. About a mile south lies West Bay, offering two good bathing beaches. Fishing and sailing.

West Bay: Bridport, Dorset

Chesil Bank   C9
Dorset. This sixteen-mile-long blue clay reef connects Abbotsbury and Portland. A huge sea wall of shingle constantly cast up by stormy seas and south-westerly gales encloses a stretch of water known as the Fleet (where Barnes Wallis tested his 'bouncing bomb' in WW II). Plentiful mackerel close to the shore. Treacherous currents make swimming hazardous.

Christchurch   E8
Hants. Pop 31,000. EC Wed. This old monastic town between the estuaries of the rivers Avon and Stour has a splendid priory, situated behind Christchurch Quay, built by the Saxons, with later additions up to Renaissance times. Nearby is the Red House Museum, housing examples of the wild life of the area. Sand and safe swimming in Christchurch Bay.

Cowes   G8
IOW. Pop 19,000. EC Wed. Today the internationally-famous hub of the British yachting world, Cowes has been strongly connected with the Royal Navy since the great ships were built and fitted here in the 18thC. The Royal Yacht Squadron on Victoria Parade retains the circular gun platform which is all that remains of Cowes Castle, built by Henry VIII. Cowes Week at the beginning of August is the peak of the May to September yacht-racing season. East Cowes is the centre of the hovercraft industry.
For those inclining towards Victoriana rather than yachts, Osborne House is only a mile away. Prince Albert conceived the design as an Italian villa, in close collaboration with Thomas Cubitt. After Queen Victoria's death here in 1901, the house was given to the nation, who in regular droves visit the state and private apartments, and the Royal playhouse known as the Swiss Cottage, which houses in miniature everything from portraits and royal garden tools to stuffed peacocks and crocodiles. Shingle beaches, some swimming.

Hamble   G7
Hants. Pop 3,000. Although it has been a popular yachting centre for decades, this village is still appealingly unpretentious. The old village centre can be approached by the waterside walk. Try some of the local crab and lobster. Marshy foreshore.

Hayling Island   H8
Hants. Pop 13,200. EC Wed. This four-mile-square island of flat fields and straggling hamlets is between the waters of Hangstone and Chichester harbours. The object of intensive seaside development in the early 1930s, it is a popular holiday centre. Excellent beach. Sailing, sea fishing.

Lulworth Cove   D9
Dorset. Pop 1,300. EC Wed. This famous beauty spot in West Lulworth is much frequented by tourists. The three-mile-long bay, almost enclosed by the surrounding cliffs, offers splendid bathing facilities. Nearby is Durdle Door, a natural limestone arch jutting right out to sea. A good place to collect fossils.

Lyme Regis   A8
Dorset. Pop 3,400. EC Thur. This one-time port lies sheltered by The Cobb, an ancient, curved breakwater, which creates a small artificial harbour. It has existed since the reign of Edward I when Lyme was granted its royal title. The museum houses many relics of the attempted rebellion by the Duke of Monmouth in 1685. Fine views from the Golden Cap (617 feet), the highest cliff in southern England. Sailing and water-skiing from Lyme Bay. Some sandy beaches at low tide.

Lyme Regis, Dorset.

Newtown   G8
IOW. Today this romantic, pretty village, the most ancient borough of the island, belies its former glory. Only a small 17thC Town Hall remains. Oyster-fishing. Sandy beaches at Newtown Bay.

Poole   E8
Dorset. Pop 111,000. EC Wed. Poole is by far Dorset's largest town with residential and industrial suburbs surrounding the huge 60-mile-round natural harbour which forms the hub of the town. The quayside is an attractive setting for the busy trading vessels, shipbuilding yards and the manufacture of famous Poole Pottery.
The harbour forms the recreational centre, offering facilities for boating, shark fishing and trips round the harbour islands. Take a boat to Brownsea Island, a naturalist's

haven protected by the National Trust, offering splendid views of the Dorset coast. Poole Bay has long beaches of firm white sand.

Portland Bill   C9
Dorset. The Bill projects from the narrow, rugged length of limestone known as the Isle of Portland. The inhabitants of this dramatic land which is devoid of almost all vegetation are a race unto themselves. An impressive lighthouse on the Bill is a popular haunt for bird watchers. Famous Portland Stone was quarried here for St Paul's Cathedral. Good bathing from Church Ope Cove.

Portsmouth   H8
Hants. Pop 200,000. EC Mon, Wed, Thur. MD Fri, Sat. The visitor should first drive to Portsmouth Heights to view a vast panorama of dockyards and military bases. Resolute penetration through tedious miles of 19thC terraced cottages toward the Guildhall and Old Portsmouth will be much rewarded. Nelson's perfectly preserved 18thC oaken flagship the 'Victory' is essential viewing. The residential district of Southsea still retains an Edwardian seaside charm, complete with old paddle steamers, chugging across the blue Solent water to the Isle of Wight. Sand and shingle beaches.

Ryde   H8
IOW. Pop 23,200. EC Thur. Overlooking the Solent, Ryde is the principal point of entry to the island. A thoroughly modern resort whose streets clamber up Ashley Down. Unremarkable architecturally, the town is popular with holidaymakers, with its good entertainment facilities for all the family. Five miles of sandy beaches.

Sandown   H9
IOW. Pop 16,000. EC. Wed. A flourishing holiday resort, commanding golden miles of sand between Culver Cliff and Luccombe Chine. It owes much of its popularity to the excellent sandy beaches, the amusement parks and the mile-long Esplanade, well furnished with every kind of traditional seaside entertainment.

Seaview   H8
IOW. Pop 1,300. EC Thur. Situated on a small promontory at the north-eastern corner of the island, Seaview is noted for its prawns and lobsters. A favourite resort for a spot of peace. Good bathing, from sandy beaches.

Shanklin   H9
IOW. Pop 16,000. EC Wed. Cliff-top hotels overlook this elegant town. Here Keats wrote part of 'Endymion'. Shanklin Chine and the Crab Hotel in the Old Village are particular tourist attractions. Sheltered sandy beaches. Golf and sea-fishing.

Southampton   G7
Hants. Pop 212,000. EC Mon, Wed, Thur. Despite extensive devastation during the Second World War, Southampton is rapidly establishing itself as a regional capital of an important part of England. Maintaining its pre-eminence as a passenger port, it is also a commercial and industrial centre with a modern university and an impressive Civic Centre. There is an historically interesting walk along the ancient city walls and many riverside walks. Sand and shingle beach at nearby Lepe.

Ventnor   H9
IOW. Pop 7,000. EC Wed. Older yet more discreet than its later rivals this resort is noted for its climate and continental appearance. The esplanade is not long but holiday visitors are well catered for. Ventnor is sheltered by St Boniface Down, the highest point on the Island (785 feet). Fine sheltered walks can be taken along the six miles of the Undercliff, westwards towards the lighthouse at St Catherine's Point. Sandy beaches.

Weymouth   C9
Dorset. Pop 42,000. EC Wed. MD Sat. A jolly seaside town which became fashionable in the 18thC among the rich and royal sea-bathers. An elegant promenade of Georgian and early Victorian houses with a statue of George III in the centre. Safe bathing and sandy beaches.

Yarmouth   F8
IOW. Pop 1,000. EC Wed. This cheery small harbour, ever busy with island visitors arriving by ferry, has a wildly continental ambience. A 16thC castle is a focal point of historical and architectural interest. Steep sand and shingle beach.

Yarmouth, Isle of Wight.

The Channel Islands

Five very different islands all trying to keep their individual qualities and all engrossed in keeping up appearances for the tourist. Although the Channel Islands are the nearest bit of Britain to France, they are deeply English with a slight continental veneer.
There are plenty of air services from London and other airports to Jersey and Guernsey, and the Sealink ferries carry cars and passengers from Weymouth. The climate is sunny and frosts are rare. Cigarettes, perfume and spirits are duty free.

Jersey   K10
The largest of the Channel Islands with a stunning coastline, superb sands and a rich assortment of places to stay.
All along the north coast the cliff scenery is splendid; a good inland route makes a change along the Route du Nord leading to St John. Don't miss Bouley Bay among the wooded hills, and, inland, Gerald Durrell's delightful zoo.
On the south coast Gorey is a bright little fishing village dominated by the mighty Mont Orguil Castle. Visit the pottery.
St Aubin's Bay has over three miles of sands with safe bathing linked by the coast road to St Helier. Superb walk to the rocks at Corbière along the old rail track. Shingle beaches at Belcroute Bay, overhung by trees and deep cut out of the red rock; a good beach at Portelet Bay.
St Brelade's Bay. If you had to choose the best beach in Jersey, this would be it. A fine two-mile sweep of sand – with small hotels among the pines. Good bathing, boating, water skiing.
St Helier is the main town and port with some modern development. The old quarter round the harbour with its covered market is the best part to wander around, and at night there is dancing, cabaret and night clubs. The Napoleonic fortifications at Fort Regent are now converted into an entertainment centre with swimming pools, squash courts and a solarium.
St Ouen's Bay is on the west and full of bouncing breakers ideal for surfing – there's five miles of sand backed by grass and duneland.

Guernsey   J9
You fly in over acres of greenhouses where Guernsey tomatoes are grown in the north of the island, and to the south-west the green hills with their cliffs drop down to magnificent beaches.
The best surfing is at Vazon Bay with its vast stretches of sand. Rock pools are fun for the children at Cobo and in the north the silver sands at L'Ancress make an ideal sheltered family beach.
In Guernsey the hotels tend not to be right on the beaches and the local buses are the most efficient local transport to the sea. A picnic lunch and a whole day by the sea is very much the Guernsey pattern.

Fermain Bay. Lying south of St Peter Port, the bay has a fine Martello Tower and wooded cliffs.

Petit Bot is a popular southern bay reached down a winding lane; at low tide there's plenty of fine sand.

St Peter Port, the capital, tumbles down the hillside, all grey and white until the town stops on the waterfront, at the spectacular harbour full of yachts and inter-island boats. Beaches are good and on a rare dull day you can spend hours in the covered French-style market.

Alderney   K9
A mere quarter of an hour from Guernsey in one of Aurigny's tiny butterfly planes, and you can be on this simple and unspoilt island. Only three and a half miles long and a mile or so wide, it's a peaceful paradise if you like the sea, cliffs and sea birds.
Miles of cliff and beach walks; on the eastern and northern side of the island are several good safe beaches of rock and fine sand: Longy Bay, Corblets Bay, Safe Bay and Brayne Bay.
St Anne is the only town – cobbled streets, an attractive church and some 15thC buildings around Marais Square. Lots of the houses in St Anne have been discreetly converted by exiles from England.

Sark   J10
Small, secret and still supervised by the Dame of Sark from the Seigneurie. This small island is reached by the sturdy steamer. No motor traffic is allowed. Perfect escape if you like stiff walks and exploring coves and caves. A haven that really does offer the visitor complete refuge from the 20thC.

Herm   J9
Take a twenty minute ride by motor launch from St Peter Port, Guernsey, to this tiny, enchanted island. Within its one and a half mile length the scenery changes from steep cliffs and bracken-covered hills in the south, to duneland and long sandy beaches towards the north. Shell Beach and Belvoir Bay are the popular beaches, leaving the rest of the island to more intrepid explorers.

Inland towns and villages

Banbury   G1
Oxon. Pop 31,000. EC Tue. MD Tue, Sat. Immortalised in nursery rhyme and famous for its original spiced cakes, this quaint town is now a thriving industrial centre. Much of the original Banbury including the cross itself has disappeared. The present cross is only one hundred years old.

Bibury   E3
Glos. Pop 700. In the Coln Valley the road runs into the pretty village of Bibury. At right angles to the river stands a row of stone-built weavers' cottages, Arlington Row, now the property of the National Trust. A partly Saxon church stands next to 17thC Bibury Court.

Blandford Forum   D8
Dorset. Pop 3,700. EC Wed. MD Thur. Set on the River Stour, this town is now mainly Georgian, older buildings having been eradicated by a series of fires. The church of SS Peter and Paul and the Town Hall are particularly fine period buildings.

Bourton-on-the-Water   E2
Glos. Pop 2,250. EC Sat. Literally 'on-the-water' – the Windrush flows right through the centre of this beautiful village. The picturesque low-arched bridges only just clear the water. The broad village green lying parallel to the river extends to the south where it is flanked by Cotswold stone houses. Now nearly spoilt as a centre for tourists. It features an inland marine aquarium, a collection of tropical birds and the famous model village.

Bradford-on-Avon   D5
Wilts. Pop 8,000. EC Wed, Sat. This pleasant town has the fine Saxon church of St Lawrence. The 12thC parish church houses the earliest English Bible used in a church–a reprint in 1572 of the 1568 Bishop' Bible. The Tithe Barn now houses a museum of Wiltshire agricultural implements.

Burford   F2
Oxon. Pop 1,400. EC Wed. A Cotswold stone village that has retained its quiet beauty. Visit the unusual Norman church which now has a spire and is decorated with good carvings. In the Tolsey (old toll house) there is a museum which illustrates the history of England as it affected a small country town. The quietly flowing Windrush River is crossed by a narrow, three-arched stone bridge.

Burford, Oxfordshire

Castle Combe   D4
Wilts. Pop 500. EC Tue, Sat. A splendid village with a 15thC market cross at its centre. The Manor House dates from 1664. Recently famous as a film setting for a typical English village in 'Dr Doolittle'.

Castle Combe : Wiltshire

Cheltenham   D2
Glos. Pop 76,000. EC Wed. MD Thur. An air of refined graciousness pervades this quiet residential Regency town. Cheltenham's former popularity as a spa was established by George III. Today, it is a prosperous commercial and educational centre, long associated with sport and the arts, though the waters can still be taken at the Pump Room in Pittville Park, an elegant building ideally situated amidst flower displays and specimen trees. The broad, tree-lined Promenade is an excellent shopping centre.

The Promenade : Cheltenham

Chipping Campden   E1
Glos. Pop 2,000. EC Thur, Sat. The most northerly of the Cotswold towns and probably the most beautiful architecturally. Its early prosperity owed much to the patronage of a wealthy wool merchant at whose expense the striking parish church was built, with a fine 120-foot high tower. The finest building though is the 17thC Market Hall.

Chipping Norton   F1
Oxon. Pop. 4,800. EC Thur. MD Wed. An abundance of old Cotswold houses adorns the highest town in the county (700 feet). Hospitable coaching inns, for example the Crown and the White Hart, still offer rest and refreshment to the visitor.

Cirencester   E3
Glos. Pop 14,500. EC Thur. MD Fri. In Roman times, as Corinium, this was Britain's second largest town, and a major strategic and trading centre. Hence the wealth of Roman remains – a never-ending source of joy to all itinerant archaeologists. A unique attraction is the direct access from the town to Earl Bathurst's vast 18thC landscaped park, with its central broad avenue, bordered by chestnuts.

Cookham　　　　　　　　　　　　　**J4**
Berks. Pop 5,500. EC Wed, Thur.
Immortalised by Sir Stanley Spencer,
whose paintings may be seen in the old village
hall. Cookham represents all that is best in
Thames-side villages.

Corsham　　　　　　　　　　　　　**D4**
Wilts. Pop 10,000. EC Wed. A pleasing
village with an interesting restored church –
St Bartholomew's – and many attractive
houses. Of note is Corsham Court, an
Elizabethan mansion with Georgian
embellishments, and parkland laid out by
Capability Brown.

Dorchester　　　　　　　　　　　　**C8**
Dorset. Pop 13,800. EC Thur. MD Wed. A
truly historic town with antecedents in the
stone, bronze, and iron ages. King John
used it as a hunting centre and in 1685,
Judge Jeffreys held his 'Bloody Assizes'
here. Much loved and written of by Thomas
Hardy, Dorchester has a county museum, a
military museum and an interesting old
Shire Hall.

Dorchester-on-Thames　　　　　　　**H3**
Oxon. A large village that still has the air of
distinction appropriate to one of the oldest
English cities. The large abbey church is
worth seeing for its Decorated architecture;
in the Jesse window behind the altar the
stonework and glass reach new heights of
curvy splendour. The recumbent figure of
a knight, probably carved in 1300, has a
very modern feel. Good antique shops in
the main street.

Farringford　　　　　　　　　　　　**F8**
IOW. The home of Tennyson for many
years, the house is now a hotel. Here he
wrote 'Maud', 'Enoch Arden' and the
'Idylls of the King'.

Gloucester　　　　　　　　　　　　**D2**
Glos. Pop 90,100. EC Thur. MD Mon, Sat.
Now a busy manufacturing centre, its
earlier pre-eminence as an inland port was
created by the construction of the canal
between Gloucester and Sharpness in 1827.
The city is cruciform in design, with four
main 'gate' streets, preserving an abundance
of historical features.

Godshill　　　　　　　　　　　　　**G9**
IOW. Pop 1,400. EC Sat. A very well kept
high village on the road to Ventnor,
popular for delicious cream teas. The early
15thC church has great charm and fine
detail. Nearby is Appuldurcombe House,
now a preserved Palladian shell set in gardens
laid out by Capability Brown.

Goring　　　　　　　　　　　　　　**H4**
Oxon. Pop 2,100. This village lies in the gap
cut through the Chilterns by the Thames;
the deep valley of hanging woods gives the
river a dramatic setting. The church at
Goring is worth a special visit for its
Norman tower, old bell (1290), and two
good brasses.

Henley-on-Thames　　　　　　　　　**H4**
Oxon. Pop 11,400. EC Wed. MD Thur. This
market town really comes to life in the first
week of July when the famous regatta is held
on the river. Henley has an air of slightly
pompous prosperity in the centre; the
superbly elegant 18thC bridge has a carved
head of Father Thames looking downstream,
and a similar head of Isis looking upstream.
Fishing and boating.

Hurley　　　　　　　　　　　　　　**J4**
Berks. Pop 2,000. EC Wed. A pleasant
riverside village complete with half-timbered
houses and Norman church. A good spot to
hire a punt and wander down the Thames.
Full of calm riverside beauty, now a haunt
of the rich.

Lacock　　　　　　　　　　　　　　**D4**
Wilts. Pop 1,400. EC Mon. A fine village
with 15th-18thC houses. The church of St
Cyriac has 14thC origins, and Lacock
Abbey was founded in 1229 for Augustinian
canonesses. It later became the centre
where William Talbot laid the foundations
of modern photography.

Maidenhead　　　　　　　　　　　　**J4**
Berks. Pop 48,300. EC Thur. MD Fri. Now a
commuters' town, but in an unrivalled
setting on this beautiful stretch of the

Thames. Close by are the beechwoods of
Cliveden, the famous Boulter's Lock, and
the village of Taplow. Maidenhead looks
best from the river and it is a good place to
shop. Note the unusual modern library.

Marlborough　　　　　　　　　　　**F4**
Wilts. Pop 6,000. EC Wed. MD Wed, Sat.
Renowned for its long and wide High Street,
this is the home of the famous public school.
A good centre for visiting the Savernake
Forest.

Marlborough, Wiltshire

Milton Abbas　　　　　　　　　　　**D8**
Dorset. Pop 600. EC Wed. A very pretty,
mostly thatched village built in the 17thC
by the first Earl of Dorchester to replace the
market town of Milton Abbas which was
demolished as it spoilt his Lordship's view.
The abbey was founded in 935, but the
present building dates from the 15thC.

Milton Abbas: Dorset

Moreton-in-Marsh　　　　　　　　　**F1**
Glos. Pop 2,500. EC Wed. The Roman
Fosse Way runs straight through the centre
of this cosy, small, wool town, which is now
the administrative centre of the North
Cotswolds. Nearby is the Four Shires Stone,
which until 1931 marked the intersection of
the boundaries of Gloucestershire,
Warwickshire, Oxfordshire and
Worcestershire.

Newport　　　　　　　　　　　　　**G8**
IOW. Pop 22,300. EC Thur. MD Tue. The
island's capital and main harbour, at the
head of the tidal estuary of the River
Medina. The town's charter dates from the
12thC and it retains much of its former
character. Charles I was held in exile here.
The Guildhall, erected in 1816, was
designed by John Nash. To the north of
Newport lies Parkhurst Forest, the island's
only significant belt of woods, near the
prison.

Oxford　　　　　　　　　　　　　　**G3**
Oxon. Pop 114,000. A beautiful city and
university. The main cross road in the city
centre is known as Carfax; in the centre is
the tower that was once part of St Martin's
Church. Climb up to the top, and amongst
the spires of Oxford you get a good idea of
the layout of the town.
Just opposite St Aldates Street is the main
gate (Tom Tower) of Christ Church, with
Oxford's largest college quadrangle. Christ
Church Hall (1529) is one of the loveliest
in the University, lined with solemn
portraits of distinguished alumni. Don't
miss the new art gallery at Christ Church.
Close by the hall is the entrance to the
cathedral which is also the college chapel.
Along Merton Street is Corpus Christi
College (1517), with its amazing sun-dial

River Isis at Oxford.

Radcliffe Camera: Oxford.

S. Mary: Oxford.

in the quad. A tiny street between Corpus and Merton colleges takes you to Christ Church-Meadow, a glorious green space that lies between the River Thames, the colleges, and the busy High Street. Merton College's statutes go back to 1264 and the college has the oldest library in England. It still keeps some of its books chained.
Near the end of Merton Street is the Botanic Garden, and a rose garden commemorating the research workers who discovered the importance of penicillin. Opposite is Magdalen College with its glorious tower where Oxford choristers greet May Day from the roof. Magdalen must be the only college in the world to have its own deer park. Along the High Street you pass Queen's, All Souls, and University colleges. Take a special look at Brasenose College which has a subtle modern court which blends perfectly with the ancient fabric. New College was founded in 1379 and has a particularly fine chapel. Through a gateway at the end of New College Lane is the Sheldonian Theatre built in 1669 by Sir Christopher Wren and surrounded by giant sculpted heads of Roman emperors. It is used for university ceremonies and concerts. Behind the Sheldonian is the Divinity School (c1427-90), a rare, perfect example of 15thC Perpendicular architecture.

Sedilia: Merton Couege, Oxford.

Sedilia:
S Mary, Oxford.

Along Broad Street is Blackwell's world renowned bookshop; next to it is Trinity, a college with some unusual modern buildings. Balliol, Jesus (where Lawrence of Arabia was an undergraduate), Exeter and Lincoln colleges are all worth visiting.
There are so many treasures in Oxford that you will have to return; don't miss the Victorian red-brick splendours of Keble, or the cool modern academicism of St Catherine's College, designed by the Danish architect Arne Jacobsen. Oxford is more than just its buildings, it is a city with a unique atmosphere of learning and pleasure. Glide slowly down the Thames in a punt on a lazy summer afternoon and you could be in a beautiful dream.

Oxford

Paradise   **D2**
Glos. Just north of Painswick on the Cheltenham Road lies this charming hamlet, named by Charles I. Complete with the Adam and Eve Inn, it lies parallel to the beautiful Slad Valley.

Romsey   **F7**
Hants. Pop 10,100. EC Wed. Set in the heart of the New Forest, this market town has a fine Abbey church founded as a nunnery in the 10thC. Also of interest is King John's House, a 13thC hunting lodge with good carving.

Salisbury   **E6**
Wilts. Pop 36,400. EC Wed. MD Tue, Sat. A truly splendid cathedral town, with numerous fine buildings, especially in the Cathedral Close. The Salisbury and South Wiltshire Museum houses most of the objects found during excavations of nearby Stonehenge.

Selborne   **H6**
Hants. Pop 1,000. EC Wed. The home of Gilbert White, the naturalist, this pleasant place houses his museum and the Oates Memorial Museum. The church of St Mary was restored by White's great-nephew in the 19thC.

Sherborne   **C7**
Dorset. Pop 9,300. EC Wed. MD Thur. A fine country town housing an abbey, a school founded by Edward VI, two castles and a thriving dairy industry, Sherborne Castle was built by Sir Walter Raleigh, and in 1688 William of Orange made his Proclamation from it.

Stow-on-the-Wold   **F2**
Glos. Pop 1,800. EC Wed. Delightfully rural, this one-time centre of the wool industry grew in geographical significance in the middle ages. Several features of historical interest remain – the old market cross and stocks stand in the market square, just east of Fosse Way. Important annual horse fairs. Good antique shops.

Streatley   **H4**
Berks. Pop 800. Intact and unspoilt, discreetly Georgian, possessing a unique village hall converted from a 19thC malthouse. Ascent of Streatley Hill will afford a fine vista towards the Thames.

Stroud   **D3**
Glos. Pop 19,100. EC Thur. MD Sat. The largest town in this Southern Cotswold region, Stroud is an important business centre. Situated in the main valley of the River Frome, it has since Tudor times been noted for its fine quality cloth. The characteristically steep, narrow streets are disappearing in the course of urban redevelopment.

Tewkesbury   **D1**
Glos. Pop 8,800. EC Thur. MD Wed, Sat. The construction of the M5 motorway has relieved this ancient town of much congestion and noise. Strategically sited at the confluence of the rivers Avon and Severn, it was the scene of a Yorkist victory in 1471, when many Lancastrians were massacred in a field known to this day as 'Bloody Field'. Narrow alleyways, Elizabethan timber-framed houses and ancient inns are all dominated by the massive 12thC abbey church.

Tewkesbury

Wantage   **G3**
Berks. Pop 8,000. EC Thur. MD Wed, Sat. Once notorious for dubious bloodsports and nefarious activities, Wantage has now become respectable. The birthplace of

Alfred the Great, commemorated by a noble statue in the market square. Once a sheep-trading centre. The entrances to the alms-houses have been paved with sheep's knuckle-bones. More bones (human) and tombs to be found in the 13thC church of SS Peter and Paul.

Whippingham G8
IOW. A Victorian shrine closely associated with Queen Victoria and Prince Albert., The church, which Albert helped to design, was attended by the royal family during their stays at Osborne.

Winchester G6
Hants. Pop 31,000. EC Thur. MD Mon. This was King Alfred's capital, but it dates from pre-Roman times. Set at the beginning of the Pilgrims' Way, the town is full of interest, including its castle, cathedral, the Royal Green Jacket Museum, the West Gate Museum, and Winchester College.

Windsor J4
Berks. Pop 30,000. EC Wed. MD Sat. Although overshadowed by the great royal castle, the town of Windsor asserts an individual dignity. Wren's Guildhall exhibits rare paintings and a history of Windsor. Across the Thames lie the playing fields of Eton College, founded in 1440.

Windsor Castle.

Hill figures

You get a strong feeling of the presence of early man in this region, not just earthworks but huge men and creatures formed in the chalk.

Alton Barnes Horse E5
Wilts. 1 mile n of Alton Barnes. A sleek, chalk-white creature with slim legs and head, poised for a quick canter above the Vale of Pewsey. 162 feet long.

Cerne Abbas Giant C8
Giant Hill, Dorset. ½ mile nw of Cerne Abbas. This naked figure wielding a mighty caveman's club is thought to be a fertility symbol. Above on the hilltop is the enclosure where the rites of spring were performed on May Day. 180 feet high and 45 feet wide.

Cherhill Horse E4
Wilts. 4 miles e of Calne, nr Cherhill. A fine figure of a white horse with a noble eye four feet in diameter, and once inlaid with up-turned bottles. Souvenir-hunters had carried away the bottles by 1872. 140 feet across.

Laverstock Panda E6
Wilts. 1 mile n of Salisbury off A30. In honour of the union (unsuccessful) between Chi-Chi and An-An at the London Zoo this cuddly panda head mysteriously made its appearance at Laverstock in 1969. 55 feet by 40 feet.

Pewsey New Horse E5
Wilts. 12 miles s of Pewsey. Last of the Wiltshire horses, the trotting figure seems to be heading cautiously along Pewsey Hill. 65 feet long, and cut in 1937 to commemorate the coronation of George VI.

Uffington White Horse F3
Berks. 2 miles s of Uffington. Popular legend has it that the white horse is associated with

King Alfred's victory over the Danes in 871. Probably dates from 100BC; 360 feet long. Some say it's not a horse but a dragon.

Westbury Horse D5
Wilts. 1 mile sw of Bretton. Soft-eyed creature with a long tail. The original dated from the 18thC and was transformed by a Mr Gee in 1778, which act earned him the title of 'vandal'. 182 feet long.

Woolbury Horse G6
Hants. 2 miles e of Stockbridge. A small, frail figure believed to represent the mount of a local 18thC highwayman who plied the Winchester-Salisbury road. 27 feet long; outlined with rough flints.

Osmington Horse, nr Weymouth.

Famous people

Jane Austen (1775-1817) H6
Jane Austen's Home, Chawton, Hants. The author lived here 1809-17, and most of her novels, including 'Emma' and 'Persuasion', were written or rewritten in the general sitting room where the creaking swing door could warn of any approaching intruders. The red-brick house is now a museum of personal relics. *Open 11.00-16.30 daily. Closed Mon & Tue Nov-late Mar.*

Charles Dickens (1812-70) H8
393 Commercial Rd, Mile End, Portsmouth, Hants. Dickens was born here. Now restored and furnished in the style of the period. *Open 10.00-17.30 daily.*

Thomas Hardy (1840-1927) C8
Hardy's Cottage, Higher Bockhampton, Dorset. 3 miles ne of Dorchester. Wherever you turn in Wessex it is certain that Hardy was there, and has written about it. Waterston Manor, west of Puddletown, was Bathsheba's home in 'Far from the Madding Crowd'. Bere Regis is the Kingsbere of 'Tess of the d'Urbervilles', Bournemouth is Sandbourne, and Salisbury is Melchester. The small thatched cottage smothered in greenery and set in an acre of gardens at Higher Bockhampton is where Hardy was born. The study from his house at Max Gate has been reconstructed in the Dorset County Museum, Dorchester. *Cottage exterior open 13.00-18.00 Mar-late Oct. Interior by written appointment with the tenant.*

Victor Hugo (1802-85) J9
Hauteville House, 38 Hauteville St Peter Port, Guernsey, C.I. Victor Hugo lived here. Now a museum devoted to his relics, furniture, tapestries and china. *Open 10.00-16.30 (Closed Thur afternoon, Sun & B.Hols) Apr-late Sep.*

Richard Jefferies (1848-87) E4
Coate Farm, Swindon, Wilts. The son of a Wiltshire farmer, the naturalist and novelist was born in this house, not far from the ancient Ridgeway path which Jefferies featured in so many of his writings. The house is now a museum and contains manuscripts, first editions and personal items. *Open 14.00-17.00 Wed & Sat Oct-Mar & Wed, Sat & Sun Apr-Sep.*

T. E. Lawrence (1888-1935) D8
Clouds Hill, nr Wareham, Dorset. About the time Lawrence of Arabia enlisted in the Royal Tank Corps in 1923, he leased a derelict cottage, Clouds Hill, which he rebuilt and later described as being 'alone in

a dip in the moor, very quiet, very lonely, very bare . . . I don't sleep here, but come out 16.30 till 21.00 nearly every evening, and dream, or write or read by the fire, or play Beethoven and Mozart to myself in the box'.
Open 14.00–18.00 Apr–late Sep (12.00–16.00 Oct–late Mar).

Bradford-on-Avon, Wiltshire.

Catherine Parr (1512–48)   **E1**
Sudeley Castle, Glos. ½ mile s of Winchcombe off A46. This was the home of Henry VIII's sixth wife after his death and her marriage to Thomas Seymour. The castle was given to Seymour by a grant of the council. Catherine died there after giving birth to her first child. A picturesque window in the old building belongs to the room still called 'Queen Catherine's nursery'. *Open 12.00–17.30 daily.*

Stanley Spencer (1891–1959)   **J4**
King's Hall, Cookham-on-Thames, Berks. Collection devoted to the paintings, drawings and personal effects of Spencer, who was born in Cookham. *Open 10.30–18.30 Mon–Fri Apr–Oct. 11.00–17.00 Sat & Sun only Nov–Mar.*

Gilbert White (1720–93)   **H6**
The Wakes, Selborne, Hants. The home of naturalist and author of 'The Natural History of Selborne', Gilbert White. White was born in The Wakes, and died there. The 17thC house set in 29 acres is now a museum with 40,000 volumes on natural history and polar explorations in the library, and personal relics of White and Antarctic explorer Captain Oates. *Open 14.00–17.00 Sat & Sun Nov–Mar. 10.30–12.30 daily Apr–Oct. (Closed Fri & Sun morning.)*

Cathedrals, abbeys and churches

Christ Church   **E8**
Christchurch, Hants. The Priory was founded in 1150 in what was then called Twineham. Reputed to be the longest parish church in England, measuring 312 feet, the choir and towers date from the 15thC, the nave is Norman.

Gloucester Cathedral   **D2**
Gloucester, Glos. Approaching the city from the west or from the dock you always see the perpendicular tower of the cathedral. This tower was built around 1450, the last major addition to the cathedral founded in 1089 apart from the Lady Chapel which completed the rebuilding in 1499. Inside note the giant round piers in the nave, and the great stone vault at the east end that frames the curtain wall of mediaeval glass.

Oxford Cathedral   **G3**
Oxford, Oxon. Now a part of Christ Church College, but still the city's cathedral, it is a great Norman church topped by the 13thC spire. It has a solid air which has survived the rigorous Victorian improvements. Sir Gilbert Scott was responsible in the 1870s for the new east rose window and the arcade. There is glass from the 14th and 17thC and a fine 17thC organ.

St George's Chapel   **J4**
Windsor, Berks. The chapel of the Order of the Garter, decorated with feudal banners, dates from the 15thC and is vaulted and elaborately decorated, with a 19thC sculpture of a bare-breasted Princess of Wales by M. C. Wyatt.

St John the Baptist   **E3**
Cirencester, Glos. A 14thC 'wool' church with a three-storey porch which was at one time the Town Hall. The nave is of great height, and the wine-glass pulpit dates from 1450.

St Laurence   **D5**
Bradford-on-Avon, Wilts. This tiny church dates from before the Norman invasion of England, possibly late 7thC. Its height is only slightly greater than its length. By the 19thC it was used as both a cottage and a school, but it is now restored to a chapel again.

St Mary the Virgin   **E3**
Fairford, Glos. A church which is renowned for its 15thC stained glass windows, made by Henry VIII's master glass painter, Barnard Flower. The complete series of 28 illustrations represents the Christian story from Creation to Last Judgment.

St Mary the Virgin   **G3**
Iffley, Oxon. A famous 12thC church with two Norman arches and an early English sanctuary. Altogether a very fine building.

St Michael and All Angels   **H3**
Rycote, Oxon. A 15thC chapel frequented by Charles I and Queen Elizabeth when they visited the area. The interior has 15thC benches and 17thC family and royal pews. The altar piece and communion plate are also 17thC.

Salisbury Cathedral   **E6**
Salisbury, Wilts. Unique in Britain because this cathedral is the only one built as a single conception. Foundation stones were laid in 1220 and 60 years later the cathedral was complete; the only addition being the great 404-foot spire, in 1334.
The building is in complete harmony with its site, partly because it is built of Chilmark stone which was quarried only twelve miles away. Inside total perfection and a certain austerity comes from the regular consistency of dark Purbeck marble shafts and lancet windows. The Lady Chapel is where the Purbeck shafts are at their most attenuated – here the cathedral has an abstract, modern feel.

Salisbury Cathedral.

Sherborne Abbey Church   **C7**
Sherborne, Dorset. A former Benedictine foundation, now a parish church, with a Saxon doorway and Great Tom – a tower bell decorated by Cardinal Wolsey. The fan vaulting is very fine; monuments include those of the 13thC abbots.

SS Peter and Paul   **D8**
Blandford Forum, Dorset. John Bastard designed and built this fine church following the 1731 fire which destroyed much of the town. It is Georgian in style in ashlar with a square tower – an interesting period church.

Wimborne Minster   **E8**
Wimborne, Dorset. A twin-towered church which dates from Norman times. The choir stalls are Jacobean and there is a 15thC Flemish glass window. The astronomical clock in the west tower dates from 1320 and shows the sun and moon rotating around the earth.

Winchester Cathedral   **G6**
Winchester, Hants. The longest cathedral in Europe, started in 1070 when Winchester was capital of England. It was one of the richest sees in England during the middle ages and the powerful William of Wykeham enriched his cathedral by adding a veneer of the Perpendicular style on the Norman base (1371–1400). Apart from having the longest nave in Europe (560 feet), Winchester has the largest Early English retro-choir in England.

Castles and ruins

Berkeley Castle   C3
Avon. Off A38 between Bristol and Gloucester. A long range of mostly 14thC buildings that date from a remodelling of the castle in 1350 on the 12thC foundations. This is one of the oldest inhabited castles in England, still lived in by genuine Berkeleys. Don't miss the exciting cells where King Edward II was murdered, nor the ancient bowling alley where the executioners probably exercised their right arms.

Carisbrooke Castle   G8
IOW. 1¼ miles sw of Newport. Well known and well worth the climb, this twenty-acre castle stands proudly above the village. Standing on the site of a Roman fort, the keep was built by the Normans. The gatehouse was finished in 1470, and the outer walls were run up as an emergency measure in 1588 by local labour when the Armada was on its way.
Open daily Mar, Apr & Oct. 9.30–19.00. May–Sep. 9.30–16.00 Nov–Feb. Closed Sun morning.

Corfe Castle   D9
Isle of Purbeck, Dorset. There is something of a picture book quality about the gaunt ruins of the castle and the picturesque village. But an authentic excitement still comes from these great stones. Built on a conical hill on the site of the earlier castles by Edward I in 1280, it has a history of mediaeval cruelty and revenge. *Open daily Mar–Oct, afternoons only Nov–Feb.*

Corfe Castle : Dorset

Lulworth Castle   D9
East Lulworth, Dorset. This westerly corner of Purbeck is full of interest and Lulworth Castle is still a romantic spot. Set on rising ground in an opening between Flowers Barrow and Binden Down, the castle stands four-square among clumps of beeches. A square, lofty, battlemented block, Lulworth looks the essence of all castles, but it was built in the 17thC as a second home by the third Lord Howard of Binden.
Admission sometimes on application.

Portland Castle   C9
Castletown, Dorset. Like an open fan the castle presents its curved face towards Weymouth Bay. It was built in 1540 by Henry VIII as one of the many castles in a line of defence that ran from Kent to Cornwall. Henry had an obsessive fear of French invaders, and this line of sturdy castles certainly made him feel prepared for anything.
Portland is one of the best preserved of these castles. Its Portland stone ashlar has remained clean cut and sharp. Look inside at the complete range of garrison quarters and feel the presence of those tough Tudors. *Open 9.30–17.30 daily Apr & 9.30–19.00 May–Sep. Closed Sun morning.*

Sandsfoot Castle   C9
Nr Weymouth, Dorset. Built to protect Weymouth Bay as a companion to Portland Castle (qv), Sandsfoot now looks sad and worn. Constructed in 1541, the garrison quarters still remain, although the octagonal gun room has now slipped into the sea. The walls and gate tower remain intact.

Windsor Castle   J4
Windsor, Berks. The largest inhabited castle in the world, and the favourite home of the present Queen. It is the size of a small town with its own chapel, barracks and state apartments all still functioning. Its silhouette as seen from the long walk in the Great Park is mostly a 19thC creation, although the origins of the castle go right back to William the Conqueror.
When the Queen is living in one of her other palaces the inside of the castle can be thoroughly inspected. It is full of treasure.
For information tel. Windsor 68222.

Unusual buildings

Alfred's Tower   C6
Stourton, Wilts. Not content with the creation of the amazing Stourhead Gardens, Henry Hoare built splendid follies around the edge of his park in 1768. The most noticeable is this tower which rises to a height of 160 feet above the spot where King Alfred raised his standard against the Danes in 878. Triangular in shape with turrets on each corner, the structure is completely hollow, and now you cannot climb up to see the views. A statue of King Alfred stands over the entry in a little niche.

Arlington Mill   E3
Bibury, Glos. 7 miles ne of Cirencester on A433. In one of the loveliest of Cotswold villages, this mill was both a cloth mill and a corn mill, and the pretty cottages, Arlington Row, were the homes of the weavers. It stands where it has stood since it was recorded in the Domesday Book, alongside the River Coln. The existing building is mostly 17thC. It has working machinery, and a museum of arts, crafts and Victoriana. *Open 11.30–19.30 Mar–Oct. Sat & Sun Nov–Feb.*

The Great Barn   F3
Great Coxwell, Berks. Sw of Faringdon. This must be the most beautiful barn in the country. Built by monks in the 13thC as a tithe barn, its sheer size suggests that the monks did pretty well. Built of stone and roofed with stone slates, its size, 152 feet long by 51 feet high, explains why William Morris called it 'as noble as a cathedral'.
Open any reasonable time.

Houses & gardens

Ashdown House   F4
Nr Lambourn, Berks. 2½ miles s of Ashbury. A very tall house that is unusual in being made of chalk blocks. Built in 1665 for the first Earl of Craven, who dedicated it to Elizabeth, Queen of Bohemia. The house is topped by a little viewing room under a dome. There must have been a great deal of running up and down stairs as the stairway occupies about a quarter of the house. *Open 14.00–18.00 Wed Apr and Wed & 1st & 3rd Sat in month May–Sep.*

Ashdown Park : Berkshire

Athelhampton   C8
Nr Dorchester, Dorset. ½ mile e of Puddletown on A35. A very fine house that remains essentially mediaeval, surrounded by walls and courts and almost encircled by the river. Inside the house the great hall is one of the finest examples of 15thC domestic architecture left in England. *Open 14.00–18.00 Wed, Thur & Sun Apr–Sep and Good Fri & B. Hol Sun & Mon.*

Blenheim Palace
Woodstock, nr Oxford, Oxon. A handsome gift from Queen Anne to her favourite soldier, the Duke of Marlborough, to celebrate the victory at Blenheim. It has a certain marshal splendour as you will see from the heaps of trophies the architect Vanbrugh has displayed along the roof line.
Inside, it must be the most palatial of all the stately homes. Churchill was born in a small unpretentious bedroom. The garden and lake are by Capability Brown. *Open 11.30–17.00 daily Apr–late Oct.*

Blenheim Palace, Oxfordshire.

Buscot Park   F3
Berks. 3 miles nw of Faringdon. Water plays the main part in this skilfully designed garden by Harold Peto. A long grassy walk with a narrow central canal, planted with water lilies, drops in stages to the twenty-acre lake created by Capability Brown. The various levels are marked with fountains, bridges, statuary and vistas. The house is charming – 18thC in the Adam style with superb painted panels by the pre-Raphaelite Burne Jones. *Open 14.00-18.00 Wed & first Sat & Sun of Apr-Sep. Wed only Oct-Mar.*

Compton Acres   E8
Dorset. Between Bournemouth & Poole in Canford Cliffs Road. Originally expensively converted from moorland, this estate is famous for its seven separate and quite distinct gardens. One, designed, planted and decorated in the Japanese manner includes pagodas, figures and lanterns reflected in a pool crossed by stepping stones. Another, the Italian garden, features a long Roman-style pool with formal urns and statues. The semi-tropical glen contains jacarandas, eucalyptus, palms, mimosas and Himalayan rhododendrons. There are also rock and winter gardens, a heather dell, and Palm Court with its valuable marble and bronze sculpture. *Open 10.30-18.30 daily Apr-Oct. Thu-dusk Jun-Aug.*

Forde Abbey   A8
Dorset. 4 miles se of Chard. Originally a 12thC Cistercian monastery and now a private house. The gardens cover 25 acres and are full of lovely lakes. Inside the house much 12thC work remains, and don't miss the superb collection of Mortlake tapestries. *Open 14.00-18.00 Sun & Wed May-Sep & Easter Sun.*

Hidcote Manor Gardens   E2
Hidcote Bartrim, Glos. 4 miles ne of Chipping Campden. Definitely not to be missed, being one of England's most beautiful gardens with views over the Vale of Evesham. Laid out by Major Lawrence Johnston over 40 years in a series of small hedged compartments, each devoted to particular colourings or species. *Open 11.00-20.00 daily Apr-Oct. Closed Tue & Fri.*

Kiftsgate Court   E1
Mickleton, Glos. 3 miles ne of Chipping Campden. Adjacent to Hidcote, a charming garden with an exceptional collection of species and old fashioned roses. Cuttings and plants can be purchased. *Open 14.00-18.00 Thur & Sun Apr-Oct.*

Milton Manor   G3
Nr Abingdon, Berks. Wander down the pretty village street at Milton to the gates of this lovely house which is well hidden. Largely 17thC with Georgian wings, the house contains two great surprises, a chapel and a library in the elaborate Gothic taste. All the rooms are handsome and the grounds well nurtured within mellow walls. *Open 15.00-18.00 Wed May-Oct.*

Pusey House   F3
Berks. 5 miles e of Faringdon. Offering a wide variety of interest from the lovely terrace dotted with dianthus, sysirinchium and blue flax, to the elegant chinoiserie bridge skimming across the lake, whose banks are planted with waterside species. *Open Wed, Thur & Sun Apr-Jul. 14.00-18.00 daily Jul-Oct. Closed Fri.*

Rousham House   G2
Steeple Aston, Oxon. 12 miles n of Oxford. William Kent's only surviving landscape design to remain unaltered. Starting from the old bowling green, complete with original seats and Scheemakers sculpture, bear left to find the Praenoste arcade which illustrates Kent's great passion for Roman antiquity in a sylvan setting. Such is the Venus' Vale, an upper and lower cascade between which is the great pond decorated with lead figures dated 1701. Further on from the little Doric Temple note the distant Temple of the Mill and an artificial ruin, both used by Kent purely to please the eye. *Open 14.00-18.00 Wed, Sun & B Hols Apr-Sep. Gardens only 10.00-18.00 daily.*

Savill Garden   J4
Windsor Great Park, Berks. Off A30 via Englefield Green. Started in 1932 in Windsor Great Park by Sir Eric Savill as a small water garden. It has since been enlarged to cover over twenty acres of woodland water and bog gardens. The heather garden makes a colourful use of a natural valley and the Punchbowl is a perfect example of bank planting with shrubs and trees. The azaleas and Japanese maples are particularly fine. *Open 10.00-18.00 daily Mar-Oct.*

Stourhead   C6
Wilts. 3 miles nw of Mere in Stourton village. Designed to be walked round in an anti-clockwise direction, this garden, created in 1741-50 by Henry Hoare in the romantic Italian style, features magnificent conifers and a huge tulip tree. Glimpsed from the grotto with its sculpture by Rysbrack is the great lake, home of swans, ducks and crested grebe. *Open 11.00-19.00 daily.*

The Pantheon, Stourhead, Wiltshire.

Museums and galleries

Abbey Ruins Museum   D7
Park Walk, Shaftesbury, Dorset. Carved stones and tiles from a Benedictine nunnery founded by Alfred the Great. Models of the church and town before 1539. *Open 10.00-19.00 daily Apr-Sep. Closed Sun morning & Mon.*

Abingdon Borough Museum   G3
The County Hall, Abingdon, Berks. Relics from the mediaeval abbey, pewter plate, uniforms and arms from the 16th-19thC, toys, ornaments and tools from local Saxon graves, all housed in the 17thC County Hall. *Open 14.00-17.00 daily.*

Ashmolean Museum of Art and Archaeology   G3
Beaumont St, Oxford, Oxon. The oldest public museum in Britain, first opened in 1683, it is rich in Egyptian relics. Drawings by Michelangelo and Raphael, 16th and 17thC silver, bronzes, snuff-boxes, and the Hill collection of musical instruments. *Open 10.00-16.00 daily. Closed Sun morning & Sat.*

Chedworth Roman Villa & Museum   E2
Chedworth, Glos. Small museum devoted to finds from one of the best preserved Roman villas in England, 150-350. *Open 10.00-18.00 Tue-Sun Mar-Sep. Wed-Sun Oct-Dec.*

Corinium Museum   E3
Park St, Circencester, Glos. Roman antiquities from the site of Corinium Dubunnorum. Fine mosaic pavements, provincial Roman sculpture. *Open daily. Closed Sun morning May-Sep (Open 10.00-16.30. Oct-Jun. Closed Sun.)*

Devizes Museum   E5
Long St, Devizes, Wilts. Important Stourhead collection of bronze age urns, beakers, grave goods and ornaments excavated from barrows on Salisbury Plain in the early 19thC. *Open 11.00-17.00 Tue-Sat (11.00-16.00 Nov-Apr.)*

Dorset County Museum   C8
Dorchester, Dorset. Finds from the iron age fort at Maiden Castle. The Thomas Hardy Memorial collection includes manuscripts, notebooks, drawings and the reconstructed study from Hardy's house in Max Gate (Dorchester). *Open 10.00-17.00 daily. Closed Sun.*

National Motor Museum G8
Palace House, Beaulieu, Hants. One of the finest collections of vintage cars, motorcycles and bicycles in the world. 1895 Knight, 1896 Pennington and the 1865 English Bone Shaker. *Open 10.00–18.30 daily, 10.00–17.00 Oct–Apr.*

Old Town House E8
High St, Poole, Dorset. This 14thC building is now a small museum. Exhibits devoted to local history, pottery, industrial archaeology and a bronze age dug-out canoe dredged up from Poole Harbour in 1964. *Open 10.00–17.00 daily mid May–Sep. Closed Sun morning.*

Russell-Cotes Art Gallery and Museum E8
East Cliff, Bournemouth, Dorset. Items associated with Napoleon and Sir Henry Irving. Fine collection of Victorian painting, watercolours and drawings. *Open daily. Closed Sun morning.*

St Peter's Bunker Museum K10
St Peter's Parish, Jersey, C.I. Grisly collection of Nazi German equipment and war relics. *Open 10.00–17.00 daily Mar–Nov*

Salisbury and South Wiltshire Museum E6
St Ann St, Salisbury, Wilts. Most of the finds from Stonehenge are here. A wide selection of mediaeval pottery, a Roman mosaic pavement from Downton and the celebrated giant figure carried in the midsummer Guild Pageants. *Open daily (10.00–16.00 Oct–Apr). Closed Sun.*

The Victory Museum H8
H.M. Dockyard, Portsmouth, Hants. Relics of Lord Nelson and the Victory are housed in the oldest part of Portsmouth dockyard. Centrepiece of the museum is a panorama of the battle of Trafalgar by W. L. Wyllie. *Open 10.00–17.00 daily. 10.00–16.00 Nov–Feb. Closed Sun morning.*

Botanical gardens

Exbury G8
Hants. 4 miles se of Beaulieu. A world-renowned garden planted by the late Lionel de Rothschild in 1918. Noted for the Exbury strain of hybrid azaleas and rhododendrons. The breeding of this strain was started by Anthony Waterer some 40 years ago at Knaphill nursery and forms the basis of the comprehensive collection seen today. *Open daily Apr–Jun. 14.00–19.00.*

University Botanic Garden G3
High St, Oxford. The oldest botanic garden in Britain, founded by Henry, Lord Danvers, in 1621. Six acres pleasantly situated by the river. Fine species collections of rare plants. Entrance arch by Inigo Jones. *Open 8.00–17.00 Mon–Sat. 10.00–12.00 & 14.00–18.00 Sun.*

Westonbirt Arboretum D3
Glos. 3 miles sw of Tetbury. Here, in one of the world's oldest arboreta, we find the greatest variety of trees and shrubs in the British Isles, shown to their best advantage by the skilful planting and foresight of Robert Halford who began the garden in 1829 on rough pastureland. *Open 10.00–20.00 or dusk daily.*

Zoos, aquaria and aviaries

The Birdland Zoo Gardens E2
Bourton-on-the-Water, Glos. One of the major bird collections in Britain, gathered in the Cotswolds. Among the 600 birds many are rare and seldom seen in captivity. Leadbeater's cockatoos, great black cockatoos, purple-crowned turacos. Tropical house and penguin pool. *Open 10.00–18.00 Mar–Oct. 10.00–16.00 Dec–Feb*

Cotswold Wildlife Park F2
Oxon, 3½ miles s of Burford off A361. A large walk-through aviary in the garden; the animals are kept in natural surroundings. Look out for the red pandas from the eastern Himalayas. *Open 10.00–18.00 (or dusk) daily.*

Jersey Zoological Park K10
Les Augres Manor, Trinity, Jersey, C.I. A zoo specializing in threatened species and founded by Gerald Durrell, author and animal-lover. The collection includes gorillas, orang-utans, a colony of black and white colobus monkeys, pigmy shrews, fennec foxes and volcano rabbits from Mexico. Look out for the lovely lizard native to this island. *Open 10.00–dusk daily.*

The Lions of Longleat D6
Longleat Park, Warminster, Wilts. This famous lion reserve also includes herds of giraffe, zebra and antelope in the 200-acre Longleat park. Admission by private car or coach. Take a trip on the Safari Boat – you can buy buckets of fish to feed the sea lions while you float around the lake. *Open daily.*

Slimbridge Wild Fowl Trust C3
Slimbridge, Glos. 2 miles n of Berkeley Rd. Finest collection of wild fowl in the world, founded by Peter Scott in 1946. Rare species include Aleutian Canada geese, king and spectacled eiders, harlequin, Hawaiian geese. There are six observation towers and fifteen hides in the sea wall for visitors. *Open daily. Closed Sun morning.*

Windsor Safari Park J4
St Leonard's, Royal Windsor, Berks. 100-acre zoo first opened in 1969, with lots of things to see and do. Dolphinarium, monkey jungle, children's zoo. *Open 10.00–dusk daily.*

Nature trails and reserves

Aston Rowant National Nature Reserve Trail H3
Aston Rowant, Oxon. Start at car park at the reserve. Mainly of botanical interest, but a good selection of commoner species may be seen along this beechwood and chalk grassland trail, 1½ miles. A guide is available from 5 Hazelton Close, Southern Rd, Thame.

Brownsea Island Nature Reserve E8
Brownsea Island, Dorset. Heath, woodland, marsh, lake and shore birds at all seasons, breeding species include heron, terns and nightjar. Access via boats from Sandbanks Ferry or Poole Quay; restricted private landing. Guided tours on certain days. There is also a nature trail (1½ miles), starting from Brownsea Island Quay. *Open Apr–Sep.*

Farlington Marshes Nature Reserve H8
Hants. Part of Langstone Harbour and a splendid area for waders and winter wildfowl, especially brent geese. Access near junction of A27 with A2030; no permit required.

Forest of Dean Nature Trails C2
Glos. As many as nine trails may be available in any year. Two of these are: Speech House Forest Trail (2¾ or 1¾ miles), beginning either at Speech House or the Beechenhurst Picnic Place; and Edge End Forest Trail (3½ or 2½ miles), which starts at the Edge End picnic place. Both provide a good cross-selection of typical forest birds. (See also 'Bird Watching').

Hengistbury Head Nature Trail F8
Hants. Start at Ranger's Cottage at Hengistbury Head. Birds of heathland, oak woodland, saltmarsh and shore. Also of geological interest. 2 miles. Guide available at the start of trail.

New Grounds Nature Reserve C3
Slimbridge, Glos. Follow sign off A38 s of Cambridge. Not only one of the world's best waterfowl collections but headquarters of the Wildfowl Trust and its research branch. Captive birds augmented by large numbers of Bewick's swans and duck, including pintail in winter, with spectacular flocks of white-fronted geese on adjoining Dumbles. Migrant waders. Peregrine and water rail regular in winter. Full details from the Wildfowl Trust, Slimbridge, Glos.

Radipole Lake Reserve C9
Weymouth, Dorset. Fine area of lake and reed-bed, with breeding reed warblers and bearded tits and a wide selection of passage

migrants and winter wildfowl. Public access at southern end allows good views of much of the area, and there is a nature trail starting at the south end of the lake. Details of restricted reserve area from RSPB, The Lodge, Sandy, Beds.

River Medina G8
Newport, IOW. Start at Newport Quay. Mainly shore birds plus cormorant, heron, kingfisher, etc. 3 miles. Leaflets from IOW Tourist Board, 21 High St, Newport IOW.

RSPB Reserve E8
Arne, nr Wareham, Dorset. Dorset heathland with breeding nightjar, stonechat and Dartford warbler; good selection of wildfowl and waders in autumn and winter. Access strictly by permit only (except at Shipstal). Details from RSPB, The Lodge, Sandy, Beds.

Thorncombe Wood Nature Trail C8
Dorset. Higher Bockhampton, e of Dorchester, off A35. Typical birds of mixed woodland. 2½ miles. Leaflet available at the start of trail. *Open Apr–Sep.*

Birdwatching

Forest of Dean C2
Glos. An outstanding forest area of the region, also well served by roads and free of access in many areas. Full details of nature trails are available from The Forestry Commission, Crown Offices, Coleford, Glos. As well as most of the typical woodland birds, the forest has breeding buzzard, sparrowhawk, nightjar, raven, wood warbler, redstart and pied flycatcher, with dipper and grey wagtail on its streams.

Langstone Harbour H8
Hants. A large area of intertidal mud and salt marsh between Portsmouth and Hayling Island, which can be examined from various points around its boundary. Excellent for waders at all seasons, but especially autumn and winter, and notable for its winter wildfowl which include duck, large numbers of brent geese, divers and grebes.

New Forest F7
Hants. One of Britain's most outstanding woodland areas, with added heathland, with a rich variety of typical species and breeding specialities such as wood warbler, hawfinch, hobby, sparrowhawk, buzzard, honey buzzard, stonechat, warblers, nightjar, red-backed shrike and woodlark. The forest is crossed by various roads and access is unrestricted at many places. In addition there are forest nature reserves and nature trails. The Forestry Commission or the Nature Conservancy at Red Lodge, Lyndhurst, for full details.

Poole Harbour E8
Dorset. This vast area lies west of Bournemouth and Poole and, in spite of various developments, is very good for birds – grebes, duck and waders in winter and autumn being the main attractions. Studland, Arne and Brownsea overlook the area, but additional vantage points include South Haven Point, the caravan site at Rockley Sands and the Shore Road north of the ferry.

Portland Bill C9
Dorset. Easily reached and well signposted from Weymouth, this is a fine bird-watching area. Here seabirds include auks, shag, kittiwake, and fulmar in summer. Spring and autumn migration produces a wide variety of passerines, often including rarities. Portland Bird Observatory and Field Centre makes an ideal base for the serious bird watcher: details from The Warden, Old Lower Light, Portland, Dorset.

Salisbury Plain E6
Wilts. An area of chalk downland and associated belts of trees. The A360 between West Lavington and Shewton, plus the minor road to the east, are good viewpoints. Notable breeding birds to look out for include hobby, buzzard, stone curlew and wheatear, and quail.

Virginia Water J4
Berks. This area is within easy reach of London, lying south-west of Egham and north of the A30. The large lake is good for waterfowl and is well known as a favourite site for the feral Mandarin duck. The surrounding woodland has a good variety of birds, including woodcock, woodpeckers and hawfinch.

Brass rubbing

The following is a short list of churches that have brasses for rubbing. Permission is almost invariably required.
Berkshire. Childrey, Shottesbrooke, Sparsholt, Windsor (St George's Chapel).
Dorset. Thornocombe, Puddletown, Shapwick.
Gloucestershire. Chipping Campden, Cirencester, Deerhurst, Northleach, Wotton-under-Edge ('Woolmen' figure brasses at Cirencester and Northleach), Minchinhampton, Fairford.
Hampshire and the Isle of Wight. Crondall, Freshwater, Havant, Headbourne Worthy, King's Somborne, Ringwood, Thruxton, Winchester (St Cross).
Oxfordshire. Brightwell Baldwin, Burford, Chinnor, Dorchester, Great Tew, Mapledurham, Oddington, Oxford (Merton College Chapel and New College Chapel), Thame.
Wiltshire. Clyffe Pypard, Dauntsey, Mere, Salisbury Cathedral.

Fossils

Visit the local museum. Its fossil collection usually states where individual fossils have been found. When visiting quarries always seek permission to enter if they look privately owned or worked. Be careful of falls of rock.

Aust Glos.
The cliffs immediately under the eastern side of the Severn Bridge are full of Rhaetic fish bones and remains, small oyster and mussel shells.

Barton-on-Sea Hants.
Cliff sections crowded with Eocene fossils.

Cheltenham Glos.
Crickley and Leckhampton Hills for oolite fossils in quarries wherever you can find them.

Cotswolds Glos.
Many rich fossil-bearing exposures. Try around Cirencester, Halmore, Mobley, Purton, Woodford and Whitfield.

Dorset Coast
The whole succession of Jurassic rocks and fossils is splendidly displayed in the foreshore and cliffs from the Devon border to Swanage.

Durlston Bay nr Swanage, Dorset.
Masses of freshwater shells and small crustacea. A rare possibility here in a thin bed is to find fossils of primitive mammals, dwarf crocodiles and fishes; occasionally fossil insects can be found.

Faringdon Berks. F3
Pits of highly fossiliferous sponge gravels in this district are abundant with sponges, bryozoa, brachiopods and echinoids.

Isle of Wight F9
The cliffs of Alum Bay, Whitecliff Bay, Headon Hill and Colwell Bay yield many fossils of the Caenozoic period. The coast near Atherfield Point, of greensand, is full of large bivalves. At Brook Point is a mass of prostrate fossil tree trunks much broken up by wave action.

Kirtlington Oxon. G2
Quarries have thick beds largely of brachiopods.

Langton Herring Dorset. C9
Exposed at Herbury, the great oolite clays provide a bed full of brachiopods and oysters.

Lyme Regis and Charmouth
Dorset. **A8**
The fossil collector's paradise. Ammonites of all sizes abound in the lias; some on the foreshore are incredibly two or three feet in size. Belemites, crinoids and molluscs, and the occasional tooth or vertebra of the large marine reptiles can also be found. Visit Lyme Regis Museum. This town is famous for fossil collector Mary Anning, who in the late 19thC extracted fabulous large skeletons from its cliffs.

Minchinhampton Common
Glos. **D3**
The quarries here have yielded well preserved shells in a matrix of white oolite limestone which are to be found in many museums.

Oxford Area Oxon. **G3**
Quarries in the Oxford area yield large upper Jurassic fauna of ammonitees, oysters, brachiopods, corals, gastropods and occasional bones. Beckley Headington, Kidlington, Kirtlington and Littlemore.

Wiltshire **F4**
Most of Wiltshire is chalk and many fossils can be found in quarries and road cuttings in Alderbury, Downton, Fyfield, Marlborough, Oare and Pitton.

Forests

Forest of Dean **C2**
Glos. In west Gloucestershire, between the rivers Severn and Wye, the Royal Forest of Dean stands on a high plateau, surrounded by splendid views, especially at Symonds Yat Rock. Here are mighty oaks, planted by Nelson for warship timbers, tall beeches and ash trees, and a full range of coniferous trees from Europe and North America. Mines and quarries for coal, iron ore, lime and sandstone, scarcely used today, date from Roman times. Herds of half-wild sheep graze the roadsides.

New Forest **F7**
Hants. In 1079 William the Conqueror created this Royal Forest, now occupying 100 square miles of south-west Hampshire between Southampton and Bournemouth, as hunting country for red deer, still present today. Three-fifths is open heath, providing pastures for herds of half-wild ponies and young cattle owned by the Commoners, who are peasant farmers holding historic rights. Two-fifths is woodland with vereran picturesque oaks and beeches, giant hollies and well-tended plantations of Scots pine and Oregon Douglas fir. Many Forestry Commission camp sites, car parks, picnic points, and way-marked trails. Magnificent riding country.

Savernake Forest **F4**
Wilts. Set high on the Wiltshire Downs east and south of Marlborough, Savernake was once a Royal Forest, and later a nobleman's chase for hunting spotted fallow deer. Today the Forestry Commission tends its magnificent groves of beeches, and provides access to woodland walks from car parks with picnic places.

Hills

Berkshire Downs **G4**
Berks. An expanse of lonely chalk uplands, 800 feet high, between Abingdon in the Thames Valley and Newbury on the River Kennet. Traversed by the wide Ridgeway, an ancient drovers track for bringing cattle to London from the west. On the north face is the famous White Horse of Uffington, a figure first carved in chalk by Celtic tribesmen, and renewed by King Alfred.

Christmas Common **H3**
Oxon. Nearly 800 feet above sea level, this hilltop village stands on the Chiltern ridge above Watlington in south-east Oxfordshire. From the steep chalk escarpment at Watlington Hill, a National Trust property nearby, views extend north

and west over the broad Thames Valley. Slopes on either side are clad in tall beechwoods, some privately owned, others part of the national Chilterns Forest. Quaint thatched cottages, walled with flint or 'cob', abound.

Cleeve Hill **E1**
Glos. Five miles north-east of Cheltenham, Cleeve Hill is the highest of the Cotswolds. Its windy summit commands magnificent views west over the Vales of Gloucester and Worcester to the Malvern Hills and the Forest of Dean. Eastwards the Midlands open out, with nothing to challenge Cleeve's 1,083 feet anywhere across England.

Cotswolds **D3**
Magnificent range of limestone hills running for 70 miles north-east from Bristol past Gloucester to Banbury in Oxfordshire, with a general height of 800 feet. Their steep scarp slopes, facing the Severn Vale to the north-west, are threaded by winding valleys clothed in tall beechwoods.

Dorset Downs **C8**
Dorset. Range of chalk hills, 600 feet in general height, running north-east for 40 miles from Dorchester towards Salisbury, Wiltshire. Green pastoral country, grazed by countless sheep and cattle, and broken by the deep valleys of 'winter bournes', streams that flow only after heavy winter rains. Includes the well-wooded Cranborne Chase, featured in Thomas Hardy's novel 'Tess of the D'Urbervilles'.

Hampshire Downs **G6**
Hants. Surrounding the county town of Winchester, the Hampshire Downs form rolling uplands with a dry chalk soil. Old drove roads, now modernised, run through green pastures and fertile arable fields, broken by straight shelter belts of beech. The few market towns, Andover, Basingstoke, Alton and Petersfield, stand in river valleys.

Inkpen Beacon **F5**
Berks. Relics of past and present jostle each other on this 974-foot chalk summit, set near the meeting point of Berkshire, Hampshire and Wiltshire, ten miles south-west of Newbury. Has an iron-age fort, prehistoric and modern trackways, Celtic fields, a mediaeval gibbet, and tractor ploughing for wheat on the downland summit. Wide views over the Thames and Kennet valleys; tricky road up.

Liddington Castle **F4**
Wilts. Highest of the Wiltshire Downs, this prominent sheep-grazed summit rises to 910 feet, standing sentinel over the bustling 'new town' of Swindon five miles north. Close by, at Coate Farm, is Richard Jefferies country, where the famous 19thC naturalist wrote his inspired prose-poems, based on intimate first-hand observations of the countryside.

Marlborough Downs **E4**
Wilts. Between the old towns of Marlborough and Calne, on the London to Bristol highway, A4, these high chalk hills rise to nearly 900 feet and provide grand country for riding, or training racehorses. Their unique concentration of ancient monuments includes the Avebury stone circle, Silbury Hill and the Wansdyke, a prehistoric boundary ditch, fifteen miles long.

Pilsdon Pen **B8**
Dorset. At 908 feet Pilsdon Pen is the highest of the dramatic range of sandstone and limestone hills that give a mountainous aspect to west Dorset. Standing close to the B3164 road from Axminster to Beaminster, it commands the fertile Marshwood Vale, where higgledy-piggledy hillside fields are flanked by odd-shaped woods of pine, oak and larch.

Meadows & marshes

Avon Water Meadows **E6**
From Salisbury in Wiltshire, south to its mouth at Christchurch in Hampshire, the River Avon is bordered by unique water meadows. Artificially drained, these

meadows were formerly artificially flooded, too.

Cricklade Meadows E3
Wilts. Though the land around Cricklade, on the old Roman road (A419) lies high in the Thames Valley, it is level and must be artificially drained to provide pasturage. Towards Fairford, Gloucestershire, on A417 to the north, large gravel pits now filled with surface water are being landscaped as boating lakes. Lechlade, an old stone village, marks the limit of Thames navigation. 'Lade', an Anglo-Saxon word, signifies 'ditch'.

Lymington Saltings and Beaulieu River F8
Hants. At the mouth of the Lymington River, in Hampshire's New Forest, flat salt marshes were formerly enclosed at high tide, so that brine evaporated, leaving dry salt. Best seen from the ferry to Yarmouth, Isle of Wight. Beaulieu, six miles east, has an old tide-mill on the Beaulieu River; also the famous Bucklers' Hard, a steep gravel beach on which wooden warships were built, then slid downhill into the water. Good inland yacht anchorage.

Salisbury Plain E6
Wilts. A broad expanse of grassland on a chalk subsoil, occupying some 250 square miles of uplands north of Salisbury. Used today mainly for military training. The Plain is dominated by Stonehenge, Britain's finest prehistoric stone circle.

Thames Valley G3
From its well-head source high on the Cotswolds near Tetbury, Gloucestershire, the stripling Thames winds gradually down past Oxford to cross the Chiltern Hills through the Goring Gap, close to Reading, Berkshire. Its upper vale is a broad grassy plain, studded with tall elms and quaint lopped willow trees.

Vale of Berkeley C3
Glos. A level lowland plain running north-west from Bristol along the course of the River Severn. It extends beyond Gloucester, to Tewkesbury. Fifty miles long, though never more than ten miles wide, it is framed by the steep Cotswolds on the east, and the Forest of Dean and the Malvern Hills to the west.

Rivers

The Bristol Avon D4
Rising near Malmesbury, the 'Bristol' Avon follows a broad vale past Chippenham and Melksham to Bradford-on-Avon, where it enters its remarkable deep narrow valley cutting through the Cotswolds to join the Severn and out to sea at Avonmouth. Small craft can sail up it as far as Bath, and below Bristol ocean steamers cruise up through the Avon Gorge on its tidal flow. A splendid suspension bridge crosses from one limestone bluff to another at Clifton, west of Bristol.

The Hampshire Avon E6
Despite its name, this river rises near Devizes in Wiltshire, flows through the fertile Vale of Pewsey, and then crosses Salisbury Plain southwards in a long narrow hollow to Amesbury, just below Stonehenge. Below Salisbury, where its water meadows form a fitting flat setting to the tall cathedral spire, it meanders down a narrow valley of drained pastures, just west of the New Forest heights, reaching the English Channel at Christchurch.

The Severn B3
Glos. The Severn, Britain's longest river, comes down from Shropshire and the far Welsh hills past Worcester. It is navigable by barges and pleasure craft throughout Gloucestershire, and below Gloucester, the ancient bridgehead, it becomes tidal, broadening out to its great estuary. This is crossed, near Chepstow, by a four-mile railway tunnel and the magnificent modern suspension bridge, one and a half miles long overall.

The Stour D8
Dorset. Rising from a beautifully landscaped lake in the National Trust's property of Stourhead, south-west of Mere in Wiltshire, the Stour meanders south across the fertile flat clays of Blackmoor Vale to Sturminster Newton in Dorset. Then it cuts right through the high range of the white chalk Dorset Downs at Blandford Forum, emerging at Wimborne Minster to wind behind Bournemouth to Christchurch harbour on the Hampshire coast. A fine trout stream, with some salmon.

Test and Itchen G7
Hants. Small rivers these, flowing down narrow valleys in the Hampshire chalk downs, the Test from Whitchurch and Romsey, and the Itchen through Winchester. Flowing on either side of Southampton, they unite there as Southampton Water, a broad tidal estuary that can safely carry the world's largest passenger ships up to the busy docks and landing stages.

Thames headwaters G3
Oxfordshire, Berkshire, east Gloucestershire and north Wiltshire are all drained by the great river Thames or its tributaries, flowing slowly south-east past Reading towards London and the North Sea. Near Oxford the main Thames, or Isis, stream is joined by the Windrush, Evenlode and Cherwell rivers from the north, and at Reading the Kennet comes in from the west. In past centuries the Thames was a major trade route; its flow was controlled by locks, and sturdy horses trod its towpaths, pulling barges. Today it is thronged with pleasure craft, which penetrate upstream as far as Lechlade in Gloucestershire, 350 feet above sea level. The Thames' source is a well beside the Cotswold highway, A473, four miles south-west of Cirencester.

Canals

The Gloucester and Sharpness Canal D2
A sixteen mile ship canal from Sharpness to Gloucester, this was the world's biggest canal (in cross-sectional dimensions) when built by Thomas Telford in the 19thC. It was constructed to avoid the dangerously shallow and twisting course of the tidal River Severn, and still carries plenty of tankers and coastal barges. There are only two locks (one at each end) but plenty of swingbridges.

The Kennet and Avon Canal E5
This superb waterway linking London with Bristol is not at the moment fully navigable. and is the subject of a massive restoration effort by volunteers, who are steadily reopening more locks and more miles of navigable waters every year. It runs through delightful countryside, passing handsome towns like Hungerford, Devizes and Bath, and is ideal for walking. Things to see: outside Bath the elegant Dundas Aqueduct, carrying the canal over the River Avon. At Devizes a flight of 29 abandoned locks on a single hillside, and the bridges in the town are architectural gems.

The Oxford Canal G3
A very pretty narrow canal running north from Oxford to Banbury, Rugby and

The Oxford Canal at Chalgrove.

Coventry, it opened up in 1790 a continuous transport link from Birmingham to London via the Thames. It thus had the same effect as the opening of the London to Birmingham railway in the 1840s and the M1 motorway in 1959. Engineered by James Brindley, the most famous of the early canal engineers, it winds about the countryside in a way that only Brindley's canals do. It is navigable throughout, and very popular among pleasure boaters.

The Thames and Severn Canal   E3
Disused since 1927, this used to run from Lechlade on the River Thames to Cirencester, Stroud and the Severn Valley, piercing the Cotswold escarpment with a mighty tunnel. Two and a quarter miles long, the Sapperton Tunnel excited comment around the country in its day—it was even visited by the inquisitive King George III—and it remains the second longest canal tunnel ever built in Britain. The tunnel is easy to find just off the Fosse Way south of Cirencester close to the source of the River Thames. There are fine portals at either end, and a canal pub still stands by the eastern entrance.

Archaeology

Avebury   E4
Wilts. The largest of the great bronze age henge monuments, of which Stonehenge is the best known. Avebury includes stone circles and earthworks. From it the West Kennet Stone Avenue runs south-eastwards, linking it with a second henge at The Sanctuary. *Open any reasonable time.*

Chedworth Villa   E2
Chedworth, Glos. Chedworth is a classic example of a Romano-British country villa, and almost the whole of the main building complex is visible. Two suites of baths survive, showing the usual method of Roman heating through piles laid between the short tile columns that supported the floor. There are several mosaic floors; the finest has figures of nymphs and satyrs, with the four seasons in the corners. The north-east corner of the site contains a 'nymphaeum', an ornamental fountain structure built over a spring. Finds from the excavations are displayed in the site museum. *Open 10.00–18.00 daily. Closed Mon and early Oct & Jan.*

Cirencester   E3
Glos. After London, Corinium was the largest city in Roman Britain, and a series of summer excavations is at present in progress. Sections of the city wall have been preserved in the abbey gardens; the amphitheatre is visible on waste land in the south-west of the town. The Corinium Museum has a fine collection of mosaics, stone architectural decoration, and small objects.

Dorchester   C8
Dorset. Roman Durnovaria. Fragments of the town walls and ditches are visible; the Roman amphitheatre, adapted from a late neolithic or bronze age henge monument, survives on the outskirts of the town. The Dorset County Museum houses local prehistoric and Roman finds.

Hod Hill   D7
Nr Blandford Forum, Dorset. Like Maiden Castle, Hod Hill belonged to the series of iron age hill forts taken by Roman forces (led by the future Emperor Vespasian) during the conquest period. At Hod Hill, a Roman garrison was installed in a small fort built into the north-west corner of the hill fort; the outlines of this are still visible.

Maiden Castle   C8
Nr Dorchester, Dorset. One of the most impressive of the great hill forts constructed during the iron age. The complex system of earth ramparts and ditches, and the elaborate entrance defences, are still clearly visible. Excavation has provided dramatic evidence of the Roman siege in 43, including a skeleton with a catapult bolt lodged in the spine. The defended circuit also contains an earlier

neolithic camp, marked by ditches with causeways across, and traces of a late Roman temple of the 4thC. Finds from the site are now in Dorchester Museum. *Open any reasonable time.*

Old Sarum   E6
Nr Salisbury, Wilts. Old Sarum was abandoned as a cathedral city and the See moved to Salisbury (New Sarum) in 1217, after which the former site slowly decayed. The earliest visible remains are the outer earth ramparts of an iron age hill fort; there is some evidence of Roman occupation, but Roman Sorviodunum may lie on lower ground to the west, since Roman policy was to move local peoples away from defensible sites. Later a Saxon town was established on the hill, followed by a Norman town with cathedral and castle; it is these Norman remains which dominate today. *Open 9.30–17.30 daily Apr & 9.30–19.00 May–Sep. (9.30–17.30 Mar & Oct. 9.30–16.00 Nov–Feb. Closed Sun morning.)*

Portchester Castle   H8
Portchester, Hants. Portchester is the most westerly in the series of 'Saxon Shore' forts built by the Romans in the later 3rdC, and the only one to retain its former commanding position over the sea. The entire wall-circuit survives, with much mediaeval retouching, and most of the massive semi-circular bastions and gate-towers. The site was adapted as a castle by the Normans, and a keep constructed in the north-west corner. *Open 9.30–17.00 daily Apr & 9.30–19.00 May–Sep. (9.30–17.30 Mar & Oct. 9.30–16.00 Nov–Feb. Closed Sun morning.)*

Silbury Hill   E4
Silbury, Wilts. The large mound at Silbury dates from the late neolithic or early bronze age. Its purpose is unknown, but it may form part of the contemporary Avebury religious complex.

Stonehenge   E6
Nr Amesbury, Wilts. The most famous of Britain's prehistoric monuments. Stonehenge has given rise to innumerable theories as to its use. The henge was constructed in several phases during the early bronze age; the circle and horseshoe now standing date from c1500 BC. The massive blue-stones and sarsen stones that make up the circles are not native to the area and may have been carried by earlier glacial action rather than by any feat of ancient engineering. Contrary to popular belief, the Druids, who did not reach Britain till the 3rdC BC, had no connection with the henge; however, some religious explanation for the site is likely. Some of the vertical and cross stones still show the mortice and tenon shapings by which they were held in place. *Open 9.30–17.30 daily Apr & 9.30–19.00 May–Sep. (9.30–17.30 Mar & Oct. 9.30–16.00 Nov–Feb. Closed Sun morning.)*

Stonehenge.

Wallingford   H3
Berks. During the latter part of King Alfred's reign and that of his son Edward the Elder (late 9th-early 10thC), a system of fortified strong-points (*burhs*) was established in southern England against the Danes. Wallingford was one of the largest of these, intended to protect a Thames crossing of great strategic importance. The town was defended within a rectangular enclosure of earth bank and ditch; the remains of these can be seen in the public park. *Accessible during park hours.*

West Kennet Long Barrow E4

West Kennet, Wilts. The long barrow is a characteristic tomb used during the neolithic period, consisting of a stone-built chamber and entrance passage covered with a long earth mound. West Kennet is one of the best-preserved of these, its chamber surviving intact and much of the walling still standing – despite the massive size of the blocks and the absence of any mortaring. *Accessible any time by footpath.*

Footpaths and ancient ways

Harrow Way

The Harrow, or Hoar, Way was once the main route from Dover to the Devon coast. In mediaeval times the Pilgrims' Way took over the eastern section of the route, but in the west the ghosts of Celtic commercial travellers still haunt the green way.
From Dover to near Basingstoke, Hampshire, the Way passes over the Downs to Weyhill and the site of the sheep fair where the Mayor of Casterbridge sold his wife. On to Salisbury Plain, close by Stonehenge, to Steeple Langford, Wiltshire, and Alfred's Tower (800 feet) overlooking Stourton and Kilmington. In Dorset, within three miles of Cerne Abbas, the Way joins the Ridgeway en route for

Icknield Way

Reputed to be the oldest trade route in England, the Icknield Way once stretched from the Wash to the Channel. Today it can be traced from Thetford in Norfolk to Cambridge, then to Letchworth and Tring in Hertfordshire, over the Thames near Streatley and along the line of the Berkshire Downs to the source of the Kennet in Wiltshire.
Most of the road has been Romanised, and the eastern section of the Way has either disappeared altogether or become a metal road, but there are still miles upon miles of beautiful walking country to explore. One of the finest sections to walk is along the green road from Upton to Wantage. On the Berkshire Downs the Way passes Blewbury, where Kenneth Grahame used to live.

The Ridgeway Path

This is one of the long-distance paths designated by the Countryside Commission. The path runs for 85 miles from near Avebury, in Wiltshire, by Barbury, Liddington, Uffington, Segsbury, Streatley, Princes Risborough to Ivinghoe Beacon in Buckinghamshire. It follows in part the prehistoric trackways that were the trade routes of ancient Britons and ancient drovers tracks. There are a number of burial mounds, long barrows, round barrows and iron age hill forts to explore along the way There are fine views across the North Wessex Downs and the Chilterns. At Hackpen Hill the path reaches a height of 900 feet before it slips down to Barbury Castle below. Near Goring the downlands rise to over 700 feet with spectacular views over the Vale of the White Horse to the north. At Britwell the path joins the Icknield Way for ten miles across Oxfordshire to the borders of Buckingham, and then on to Ivinghoe Beacon.

Regional sports

Cricket

Broadhalfpenny Down, two miles north-east of Hambledon on the B2150 from Havant, is widely regarded as the birthplace of cricket as it is known today. The Hampshire County Cricket Club continues the tradition and is one of the country's leading cricket teams. The county ground is at Banister Park, Northlands Road, Southampton, but they do use other pitches in the county for big matches. Details from the Secretary at Banister Park or Tel 23286.

Fishing

England's most famous trout stream, the River Test, flows through some of Hampshire's least spoilt countryside. Not surprisingly fishing here is expensive and mostly privately owned. Day tickets can, however, be obtained from the Greyhound Hotel, Stockbridge, nine miles north-west of Winchester.

Sailing

Dorset and Hampshire is the premier maritime playground in the world – with apologies to no one!

Poole Harbour, Dorset. This is the second biggest natural harbour in the world (Sydney, Australia, being the biggest). Superb dinghy sailing with good breezes uncluttered by trees and buildings. Parkstone Yacht Club races a wide variety of dinghies and will accept temporary members for a small monthly subscription. Contact the Secretary.
The Solent is the area of water bounded by the Hampshire and Dorset coast, and the northern coast of the Isle of Wight. There are yacht clubs dotted along every inlet from Lymington in the west to Chichester and Langstone Harbours in the east. Moorings for yachts and cruisers are expensive and the waiting lists are long.
Many clubs have temporary membership schemes, but the visitor is advised to obtain a list of clubs' secretaries from the Secretary, Royal Yachting Association, 5 Buckingham Gate, London SW1.
Cowes Week. This gigantic international festival of sail takes place at the beginning of August. Races are staged by individual Solent yacht clubs, but the whole thing is organised by a central committee. By tradition all the big classes of yachts are started from a line extending to seaward from the Royal Yacht Squadron Club House at Cowes.

Sailing near Cowes.

The Severn Bore

Glos. The Bore is an occasional tidal wave which races up the River Severn at speeds around ten to twelve miles per hour and at a height varying from six to ten feet. In recent years it has become a great challenge to surfers who have a wave they can ride (in theory!) for six or seven miles.
A favourite starting point is the Bird in Hand Pub near Minsterworth where the A48 Gloucester/Chepstow road runs along the river bank for about one and a half miles.

Skin Diving

Swanage, Dorset. There is a diving school on the pier where you can take instruction and hire all the gear. Good safe diving.
Chesil Cove, Portland, Dorset. Exciting diving, deep and interesting. Wrecks and lots of life. Good facilities at Ron Parry's dive shop.

Festivals

For information and tickets for festivals go to the local information centre or ticket agent.

The Cheltenham Festival D2

Cheltenham, Glos. One of the most important festivals in Britain with many first-performance successes. The theme is new works by British composers, though equal time is given to established works. Peter Fricker's 1st symphony was first conducted here by Sir John Barbirolli. *Early Jul.*

Purbeck Festival of Music E9

Isle of Purbeck, Dorset. A free and easy

miniature Glyndebourne in the Isle of Purbeck, with concerts given in the local village churches and country houses by amateurs and professionals. Wine and cheese and evening dress. *Early Aug.*

Southern Cathedrals Festival   G6
Festival of music presented by the combined choirs of Chichester, Salisbury and Winchester Cathedrals, and held each year consecutively in each cathedral every three years. *Late Jul.*

Stroud Festival   D3
Stroud, Glos. Festival of religious drama and the arts, with a tradition of mixing professional and amateur performances. There are exhibitions of local arts and crafts and poetry readings. *Late Oct.*

Windsor Festival   J4
Windsor, Berks. Festivals at Windsor date from the 14thC jousting contests. Now the entertainment is strictly musical – with concerts and recitals by some of the world's leading musicians and singers. *Late Sep-Oct.*

Fun things

Alum Bay Sand   F9
Alum Bay, IOW. Go right down to the west end of the island near the Needles, and take one of those tall thin glass instant coffee jars with you. The cliffs at Alum Bay are famous for their multi-coloured layers of sandstone. There are twelve distinct shades, and with a bit of care and perseverance these can be coaxed into layers in your coffee jar, thus providing an attractive souvenir.

Bourton-on-the-Water Model Village   E2
Bourton-on-the-Water, Glos. A delightful model of an equally attractive village. Both model and subject are built from the warm Cotswold stone, and the similarity between the two is quite staggering. *Open 9.00–dusk daily.*

Canal race: Devizes to Westminster   E5
Devizes, Wilts. The Kennet and Avon Canal, built to link London to Bristol, is the route of an exciting and arduous canoe race from Devizes to Westminster. The toughest canoe race in the world; 125 miles non-stop in under nineteen hours. The record is held by the Services. Because of the state of the canal in many places the first man home has to be as good with his feet as with a paddle. Parts are dry and canoe has to be carried for as much as one mile. *Easter.*

The Falconry Centre   C2
Newent, Glos. A magnificent collection of about 32 species of birds of prey. Fine museum, and courses given in the art of falconry. *Open 10.30–17.30 daily. Closed Tue.*

Great Western Railway Museum   F3
Faringdon Rd, Swindon, Wilts. Brunel, the great engineer, pioneered the GWR in the early days of steam. Historic locomotives of the time are shown with an interesting collection of Brunel mementoes. *Open 10.00–17.00 daily. Closed Sun. morning.*

Hotels

The following indicates the price range of a single room per night:
£ inexpensive
££ medium priced
£££ expensive

Ascot, Berks
Berystede Hotel, Bagshot Rd, Sunninghill. Tel 23311. A Victorian country house in several acres of parkland. Spacious and comfortable. *££.*

Bilbury, Glos.   B4
Grand Spa Hotel, Sion Hill, Clifton. Tel 38955. A well established hotel set high on the Avon gorge. *££.*

Bournemouth, Dorset   E8
Royal Bath Hotel, Bath Rd. Tel 25555. A 'Grand' hotel with chandeliers and ornamental ceilings. Elegant and comfortable. *££.*

Bucklers' Hard, Hants.   G8
Master Builder's House Hotel, Beaulieu. Tel 253. An Adam fireplace, flagstones and beams in the bar and a ghost are among the features of this famous Shipbuilder's house. *£.*

Castle Combe, Wilts   D4
Manor House Hotel. Tel 782206. A spacious mediaeval manor with good antiques in the public rooms. Two of the bedrooms have four-posters. *££.*

Cheltenham, Glos   D2
Malvern View Hotel, Cleeve Hill. Tel Bishop's Cleeve 2017. Beautiful antiques and fine modern paintings enhance the interior of this stone house. Magnificent views of the Malvern Hills. *££. No children under 6.*

Chipping Norton, Oxon   F1
Crown and Cushion Hotel, High St. Tel 2533. An attractive and cheerful coaching inn with a friendly atmosphere. *£.*

Cirencester, Glos   E3
Stratton House Hotel. Tel 3836. A 17thC manor house in well tended grounds. A fine oak-beamed smokeroom acts as the bar. *£.*

Freshwater, IOW   F8
Farringford Hotel, Bedbury Lane. Tel 2500. This former home of Lord Tennyson is surrounded by 200 acres of landscaped garden and parkland. Well appointed public rooms include the poet's library. *££.*

Hurley, Berks   J4
Ye Olde Bell Hotel, nr Maidenhead. Tel Littlewick Green 4244. Reputedly England's oldest inn. The heavily beamed flagstoned lounge has cottage style furnishings. *£££.*

Lyndhurst, Hants   F7
Crown Hotel, High St. Tel 2722. A fine Georgian country house hotel, set in parkland. Public rooms house antiques. Personal service. *£.*

Moreton-in-Marsh, Glos   F1
Redesdale Arms Hotel. Tel 50308. A tastefully modernised Cotswold stone coaching house. The flagstoned courtyard is an ideal setting for drinks in the warmer weather. *££.*

Oxford,   G3
Randolph Hotel, Beaumont St. Tel 47481. Dignified, modernised 19thC Gothic, in the heart of the city. *£££.*

Salisbury, Wilts   E6
King's Arms Inn, St John's St. Tel 27629. An attractive half-timbered inn with fine antique furniture in the public rooms. *£.*

Rose and Crown Hotel, Harnham. Tel 27908. A well situated 13thC inn with distant views of the cathedral. *££.*

Shaftesbury, Dorset   D7
Grosvenor Hotel, The Commons. Tel 2282. A pleasant hotel in the market square. Public rooms display antique furniture. *££.*

Silchester, Hants   H5
Romans Hotel, nr Reading. Tel 700421. An ideal family retreat with lovely grounds and sports facilities, swimming pool and tennis courts. *££.*

Southampton, Hants   G7
Dolphin Hotel, 34 High St. Tel 26178. A well situated hotel, both for liner passengers and businessmen. Sedate and comfortable. *££.*

Sutton Benger, Wilts   D4
Bell House Hotel, nr Chippenham. Tel Seagry 401. An elegant hotel, tastefully furnished with antiques. Luxurious individually styled bedrooms. Excellent food. *££.*

Westonbirt, Glos   D3
Hare and Hounds Hotel, nr Tetbury. Tel 233. Set in ten acres of land, this Tudor style hotel is ideal for families. *£.*

Weston-on-the-Green, Oxon   G2
Weston Manor Hotel, nr Oxford. Tel Bletchington 621. A splendid manor steeped in history. A fine 'Great Hall' and a ghost are among its attractions. *££.*

Winchester, Hants   G6
Wessex Hotel, Paternoster Row. Tel 61611. A good modern hotel which blends well with the cathedral. There is a fine John Piper screen. *£££.*

Windsor, Berks **J4**
Old House Hotel, Thames St. Tel 61354.
Built and lived in by Wren in 1676, and
decorated and furnished in the style of the
period. Good views of the river and the
castle. ££.

Regional food and drink

Bacon and Sausages
Wiltshire is traditionally a 'pig' county.
Bacon and hams were cured not only from
the local Wessex saddlebacks, but also from
overseas pigs who rested on the Downs en
route for London from Bristol. A sausage
industry has now been built up on this
historical base.

Cakes
The English fascination with wrapping food
in pastry is not confined to Cornwall.
Banbury Cakes and Clifton Puffs are
examples of mixed-dried fruit pastries which
are prepared in this way. Lardy Cakes
abound in Wiltshire towns, lard traditionally
coming from the local Wiltshire pigs.

Channel Islands food
The milk from the famous Jersey and
Guernsey breeds of cow is delicious, with
thick yellow cream. The islands are also
famous for fish and particularly lobsters.
There is a soup made from conger eels which
are landed here.

Cheeses
Caerphilly. Although originating from
Glamorgan, it is now made in the west
country, and is a very mild-flavoured small,
white cheese.
Cheddar. One of the most famous
British cheeses which, although produced all
over the world, is still made in this area, of
which Shepton Mallet is the centre of the
cheese industry. A pale yellow cheese of
firm texture.
Double Gloucester. A smooth-textured
honey-coloured or light red cheese with a
somewhat fuller flavour than cheddar.
Dorset Blue Vinny. A strong tasting, deep
blue veined cheese with a stiff crumbly
texture. It is made from partly skimmed
milk which is unusual in this country. Eat
it with a local crispbread roll called 'Dorset
knobs'.
Pork. From Wiltshire, this is a type
of brawn made from pork hocks.

Restaurants

Restaurants
£   inexpensive
££   medium priced
£££   expensive

Amesbury, Wilts **E6**
Antrobus Arms, Church St. Tel 3163.
Regency hotel. English. LD. ££. Book.

Bishop's Cleeve, Glos **D1**
*Cleeveway House, Evesham Rd (A435). Tel
2585.* 17thC Cotswold house. Individual
cooking to high standards. Franco-British.
LD. Closed Sun & Mon. ££. Book.

Burford, Oxon **F2**
Bay Tree, Sheep St. Tel 3137. 16thC inn
with family atmosphere. Traditional
English. Garden. LD. ££. Book.

Burghfield, Berks **H4**
*Knight's Farm Restaurant, 2½ miles sw of
Reading off Newbury Rd.* Tel Reading 52366.
Mainly English and French. LD. Closed Sun
D & Mon LD. £££. Book.

Chinnor, Oxon **H3**
*Sir Charles Napier Inn, Spriggs Holly. Tel
Radnage 3011.* Cosy, informal inn. Mainly
English and French. Music and dancing
some evenings. LD. Closed D Sun.

Christchurch, Dorset **E8**
Splinters, 12 Church St. Tel 3454. Informal.
Bistro cooking. D. Closed Sun. ££. Book.

Fairford, Glos **E3**
Pink's, London Rd. Tel 355. Galleried stable
restaurant. French and English. LD. Closed
Sun D, Mon L. £££L, £££D. Book.

Kintbury, Berks **G4**
Dundas Arms. Tel 263. Pleasant inn flanked

by the River Kennet and the Kennet and
Avon Canal. Mainly French. D. Closed
Sun & Mon D. £££. Book.

Lymington, Hants **F8**
Limpets, 9 Gosport St. Tel 75595. Small
French restaurant with a very friendly
atmosphere. Speciality limpets! D. Closed
Mon. L served Sun in winter. ££.

Milford-on-Sea, Hants **F8**
Mill House Restaurant, 1 High St. Tel 2611.
Popular little restaurant. Elaborate menus,
mainly French. LD. Closed Sun D & Mon.
££. Book.

Newbury, Berks **G4**
La Riviera, 26 The Broadway. Tel 47499.
Friendly. Greek and Italian. LD. Closed
Wed LD. ££. Book.

Oxford, Oxon **G3**
*Restaurant Elizabeth, 84 St Aldates. Tel
42230.* Established. Popular. Mainly French.
LD. Closed Mon–Sat L. £££. Book.

La Sorbonne, 130a High St. Tel 41320.
Situated on the first floor of a pleasant
17thC building. Excellent French cooking.
LD. Closed Sun. ££. Book.

Plush, Dorset
Brace of Pheasants. Tel Piddletrenthide 357.
Former village forge. Good bar snacks.
English, some French. LD. Closed Sun &
Mon. ££. Book D.

Ramsbury, Wilts **H4**
Bell Inn. Tel 230. Pub/restaurant in the
centre of the village. Individual cooking.
Mainly English. LD. Closed Sun D & Mon.
£££. Book D.

Salisbury, Wilts **E6**
*Crane's Restaurant, 90-92 Crane St. Tel.
3471.* Outstanding French-provincial
cooking. LD. Closed Sun & Mon. ££. Book.

Silchester, Hants **H5**
Romans. Tel 700421. Small, friendly hotel.
Mainly English but some French. Varied
menus. LD. Closed Sat L & Sun D. ££.
Book..

Stroud, Glos **D3**
Mr Baillie's, 203 Slad Rd. Tel 5331.
Victorian country mansion set in pleasant
gardens. Imaginatively cooked English
dishes, good wine selection. Closed Mon &
D Sun. ££. Book.

Sturminster Newton, Dorset **C7**
*Plumber Manor, Hazelbury Bryan Rd. Tel
72507.* 17thC manor house set in 15 acres of
parkland. International menu. D. Closed
Mon & Sun Nov–Mar. ££. Book.

Tetbury, Glos **D3**
The Close, 8 Long St. Tel 52272. Handsome
Cotswold house. Comfortable with English
and French cooking to high standards. Well
thought-out menus. LD. £££. Book D.

Thornbury, Avon **C3**
Thornbury Castle. Tel 412647. 16thC castle.
Outstanding wines and elaborate food.
Formal atmosphere. LD. Closed Mon &
Sun D. £££. Book.

Weymouth, Dorset **C9**
*Sea Cow Bistro, 7 Custom House Quay. Tel
3524.* Friendly, informal restaurant. Local
fish and straightforward cooking. LD.
Closed Sat & Sun. ££. Book.

Wickham, Hants **G7**
*Old House Restaurant, The Square. Tel
833049.* Pleasantly renovated Georgian
house. French cooking to a high standard,
try the home-made soups. LD. Closed Sun,
L Mon. ££. Book.

Winchester, Hants **G6**
Old Chesil Rectory, 1 Chesil St. Tel 3177.
Old converted shop. Authentic Italian. LD.
Closed Mon. £££. Book.

Woodstock, Oxon **G2**
Bear Hotel, Park St. Tel 811511. Popular
ancient inn. English traditional. The set
menus are the best. LD. £££. Book D.

London's Country and Coast

This part of England depends largely on London but that doesn't mean it has been totally urbanised. Kent, Surrey and Sussex have some of the country's loveliest countryside; you can feel that men have cultivated it for centuries and that it has been inhabited for a very long time. The Romans lived here, St Augustine landed in Kent, the Saxons and the Normans made their presence felt. Arriving by sea from Europe, you will see all the basic Englishness of this part of the world; from the white cliffs at Dover to the trim hedges, rolling downland and cosy cottages. Now Britain is part of the European Community this is, more than ever, England's doorstep to the continent. Vulnerable and lovely countryside needs constant watching and the ancient towns and villages need vigilant care to save them from the advance of the metropolis, the motorways, and the juggernauts.

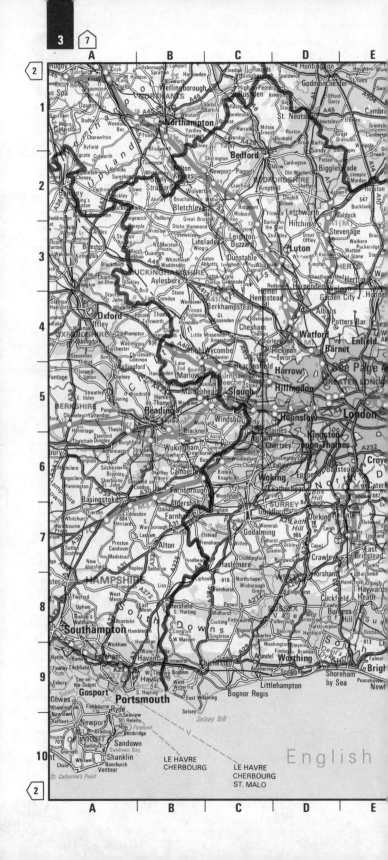

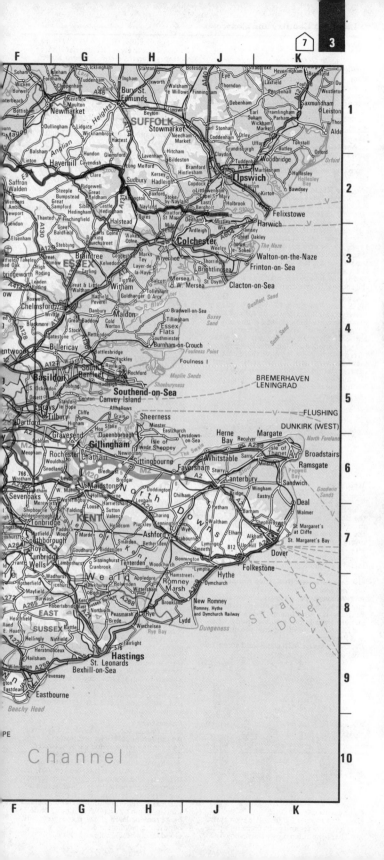

The coast

Allhallows
G5
Kent. Pop 600. A weird and wonderful Thames estuary spot, once destined to be a Londoner's holiday resort: it never quite made it. Now it's the hinterland of industry and oil refineries – when the tide goes out there are miles of mud and vast numbers of sea birds. Beach: shingle and mud.

Beachy Head
F9
E. Sussex. 500-foot-high chalk cliffs topped with smooth turf. To glance over the edge at the tiny lighthouse is a dizzy experience. Take care of the unfenced Lovers Leap. No beaches.

Bognor Regis
C9
W. Sussex. Pop 34,400. EC Wed. Oddly disconnected, Queen Victoria's 'dear little Bognor' was developed on a quiet scale in the 1820s a mile away from the original village of Bersted. A sneakish imitation of the bigger resorts but of modest ambition. Probably the original of Jane Austen's 'Sanditon'. Unselfconsciously developed for the well-to-do, it didn't really fill up until the 20thC.
Sandy beach with safe bathing except near the rocks at the western end.

Bosham
B9
W. Sussex. Pop 3,200. EC Wed. A full stop between two inlets of sea; flint, brick and tile-hung cottages huddled delightfully round the water's edge in Chichester harbour. The road on the south side of the village is flooded at high tide. From the tarred buildings on the quay there are fine views to the estuary. The Bayeux Tapestry depicts Harold setting sail from here to Normandy.
Swimming is dangerous near the harbour.

Bosham

Brighton
E9
E. Sussex. Pop 160,000. EC Wed, Thur. Like its more sedate neighbour, Hove, Brighton is a brilliant, beautiful town: the essence of the English seaside. There's almost too much to do, the three miles of promenade by the sea have everything: indoor and outdoor pools, two piers, the world's first electric railway, waxworks and an aquarium. The town was built for relaxation and the Royal Pavilion was the Prince Regent's pleasure dome. A visit is a must; nowhere else in the west are there such sumptuous oriental rooms. The town is full of marvellous shops, antiques, Victorian churches, cinemas, parks and gardens. Brighton is a humdinger of a place and only an hour from London on fast trains. Visit the Lanes, Churchill Square, the museum and Preston Park.
Beaches: shingle with some sand at low tide; life guards.

Brighton: Regency Square

Broadstairs
K6
Kent. Pop 20,000. EC Wed. Uneven 19thC terraces, cottages and pubs focus on a pint-sized harbour hugged by a horseshoe of squat chalk cliffs. Here, in Bleak House, Dickens wrote David Copperfield. More cottagey than the rest is Harbour Street, twisting its way through York Gate to a sandy foreshore.
The North Foreland Lighthouse, built in the late 17thC, is worth a look.

Clacton-on-Sea
J3
Essex. Pop 38,000. EC Wed. MD Tue. Since the Victorians popularised the English seaside, Clacton has grown from a collection of villages into a thriving resort. The 1870s produced the Royal and Grand Hotels and the obligatory Marine Parade. Cheerful and busy, the pier has a switch-back and all the amusements you need; there are band concerts and crazy golf.
Beach: long, sandy with diving boards and platforms.

Cuckmere Haven
F9
E. Sussex. Beautiful estuary between white cliffs with an unspoilt shingle beach where bathing is safe away from the river. The valley of flat meadows is a real haven of peace, but likely to become an organised country park.

Deal
K6
Kent. Pop 25,500. EC Thur. A trio of Tudor castles, a steep shingle beach, the beat of military marches from the Royal School of Music, and one of Britain's most modern piers. One of the Cinque Ports, it was planned as two parallel roads front and rear, with a mesh of alleys criss-crossing the gap, and Middle Street snaking between the lot. It is claimed as the landing place for Julius Caesar's invasions. Of interest is the church of St Leonard, with distinctive cupola and splendid Pilot's Gallery (1685).
The steep beach, ideal for fishing, is safe only if swimmers stay close in.

Dover
K7
Kent. Pop 34,000. EC Wed. MD Sat. The front door to Europe, breezy and businesslike, it spills inland from the harbour up a valley between chunks of chalk headland. To the left are the famous white cliffs, whilst to the right is the mighty castle, dominating both town and harbour.
The 13thC hostel for pilgrims, the Maison Dieu Hall and the Roman lighthouse are fascinating. Safe bathing with sand and shingle beach.

Dungeness
J8
Kent. A windy promontory pointing into the English Channel; Dungeness is a ledge of gravel that is still growing. A quiet and lonely spot, although it has a seagull sanctuary, a lighthouse and two nuclear power stations.
Beaches: shingle, fishing safer than bathing. Strong currents.

Eastbourne
F9
E. Sussex. Pop 70,500. EC Wed. An elegant resort of Georgian and Victorian character with a sea front of grey/white buildings like a bit of Beachy Head lining the shingle beach. Wooden groynes split the shingle beach into compartments; safe bathing.

Faversham
H6
Kent. Pop 15,000. EC Thur. MD Wed, Fri, Sat. A market town, formerly a flourishing port, hung round a navigable creek of the Swale estuary. Dignified Georgian fronts to the houses hide fine 16thC details. The best are in Abbey Street and Court Street.
Shingle beach at Graveney Marshes to the north-east.
Sparkling Guildhall in Market Place; look out for the interesting restoration of the gunpowder mill.

Folkestone
J7
Kent. Pop 44,000. EC Wed. MD Tue, Fri. An important cross-channel port of unassuming terraces and gardens carved from the wooded chalk cliffs, it was developed in the middle of the last century as a popular seaside resort. Narrow old streets wind down to the original fishermen's quarters near the harbour. On the cliffs is one of the 74 Martello towers, part of a chain of small forts built to defend England from invasion by Napoleon. The 1½-mile long promenade, the Leas, is complete with bandstand, pavilion and gardens.
Good sandy beach, safe and clean.

Folkestone

Harwich   J2
Essex. Pop 15,000. EC Wed. A port for more
than ten centuries, the kind of place you
usually pass through on the way to board a
ship. A mediaeval street pattern with some
Georgian houses and weather-boarded inns.
Ships provide constantly moving scenery,
the largest car ferries from Holland docking
at Parkeston Quay. Lighthouses and a late
17thC treadmill crane are reminders of
harsher seafaring days. Dovercourt is the
seaside area but it lacks the energy of the
port.
Bathing on sandy beaches.

Hastings and St Leonards   G9
E. Sussex. Pop 74,000. EC Wed. The old
town of Hastings is one of the Cinque Ports.
It is an intriguing collection of bent-backed
houses and narrow twisting streets. On a
sweep of the beach beneath the rugged cliffs
are gangling timber-framed fishing huts –
as elegant as the giants of La Mancha.
Modern Hastings is a string of ice cream
parlours and boarding houses but it has one
gem, Pelham Crescent, one of the most
elegant crescents on the south coast. On the
cliffs are the ruins of the Norman castle. Six
miles to the north-west is Battle, the spot
where William the Conqueror defeated
Harold in 1066.
St Leonards adjoins Hastings and is a unique
example of a Regency new town planned and
developed in the 1830s by James and
Decimus Burton. Fashionable in the 19thC,
its heart is the Royal Victoria Hotel on the
sea front. A long valley of landscaped
gardens climbs up from the sea front dotted
with stately houses.
Look out for North Lodge, once the home of
writer Rider Haggard, and the fairy-tale
Gothic Clock House.
Beach: long – sand and shingle; safe
bathing.

Pelham Crescent, Hastings

Hythe   J7
Kent. Pop 12,000. EC Wed. The old part of
Hythe, like Rye, is a port in mothballs and
another of the original Cinque Ports. It lies
half a mile inland in a commanding position
riding a steep hill. A leafy place of narrow
streets, with mellow 18thC buildings
dominated by a large church with a
celebrated 13thC chancel. Near the
foreshore the mood changes from the
homespun grid of streets on the hill to
seaside-suburban. The home of the
Romney, Hythe and Dymchurch Railway,
the world's smallest public steam railway.
Boating on the Royal Military Canal.
A shingle and sand beach.

Littlehampton   C9
W. Sussex. Pop 19,000. EC Wed. Little
Victorian resort at the mouth of the fast
flowing River Arun with excellent boatyards.
Miles of safe, sandy beaches, particularly
good across the river.

Maldon   G4
Essex. Pop 14,000. EC Wed. MD Thur, Sat.
A tight little town on one of the few hills in
Essex. The liveliest part of the town is by
the River Blackwater where fishing and
sailing boats cluster round the Hythe. Of
interest are good 15thC buildings in the
High Street, and the triangular tower of All
Saints Church. A very nautical air pervades
although the town is twelve miles from the
open sea.

Margate   K5
Kent. Pop 50,000. EC Thur. MD Thur, Fri.
A bit of a dog's dinner now, but once
popular with wealthy Victorians. The arrival
of the Saturday Boat, which brought
Londoners down for the weekend, was a
great social event. This was the first of the
villages on the Isle of Thanet to develop as a
seaside resort. It was a local Quaker who
invented the bathing machine in 1753.
Development began in earnest in 1769 when
Cecil Square was laid out. It soon became a
resort for the 'nobility and persons of fashion'
In humbler streets behind the front there is a
fantastic 19thC folly on Grotto Hill. On the
front is Dreamland, a razzmatazz Disney-
style amusement park.
Wide sandy beach in front of a lively
promenade with safe bathing.

Ramsgate   K6
Kent. Pop 40,000. EC Thur. MD Fri. One of
the Cinque Ports, it is now a miniature
Monte Carlo sprawled over two chalk cliffs
with an artificial harbour for small boats. It
figured prominently in the evacuation of
Dunkirk in 1940 when 80,000 soldiers were
landed at the port. West of the harbour are
white cliffs capped by promenades and
lawns. It has one of the finest Victorian
churches in England, designed by Pugin.
Long sandy beach to the east of the harbour.
Safe bathing.

Ramsgate

Rochester   G6
Kent. Pop 56,000. EC Wed. MD Fri. An
endearing but shabby town, once a Roman
settlement by a ford across the River
Medway. The town grew in importance
when it was made a bishopric by St
Augustine in 604. The present cathedral was
begun in 1077 on the site of his church. Also
a busy thriving port.
Rochester is dominated by the Norman
castle, set on a low cliff above the river, with
one of the finest and best preserved keeps in
England. It was at Gad's Hill, on the north-
west outskirts of the town, that Charles
Dickens made his home. Note the Tudor
building in King's School; and Restoration
House, built 1587, where Charles II stayed
on his way to London to claim his throne.

Rye   H8
E. Sussex. Pop 4,500. EC Tue. MD Thur. Set
above a hill of sandstone rock, the Rye
roofscapes leap-frog over each other in an
ever-ascending scale to the single point of a
church spire, like the galloping rhythm of a
sea shanty. A Cinque Port once washed by
the sea, the town is now marooned in the
flatness of the Sussex landscape, with the sea
a thin line on the horizon. There is still some
of the smugglers' swagger left in secret
corners. Of interest – 18thC Water House,
Town Hall, Ypres Tower, Lamb House,
Mermaid Inn and 12thC church.
Safe bathing in calm weather from the
shingle beach between Rye Harbour and
Winchelsea Beach.

Rye Harbour

St Margaret's Bay   K7
Kent. The place to start if you want to swim
across the Channel, as this bay is the nearest
point to France. High chalk cliffs all round;
shingle beach.

Sandwich   K6
Kent. Pop 4,500. EC Wed. MD Thur. A
picturesque town, one of the original Cinque
Ports and the chief harbour for the export of
wool in the 13thC. It was nearly ruined by
the silting up of the River Wansum in the

15thC and 16thC. Later prosperity was based on the Protestant clothworkers who arrived from France and Holland in 1560. Look at the quaint mid-16thC gatehouse with drawbridge.
Safe swimming at Sandwich Bay to the east. A sandy beach, one mile wide at low tide.

Selsey Bill   **C9**
W. Sussex. Fast eroding Channel headland with good fishing from a shingle beach. Once an island in ancient times. There is a tiny village almost engulfed by holiday camps. Since the discovery of a Greek amphora offshore, skin diving has become popular. The Saxons landed here in 477; so did St Wilfred when he aimed to convert the Saxons to Christianity.

Southend   **H5**
Essex. Pop 163,000. EC Wed. MD Tue, Thur. Only Blackpool can compare with Southend. It is London's nearest seaside and everything is on a big scale. The pier is the largest in the world.
The domed Kursaal is the centre of a vast amusement park. At night the Golden Mile is England's answer to Sunset Strip. As the town has grown it has consumed surrounding villages which remain, like Leigh-on-Sea, as quiet oases. When the town is full of day visitors it's a roaring, randy place not suitable for the sensitive, but great if you like cockles. Don't miss the floral clock as it must be the largest ever seen.
A sand and shingle beach, but muddy in places.

Whitstable   **J6**
Kent. Pop 25,000. EC Wed. Famous since Roman times for its oysters and as the harbour of Canterbury, it stands unselfconsciously on the southern side of the wide Thames Estuary. Developed first inland around its parish church, it spread out along the High Street to the shore itself. The transition from bay windows and brickwork to shipyards and sail lofts round old inns and narrow streets is sharp and hearty. And finally there is the sea, framed in weather-boarding or rigging and just about as exhilarating as ever in this cheerful Charlie of a town.
Stroll along the Sea Wall and Island Wall and the Street, a unique finger of land jutting out to sea. Safest place along the Kent coast for bathing. Shingle and sand beach.

whitstable

Winchelsea   **H8**
E. Sussex. EC Wed. Late 13thC town replacing the original town swallowed by the sea in a series of violent storms. Only half built, it stands on a hill, an affluent backwater of green grass verges and genteel Georgian houses. Defoe described it as the skeleton of an ancient city rather than a real town. Made a Cinque Port in 1336, it's in a dry dock of grass green country.
Among notable features are three gates surviving from 13thC defences; the much restored Court Hall; the 14thC decorated parish church with some fine canopied tombs; and the ruins of a Franciscan priory chapel.
Long shingle beach to the south. Submerged obstacles and mud holes on the beach, but otherwise safe.

Worthing   **D9**
W. Sussex. Pop 88,000. EC Wed. MD Thur. An ugly muffin of a town; a place of brave beginnings and ignoble endings. Georgian and Victorian terraces heave-ho with gimcrack modern. Unable to make up its mind whether to be Bournemouth or Brighton, it ended up as a sort of Mae West of the south coast. There is a 960-foot long pier.
The long shingle and sand beach is safe for bathing.

Inland towns and villages

Alfriston   **F9**
E. Sussex. Pop 700. EC Wed. A muddle of half-timbered houses by the River Cuckmere under the shadow of the South Downs. The great church, its heart, sits astride an ancient Anglo-Saxon mound. Pre-heyday of the smugglers is the 14thC wattle-and-daub rectory, whilst the 15thC Star Inn is one of the oldest in England. To visit: a Saxon cemetery, long barrow and round barrow behind the little town.

Ampthill   **C2**
Beds. Pop 5,500 EC Tue. MD Thur. One of the best towns in Bedfordshire with some splendid 18thC houses. The castle where Henry VIII sent Katherine of Aragon to await her divorce has gone, but you can still walk beneath the 300-year-old oaks in Ampthill Park.
Look out for Avenue House in Church Street, a fine 1780 house with a magnificent garden.

Arundel   **C9**
W. Sussex. Pop 2,500. EC Wed. An important town before the Conquest, it's now predominantly Victorian. The mighty Norman castle has all the textbook bits, crenellated keeps, embattled barbican towers and wooden drawbridge intact. Overlooking the valley of the River Arun with the town at its feet and backed by beech woods, it was painted by Turner and Constable.
The grandiose French Gothic of the Victorian cathedral adds light relief.
Of interest – 14thC church of St Nicholas and remains of the 12thC priory.

Aylesbury   **B3**
Bucks. Pop 41,000. EC Thur. MD Wed, Sat. County town of Buckinghamshire; home of the plump white ducks and centre of the broad fertile Vale of Aylesbury. It is gaining in importance as a cruising centre for the Aylesbury arm of the Grand Union Canal. Now ringed with modern roads, an enormous new county office rears its vacuous head over the town centre. The 15thC King's Head is a marvellous inn: you can even take a drink sitting in Cromwell's chair.
To visit: Roman exhibits at the Bucks County Museum, and the church of St Mary.

Bedford   **C2**
Beds. Pop 73,000. EC Thur. MD Sat. An unassuming town happily related to the River Ouse, which, flanked by gardens, wanders through the town. The nearby village of Elstow is where John Bunyan was born in 1628, and the Moot Hall houses a good Bunyan exhibition. In the library at Bedford manuscripts relating to Bunyan and The Pilgrims' Progress can be seen.
Of interest are the Bedford Museum and the Cecil Higgins Art Gallery.

Biddenden   **G7**
Kent. Pop 2,000. EC Wed. An essay in half-timbering with ancient weavers' cottages and the mediaeval Cloth Hall, set in the Weald of Kent along a homely village street, short and very perfect, cobwebs and all.
15thC Vane Court and 16thC Castwisell Manor are worth seeing.

Bishop's Stortford   **F3**
Herts. Pop 22,000. EC Wed. MD Thur, Sat. Worth a visit for its maltings (where barley was prepared and stored for beer making) red brick and white weather-boarding with fine towers.

Canterbury   **J6**
Kent. Pop 36,000. EC Thur. MD Wed, Sat. Originally a large Roman town sited on sloping ground where Watling Street forded the River Stour. A centre for pilgrims from all over Europe following Becket's death in 1170 until the destruction of the martyr's shrine by Henry VIII. It was also a refuge for many Flemish and Huguenot immigrants in the late 16thC.
The good things that remain stand out like a crisp spring morning – the hugger-mugger of Mercury Lane down which the cathedral peeps; Christ Church gate sculpted in ceremonial pomp adds a touch of dignity to the small market place. Go through the gate into the solitude of the cathedral precinct

with lofty bent-backed houses and then –
wham! – the cathedral – Colossus itself, a
sort of architectural King Kong, William of
Sens gone madly
grand. And all
around, in long-
forgotten corners,
memories of
Chaucer, Falstaff
and Cobbett
whisper gently.
Telling remains of
14thC and 15thC
city walls and the
14thC Westgate,
intact; ruins of a
Norman castle;
excavations of a
Roman town house;
16thC weavers'
house; and 17thC
Falstaff Hotel.
Associations with
Chaucer's Canter-
bury Tales (c1387).

Canterbury

Castle Hedingham   G2
Essex. Pop 1,000. One of the mightiest
castles of East Anglia and still standing high
above the old trees as a reminder of Norman
power. Built by the powerful de Vere family
in 1140, the keep is one of the best preserved
examples in England. Very little could
penetrate walls eleven feet thick, whilst
100-foot-high towers would repel any
invader.
Over the moat a 15thC bridge leads into a
Norman interior with original zigzag
decoration. A Norman church and some
mediaeval and Georgian houses make up the
best parts of this tiny town.

Chalfont St Giles   C4
Bucks. Pop 7,000. EC Thur. John Milton
moved here in 1665 to escape the London
plague. Worth a visit today to see his tiny
cottage, now a museum, where he wrote his
epic poems, Paradise Lost and Paradise
Regained. The village green looks
prosperous and there are good shops. The
church of St Giles has some wall paintings
from the middle ages.

Chelmsford   G4
*Essex. Pop 58,000. EC Wed. MD Tue, Fri,
Sat.* The county town; not as steeped in
history as neighbouring Colchester but a
busy modern centre. The late mediaeval
parish church is now the cathedral and has
been restored and extended. The nearby
village of Writtle is worth a side trip for its
lovely pond and green. Visit the Chelmsford
and Essex museum and the Shire Hall.

Chichester   C9
W. Sussex. Pop 21,000. EC Thur. MD Wed.
A Roman, mediaeval and Georgian city
dominated by the remains of the Roman
plan – two long, straight main streets
crossing at right angles. At their junction
stands the fine 16thC Market Cross,
originally the focus of a market place.
An uncomplicated town of stately
buildings, its cathedral stands to one
side of West Street and is not, like other
cathedrals, a focal point within a close.
In the Bishop's Palace, the chapel and walls
of the great kitchen are 13thC and the
gateway 14thC. The 18thC Pallant House
and the Council House are stimulating.
Nearby is the Roman palace of Fishbourne.
Don't miss the good Festival Theatre.

Chiddingfold   C7
Surrey. Pop 2,700. EC Wed. Once one of the
centres of the mediaeval glass-making
industry set in the Weald near the Sussex
border, it's a large handsome village with a
row of bulky tile-hung Georgian cottages
facing a triangular green with a pond and a
14thC church.
The 15thC Crown Inn in half-timbering and

the elegant old Manor House of 1762 are
interesting.

Chiddingstone   F7
Kent. Pop 900. Almost too good to be true,
more a film set than a real place. The street
is a dog-leg around the textbook Gothic of
church and graveyard. It has a whisper you
may not catch of 16th and 17thC England;
timber-framed buildings with barge-
boarded gables and pendants, brick nogging
and all the niceties of Tudor England.
Interesting 18thC rectory; also Chiddingstone Castle, a 19thC restoration with
Stuart and Jacobite pictures and an Ancient
Egypt collection.

Chilham   J6
Kent. Pop 1,500. EC Thur. Reached by
narrow lanes, a handful of buildings grouped
casually around a small square on a narrow
plateau of land between church and castle.
Jostling picturesqueness with more than a
smattering of the feudalism of the middle
ages. Fine views through limes to the rolling
country around the River Stour.
Chilham Castle was built in 1616 by Inigo
Jones around a 12thC Norman keep.
Tantalising Neolithic long barrow and, at
Dane Street, several handsomely grouped
farms with oasts and half-timbered
farmhouses.

Colchester   H3
Essex. Pop 80,000. EC Thur. MD Sat. One
of the oldest towns in Britain. Colonised by
the Romans under Claudius in 49, it was
here that Queen Boadicea, in 61, led the
local tribes in a major revolt against the
Romans. The city walls are the chief visible
reminder of Colchester's Roman past,
particularly the massive Balkerne Gate. The
museum has a mass of Roman relics including
a touching gravestone of a centurion. The
keep is the largest in Europe, massive and
splendid.
The town hugs the hill, its outline
punctuated by the tower of the florid
Edwardian town hall and the crazily huge
Victorian water tower. Fine streets of 17thC
and 18thC houses have been progressively
sacked by developers. Go soon before the
whole town becomes a multi-storey car park.
Visit Bourne Hill, the 16thC mill, Holy
Trinity church with its Saxon tower, and the
Minories Art Gallery for drawings by
Constable.

Dedham   H2
Essex. Pop 1,700. EC Wed. Genteel and
spacious, it is the best little town in Essex.
Wander among the good houses along the
High Street and Mill Lane towards the
River Stour. St Mary's church (1500) was
often painted by John Constable.

Farnham   B7
Surrey. Pop 31,500. EC Wed. A good
Georgian base topped by the domestic brick
buildings and Wayneflete Tower of
Farnham Castle. Two Georgian streets,
West and Castle, are full of fine houses; note
especially Willmer House, now a museum
and a vigorous example of Farnham
Baroque. Birthplace of that jolly radical
William Cobbett.

Finchingfield   G2
Essex. Pop 800. EC Wed. This is it, a perfect
English village, with a church on the hill,
duckpond, village green, haphazard lanes
and gabled Guildhall – even a windmill to
the north.

Godstone   E6
Surrey. Pop 5,500. EC Wed. A cracking
village green, unspoilt and only nineteen
miles from London. A little church, with a
pretty shingled spire, sits among the trees.
Some jolly almshouses by the church have a
domestic chapel with a cosy fireplace in the
nave to warm the inmates.

Finchingfield.

Goudhurst   G7
Kent. Pop 3,000. EC Wed. Surrounded by orchards and hop gardens, it climbs a hill with the village pond at the bottom and the fat sandstone church, a mixture of Classical and Gothic, at the top. The whole place is an encyclopaedia of Wealden building. Scrutinize the 16thC Church House and discreetly handsome inn.

Goudhurst

Great Bardfield   G2
Essex. Pop 1,000. There are three Bardfields; Great, Little and Bardfield Saling, all edged by the River Pant. Great Bardfield has a broad, sloping High Street, with a nice variety of mediaeval and Georgian houses. The 16thC museum has a good show of local crafts. A popular place for artists, it retains a bohemian air. Visit the church and Cottage Museum.

Haddenham   B4
Bucks. Pop 2,300. EC Wed. Unusual combination of good modern houses and fine old ones, built with the traditional local material, wicherts (a chalky marl mixed with straw and water). Church and village pond on the edge of the green.

Hambleden   B5
Bucks. Pop 1,600. The full feudal scene, from manor house to village pump. Look into the museum for Roman farm implements found nearby. Don't miss the great weather-boarded water mill, one of the few left along the Thames.

Harlow (New town)   F3
Essex. Pop 80,000. EC Wed. MD Tue, Fri, Sat. One of the first of Britain's new towns started after the war in 1947 to provide homes and jobs for Londoners. Planned by Sir Frederick Gibberd it pioneered pedestrian shopping areas, landscaping schemes for a whole town, and the first tower block of flats in Britain. The effect is dull but the planning good, and as the trees grow it may even become a pleasant place. Good modern sculpture by Moore, Rodin and Hepworth.

Hatfield   D4
Herts. Pop 25,000. EC Mon, Thur. MD Wed, Sat. Hatfield new town has grown up only since 1947, but across the railway in old Hatfield small, plain Georgian houses mount the hill crowned by the Jacobean home of the Cecils. Inside the gates of Hatfield House a heady feeling of Elizabethan splendour survives, keeping the 20thC firmly at bay. Visit the church also.

Lewes   E9
E. Sussex. Pop 14,000. EC Wed. MD Mon, Tue. A jolly place, half in a hollow and half up a hill, dominated by a castle, with the Downs rising all about it and the Channel another bend away. It's very much the county town. Important already in Saxon times, it was the site of the first Clunaic priory in England. The curious 16thC house at Southover was given to Anne of Cleves by Henry VIII after their divorce in 1540. It houses a collection of furniture, costumes and household equipment.

Little Gaddesden   C3
Herts. Pop 1,200. A manor house of 1576 with trimmed yew gardens; magnificent sweeps of beechwoods; and a 19thC Gothic extravaganza; all are found around this village. Ashridge House was rebuilt in 1809 by James Wyatt, and inside the chapel and dizzily high tower are superb examples of Wyatt's romantic Gothic work.

The Mardens   B8
W. Sussex. Four tiny hamlets – hardly anything to them, but they have that indefinable something. East Marden, a handful of flint cottages and church in a cup-shaped hollow; North and Up Marden, church, farms and trees, whilst West Marden is larger with no church, but an armful of delightful flint cottages straggling up a hill. Lovely 13thC church at Up Marden, simple and dignified.

Marlow   B5
Bucks. Pop 12,000. EC Wed. Walk straight on to the suspension bridge to catch the essence of Marlow. Here the Thames is at its best, crowded with weekend boatmen and swans. At the elegant inn, the Compleat Angler, you can enjoy a riverside meal and then a stroll along the towpath or through the little Georgian and gabled town for tea. Makes a perfect English afternoon.

Mistley   J2
Essex. Pop 2,100. EC Wed. An Essex town with strong leanings towards Suffolk. It stands on the Stour, where at high tide the river is over a mile wide, and in autumn is graced by gatherings of hundreds of mute swans. Attempts to turn the town into an 18thC spa failed; only two elegant Adam towers remain looking incongruous among the sturdy Victorian maltings. A tree-lined walk takes you into Manningtree, a neat Georgian neighbour.

Mistley, Essex: The Adam Towers.

Much Hadham   E3
Herts. Pop 2,100. EC Wed. Essence of English country life as it is lived – by some. A street of sustained quality, full of terrific 18thC houses and 16thC and 17thC cottages. A country gentleman's house (1740) has the best name in the village, The Lordship, and it lives up to it.

Old Warden   D2
Beds. Pop 500. A model village full of pretty thatched cottages, built for his tenants by the Victorian Lord Ongley. But the real reason for a visit here is the Shuttleworth Collection of old aeroplanes on the airfield 1½ miles north-east of the village. On an exhibition day you might well see a genuine 1909 Bleriot actually flying.

Saffron Walden   F2
Essex. Pop 10,000. EC Thur. MD Tue, Sat. Once a very prosperous town, its wealth coming from the wool trade in the middle ages. Three splendid pubs, the Sun Inn, the Cross Keys and the Rose and Crown. The nature reserve at Hales Wood lies three miles to the north-east. The great Jacobean mansion of Audley End lies a mile to the west in a beautiful landscaped park. Its Great Hall and good picture collection are well worth a visit.

St Albans   D4
Herts. Pop 52,000. EC Thur. MD Sat. Now a busy centre of commuter territory, but you don't have to look far to find over 2,000 years of history. Start with Verulamium, the Roman city, now almost completely excavated: the hypocaust (Roman underfloor heating), mosaic floors, semi-circular theatre and fine Roman walls make you wonder how far the modern city really has advanced. The dominant feature of St Albans is the great abbey, with its long nave and stubby tower. Some rare, recently uncovered, mediaeval wall paintings cheer the solemn atmosphere of the Norman nave. The town's modern growth has emasculated much of the city; the High Street could be renamed 'Main Street, Anywhere'.
Visit St Michael's Saxon church, Romeland and Fishpool Streets and Gorhambury House.

Shoreham   F6
Kent. Pop 1,900. As cheerful as red faces in country pubs, it huddles as snugly as possible in the saddle of land between long and high chalk ridges thickly wooded with beech and oak. By the old ford across the River Darent, half a mile from the main road, stands the

house where Samuel Palmer, the painter, lived, during his most creative period in the 1830s.
For the open-eyed – Old George Inn and Filston Hall, a delightful and unusual 17thC moated house.

Smarden H7
Kent. Pop 1,000. Modest half-timbered cottages, at once both gentle and kind, terrace the street. The 14thC stone church at the west end has a charming lych gate. Fine examples of half-timbering in the Dragon House and Chessenden. Interesting farmhouses in Hamden (1¼ miles south-east), and Watch House (1½ miles north-west).

Stoke Poges C5
Bucks. Pop 4,000. EC Wed. Golf courses and the churchyard which inspired Thomas Gray's 'Elegy'. The monument to Gray is in a meadow by the church; 18thC Stoke Park with landscaped park is now a golf club.

Tenterden H7
Kent. Pop 6,000. EC Wed. MD Fri. The finest example of a traditional weather-boarded and tile-hung Kentish town. A tiny settlement in Roman times, it wasn't until Edward III encouraged the Flemish weavers to settle in England in the 14thC that the town prospered. A small market town situated on a ridge of high ground, it is one very long High Street, with a mixture of trees, pavements and wide grass verges. The church punctuates the High Street in time for you to catch your second breath. Basic character remarkably well preserved. 14thC Pittlesden Gatehouse is impressive. Also 18thC Westfield House and 19thC Town Hall. Some fine 18thC headstones in the churchyard.

Tenterden, Kent

Thaxted F2
Essex. Pop 2,000. EC Wed. A modest, harmonious town of white plastered houses and a beautiful church that must be seen. The Guildhall is a jovial expression of 15thC merchant competence.

Thaxted : The Guildhall

Tunbridge Wells F7
Kent. Pop 44,500. EC Wed. A rural hamlet at the turn of the 19thC when people first took the waters from its chalybeate spring, it was rapidly developed into a fine Regency spa. *Raison d'être*, the Pantiles, a colonnaded promenade with raised music gallery and lime trees, first laid out in 1638 – the perfect pedestrian precinct.
See Calverley Crescent, built in the 1830s by Decimus Burton, and the 17thC church of King Charles the Martyr with fine plaster ceiling, wooden cupola and clock of 1759.

Ware E3
Herts. Pop 14,700. EC Thur. MD Tue. A water-mills-and-malthouses sort of town, with the long High Street following the River Lea. It is a good gabled street which widens at the Regency Old Town Hall. Here Lady Jane Grey was declared queen in 1553. The church and nearby Fanhams Hall are worth visiting.

Welwyn Garden City D3
Herts. Pop 40,000. EC Wed. The spirit of reformer Ebenezer Howard lives on at

Welwyn. He wanted to build clusters of towns that combined the virtues of town and country. The town centre is worth a look. Generously planned and planted, it's now more garden than city.

Westerham E6
Kent. Pop 4,200. EC Wed. A small country market town on a hill at the end of the Darent Valley. Houses muddle round the tapering green with the church as focal point. The birth place of General Wolfe (1727), and the home of Winston Churchill until his death.
Of interest – Quebec House, Squerryes Court and Chartwell.

Regional oddities

Cinque Ports
The principal bastions of England during the mediaeval wars with France, these five ports were Hastings, Romney, Hythe, Dover and Sandwich. Rye and Winchelsea were made Cinque Ports in the 14thC, and the correct description of the confederation is 'The Cinque Ports and the Two Ancient Towns'. They supplied 57 ships furnished and manned in return for privileges and concessions granted by the King.

Hill Figures
Ditchling Cross. Sussex. 5 miles nw of Lewes. Dating from the Battle of Lewes in 1264, when Simon de Montfort defeated Henry III, it is a Greek type of cross 100 feet wide.
Litlington Horse. Sussex. Hindover Hill, nr Litlington. The present white horse, carved in the chalk hill, dates from about 1925. An earlier figure was cut for the coronation of Queen Victoria, but no trace remains.
Whipsnade White Lion. Beds. 1 mile n of Dagnall. Cut into the chalk face of Dunstable Downs, it is 500 feet long and edged in cement. Modern.
Wilmington Long Man. Wilmington, Sussex. Carved into the chalk north face of Windover Hill overlooking the village, the gigantic threatening figure 226 feet high holds a staff in each hand. Origin unknown, but probably Saxon.
Wye Crown. Kent. 1 mile se of Wye. Cut to celebrate the coronation of Edward VII in 1902, it is 240 feet wide.

Martello Towers
Kent and Sussex. A chain of small forts built by the Royal Engineers between 1810 and 1812 as a defensive line between Seaford and Folkestone against invasion by Napoleon. Two-storeyed brick-built towers with a gun mounted on a revolving platform, they are about 30 feet high, fifteen feet in diameter and six feet thick.
The design was based on the *Torre della Mortella* on the island of Corsica which impressed the English in the campaign of 1794. Each tower housed a garrison of 25 men in the upper part, with stores and ammunition below.

Oast Houses
Commonly found in Kent and Sussex they date back to the 16thC when brewing with hops was first practised in England. Formerly picked by hand, the hops ripen in late August or September. The green cones are dried to a ten per cent moisture content by hot air for eight to ten hours in a special kiln, the oast house. This is usually circular, with a cowl on top which turns with the wind whilst a vent controls the ventilation. After drying, the hops are taken from the kiln, cooled, and pressed into sacks.
Hops are grown in the south-east chiefly in the Medway valley from Tonbridge through to Staplehurst, and in a belt from Faversham to Canterbury. Some of the best examples of the many thousands of oast houses are at Belting Hadlow, Cobham and Boughton, Kent.

Chiddingstone, Kent   Boughton, Kent

Tower mill, Shipley, Sussex X   Post & Tower Mills – Jack and Jill at Clayton, Sussex

Windmills

Good examples of post mills are at Chillenden, Kent and Clayton, Sussex. At Outward, five miles south-east of Redhill, Surrey, is the oldest working windmill in Britain, which was built in 1665.
Examples of smock mills are at Cranbrook, Kent, Shipley, Sussex, and Stansted Mountfitchet, Essex.
Fine 55-foot-high tower-windmill in working order at Polegate, 4 miles north of Eastbourne, Sussex.

Bourn mill, Cambs   mill at Outham, Kent

The Yeoman's House

Kent. There was an abundance of oak in mediaeval times in Kent, and the technique of timber framing was simple, so this type of house became a standard design for the prosperous farmer. The house often included a central hall with a tall window under jutting eaves. These eaves were supported by diagonal bracing from the inner sides of the projecting upper storeys. Typical examples are Hawkenbury Farm, near Staplehurst, Stoneacre, Otham, and Old Bell Farm, Harrietsham. But you can see others in most villages in the county.

Yeoman's House

Famous people

Anne Boleyn (1507-36)   **E7**
Hever Castle, Hever, Kent. A warm brick Tudor castle where Anne was born, still moated and wearing well. Now extended and improved by the Astor family, it is surrounded by beautiful gardens and a collection of Italian sculpture. Anne Boleyn was a lady of Henry VIII's court and she became his second wife. She only enjoyed Henry's company for three years. He tired of her, and she was beheaded. Hever has all the atmosphere of those dangerously elegant days.
Open 13.00-19.00 Wed, Fri, Sun & B. Hols Apr-Sep.

Winston Churchill (1874-1965)   **E7**
Chartwell, nr Westerham, Kent. This house is where Churchill recharged his batteries during his wartime leadership, and it is the place he loved above all others. The house is not particularly distinguished, but it has long views over the Kentish Weald and is full of associations, as the National Trust is careful to keep the house as it was when Churchill lived there. You can see the study where he wrote (usually writing standing up at a special desk), and rooms full of his own oil paintings. In the gardens is the fishpond

where the elder statesman fed his carp, and you can examine the long wall which he built with his own hands, as a relaxing therapy after troubled wartime days. *Open 14.00-18.00 Wed & Thur (11.00-18.00 Sat, Sun & B. Hols) Mar-Nov.*

Charles Darwin (1809-82)   **E6**
Downe House, Downe, Kent. Where Darwin lived from 1842 onwards, worked and wrote his controversial 'Origin of Species'. *Open 13.00-18.00 daily. Closed Fri & Mon.*

Benjamin Disraeli (1804-81)   **C4**
Hughenden Manor, High Wycombe, Bucks. Disraeli lived here from 1847 until his death in 1881. Contains much of his furniture, pictures, books and relics. *Open daily 14.00-18.00. Feb-Nov. Closed Mon & Tues.*

Henry James (1846-1916)   **H8**
Lamb House, Rye, E. Sussex. Henry James felt that England fulfilled all his dreams of European civilisation, and Rye is very near perfection as an English town. After a spell in London, James moved to Rye where he bought the elegant simple 18thC Lamb House. *Open 14.00-18.00 Wed & Sat Apr-Oct.*

Rudyard Kipling (1865-1936)   **G8**
Bateman's, Burwash, E. Sussex. Built in 1634, the house contains furniture and relics of the writer. The surroundings are described in 'Puck of Pook's Hill'. *Open 11.00-18.00 Mon-Thur & 14.00-18.00 Sat, Sun & Good Fri.*

Samuel Palmer (1805-81)   **F6**
Shoreham, Kent. The Water House, Shoreham, is where Palmer lived from the 1830s. One of England's finest pastoral painters, he was inspired by the peace and beauty of the countryside around Shoreham. His Shoreham period was the most productive and creative of his life and the atmosphere of his Valley of Vision can still be sensed in this Kent village. Although his house is not open to the public a visit to this village gives you all the background you need.

George Bernard Shaw (1856-1950) **D3**
Shaw's Corner, Ayot St Lawrence, Herts. This brilliant, witty playwright moved to Ayot St Lawrence in 1906. The house is a simple, relatively modern one in this quiet corner of Hertfordshire. Shaw's rooms are exactly as he left them, and his study and desk still keep the dry Fabian air of learning coupled with hard work. The village has a good inn and the beautiful Brocket Park is nearby. *Open 11.00-18.00 daily. Closed Mon & mid-Dec-mid-Jan.*

General Wolfe (1727-59)   **E7**
Quebec House, Westerham, Kent. A mainly 17thC house where Wolfe spent his early years. Contains a collection of 'Wolfiana'. *Open 14.00-18.00 Tues, Wed & Sun Mar-Oct. Daily. B. Hol Mon.*

neickham, Quebec House

Cathedrals, abbeys & churches

Canterbury Cathedral   **J6**
Canterbury, Kent. Mecca for pilgrims in the middle ages who visited the shrine of St Thomas Becket. The place of Becket's martyrdom is marked by a plaque on the floor.
The cathedral was founded in 597, but nothing built before the Conquest survives. William of Sens, the great master-mason of the early Gothic style, was the architect of the choir and apse. A man of great ability and an ingenious workman in wood and stone, his design was as revolutionary in England as that of St Denis in France. Henry Yevele designed the nave in 1374. Externally the cathedral is dominated by the

Bell Harry Tower designed by John Wastell in the late 15thC. In the Trinity Chapel on the south side is the magnificent tomb of Edward the Black Prince, Edward III's son who died in 1376. Canterbury is a treasure house of 13thC stained glass; the chapter house has a fine wooden ceiling; and the Perpendicular cloisters on the north are as straight as churchmen.

Chichester Cathedral   C9
Chichester, W. Sussex. Founded in 1080 it was much altered after the great fire of 1187 although the leisurely bay-to-bay rhythm of the original 12thC building has been preserved. Romanesque from end to end, it's an imposing gesture in the flat landscape around, with the Downs a gently rising backcloth. Note the double aisles, resulting from former lateral chapels, fine central spire, Norman nave and Transitional retrochoir. The detached bell-tower is the only example in an English cathedral. Look out for the modern tapestry by John Piper and painting by Graham Sutherland.

Greenstead-Juxta-Ongar   F4
Essex. Famous as the only surviving log church in England, dated 1013. The nave is built of oak trees split vertically and set in an oak sill. The tower is timber too, weather-boarded outside with a sturdy spire.

Rochester Cathedral   G6
Rochester, Kent. Unassuming cathedral on the edge of the old city, facing eastward across the Medway to the low line of the Kentish hills. Modest in appearance and dimension, its nave is plain Norman. Gradually developed from 1179 to 1240, whilst the central tower was built in 1904. Externally it has little distinctive craftmanship with the exception of a fine Norman doorway on the west. Inside, note the walled choir and several good tombs.

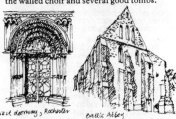

west doorway, Rochester   *Battle Abbey*

St Albans Abbey   D4
St Albans, Herts. 11thC at its heart, the abbey has grown irregularly, resulting in the second longest nave in England. Built around the shrine of St Alban, the first English martyr, the central tower used red Roman bricks taken from Roman sites nearby. On the Norman nave piers are a rare series of mediaeval wall paintings that were covered with whitewash for centuries.

St Bartholomew   E9
Brighton, E. Sussex. This is the kind of church that brings you to your knees. A great Noah's Ark of brick, rising to 135 feet, out-topping even Westminster Abbey. Inside, the local architect Edmund Scott built a completely plain brick church, unusual particularly for the 1870s, in that it depends only on size and proportion for its effect. The scale is Byzantine around the high altar with sumptuous plain slabs of marble and a dauntingly simple baldachino. Perfect 'arts and crafts' candlesticks and metalwork – the silver altar in the Lady Chapel is refined late

Victorian work at its richest. This is a church that overwhelms with its own terrifying but simple grandeur.

St Lawrence Church   F4
Blackmore, Essex. A carpenter's paradise – one of the most impressive timber towers in England. Go inside and look up the tower: a mass of great beams lead up to the belfry.

St Mary's   D8
Sompting, W. Sussex. A famous 11thC church with a Saxon tower on the south slope of the Sussex Downs. The tower is topped by a Rhenish Helm spire which is unique in England. The rest of the church is late 12thC with good stone vaults and the whole place still has an untouched air of peaceful holiness.

Waltham Abbey   E4
Waltham Abbey, Essex. King Harold was buried here after his defeat at the Battle of Hastings in 1066. The Norman nave remains but is a mere fragment of the great abbey. There is a massive majesty about the great stone piers and this has been enhanced by some good Victorian glass. The Burne-Jones east window is worth a special look.

Castles & ruins

Battle Abbey   G8
Battle, E. Sussex. It was before the Battle of Hastings that William of Normandy vowed he would build an abbey should victory be his. The large abbey was consecrated in 1094 in the presence of William Rufus. Now only a few ruins remain, but it is very impressive. The high altar stands on the actual spot where King Harold fell in 1066. Note the Decorated style gatehouse, it is one of the finest in England. *Open daily. Closed Sat afternoon and Sun Sep–mid-July.*

Bodiam Castle   G8
Bodiam, E. Sussex. Ten miles north-west of Winchelsea, it stands in a moat of water lilies. Built in 1385 under the licence of Richard II in case of possible invasion by France. Octagonal in plan, it is approached over an oak bridge which spans the moat. An intruder would then be under fire from the towers and have to pass the barbican and cross a ten-foot moat, in order to storm the main gatehouse. It looks intact but is only a shell – a roofless but well preserved ruin. *Open 10.00–19.00 daily Apr–Sep. Closed Sun Oct–Mar.*

Bodiam Castle

Deal Castle   K6
Deal, Kent. A squat castle within thick walls, it was the middle one of three castles, built by Henry VIII, to protect shipping in the Downs and inside the treacherous Goodwin Sands. Part of a package deal of 20 forts built in 1540 as a defensive system in case of invasion (prompted by the Pope's call for a crusade against England following Henry's break with the Church of Rome). It was the largest and most elaborate of all his forts, planned like a Tudor rose, and sunk within a moat. *Open 9.30–17.30 daily Apr and 9.30–19.00 May–Sep (9.30–17.30 Mar and Oct, 9.30–16.00 Nov–Feb. Closed Sun morning).*

Dover Castle   K7
Dover, Kent. The castle commands this important harbour at the start of the shortest sea route to the continent. For centuries Dover was the key to England, and vast sums were spent on its fortifications. The main fortifications of the castle belong to the late 12th–13thC; the fine rectangular keep was built in the 1180s – the first time that concentrically arranged fortifications had been used in England. The circuit of enclosing walls was altered during the Napoleonic period when the tops of the

towers were cut and the stumps strengthened for gun emplacements. High up on the white cliffs it stands frowning like a clap of thunder. Don't fall off. *Open 9.30–17.30 daily Apr & 9.30–19.00 May–Sep. (9.30–17.30 Mar & Oct. 9.30–16.00 Nov–Feb. Closed Sun morning.)*

The keep, Dover Castle

Herstmonceux Castle   F8
Herstmonceux, E. Sussex. With imposing towers and battlemented façade of magnificent brickwork surrounded by a moat, its external regularity is reminiscent of the earlier Bodiam. Built in 1440 by Sir Roger Fiennes, a civil servant under Henry VI, it is richly evocative of Tudor England. Main feature, a massive gateway. Dismantled in 1777, it remained a ruin until extensively restored in 1933. *Open 14.00– 17.00 Mon–Fri & 10.30–17.00 Sat & Sun Apr–Sep.*

Unusual buildings

Bull's Tower   G2
Pentlow, Essex. This folly is a 75 foot high brick tower, with narrow windows decorated with crosses and diamonds of dark bricks. Built in 1859 as a memorial.

De La Warr Pavilion   G9
Bexhill-on-Sea, E. Sussex. Built in 1933–6 and designed by Eric Mendelsohn, a leading German architect, and Chermayeff. Amply glazed, this pioneering product of the Jazz Age, with its clean long lines towards the sea, is the Fred Astaire of them all.

Eton College   C5
Eton, Bucks. England's most exclusive school, still breeding an élite now based more on cash than on birth. Worth a visit for its range of courts and lovely chapel which retains some rare wall paintings dating from 1479. The college and its neighbour Windsor Castle across the river are the last remnants of the feudal past, and they're both still thriving. *Main college building usually open.*

Eton College

Gothic Temple   B2
Stowe Park, Stowe, Bucks. Designed by Gibbs in 1713, it is triangular in plan with hexagonal turrets at the corners, the walls between having castellated gables. The first floor has a gallery with tall Gothic windows looking out on to Stowe Park. Now in the grounds of a school, but often open.

Lancing College   D9
Lancing, W. Sussex. Founded by Nathaniel Woodward, it was built high up on a beautiful exposed site in 1848. Designed by R.C. Carpenter in the Gothic tradition with the right mixture of competence, sincerity and common sense. The triumph is the chapel, a massive monument more French than France. *Usually open.*

Lancing College Chapel.

The Piers   E9
Brighton, E. Sussex. The one original contribution to the seaside, beach and sea

apart, were these elegant cast iron insects striding out to sea. No seaside resort is a proper one without a pier. Like the best of Mississippi paddle steamers, but permanently tethered to the land, they were for landlubbers and sailors alike. Brighton, not to be outdone has two piers. West Pier was built in 1868 and Palace Pier in 1891. Now closed, the West Pier is sedately classical in style. The Palace Pier, more delightfully vulgar, swells out into a spacious platform of sun decks, an amusement hall, peep shows and a shopping arcade. Unashamedly grand with elaborate facades, white columns and golden-domed towers.

Royal Holloway College   C5
Surrey. S. of Egham on A30. This is the largest, jolliest Victorian building in the Home Counties – built as a ladies' college in 1879 by a rich industrialist, it is modelled on Chambord in the Loire. Its sheer size is staggering – every young lady had two rooms. Now they admit men and it's not quite the same.

Royal Pavilion   E9
Brighton, E. Sussex. Originally a house leased by the Prince of Wales in 1786 and redesigned by Henry Holland in an attractive classical design with central rotunda and dome. In the early 19thC tastes changed. There was a diversion from the neo-classical to the architecture of India, China and Egypt as well as doodling in castellated houses, rustic cottages and Italianate villas. Nash, commissioned to redesign the house, began in 1816 by throwing over the outline of Holland's building a richly oriental fancy dress with pinnacles, minarets and imposing onion-shaped domes. He mixed his motifs lavishly, especially inside, where the interiors are both Chinese and Gothic. Externally, it's more sedately Indian with the delicate pierced stonework and well-fed domes, an apparition in lime-green and cream (colours you always seem to come face to face with wherever you walk in Brighton). *Open daily (10.00–20.00 Jul–Sep).*

Sham Church Folly   C7
Peper Harrow, Surrey. A beautiful sham church ruin built by Lord Middleton in the mid-19thC in the form of a ruined east wall incorporating a genuine Decorated window in grey stone.

Shell Room and Grotto   C2
Woburn Abbey, Woburn, Beds. Like a large stone igloo, with unglazed windows, star patterned floor and richly decorated walls. it is set in the garden near the Chinese Dairy. Built in the 18thC.

University of Sussex   E9
nr. Brighton, E. Sussex. Early 1960s. The best thing to hit Brighton since the Royal Pavilion – not so much for the architecture, which has a little too much of the Mantovanis, but for the aura. The best of the Oxbridge collegiate trappings (quad-rangles and water) are gathered together in superb rolling downland with a backcloth of Rowland Hilder beeches. It's the students' first choice after Oxford or Cambridge. Has a round chapel based on the beehive tombs at Mycenae.

Houses & gardens

Ascott House   C3
Wing, Bucks. A former hunting lodge set in charming grounds planted with unusual trees, thousands of naturalised bulbs and with a French formal garden. The house contains a treasure of French and Chippendale furniture, oriental porcelain, and paintings by Hogarth, Rubens and Gainsborough; all given to the National Trust by the Rothschilds. *Open 14.00–18.00 Wed, Sat & B. Hol Mon Apr–Sep. (also Sun Jul & Aug.)*

Crittenden House   G7
Matfield, Kent. A charming Kentish farmhouse garden surrounded by orchards. A cornucopia of ideas; a particularly

interesting one is the conversion of old pits into water gardens. *Open 14.00–19.00 various Sun Apr–Aug; various Mon Apr & May.*

Great Dixter G8
Northiam, E. Sussex. 15thC half-timbered manor house. The gardens, designed by Sir Edwin Lutyens, are a connoisseur's delight full of fascinating plants, colour and fragrance – yew hedges, topiary and flower borders; naturalised daffodils and fritillaries; peonies, fuchsias, rose garden. *Open 14.00–17.00 daily Apr–mid-Oct. Closed Mon.*

Hatfield House D4
Hatfield, Herts. One of the four or five major Jacobean houses in the country. E-shaped plan, with a plain front and lavish carving and stonework on the garden side. Traditional Great Hall with minstrels' gallery; the great staircase is superbly carved and covered with figures of cherubs and trophies. Full of tapestries and fine furniture as well as a collection of Queen Elizabeth I's belongings, including her silk stockings and gardening hat. *Open 12.00–17.00 Tue–Sun late Mar–Oct. (Open B. Hol Mon.)*

Hever Castle E7
Kent. 3 miles se of Edenbridge off B2026. Small quadrangular castellated house with a surrounding moat, rebuilt 1462. Many recent additions and alterations but the exterior is unchanged. Home of Henry VIII's second wife, Anne Boleyn, it has a fine gateway and drawbridge and magnificent gardens with a 35-acre lake. *Open 13.00–19.00 Wed, Fri, Sun & B. Hols. Apr–Sep.*

Ightham Mote F6
Ivy Hatch, Kent. Set among trees and meadows, with peacocks in the gardens, a well preserved manor house of varied domestic styles blended ingeniously into a mediaeval and Tudor whole, with moat still encircling the house. The mediaeval part is the 14thC Hall, situated in the east wing and entered from a courtyard. *Open 14.00–17.00 Fri.*

Knole House F6
Sevenoaks, Kent. Half a mile from Sevenoaks and set on a flat plateau of land in the undulating blanket of a large park of deer, old oaks and beeches. This imposing large house, richly decorated and furnished, has one of the finest of Jacobean staircases. Built around three main courtyards with an entrance gate tower, it is one of a number of Jacobean great houses built, or extensively remodelled, during the early part of the 17thC. Originally an old manor house patched up by the Archbishop of Canterbury in 1456. The Archbishop then built himself a great new palace. Seized by Henry VIII in 1532 and substantially extended. The estate was granted to Sir Thomas Sackville in 1566 by Elizabeth I, and in 1604 he undertook the major remodelling of the whole estate. Virginia Woolf used it as a model for the house in her novel 'Orlando', the manuscript of which can be seen in the main entrance hall. Paintings by Van Dyck and Reynolds are amongst the collection. *Open Wed–Sat & B. Hols Mar–Dec (10.00–15.30 Nov–Mar).*

Layer Marney Tower H3
nr Colchester, Essex. 1 mile s of B1022. The tallest Tudor gatehouse in England stands eight storeys high in brick with unique terracotta trimmings. Surrounded by yew hedges and rose gardens. *Open 14.00–18.00 Sun & Thur Apr–Oct (11.00–18.00 B. Hols). Also Tue July & Aug.*

Luton Hoo D3
Luton, Beds. Stands in a great park landscaped by Capability Brown. The view of the lakes from the house is a triumph of 18thC landscape art. The house was originally designed by Robert Adam but a series of fires and alterations make his work

hard to find. The body of the main house is now the creation of Mewes and Davis, architects of the London Ritz Hotel. The house stands today as a daunting display of Edwardian wealth, and houses a collection of treasures from mediaeval religious art to Fabergé's fabulous more worldly trinkets. *Open 11.00–18.00 mid-Apr–Sep daily except Tue, Fri & Sun morning.*

Nymans Gardens E8
W. Sussex. S of Handcross 1 mile along B2114. A garden famous for its rhododendrons, magnolias and camellias. Especially noted for the shrub *eucryphia nymansay*, first raised here in 1915. Of interest to homesick Antipodians is the Tasmanian garden. National Trust. *Open 14.00–19.00 Tue–Thur, 11.00–19.00 Sun & B. Hols Apr–Oct.*

The Orchard D4
Chorleywood, Herts. Up in Shire Lane is the house that C. A. Voysey built for himself in 1901. It is a model of the quiet domesticity that is so typical of the English character. The gables and tall chimneys are pure and simple shapes, while inside the hall, the fireplace and even the door hinges are delicate examples of Voysey's style. *Private.*

Parham House C8
Amberley, W. Sussex. An Elizabethan mansion begun in 1577 by Sir Thomas Parham who sailed with Drake to Cadiz. As sober as Sunday, a Tudor house in a Tudor landscape of big trees, bracken and deer, facing the bare Downs with a church on the lawn. There is a Great Hall with unusually tall mullioned windows and plastered ceiling; straightforward, but welcoming. Elizabethan, Jacobean and Georgian portraits. Fine walled gardens. *Open 14.00–17.30 Sun, Wed, Thur & B. Hols Apr–Sep.*

Paycocke's G3
Coggeshall, Essex. One of the best examples in England of a merchant's house of 1500. Terrific timbers and carving, and the inside glows with a collection of 16thC and 17thC furniture. National Trust. *Open 14.00–17.30 Wed, Thur, Sun & B. Hols Apr–Sep.*

Penshurst Place F7
Penshurst, Kent. The birthplace of Sir Philip Sidney (1554–86), soldier, poet and statesman. A typical, well preserved mediaeval manor house enlarged and added to in the Elizabethan period. A fine 14thC hall intact with screen at one end and dais at the other. Furniture, portraits and armour from the 15thC onwards. Terraced formal gardens, begun in 1560. *Open 14.00–18.00 daily (except Mon & Fri) Apr–Sep. Tel Penshurst 307.*

Penshurst Place

Polesden Lacey D6
Surrey. 3 miles nw of Dorking via A246. One of the loveliest gardens near London, with herbaceous borders, terraces and beech walks. Stroll along the terrace to see the superb view of Ranmore woods – English landscape at its best. *Open 11.00–18.00 Wed, Thu & Sat, Sun & B. Hols Mar–Nov. 14.00–18.00 Sat & Sun Nov.*

St Osyth Priory J3
Essex. 4 miles w of Clacton on B1027. Glorious collection of monastic buildings around smooth lawns and gravel paths. No monks tread the cloister here, only peacocks; and inside, the present owner's sophisticated collection of jade is a far cry from monastic simplicity. Go for the great gatehouse, alive with sparkling flint patterns. *Open 10.00–18.00 daily May–Sep.*

Sissinghurst Castle G7
Kent. Off A202 e of Sissinghurst. The creation of Victoria Sackville-West and Harold Nicolson, it is one of England's loveliest sights incorporating small, highly individual walled gardens within a formal plan. Worth noting are the White Garden, herb garden and old fashioned cottage garden. It belongs to the National Trust. *Open 12.00–1830 (10.00–18.30 Sat, Sun & B. Hols) Apr–mid-Oct.*

Stowe Park **B2**
Stowe, Bucks. England's genius for landscape gardening can be seen in all its splendour at Stowe. A verdant landscape full of elegant temples and monuments. Don't miss the Temple of British Worthies where even King William III acquires a Greco-Roman look. *Open 14.00–18.00 Jan–Apr & late Jul–Aug.*

Uppark House **B8**
South Harting, nr Petersfield, W. Sussex. A red brick house with stone dressings built between 1685 and 1690 up the top of a valley within a mile of the crest of the North Downs. A Wren styled country house, comfortable to look at with landscaped grounds designed by Humphrey Repton in the 19thC, with pastures in one long sweep to the house walls like fitted carpets. Inside an unusually complete preservation of an 18thC interior. *Open 14.00–18.00 Wed, Thur, Sun & B.Hols Apr–Sep.*

Woburn Abbey **C2**
Woburn, Beds. One of the stateliest stately homes of England, and even the incredible commercialisation cannot detract from the gracious view of the west front when you first see it across the landscaped park. Part of the house was demolished in 1950 but more than enough remains, including the richly decorated state rooms with Rococo ceilings. In the park is an amazing collection of buildings – stately trimmings for a stately home, including a Chinese dairy, grotto, ice house, sculpture gallery and of course a maze. *Open 11.30–18.15 (11.30–19.00 Sun) Apr–Oct. 13.00–16.45 daily Oct–Mar.*

Wrest Park **D2**
Silsoe, Beds. For England it is an unusually formal canal garden; from 1706 it was laid out in radiating beds and canals, with long vistas leading to a series of garden ornaments. *Open 10.00–19.00 Sat, Sun & B. Hols Apr–Oct. (Grounds only.)*

Museums & galleries

Anne of Cleves House **E9**
High St, Southover, Lewes, E. Sussex. Picturesque half-timbered 16thC house holds an interesting collection of furniture, costumes, household equipment, ironwork and the Potter collection of chalk fossils. *Open 10.30–17.30 Mon–Sat & also 14.30–17.30 Sun Apr–Oct.*

Brighton Museum and Art Gallery **E8**
Brighton, E. Sussex. A fine collection illustrating Sussex archaeology and history; the Willett Collection of English pottery; 18thC furniture; British paintings of 19thC–early 20thC; watercolours and drawings. *Open 10.00–19.00 Mon–Fri (10.00–17.00 Sat. 14.00–17.00 Sun.)*

Chelmsford and Essex Museum **G4**
Oaklands Park, Chelmsford, Essex. A mixed bag of a museum. Tunstill Collection of English drinking glasses; collection of eggs; 300-odd specimens of British birds; and a good collection of Roman Essex finds. *Open 10.00–17.00 daily. Closed Sun morning.*

Colchester and Essex Museum **H3**
Colchester, Essex. The Castle, a mighty Norman keep built on the foundations of a Roman temple, houses an impressive archaeological collection from Essex and Roman Colchester dating from the stone age to the 17thC. *Open 10.00–17.00 daily. Sun 14.30–17.00 (Apr–Sep only).*

Elstow Moot Hall **C2**
Elstow, nr Bedford, Beds. Once used as a meeting-place and Sunday School of the Bunyan congregation, it now contains a fine 17thC collection associated with John Bunyan. *Open 10.00–17.00 Tue–Sat and Sun afternoon.*

Potter's Museum **D8**
Bramber, W. Sussex. Macabre but enchanting taxidermy collection, first opened in 1861. It includes a series of tableaux of stuffed kittens, red squirrels, rabbits and rats in such settings as 'The Cock Robin Story'. *Open 11.00–20.00 daily.*

Royal Tunbridge Wells Museum and Art Gallery **F7**
Civic Centre, Tunbridge Wells, Kent. Delightful Victoriana – a permanent collection of paintings, garments worn by Queen Victoria, dolls, huge dolls' house, bygones, prints of old Tunbridge Wells. *Open 10.00–17.30 daily. Closed Sun & B. Hols.*

Smallhythe Place **H7**
Kent. 2 miles s of Tenterden on e side of B2082. Cosy half-timbered house of 1480, once owned by Dame Ellen Terry and now a memorial to her. The museum also includes relics of Irving, Mrs Siddons, David Garrick, other actors and actresses. *Open daily Mar–Oct. Closed Tue & Fri.*

The Towner Art Gallery **F9**
Borough Lane, Eastbourne, E. Sussex. Good collection of paintings depicting Sussex scenes; delightful Georgian caricatures and the Bell collection of British butterflies. *Open 10.00–18.00 daily. Closed Sun morning.*

Weald and Downland Open Air Museum **C9**
Singleton, W. Sussex. 5 miles n of Chichester on A286. A fantastic collection of historic 14thC–19thC buildings saved from destruction and re-erected at the foot of St Roche's Hill in 37 acres of meadows and woodlands. Includes two mediaeval farm-houses and a 16thC treadwheel. Nature trail and attractive picnic sites. *Open 11.00–18.00 Easter–Sep. Closed Mon.*

Botanical gardens

Bedgebury National Pinetum **G7**
Goudhurst, Kent. First planted in 1924, the forest consists of over 200 species of temperate zone cone-bearing trees laid out in genera. Of great use to foresters and botanists, it is sited in the lovely undulating countryside of the Weald of Kent. *Open daily.*

Sheffield Park Garden **F8**
E. Sussex. 5 miles nw of Uckfield. A perfect English country environment. 142 acres of woods, parkland, gardens and five lakes, on different levels, originally laid out in the 18thC. There are colourful rhododendrons and azaleas, rare specimen conifers and eucalyptus; waterlilies, daffodils and bluebells. *Open 11.00–19.00 daily May–Sep (closed Mon & Sun morning). 11.00–17.00 Oct & Nov, Wed, Sat & Sun Apr.*

Wakehurst Place Garden **E8**
E. Sussex, 1½ miles nw of Ardingly on B2028. Owned by the National Trust and used as an extension of the Botanical Gardens at Kew, Wakehurst offers 476 acres of woodlands and gardens. A haven of exotic plants, trees and shrubs; ponds and lakes are linked by a watercourse. *Open 13.00–17.00 daily Oct & Feb (14.00–18.00 Mar). Open 14.00–18.00 Mon–Fri (14.00–19.00 Sat, Sun & B. Hols) Apr–Sep. 12.00–16.00 Nov–Jan.*

Wisley Garden **C6**
Wisley, Ripley, Surrey. This is the back garden of the Royal Horticultural Society where every possible form of gardening is indulged; there are experimental laboratories and gardens, and perfect examples of planting to delight and encourage all gardeners, from allotment holder to expert. Greenhouses and pinetum, rock garden and dazzling masses of azaleas, camellias, roses and rhododendrons. *Open 10.00–19.30 (16.30 winter) daily. Closed Sun morning.*

Zoos, aquaria & aviaries

Birdworld Zoological Gardens **B7**
Hold Pond, nr Farnham, Surrey. An attractive setting for a fine tropical bird collection. *Open 9.30–18.00 daily.*

Brighton Aquarium & Dolphinarium **E9**
Marine Parade, E. Sussex. Over 80 tanks illustrating marine life, also very agile and intelligent dolphins. *Open 9.00–18.30 daily. Tel 64233.*

Chessington Zoo **D6**
Chessington, Surrey. This constantly
expanding zoo is always good for children.
There are plenty of gardens, a miniature
railway and the best thing is a splashy hippo
wallow. Landscaped enclosures for tigers,
leopards, pumas, penguin pool and a fine
ape house. *Open 9.30–17.30 daily (10.00–
16.00 Nov–Feb).*

Colchester Zoo **H3**
Stanway Hall, Colchester, Essex. This is the
only general zoo in East Anglia, especially
good for big cats: lions, tigers and leopards.
also black panthers and cheetahs. *Open
9.30–19.30 daily.*

**Flamingo Gardens and
Tropical Bird Zoo** **C1**
Weston Underwood, Olney, Bucks. This is
one of the best collections of storks and
flamingos in Britain. *Open 14.00–20.00 Sun,
Wed, Thur, Sat Apr–Sep.*

Mole Hall Wildlife Park **F2**
Widdington, Newport, Essex. In this small
mixed collection, around a moated
Elizabethan house are some very rare woolly
monkeys. *Open 10.30–18.00 daily.*

Whipsnade Park Zoo **C3**
Whipsnade, nr Dunstable, Beds. 500 acres of
animal park, good for wild horses, white
rhinos, deer and gazelle. It is run by the
London zoo. *Open 10.00–19.00 daily.*

Woburn Abbey Zoo Park **C2**
Woburn Park, Woburn, Beds. A world famous
collection of rare deer, it has now become
the Woburn Wild Animal Kingdom, the
largest game reserve outside Africa. *Open
daily 10.30–17.45 Apr–Aug. 11.00–17.15
Sep–Oct. 12.00–16.00 Nov–Mar.*

Nature trails & reserves

Black Down Nature Trail
*W. Sussex. 1 mile se of Haslemere, off
Tennyson's Lane.* Highest spot in the county
with superb views to the South Downs;
there are Scots pine, and oak woods, deer,
meadow pipits, yellow hammers. *Open daily.*

Coombe Hill
*Aston Clinton, Bucks. 17 miles w of Wendover
s of B4010, leading from Chequers Court.*
This is a nature trail with the highest
viewpoint of the Chilterns. There are
spectacular views of Aylesbury and the
woods surrounding Chequers. *Open daily.*

East Head Nature Walk
West Wittering, W. Sussex. There is a
circular walk round the beach and sand
dunes of this spit of land east of Chichester
harbour. Dune reclamation work, mud flats
and a fine assortment of wildlife can be seen
along this coast. Start behind the beach west
of West Wittering. *Open daily.*

Hatfield Forest
Nr Bishop's Stortford, Essex. Forest and
lakes rich in wildlife. Fallow deer, badgers,
tufted duck and teal. The trail starts at the
Shell House by the lake. *Turn off B183 ½ mile
w of Hatfield Broad Oak – entrance 2 miles.
Open daily.*

Kingley Vale National Nature Reserve
West Stoke, Chichester, W. Sussex. Largely
chalk downland, it has possibly the finest
yew wood in Europe. The trees are so large
and cast such deep shadows that only very
special flora grow there. *Open daily.*

Maulden Wood
Ampthill, Beds. A mixed coniferous and lush
broad-leaved forest. The trail begins 1 mile
north of Clophill on the A6, the main
London-Bedford road. *Open daily.*

The Punch Bowl Nature Trail
*Nr Hindhead, Surrey. 150 yards n of traffic
light on A3.* In the magnificent open
countryside of sandy soil, heath and gorse,
with oaks on the higher ground and oaks on
the lower ground, the trail starts at the
National Trust car park.

Bird watching

Abberton Resevoir
Essex. 4 miles from Colchester on the B1026.
Has the largest collection of wildfowl in
Britain: widgeon, Bewick's swan, smew,
black tern, red-crested pochard. Access to
the reservoir is restricted, but there are
excellent views of the area from the nearby
roads.

Beachy Head
E. Sussex. S of Eastdean off A259. This chalk
headland (575 feet) is a magnificent spot from
which to observe offshore sea birds: divers,
terns, gulls, warblers, flycatchers. It is the
centre for migration studies in Sussex.

Blackwater Estuary
Essex. Off the B1026 nr Goldhanger. A good
spot for wildfowl, it has Brent geese,
widgeon, shelduck, red shank and godwits.
The best place to start is from the Bradwell
Bird Observatory on the southern shore near
Dengie Flats.

Dungeness
Kent. S of Lydd on the ring road. A bleak
promontory of shingle, gorse and brambles
which juts into the Channel. A good spot to
study bird migration; more than 6,000 birds
are ringed here every year. Divers, common
and herring gulls, Arctic and roseate terns,
waders.

Swale Estuary, Isle of Sheppey
Kent. This huge area of mudflats, salt and
freshwater marsh, is marvellous for wildfowl
along the sea walls, and freshwater waders on
Windmill Creek. Sea duck off Shell Ness.

Tring Reservoirs
Herts. 2 miles n of Tring. Once a marshland,
it lies at the foot of the Chilterns. Famous
for the breeding of the little ringed plover,
it is now a National Nature Reserve. Tufted
duck, goosander, waders, black terns, great
crested grebe.

Brass rubbing

The following is a short list of churches that
have brasses for rubbing. Permission is
almost invariably required.
Bedfordshire. Cople, Elstow, Shillington,
Wymington.
Buckinghamshire. Drayton Beauchamp,
Eldesborough, Eton College Chapel,
Hambleden, Lillingstone Lovell, Stoke
Poges, Thornton, Twyford, Upper
Winchendon, Waddesdon.
Essex. Aveley, Chrishall, Latton, Little
Easton, Little Horkesley, Pebmarsh,
Stifford, Wivenhoe;
Hertfordshire. Berkhamsted, North Mimms,
St Albans Abbey, St Albans (St Michael's),
Sawbridgeworth, Standon, Watford,
Watton-at-Stone.
Kent. Chartham, Cobham (eighteen
exceptionally fine brasses), East Sutton,
Graveney, Hever, Minster in Sheppey,
Northfleet, Saltwood, Upper Hardres,
Woodchurch.
Surrey. Beddington, Crowhurst, East
Horsley, Stoke d'Abernon.
Sussex. Battle, Cowfold, Etchingham,
Fletching, Hurstmonceux, Trotton, West
Grinstead.

Fossil hunting

Visit the local museum. Its fossil collection
usually states where individual fossils have
been found. When visiting quarries always
seek permission to enter if they look
privately owned or worked. Be careful of
falls of rock.

Bognor Regis W. Sussex
On the foreshore at low tide can be found
Eocene lamellibranchs, corals, crustaceans,
fish bones, etc.

Leighton Buzzard Beds.
Nearby pits and quarries contain ventricles
of fossiliferous limestone up to ten feet in

length containing brachiopods, shells, ammonites, etc.

North Downs Kent and Surrey
The chalk yields echinoids, brachiopods, sponges and ammonites. There are many quarries at the base of the chalk escarpment along the Pilgrims Way (vast and awesome pits at Snodland and Burham). Also search the cliffs between Folkestone and Dover (look in the gault of the famous landslip area of the Warren whilst you are here).

Sevenoaks Kent
Pits of gault clay at Greatness and at Ford Place near Wrotham contain ammonites, belemnites, gasteropods, marine worms and the occasional shark's tooth. Avoid a wet day – it gets sticky!

Swanscombe Kent
Pleistocene bones and artefacts in nearby gravel pits.

South Downs Sussex
Chalk pits under the ridge of the South Downs, notably at Arundel, Boxgrove, Burpham, Durrington, Friston, Houghton, Lavant, Lewes, Offham, Singleton.

Walton-on-the-Naze Essex
The coastal cliffs of Red Crag give shark's teeth, gastropods, lamellibranchs.

Forests

Ashdown Forest E7
E. Sussex. Part of what was once the huge Roman Wealden forest of Anderida. There are 20 undulating square miles of wild heath, moorland, woodland and rocky outcrops. Iron country with hammer ponds in the valleys.

Burnham Beeches C5
Bucks. 3 miles e of Maidenhead. 600 acres with huge beech trees, it was once part of a vast forest that extended over the Chiltern Hills.

Epping Forest E4
Essex. 5,600 acres on the fringe of Greater London. A remnant of the vast hunting reserve for Saxon, Norman and Tudor kings, it was bought by the Corporation of the City of London in 1882. A place of sunlit glades, rough heaths and great hornbeam trees, it was much loved by poets like John Clare and Tennyson.

Hills

Box Hill D6
Nr Dorking, Surrey. A picnic spot on the North Downs popular since the reign of Charles II. John Evelyn, the diarist, praised its yews and box trees. It is one of the best viewpoints in Surrey. Many of the trees were cut in the 18thC when box wood was used for wood engraving blocks.

Chiltern Hills
Bucks. A ridge of chalk that runs across the southern half of Buckinghamshire, with fine views, magnificent beechwoods and hospitable villages.

Devils Dyke D8
Nr Brighton, E. Sussex. A V-shaped cleft in the Downs with long views across the Weald. Legend has it that the devil, in an effort to quell the growth of Christianity, began to dig a trench through which the English Channel would flood the Weald. A woman watching him held up a candle and the devil fled, mistaking it for the rising sun.

Leith Hill D7
Surrey. 4 miles sw of Dorking. A long, high ridge of woodland with magnificent views and a 65-foot-high ragstone tower with brick surrounds. There are exhilarating walks along the top of the ridge.

North Downs
There are steep ridges of heavily wooded chalk facing the South Downs across the rolling landscape of the Weald of Kent and Sussex. The rivers Wey, Mole, Darent,

Medway and Stour cut through them. Their highest section lies between the Medway and Mole, whilst the eastern end is marked by the white cliffs of Dover. Westward they run into the Hog's Back.

Seven Sisters F9
Nr Eastbourne, E. Sussex. These seven dramatic chalk cliffs over 500 feet high are the culmination of the South Downs. They are criss-crossed by fine walking tracks.

South Downs
Less wooded than the North Downs, they are cut by the rivers Arun, Adur, Ouse and Cuckmere. Southwest of Petersfield the Hampshire and South Downs meet. Higher and more wooded from there to Arundel, the South Downs end splendidly in the east at the Seven Sisters and Beachy Head.

Meadows & marshes

Essex Flats
South Essex. Once closely forested with oaks in the middle ages, now a large tract of low-lying land sliding muddily into the North Sea beyond marshes and creeks.

Romney Marsh
Kent. S of Ashford. A large flat expanse, now largely drained and used for sheep farming. Traversed by weedy dykes, it is dank and cold in winter, whilst heavy mists often descend on mid-summer evenings. Ideal area for smuggling until early in the 19thC. Sharp views to Rye and Winchelsea.

Runnymede
Surrey. Upstream from where the Colne enters the River Thames is the level meadow of Runnymede. It was here King John sealed the draft of Magna Carta in 1215. The memorial to President John F. Kennedy is on a hill above Runnymede.

Rivers

The Mole
Surrey. The Mole, a typical Surrey stream, rises on the Wealden Ridge near Gatwick Airport, and crosses the clay plain to Dorking. Then, between that town and Leatherhead, it follows the steep-sided Mole Gap through the chalky North Downs, clad in beautiful beechwoods, to join the Thames at Molesey.

The Ouse
Beds. Most of Bedfordshire lies in the basin of the Ouse, which is navigable all the way from Bedford town for 60 miles north to King's Lynn, a seaport on the Wash. A good boating and fishing river, it has been canalized throughout its lower course to protect the fertile fens from winter floods.

The Ouse
Sussex. A typical Sussex river, the Ouse rises in the Wealden clay near Haywards Heath, then crosses a flat clay plain to the county town of Lewes. Cutting a deep gap through the chalk ridge of the South Downs, it joins the sea at Newhaven, a leading harbour for cross-Channel ferries.

The Stour
Kent. Starting near Hythe, close to the south coast, the curious Stour winds north through Ashford and Wye, cutting a picturesque gap through the North Downs chalk hills. At the cathedral city of Canterbury it becomes navigable, following on eastwards through level pastures to Sandwich, an ancient Cinque Port on Kent's eastern shore.

The Thames
The Thames and its tributaries drain the central region of the aptly named London Basin. Its main stream, made navigable by a system of locks and weirs, forms Buckinghamshire's southern boundary, with boating centres at Henley and Marlow in Buckinghamshire, and also at Kingston-on-Thames and Richmond in Surrey. There, becoming tidal, it plunges into metropolitan London, emerging near Tilbury as a great, commercial, tidal but polluted river bearing

huge cargo ships, tankers and passenger-carrying craft. The Thames' main northern tributaries, which run south from the Chiltern chalk hills across the clay basin, are the Colne which drains western Hertfordshire, including St Albans, and the Lea, which flows through Luton (once Lea-town) and Hertford.

Canals

The Grand Union Canal
This is one of the better-known waterways of the south-east, and forms the busy trunk route from London to the Midlands. The canal begins at a junction with the Thames in Brentford, then undertakes a steady climb through 55 locks to cross the Chilterns escarpment near Tring, where a complicated system of reservoirs, streams and pumping engines exists to defend the three-mile summit level against the constant loss of water incurred by the passage of boats through locks at either end. From here the canal drops down to the Vale of Aylesbury and the gentle farming landscape of Buckinghamshire. At Wolverton, on the Buckinghamshire/Northamptonshire border, the Grand Union crosses the River Ouse on an iron aqueduct and then begins the climb up to the Northamptonshire Heights.
Best places to see the canal: Berkhamsted, with its houseboats and barges, locks and canal pubs; Wolverton, with the aqueduct over the Ouse; and Marsworth, with its locks, canal junctions, reservoirs, workshops and canal pubs. An excellent and fascinating nine-mile walk would be to start at Tring Station and go down to Marsworth, then down the sixteen narrow locks of the Aylesbury Arm to the basin in the town. The station is nearby.

The Royal Military Canal
This is one of the most amazing canals in England. It was in fact built by the British Government in the time of the Napoleonic Wars to form a line of defence against possible invasion and at the same time to form a useful military transport route for the garrisons based on the south coast. The canal starts at Shorncliffe (just west of Folkestone) and extends through Hythe and Rye to the sea near Winchelsea, thus describing a 30-mile arc around the great Romney Marsh. After the Battle of Trafalgar it became clear that the canal would be unlikely to be required for military purposes, but it was maintained just in case. It is now, of course, disused but in a reasonable state of repair.

The Thames and Medway Canal
This long-defunct waterway runs from Gravesend to Strood, and used to offer traders an attractive alternative to the much longer route down the Thames Estuary and round the Isle of Grain. Principal traffic on the canal was carried in sailing barges, which would drop their masts and be hauled along the canal – often by men. The most interesting feature of the canal was – and is – the great tunnel between Higham and Strood, which carves its way through the ridge dividing the Thames and Medway estuaries. As built, the 4,100-yard tunnel was so long it became a severe bottleneck to barge traffic, which could only be worked through one way at a time. So the centre of the tunnel was excavated from the top, and a lay-by 200 yards long was created. The one tunnel thus became two relatively short tunnels, and the traffic flow was much improved. Later, when the railway from Gravesend to Rochester was built, the canal company was bought out and the two tunnels drained and converted into railway tunnels. Observant passengers on this line can still notice the unusual tunnel entrances and the brief five-second glimpse of daylight separating the tunnels.

The Wey and Arun Junction Canal
The Wey and Arun, which was built early in the 19thC to connect the River Wey near Guildford, Surrey to the Arun near Pulborough, Sussex, used to provide a fascinating waterway route from the Thames to the south coast at Littlehampton, Sussex.

A branch was also built from the Arun to Chichester Harbour, thus giving an inland route right through from London to Portsmouth. The canal did not thrive, however, and through navigation has been impossible for over 100 years, during which time the locks have become heavily overgrown, the aqueducts have collapsed, and the bridges have mostly been dropped. The canal is not entirely forgotten, for a canal society is now working to restore at least parts of it, but even seasoned canal-spotters have difficulty in tracing the route of the once busy navigation.
1-inch O.S. maps are essential for any exploration of the Wey and Arun Canal. There are plenty of ruined locks, many of them tucked away in woods, as at Dunsfold. And near Pulborough the energetic may even discover an abandoned tunnel.

Archaeological sites

Bignor Villa   C8
Nr. Petworth, W. Sussex. Roman villa built during the early 4thC on the site of an earlier house. It includes an unusually fine series of mosaics, one of them showing cupids in a gladiatorial combat. *Open Tue–Sun & B. Hols Mar–Oct (also Mon in Aug & Sun in Nov).*

Chanctonbury Ring   D8
W. Sussex. 1 mile se of Washington. On the crest of the South Downs, a magical ring of beech trees planted in 1760 around an iron age hill fort. Occupied by the Romans in the 3rdC and 4thC, there are the remains of Roman buildings in the middle.

Cissbury Ring   D9
W. Sussex. 1 mile e of Findon. This iron age hill fort is an elongated oval defended by a great rampart and external ditch, with a smaller counterscarp bank outside the ditch. It was not used during Roman times, but hastily refortified with a turf bank during the early part of the dark ages. Views to the Isle of Wight and Beachy Head.

Colchester   H3
Essex. Camulodunum was the first Roman city built in Britain under Claudius in 49-50. Excavations this century have uncovered a Roman street with a courtyard house in Castle Park; a temple, possibly to Mithras, was also found. The museum possesses the largest number of Roman relics gathered from a single site in Britain, and the castle which houses it is built on the foundations of the Roman temple to Claudius. The Roman Balkerne Gate is still visible.

Fishbourne Roman Palace   C9
Salthill Rd, Fishbourne, Chichester, W. Sussex. An outstanding Roman building covering an area of 250,000 square feet, built between 71 and 80 at the head of the eastern arm of Fishbourne Creek. One wing of the building, with mosaic floors, and much of the Pompeii-like gardens have been conserved. Finds are housed in the museum on site. *Open 10.00–19.00 daily Jun–Aug (10.00–18.00 May & Sep. 10.00–16.00 Mar, Apr & Oct & Sat & Sun Nov).*

Lullingstone Villa   F6
Kent. ½ mile sw of Eynsford. Set on high ground to the west of the River Darent, with chalk ridges rising above it. Excavations have revealed much of this remarkable Roman villa. It has what must be one of the earliest private Christian chapels in Britain. Fine mosaic floor and other decorative features. *Open daily.*

Pevensey Castle   G9
Pevensey Bay, E. Sussex. Here the two different Roman and Norman worlds are juxtaposed. Centuries after the Romans had left, the great walls were still strong enough for the Norman kings to build castles within them. The twelve-foot-thick walls, enclosing about ten acres, were considerably larger than most of the 'Saxon Shore' forts. The solid round-fronted bastions were irregularly spaced, but in such a way as to ensure that the wall between could be covered by cross-fire. *Open daily. Closed Sun morning.*

Richborough Castle K6

Kent. Off A257 ½ mile n of Sandwich.
Landing place of the Roman legions during
the Claudian invasion of 43. The walls now
standing are those of the 'Saxon Shore' fort
of the late 3rdC. Inside are visible ditches of
an earlier 3rdC fort, and the foundations of a
massive monument, built in the late 1stC,
from which bronze letters and imported
marble have been recovered. With Reculver,
of which little is now visible, Richborough
guarded the Channel between the Isle of
Thanet and the mainland. A site museum
houses excavation finds. *Open 9.30–17.30
daily Apr & 9.30–19.00 May–Sep. (9.30–
17.30 Mar & Oct. 9.30–16.00 Nov–Feb.
Closed Sun morning.)*

Roman Forts of the Saxon Shore

Girdling the coast of south-east Britain from
Brancaster in Norfolk to Portchester in
Hampshire was a chain of mighty Roman
forts. There were at least ten forts of which
nine survive, at Brancaster, Burgh Castle,
Bradwell, Reculver, Richborough, Dover,
Lympne, Pevensey and Portchester. All are
near the sea, usually at strategic points
guarding the natural gateways of south-
eastern Britain. Each could hold a substantial
garrison, and adjoined a harbour from which
a Roman fleet could operate.

Verulamium D4

St Michael's, St Albans, Herts. One of the
finest Roman towns in England with many
excellent buildings and sites. The centre was
destroyed by Boadicea during the Icenian
revolt. There are fascinating remains of the
theatre with its colonnaded stage and
auditorium, and of the town walls, which are
visible. The Verulamium Museum houses a
fine collection of iron age and Roman
material. *Open daily. Closed Sun morning
(10.00–16.00 Nov–Mar).*

Footpaths & ancient ways

North Downs Way

140 miles of footpath across Surrey and Kent
which coincides with part of the old
Pilgrim's Way, and runs along the escarpment of the North Downs. Recently created
a long-distance footpath, it begins at
Farnham, passing near Guildford, Dorking,
Caterham, Wrotham, Chatham, Ashford,
Folkestone, Dover, and then turns in a wide
loop to Canterbury.
There are fine views southwards along the
escarpment, rising to a height of over 700 feet
at Netley Heath. The path leads over the
cliff tops between Folkestone and Dover,
and there is an alternate route around
Lydden Spout Ranges to use on shooting
days.

Pilgrims' Way

Stretching for 120 miles across Hampshire,
Surrey and Kent, the Pilgrims' Way leads
from Winchester to Canterbury, once the
centre of mediaeval pilgrimage, where stood
the shrine of St Thomas Becket. It follows
the trackway, once the route of neolithic
tribesmen, that ran from the Straits of Dover
to Stonehenge and beyond.
The Way passes by Alton, Farnham,
Guildford, Dorking, Redhill and Charing
and along the lower slopes of the escarpment
of the North Downs. Much of it is motor
road today, especially in Hampshire. In
Surrey and Kent, however, there are miles of
country lanes bordered by hedgerows. But
for the rest the Way leads across fields and
skirts woodlands along shaded paths. In
Sandy Lane, West Warren, it has become a
hollow path rubbed away by centuries of
pilgrim feet. In high summer the nettles
grow six feet high and hawthorn, blackthorn,
wild roses and barbed wire can bar the way.
There are fine views from the top of
Martha's Hill, one mile north of Chilworth,
and the Way descends from there into the
wood north-east of Shere, below Ranmore,
emerging on Box Hill above Dorking.
Villages along the Pilgrims' Way, like
Chilham, still have their feudal aura intact.
The best months to walk are April, May and
June.

South Downs Way

The country's first long-distance bridleway,
and escape route for the asphalt-weary, set
aside for walkers, horse-riders and cyclists.
It stretches for 80 miles across Sussex from
Eastbourne to the Hampshire boundary in
the west, following the South Downs with
expansive views over the Weald for most of
the way. Also good viewpoints at Windover
Hill, Firle Beacon and Ditchling Beacon. To
the south are rolling hills with an occasional
glimpse of the sea.
Westward the path leads through woodlands
of deciduous and mixed forest. Fine views
from Rackham and Bignor Hills, Cocking
Down and Harting Down.

Regional sports

Bat and Trap

Canterbury, Kent. This game is one of
cricket's ancestors and has been played
around Canterbury for at least 180 years. It
is played on a grass pitch 21 yards long. A
batsman has to hit a ball through two posts
13½ feet apart. The ball is bowled underarm
at the trap, which is a block of wood with a
wooden plank pivoted like a see-saw. The
batsman tees the ball up by hitting the trap
and then the ball.
There are 46 active teams round Canterbury,
playing from mid-April to mid-September.
See the game played at the Golden Lion,
Broad Oak or round Canterbury at the
Rising Sun, Royal Artillery, Ye Olde
Beverly, and Brewers Delight.

Cricket

Hampshire may have given birth to the
rules of cricket, but nowhere is it played
more widely than in Kent, as the number of
towns which run cricket festivals bears
witness. Much of England's cricketing
strength and following is drawn from
south-east England. Kent, Sussex, Surrey
and Essex all run first class teams. County
grounds are as follows:
Kent County Cricket Club. St Lawrence
Ground, Old Dover St, Canterbury, Kent.
Tel 63421.
Essex County Cricket Club. New Writtle St,
Chelmsford, Essex. Tel 54533.
Surrey County Cricket Club. The Oval,
Kennington, London. Tel 01-735 2424.
Sussex County Cricket Club. Eaton Rd, Hove,
Sussex. Tel Brighton 732161.

Gliding

Dunstable Downs, Beds. Here you will find,
on the steep north-west-facing slopes of the
Chiltern Hills, the regular steady thermal
lifts required to make an ideal launching
ground for gliders. Flights and instruction
can be arranged from the club on the Downs.

Motor Racing

Brands Hatch, nr Farningham, Kent. Shares
with Silverstone the distinction of staging
the British Grand Prix for Formula One
racing cars in July, Brands being the venue
in even-numbered years. The circuit is in
constant weekend use for both motor car and
cycle racing. Embryo Fangios can use the
circuit on most Saturday afternoons, and all
day on the first Wednesday of every month if
they are in possession of an RAC
competition licence and a crash helmet.
Tuition is also available.

Polo

Cowdray Park, Midhurst, W. Sussex. This
game on horseback originated in India and
was brought back to England by the British
Army, amongst whom it was very popular.
The cost of the game these days is
astronomical and none but the very wealthy
can afford to play. It is, nevertheless, a most
attractive spectator sport. Matches are
played at weekends Apr-Aug.

Racing

Goodwood, W. Sussex. In the magnificent
scenery of the South Downs, the 'Glorious
Goodwood' meeting starts on the last
Tuesday in July and is among the main
events in the racing calendar.
Epsom, Surrey. This is the race course on the
North Downs where the famous Derby and

Oaks are run in early June. It is only in comparatively recent times that Parliament has stopped taking the day off on Derby Day. There are other meetings in April and August.

Stoolball
Midhurst, W. Sussex. Around Midhurst, the old Sussex game of stoolball is still played. The game goes back to the 15thC and remained popular throughout the country until the 18thC when its place was taken by cricket. The games are similar, with eleven players each side; but in stoolball the ball is bowled underarm, the bat is like a table tennis bat, and the wicket is a stool, one foot square mounted on a stake 4 feet 8 inches from the ground. A stoolball player can be out 'body before wicket' as distinct from cricket's 'leg before'. The game is played during the evenings throughout the summer.

Festivals

For information and tickets for festivals apply to the local information centre or ticket agent.

Brighton Festival
Brighton, E. Sussex. An early summer festival of music, theatre and the visual arts. *May.*

Chichester Festival Theatre Season
Chichester, W. Sussex. A much acclaimed festival season of plays, presented by a guest director and a company of distinguished actors, and performed in the bright modern Festival Theatre. *May–Sep.*

Glyndebourne Festival Opera
Glyndebourne, E. Sussex. One of the leading opera festivals in the world. An 800-seat opera house built alongside the home of Audrey and John Christie. Formal dress is the ritual, like the picnic supper in the gardens on the edge of the Downs. *May–Aug.*

Haslemere Festival
Haslemere, Surrey. A festival of early music played on 16thC, 17thC and 18thC instruments. Other old instruments can be viewed in the Haslemere Museum. Pay a visit to the workshops. *July.*

Little Missenden Festival
Little Missenden, Bucks. A village festival of music and arts in the Chilterns. Concerts are given in the mediaeval church. *Oct.*

Stour Music Festival
Wye environs, Kent. Unusual festival held in the heart of Kent. Rarely heard early music is performed in the local parish churches and country houses. Modern painting exhibition usually held in the church. *June.*

Tilford Bach Festival
Tilford, Surrey. The music of Bach and his contemporaries is performed in the parish church of Tilford. *May.*

Fun things

Audley End House Railway   F2
Audley End, Essex. Off the A11, 1 mile w of Saffron Walden. A 10¼ inch gauge miniature railway runs for nearly a mile through the wooded park, crossing twice over the River Tam. There are two steam locomotives and one diesel. *Open 10.00–17.30 daily Apr–Oct. Closed Mon.*

Bekonscot Model Village   C5
Warwick Rd, Beaconsfield, Bucks. A superb miniature village of half-timbered villas and a few Georgian houses, inhabited by model villagers. The scale is not always consistent but the effect is delightful. There is also a miniature railway. *Open 10.00–18.00 daily.*

Bluebell Railway   E8
Horsted Keynes, E. Sussex. One of the first standard gauge lines to be taken over by a preservation society. The railway runs to Sheffield Park Station five miles away. A very fine cross section of vintage and British Rail Steam Locomotives are operated. Beautiful scenery. *Open most weekends & daily Jun–Sep.*

Dreamland Funfair   K5
Margate, Kent. This rivals in size its opposite number across the Thames Estuary at Southend. There are 20 acres of amusements. Recommended are the big dipper, dodgems and caterpillar. Sited by the sea front.

Hell Fire Caves   B4
Bucks. 2 miles nw of High Wycombe. These caves, cut out of chalk, achieved great notoriety in the 18thC as the headquarters of the 'Hell Fire Club', a depraved aristocratic set whose interest in Satanism terrorised the local area.

Marbles   Y7
Crawley, W. Sussex. Nearby Tinsley Green is the venue of the All England Marbles Championship. The event takes place outside a pub called the Greyhound on Good Friday every year.

North Foreland Lighthouse   K6
Nr Broadstairs, Kent (1½ miles n). Open usually in afternoon except Sunday and in fog. Permission from keeper required. Tel Thanet 61869.

The Romney, Hythe and Dymchurch Railway   J8
New Romney, Kent. The railway runs 13½ miles from New Romney to Dungeness Lighthouse. A 15-inch gauge line, it has an impressive collection of steam engines operating on a frequent and regular service during the summer months. Scenically the Romney Marshes may not be to everyone's taste, but the lonely atmosphere so close to civilization is intriguing.

The Shuttleworth Collection   D2
Old Warden, Beds. 4 miles w of Biggleswade, 2½ miles off A1. About 50 historic aeroplanes including a Hawker Hurricane and Spitfire of World War II and a World War I Bristol Fighter.

Hotels

The following indicates the price range of a single room per night:
£   inexpensive
££   medium priced
£££   expensive

Alfriston E. Sussex   F9
Star Inn, nr Polegate. Tel 495. 15thC inn with modern comforts behind heavily carved facade. Good cuisine. *££.*

Brighton E. Sussex   E9
Hotel Metropole, King's Rd. Tel 775432. A grand Victorian hotel now modernised with health hydro and a rooftop Starlit Room restaurant; good French cooking. *£££.*

Burnham-on-Crouch Essex   H4
Ye Olde White Hart Hotel, The Quay. Tel Maldon 782106. Victorian yachting hotel with its own jetty. *£.*

Canterbury Kent   J6
Falstaff Hotel, St Dunstan's St, Westgate. Tel 62138. 15thC pilgrims' inn. Comfortable beamed rooms offer a warm welcome. *£.*

Chichester W. Sussex   C9
Dolphin and Anchor Hotel, West St. Tel 85121. Two coaching inns run together make an attractive stopping off point opposite the cathedral. Sauna bath. *££.*

Churt Surrey   B7
Frensham Pond Hotel, nr Farnham. Tel Frensham 3175. Country home comfort in peaceful setting; bedrooms have period furniture and colour tv. Good food. *£££.*

Climping W. Sussex   C9
Bailiffscourt Hotel, Bailiffscourt. Tel Littlehampton 3952. A marvellous and unique hotel. A careful reconstruction of a mediaeval manor set in 1,000 acres with a private beach. Combines ancient splendour with modern luxury. Personal service. *££.*

Colchester Essex   H3
George Hotel, High St. Tel 78494. Retains much of its original 14thC charm with ample comfort. There is a leafy 300-year-old vine in the courtyard, whilst a section of old Roman street emerges in the cellar bar. *£.*

Deal Kent   **K6**
Royal Hotel, Beach St. Tel 5555. Right on the beach, quaint historical hotel loved by Churchill. Excellent cuisine using local fish and fresh vegetables. Good centre for Cinque Ports. No dogs. *£.*

Dorking Surrey   **D7**
Burford Bridge Hotel, Box Hill. Tel 4561. Close to Box Hill with its own swimming pool and gardens. Easy access from London. *££.*

East Grinstead W. Sussex   **E7**
Gravetye Manor Hotel. Tel Sharpthorne 810567. 30 acres of landscaped garden enclosed by 1,000 acres of forest surround this large, comfortable Elizabethan manor house. *£££.*

Haslemere Surrey   **C7**
Georgian Hotel, High St. Tel 51555. Pleasant Regency style hotel with two squash courts, sauna bath and log fires. *£.*

Hertingfordbury Herts   **E3**
White Horse Inn. Tel Hertford 56791. A combination of old and new with a pleasant garden. Well situated in a pretty village. *££.*

Marlow Bucks   **B5**
Compleat Angler Hotel. Tel 4444. Alongside Marlow's elegant suspension bridge it stands on a beautiful stretch of the Thames. A ritzy and very luxurious hotel with its own special restaurant, 'Le Valaisan'. *£££.*

Rye E. Sussex   **H8**
Mermaid Hotel, Mermaid St. Tel 3065. Visited by Queen Elizabeth I in 1573, this 15thC inn with authentic timbers embodies the best of the smugglers' swagger with modern comforts and log fires. No dogs. *£.*

St Albans Herts   **D4**
Sopwell House Hotel, Cottonmill Lane. Tel 64477. With period furniture and furnishings, original ceilings and flagstones intact, this yellow-painted Georgian mansion is just outside the Roman city. *££.*

Regional food & drink

Aylesbury Harvest Pie
Young rabbit stuffed with prunes, baked with bacon and onions and garnished with forcemeat balls.

Biddenden Cakes
Cakes, distributed at Easter, with an impression of Siamese twin girls who, 400 years ago, left land to provide for the poor of this Kent village.

Brown Shrimps
Native to the Kent coast, they are the same natural transparent colour as other shrimps, but turn brown when cooked. Easily caught at low tide at Camber Sands.

Cobnuts
In the autumn, Kent Cobnuts, oval nuts wrapped in a green husk, are harvested. A smaller, wild variety can be found in hedgerows.

Dover Sole
Can be bought fresh in most eastern Kentish seaside towns, but a good place to buy this and other excellent fish still kicking is Hastings Fish Market.

Dunmow Flitch
A side of bacon which is awarded to the couple who can vouch that they have not quarrelled for a year and a day nor regretted their marriage. The Flitch ceremony takes place each Whit Monday at Dunmow, Essex.

Epping Sausage
Skinless sausage of pork and beef suet heavily flavoured with sage and spiced with thyme, marjoram and nutmeg.

Kentish Cider Wine and Barley Wine
Kentish cider (from the vast acreages of apple orchards) is sweet and very strong. Both this and barley wine are obtainable in the Weald of Kent in many inns. Barley Wine is extremely powerful stuff.

Whitstable Oysters
Whitstable has been famous for oysters since Roman times. Today the Royal Whitstable Native Oyster is world-renowned.

Restaurants

The following indicates the price range for a meal.
£   inexpensive
££   medium priced
£££ expensive

Aston Clinton Bucks   **C3**
Bell Inn, on the A41. Tel Aylesbury 630252. Franco-British. Exceptional wines. *LD £££. Book.*

Biddenden Kent   **G7**
Ye Maydes, 15 High St. Tel 306. French, informal. Fixed-price menus – changed frequently. *LD. Closed Sun D & Mon. ££. Book.*

Billingshurst W. Sussex   **D8**
XVth Century, 42 High St. Tel 2652. Small restaurant in 15thC cottage. Home-made English dishes. *D. Closed Sun. ££. Book.*

Brighton E. Sussex   **E9**
Le Francais, 1 Paston Place, Kemp Town. Tel 680716. Self-assured French. *D. Closed Sun. £££. Book.*

Brighton E. Sussex   **E9**
Tureen, 31 Upper North St. Tel 28939. Informal bistro cooking. *LD. Closed Sun & Mon. £L. ££D. Book.*

Burham Kent   **G6**
Toastmaster's Inn, Church St. Tel Medway 61299 Friendly inn on a village street. Outstanding wine list. French-provincial food. *LD. Closed Mon. £££. Book.*

Chichester W. Sussex   **C9**
Little London, 38 Little London, off East St. Tel 84899. Near Chichester Museum. Mainly French, caters for after-theatre parties. *LD. Closed Sun & Mon. £L. ££D. Book.*

Dedham Essex   **J2**
Le Talbooth, Gun Hill. Tel Colchester 323150. Tudor hotel near the river. Franco-British. *LD. £££. Book.*

Dorking Surrey   **D7**
Little Dudley House, 77 South St. Tel 2652. Family-run. Mainly English. *LD. Closed Sun. £L. ££D. Book.*

East Grinstead W. Sussex   **E7**
Gravetye Manor, B2110 sw of town, 2 miles from Turner's Hill. Tel Sharpthorne 810567. 16thC house with attractive grounds. Elaborate menus, notable wines. *LD. £££. Book.*

Felsted Essex   **G3**
Boote House. Tel Great Dunmow 820279. Family-run. Imaginative menus. *D. Closed Sun & Mon. ££. Book.*

Folkestone Kent   **J7**
Emilio's Restaurant Portofino, 124 Sandgate Rd. Tel 55762 & 55866. Italian. Attentive service. *LD. Closed Mon. £L. ££D. Book.*

Jevington E. Sussex   **F9**
Hungry Monk. Tel Polegate 2178. Family-run, friendly. Fixed-price menus. Franco-British. *LD. L. £L.*

Lewes E. Sussex   **E9**
Trumps, 20 Station Rd. Tel 3906. Small, fashionable restaurant with English and French cooking and friendly service. *D. Closed Sun & Mon. ££.*

Midhurst W. Sussex   **C8**
Mida Restaurant. Tel 3284. Tiny restaurant in the main street. Serious French cooking. Last orders 22.30. *LD. Closed Sun L & Mon. £££. Book.*

Westerham Kent   **E7**
Le Marquis de Montcalm, Quebec Square. Tel 62139. Sevenoaks side of town. French cooking to high standards. Ambitious menu. Also *D. £££. L cheap. Book.*

Worthing W. Sussex   **D9**
Paragon, 10 Brunswick Rd. Tel 33367. Good French and Italian dishes. Cheerful atmosphere. *LD. Closed Sun & Tues. ££.*

Wye Kent   **H7**
Wife of Bath, 4 Upper Bridge St. Tel 812540. Edwardian house. Set menus changed weekly – individual cooking. Mainly French. *LD. Closed Sun & Mon. ££. Book.*

London

As well as being Europe's biggest city, London is by far the most varied and fascinating place in the world. Topographically London is a twenty mile shallow basin with the Thames crossing its middle. It is a collection of a thousand villages that somehow got joined together, and although eroded by the spread of anonymous development somehow these village centres remain. The city of London still has a separate identity despite massive rebuilding – only just curbed in time: you can still see St Paul's from the river. London grows and changes daily; it has immense vitality, friendly people, some of the most interesting shops ever and is full of theatres, museums, libraries, odd squares, quiet parks and some unexpected surprises.

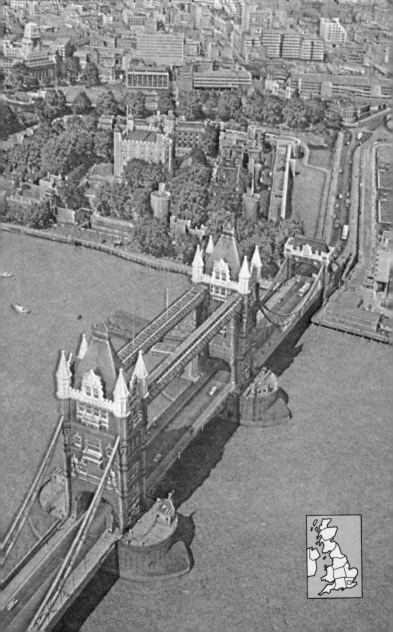

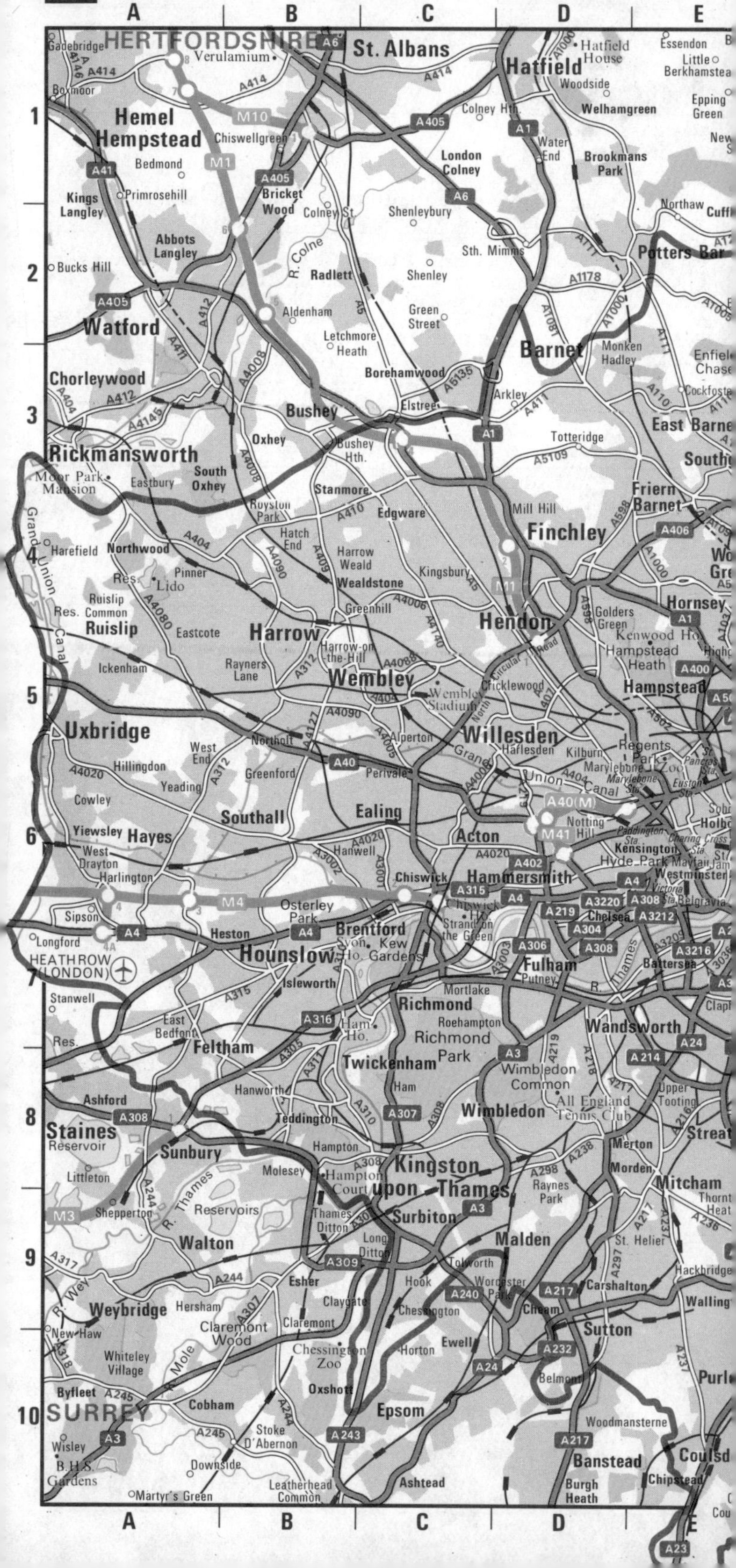

4

HERTFORDSHIRE

Gadebridge
Boxmoor
A414
Verulamium
A6
St. Albans
A414
Hatfield
Hatfield House
Essendon
Little Berkhamstea
Epping Green

1
Hemel Hempstead
A41
Bedmond
Primrosehill
M10
A414
Chiswellgreen
A405
M1
Colney Hth.
A1
A405
London Colney
Water End
Welhamgreen
Brookmans Park
New S

Kings Langley
Bucks Hill
Abbots Langley
A405
Bricket Wood
Colney St
R. Colne
Radlett
Shenleybury
Shenley
A6
Sth. Mimms
A1178
A1081
A1000
Potters Bar
Northaw
Cuff
A1

2
Watford
A411
A412
A4008
Aldenham
Letchmore Heath
Green Street
A411
Barnet
Monken Hadley
A411
Enfiel Chase
Cockfoste

Chorleywood
A412
A404
Bushey
Oxhey
Bushey Hth.
Borehamwood
A5135
Elstree
Arkley
A1
Totteridge
A110
East Barne

3
Rickmansworth
A4145
A404
Moor Park Mansion
Eastbury
South Oxhey
Royston Park
Stanmore
A410
Edgware
A5109
Mill Hill
Friern Barnet
South

Harefield
Northwood
A404
Pinner
Hatch End
Harrow Weald
A4090
Wealdstone
Greenhill
A4006
Kingsbury
M1
Finchley
A406
A598
Wo Gre

4
Ruislip
Res.
Lido
A4080
Eastcote
Ickenham
Harrow
Rayners Lane
A312
Harrow-on-the-Hill
A4088
Wembley
Wembley Stadium
A404
Cricklewood
Hendon
Circular Road
Golders Green
A1
Kenwood Ho
Hampstead Heath
High
Hornsey
A400
Hampstead
A50

5
Uxbridge
A4020
Hillingdon
Cowley
Yeading
West End
Northolt
A312
Greenford
A40
Perivale
A4090
A4005
Alperton
Willesden
Harlesden
Kilburn
Marylebone
Grand Union Canal
A404
Regents Park
London Zoo
Euston
Pancras
Sob
Holb

6
Hayes
West Drayton
Harlington
Sipson
Yiewsley
A4020
Southall
Hanwell
A4020
Ealing
Acton
A40(M)
M41
Notting Hill
A402
Paddington
A40(M)
Kensington
Hyde Park
Charing Cross
Westminster
Victoria

Longford
A4
HEATHROW (LONDON)
Heston
Osterley Park
A4
Brentford
Syon Ho.
Kew Ho. Gardens
Chiswick
A315
Strand on the Green
Hammersmith
A4
A315
A219
A3220
A308
A3212
Chelsea
A304
Battersea
A3216

7
Stanwell
Res.
East Bedfont
A315
Isleworth
Hounslow
Mortlake
Putney
A306
Fulham
Thames R.
A3
Wandsworth
A214
A24
A3
Clap

Ashford
Feltham
Hanworth
A316
Ham Ho.
Richmond
Roehampton
Richmond Park
A3
A219
Wimbledon Common
Upper Tooting
A217

8
Staines Reservoir
A308
Littleton
M3
Shepperton
Sunbury
A308
Teddington
Twickenham
Ham
A310
A307
Wimbledon
All England Tennis Club
Merton
A238
Mitcham
Streat

9
Weybridge
New Haw
A317
Walton
R. Thames
Reservoirs
Hersham
A244
Esher
Molesey
Thames Ditton
Hampton
Hampton Court
A308
Long Ditton
A309
Kingston upon Thames
Surbiton
A3
Malden
Raynes Park
A298
A238
A297
St. Helier
Morden
A217
Hackbridge
Walling

Claremont Wood
Claremont
Claygate
Chessington
Hook
Tolworth
Worcester Park
Ewell
A240
A24
Cheam
A217
Carshalton
Sutton

10
SURREY
Byfleet
A245
A3
Wisley
B.H.S. Gardens
Martyr's Green
Cobham
Downside
A245
Stoke D'Abernon
Leatherhead Common
Oxshott
A243
Epsom
Ashtead
A24
A232
Woodmansterne
Banstead
Burgh Heath
A217
Belmen
Coulsd
Chipstea
A23

F G H J K

Hoddesdon
Hacketts
Broxbourne
Wormley
Appleby St.
Oak
Cheshunt
museum
Fortyhill
nfield
nchmore Hill
Edmonton
Tottenham
Walthamstow
Leyton
Hackney
lington
Shoreditch
Bethnal Green
City London
Liverpool St.
Fenchurch Street Sta.
wark
Bermondsey
Deptford
erwell
New Cross
Dulwich
South Circular Road
Sydenham
wood
Penge
Selhurst
roydon
South Croydon
Addiscombe
Hamsey Green
eleaze

Roydon Hamlet
Lower Nazeing
Nazeing
Bumbles Green
Res.
Upshire
High Beach
Epping Forest
Queen Elizabeth's Hunting Lodge
Buckhurst Hill
Chingford
Woodford
A406
Wanstead
A116
Forest Gate
Manor Park
Stratford
W. Ham
Stepney
Poplar
Rotherhithe Tunnel
Blackwall Tunnel
Blackheath Village
Kidbrooke
Lewisham
Hither Green
Catford
Grove Park
Mottingham
Chislehurst
Beckenham
National Recreation Centre
Bromley
Bickley
Eden Park
West Wickham
Hayes
Keston
New Addington
Selsdon
Sanderstead
Farleigh
Warlingham

Gt. Parndon
Harlow
Hastingwood
Thornwood Common
M11
A1161
North Weald Bassett
Epping Upland
Epping Green
Epping
Coopersale Common
Ivychimneys
Theydon Bois
Fiddlers Hamlet
Birch Hall
Epping Forest
Abridge
Loughton
Chigwell
Lambourne End
Grange Hill
Hainault
Chigwell Row
Mark's Gate
Aldborough Hatch
Collier Row
Barkingside
Newbury Park
A12
Seven Kings
A1083
Beacontree
Ilford
A124
Barking
E. Ham
Beckton
Creekmouth
Woolwich
Charlton
Greenwich
Maritime Museum
Plumstead
Thamesmead
Abbey Wood
Belvedere
Welling
Palace Eltham
New Eltham
Sidcup
Foots Cray
Caves
A20
St. Paul's Cray
Petts Wood
St. Mary Cray
Orpington
Bromley Common
Farnborough
Green St. Green
Pratts Bottom
Downe
Cudham
Biggin Hill
Knockholt Pound
Westerham Hill
Chevening

Potter Street
Foster St.
High Laver
Little Laver
Magdalen Laver
Moreton
Fyfield
Bobbingworth
Shelley
A122
Greensted
Toothill
Chipping Ongar
High Ongar
A128
ESSEX
Stapleford Tawney
Stanford Rivers
Little End
Kelvedon Hatch
R. Roding
Navestock
Navestock Side
Stapleford Abbotts
Bournebridge
Havering-atte-Bower
Noak Hill
South Weald
A12
Harold Hill
Harold Wood
Squirrel's Heath
Gidea Park
Romford
A124
Hornchurch
Emerson Park
Cranha
Rush Green
Elm Park
Upminster
Corbets Tey
Dagenham
A13
South Hornchurch
Rainham
Wennington
Purfleet
Belhas
Aveley
R. Thames
Erith
Slade Green
Tunnel
A282
Dartford
Stone
A226
Crayford
A2
Bexley
A223
Coldblow
North Cray
Wilmington
Hextable
Hawley
Darenth
South Darenth
M25
Sutton at Hone
Swanley
Horton Kirby
Crockenhill
Roman Villa
Lullingstone Castle
Well Hill
Chelsfield
Badger's Mount
Shoreham
Knockholt
Chevening Park
Otford
A225
Eynsford Castle
Eynsford
M20
Farningham
KENT
Brands Hatch
West Kingsdown
Kemsing
Heaverham
Halstead

F G H J K

Districts

Bank EC2　　　　　　　　　　　　F6
The commercial centre of London, this is the home of the Bank of England, the Royal Exchange, Mansion House, the Stock Exchange. Just south is Wren's Monument to the Great Fire of 1666.

Bankside SE1　　　　　　　　　　F6
Southwark. The Thames-side walk has the finest views of St Paul's and the City. An area of warehouses, docks, the Anchor pub, and the power station looking like a giant, forbidding fortress.
Near the site of Shakespeare's original theatre is the new Globe Playhouse, looking like a demented scaffolding under canvas. The summer festival is the beginning of an exciting effort to create a World Centre for Shakespeare studies in Southwark.

Belgravia SW1　　　　　　　　　　E6
Handsome Regency squares and mews: Eaton Square, Chester Square, Belgrave Square. Designed and built by Thomas Cubitt, 1825 onwards.

Blackheath Village SE3　　　　　G7
The Hampstead of the south with a broad common once popular with highwaymen, and a cosy row of village shops and houses in the vale.

Chelsea SW3　　　　　　　　　　　E6
It's the people not the buildings that attract, though most of the wanderers along the King's Road are probably tourists too. Some lovely Georgian cottages and typical late Victorian houses. Cheyne Walk and Tite Street were the places to live, with neighbours such as Carlyle, Rossetti, Turner and Oscar Wilde. Georgian houses and some house boats along the waterfront.

Chiswick W4　　　　　　　　　　　C6
The Georgian houses along the waterfront stretch from Kew Bridge to Hammersmith. Originally there were three 18thC mansions with grounds down to the river – Grove House, Sutton Court and Chiswick House. The latter only remains. Lord Burlington and William Kent who were largely responsible for the elegance of Chiswick are buried in St Nicholas' church. Chiswick Mall is still reminiscent of the wealthy riverside village.

The City EC4　　　　　　　　　　　F6
Known as 'the square mile', this was Norman London. Wren's great St Paul's Cathedral stands on the Ludgate Hill with commercial London spreading out around her. Wander down the alleyways off Carter Lane and you will get a taste of London before the Great Fire.

Covent Garden WC2　　　　　　　E6
Originally designed by Inigo Jones as a residential square in 1638; the market buildings were erected in 1831. The smell of flowers, fruit and vegetables has faded from the steps of the Royal Opera House and Drury Lane now that the market has moved. The area is now packed with fashionable craft shops, restaurants and artists' studios.

Croydon Surrey　　　　　　　　　F9
The town centre is a massive concrete 'metropolis'. Good facilities for shopping, but ugly. Fairfield Hall is the theatre complex with some excellent productions.

Royal Naval College, Greenwich

Greenwich SE10　　　　　　　　　G7
The church which had a vast number of mediaeval relics was completely burnt out during World War II and most were lost including the famous 'Tallis Organ' (Thomas Tallis musician, 1510-85, is buried here).
In the park the Queen's House, a perfect example of neo-classical architecture by Inigo Jones, houses the Maritime Museum.

Marked on the path in front of the Observatory (also in the park but no longer in use) is the zero meridian from which was calculated the Greenwich Mean Time. In 1831 Charles Darwin, grandson of Erasmus, set off aboard 'The Beagle' on a scientific expedition to South America. The 'Cutty Sark', one of the original tea-clippers, and Chichester's boat 'Gypsy Moth' are in dock near the pier.
Up to the 19thC the only dock system in existence was on the South Bank where the Great Howland dock had been built in 1696 to take the Greenland whalers. Most ships had to dock at the 'legal quays' where all cargo had to be disembarked between dawn and dusk. The India group of docks were opened in 1802 to cope with increased traffic and combat the smuggling which was rife as a result of the overcrowding at the legal quays. The royal docks followed from 1855. In 1909 the three companies which owned these dock areas privately merged into the Port of London Authority, which then had complete control.
After World War II the Old Granary at Shooter's Hill became the PLA's private radio station. Since then international VHF and UHF have been installed centred on Greenwich and known as the Thames Navigation Service. Radar was introduced into the port system in 1955 and covers the whole river down to the estuary mouth.

Hammersmith W6　　　　　　　　D6
The riverside Mall stretching from Hammersmith to Chiswick is the place to visit, with its boathouses, pubs and terraces of Georgian houses, including Kelmscott House where William Morris lived and founded his printing press.

Hampstead Village NW3　　　　　E5
Still very much a village of Georgian houses and alleyways. Church Row, Holly Mount

and Regency houses on Downshire Hill, including Keats' house, are notable.

Highgate N6　　　　　　　　　　　E5
A picturesque cluster of Victorian and Georgian houses on top of a hill over-run by traffic.

Kensington W8　　　　　　　　　　D6
Kensington High Street is the main thoroughfare – a busy shopping area. The more interesting Church Street runs north with its antique shops and stolid stucco buildings. South Kensington centres around Exhibition Road with its massive Victorian hulks of museums.

Kew Green Surrey　　　　　　　　C7
Elegant 18thC houses around a triangular green. Gainsborough is buried nearby in the churchyard of St Anne's.

Kew Green.

Kingston-upon-Thames Surrey **C8**
An ancient market town with a gaudy
Victorian market hall. Clattern Bridge dates
from the 12thC.

Marylebone W1 **E6**
Nestled between Regent's Park, Oxford
Street and Edgware Road, a mainly
residential area with many fine 18thC streets
and squares. Baker Street is here, home of
that gentleman with the deerstalker, ulster
and pipe. But Marylebone High Street is the
centre of the once village – a narrow,
winding street.

Mayfair W1 **E6**
An elegant quarter of boutiques, bow-fronts
and Georgian and 19thC houses, bounded
by Park Lane, Oxford Street, Regent Street
and Piccadilly. Savile Row, Bond Street,
Burlington Arcade, Berkeley and Grosvenor
Squares and Shepherd's Market are all here.
Wander down South Audley Street or stop
in at Sotheby's auction rooms in New Bond
Street.

Notting Hill W11 **D6**
An area of decayed elegance with many
stucco buildings and tree-shaded squares.
The main attraction is the Portobello Road
market – few antiques these days, but much
junk. Christie's house in Rillington Place has
gone, but his exploits are immortalised in the
Chamber of Horrors at Madame Tussaud's.

Richmond Surrey **C7**
A pleasant almost rural town which has had
long associations with royalty. Richmond
Palace was a favourite palace of Elizabeth I.
Other famous residents included Joshua
Reynolds, first president of the Royal
Academy, who had a weekend house here.
Leonard and Virginia Woolf lived at
Suffield House and set up the Hogarth
Press (publishing among other things the
early works of T. S. Eliot). The park of
2,000 acres has good herds of deer. Private
shooting was stopped in 1904.

St James's SW1 **E6**
Once the precinct of the court of Charles II,
and later developed in the 18thC. Famous
for its clubs along Pall Mall, shops along
Piccadilly and Jermyn and St James's Streets,
and a quiet air of aristocratic self-assurance.

Soho W1 **E6**
A notorious and lively place of 18thC streets
and undistinguished modern replacements.
Old Compton Street is its exotic heart with
superb food and wine shops; Wardour Street
is the centre of the film industry;
'Chinatown' is around Gerrard Street; and
Carnaby Street is for the purveyors of cheap
trendy gear. Strip clubs abound.

Spitalfields E1 **F6**
The infamous haunt of Jack the Ripper. The
fruit and vegetable market remains, for the
moment, in the centre of a once thriving area
of artisans built up in the 17th & 18thC.
Fournier Street has some fine examples of
18thC popular design. Wilkes Street is a
haunted row of derelicts beside Hawksmoor's
Christ Church, recently rescued from a
certain death.

Strand on the Green W4 **C7**
Once a quiet river-side village. Some fine
Georgian houses.

West End WC2 **E6**
Piccadilly Circus and Leicester Square are the
hub of London night – with endless cinemas
and theatres along Shaftesbury Avenue,
and strip clubs and restaurants spilling over
from neighbouring Soho. Frenetic,
cosmopolitan and crowded.

Whitehall SW1 **E6**
A wide thoroughfare used for ceremonial
and state processions – with Trafalgar
Square at one end and the Houses of
Parliament and Westminster Abbey at the
other. In between are government offices
including the Foreign Office, the Admiralty
and the Home Office. Leading off Whitehall
is Downing Street. The Horse Guards
is a big tourist attraction.

The Horse Guards

Streets

Bond Street W1 **E6**
Mayfair's fashionable High Street.
Originally laid out in the 1680s it no longer
has any architectural distinction but is noted
for its art dealers' galleries, fashion and
quality shops.

Bow Lane EC4 **F6**
A huddled curve of Dickensiana full of small
shops and cafes, squeezing nimbly past St
Mary-le-Bow.

Burlington Arcade W1 **E6**
Piccadilly. 1819 Regency shopping
promenade with original shop windows.
Still employs a beadle to preserve the
gracious atmosphere.

Carnaby Street W1 **E6**
Neon-lit extravaganza; now a pedestrian
walk.

Cheyne Walk SW3 **E6**
One of the most famous streets in London.
Fronting the river. Turner, Whistler and
Rossetti lived here.

Chiswick Mall W4 **C6**
17th-18thC riverside houses.

Downing Street SW1 **E6**
A 17thC street with houses built by Sir
George Downing. No. 10 is the official
residence of the Prime Minister; No. 11 of
the Chancellor of the Exchequer.

Fleet Street EC4 **F6**
London's 'street of ink'. Has been associated
with printing since the days of Caxton. All
national and most provincial newspapers
have their offices in or near it.

Hammersmith Mall W6 **D6**
Upper & Lower Mall. Boathouses, riverside
pubs and terraces of Georgian houses,
including Kelmscott House (1780) where
William Morris lived and founded his
printing press.

Kensington Palace Gardens W8 **D6**
A street of prosperous town mansions in the
grand Italianate style, laid out by
Pennethorne in 1843, but continued by other
famous architects. No. 8a is by Owen Jones
and Decimus Burton; No. 12a James
Murray; Nos. 18-20 by Banks and Barry;
No. 13 by C. J. Richardson.

Kings Road SW1 **E6**
Chelsea's enticing hotch-potch, as colourful
as a rainbow and as sociable as the telephone
directory.

Admiralty Arch

The Mall W1 **E6**
Processional way laid out by Sir Aston Webb
as a national memorial to Queen Victoria.

Oxford Street W1 **E6**
An exhausting and exasperating mall of
department stores amidst the rat race.

Pall Mall SW1 **E6**
Early 19thC opulence. This fine street and
its surroundings express the confidence and
wealth of the London of this period. Pall
Mall itself contains two fine buildings by
Sir Charles Barry; the Travellers Club,
1829-32 (Italian-Renaissance revival), and
his more mature Reform Club 1837-41.

Reform Club   The Athenaeum Club

Piccadilly W1 **E6**
A straight mile of polished complexities. Of
interest—Apsley House; Burligion House;
the Ritz; view to St James's Palace.

Queen Anne's Gate SW1   **E6**
Quiet, completely preserved 18thC street
in its original state. Statue of Queen Anne
near No. 13.

Regent Street W1   **E6**
Planned by John Nash in the early 19thC as
part of one dashing curve from St James to
Regent's Park. Much altered grandeur with
de luxe shops and offices.

Royal Opera Arcade   **E6**
Between Pall Mall and Charles II St SW1.
John Nash 1816, London's earliest arcade.
Pure Regency; bow-fronted shops, glass
domed vaults and elegant lamps.

St James's Street SW1   **E6**
Contains some of its original 18thC houses
and shopfronts. Boodles (No. 28) 1775 by
J. Crunden; Brooks's (No. 60) 1776 by
Henry Holland.

Shaftesbury Avenue W1   **E6**
An enticing curve of colour and exotica built
in 1880 with a liberal sprinkling of theatres.

Strand WC2   **E6**
Once a 'strand' – a walk along the river
bordered in Stuart times with mansions
and gardens down to the river. Their names
still survive in the streets: Bedford,
Buckingham, Villiers.

Wardour Street W1   **E6**
The stronghold of celluloid glamour hidden
behind dour filing-cabinet blocks.

Woburn Walk WC1   **E6**
Built by Cubitt in 1822 it's an elegant stucco
terrace of bow-fronted shops.

Markets

Berwick Street   **E6**
Soho W1. Well-known Soho street market.
Fruits, vegetables and general. *Open 8.00–
19.00. Closed Thur afternoon & Sun.*

Billingsgate   **F6**
Lower Thames St EC3. Market building
1876. London's fish market. Once a port
(nearly all fish now comes by land). Porters,
famous for their strong language and their
unique leather hats on which they carry fish
boxes. *Open from 6.00 daily. Sun–
Shellfish only.*

Caledonian Market   **F6**
Bermondsey St SE1. Antiques. *6.00–13.00
Fri.*

Camden Passage   **F5**
Islington High St N1. Small market of
antique stalls and shops in what is now a
fashionable locality. *Open 10.30–17.30
Mon–Sat.*

Covent Garden Market WC2   **E6**
Originally designed by Inigo Jones as a
residential square in 1638, the market
buildings were erected in 1831. The glass
Floral Hall, 1859, is by E. M. Barry;
other market halls 1831–33 by Charles
Fowler. The market moved to Nine Elms
in 1974.

High Street   **G4**
Walthamstow E17. Over a mile of stalls and
shops selling literally everything. Crowded
and noisy. *Open 8.00–17.00 Mon–Fri.
8.00–19.00 Sat. Closed Wed afternoon &
Sun.*

Leadenhall Market   **F6**
Gracechurch St EC3. Impressive Victorian
glass and iron hall, 1881, housing the
poultry market.

Leather Lane   **E6**
Holborn EC1. General. *Open 11.00–14.00.
Closed Sat & Sun.*

Petticoat Lane   **F6**
Middlesex St E1. Busy bustling colourful
street of stalls. Sells clothes and anything of
popular market value. *9.00–14.00 Sun.*

Portobello Road   **D6**
Off Westbourne Park W11. The nearest tube
is Ladbroke Grove. Half the street is full of
antique stalls and the other half of fruit and
vegetables dividing roughly at the Finch's
pub. Further up there are 'junk' stalls and
some boutiques. *Sat all day.*

Covent Garden Market.

Royal Standard Antiques Market   **G7**
*The Car Park, Royal Standard Hotel,
Vanbrugh Park, Blackheath.* Antique market
with a variety of stalls. *All day Sat.*

Smithfield Market (Wholesale)   **F6**
Charterhouse St EC1. The largest meat
market in the world (ten acres). The
Italianate-style market buildings with some
ornamental ironwork were designed by
Horace Jones and erected 1868 and 1899.
Open from 5.00 Mon–Sat.

Spitalfields (Wholesale)   **F6**
Commercial St E1. Nr Liverpool St Station.
Five acres of fruit, vegetables and flower
market. *From 4.30 Mon–Sat.*

Courts and squares

Ball Court   **F6**
Next to 39 Cornhill EC3. Straight out of
Dickens. Simpson's Chop House built in
1757.

Bayswater W2   **D6**
Unpretentious Georgian squares and
terraces built 1830-60.

Berkeley Square W1   **E6**
The adman's habitat full of grand trees and
blandly indifferent buildings.

Bloomsbury Squares WC1   **E6**
Elegant Georgian houses and squares;
Bedford Square, Russell Square, Tavistock
Square. Built by Thomas Cubitt, mid
19thC.

Cadogan Square SW1   **E6**
A typical 19thC Chelsea square of red-
brick houses.

Fitzroy Square W1   **E6**
The south and east sides by Robert Adam
1790–94.

Leicester Square W1   **E6**
Laid out originally as a Dutch garden in
1720, it's now a leafy and electric foyer to the
cinema world.

Sloane Square SW1   **E6**
An uninhibited plug hole for the King's
Road.

Trafalgar Square WC2   **E6**
Laid out by Sir Charles Barry, 1829.
Nelson's column (granite) by William
Railton 1840. Statue by Baily. Bronze lions
by Landseer 1868. Fountains by Lutyens
1948. Famous for its pigeons and
political demonstrations.

Wardrobe Place EC4   **E6**
A tiny 18thC world of gas lamps, planes and
18thC brick tucked quietly behind a slice of
city backside.

*monument
Duke of York's column*

Nelson's column

London oddities

Cockney   F6
Rhyming slang was evolved in the East End supposedly by villains in the 1830s, and continues as a living thing. It consists of a repertoire of phrases rhyming with words which they replace:

belch	Raquel Welch
believe	Adam and Eve
boozer	battle cruiser
breasts (tits)	Bristol Cities
copper	bottle and stopper
deaf	Mutt 'n' Jeff
dinner	Lilley and Skinner
dole	sausage roll
dope	bar of soap
drunk	elephant's trunk
ear	bottle of beer
eyes	mince pies
head	loaf of bread
house	cat and mouse
knickers	Alan Whickers
lips	apple pips
the missus	cheese and kisses
phone	eau de Cologne
queer	ginger beer
road	frog and toad
scotch	pimple and blotch
shirt	Dickie Dirt
sky	apple pie
son	currant bun
steak	Joe Blake
table	Cain and Abel
stairs	apples and pears
teeth	Hampstead Heath
thief	tea leaf
waiter	hot potato

Famous people

Thomas Carlyle (1795–1881)   E6
24 Cheyne Row SW3. The writer lived here for 47 years, where he wrote many of his best works.
A tall, narrow building stuffed with original furnishings and relics. Cosy and lived in. *Open 11.00–13.00 & 14.00–18.00 Wed–Sat. Closed Sun morning.*

Charles Darwin (1809–82)   H10
Downe House, Downe, Kent. The home of the Victorian naturalist for 40 years. This is where he wrote 'The Origin of the Species'. *Open 13.00–18.00. Closed Mon & Fri.*

Charles Dickens (1812–70)   E6
48 Doughty St WC1. 19thC terrace house with relics of Dickens' life and writings. He lived here from 1837 to 1839. *Open 10.00–17.00 daily. Closed Sun & B. Hols.*

William Hogarth (1697–1764)   C6
Hogarth Lane, Great West Rd W4. This 17thC country villa was the home of the master of British caricature from 1749 until his death. He is buried nearby in the churchyard of St Nicholas. *Open 11.00–18.00 Apr–Oct, 11.00–16.00 Oct–Mar. Closed Sun morning.*

Dr Samuel Johnson (1709–84)   E6
17 Gough Square, Fleet St EC4. A simple 17thC brick house where he lived 1748–59, and wrote the 'Dictionary' in the attic. Relics and portraits. *Open 10.30–17.00 May–Sep. 10.30–16.30 Oct–Apr. Closed Sun.*

John Keats (1795–1821)   E5
Wentworth Place, Keats Grove NW3. The poet lived here during his prolific period 1818–20. *Open 10.00–18.00 daily. Closed Sun.*

Karl Marx (1818–83)   E6
His home at 28 Dean Street is marked by a blue plaque, but the place to see is seat No. G7 in the Reading Room of the British Museum, where he wrote 'Das Kapital'. Devotees also pilgrimage to his grave in Highgate Cemetery. *Cemetery open 9.00–17.00 Mon–Sat. 14.00–17.00 Sun.*

William Morris (1834–96)   G4
Water House, Lloyd Park, Forest Rd E17. The Georgian mansion where Morris spent his boyhood. Now a museum and gallery: textiles, wallpapers and designs by Morris and the pre-Raphaelites. *Open 10.00–17.00*

(10.00–20.00 Tue & Thur Apr–Sep.) Closed Sun except 1st Sun each month.

Horace Walpole (1717–97)   C8
Strawberry Hill, Waldegrave Rd, Twickenham. The original 'Castle of Otranto' – a Gothic-Rococo fantasy created out of a simple 18thC country villa by Walpole and his friends, the 'Committee of Taste'. Now St Mary's Training College. *Visits by appointment only.*

Duke of Wellington (1769–1852)   E6
Apsley House, 149 Piccadilly W1. Known as 'No. 1 London', this was the home of Wellington until his death. Full of silver plate, snuff boxes, porcelain, medals and an eleven-foot-high nude statue of Napoleon. *Open daily. Closed Sun morning.*

Cathedrals, abbeys & churches

All Hallows-by-the-Tower   F6
Byward St EC3. Foundations date from 675 audaciously restored by Lord Mottistone after bombing. Fine copper steeple. Crypt museum with Roman pavement. *Open Sat & Sun or by arrangement with Verger.*

All Souls Langham Place   E6
Langham Place W1. John Nash 1822–24. Corinthian columns with needle spire. Restored after bomb damage.

Brompton Oratory   D6
Brompton Rd SW7. Large Italian Renaissance-style church designed by H. Gribble, 1884. Fine marbled interior and original statues from the Cathedral of Siena.

Chapel Royal of St John   C6
White Tower, Tower of London EC3. The oldest church in London, c1085, original Norman.

Christchurch Spitalfields   F6
Commercial St E1. Fine church by Hawksmoor. 1723–25.

Grosvenor Chapel   E6
South Audley St W1. 'Colonial'-looking chapel built 1730. Decorations by Comper added in 1912.

Holy Trinity   E6
Sloane St SW1. By Sedding in 1890. London's most elaborate church of the 'Arts and Crafts' movement.

The Queen's Chapel, St James's Palace   E6
Marlborough Rd SW1. Built by Inigo Jones 1623. Fine restored woodwork and coffered ceiling. *Open on application to the Administrative Officer, Marlborough House, SW1.*

St Andrew-by-the-Wardrobe   F6
Queen Victoria St EC4. Fine city church by Wren, 1635–95. Restored after bomb damage, 1959–61.

st Andrew by the Wardrobe   st Lawrence Jewry

St Andrew Undershaft   F6
Leadenhall St EC3. Rebuilt 1532. Altar rails by Tijou, font by Nicholas Stone. Monument to John Stow, London's first historian.

St Bartholomew-the-Great   F6
West Smithfield EC1. Norman choir of Augustinian Priory 1123 with later Lady Chapel: the only pre-Reformation font in the City. Tomb of founder (who also founded St Bartholomew's Hospital) and other fine monuments.

St Mary-le-Strand, St Clement Danes, The Strand, St Martin-in-the-Field

St Bride F6
Fleet St EC4. Wren 1670–84. Famous spire 1701–04. Restored after bomb damage. Fine city church.

St Clement Danes E6
Strand WC2. First built for the Danes 9thC. Spire by Gibbs. Rebuilt by Wren 1681.

St Clement near Eastcheap F6
Clements Lane, King William St EC4. Wren 1687. Restored by Butterfield 1872, and by Comper 1933. Notable 17thC woodwork and fine organ 1695.

St Cyprian E6
Clarence Gate NW1. Outstanding example of a complete church by Comper in his early style, 1903.

St Ethelburga F6
68–70 Bishopsgate EC2. Tiny church, late 14thC restored by Comper. Fine mural by Hans Feibusch (1693) on East Wall. One of the City 'Guild churches' whose special concern is with mental and spiritual health.

St George Bloomsbury E6
Bloomsbury Way WC1. Hawksmoor, 1731. Statue of George I on top of steeple. Restored in 1870. Six-column Corinthian portico. Classical interior.

St George's Hanover Square E6
Hanover Square W1. Classical church by John James 1721–24. Restored by Blomfeld in 1894. Original of 'Last Supper' by Kent.

St George's Southwark F6
Borough High St SE1. A Georgian building with fine ornamental plaster ceiling. 'Little Dorrit's' church. Rebuilt 1734–36 by J. Price.

St Giles Cripplegate F6
Fore St EC2. 14thC church restored 1952 after bombing. Contains Milton's grave. Remains of London Wall in churchyard.

St Helen's Bishopsgate F6
Great St Helen's EC3. The 'Westminster Abbey of the City' built about 1212.

St James Garlickhythe F6
Garlick Hill EC4. Fine city church by Wren, 1687. Well-restored steeple 1713. Good ironwork.

St James's Piccadilly E6
Piccadilly W1. By Sir Christopher Wren 1684. Restored by Sir Albert Richardson in 1954 after serious bomb damage. Reredos, organ casing and font by Grinling Gibbons. Famous 'Father Smith' organ presented by Queen Mary in 1691 and brought from Whitehall Palace.

St Lawrence Jewry F6
Gresham St EC2. Wren, 1670–86. Restored in 1957. Replicas of steeple and original Wren ceiling.

St Leonard Shoreditch F6
Between 118 & 119 High St E1. Rebuilt 1736–40 by Dance senior. Fine steeple. *Open 12.30–14.00 Wed.*

St Luke Chelsea E6
Sydney St SW3. Savage, 1824. Sumptuous early-Gothic revival.

St Magnus the Martyr F6
Lower Thames St EC3. Wren, 1671–87. Restored by Lawrence King. One of Wren's finest steeples, 185 feet high, added 1705–06. Anglo-Catholic. Baroque interior.

St Margaret Lothbury F6
Lothbury EC2. Wren 1686–93, steeple 1698–1700. Fine fittings, including an open-work screen. Bust of Ann Simpson by Nollekens.

St Margaret's Westminster E6
Parliament Square SW1. Rebuilt 1504–18. Splendid early 16thC east window and an excellent series of stained glass windows by John Piper. The parish church of the House of Commons.

St Martin-in-the-Fields E6
Trafalgar Square WC2. James Gibbs, 1726. Famous spire and portico. Fine Venetian east window and white and gold moulded plaster ceiling.

St Mary Abchurch F6
Abchurch Yard EC4. Wren 1681–87. Fine ceiling by William Snow. Reredos by Grinling Gibbons.

St Mary Aldermary F6
Watling St EC4. Late Gothic rebuilt by Wren. Early 18thC. Fine fan vaulting with saucer domes.

St Mary-at-Hill F6
Lovat Lane EC3. Wren 1676. Tower 1788. Box pews and magnificent fittings.

St Maryiebone Parish Church E6
Marylebone Rd NW1. Thomas Hardwick, 1813–17. Thomas Harris added the chance in 1884. Imposing white and gold interior.

St Mary-le-Bow F6
Cheapside EC2. The church of 'Bow Bells' fame by Wren, 1680. Restored by Lawrence King after bomb damage. Superb steeple.

St Mary-le-Strand E6
Strand WC2. James Gibbs, 1714–17. A perfect small Baroque church in the middle of the road.

St Mary Woolnoth F6
(Guild Church)
Junction of Lombard St & King William St EC3. Remarkable 1716–27 Baroque church by Hawksmoor. Church of England services on weekdays.

St Olave Hart Street F6
8 Hart St EC3. Pre-'fire', Samuel Pepys' church, 1450. Restored by Glanfield after bomb damage. Fine vestry and crypt.

St Paul's Cathedral F6
EC4. Wren's greatest work: built 1675–1710, replacing the previous church destroyed by the Great Fire. Superb dome and porches. Contains magnificent stalls by Grinling Gibbons. Ironwork by Tijuo, paintings by Thornhill and mosaics by Salviati and Stephens.

St Paul's Cathedral

St Paul Covent Garden E6
Covent Garden WC2. Fine 'ecclesiastical barn' by Inigo Jones. Rebuilt by T. Hardwick after fire of 1795. Pleasant gardens at western (entrance) end.

St Peter-upon-Cornhill F6
Bishopsgate Corner EC2. Very fine church by Wren 1677–87. Oldest church site in City, reputedly 179. Organ (built by Schmidt) famous for Elizabethan music. Fine carved screen. 14th and 15thC plays performed at Christmas.

St Stephen Walbrook, St Bride Fleet Street, St Magnus the Martyr

St Stephen Walbrook   F6
Walbrook EC4. Masterpiece by Wren, 1672–79; steeple 1714–17. Dome, with eight arches, supported by Corinthian pillars, all beautifully restored.

SS Anne & Agnes   F6
Gresham St EC2. Wren 1676–87. Attractive church restored after bomb damage.

Southwark Cathedral   F6
Borough High St SE1. Much restored. Built by Augustinian Canons 1206. Beautiful early English choir and retrochoir. Tower built c1520, nave by Blomfield 1894–97. Contains work by Comper (altar screen).

The Temple Church   F6
Inner Temple Lane EC4. Completely restored. 12thC round nave and 13thC choir. Fine recumbent effigies. Reredos by Wren.

Westminster Abbey.

Westminster Abbey   E6
Broad Sanctuary SW1. (The Collegiate Church of St Peter in Westminster). Original church by Edward the Confessor 1065. Rebuilding commenced by Henry III in 1245 who was largely influenced by the new French cathedrals. Completed by Henry Yevele and others 1376–1506 (towers incomplete and finished by Hawksmoor 1734). Henry VII Chapel added 1503; fine 'Perpendicular' with wonderful fan vaulting.

Westminster Roman Catholic Cathedral   E6
Ashley Place SW1. Early Christian Byzantine-style church by J.F. Bentley, 1903. The most important Roman Catholic church in England. Fine marbled interior.

Historic buildings

Abbey Mills Pumping Station   G5
Abbey Lane E15. An unusual building of cupolas and domes built in 1865 to pump the 83 miles of sewers draining the 100 square miles of the City of London.

Albany   E6
Piccadilly W1. Patrician Georgian mansion by Sir William Chambers 1770. Now privately owned residences with quiet public forecourt.

Bank of England   F6
Threadneedle St EC2. The vaults hold the nation's gold reserves. Outer walls are still the original design by Sir John Soane, architect to the Bank from 1788–1833. Rebuilt by Sir H. Baker 1925–33.

Banqueting House E6
Whitehall W1. 1619–25. 17thC Palladian style by Inigo Jones. Rubens ceilings 1630. *Open 10.00–17.00 (Sun 14.00–18.00). Closed B. Hols.*

Banqueting Hall, Whitehall.

Boston Manor House   C6
Boston Manor Rd, Brentford, Middx. Tudor and Jacobean mansion with park and gardens. *Open 14.30–17.00 Sat May–late Sep.*

Burlington House   E6
Piccadilly W1. Victorian-Renaissance facade on one of the great 18thC palaces. Houses the Royal Academy and various royal societies.

Carlton House Terrace SW1   E6
A magnificent sweep of columns by John Nash 1827–32.

Charlton House   G7
Charlton Rd SE7. Perfect small red-brick Jacobean manor house on an 'H' plan, built 1607–12. Fine ceilings, staircase and some bizarre chimneypieces. *Open by appointment only. Contact warden.*

Chelsea Royal Hospital   E6
Chelsea Embankment SW3. A hospital for old soldiers. Fine, austere building 1682 by Wren. Stables 1814 by Sir John Soane.

Chiswick House   C6
Burlington Lane W4. Lovely Palladian villa built in the grand manner by the 3rd Earl of Burlington 1725–30. Fine interiors and gardens by William Kent. *Open 9.30–17.30 daily Apr, Mar & Oct. 9.30–19.00 May–Sep. Closed Mon & Tues Oct–Mar.*

Chiswick House

Clarence House   E6
Stable Yard Gate SW1. Mansion by Nash 1825. Now the home of the Queen Mother.

Crewe House   E6
15 Curzon St W1. Georgian town house, 1735 by Edward Shepherd who gave his name to Shepherd's Market nearby. It was for many years the home of the Marquess of Crewe.

Fribourg & Trever   E6
34 Haymarket SW1. Fine old shop front. Unaltered, it has been a tobacconist since 1720.

Fulham Gasometer   D7
Fulham Gasworks SW6. The oldest gas-holder in the world; built in 1830 by Winsor & Mindock. Diameter 100 feet; capacity a quarter million cubic feet. An extraordinary piece of early industrial engineering.

Gray's Inn   E6
Holborn WC1. Entrance from passage next to 22 High Holborn. An Inn of Court since the 14thC. The Hall (16thC) and 'buildings' restored after bomb damage. Gardens were laid out by Francis Bacon. *Hall open by appointment only. Gardens 12.00–14.00 June & July. 8.00–18.00 Aug. Closed Sat.*

Guildhall   F6
Off Gresham St EC2. 15thC with facade by George Dance 1789 and later restorations by Sir Giles Gilbert Scott. The Great Hall is used for ceremonial occasions. Mediaeval groined vaulting in crypts. Library Art Gallery; museum of clocks and watches. *Open 10.00–17.00 daily. Closed Sun except afternoon May–Sep.*

Gunnersbury Park   C6
Acton W3. Regency house of the Rothschilds. Museum of local history, including transport. Park. *Open 14.00–17.00 Mon–Fri; 14.00–18.00 Sat & Sun Apr–Sep. 14.00–16.00 daily Oct–Mar.*

Hall Place   J7
Bexley, Kent. Nr junction of A2 & A223. Splendid topiary in the shape of the Queen's Beasts. Rose, rock and herb gardens. *Open 10.00–17.00 Mon–Fri Apr–Oct. Closed Sat & Sun morning.*

Holland House   D6
Off Kensington High St W8. One wing only left of this mansion by Thorpe 1607. In Holland Park (50 acres).

Houses of Parliament

Houses of Parliament E6
St Margaret St SW1. Victorian-Gothic building 1840-68 by Sir Charles Barry and A.W.N. Pugin. Westminster Hall was built in 1099 as the Great Hall of William Rufus' new palace: the roof dates from the late 14thC. *Tour of Parliament, admission at Sovereign's entrance, House of Lords.*

Inns of Chancery E6
Before the 18thC a student of law had first to go through one of the nine Inns of Chancery then existing.
They have now mostly disappeared. Staple Inn, High Holborn, remains a fine Elizabethan building. Others survive only as names. Clifford Inn, Thavies Inn and Furnival Inn.

Kenwood House (Iveagh Bequest) E5
Hampstead Lane NW3. Robert Adam house and interior 1767-69. English 18thC paintings and furniture. Fine Rembrandt, Hals and Vermeer. Gardens and wooded estate of 200 acres. *Open 10.00-19.00 Apr-Sep. 10.00-16.00 Oct-Mar. Closed Sun morning.*

King's Cross Station E5
Euston Rd NW1. Functional. 1851 by Lewis Cubitt.

Lancaster House E6
Stable Yard, St James's SW1. Early Victorian London town house. Lavish state apartments and painted ceilings. *Used for official functions.*

Law Courts E6
Strand WC2. Massive Victorian-Gothic building, housing the Royal Courts of Justice. *Open to public 10.00-16.30 Mon-Fri. Closed Aug & Sep.*

Lincoln's Inn E6
Lincoln's Inn WC2. An Inn of Court, 17thC New Square, gardens, barrister chambers and solicitors offices. A chapel by Inigo Jones (1623) and the 15thC Old Hall, Great Hall was built in 1845. The 'stone buildings' are by Sir Robert Taylor and were begun in 1774. Still has Dickens atmosphere. *Apply to Gatehouse in Chancery Lane for admission to Hall and chapel, Mon-Fri.*

Lincoln's Inn Fields WC2 E6
Seven acres of gardens laid out by Inigo Jones 1618. Once a famous duelling ground, now office workers play competition games. Nos. 12-14 built 1792 by Sir John Soane. Nos. 57-8 built 1730 by Henry Joynes. Nos. 59 & 60 built 1640 by Inigo Jones.

Mansion House F6
Opposite Bank of England EC2. Official residence of the Lord Mayor. Palladian building by George Dance 1739. Completed 1752. *Open alternate Sat mornings by appointment only. Parties limited to 30.*

Mansion House

Marlborough House E6
Marlborough Gate, Pall Mall SW1. Designed by Wren 1710. Contains a painted ceiling by Genti Peschi which was originally designed for the Queen's House at Greenwich. The simple classical-style Queen's Chapel in the grounds is by Inigo Jones, 1626. *Not open to the public.*

Old Curiosity Shop E6
13-14 Portsmouth St WC2. Tudor house built 1567 and now an antique shop. Immortalised by Dickens in 'The Old Curiosity Shop.' *Open daily.*

Old Swan House E6
17 Chelsea Embankment SW3. Late 19thC house by R. Norman Shaw.

Osterley Park House B7
Thornbury Rd, Osterley, Middx. Remodelled by Robert Adam 1761-78 on an already fine Elizabethan building built round a courtyard. The magnificent interiors with furniture, mirrors, carpets and tapestry all show the elegance and richness of Adam's genius. *Open 14.00-18.00 daily Apr-Sep. 12.00-16.00 Oct-Mar. Closed Mon except B. Hols. Park open all year.*

Paddington Station D6
Praed St W2. 1850-52. 'Railway-cathedral' engineering at its best by Brunel; the Gothic ornament by Wyatt and Owen Jones; the Renaissance-style hotel by Hardwick.

The Queen's House G7
Romney Rd SE10. Now part of the National Maritime Museum. Built by Inigo Jones 1619 for the Queen of Denmark. *Open 10.00-18.00 daily. Closed Sun morning.*

Queen's House, Greenwich

The Red House
Bexleyheath, Kent. A reaction from everything implied in mid-Victorian design. Built in 1859 by Philip Webb for William Morris as an embodiment of the honesty and decency Morris and the pre-Raphaelite brotherhood sought to convey in crafts. Pared-down Gothic in two storeys it lacks just that little bit of 'oomph'. *Private.*

Royal Exchange F6
Corner of Threadneedle St and Cornhill EC3. Built in 1884 by Tite. The third building on this site. Originally founded as a market for merchants and craftsmen in 1564, and destroyed in the Great Fire. The second building was also burnt down in 1838. Ambulatory containing statues and mural painting and courtyard. *Open 10.00-16.00 Mon-Fri. 10.00-12.00 Sat. Closed Sun & B. Hols.*

Royal Hospital G7
Greenwich SE10. Now the Royal Naval College; the site of the former royal palace for the Tudor sovereigns. A fine and interesting group of classical buildings by Webb 1664, Wren 1692 and Vanbrugh 1728. Chapel by James 'Athenian' Stuart 1789 and Painted Hall by Thornhill. *Open 14.30-17.00 daily. Closed Thur.*

St Pancras Station E5
Euston Rd NW1. Victorian-Gothic. 1868 by Sir George Gilbert Scott.

Sudbrook Cottage C8
Petersham Rd, Ham Common, nr Richmond. The garden of Beverley Nichols made famous by his writings; rhododendrons, azaleas, flowering shrubs. *Open occasionally in Spring.*

Syon House B7
Park Rd, Brentford, Middx. The exterior is the original convent building of the 15thC but the interior 1762-69 is wholly and brilliantly by Robert Adam. The imaginative elegance and variety in each room is unsurpassed. Garden by Capability Brown. Do not miss Syon Lodge nearby – Crowther's showplace of acres of garden ornaments. *Open 13.00-17.00 Mon-Fri mid Apr-late Jul. Sun-Thur late Jul-Oct. 11.00-17.00 B. Hol Mon.*

Syon House

The Temple F6
Inner Temple, Crown Office Row EC4. Middle Temple, Middle Temple Lane EC4.

Both are Inns of Court. Enter by Wren's gatehouse, 1685, in Middle Temple Lane. An extensive area of courtyards, alleys, gardens and warm brick buildings. Middle Hall 1570. The Temple Church is an early Gothic 'round church' built by the Templars 12th-13thC. *Inner Temple open 10.00-11.30 & 16.30-18.00. Closed Sat, Sun, B. Hols and legal vacations. Middle Temple open 10.00-16.30 Mon-Fri. Closed Sat, Sun, B. Hols and during examinations.*

The Tower of London

The Tower of London   F6
Tower Hill EC3. A keep, a prison and still a fortress. Famous for the Bloody Tower, Traitors' Gate, the ravens, Crown Jewels and the Yeoman warders. Norman Chapel of St John. Museum. *Open 9.30-17.00 daily (closed Sun morning) Mar-Oct. 9.30-16.00 daily (closed Sun) Nov-Feb.*

Vanbrugh Castle   G7
3 Westcombe Park Rd, Maze Hill SE3. Sir John Vanbrugh's own house 1717-26. *By appointment only.*

Watermen's Hall   F6
18 St Mary at Hill EC3. Adam-style front surviving from 1780. Unexpectedly beautiful amid drab surroundings.

York Watergate   E6
Watergate Walk, off Villiers St WC2. Built in 1626 by Nicholas Stone as the watergate to York House. It marks the position of the north bank of the Thames before the construction of the Victoria Embankment in 1862. The arms and motto are those of the Villiers family.

Modern architecture

Barbican Project   F6
London Wall EC1. Chamberlain Powell & Bon, 1955-73. This ambitious and competition winning scheme heralds the return of people to the city. Including pedestrian decks, water gardens and several cultural and educational institutions, this scheme is a splendid example of the architectonic environment.

Economist Building   E6
25 St James's St SW1. Alison & Peter Smithson, 1965-66. A very beautiful and harmonious group of buildings with its own raised piazza. The design was intended to demonstrate a general principle for the redevelopment of dense commercial areas and is a rare example of new building in an area with the traditional street pattern where the abandonment of the street frontage is not regretted.

Highpoint Flats   E5
North Hill, Highgate N6. Lubetkin & Tecton, 1935 and 1938. Two blocks of flats which have provided one of the yardsticks of good modern architecture over the last 30 years.

South Bank Arts Centre   F6
Between Waterloo Bridge and Hungerford Footbridge SE1. GLC Architect's Department. 1951-72. Has now completed the third stage of its development with the opening of the National Theatre. Conceived as a project to revitalise the South Bank of the river, these buildings form a linear statement of three phases in British Architecture from 1951 to the present day.

Bridges

Albert Bridge   E6
Unusual rigid chain suspension. Built by Ordish 1875.

The Albert Bridge

Battersea Bridge   E7
The old Battersea Bridge of 1772 was a picturesque wooden structure much painted by Whistler and Turner. Replaced in 1890 by Sir Joseph Bazalgette's iron bridge.

Chelsea Bridge   E6
Open 1858. Rebuilt as a suspension bridge by LCC, 1937.

Hammersmith Bridge   D6
Sir Joseph Bazalgette's suspension bridge, 1887. Has a distinct personality of its own. This flows from the partly gilt iron pylons crowned with fussy pavilion tops, all of which bestow a sense of frivolity on the bridge.

Hammersmith Bridge

Kew Bridge   C7
The bridge was opened by Edward VII in 1903 and is officially called the King Edward VII bridge. Designed by Sir John Wolfe Barry and Cuthbert Brereton it replaced the earlier 18thC bridge and is a fine stone structure with three spans.

London Bridge   F6
The site of many replacements. Wooden construction until 13thC; the famous stone bridge that followed carried houses and shops. Granite bridge built in 1832 by Rennie was shipped off to Lake Havasu City, Arizona in 1971. Latest construction completed 1973.

Putney Bridge   D7
The wooden toll bridge of 1729 which had become unsafe was replaced by this bridge by Sir Joseph Bazalgette in 1884.

Richmond Bridge

Richmond Bridge   C7
Built in the classical style by James Paine, 1777. It replaced the earlier horse ferry and was a toll bridge until 1859.

Tower Bridge   F6
Victorian-Gothic towers with hydraulic twin drawbridge. Jones and Wolfe Barry, 1894.

Tower Bridge

Waterloo Bridge   E6
Concrete. Fine design by Sir Giles Gilbert Scott, 1940-45.

Westminster Bridge   E6
Graceful cast iron. Thomas Page 1862.

Palaces

Buckingham Palace   E6
St James's Park SW1. The permanent London palace of the reigning sovereign. Originally built 1705; remodelled by Nash 1825; refaced 1913 by Sir Aston Webb.

Eltham Palace   **H7**
Off CourtYard, Eltham SE9. 15thC royal
palace until Henry VIII. Great Hall with
hammer-beam roof and a very fine 14thC
bridge over the moat.

Fulham Palace   **D7**
Fulham Palace Rd SW6. Official residence
of the Bishop of London. 16thC building
with riverside park. *Open 1 day only in Apr,
otherwise by appointment only.*

Hampton Court Palace

Hampton Court Palace   **B8**
Hampton Court, Middx. Royal palace built
1514 for Cardinal Wolsey with later
additions by Henry VIII and Wren.
Sumptuous state rooms painted by
Vanbrugh, Verrio and Thornhill. Famous
picture gallery of Italian masterpieces.
Orangery, mellow courtyards, the 'great
vine' and the maze. The formal gardens are
probably among the greatest in the world.
Exotic plants from 16thC. *Open 9.30-18.00
(11.00-18.00 Sun) May-Sep. 9.30-16.00 Nov-
Feb. 9.30-17.00 (14.00-17.00 Sun) Mar, Apr
& Oct.*

Jewel Tower   **E6**
Old PalaceYard SW1. 14thC fragment of the
old Palace of Westminster. *Open 10.30-18.30
Mar-Sep. 10.30-16.00 Oct-Feb.*

Kensington Palace

Kensington Palace   **D6**
Kensington Gardens W8. Simple and
charming building acquired by William III
in 1689 as a palace. Exterior altered by Wren,
interior by William Kent. Queen Victoria
and Queen Mary were born here. Now the
London Museum. The warm brick
Orangery was built 1704 by Hawksmoor.
*Some rooms open 10.00-18.00 Mar-Sep.
10.00-17.00 Oct & Feb. 10.00-16.00 Nov-
Jan. Closed Sun morning.*

Kew Palace   **C7**
Kew, Surrey. Small red-brick house Dutch
style, 1631. Souvenirs of George III and a
collection of animal and bird pictures. *Open
11.00-17.30 daily Apr-Sep. Closed Sun
morning.*

Lambeth Palace   **E6**
Lambeth Palace Rd SW1. The London
residence of the Archbishop of Canterbury.
15thC. Fine mediaeval crypt and 17thC hall.
Portraits 16th-19thC. *Great Hall only open
4 days a year. Library open for readers daily.
Closed Sun.*

Old Palace   **F9**
Old Palace Rd, Croydon, Surrey. Seat of the
Archbishop of Canterbury for 1,000 years.
Tudor chapel. *Open various dates Mar-May
& Jul.*

St James's Palace   **E6**
Pall Mall SW1. Built by
Henry VIII with many
later additions. Still
officially a royal
residence. Ceiling of
Chapel Royal by
Holbein. *No admission
to palace. Entry to
courtyards only.*

St James's Palace

Cemeteries

Highgate   **E5**
Swains Lane N6. Overgrown and sinister,
with crumbling vaults and sepulchres. The
Rosettis are buried here; also George Eliot
and Herbert Spencer. The older part is now
closed because of vandalism but Karl Marx,
the most famous resident, is lying in the
newer section. Visitors welcome.

Kensal Green NW10   **D5**
Old and shady with many familiar names
engraved on the 77 acres of tombstones,
including Thackeray, Wilkie Collins and
Anthony Trollope.

Nunhead Cemetery   **F7**
Ivydale Rd SE15. Like Highgate plagued by
vandals but it's a marvellous haunted place
set in a large wooded park with many gloomy
family vaults.

St Anne's   **E6**
Wardour St W1. King Theodore of Corsica
was buried here (1756); so was William
Hazlitt. A sad place these days, much
neglected.

St George's Gardens   **E6**
Gray's Inn Rd WC1. A small, overgrown
graveyard garden, with underground
passages and vaults.

St John's   **E5**
Church Row NW3. The parish church of
Hampstead. An overcrowded friendly village
churchyard. Constable is buried in the
south-east corner. In the cemetry north of
the road are George du Maurier, Sir Herbert
Beerbohm Tree and Sir Walter Besant.

St Mary Magdalen R.C. Church C7
Mortlake SW13. Sir Richard Burton,
explorer and linguist, is buried here in a
grand Arab tent-shaped tomb with Cararra
marble interior. Nothing else equals it.

Museums & galleries

British Museum   **E6**
Great Russell St WC1. One of the largest and
greatest museums in the world. Famous
collections of Egyptian, Assyrian, Greek and
Roman, British, Oriental and Asian
antiquities. Egyptian mummies, the colossal
Assyrian bulls and lions in the Nimrud
gallery, Cambodian and Chinese collections,
the Elgin Marbles and the Rosetta Stone.
Building 1823-47 by Sir Robert Smirke: the
domed reading room roof is by Sidney
Smirke. *Open 10.00-17.00 daily. Closed
Sun morning.*

Courtauld Institute Galleries   **E6**
Woburn Square WC1. The Courtauld
Collection of French Impressionists
(including fine paintings by Cezanne, Van
Gogh, Gauguin) and the Lee,
Gambier-Parry and Fry collections. *Open
10.00-17.00 daily. Closed Sun morning.*

Geological Museum   **D6**
Exhibition Rd SW7. Physical and economic
geology and mineralogy of the world;
regional geology of Britain. Models,
dioramas and a large collection of gems,
stones and fossils. *Open 10.00-18.00 daily.
Closed Sun morning.*

Hayward Gallery   **E6**
Belvedere Rd SE1. Changing exhibitions of
major works of art arranged by the Arts
Council. Fine modern building and river
setting. *Open 10.00-20.00 Mon-Fri. 10.00-
18.00 Sat. 12.00-18.00 Sun.*

Imperial War Museum   **E6**
Lambeth Rd SE1. Very popular national
museum of all aspects of war since 1914.
Collection of models, weapons, paintings,
relics, The building was once a lunatic
asylum. *Open daily. Closed Sun morning.*

Museum of London   **F6**
150 London Wall EC2. London's new
museum. The life and history of London
from Roman times to the present day.
Antiquities, costume, pictures, coronation
robes, the London theatre, toys and games,
fire engines. Also 'Orangery' and gardens.
Open daily. Closed Sun morning & Mon.

Museum of Mankind   **E6**
Burlington Gdns W1. Exhibitions on various
aspects of ethnography. Concentrates on the
art and culture of pre-industrial societies.
Open 10.00-17.00 daily. Closed Sun morning.

National Army Museum   **E6**
Royal Hospital Rd SW3. The story of the
Army 1480-1914, its triumphs and disasters,
its professional and social life all over the
world. Uniforms, pictures, weapons and
personal relics. *Open daily. Closed Sun
morning.*

National Gallery   **E6**
Trafalgar Square WC2. Very fine
representative collection of famous pictures.
Rich in early Italian (Leonardo da Vinci,
Raphael, Botticelli, and Titian). Dutch and
Flemish (Rembrandt, Rubens, Frans Hals,
Van Dyck). Spanish 15th–18thC (Velasquez
and El Greco). British 18th and 19thC
(Constable, Turner, Gainsborough and
Reynolds). Building 1838 by W. Wilkins.
*Open daily (10.00–21.00 Tue & Thur Jun–
Sep). Closed Sun morning.*

National Maritime Museum   **G7**
Romney Rd SE10. The finest maritime
collection in Britain. Ship models, paintings.
navigational instruments, costumes and
weapons. Incorporates the Queen's House
by Inigo Jones 1616 and the Old Royal
Observatory. *Open 10.00–17.00 daily. Closed
Sun morning.*

National Portrait Gallery   **E6**
2 St Martin's Place WC2. Historical
collection of contemporary portraits of
famous British men and women from early
9thC to the present day. *Open 10.00–17.00
daily. Closed Sun morning.*

Natural History Museum   **D6**
Cromwell Rd SW7. The national collections
of zoology, entomology, palaeontology and
botany. Particularly notable is the bird
gallery, the 90-foot model blue whale and the
great dinosaur models. Built 1881 by
A. Waterhouse. *Open daily. Closed Sun
morning.*

Science Museum   **D6**
Exhibition Rd SW7. The history of science
and its application to industry. A large
collection of very fine engineering models,
steam engines, motor cars, aeroplanes and
children's gallery. *Open daily. Closed Sun
morning.*

Sir John Soane's Museum,   **E6**
13 Lincoln's Inn Fields WC2. Soane's
personal collection of antiquities, paintings
and drawings including Hogarth's 'Election'
and the 'Rake's Progress'. Building
designed by Soane 1812. *Open daily. Closed
Sun & Mon.*

Tate Gallery   **E6**
Millbank SW1. Representative collections of
British painting from the 16thC to the
present. Blake, Turner, Hogarth, the
pre-Raphaelites, Ben Nicholson, Spenser
and Francis Bacon; also Picasso, Chagall,
Mondrian, Moore, Hepworth, Degas. Built
1897 by Sidney R. J. Smith. *Open
10.00–18.00 daily. Closed Sun morning.*

Victoria & Albert Museum   **D6**
Cromwell Rd SW7. A museum of decorative
art, comprising vast collections from all
categories, countries and ages. Over ten
acres of museum! It includes important
collections of paintings, sculpture, graphics
and typography, armour and weapons,
carpets, ceramics, clocks, costumes, fabrics,
furniture, jewellery, metalwork and musical
instruments. *Open 10.00–18.00 daily. Closed
Sun morning.*

Wallace Collection   **E6**
Hertford House, Manchester Square W1. A
private collection of outstanding works of art
which were bequeathed to the nation by
Lady Wallace in 1897. Splendid
representation of the French 17th and
18thC; also several Rembrandts, a Titian,
some Rubens, and paintings by Canaletto
and Guardi. French furniture; Sevres
porcelain; Majolica; Limoges enamel and
armour. *Open 10.00–17.00 daily. Closed Sun
morning.*

Whitechapel Art Gallery   **F5**
80 Whitechapel High St E1. Frequent public
exhibitions of great interest. The
Whitechapel has successfully introduced
new ideas in modern art into London. *Open
11.00–18.00 Tue–Sat. Closed Sun morning &
Mon.*

Botanical gardens

Avery Hill   **H7**
Bexley Rd SE9. A second smaller Kew.

Good collection of tropical and temperate
Asian and Australasian plants in
glasshouses, including a selection of
economic crops. *Open 11.00–17.00 Apr–Oct
(11.00–18.00 Sat, Sun & B Hols). 13.00–
17.00 Nov–Mar.*

Chelsea Physic Garden   **E6**
Swan Walk, Chelsea SW3. Founded in 1673
by the Society of Apothecaries; second
oldest botanical garden in Britain. Contains
fine old trees. Garden open to students and
teachers; not open to general public.

Royal Botanic Gardens, Kew   **C7**
Kew Rd, Richmond, Surrey. One of the
world's great botanic gardens. Famous for
its natural collections, identification of rare
plants, economic botany and scientific
research. Nearly 300 acres of pure aesthetic
pleasure. Arboretum; alpine, water and
rhododendron gardens. Magnificent tropical,
orchid, palm and Australasian houses.
Herbarium contains Sir Joseph Hooker's
famous H.M.S. 'Erebus' and Indian plant
collections. The orangery and pagoda were
designed by Sir William Chambers (1760),
and the glass palm house (1844–48) by
Decimus Burton. *Open 10.00–20.00 or
dusk.*

Palm House, Kew Gardens.

Zoos & aquaria

The London Zoo Aquarium   **E5**
Zoological Gardens, Regent's Park NW1.
Marine and tropical halls; excellently lit and
displayed. A well-stocked aquarium of both
sea and freshwater fish and amphibians from
European and tropical waters. Particularly
notable are the fine sea fish, the octopus,
stingrays and sharks. *Open daily.*

London Zoo   **E5**
*The Zoological Society of London, Zoological
Gardens, Regent's Park, NW1.* Founded to
collect 'new and curious' animals for
scientific study; now a beloved part of
London life. A.A. Milne came to see *the*
Winnie bear. The Royal Family found a
home here for exotic four-legged gifts. A
veritable Ark, the 7,000 animals include one
of every kind. Of interest: world's first
reptile and insect houses; Lord Snowdon's
Aviary; 'Moonlight World' of nocturnal
animals. *Open daily. Tel 01-722 3333.*

Brass rubbing

The following is a short list of churches that
have brasses for rubbing. Permission is
almost invariably required.
London. Bishopsgate (St Helen's);
Camberwell (St Giles); City (All Hallows by
the Tower; St Dunstan-in-the-West);
Enfield; Fulham; Harrow; Hillingdon;
Wandsworth; Westminster Abbey.

Parks

Clapham Common SW4   E7
A fair example of the broad village greens of
South London. There are others at
Wandsworth, Tooting, Streatham and
Mitcham, and together they give an illusion
of green space, sorely needed around a great
shapeless city. They owe their survival as
public open spaces to their former use as
grazing grounds for the villagers' cattle,
before suburbia swallowed up the last South
London farms.

Danson Park   J7
Bexleyheath,Kent. Water and rock gardens
set in a Capability Brown landscape. Also a
charming Old English rose garden. *Open
daily.*

Dulwich Park

Dulwich Park SE21   F7
Just east of Dulwich Village, it holds fine
trees, landscaped lawns and flower beds and
a winding lake. Famous for its
rhododendrons and azaleas. A favourite
garden of the late Queen Mary. *Open
7.30-dusk Nov-Mar. 7.00-22.00 Apr-Oct.*

Greenwich Park SE10   G7
A royal park of 200 acres with pleasant
avenues lined with chestnut trees, sloping
down to the Thames. Impressive views of
the river, the shipping and the two classical
buildings: the Queen's House by Inigo Jones
and the Royal Naval College (once a Tudor
Royal Palace). Contains also the old Royal
Observatory and its pleasant garden.
Thirteen acres of wooded deer park, a bird
sanctuary and bronze age tumuli. *Open
7.00-20.00 Apr-Oct. 7.00-dusk Nov-Mar.*

Hampstead Heath NW3   E5
High, open and hilly, 800 acres of park and
woods. Penned deer and foxes sometimes
can be seen. Crowded on Bank Holidays
with visitors to the famous fair and the three
equally famous pubs – the Bull & Bush, The
Spaniards and Jack Straw's Castle. Includes
Parliament Hill, Golders Hill (containing a
fine 'English' town garden), and Kenwood.
Ponds and bandstand, tennis and athletics.
Open 24 hours.

Hampton Court   B8
Hampton Court, Middx. 1,100 acres of royal
park bounded on two sides by the Thames.
Hampton is the formal park of a great Tudor
palace with ancient courts, superb flower
gardens and the famous 'great vine' and
maze planted during Queen Anne's reign.
Open 7.45-dusk.

Holland Park W8   D6
Behind Kensington High St. 55 acres of calm
and secluded lawns and gardens with
peacocks. Once the private park of Holland
House (partially restored after bombing
during the war). Open-air theatre in
summer. *Open 7.30-22.00 Apr-Oct.
7.30-dusk Nov-Mar.*

Hyde Park W1   E6
A royal park since 1536, it was once part of
the forest reserved by Henry VIII for
hunting wild boar and bulls. It is now a
pleasant 340 acres of parkland, walks, Rotten
Row with horseriders and the Serpentine – a
fine natural lake for fishing, boating and
swimming. The famous 'Speakers' Corner'
is near Marble Arch. *Open 5.00-24.00*

Kensington Gardens W2   D6
A formal and elegant addition to Hyde Park.
275 acres of Royal park containing William
III's lovely Kensington Palace, Queen
Anne's Orangery, the peaceful 'Sunken
Garden' nearby, the Round Pond with its
busy model sailing-boats and on the south,
the magnificently Victorian 'Albert
Memorial'. *Open 5.00-dusk daily.*

Primrose Hill NW8   E5
A very minor royal park of simple grassy hill
200 feet high giving a fine view over London.
Open 24 hours.

Regent's Park NW1   E5
A royal park of 470 acres, originally part of
Henry VIII's great hunting forest in the
16thC. The Prince Regent in 1811 planned
to connect the park (and a new palace) via
the newly built Regent Street to Carlton
House. Although never fully completed the
design by John Nash (1812-26) is of great
distinction, the park being surrounded by
handsome Regency terraces and imposing
gateways. Contains also the Zoo, the
Regent's Canal. a fine boating lake with 30
species of birds and the very fine Queen
Mary's rose garden within Nash's Inner
Circle. Open -air theatre. *Open 6.00-dusk.*

Nash Terraces, Regent's Park.

Richmond Park   C7
Surrey. A royal park of 2,500 acres first
enclosed as a hunting ground by Charles I in
1637. Retains all the qualities of a great
English feudal estate – a natural open park of
spinneys and plantations, bracken and
ancient oaks (survivors of the great oak
forests of the middle ages) and over 600 red
and fallow deer. *Open 7.00-dusk daily.*

St James's Park
& Green Park SW1   E6
The oldest royal park, acquired in 1532 by
Henry VIII, laid out in imitation 'Versailles'
style by Charles II; finally redesigned in the
grand manner for George IV by John Nash
in the 1820s. A most attractive park, with
fine promenades and walks, and a romantic
Chinese-style lake, bridge, and weeping
willows. The bird sanctuary on Duck Island
has some magnificent pelicans and over
twenty species of duck and geese. *Open
5.00-24.00*

St James's Park.

Shooters Hill SE18   G7
Hundreds of acres of woods and open
parkland containing Oxleas Woods,
Jackwood and Eltham Parks. Castlewood has
a folly erected 1784 to Sir William James for
his exploits in India. *Open 24 hours.*

Streatham Common SW16   E8
The Rookery was formerly the garden of an
18thC mansion; rockery, wild garden, a
'white' garden and splendid old cedars. *Open
24 hours.*

Victoria Embankment WC2   **E6**
The joy of the lunchtime office worker on a
fine summer day. Banked flowers, a band,
shady trees, deckchairs and a crowded
open-air cafe.

Wimbledon Common SW19   **D8**
1,100 acres including Putney Heath,
comprising wild woodland, open heath and
several ponds. Golf courses; sixteen miles of
horse rides; playing fields; bronze age
remains; rare and British flora. Protected by
the act of 1871 as a 'wild area' for
perpetuity. *Open 24 hours.*

London's river

To every Londoner the 'river' can mean only
one thing, the Thames. From Putney
upstream to Hampton Court you can explore
the Thames' green banks by a footpath that
was used, until a century ago, by sturdy
horses towing barges. From Putney down to
Tower Bridge there are frequent
embankments or parks beside public roads,
and one bank or the other is usually
accessible. Below Tower Bridge, right down
to Woolwich, the great river is usually
hidden away behind high dock walls, and
only exceptionally, as at Greenwich Park,
will you get any worth-while view from the
land. But the best way to view any great
river is from a boat. All through the summer
tourist craft sail from Westminster Pier,
Charing Cross Pier, and the Tower of
London, taking people upstream to
Hampton Court, or downstream as far as
Greenwich, at a leisurely speed ideal for
sightseeing.
Following the Thames downstream from
Hampton Court Bridge, where there is a
large boating centre, you pass first the trees
and lawns of Hampton Court Park and then,
below Kingston Bridge, reach Teddington
Lock. The river flows on north past the
green, tree-lined meadows of Ham and
Petersham to Richmond, another boating
centre. Climb Richmond Hill for its glorious
view south-west up the river. Below
Richmond's bridges there is a tidal barrage
and lock, used only at low tide. Flowing
between Syon Park and Kew Gardens the
Thames keeps its rural aspect right down to
Kew Bridge. Even along the famous Oxford
and Cambridge boat-race course from
Barnes to Putney – the crews row the other
way, upstream – the river makes a rural oasis
winding through suburban West London.
Now a tamed, urban river, confined between
stone embankments and crossed by a dozen
bridges, the Thames flows on through the
heart of London past the Houses of
Parliament on its Westminster banks, and
the Tower of London beside the City. Until
1970 ocean-going steamers came daily up
the Thames, passing through Tower Bridge
to the busy Pool of London below London
Bridge. Today only a few oil tankers, craft
carrying coal for power stations, and strings
of barges drawn by tugs, use this once active
commercial artery. Only the hidden
downstream docks harbour larger shipping.

River Trips
Trips down river to Greenwich from
Charing Cross Pier, Tower Pier and
Westminster Pier. Trips up river to
Battersea and Hampton Court. *Apr-Oct.*

Canals

It is only recently that the canals of the
metropolis have ceased to perform their
erstwhile function as carriers of goods in and
out of London. Nowadays the River Thames
carries less freight than ever before, and even
the London Docks are handling less and less
traffic. The Surrey Docks are now closed
down, and the Surrey Canal that served
them is closed too.
London's main canal however, the Regent's
Canal, is still in good condition, and although
trade has virtually finished, it is used a little

by any pleasure boats whose owners can
decipher the complicated lock opening
hours. However it is more useful as a local
amenity for residents in areas with little
'public open space'. To these people the
canal is a thing of beauty and quiet, a
reminder of the past and a fascinating
contrast in every way to the humdrum facts
of their everyday life.
Best places to see the canal are Paddington,
where 'Little Venice' entices the towpath
walker; Regent's Park, where you can walk
along the tree-lined cutting and go right
through the Zoo; Camden, where the locks
start the 90 foot drop to the river; and
Islington, where there is a half-mile long
tunnel and another lock by the great City
Road Basin. Here the towpath has been
recently opened up to strollers, and local
children learn to row and sail from the youth
club based on an old timber barge moored in
the Basin. Below here the towpath is closed,
and the canal is still a secret highway.
Regent's Canal Dock itself is silent and
empty of ships.

Jason's Trips   **D6**
*Canaletto Gallery, opposite 60 Blomfield Rd
W9.* Trips along Regent's Canal and Grand
Union Canal in the traditional canal narrow
boat 'Jason'. Advisable to book. *Apr-Oct.*

Archaeology

All Hallows-by-the-Tower   **F6**
Byward St EC3. The crypt of this church
has a Roman mosaic floor, composed of
plain red tesserae, dating from the later
2ndC. A gully runs across the pavement, and
probably marks the position of a partition
wall. The crypt also has a collection of
Roman pottery, masonry fragments, and
pieces of two Saxon crosses. *Apply to Verger
for admission.*

Bank of England   **F6**
Threadneedle St EC2. The Bank of England
stands on one of the most archaeologically
fertile areas of London, and has produced
many Roman finds. One of these, a mosaic
floor, has been restored and relaid at the foot
of the main staircase, and can be seen by the
public during business hours.

City Wall   **F6**
The wall of Roman Londinium was begun
c200, and continued in use, with much
rebuilding and addition, through the middle
ages. In the north-west corner, the wall
incorporated the two outward walls of the
Roman fort, which were thickened to bring
them into line (see Cripplegate Fort for
sections showing this). Gate-houses were
built where roads left the city, and during
the later 3rd and 4thC several semi-circular
bastions were added at intervals to the face,
though most of the surviving bastions are
probably mediaeval.
The Wall, with the base of a bastion, can be
seen in the Tower of London, behind the
ruined Wardrobe Tower. Other stretches,
with mediaeval rebuilding, can be seen in
Wakefield Gardens (opposite the Tower), at
8-10 Cooper's Row, and (with permission
from the Postmaster) in the G.P.O. St
Martin's-le-Grand.

Cripplegate Roman Fort F6
The fort was discovered during post-war excavations, and apparently dates from the early 2ndC. Although built to the standard Roman pattern, it was a barracks for soldiers engaged on the ceremonial and guard-duties connected with a capital city and the presence of an Imperial governor, rather than a defensible military base.
Sections of the stone wall, which originally had a ditch in front and a strong bank behind can be seen in Noble Street and, with later Roman thickening to bring its defences into line with the city wall and some mediaeval rebuilding, in St Alphage Churchyard, and to the south of St Giles Cripplegate. The Noble Street section also has an internal corner tower and an interval turret along the circuit. Part of the West Gate can be seen under London Wall. *Open 12.30–14.00 Mon–Sat. For access at other times apply to Guildhall.*

Roman Bath-House F6
Lower Thames St. Excavations on this site revealed a late Roman house, and part of the connected bath-suite has been preserved. This includes a wall with an apse, and the tile piers that originally supported the floor and allowed the circulation of hot air underneath. *By arrangement with Guildhall Museum.*

St Brides F6
Fleet St. The fragmentary remains of a Roman mosaic pavement, composed of red and a few yellow tesserae, can be seen at the east end of the crypt. The building that contained it extended beyond the church, and lay outside the Roman city.

Temple of Mithras F6
Queen Victoria St. The Roman temple dedicated to the Persian god Mithras was the most spectacular of the finds made during excavation of the City bomb-sites after the War. Originally it lay on low ground by the Walbrook, but has now been rebuilt, using the original materials, in front of Temple Court; the Roman earth floor has been replaced with paving. The worship of Mithras was confined to men, and was apparently favoured particularly by merchants and soldiers; the London temple is the only one at present known in Britain that is not associated with a fort. 'Mithraea' are always small, with a central nave and flanking aisles; the focus was a representation of Mithras slaying the Bull, and a sculpture depicting this was found in the late 19thC when the temple was still unknown – it is now housed in the London Museum. The temple excavations produced the finest group of imported sculptures found in Roman Britain, and a unique decorated silver canister; these objects are now displayed in Guildhall Museum.

Sport

Archery E6
Twenty-one archery clubs in the county of London, each having its own ground. Grounds at Duke of York's headquarters, Crystal Palace, Duke's Meadow, Dulwich and Regent's Park. County of London championships held at Bowings sports ground, Earlsfield SW7. *Last Sun in Aug.*

Badminton C5
All England championship at Wembley in March; also tournaments at Wimbledon, Epsom, Eltham, Crystal Palace, Leyton and Sydenham. All England junior championship held at Wimbledon in January.

Boxing E6
ABA championships held in May. Fights take place at: Wembley, Olympia, Earl's Court, Lime Grove and the Royal Albert Hall. Also at West Ham, Bermondsey, Shoreditch and Walworth town halls. For details of forthcoming bouts consult 'Boxing News'.

Cricket D6
County matches and Test matches at Lord's and the Oval. For latest Test scores dial 160. *The season is from mid Apr–early Sep.*

Cycling C5
Once a predominantly continental sport, now becoming increasingly popular in Britain. The professional, spectacular and incredibly fast six-day indoor events staged at Wembley are well worth a visit, even for the uninitiated. Details from British Cycling Federation. Banked circuit at Herne Hill.

Football C5
The FA Cup final is held at the Empire Stadium, Wembley, about the second Sat in May. Stadium holds 100,000 people under cover.

Greyhound Racing
Win, or lose, a fortune betting on 'the dogs'.
White City Stadium D6
Wood Lane W12. Tel 01-743 5544. *Thur & Sat.*
Wimbledon Stadium D8
Plough Lane SW17. Tel 01-946 5361. *Wed & Fri.*

Lawn Tennis E6
Public courts in about 60 London parks. Tournaments are held at Beckenham (Kent championships second week in June); Chingford (Connaught Club's Hard Court Tournament, second half of April); Hurlingham (first half of May); Cumberland Club NW6 (mid Apr); Sutton (Surrey Hard Court championships, fourth week of Apr).
*All England Lawn Tennis & D8
Croquet Club.* Church Rd SW19. (01) 946 2244. Stages the Wimbledon Fortnight (perhaps the world's top event) in the last week of June and first week of July.
Queen's Club. Paliser Rd W14. Stages the London championships in the third week of June and the covered court championships Oct–Nov.

Polo C8
Played at Ham House, Richmond, on summer Sundays. Richmond Park (nr Roehampton Gate) Tue & Thur evenings and Saturday afternoons in summer.

Real Tennis D7
This interesting game is in danger of becoming extinct and there are only five clubs in the London area. A trial game can be played at: *Queen's Club* Paliser Rd W14. (01) 385 3421.

Rowing D7
Events take place in the summer months, the most notable being the Oxford and Cambridge boat race from Putney to Mortlake in Mar or Apr. Other events are the Head of the River event on the Thames; the Schools Head of the River race from Chiswick to Putney; the Sculling Head of the River from Mortlake to Putney; the Wingfield Sculls between Putney and Mortlake. Important regattas are held at Brent (Welsh Harp reservoir, Whit Mon) Chiswick, Hammersmith, Henley, Kingston, Putney (including the Metropolitan regatta) Richmond, Twickenham, Walton.

Rugby Football C8
The principal association connected with the game of rugby is:
Rugby Football Union Whitton Rd, Twickenham, Middx. Twickenham is the home and headquarters of rugby and the important matches including Internationals are played there.

Show Jumping C5
The two major events are the Royal International Horse Show at Wembley in July and the Horse of the Year Show at Wembley in October. There are also notable events staged at Windsor, Richmond and Clapham Common.

Skittles E5
Freemason's Arms, 32 Downshire Hill NW3. (01) 435 4498. Played with a 'cheese', this is the original game of skittles. Must provide your own 'sticker'. *20.00 Tue, Thur & Sat.*

Stock-car racing
Controlled by the RAC. Noisy, colourful, exciting and slightly dangerous. Contrary to popular opinion, the drivers do actually try to avoid hitting each other (except in 'banger' racing). Events mostly staged Saturday evenings in the summer:
Harringay Stadium F4
Green Lanes N4. (01) 800 3474.
Wimbledon Stadium D8
Plough Lane SW17. (01) 946 5361.

Festivals

For information and tickets for festivals go to the local information centre or ticket agent.

Aldwych World Theatre   **E6**
Aldwych Theatre, 49 Aldwych WC2.
Production of classics and outstanding modern plays by theatre companies from all over the world. All performances in original language (audio translators for audience). *Usually mid Apr–Jun.*

Camden Festival   **E5**
St Pancras Library, 100 Euston Rd NW1.
Rarely performed music and opera; also well-known choral and symphony concerts. Art exhibitions, poetry and drama. *Three weeks usually late Apr–late May.*

City of London Festival   **F6**
Music festival with great choirs and orchestras. Also chamber music and recitals. Concerts in St Paul's Cathedral, the Guildhall and the Mansion House. Exhibitions in City livery companies. Some outdoor activities and processions. Ox roasting. *Two weeks mid Jul.*

Greenwich Festival   **G7**
Greenwich SE18. Celebrates the borough's past and present with dancing, concerts, banquets, exhibitions, competitions – fun with a home-grown flavour but 'local' talent is often internationally known. Events in most borough towns. *Mid Jun.*

London Film Festival   **E6**
National Film Theatre, South Bank SE1.
Many people's only chance to see some of the best British and foreign films of the year. *Two weeks mid Nov.*

Theatreland

CINEMAS

Academy One, Two & Three   **E6**
165 Oxford St W1. Academy One
(01) 437 2981. Academy Two *(01) 437 5129.*
Academy Three *(01) 437 8819.* Latest continental and festival successes with occasional revivals. Has outstandingly good restaurant. *(01) 437 8774.*

Carlton   **E6**
Haymarket SW1. (01) 930 3711. Long-running British and American releases.

Casino Cinerama   **E6**
Old Compton St W1. (01) 437 6877.
Cinerama 'blockbusters'. All seats bookable.

Cinecenta   **E6**
Panton St SW1. (01) 930 0631. Four small cinemas under one roof showing very new films.

Classic   **E6**
98 Baker St W1. (01) 935 8836. Good (often ancient) selected revivals.

Columbia   **E6**
93 Shaftesbury Avenue W1. (01) 734 5414.
Selected long-running releases in plushy new cinema.

Curzon   **E6**
Curzon St W1. (01) 499 3737. Specially selected new films in very lush surroundings.

Dominion   **E6**
Tottenham Court Rd W1. (01) 580 9562.
Long-running spectaculars.

Empire   **E6**
Leicester Square WC2. (01) 437 1234.
Bookable first releases in cavernous 'movie palace'. Adjustable seats, perfect vision.

Everyman   **E5**
Holly Bush Vale, opposite Hampstead Tube Station NW3. (01) 435 1525. Weekly classic revivals.

Leicester Square Theatre   **E6**
Leicester Square WC2. (01) 930 5252. First releases in a vast 'movie palace'.

London Pavilion   **E6**
3 Piccadilly Circus W1. (01) 437 2982.
Popular and sensational films. New releases.

National Film Theatre   **E6**
South Bank SE1. (01) 928 3232. Members only except weekends. Serious museum studies of directors, styles, stars, retrospectives and movie history. Two cinemas.

Odeon   **E6**
Leicester Square WC2. (01) 930 6111.
Latest hand-picked releases.

Odeon   **E6**
St Martin's Lane WC2. (01) 836 0691.
Popular 'road show' releases in new intimate cinema. Advance booking.

Paris Pullman   **D6**
65 Drayton Gardens SW10. (01) 373 5898.
New foreign subtitled releases and revivals. Coffee bar club.

Warner   **E6**
Leicester Square WC2. (01) 439 0791. Two cinemas in one showing new Warner general releases.

CONCERT HALLS

Purcell Room   **E6**
South Bank SE1. (01) 928 3191. Chamber music and solo concerts. Generally performances which require more intimate surroundings.

Queen Elizabeth Hall   **E6**
South Bank SE1. (01) 928 3191. Symphony, orchestral and large band concerts. Also special events such as Poetry International take place here.

Royal Albert Hall   **E6**
Kensington Gore SW7. (01) 589 8212.
Victorian domed hall named after Prince Albert, built 1871. Orchestral, choral, pop concerts and public meetings. Famous for the 'Proms'.

Royal Festival Hall   **E6**
South Bank SE1. (01) 928 3191. Built in 1951 for the Festival of Britain. Seats 3,000. Orchestral and choral concerts.

Opera, Ballet and Musicals

Coliseum   **E6**
St Martin's Lane WC2. (01) 836 3161.
Largest London theatre seating 2,700. Now houses both the resident Sadler's Wells Company and the touring one.

Covent Garden   **E6**
Royal Opera House, Bow St WC2.
(01) 240 1066. World-famous Royal Ballet and Opera company with an international reputation.

Drury Lane (Theatre Royal)   **E6**
Catherine St WC2. (01) 836 8108. Opened under royal charter by Thomas Killigrew in 1663 and has been burnt down and rebuilt four times. Nell Gwynne sold oranges there; Garrick, Mrs Siddons, Kean and others played there. General policy now is vast productions of musical plays.

Sadler's Wells   **E6**
Rosebury Avenue EC1. (01) 837 1672. Once a spa (the original well discovered by Thomas Sadler is under a trap-door at the back of the stalls). Birthplace of the Royal Ballet company; now used by visiting opera and ballet companies. See also Coliseum.

THEATRES

Aldwych   **E6**
Aldwych WC2. (01) 836 6404. Winter home of the Royal Shakespeare Company. Summer season is the World Theatre.

Ambassadors   **E6**
West St WC2. (01) 836 1171. Small theatre – billed 'The Mousetrap' from 1952–75.

Duke of York's   **E6**
St Martin's Lane WC2. (01) 836 5122. Built by 'Mad (Violet) Melnotte' in 1892. Associated with names like Frohman, G.B. Shaw, Granville Barker, Chaplin and the Ballet Rambert. Straight plays and comedies.

Haymarket (Theatre Royal)   E6
Haymarket SW1. (01) 930 9832. Elegant theatre.

Mermaid   E6
Puddle Dock, Blackfriars EC4. (01) 248 7656. Converted river warehouse with an open staged theatre. Excellent restaurants and bar. Unusual productions in a unique setting. Membership entitles you to reduced-price previews.

National Theatre   E6
South Bank, Waterloo SE1. The National Company provide top quality plays in the three theatres in the new complex. Book well in advance but some seats are available on the day of performance.

Palladium   E6
8 Argyll St W1. (01) 437 7373. Second in size to the Coliseum and houses top variety shows and the annual Royal Command Performance.

Round House   E5
Chalk Farm Rd NW1. (01) 485 8073. An exciting experimental theatre in a converted railway shed. Only 50% of the seats are bookable in advance. Usually packed to capacity.

Royal Court   E6
Sloane Square SW1. (01) 730 1745. Home of the English Stage Company which produces many major experimental plays.

Savoy   E6
Strand WC2. (01) 836 8888. Entrance is in the forecourt of the Savoy Hotel. It was the first London theatre to be fully electrically lit. Produces a variety of plays, comedies and musicals.

Theatre Royal   G5
Salway Rd, Stratford E15. (01) 534 0310. Joan Littlewood's East End theatre workshop showing new plays and musicals.

Whitehall   E6
14 Whitehall SW1. (01) 930 6692. Brian Rix played his particular brand of farce here for many years. The theatre specialises in popular theatre.

Fun things

The Changing of the Queen's Guard   E6
Buckingham Palace SW1. The new Guard, following the band, arrives from Chelsea or Wellington Barracks for the ceremony lasting half an hour. Not held in bad weather. *11.30.* If Royal standard is not flying, then held at St James's Palace at *11.30. St James's Palace SW1.* The old Guard leaves St James's for Buckingham Palace at *11.15.* Small ceremony.

The Changing of the Queen's Life Guard   E6
Horse Guards Arch, Whitehall SW1. The ceremony popularly known as 'the changing of the Guard' lasts 20 mins. *11.00 (Sun 10.00).* The Guard is also inspected on foot at *16.00.*

The 'Cutty Sark'   G6
King William Walk SE10. Stands in dry dock. One of the great sailing tea clippers, built 1869. Museum. *Open 11.00–18.00 daily Apr–Sep, 11.00–17.00 Oct–Mar. Closed Sun morning.*

HMS 'Discovery'   E6
Victoria Embankment WC2. Captain Scott's 1901–04 Antarctica vessel. Scott relics. *Open 13.00–16.30.* Other moored ships nearby are HMS 'Chrysanthemum' and HMS 'President' (naval training vessels) and the 'Wellington' belonging to the Master Mariners.

Doggets Coat & Badge Race   F6
The Thames, London Bridge to Chelsea. Rowing race for Thames Watermen, originated in 1715. Sometimes called the 'Waterman's Derby'. *Mid Jul or early Aug. No fixed date.*

HMS Discovery.

Lord Mayor's Procession and Show   F6
The newly elected Lord Mayor is driven in his state coach from the Guildhall to the Law Courts to be received by the Lord Chief Justice. The biggest ceremonial event in the City. *2nd Sat Nov.*

Oxford v Cambridge Boat Race   D7
River Thames, Putney to Mortlake. Mar or Apr.

Post Office Tower   E6
Maple St W1. The highest restaurant in London, revolving slowly and giving an ever-changing view over Regent's Park, central and outer London: from Epping Forest in the east to the Surrey hills in the west.

The Post Office Tower

Round Pond   D6
Kensington Gardens W2. Model yachts abound, usually sailed by proud fathers. Kite flying nearby at weekends.

Royal Tournament   D6
Earl's Court SW5. Impressive military spectacle with marching displays and massed brass bands. *2 weeks mid Jul. No fixed date.*

Swan Upping   F6
Starts: London Bridge (Temple Stairs) 9.00–9.30. The three Swan Masters of the owners of all the Thames' swans (HM Queen the Dyers' Company and the Vintners' Company) boat up-river to Henley taking a census of the swans. *Mid Jul or Aug. No fixed date.*

The Tower of London   F6
Tower Hill EC3. A keep, a prison and still a fortress. Famous for the Bloody Tower, Traitors' Gate, the ravens, Crown Jewels and the Yeoman warders. Norman Chapel of St John. Museum. *Open 9.30–17.00 daily Mar–Oct (closed Sun morning). 9.30–16.00 Nov–Feb (closed Sun).*

Trooping the Colour   E6
The route is from Buckingham Palace SW1 along the Mall to Horse Guards Parade, Whitehall, and back again. The Queen's official birthday. Pageantry at its best. *Sat nearest 11th June.*

Windmills   D8
There is a famous windmill on Wimbledon Common; a pumping mill on Wandsworth Common on the corner of Windmill Road; an elegant tower mill, built 1816 at Blenheim Gardens, Brixton.

Hotels

This is a small selection of a vast number of hotels in London. The following indicates the price range of a single room per night:
£   inexpensive
££   medium priced
£££   expensive

Brown's Hotel   E6
Dover St W1. Tel 01 493 6020. A traditional family hotel with good friendly service. *£££*.

Cadogan Hotel   E6
75 Sloane St SW1. Tel 01 235 7141. Oscar Wilde was arrested here. Well situated for Harrods. *£££*.

Claridges   E6
Brook St W1. Tel 01 629 8860. A truly dignified hotel situated near Oxford Street. Excellent food and service. *£££*.

Cora Hotel   E6
Upper Woburn Place WC1. Tel 01 387 5111. Comfortable and well-situated for Euston Station. Modernised. *££*.

Eccleston Hotel   E6
Eccleston Square SW1. Tel 01 834 8042. Conveniently placed hotel for air, rail and coach termini. *££*.

Epping Forest Motel   H1
Epping High St, Epping, Essex. Tel 3134. A well-situated motel on the A11, fifteen miles from London. *££*.

Great Western Royal Hotel   D6
Paddington W2. Tel 01 723 8064. A Victorian railway hotel carefully modernised. Efficient service *££*.

Green Park Hotel   E6
Half Moon St W1. Tel 01 629 7522. Modernised and adjacent to Piccadilly. Efficient service. Sauna. *£*.

Hilton   E6
22 Park Lane W1. Tel 01 493 8000. A modern international hotel overlooking Hyde Park with many amenities. Good food. *£££*.

Hotel Russell   E6
Russell Square WC1. Tel 01 837 6470. A comfortable Edwardian hotel with well-modernised bedrooms. Fine entrance and lounge. *££*.

Hotel Trianon   D6
101 Lexham Gdns. W8. Tel 01 370 6274. An inexpensive but simple hotel close to West London Air Terminal. Popular with Australians. *£*.

Maggie's Place Hotel   D6
21 Avonmore Rd W14. Tel 01 603 2389. A comfortable bed and breakfast hotel in Kensington. Ideal for those on a budget. *£*.

Mandeville Hotel   E6
Mandeville Place W1. Tel 01 935 5599. Comfortable and efficient; close to Oxford and Bond Streets. *££*.

Milestone Hotel   D6
Kensington Court W8. Tel 01 937 0991. Conveniently situated for Knightsbridge and the Albert Hall, this Victorian hotel is opposite Kensington Gardens. *££*.

Selsdon Park Hotel (Sanderstead)   F9
Addington Rd, South Croydon. Tel 01 657 8811. Set in 200 acres of parkland. Many amenities including a solarium, golf course and riding. *££*.

Skyway Hotel   A6
London Airport, Bath Rd, Hayes, Middx. Tel 01 759 6311. A modern hotel which caters to the needs of the jet-age traveller. *££*.

Water Gardens Hotel   E6
74 Courtfield Rd SW5. Tel 01 373 8594. Each apartment in this modern hotel includes a colour TV, telephone and radio. There is an adequate restaurant and sauna. *££*.

Pubs

Most London pubs are 19thC but can be up to 400 years old. They take on the character and needs of the locality and are aptly called 'locals'. Of the 7,000 pubs in London we have selected the following on the basis of particularly interesting aspects which make them stand out from the rest. But many others can be found by the thirsty and curious.

Blackfriar   F6
174 Queen Victoria St EC4. Tel (01) 236 5650. Triangular-shaped building in the shadow of Blackfriars railway bridge. Unique 'Art Nouveau' interior. Associated with the old Dominican priory.

Cheshire Cheese   F6
145 Fleet St EC4. Tel (01) 353 6170. Rebuilt after the Great Fire. Low-ceilinged tavern. Excellent English food.

Cock Tavern   F6
22 Fleet St EC4. Tel (01) 353 8570. Small but good journalists' tavern with literary associations. Three dining rooms. Good English steak and kidney puddings and pies upstairs.

Grenadier   E6
18 Wilton Row SW1. Tel (01) 235 3074. Mews pub with ceiling covered with wine labels. Duke of Wellington played cards here.

Hoop and Grapes   F6
47 Aldgate High St EC3. (01) 481 1375. The oldest licensed house in London – it missed the Great Fire by 50 yards, *Closed Sat & late Sun.*

Nag's Head   E6
10 James St, Covent Garden WC2. Tel (01) 836 4678. Theatrical and market pub. Theatre playbills and prints.

Olde Mitre Tavern   E6
1 Ely Court, Hatton Garden EC1. Tel (01) 405 4751. Built in 1546 by the Bishops of Ely for their servants. Associations with Queen, Elizabeth and Dr Johnson.

Prospect of Whitby   F6
57 Wapping Wall E1. Tel (01) 709 1095. 600-year-old smuggler's haunt next door to Execution Dock. Terrace overlooking the Thames. Associations with Pepys.

Salisbury   E6
90 St Martin's Lane WC2. Tel (01) 836 5863 Ornate Victorian pub.

Spaniards Inn   E5
Spaniards Rd NW3. Tel (01) 455 3276. Popular 18thC tavern opposite the old toll-house on Hampstead Heath. Associations with Dick Turpin, Byron, Shelley, Keats, and Reynolds.

Trafalgar Tavern   G6
Park Row SE10. Tel (01) 858 2437. An old waterfront tavern. Try the upstairs bar with the 18thC man-of-war decor.

Regional food

Boiled beef and carrots
This favourite cockney dish of cured and boiled beef – either brisket or silverside, is accompanied by carrots, pease pudding and dumplings.

Chelsea bun
This yeast-raised sugary currant bun was originally made to counter the popularity of the Bath bun in the 18thC.

Eel pie
The eels were traditionally fished from the Thames between Kingston and Richmond and the pie gave its name to Eel Pie Island. Many local recipes exist, the most popular being of eels, lemon, parsley and shallots.

Jellied eels
One of the delights of London street markets are the fish stalls where it is possible to buy prawns, cockles, mussels and the East Enders' favourite – jellied eels.

Whitebait
This, another traditional Thames fish, was caught especially near Greenwich. Alas, no more, but the tradition of eating whitebait at Greenwich persists.

Restaurants

£ inexpensive
££ medium priced
£££ expensive

L'Artiste Affamé D6
243 Old Brompton Rd SW5. Tel 01-373 1659.
French provincial food in a candle lit, plain,
well scrubbed restaurant. D. Closed Sun. ££.

Bertorelli's E6
19 Charlotte St W1. Tel 01-636 4174.
70-72 Queensway W2. 01-229 3160. Busy
straight-forward Italian eating places. Good
food at reasonable prices. LD. Closed Sun. £.

Bloom's F6
90 Whitechapel High St E1. Tel 01-247 6001.
Exuberant, kosher restaurant. Handy for
Bethnal Green Market and Whitechapel
Art Gallery. Go early on a Sunday. LD.
Closed Fri afternoon, Sat & Jewish Hols.
£. No bookings.

Brompton Grill D6
243 Brompton Rd SW3. Tel 01-589 8005.
An elegantly decorated restaurant serving
good French food. LD. Closed Sun L. ££.

Carrier's E5
2 Camden Passage N1. Tel 01-226 5353.
Robert Carrier's famous restaurant.
Individual cooking to high standards. LD.
Closed Sun. £££. Book.

Casa Cominetti G7
129 Rushey Green SE6. Tel 01-697 2314.
Friendly, family restaurant. Italian cooking.
LD. Closed Sunday D. ££. Book.

Chanterelle D6
119 Old Brompton Rd SW7. Tel 01-373 7390.
Attractive decor, friendly service. Dim lights
and huge helpings. LD. Closed Sun L. ££.

Chelsea Rendezvous D6
4 Sydney St SW3. Tel 01-352. 9519
Popular with young people, usually
crowded. Good Chinese food and happy
atmosphere. LD. Closed Christmas. ££. Book.

Chez Solange E6
35 Cranbourn St WC2. Tel 01-836 0542.
Busy but roomy. Typical French cuisine
with cheeful service. LD. Closed Sun. ££.

Cranks Salad Table E6
Marshall St W1. Tel 01-437 9431. Popular
vegetarian restaurant. LD. Closed Sun. £.
No bookings.

L'Escargot Bienvenu E6
48 Greek St W1. Tel 01--437 4460. Typical
bourgeois French cuisine and decor. LD.
Closed Sun L. & Sun. ££.

L'Etoile E6
30 Charlotte St W1. Tel 01-636 7189.
Typically French in atmosphere and style.
Top-quality food and attentive service.
LD. Closed Sat, Sun and Aug. ££.

Gay Hussar E6
2 Greek St W1. Tel 01-437 0973. Robust
Hungarian restaurant. Set lunches good
value. LD. Closed Sun. ££. Book.

The Gaylord E6
79-81 Mortimer St W1. Tel 01-580 3615.
Authentic Punjabi food. Spices added
individually to each dish giving some
delectable flavours. LD. £.

Gennaro's E6
44 Dean St W1. Tel 01-437 3950. Busts of
Roman heroes and contemporary figures.
Antique cutlery. Wide menu of good
Italian dishes. LD. Closed Sun. ££.

Hellenic E6
30 Thayer St W1. Tel 01-935 1257.
Popular Greek restaurant, cheerful waiters
ensure an informal atmosphere. Crowded at
lunchtimes. LD. Closed Sun. £.

Au Jardin des Gourmets E6
5 Greek St W1. Tel 01-437 1816.
Unassuming but impeccable French
classical cuisine. Good wines. LD. Closed
Sat L. & Sun. ££.

Kettners E6
29 Romilly St W1. Tel 01-437 3437. A
100-year-old comfortably plush
establishment with courteous leisurely
service. French cuisine. Try their daily
special dish. LD. £££.

Lee Ho Fook E6
15 Gerrard St W1. Tel 01-736 9578. A
Chinese restaurant patronised by Chinese.
The most authentic Cantonese food in the
West End. LD. ££.

Manzi's E6
1-2 Leicester St WC2. Tel 01-437 4864.
Typical busy provincial Italian fish
restaurant with bar and marble-topped
tables. LD. Closed Sun L. ££.

Masako E6
6-8 St Christopher's Place W1. Tel
01-935 1579. The first Japanese restaurant
in London. Service by graceful and
charming Japanese girls in kimonos.
Completely oriental atmosphere. Try the
complete dinner. LD. Closed Sun. ££.

Mirabelle E6
56 Curzon St W1. Tel 01-499 4636. A
world famous luxury restaurant. Renowned
for fine cooking and a magnificent wine
cellar. LD. Closed Sun. £££.

Mon Plaisir E6
21 Monmouth St WC2. Tel 01-836 7243.
Small, spartan, typically French bistro with
'slate' menu. Unobsequious but friendly
service. D. Closed Sat & Sun. ££.

Overton's E6
5 St James's St SW1. Tel 01-839 3774.
Long-established fish restaurant of
character. 'Old world' atmosphere in the
nicest sense. LD. Closed Sun. Minimum
charge L. ££.

Parkes E6
4 Beauchamp Place SW3. Tel 01-589 1390.
Cooking of outstanding distinction. Small
and expensive. LD. Closed Sun. £££.

Raw Deal E6
65 York St W1. Tel 01-262 4841. Hot
dishes, special food for slimmers. Fruit and
vegetables all organically grown. LD.
Closed Sun. £.

Rules E6
35 Maiden Lane WC2. Tel 01-836 5314.
Traditional British food. Historic 16thC
building. LD. Closed Sat & Sun. £££. Book.

Sheekey's E6
28-32 St Martin's Court WC2. Tel 01-836
4118. Excellently cooked and served fish –
mostly steamed – with salad and potato.
Crowded. LD. Closed Sun & Sat D. ££.

Simpson's-in-the-Strand E6
100 Strand WC2. Tel 01-836 9112. A famous
restaurant with an Edwardian club
atmosphere. The attentive service and the
large carvings from enormous joints of beef
and lamb are its best feature. Only order
English food. Vegetables sometimes
disappointing. LD. Closed Sun. ££.

Stone's Chop House E6
Panton St SW1. Tel 01-930 0037.
Victorian chop house, rebuilt after the war
and given authentic atmosphere with brass,
black leather seating and Victoriana.
Excellent English cooking, generous
helpings. LD. Closed Sun. ££.

The Swiss Centre E6
2 New Coventry St (Leicester Square) W1.
Tel 01-734 1291. Four different restaurants.
Imaginative decoration. ££.

Tandoori D7
153 Fulham Rd SW3. Tel 01-589 7749.
North-west frontier cooking of very high
quality by Pathan chefs in the traditional
clay ovens. Pleasant decor with soft music.
D. ££. (L. served Sun.)

Tiberio E6
22 Queen St W1. Tel 01-629 3561. Top
quality Roman cooking in popular, crowded
atmosphere. Band for dancing 23.30–3.00.
LD. Closed Sat & Sun. £££.

White Tower E6
1 Percy St W1. Tel 01-636 8141. Elegant;
first class cuisine. Agreeable and leisurely
service. LD. Closed Sat & Sun. ££.

Wiltons E6
27 Bury St SW1. Tel 01-930 8391.
Traditional British cooking to high standards
in this grand old Victorian building. LD.
Closed Fri D, Sat & Sun. £££. Book.

Wales

Wales is a fiercely independent part of the United Kingdom and there can be no question of its difference. Ringed with great castles, impressive remnants of the days when the Celtic fringe had to be kept under control, Wales offers a feast of scenery. From the valleys and Black Mountains in the south to the glories of Snowdonia in the north, it has so much to offer those who enjoy the outdoors. The coast is varied; there are miles of flat sand and splendid cliffs on the Gower, and at Conway the mountains come so close to the sea that the road takes to a tunnel. Sail from Solva into St Bride's Bay and you are amongst the magnificent Dyfed coastal scenery.

The people are as delightful as their country; talkative and musical with an attractive lilting accent they have preserved their own language and traditions. Sturdy from generations of mining and tough hill farming; they are a great contrast to their more effete English neighbours.

A B C D E

Carmel Head
Penrhyn Bay
Holyhead Bay
Bull Bay
Cemaes Bay 418
Amlwch
Anglesey
Llanfachraeth
Bodedern
Llanerchymedd
Moelfre
Red Wharf Bay
Holyhead
Holy Island
Rhoscolyn
Gwalchmai
Llangefni
Benllech
Pentraeth
Penmon
Llanfaelog
Menai Bridge
Talwrn
Beaumaris
Llangoed
Penm...
Rhosneigr
Bangor
Plas Newydd
Bethe...
Aberffraw
Bryn-Siencyn
Port Dinorwic
A55 A...
Newborough
Llanberis
Deiniol...
Caernarfon
Newborough Warren
Llanrug
Lake Railway
Betws-y...
Caernarfon Bay
Llandwrog
Snowdo...
Talysarn
Garmon

Dry Island
Rhoscolyn
Llangefni
Gwalchmai
Rhosneigr
Porth Nobla
Aberffraw
Newborough
Newborough Warren
Menai Bridge
Bryn-Siencyn
Port...
Llanberis
Lake Rai...
Llanberis
Snow...
Betws...
Garmon
Talysarn
Llanllyfni

Caernarfon Bay
Caernarfon
Llandwrog
Clynnog-fawr
1849
Llithfaen
Llanaelhaearn
Trwyn y Gorfach
Carreg Ddu
Chwilog
Porthmadoc
256...
Tremad...
Criccieth
Tremadog Bay
Tudweiliog
Nefyn
Edern
Bodfuan
Dinas
Llŷn
Porthmadoc
Pwllheli
Sarn
Llanbedrog
Llandanwg
Meillteyrn
Aberdaron
Abersoch
Rhiw
Llanengan
Porth Neigwl
Dyffryn
Ardudw...
Bardsey Sound
Trwyn Cilan
Bardsey I.

Llan...
Bar...
Barm...
Fai...
Llwyng...
Tyw...

Cardigan
Bay
Ab...
Aberystwy...

Llanrhystyd
Llanon
Aberaeron
New Quay
Llanarth
ROSS LARE
Llandysiliogogo
Llwyndafydd
Llangranog
Ystrad Aeron
Mydroilyn
Cribyn
Aberporth
Verwig
Ffostrasol
Llanwenog
Cemaes Head
St Dogmaels
Cardigan
Beulah
A475
Ceibwr Bay
Moylgrove
Llandyssul
Llan...
Dinas Head
Fishguard Bay
A475
Strumble Head
Dinas
Eglwyswrw
Pepcader...
DYFE...
Goodwick
Newport
Goneath
Newcastle Emlyn
Rhos
Abergorle...
St Nicholas
Fishguard
A48
Boncath
Porth-gain
Mathry
Llanychaer
Preseli Mts.
Crymmych
Cynwyl Elfed
Brechfa
St David's Head
Letterston
-1760
Llanfyrnach
Puncheston
Llanglydwen
Cynwyl Elfed
St David
Llanrian
Llanycefn
Llanboidy
Carmarthen
A40
Ramsey I.
Solva
Treffgarne
Clarbeston
Llandd...
Newgale
Roch
A478
Cwmffrwd
Nolton
Camrose
Llawhaden
Narberth
Langain
A48
Druidston
Whitland
St Clears
Llandefaelog
Broadhaven
Haverfordwest
Red Roses
Llanstephan
Pontyates
Tumble
St Brides Bay
A40
Templeton
Laugharne
Llansaint
Skomer I.
St Brides
Walton West
Johnston
Kilgetty
Pendine
Kidwelly
Llannon
Marloes
Sandy Haven
Rosemarket
Saundersfoot
Burry Port
He...
Dale
Milford Haven
Neyland
Carmarthen Bay
Pembrey
Llangennech
Skokholm I.
St Ann's Head
Carew
Pembroke Dock
Penally
Pembrey
Llanelli
Gorse...
Angle
Pembroke
Tenby
Llanmadoc
Llangennech
Castlemartin
Manorbier
Caldey I.
Llanrhidian
Bosherston
Reynoldston
Linney Head
St Govan's Head
Rhossili
Oxwich
Worms Head
Porteynon
CORK
Mumbles Bay

A B C D E

1

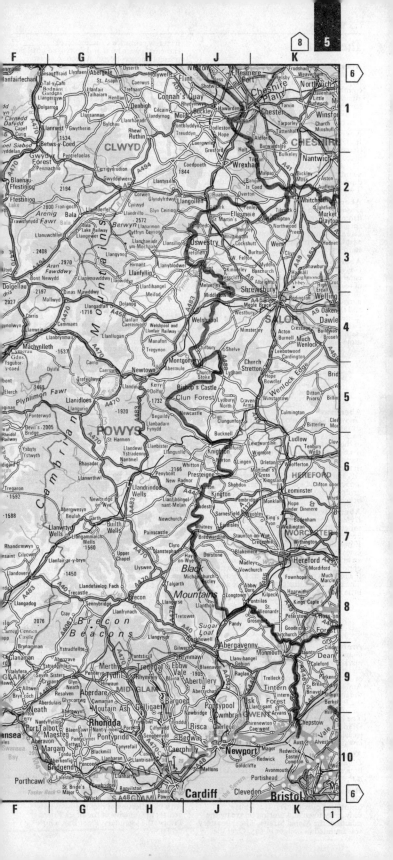

The coast

Aberaeron E6
Dyfed. Pop 1,300. EC Thur. An elegant
Regency new town built in the 19thC with
comfort, care and spaciousness; the plan is
attributed to John Nash. It has a colourful
harbour, broad streets and handsome
houses, all pastel-washed. There are shingle
beaches on either side of the harbour.

Aberavon F10
W. Glamorgan. A wilderness of duneland
transformed into a monumental pleasure
place of electric fervour. There is an
Olympic-standard indoor freshwater
swimming pool, other sports facilities, a big
dipper and scenic railway for the children.
Two miles of firm safe sandy beach.

Aberdaron C3
Gwynedd. Pop 1,200. EC Wed. A remote
fishing village of white cottages and a
sprightly 6thC church. Y Gegin Fawr, a
cafe and souvenir shop, was built in the
14thC as a resting place for pilgrims to
Bardsey.

Aberdovey E4
Gwynedd. Pop 1,100. EC Wed. An
enterprising place. Simple, elegant, yet full
of real life. A collection of neat colourful
shops and houses perch gingerly on a
narrow strip of land between the mountains
and the sea. Charles Dibdin's 18thC opera
'Liberty Hall' made famous the song 'The
Bells of Aberdovey'.
Bathing is safe from the long, sandy,
dune-backed beach north of the village.

Aberffraw A2
Gwynedd. Pop 1,400. Spick-and-span
cottages and an ancient hump-backed
pack-horse bridge. It was here the Britons
of the west rallied under Maglocunos to halt
the Saxon onslaught. On an island in the bay
stands the church of St. Cwyfan. Founded
in the 7thC it was restored in 1893.
Of interest – Barclodiad-y-Gawres, a
4,000-year-old burial chamber. South of the
bridge grassy dunes lead to a quiet sandy
beach.

Aberystwyth E5
Dyfed. Pop 10,700. EC Wed. MD Mon. A
sober and dignified place strung out along a
broad promenade with prim Victorian and
Edwardian buildings. At the north end is
Constitution Hill, bruised and battered like
an upended and camouflaged helmet. At the
opposite end is a grassy hillock crowned with
the remains of a 12th and 13thC castle.
The beach is of fine gravel, shingle and a
little sand.

Amlwch B1
Gwynedd. Pop 3,700. EC Wed. A diffident
market town and holiday resort with a
down-at-heel yet spirited harbour
overlooked by a ruined windmill. In 1768
Amlwch was a small fishing hamlet. With
the discovery of huge deposits of copper in
the Parys Mountain in the late 18thC it
rapidly became a busy and prosperous town.
The boom years ended in the 19thC.
Of interest – Llaneilian church, one of the
treasures of Anglesey. Small sandy beach at
low tide. Excellent bathing and boating.

Angle B9
Dyfed. Pop 300. A quaintly shy cluster of
houses along a silent village street. At the end
is the muddy sand of Angle Bay.

Bangor E1
Gwynedd. Pop 16,000. EC Wed. A place of
unfulfilled possibilities. It is a busy
university town and touring centre by the
mouth of the Menai Straits. The monastery
was founded in Bangor in 525. Over the

next few centuries a succession of
cathedrals were built and destroyed until the
present one was begun in 1496. A squat
building in a low-lying site it was restored
by Sir Gilbert Scott in 1866–80. Of
interest – the Menai Suspension Bridge; the
unique Bible Garden.
The beach is mainly shingle. Bathing is safe
on the incoming tide.

Barmouth E3
Gwynedd. Pop 2,100. EC Wed. A collection
of ordinary things made special as they
cluster uniquely together between a curve of
the sea, a pock-marked hill, and the
Mawddach Estuary. Barmouth is a twisting
narrow place, grey and Victorian, with
bay-windowed joviality.
An impassive promenade sweeps round to a
boat-filled river-mouth harbour. Of
interest – Ty Gwyn yn Y Bermo (White
House in Barmouth) said to have been built
by the Earl of Richmond who later became
Henry VII.
Long sandy beach.

Barmouth

Beaumaris B2
Gwynedd. Pop 2,100. EC Wed. Reached
through the shadow between high ground
and the sea, it is an irresistable place
wrapped round a curve of flat land which
juts into Conway Bay. The curve itself is
emphasised by cliff-white terraces with bay
windows. Across the waters are the foothills
and mountains of Caernarvonshire, misty in
the distance. Yachts moor in the bay where
wooden warships once anchored to deliver
supplies to the 13thC castle. Of interest – the
15thC Tudor House in the main street; the
old gaol built in 1614.
A mainly shingle beach leads to areas of
sand at low tide. Bathing is safe on the
incoming tide.

Benllech B1
Gwynedd. Pop 1,500. EC Thur. Set on
Anglesey's east coast, Benllech is a popular
holiday village. Nothing special, but bags of
spirit, like a plain girl doing a fandango.
The beach is long and sandy. It shelves
gently and bathing is safe.

Bontddu F3
Gwynedd. EC Wed. An attractive small-
scale village, washed in along the northern
shore of the pine-clad Mawddach Estuary.

Broad Haven B8
Dyfed. Pop 300. A popular beach with fine
sand flanked by cliffs and rock pools.

Caernarvon E1
Gwynedd. Pop 9,300. EC Thur. MD Sat. A
small grey town wrapped round a hilltop
square. The boisterous castle was one of the
mightiest of 13thC Europe.
Business and tourist centre of Snowdonia,
Caernarvon stands on the western end of the
Menai Strait where the River Seiont flows
into the sea. Of interest – remains of a
Roman fort; the Menai Suspension Bridge.

Cardiff H10
*S. Glamorgan. Pop 278,200. EC Wed.
MD Mon.* Straddling the River Taff is this
expressive and lively place full of pubs and
bars and spacious streets.
A large seaport and the capital of Wales,
Cardiff has a history going back to Roman
times. It was a Norman centre of military
strength and justice, and during the Civil
Wars it was stoutly Royalist. By the middle
of the 19thC it was already a prosperous
port and has remained implacably Victorian
at heart ever since.
Of interest – Llandaff Cathedral, rebuilt
after the blitz; St John's Church built in the
15thC; the huge castle; the Edwardian Civic
Centre; Cardiff Arms Park; St Fagan's Folk
Museum; the National Museum of Wales,
with its collection of pictures by Welsh
artists; the remains of the Black Friars
Priory; the legendary Tiger Bay, a little
arid now.

Cardigan C7
Dyfed. Pop 3,800 EC Wed. MD Mon. A sharp-edged place full of vigour. Once an important sea-port closed by the silting up of its river. Now it is a bustling market town sitting astride the River Teifi amongst the rich farms and forests of Cardiganshire. Of interest – the ancient bridge; the remains of a 12thC castle; the abbey ruins; the local market.

Ceibwr Bay C7
Dyfed. A shingle cove of anonymous quietness at the foot of towering cliffs. Grey seals can sometimes be seen.

Cemaes Bay A1
Gwynedd. Pop 800. A handful of whitewashed cottages grouped round narrow streets and a small harbour. The whole place is simple and unadorned. At Wylfa Head across the bay is the new nuclear power station.
The sandy beach is completely covered at high tide.

Clynnog Fawr D2
Gwynedd. Pop 900. Sentimentally small-scale, a handful of whitewashed cottages and the church of St Beuno, founded in the 7thC and a resting place for pilgrims to Bardsey Island. A quiet shingle beach is reached by a pleasant lane.

Colwyn Bay G1
Clwyd. Pop 25,500. EC Wed. A broad, impassive place in a half-moon curve of the bay. At the turn of the century it was a placid cluster of fishermen's huts. Now it's a bustling resort with a lively pier and pleasant promenade.
Sandy beach with a sheltered bay good for water sports.

Conwy F1
Gwynedd. Pop 12,200. EC Wed. MD Tue, Sat. An ordinary town transformed by its setting. Conwy is disarmingly wrapped round the side of a ridge above a harbour and estuary. Everything here is subservient to the castle, a genteel monster full of brute force. Of interest – Telford's elegant suspension bridge built in 1826; Robert Stephenson's tubular bridge; a house on the quay reputed to be the smallest in Britain; the 14thC church of St Mary; the 12thC abbey; Plas Mawr, the Elizabethan mansion built 1585. Fast currents make the estuary unsafe for bathing. Bathing is safe from Morfa beach 1¼ miles north-west.

Criccieth E2
Gwynedd. Pop 1,500. EC Wed. A family resort dominated by an expressively silent 13th C castle which stands on a grassy headland with incomparable views of Cardigan Bay. Of interest – community hymn-singing which takes place on Sunday evenings in summer at the bottom of Mona Terrace; the church of St Catherine; Brynawelon, home of Lloyd George.
The beach is a curve of shingle and low tide sand.

Criccieth

Dale B9
Dyfed. Pop 300. A sheltered line of colour-washed cottages in a picturesque cubby-hole inside the entrance to Milford Haven. Of interest – Dale Fort, built in the 19thC. Surrounded by numerous fine sandy beaches.

Druidston B8
Dyfed. A sandy beach backed by sheer cliffs. On-shore winds create ideal conditions for surfing.

Fishguard B7
Dyfed. Pop 4,900. EC Wed. MD Thur. Lower Fishguard is a huddle of old wharfs and cottages round a small harbour. Perched on top of the tree-covered headland above is Fishguard proper, exact and alert like a clock spring. Of interest – the Royal Oak Inn in the square; Tregwynt, one and a half miles south, has an interesting old mill producing fine Welsh weaves.

Harlech E3
Gwynedd. Pop 1,300. EC Wed. Like many of the great castle towns in Wales, Harlech is small. Cottage-high grey buildings play piggy-back on the monstrous rock shoulders of the stone-built castle. There are sharp views between buildings to an almost table-flat valley. Beyond are the mountains of Snowdonia, misty in the distance.
The long sandy beach sweeps north to the mouth of the Glaslyn Estuary where swift currents make bathing dangerous.

Holyhead A1
Gwynedd. Pop 10,600. EC Tue. MD Sat. A heavy-weight place complicated and involved like the local gossip. A mixture of sandy bays, industry and bustling port. This is the terminus for Dublin-bound ferries; the harbour is protected by Britain's longest breakwater. Have a look at South Stack's famous lighthouse.
Newry Beach, a stretch of clean shingle, runs from the landward end of the breakwater towards Salt Island.

Laugharne D9
Dyfed. Pop 1,000. A quiet place; if you planted dynamite something might happen. Pronounced 'Larn' it is one of the most charming small towns in Wales. Smudged round the mouth of the River Taf, with the green hills of the Llanstephan Peninsula staring out across the water, Laugharne is a street of Georgian houses, an 18thC town hall, a 12thC castle and a shingle foreshore. Dylan Thomas lived and worked here in the Boat House wedged between the hillside and the river bank along the cliff walk behind the castle.
Of interest – the unpretentious grave of Dylan Thomas in the churchyard; Brown's Hotel, the poet's favourite. Not far from a good sandy beach.

Llandanwg E3
Gwynedd. Pop 1,400. A sandy rock-scattered beach of expressive emptiness. Half-buried in the dunes is a small-scale and derelict church. Parts date from the 6thC.
Except on the ebb tide the bathing is safe.

Llandudno F1
Gwynedd. Pop 17,700. EC Wed. A splendid place full of smug and electric bonhomie. This is the resort where Lewis Carroll – the Rev Charles Dodgson – met the little girl who inspired 'Alice in Wonderland'. The pier is something special – it's as if Battersea Fun Fair had exploded and the remaining bits had congealed into a misshapen box of amusement and been set on a sea of spidery legs. Of interest – Professor Codman's Wooden Headed Follies; a funicular ride up the Great Orme's Head. The beach is a gentle arc of golden sand, limestone headlands at either end, and elegant shoulder-to-shoulder hotels in the middle.

Llandudno

Llangrannog D7
Dyfed. Pop 200. A colourful village with houses tumbling cheerfully to the beach between a cleft in the high cliffs. Safe bathing and good sea fishing.

Llanstephan D9
Dyfed. Pop 1,000. Backed by harp-shaped hills, it is a granny knot of cobwebbed lanes on a hilltop. Llanstephan lies on the west side of the estuary of the Towy. Down at the water's edge is the ruined castle. Of interest – St Anthony's Well. Bathing is safe on the incoming tide.

Manorbier C9
Dyfed. Pop 1,170. EC Sat. A companionable village grouped round an impressive Norman castle which spits hell and high water across a broad green valley to the open sea. The beach is sandy with a scattering of shingle.

Mewslade Bay   **D10**
W. Glamorgan. A delightful little bay
sheltered by high cliffs. The sandy beach is
completely covered at high tide.

Milford Haven   **B9**
Dyfed. Pop 13,700. EC Thur. MD Fri.
Designed and built in the late 18thC on
steeply sloping ground around a little
harbour, it is a neat place of starched and
pressed gentility. There are magnificent
views of the busy waterway. Oil tankers of
over 250,000 tons berth at the jetties which
reach out into the main stream.

Moelfre   **B1**
Gwynedd. Pop 200. A vigorous, salt-aired
fishing village famed for the skill and
courage of its lifeboatmen. Almost 900 lives
have been saved since the station was
founded in 1830. Safe bathing from a
shingle beach.

Newgale   **A8**
Dyfed. A lonely sandy beach with curving
breakers.

Newport   **J10**
Dyfed. Pop 1,060. EC Wed. A place of
bent-backed charm, an ancient castled town
carved out of the Welsh domains by Martin
de Tours in 1093. Of interest – pre-Christian
hut circles on Carn Ingli Common. There
are two fine beaches – Draeth and Parrog,
the town beach with a picturesque quay.

New Quay   **D6**
Dyfed. Pop 700. EC Wed. Steep, twisting
narrow streets with everything jammed
together in a delightful free-for-all around a
sheltered harbour. New Quay was a bustling
port and ship-building centre in the early
19thC. The coastal trade was superceded
by the railways towards the end of that
century.
By the 1920s the port had become an
attractive holiday centre. The poet Dylan
Thomas lived here in the 1940s. East of the
harbour is a sandy crescent of sheltered
beach one and a half miles long.

New Quay

Pendine   **D9**
Dyfed. Pop 300. Six miles of flat, firm sand-
backed dunes. The beach was used for
successful attempts on the world land speed
record in the 1920s by Sir Malcolm Thomas
and J. G. Parry-Thomas.

Penmaenmawr   **F1**
Gwynedd. Pop 4,000. EC Wed. A busy little
resort backed by the Caernarvonshire
mountains, and hanging down the side of the
hills between the great headlands of
Penmaenbach and Penmaenmawr. This was
the site of a stone age axe factory. Of
interest – Puffin Island off the eastern tip of
Anglesey.
The long sandy beach is backed by shingle
and a railway line. At Penmaenmawr the line
is separated from the shore by a broad,
traffic-free promenade. Good bathing.

Port Eynon   **E10**
W. Glamorgan. Pop 250. A village full of
quiet picturesqueness, with a sandy
dune-backed beach flanked by high cliffs.

Porthcawl   **F10**
Mid Glamorgan. Pop 14,100. EC Wed.
Porthcawl was developed originally as a
19thC coaling port now a teeming giant full
of family fun. The 3,000 caravan park is one
of the largest in Europe. Sandy beaches with
occasional outbreaks of rock.

Porthgain   **A8**
Dyfed. Pop 150. A tiny inlet with a snug
harbour brim-full of atmosphere. There are
several small shingle coves to the east.

Porth Nobla   **D1**
Gwynedd. Miles of golden sand ending
beneath a rocky headland.

Porth Penrhyn-Mawr   **A1**
Gwynedd. An anonymously quiet shingle
beach flanked by low grassy headlands at the
end of a country lane.

Porthmadog   **E2**
Gwynedd. Pop 3,900. EC Wed. An anthology
of solid 19thC comfort with broad tree-lined
streets and a high-spirited harbour.
Conceived in 1807 by William Alexander
Madocks on 7,000 acres of reclaimed land.
The town became a thriving port with
locally built sailing ships carrying slate to
many parts of the world. Have a ride on the
Ffestiniog Narrow Gauge Railway.
Good bathing at Black Rock Sands, except
at the south-eastern end of the beach where
there are swift currents.

Portmadoc

Prestatyn   North **H1**
Clwyd. Pop 15,480. EC Thur. A popular
holiday resort. Until the late 19thC it was a
lead mining centre. 700-foot-high hills
provide a green partially wooded backdrop.
The area known as Central Beach is
overlooked by a broad traffic-free promenade
flanked by dunes.
Of interest – Dyserth, an old world village
with a waterfall at its centre; Edward I's
castle of Rhuddlan, three and a half miles
west.
Three miles of sandy beach. A 300-yard
stretch near the western end of the
promenade is clearly marked with flags and
recommended for swimming.

Rhoscolyn   **A2**
Gwynedd. Pop 300. The epitome of
picturesqueness – sand sheltered by rocky
headlands and reached by a narrow lane
between high grassy banks. The village is a
quarter of a mile away.

Rhosili   **D10**
W. Glamorgan. Pop 300. An expansive
sweep of golden sands reached from a
clifftop village. Good surfing.

Rhyl   North **G1**
Clwyd. Pop 21,700. EC Thur. A magnet for
Merseyside and the East Midlands, Rhyl is
an electric hive of activity with a heaving
mass of fun-seekers.
Of interest – Royal Floral Hall, complete
with children's zoo; the bathing beauty
contests. Long sandy beach.

St David's   **A8**
Dyfed. Pop 1,700. EC Wed. A pint-sized
city set on a small stream near the sea. Once
a considerable place it's now a delightful
'has-been' without a care. The cathedral,
nestling in a valley, was begun in the late
12th C. Across a brook are the ruins of the
Bishop's Palace. Built by Bishop Gower in
1340, it was destroyed by Bishop Barlow in
the 15thC.
Sheltered sandy beach at Caerfai Bay.

Sandy Haven   **B9**
Dyfed. Firm sand along the thickly wooded
banks of a picturesque creek.

Saundersfoot   **C9**
Dyfed. Pop 2,500. EC Wed. Everything
muddled and informal. The busy harbour
is surrounded by broad quays in a horseshoe
of hills and cliffs. The whole place is flanked
by sandy beaches.

Solva   **A8**
Dyfed. A tiny village in a picturesque
huddle along Solva Creek, it has become
one of the most popular boating centres on
St Bride's Bay. Smaus Lighthouse, lying
fifteen miles offshore, is one of the most
isolated in the world.

Swansea   **F10**
*W. Glamorgan. Pop 172,600. EC Thur. MD
Fri, Sat.* The 'ugly, lovely town' of Dylan
Thomas, full of broad impassive parks and
suburban sobriety. Made a city by Prince
Charles following his investiture as Prince of
Wales. It's the main shopping centre for
south-west Wales. Of interest – the
Guildhall's magnificent Brangwyn Hall;
Swansea's 16thC fortress; Weobley Castle
near Llandimore; 13thC Oystermouth
Castle.

Talybont   **E4**
Gwynedd. An unself-consciously pretty
village of stone-built charm. The beach lies
west of the village, three quarters of a mile
from the main road.

Tenby   **C9**
Dyfed. Pop 5,000. EC Wed. A richly
mediaeval place of close-knit narrow streets
tied round a bustling harbour in the shelter
of Castle Hill. A ruined 14thC stronghold
stands on top of the hill.
Of interest – the 15thC Tudor merchant's
house; St Mary's Church, the largest parish
church in Wales; Caldey Island.

Tywyn   **E4**
Gwynedd. Pop 3,850. EC Wed. A place of
semi-detached self-consciousness lying back
from the water's edge in the middle of a flat
plain. There's an eruption of hills all round
except to the west, where it is washed by the
sea. Originally settled by the Saxons in 516
it is now a popular holiday resort. Of interest
– St Cadfan's Church which houses
Cadfan's Stone, of early Christian origin; the
narrow gauge railway of Tal-y-llyn. Three-
mile sweep of sand and shingle beach.

Inland towns & villages

Abergavenny   **J9**
Gwent. Pop 9,400. EC Thur. MD Tue, Fri. A
big-hearted place with whiffs of elegance. Set
in a mountain-ringed valley, Abergavenny
is a large market town crammed closely
round a long twisting narrow high street.
This is the gateway to South Wales. The
Romans had a fort here; the Normans made
it an important stronghold. Of interest –
the 19thC Angel Inn; church of St Mary;
the great tithe barn of the priory.

Bala   **G2**
Gwynedd. Pop 1,600. EC Wed. MD Thur.
A discreet Victorian town straddling a wide
tree-lined street at the eastern end of
Bala Lake. It was the home of the Methodist
revival in 18thC North Wales. Of interest –
Tomen-y-Bala, a grassy mound behind the
high street and once the site of a 13thC
castle.

Beddgelert   **E2**
Gwynedd. Pop 800. EC Wed. A compact
group of stone-built inns and cottages
surrounding a diminutive bridge, it's a
mountain village as crisp as an icicle.
Of interest – the grave of Gelert; not far from
the town, Dinas Emrys, an iron age and
Roman hill fort; Hafod Lwyfog, a typical
17thC Caernarvonshire farmhouse.

Blaenau Ffestiniog   **F2**
Gwynedd. EC Thur. MD Fri. A chain-gang
sort of town, hard-bitten and pressed in by
dark mountains. Even the walls of the
buildings seem to grow out of the ground, all
rugged rock and slate and indefatigable.
Fabulous walks and exhilarating views.
Of interest – Llechwedd Slate Caverns –
you can take a tour through the slate quarry.

Brecon   **H8**
Powys. Pop 6,300. EC Wed. MD Tues, Fri.
A place of extremes in a landscape of folds
and hills. Built at the junction of the rivers
Honddu and Usk, Brecon is a prosperous
market town dominated by a 13thC priory
church; it's now the cathedral of the diocese
of Swansea and Brecon. Look at the iron
age hill-fort to the north on a hill above the
town; the remains of the 11thC castle; a
partly restored Roman fort two miles west
of the town; the large lake to the east.

Builth Wells   **H7**
Powys. Pop 1,500. EC Wed. MD Mon. A
once prosperous Victorian spa, Builth Wells
is now a sedate and sober market town set in
broad green meadows and wooded hills.
Rebuilt after a devastating fire in 1691 it
consists of one long high street running
between the 18thC bridge across the River
Wye and the mediaeval church. Of interest –
the 18thC Pump Room and the old Crown
Hotel; the stone-built wool market.

Builth Wells

Caerphilly   **H10**
S. Glamorgan. Commanding a tangle of
valleys to its north, Caerphilly is in a sense a
ruined town; the ruined castle totally
dominates the remaining handful of houses.
The town was both a former Roman fort and
a Norman citadel. Its fame now rests on the
fine white crumbly cheese which has been
copied all over the world.

Carmarthen   **D8**
Dyfed. Pop 13,100. EC Thur. MD Wed, Sat.
An animated old-world Welsh town with
bent-backed houses and narrow winding
streets crammed onto a bluff above the river
Towy. The new council offices and the old
castle dominate the picture, as they stand
growling at each other across the rooftops.
The town started life as a Roman fortress.
By the end of the 11thC Carmarthen was
really two towns; the Norman town
developed round their castle and the Welsh
town, a quarter of a mile to the east, centred
on the Augustinian priory of St John the
Evangelist. The two remained bitterly
hostile until finally fused together. Have a
look at the 13thC church of St Peter; the
Guildhall, built in 1770.

Chepstow   **K10**
Gwent. Pop 8,000. EC Wed. It seems like
any other place at first, until you enter via
the 16thC town gate and then everything
seems to happen fast. The town falls rapidly
away before you in a series of twisting streets
and roofscapes. There are views across to
wooded hills, and at the bottom of the town
is the mighty Norman castle. It is an
impressive ruin standing in a shallow cliff
on the west bank of the Wye.
Chepstow was once a busy port before the
railways and bigger ships. It is still a
flourishing market centre. Of interest – the
Norman parish church of St Mary, heavily
restored in 1871; the iron bridge across the
Wye; the 19thC bow-windowed houses in
Bridge Street; the mediaeval stocks.

Denbigh   **H1**
Clwyd. Pop 8,100. EC Thur. MD Wed.
Dominated by a smugly impressive 13thC
castle Denbigh, small-scale and mellow,
wearily climbs a limestone hill. The place is
gentle and ancient like a retired great uncle.
H. M. Stanley, explorer of Africa and the
man who found Dr Livingstone, was born
here. Of interest – the 14thC garrison chapel;
the 16thC town hall; the Hawk and Buckle
Inn with its site of an old cockpit.

Denbigh

Dolgellau   **F3**
Gwynedd. Pop 2,600. EC Wed. MD Fri. A
stone-built market town, hard as nails one
minute, dainty the next. It's a knot of
narrow streets and grey-faced houses
hemmed in by fat foothills and the massive
Cadair Idris mountain. Of interest – the
17thC bridge; Toll House; the 13thC effigy
in the church of St Mary.

Grosmont   **J8**
Gwent. Pop 600. A cobwebbed border village
standing with its 13thC castle high above the
winding Monnow River, and quietly
reminiscent of a mediaeval past of great
importance; as the 14thC church confirms.

Haverfordwest B8

Dyfed. Pop 9,100. EC Thur. MD Sat. A tight-packed place built round a 13thC square-walled fortress on high ground above the Western Cleddau river. Once an important port, it is now the county town of Pembrokeshire with a brooding mediaeval aura. Of interest – the 13thC church of St Mary with fine lancet windows; Shire Hall; the Market House; the old quay along the river; remains of the 13thC Augustinian priory.

Near to the coast and the quiet creeks of Milford Haven.

Hay-on-Wye J7

Powys. Pop 1,200. EC Tue. MD Mon, Thur. A fretted skyline of buildings clambers up a sharp slope of land to the south of a broad, shallow part of the Wye. Behind the town to the south, the Black Mountains add a touch of thunder to the town's silhouette. A one-time Roman fort and Norman castle town, it is now a busy market centre with some memorable inns. Of interest – Hay Castle, founded in 1090 but now predominantly Jacobean in style; the Three Cocks, a once important coaching stage; the nearby castle ruins at Clifford, to the north; and Longtown to the south.

Kidwelly D9

Dyfed. Pop 3,000. A small town full of mediaeval charm. Kidwelly grew up at the mouth of the Gwendraeth Fach river in the days of the Norman invasion of South Wales. Kidwelly Castle, even in ruins pretty much the strong-armed bully, dominates the town. A second settlement grew up across the river, built round the 12thC Benedictine priory. The two townships are linked by a splendid 14thC bridge. Of interest – the ruined 14thC gateway near the castle; the priory church.

Lampeter E7

Dyfed. Pop 2,200. EC Wed. MD Tue. A bustling market town built round a ford of the River Teifi. It's a slap-on-the-back sort of place in the heart of rich farmland. Lampeter is famous for the horse fair held annually in May. St David's College was founded in 1882 for training students for holy orders.

Llanddewi Brefi F6

Dyfed. Pop 500. A handful of quiet, stern-faced houses dominated by an austere church standing on a mound. Serene and dignified in lonely open landscape. Have a look at the early Christian memorial stones in the churchyard.

Llandeilo F8

Dyfed. Pop 1,780. EC Thu. MD Sat. A modest market town set in a sweep of the River Towy. As clean as a whistle, Llandeilo is all shiny-faced houses and laundered grass following a Civic Trust scheme. Of interest – ruins of the 11thC Dinefwr Castle; Dryslwyn Castle five miles west; Carreg Cennen Castle, built on a limestone hill three and a half miles to the south-east.

Llandrindod Wells H6

Powys. Pop 3,400. EC Wed. An unstructured town of Edwardian spaciousness. Standing on a 700-foot-high plateau overlooking the River Ithon, it was once the largest and most popular of Welsh spas. In late Victorian times it attracted over 80,000 visitors a year. Of interest – the well preserved Roman fort of Castell Collen above Llanyre.

Llangollen H2

Clwyd. Pop 3,100. EC Thur. MD Tue. A hard-edged place built around the singing River Dee with high ridges of land closing in on both sides. It's a place of surprises, like a Welsh ballad. The home of the International Music Eisteddfod since the Second World War. Of interest – the 14thC stone bridge; Plas Newydd, an 18thC conglomeration of bits and pieces to make a black-and-white timbered mansion; Llangollen Canal; the castle ruins; the 13thC Valle Crucis Abbey.

Llanidloes G5

Powys. Pop 2,300. EC Thur. MD Sat. A straightforward place with views out along open-ended streets to the fat green hills. An historic market town built at the junction of

Llanidloes, the market hall

the River Severn with the Clywedog river. Of interest – the 13thC church with a fine hammer-beam roof; the old market hall; the Clywedog dam and lake.

Llantrisant H10

Mid Glamorgan. A mediaeval town in the saddle between two hills, dominated by its church and the ruined tower of the castle. This was the home of the eccentric Victorian, Mr Price who, to the horror of the local inhabitants, cremated his dead son at a time when such a practice was considered barbarous. Inept new development has diluted the brimstone and fire atmosphere. Of interest – an iron age hill fort to the east.

Machynlleth F4

Powys. Pop 1,800. EC Thur. MD Wed. A small-scale market town squashed amongst hills, and spread out along a gentle High Street. Note the giant 19thC clock tower.

Machynlleth was a former Roman military station. In the early 15thC it was chosen by Owain Glyndwr to be the capital of a Wales freed from the rule of Henry IV. Of interest – the stone-built parliament house in the centre of Maen-gwyn Street; the 18thC White Lion; a Jacobean house at the upper end of Maen-gwyn Street.

Machynlleth

Monmouth K9

Gwent. Pop 7,000. EC Thur. MD Fri, alternate Mon. Standing at the point where the River Monnow flows into the Wye, it was a strategic stronghold of mediaeval Wales. It held the lower hills between the moorland heart of Wales and the wide fields of the Midlands; it mastered the outfall of the rivers whose upper reaches lead to the central passes between the Severn and the Dovey. Whoever held it could control the whole of South Wales.

This was the site of Roman Blestium, and the 12thC home of Geoffrey of Monmouth. In 1387 Henry V was born in the 11thC castle. Charles Rolls, of Rolls-Royce fame, was born at nearby Hendre. Of interest – the mediaeval fortified bridge gateway across the Monnow. It is the only one in Britain, and one of the few remaining in Europe; the 14thC church; the 18thC Shire Hall; Nelson Museum.

Monmouth – the Monnow bridge

Montgomery J4

Powys. Pop 1,000. A strong-spirited market town of bow-windowed and cobble-stoned charm, hiding beneath the bones of a 13thC castle. There are some Elizabethan, Jacobean and Georgian houses. The 14thC church has a fine rood screen. Look at the historic Rhydwhiman Ford.

Newport J10

Gwent. Pop 110,000. EC Thur. MD Fri, Sat. A busy commercial centre with everything fierce and direct. Built on the banks of the River Usk, Newport is a product of the Industrial Revolution. Of interest – the transporter bridge, which carries cars and pedestrians on a moving platform; the castle ruins; the Roman amphitheatre at nearby Caerleon.

New Radnor H6

Powys. Built to the east of Radnor Forest, it was originally walled in with a regular pattern of small-scale streets dominated by an 11thC castle. The castle was destroyed first by King John in the 13thC, rebuilt by his son, and destroyed by the Welsh prince Owain Glyndwr in the early 15thC. Of interest – two and a half miles to the east, the hamlet of old Radnor.

Newtown H5

Powys. Pop 5,610. EC Thur. MD Tue, Sat. A prosperous market town happily ensconced in the Severn Valley. Founded in the late 13thC when the then victorious King of England, Edward I, had a new town built round a small village commanding a ford across the Severn. The birthplace of Robert Owen, factory reformer and founder of the co-operative movement. Of interest – the textile museum in an original hand-loom weaving factory in Commercial Street.

Presteigne J6

Powys. Pop 1,200. EC Thur. A border town between England and Wales languishing amongst the gentle slopes and wide vales. A pleasant and peaceful place with crisp black-and-white half-timbered cottages and houses. Of interest – the church of St Andrew with Saxon and Norman work and a 16thC Flemish tapestry; the Tudor-built Radnorshire Arms; the mediaeval Duke's Arms.

Ruthin H1

Clwyd. Pop 4,300. EC Thur. A bright-eyed, excitable place, with sharp views between the buildings to distant peaks, or down twisting streets to the rolling valley floor. Of interest – the 13thC Ruthin Castle; the 14thC church; Nantclwyd House in Castle Street, a fine example of a 14thC town house; the 16thC half-timbered Exmewe Hall; the old court and prison, built 1401.

St Asaph H1

Clwyd. Pop 3,100. EC Thu. MD Thur. Dates back to Roman times. A quiet, sensible, hilltop town. The cathedral was remodelled in the 19thC by Gilbert Scott. Of interest – Pont Dafydd, a stone bridge built in 1630; the 15thC St Asaph parish church.

Tintern K9

Gwent. Pop 700. EC Wed. A riverside village of postcard possibilities. Everything is simple and straightforward and set in the lovely Wye Valley. Of interest – Tintern Abbey.

Tregaron F6

Dyfed. Pop 4,200. EC Thur. MD Alternate Tue. Backed by the lovely range of the Cambrian hills, Tregaron is a small town with a simple square – all a little apart from the world. Of interest – the iron age hill fort half a mile to the north-east; the 14thC church tower; the great Tregaron bog to the north.

Tremadog E2

Gwynedd. Pop 1,100. EC Wed. The birthplace of Lawrence of Arabia. Tremadog is a virtuous and single-minded place overshadowed by peaks. A classically planned model town built by Alexander Madocks in the early 19thC. Small-scale but spacious, its grey stone buildings stand formally round the town hall and square.

Usk J9

Gwent. Pop 2,000. EC Wed. MD Alternate Mon. A gentle-mannered town built on high ground on the east bank of the River Usk. There is a modest but broad square, whilst the ruined castle looks wistfully over broad meadowlands. Eight miles south of the Usk are the remains of a Roman fortress.

Wrexham J2

Clwyd. Pop 39,000. EC Wed. MD Mon, The centre of the North Welsh coalfield Wrexham has one surprising gem, the pit-shaft-coloured church of St Giles. Listed as one of the Seven Wonders of Wales, it's a richly sculptured masterpiece built in 1472. The wrought-iron gates to the churchyard are by the Davies brothers of Bersham. Look at Pugin's Roman Catholic church in Regent Street; the 19thC Jacobean market hall.

Regional oddities

Coracles

Shaped like a giant walnut shell, the Welsh coracle is made of willow and hazel canes covered with hides. Its design has not changed since ancient times, and it is still used for fishing salmon on the Teifi and Towy rivers.

Eisteddfod

The contests of music and poetry known as Eisteddfodau have been an outstanding feature of Welsh life for centuries. One of the earliest on a national scale was called in 1176 by Lord Rhys, one of the Welsh princes. He invited all the country's bards to his castle at Cardigan to compete against each other. Those of South Wales were found to excel in music, those of the North in verse.

The Grave of Gelert

Beddgelert, Gwynedd. Beddgelert is said to mean the Grave of Gelert. The story goes that Prince Llywelyn the Great, having left his hound Gelert to guard his infant son, returned from the chase to find the animal covered in blood. Assuming the animal had eaten his son he slew it in revenge without realising that the dog had in fact saved his son from a wolf. Both grave and story are thought to be the work of an enterprising 19thC hotelier.

Llanfairpwllgwyngyllgogerychwrn drobwllllantysyliogogogoch

Gwynedd. A descriptive, enterprising but extraordinary mouthful. The village's famous name is a combination of the local names of Llanfair and Llantysilio. Its meaning is 'St. Mary's by the White Aspen over the Whirlpool and St. Tysilio's by the red cave'. The railway station is now a café, the famous nameplate, so often snatched by jovial students, is now in the Penrhyn Castle Museum.

Portmeirion

Gwynedd. Portmeirion is a private village. An elegant and well meant misfit created as a tiny Italianate dream town. Begun in 1926 by the Welsh architect, Sir Clough Williams Ellis, it's an ornate and elaborately planned refugee camp for the discarded architectural bric-a-brac of centuries.
It all started with the 19thC house, now the hotel, at the water's edge. An elegant campanile crowns the hill with 18thC houses jammed carefully round it. Noel Coward wrote his comedy 'Blithe Spirit' in the water house between one Sunday and the next. *Open 10.00–18.00 daily.*

The Welsh language

Welsh is a celtic language related to Breton, Cornish, Irish and Scots Gaelic and has been used as a written language since about the 6thC.
Written Welsh is standard, but the phonetic spoken Welsh varies in accent in different parts of the country.

aber	– mouth of a river or stream
afon	– river
bach	– small
bryn	– hill
ban	– high place/peak
carreg/cerrig	– stone
craig	– rock
coed	– wood/trees
dyffryn	– valley
llyn	– lake
traeth	– beach
ynys	– island
bedd	– grave
capel	– chapel
eglwys	– church
plas	– mansion
castell	– castle
dinas	– city/fort
caer	– fort
hafod	– summer residence
hendre	– winter residence
newydd	– new
ty	– house
heol	– road
llwybr	– path
garth	– enclosure

Famous people

Owain Glyndwr (c1349-c1415)   H3
Sycharth, Clwyd. 2 miles ne of Llangedwyn.
Sycharth was the main residence of the
almost legendary Welsh hero. The moated
mound and bailey castle have recently been
excavated.
After Glyndwr was declared Prince of Wales
he held a parliament at Machynlleth in 1404
in what is now the Owain Glyndwr Institute,
Maen-gwyn Street. He may have lived in the
Royal House, Penrallt Street.
According to tradition, Glyndwr died and
was buried in Monnington-on-Wye. More
romantic is the fact that he was forced into
outlawry some time after 1408, disappeared,
and died in an unknown hiding-place.

David Lloyd George (1863-1945)   E2
Llanystumdwy, Gwynedd. The Prime
Minister spent his childhood in this lovely
village. He lived with his uncle at Highgate,
'on the main Criccieth road, attended the
church school, and died in his home, Ty
Newydd, close by. The Lloyd George
Memorial Museum stands in the grounds of
his estate. *Museum open 10.00-17.00 daily
late May-Sep. Closed Sat & Sun.*

Merlin   D8
Old Oak, Priory St, Carmarthen, Dyfed. King
Arthur's wizard is said to have been born in
Carmarthen. Certainly one of his favourite
haunts was on the winding River Towy. The
gnarled stump of the 'Old Oak' has been
associated with him for centuries. Merlin
prophesied that when the tree fell the town
would perish. They're both still there.

Robert Owen (1771-1858)   H5
Broad Street, Newtown, Powys. Once the
home of social reformer Robert Owen, it is
now a museum displaying books, pictures,
documents and relics relating to Owen. *Open
10-30-12.30 & 14.30-16.30 May-Sep.
Closed Sun.*

Sir Henry M. Stanley (1841-1904)   H1
St Asaph, Clwyd. Henry Morton Stanley
(born John Rowlands), of Dr Livingstone
fame, spent nine years in the workhouse here
before he set sail for America as a cabin boy.
He was born in a cottage near Denbigh
Castle which has since been torn down.

Dylan Thomas (1914-53)   D9
Boat House, Laugharne, Dyfed. The poet
lived here for many years and is buried in the
local churchyard. Every year on the 3rd July
the local Thomas Festival presents 'Under
Milk Wood'. *Boat House not open to the
public.*

Cathedrals, abbeys & churches

Aberedw Church   H7
Aberedw, Powys. Passionately primitive like
a dozen 'hail Marys', it is a 13thC Welsh
mountain church extensively restored in the
Tudor period. There is a fine late 14thC
rood screen. The north porch has a splendid
hammer-beam roof and wooden front.

Bangor Cathedral   E1
Bangor, Gwynedd. A conscientious but
lifeless artefact. Founded in 548 it was
almost wholly destroyed in the 11thC and
15thC. It was later transformed into a
Decorated building by Sir Gilbert Scott and
his son between 1868 and 1880.

Brecon Cathedral   H8
Powys. Clean cut respectability envelops this
massive cathedral. Originally the 13thC
priory church of St John the Evangelist, it
stands high above the River Honddu
dominating the narrow streets of Brecon.

Capel-y-ffin Church   J8
Capel-y-ffin, Powys. Surrounded by yews the
church is a simple cottage-like building with
a wide porch and a tower.

Clynnog Fawr Church   D2
Clynnog Fawr, Gwynedd. A noble gesture in
a coastal village of whitewashed cottages.
This is the best Gothic church west of
Conwy; a collegiate building with a porch,
carved rood screen, choir stalls and fine
timbered roof. Founded by St Beuno in the

early 7thC, it became a pilgrims' resting
place.

Llandaff Cathedral   H10
Cardiff, S. Glamorgan. A small corner of
quiet contemplation. Lying half hidden in a
hollow the cathedral stands in an untidy
village at the end of the creeping suburbs of
Cardiff. Begun in 1107, the building is all
west-of-England English, particularly the six
western arches of the nave. The west front
was completed in 1220; the elegant Lady
Chapel was added in the 13thC. The
north-west tower was added by Henry VII's
uncle. The cathedral was completely
renovated following war damage.

Llanengan Church   D3
Llanengan, Gwynedd. A square-towered
15thC miracle dressed in the best of Gothic
taste. The fine double nave is crossed by a
wonderful rood screen.

Montgomery Church   J4
Montgomery, Powys. The church has a
magnificence out of all proportion to the
town's size. Built mainly in the 13thC, it has
a rood screen of great beauty; seating stalls
complete with misericords; a notable
Renaissance tomb of Sir Richard Herbert.

St Asaph Cathedral   H1
St Asaph, Clwyd. Perched on a hilltop with
the city huddling round, it is the smallest
cathedral in Britain. Thoroughly restored by
Sir Gilbert Scott in 1869, in the most
sensitive of ways, but somehow lacking the
sort of climax one expects with a love affair.
It has had a chequered history. Founded in
537, it was destroyed by Owain Glyndwr and
later burnt by the Roundheads.

St Asaph Cathedral

St Woolos, Newport

St David's Cathedral   A8
St David's, Dyfed. Set in a shallow vale it is
an alert and sensitive miracle. The cathedral
is the third to stand on this site. Built in the
12thC of purple coloured stone, it has been a
place of pilgrimage for centuries.
In 1800 it was heavily restored by John Nash,
and by Gilbert Scott in 1862. The nave is an
intricate Norman structure. On the choir
stalls are some fascinating misericord
carvings; delicate fan vaulting above the
Holy Trinity chapel. Across a brook are the
ruins of Bishop Gower's palace built in 1340.

St Davids Cathedral

St David's Church   C9
Caldey Island, Dyfed. A single-minded and
rugged monolith as solid as a rock.
Built in that twilit Christian period
following the Roman exodus, it is a
stiff-limbed creation made to withstand the
press of gales and time.

St John's, Cardiff   St Davids, Caldey Island

St John's Church   H10
Cardiff, S. Glamorgan. A 15thC church of
small-town Perpendicular with an elegant
tower built in 1443.

St Woolas Church   **J10**
Newport, Gwent. A headstrong and righteous
church. Built in the 12thC it has a fine
Norman nave. The two outstanding features
are the Galilee Chapel and the ponderous
square tower.

Wrexham Church   **J2**
Wrexham, Clwyd. The parish church of
Wrexham, nicely sited off the High
Street. It's a lavish 15thC church in the most
prosperous of Perpendicular styles. The
tower is a splendid pinnacled landmark 135
feet high. In the churchyard is a memorial to
the much travelled Elihu Yale, one of the
founders of Yale University.

Castles and ruins

Abergavenny Castle   **J9**
Abergavenny, Gwent. Standing on the
wooded hill that dominates the town, it is a
melancholy skeleton bereft of self-defence.
Built in the 12thC, all that is visible is the
gatehouse, the mound, some of the walls, and
the foundations of the keep. The castle was
captured by Llewelyn in 1215, burned by
Owain Glyndwr in 1404, and finally slighted
by Fairfax during the Civil War. *Open 11.00-
13.00 & 14.30-17.00. Closed Sun morning &
Sun Oct-Mar.*

Aberystwyth Castle   **E5**
Aberystwyth, Dyfed. Gaunt remains stand
on a steep hill at the end of the promenade.
The castle was symmetrical in plan. There
was no keep, but it was defended by two lines
of walls and a moat. Like the other North
Wales castles it could be supplied from the
sea. A town was built alongside it as a colony
for English settlers.

Beaumaris Castle   **B2**
Beaumaris, Gwynedd. Guarding the Menai
Straits, Beaumaris is a mumbling monolith
built like a slab cake. It is the classic example
of the concentric plan. The main principle of
the design was that any enemy gaining
control of the outer curtain would be left at
the mercy of the garrison in the inner ward.
Begun in 1295, it included a sea-water moat
and a dock for shipping protected by the
outer defences of the castle. *Open 9.30-17.30
daily Apr & 9.30-19.00 May-Sep. (9.30-
17.30 Mar & Oct. 9.30-16.00 Nov-Feb.
Closed Sun morning.)*

Beaumaris Castle

Caernarvon Castle   **E1**
Caernarvon, Gwynedd. Begun in 1285 after
Edward I's successful campaign against the
Welsh. An uncompromising giant with an
aura of the Holy Land in mothballed
corners. With its weather-burnt face
mirrored in the glassy waters of Afon Seiont,
it is the most magnificent of the Edwardian
Welsh castles. Inside is the Royal Welch
Fusiliers Regimental Museum, *Open
9.30-17.30 daily Apr and 9.30-19.00 May
-Sep. (9.30-17.30 Mar & Oct. 9.30-16.00
Nov-Feb. Closed Sun morning.)*

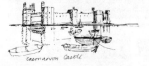

Caernarvon Castle

Caerphilly Castle   **H10**
Caerphilly, Mid Glamorgan. A muscle-bound
masterpiece armed to the teeth with
technological ingenuity. The castle is one of
the largest and finest examples of 14thC
military construction from the golden age of
castle building in Britain. It was built on
the concentric plan by Gilbert, Earl of
Gloucester in 1267. There is a rectangular
inner ward with a fat drum-tower at each

Caerphilly Castle

corner and a gatehouse in the centre of each
end wall. The outer walls were protected by
lakes formed by damming up two streams.
*Open 9.30-17.30 daily Apr & 9.30-19.00
May-Sep. (9.30-17.30 Mar & Oct. 9.30-
16.00 Nov-Feb. Closed Sun morning.)*

Cardiff Castle   **H10**
Cardiff, S. Glamorgan. The finest example
in Wales of a Norman castle on a mound
surrounded by a ditch. Built in 1093 by the
Norman war-lord Robert Fitzhamon, it was
replaced by a stone keep in the 13thC. In
the 15thC the main part of the present castle
was built including the famous octagonal
tower. Of interest – the drawing room with a
rare Louis XIII clock, the library, the great
hall, the banqueting hall and the Chaucer
Room. *Open 10.00-12.00 & 14.00-17.00,
closed Sun, Oct-Apr. 10.00-12.00 & 14.00-
19.00, closed Sun morning, May-Sep.*

Carmarthen Castle   **D8**
Carmarthen, Dyfed. A gaunt stone scarecrow
standing on a high cliff overlooking the river.
Only the gateways and towers remain of
what was once an important residence of the
princes of South Wales.

Carreg Cennen Castle   **F8**
Nr Llandeilo, Dyfed. Daringly sited on a
limestone crag high above a river valley, it's
at once sharp-fisted, tough and yet graceful
in decay. Fairly regular in plan, it was built
in the 13thC. Between the outer and inner
wards is a strong and elaborate barbican.
The passage to the inner ward lay over three
drawbridges. *Open 9.30-17.30 Mar, Apr &
Oct, 9.30-19.00 May-Sep, 9.30-16.00
Nov-Feb. Closed Sun morning.*

Castell Coch   **H10**
Mid Glamorgan. 6 miles nw of Cardiff. If you
were looking for a slightly blood-curdling
setting for a Bavarian fairy tale you couldn't
go far wrong with this turreted stone dragon.
Originally the 13thC home of the princes of
Powys, traditional allies of the English, it
was rebuilt William Burges in 1875. The
castle was planned in a triangle with round
towers at the corners. It guards the mouth of
Taffs Well Gorge.
*Open 9.30-17.30 daily
Apr & 9.30-19.00
May-Sep 9.30-17.30
Mar & Oct. 9.30-16.00
Nov-Feb. Closed
Sun morning.)*

Castell Coch

Chepstow Castle   **K10**
Chepstow, Gwent. Built on rising ground on
the west bank of the River Wye, it is a
round-shouldered bully full of arrogant
detachment. Begun in 1067 by William
FitzOsbern, Chepstow is one of the mightiest
Norman strongholds in the west. It consists
of a series of courtyards following the line
of the land. There is a hall keep, round
towers and two impressive gatehouses at
front and rear. *Open 9.30-17.30 daily Apr &
9.30-19.00 May-Sep (9.30-17.30 Mar &
Oct. 9.30-16.00 Nov-Feb. Closed Sun
morning.)*

Chepstow Castle

Chirk Castle   J2
*Nr Wrexham, Clwyd. 2 miles from Chirk on
A5.* A 13thC frontier fortress. Rectangular
in plan, it has a round tower at each corner.
In the central square are relics from the
Civil War. The chambers and dining-rooms
inside are richly evocative of the castle's
history. There is a splendid park with fine
ornamental gates by the Davies brothers of
Bersham. *Open 14.00–17.00 Tue, Thur, Sat
& Sun mid Apr–Sep. 11.00–17.00 B. Hols.*

Conwy Castle   F1
Conwy, Gwynedd. Built as a residence as well
as a fortress, it is an elegantly dressed
ruffian with eight massive drum-towers
connected by curtain walls some fifteen feet
thick. An outstanding example of Edward I's
genius for military architecture, it is sited on
broad precipitous rock beside the River
Conwy. Hiding behind it, like a child
behind apron strings, is the walled town.
*Open 9.30–17.30 daily Apr & 9.30–17.00
May–Sep. (9.30–17.30 Mar & Oct. 9.30–
16.00 Nov–Feb. Closed Sun morning.)*

Denbigh Castle   H1
Denbigh, Clwyd. A long, spidery but
handsome ruin. The original Welsh castle
was a timber building on top of a mound.
During Edward I's successful campaign of
1282 it withstood attack for a period, but
after its capture it was replaced by a stone
castle built 1282–1322. It has an impressive
gatehouse. *Open 9.30–17.30 daily Apr &
9.30–19.00 May–Sep. (9.30–17.30 Mar &
Oct. 9.30–16.00 Nov–Feb. Closed Sun
morning.)*

Harlech Castle   E3
Harlech, Gwynedd. Begun in 1283, it was
built by Edward I on a high rock
promontory overlooking what was then an
inlet of sea. Overpowering and impressive,
it was entered over a moat by a stone arch,
and over the drawbridges of an impregnable
barbican. Approximately square in plan it
has round towers at the four corners and a
central gatehouse on the east wall.

Harlech Castle

Laugharne Castle   D9
Laugharne, Dyfed. Wistful and romantic
remains wrestle under a mass of ivy. It is a
late 13thC stone-built castle standing on the
west bank of the River Taf. There was once
a strong round keep consisting of three
storeys, the top storey covered by a pointed
dome rising above the battlements.

Llanstephan Castle   D9
Llanstephan, Dyfed. An impressively
friendly ruin perched on a headland above
this Towy-mouth village. Built in the 12thC
it was captured and re-captured by the
Welsh and the English. It consisted of an
upper ward above the steepest slope, and a
lower ward protected by ditches out in the
ock. *Open any reasonable time.*

Manorbier Castle   C9
Dyfed. 5 miles sse of Pembroke off A4139. A
gentle ad-hoc ruin surrounded by all the
features of a mediaeval community: castle,
church, ponds, mill, dovecote and orchards
wrapped round the feudal seat. Built in the
early 12thC for William de Barri, it has a
series of towers linked by high curtain walls
with a clenched-fisted sort of gatehouse
complete with portcullis. *Open 11.00–18.00
Easter week & daily mid May–Sep.*

Manorbier Castle

Newport Castle   J10
Newport, Gwent. A ruin almost ecclesiastical
in appearance. It was built in 1171 along the
River Usk as part of the Norman Conquest
of the west. Enough of it survived the
Border Wars to be remodelled in the 15thC
during the Wars of the Roses. Cromwell
finally reduced it to ruins. The most
impressive part is the central tower.

Ogmore Castle   G10
3 miles sw of Bridgend, Mid Glamorgan. Once
the 12thC stronghold of the hated William
de Braose, it is now a romantic misfit more at
home with some companionable cottages
along the River Ewenny than with its bull-
necked bully boys of old. *Open 9.30–17.30
Mar, Apr & Oct, 9.30–19.00 May–Sep,
9.30–16.00 Nov–Feb. Closed Sun morning.*

Oystermouth Castle   E10
Mumbles, W. Glamorgan. Built in 1287 on a
hill with a bandstand view, the present ruin
is the second castle constructed on the site.
It was somewhat irregular in plan, with a
gatehouse, an open courtyard and keep, all
connected by high curtain walls without
towers. On the top floor was the chapel, its
piscina and traceried window still preserved.

Pembroke Castle   B9
Pembroke, Dyfed. An imperious custodian of
a rocky ridge above the River Pembroke and
surrounding marshes. Begun in the late
11thC it was an important Norman
stronghold in South Wales. It was later used
as a base for Norman operations in Ireland.
Pembroke was the Parliamentarians' first
major foothold in South Wales during the
Civil War. *Open 10.00–19.00 (Sun 11.00–
18.00) Apr–Sep. 10.00–17.00 (closed Sun)
Oct–Mar.*

Pembroke Castle

Raglan Castle   J9
Raglan, Gwent. Set between wooded slopes
and river valley it is an elegantly aloof giant
built in the old Welsh border district of
Gwent. The machicolated towers in clean,
dressed stone are 15thC. The great Yellow
Tower of Gwent is a fine example of a self-
contained fortified dwelling surrounded by
a moat. *Open 9.30–17.30 daily Apr &
9.30–19.00 May–Sep. (9.30–17.30 Mar &
Oct. 9.30–16.00 Nov–Feb. Closed Sun
morning.)*

Rhuddlan Castle   H1
Rhuddlan, Clwyd. Now a massive and
magnetic ruin, it was begun in 1277 under
Edward I. The castle stands at what was the
lowest fording place for crossing the River
Clwyd and the coastal marshes.
Concentrically planned, it had a square inner
ward with great round towers and gatehouses
at the corners. The ward was protected by
curtain walls and wet and dry moats.
*Open 9.30–17.30 daily Apr & 9.30–19.00
May–Sep. (9.30–17.30 Mar & Oct. 9.30–
16.00 Nov–Feb. Closed Sun morning.)*

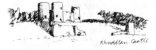

Rhuddlan Castle

Tintern Abbey   J7
Tintern, Gwent. Once a great Cistercian
abbey founded in 1131, it is now an
impressive and bare skeleton, elegant and
intricate like the winter tracery of trees.
Tintern lies in the green fields of a broad
valley at the point where the River Wye
widens. The nave is all silence and green
grass. *Open 9.30–17.30 daily Apr & 9.30–
19.00 May–Sep, (9.30–17.30 Mar–Oct.
9.30–16.00 Nov–Feb. Closed Sun. morning.)*

Valle Crucis Abbey   J2
Nr Llantysilio, Clwyd. With hills framed in
its glassless windows, it is an enviable ruin
sitting in retirement in a secluded and
sheltered site. Built in the great tradition of
the Cistercians, the abbey was founded in
1201. Its choir is said to have rivalled
Salisbury. *Open 9.30–17.30 daily Apr and
9.30–19.00 May–Sep. (9.30–17.30 Mar &
Oct 9.30–16.00 Nov–Feb. Closed Sun
morning.)*

Unusual buildings

Bangor-is-Coed Bridge **J2**
Bangor-is-Coed, Clwyd. A fine 17thC bridge said to have been designed by Inigo Jones.

City Hall **F10**
Swansea, Glamorgan. Designed by Sir Percy Thomas in 1930 with cathedral precision: an elegant symbol of civic dignity. Inside are some murals by Frank Brangwyn.

The Guildhall, Swansea

Conwy Railway Bridge **F1**
Conwy, Gwynedd. Parallel to Telford's bridge, this one was built by Robert Stephenson in 1848. It is of tubular construction in a single span; each of the two tubes is 412 feet long.

Conwy Suspension Bridge **F1**
Conwy, Gwynedd. Built over the River Conwy in 1826 by Telford, it is a suspension bridge with iron chains. Telford designed the towers in castellated form to harmonise with the mediaeval castle.

Derry Ormond Tower **E7**
Llangybi, Dyfed. Standing on high ground to the south of Derry Ormond is a circular column with slit windows. It was built in the 19thC as an eye-stopper.

Holiday cottages **E2**
Portmadog, Gwynedd. Simple, but richly evocative housing, jammed informally together along the water's edge. Built on Portmadog Quay in 1968, the housing was designed by John Phillips.

Housing, Portmadog Quay

Menai Suspension Bridge **E1**
Menai Straits. 2½ miles w of Bangor. It carries the A5 London to Holyhead road and was built when the road was continued to Gwynedd.
Designed by Telford, work on the bridge began in 1820. Although not an original idea it was the largest project of its kind undertaken at that time. The bridge is nearly half a mile in length and has a central span of 579 feet.

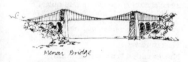

Menai Bridge

Severn Bridge **K10**
Nr Chepstow, Gwent. Designed by Sir Gilbert Roberts, the bridge was opened in 1966. The gateway to Wales, it is an elegant rainbow of steel soaring over the wide Severn. The whole bridge is over two miles in length, and the main bridge is carried on two steel towers 445 feet high.

Ty Hyll **F1**
Betws-y-Coed, Gwynedd. A 15thC building named the 'Ugly House' because of its construction: irregular-shaped stones hurriedly heaped together. At the time, any free man could obtain freehold rights on common land if he could build a fireplace and a chimney, starting at dusk and managing to have the chimney smoking by dawn. The rest of the house could then be finished at leisure.

Houses and gardens

Bodnant **F1**
Denbigh. Gwynedd, 4 miles s of Conwy. A superb terraced garden laid out in 1875 by Henry Pochin in the Italian style and developed by the Lords Aberconway. It is one of the finest gardens in the country. The Pin Mill, originally built in Gloucestershire as a pin factory, stands at one end of a long narrow pool surrounded by smooth green lawns edged with herbaceous borders and faced by an open air theatre. *Open 13.30–16.45 Tue–Thur, Sat & B. Hol. Mon Apr–Oct.*

Cymerau **F4**
Glandyfi, Dyfed. 5 miles sw of Machynlleth. A garden of medium size set in glorious country with splendid views. There is a large collection of flowering shrubs. *Open Sun 14.00–18.00 or by appointment.*

Gwrych Castle **G1**
Abergele, Clwyd. A Gothic fantasy designed by C. A. Busby in 1814. The castellated walls and turrets are pure romance. *Open daily.*

Gwyllt Gardens **E2**
Portmeirion, Gwynedd. 2 miles sw of Penrhyndeudraeth. Twenty miles of woodland walks, wild with rhododendrons, azaleas and sub-tropical species surrounding the fairyland setting of Portmeirion, perched above Cardigan Bay with Snowdon in the background. *Open 10.00–19.00 daily.*

Hafodty **E1**
Bettws Garmon in Snowdonia National Park, Gwynedd. Of particular interest are the Nant Mill Waterfalls where the migration of elvers can be seen from June to August, and salmon can be spotted leaping September to December. There are charming water and rock gardens. *Open dawn to dusk daily.*

Nanteos **F5**
Dyfed. 2½ miles se of Aberystwyth. Set in the shadow of a steeply wooded ridge it is one of the most notable of Georgian manor houses in Wales. Built in 1739, its main block is a sandstone-faced rectangle. Richard Wagner, who visited Nanteos, is said to have composed part of 'Parsifal' here. *Open 13.00–17.30 daily (13.00–22.00 Wed Jun–Sep.).*

Penrhyn Castle **E1**
Gwynedd. 1½ miles e of Bangor. A joyous joke like an elaborate Hollywood Valhalla. A vast marble neo-Norman cliché so absurd that it works. The castle is splendidly sited on a ridge at the end of the Menai Straits. In the state bedroom is the heavily carved oak bed in which Queen Victoria slept when she visited Penrhyn in 1859.

Plas Newydd **E1**
Llanfairpwll, Gwynedd. Built 1800–1810 on the site of an old house. A result of the combined efforts of James Wyatt and Joseph Potter, it is set in civilised parkland against wild views of Snowdonia. Somewhat de-Gothicised in the 1930s, it is basically classic in order and symmetry with a rumbling of romantic fervour. Occupied by H.M.S. Conway, a cadet training school for the Merchant Navy.

Plas Newydd, Llanfairpwll

Powys Castle **J4**
Welshpool, Powys. An aloof and mediaeval house standing like an abrupt red cliff in the landscape. Renovated in the 19thC by Capability Brown it has all the Italianate whims and fancies of an elaborate wedding cake. The state rooms are full of fine furniture, paintings, murals and relics of Clive of India.
The magnificent terraced gardens were completed in the 18thC at immense cost, dropping down in four stages to a lawn. *Open 14.00–18.00 Wed–Sun May–Sep.*

Museums and galleries

Bangor Art Gallery and
Museum of Welsh Antiquities   E1
*Old Canonry, College Road, Bangor,
Gwynedd.* Collections illustrating the history
of North Wales; prehistoric and Roman
antiquities, furniture, textiles and clothing.
Open daily 10.30–16.30. Closed Sun.

Glynn Vivian Art Gallery   F10
Alexandra Road, Swansea, W. Glamorgan.
Exhibits of Swansea porcelain and pottery;
a large collection of pictures with many
Welsh artists represented: Richard Wilson,
Augustus John, Kyffin Williams; bronzes by
Epstein and Barbara Hepworth. *Open daily
9.00–17.30. Closed Sun.*

Merthyr Tydfil Art Gallery
and Museum   H9
*Cyfarthfa Castle, Merthyr Tydfil, Mid
Glamorgan.* A neo-Gothic castle is the
setting for this local museum: relics of the
iron smelting and coal industries, natural
history and antiquities, a replica of a Welsh
kitchen, paintings, Swansea and Nantgarw
china, coins and medals. *Open daily.
14.00–17.00 Sun.*

The Narrow Gauge Railway
Museum   E4
Wharf Station, Tywyn, Gwynedd. Started as
a collection devoted to the old Talyllyn
Railway which was built in the 1860s, the
museum now owns a number of British and
foreign built items. Some of the wagons and
locomotives are over 100 years old. *Open
daily Apr–Oct or by appointment.*

The National Library of Wales   E5
Aberystwyth, Dyfed. One of the six copyright
libraries in Britain. Most of the collection is
related to Wales. There is also a magnificent
set of over 50 drawings by Thomas
Rowlandson. *Open daily. Closed Sun.*

The National Museum of Wales   H10
Cathays Park, Cardiff, S. Glamorgan. The
essence of Wales and the Welsh amassed
under a single roof. Geology, botany,
zoology, archaeology, industry and art are
all represented. Among the prized
possessions are the Dolgellau chalice and
paten and the Dynevor plate. *Open daily.
Closed Sun morning.*

Newport Museum and Art
Gallery   J10
John Frost Square, Newport, Gwent. Many
fine treasures here. Remains from the
Romano-British town of Caerwent, a
collection of Pontypool and Usk japan-ware,
and a superb collection of early English
water-colours. *Open daily. Closed Sun.*

Penrhyn Castle   E1
Bangor, Gwynedd. The Norman-style castle
built of Mona marble 1827-40, holds a fine
collection of over 1,000 dolls from all over
the world; also stuffed birds, animals and
insects, and a locomotive museum, including
rolling stock. *Open 14.00–17.00 Mon, Wed
and Thur Apr, May and Oct. 11.00–17.00
daily Jun–Sep (Closed Sun except 14.00–
18.00 Jul and Aug).*

Plas Newydd Museum   H2
Grapes Hill, Llangollen, Clwyd. A black-and-
white 18th C house, once the home of the
eccentric blue-stockings, the 'Ladies of
Llangollen', and now a museum with some
fine oak carvings and stained glass. *Open
10.30–19.30 Mon–Sat (11.00–16.00 Sun)
May–Sep. By appointment Oct–Apr.*

The Royal Welch Fusiliers   E1
Queen's Tower, Caernarvon Castle, Gwynedd.
The museum presents the history of the
regiment from its foundation in 1689. On
display is the hat ribbon worn by William of
Orange, 1690; officer's mitre cap, 1750;
campaign medals and portraits. *Open
9.30–17.30 daily Apr & 9.30–19.00 May–
Sep. (9.30–17.30 Mar & Oct. 9.30–16.00
Nov–Feb. Closed Sun morning.)*

Welsh Folk Museum   H10
St Fagans, nr Cardiff, S. Glamorgan. Set in
100 acres of woodland, the museum offers
cottages, farms, a woollen mill, chapel,
tollgate house, smithy, barn, cockpit, gipsy
caravan and furnished Tudor mansion, all
beautifully re-erected and preserved. Don't
miss the Gallery of National Culture with
its collections relating to Welsh life and
manners. *Open 10.00–19.00 daily July &
Aug. 10.00–18.00 Apr–Jun & Sep. 10.00–
17.00 Oct–Mar. Closed Sun morning.*

Botanical gardens

Duffryn Gardens   H10
8 miles sw of Cardiff on A48, S. Glamorgan.
Some rare trees and shrubs are included in
the 100 acres of gardens. Interesting
collection in the greenhouses. Parking for
1,000 cars. *Open 10.00–19.00 daily June–Sep.
13.00–19.00 Mar–May and Sat & Sun.*

Zoos, aquaria and aviaries

Cardiff Zoo   South H10
Weycock Rd, Barry, S. Glamorgan. A small
zoo (only eight acres) specialising in big cats
(lions, leopards and pumas). Also bears, sea
lions, monkeys, raccoons, elephants and
parrots. *Open daily.*

The Welsh Mountain Zoo and
Botanic Gardens   G1
Flagstaff Gardens, Colwyn Bay, Clwyd.
Noted especially for its free-flying birds of
prey. Displays are given daily in the summer
of hawks, falcons and vultures. There are
also bears, monkeys, lions, reptiles, Welsh
mountain goats, tropical birds, penguins,
flamingos and an elephant. *Open 10.00–dusk.*

Whitson Zoo   J10
Whitson, nr Newport, Gwent. A small zoo in
the grounds of Whitson Court. There is a
fine aquarium with more than 60 varieties of
tropical fish; wild-fowl; bears and monkeys.
Open daily.

Nature trails & reserves

Devil's Bridge Nature Trail   F5
Dyfed. Start at Hafod Arms Hotel Kiosk.
½ mile. A short but most interesting trail in
one of the best areas in Wales for seeing kites.

The Dinas Nature Trail   F7
*Dyfed. Start clearly signposted from road
from Rhandirmwyn nw of Llandovery to the
new Llyn Brianne Dam.* RSPB Information
Centre and trail on annexe to Gwenffrwd
Reserve. Buzzard, sparrowhawk, raven,
redstart, wood warbler and pied flycatcher,
with dippers on the River Towy and
possibility of kite. *Also public footpath to
Twm Shon Catti's Cave open all year.*

Marloes Sands Nature Trail   A9
*Dyfed. Start at Marloes Sands Car Park,
13 miles sw of Haverfordwest.* 2½ miles,
spectacular scenery and good for grey seals.
Birds include raven and chough, as well as
sea birds offshore. Guide from the West
Wales National Trust, Victoria Place,
Haverfordwest.

Newborough Warren National
Nature Reserve   B2
Newborough Warren, Gwynedd. Off A4080.
The whole area lies to the west, via marked
rights of way. Good all-round bird watching
and particularly good for waders at all
seasons and wildfowl in winter.

Pembrokeshire Seabird
Islands   A9
Among the best-known bird areas in Wales
and well worth visiting.
Ramsey. Daily crossings from the lifeboat
station at St. Justinian, three miles west of
St David's. Permit from boatman. No
advance booking necessary. Self-guiding
route, leaflet and map from Warden. Ideal
for day visits. Breeding birds include Manx
shearwater, auks, buzzard, and chough and
peregrine are usually present. Noted for grey
seals. RSPB Reserve. *Open Apr–Sep.
Skokholm.* Breeding Manx shearwater, storm
petrel, guillemot and razorbill and especially

good for sea watching and for a wide variety of migrants. Further details from West Wales Naturalists' Trust, 4 Victoria Place, Haverfordwest. Accommodation available at the Bird Observatory. No day visits.
Skomer. Boat from Martins Haven. Skomer is equally good for migrants, and its breeding birds include Manx shearwater, storm petrel, fulmar, auks, including puffin, chough. Nature trail, but visitors should first contact the West Wales Naturalists' Trust, as above. National Nature Reserve. *Open daily Apr–Sep.*

Rhosili Nature Trail   D10
W. Glamorgan. 15 miles w of Swansea. Start at Rhosili Car Park. 3 miles; guide from Nature Conservancy, Gower Countryside Centre, Old School Room, Oxwich. Birds include fulmar, guillemot and razorbill.

South Stack Nature Trail   A1
Gwynedd. At w side of Holyhead Island. Guided walk to lighthouse, taking in cliff flora and birds – which include razorbill, guillemot, puffin and kittiwake. Leaflets from the café at South Stack or from Gwynedd Tourist Association centres. *Open mid May–Jul.*

Tregaron Bog Nature Reserve   F6
Nr Tregaron, Dyfed. National nature reserve on the headwaters of the River Teifi, near the tiny town of Tregaron. Its impassable expanse of soft peat preserves in half-fossilised form the history of the Welsh flora since the last ice age.

Bird watching

Brecon Beacons   H8
Powys. Accessible from minor roads from Brecon, Tal-y-bont and Pontsticill, and from A470 nr Storey Arms. This wild mountain area offering in summer buzzard, red grouse, dipper, ring ouzel, wheatear, pied flycatcher and wood warbler and merlin.

Cemlyn Bay   A1
Gwynedd. Nr Tregele on A5025. Owned by the National Trust but readily seen from the track to Trwyn Cemlyn from Plas Cemlyn. Terns are present in the breeding season, while spring and autumn bring migrant waders. Waders and a good selection of wildfowl are present in winter.

Dovey Estuary   F4
Dyfed. An extensive estuary which includes a National Nature Reserve, noted for its winter wildfowl (including small numbers of white-fronted geese) and spring and autumn waders.

Great Ormes Head   North F1
Gwynedd. N along the coast road from Llandudno. This popular tourist site is very good for breeding seabirds – fulmar, kittiwake, razorbill, guillemot and puffin – and ravens are commonly seen. In addition it can be good for migrant seabirds and other species in autumn.

Milford Haven   B9
Dyfed. This is a large tidal complex with perhaps a dozen good birdwatching areas. Particularly good spots are Dale Roads (off Dale, B4327 from Haverfordwest); Hook (A4076 from Haverfordwest, left at Merlin's Bridge and left again after three miles); Landshipping Quay (via lanes from Cross Hands, A4075); Cosheston Pill (from Waterloo ne of Pembroke); and Angle Bay (footpath from B4320 at Angle).
The area is noted for passage waders and a good variety of winter waders and wildfowl, and in addition St Ann's Head is good for seabirds, raven and chough.

Snowdonia   F1
Gwynedd. Among many good areas to explore: Capel Curig (entrance opposite Corwen Hotel) for typical woodland species; the moors west of Bethesda for moorland birds; Cwm Idwal, in the Ogwen Valley, for high ground species.
Choughs breed in a few slate quarries and other summer birds likely to be seen include buzzard, red grouse, golden plover, raven, dipper, grey wagtail, wheatear, redstart, ring ouzel and pied flycatcher.

Fossil hunting

Visit the local museum. Its fossil collection usually states where individual fossils have been found. When visiting quarries always seek permission to enter if they look privately owned or worked. Be careful of falls of rock.

Dyfed
Much of the county is made up of Silurian rocks, and Llandoverian graptolites may be found, but are not common throughout. The type-area of the Llandeilo stage of the Ordovician lies in central Carmarthen where flagstones give a shelly fauna including trilobites around Llandeilo; also the Caradocian Mydrim Limestone and Birdshill Limestone near Llandeilo contain trilobites and brachiopods. Similar fossil fauna may be found in the Silurian rocks of the Llandovery stage around Llandovery and other localities in the Towy Valley.
The early Palaeozoic Cambrian rocks in the area around St David's and especially Solva Harbour contain a variety of trilobites. Access to the cliffs is difficult in many places. At Abereiddy Bay graptolites are very common in the shales. The coast around Tenby is of carboniferous limestone, as is much of the peninsula south of Milford Haven.

Glamorgan
The county is mainly of carboniferous rock. The lower carboniferous limestone is fossiliferous and can be seen in the cliffs of the Gower Peninsula and in quarries around Bridgend. The upper carboniferous is represented by the coal measures of the valleys where some fossil plants may be found. In the south fossiliferous Rhaetic and Lias are well exposed at Barry, Penarth and Lavernock with many fossil ammonites and bivalves.

North Wales
Not a highly fossiliferous area – many places have thick volcanic ash and lava deposits of Ordovician age, especially around Snowdonia. Much of Gwynedd and the Lleyn is made up of Pre-Cambrian rocks. The Cambrian Menevian beds contain many trilobites and may be seen around St Tudwal's Point on the Lleyn Peninsula. The Cambrian forms much of the upland area around Harlech; some of the beds contain fossils. The Ordovician is widespread and contains fossiliferous beds in places: a shelly limestone occurs around Arenig, and in localities around Bala. The Berwyns have many shales and slates which yield graptolites.
Silurian Wenlock shales occur in the Welshpool district with characteristic assemblages of trilobites, brachiopods and bivalves.
Fossiliferous carboniferous limestone forms a high escarpment east of Llangollen, which extends northwards into Clwyd through the Vale of Clwyd. Near Newmarket and Prestatyn are fossil shell-reefs with abundant brachiopods. The coal measures extend under the Triassic sandstone and are mined in Clwyd.

Powys
Mainly Devonian old red sandstone, normally unfossiliferous, but early fishes have been found.
Trilobites, brachiopods and bivalves can be found in the Ordovician Llandeilo beds. They may be collected in the Builth area, as can a similar assemblage from the Upper Silurian Ludlow beds.

Forests

There are remnants of ancient oak forests in some of the valleys still. They are worth looking out for; very old oaks clinging to steep hillsides and covered with silver grey lichen. They are hundreds of years old and irreplaceable – unfortunately many are being cut down.
Much of the wild open and natural countryside of the hills and mountains of Wales is fast losing its character as vast

areas are drained and planted with quick growing catch-crops of conifers. They kill the view, kill the wild environment, and lay like a dark cloud on previously lovely open hills. If allowed to continue this could destroy all the distinctive quality of the Welsh hills.

Coed-y-Brenin   F3
Gwynedd. North of the little stone town of Dolgellau in Gwynedd the tall woods of Coed-y-Brenin, or Forest of the King, rise on either side of the rushing River Mawddach.

Dyfi Valley and Forests   F5
Travelling eastwards up the broad Dyfi (or Dovey) Estuary, from Aberdyfi (Aberdovey) or Aberystwyth on the coast, you will see a multi-coloured panorama of woodlands of oak and birch, pine and larch, beech, spruce or alder, all the way to Machynlleth.

Gwydyr Forest   F1
In the Conwy Valley, centred on Betws-y-Coed, this forest of pine, larch, spruce, Douglas fir and oak has been created by the National Forestry Commission since 1920. Clothing the rugged Snowdonian foothills, it runs far up the Llugwy Valley to Capel Curig, and the Lledr Gorge to Dolwyddelan; outliers rise on bluffs far down the Conwy Valley.

Hills & mountains

The Berwyns   H2
Marching south-west from Clwyd into Gwynedd and Powys, between the valleys of the Dee and the Severn, the Berwyn range forms a wild thinly-peopled ridge of moorlands and sheep walks. Though 25 miles long, five miles wide and 2,700 feet high, they lack distinct peaks.

Black Mountains   F8
Confusingly, South Wales has two ranges both called Black Mountains or Mynydd Du. One in Dyfed, south-east of Llandovery, is a huge sheep walk interspersed with scattered hill farms, between the Towy and Tawe valleys. On the Herefordshire border, between the towns of Brecon, in Powys, and Abergavenny, in Gwent, the eastern Black Mountains rise in wilder seclusion. You can explore deep valleys, with oaks and sprucewoods running far into 2,500-foot hill ranges, where farmers still ride sturdy Welsh ponies as their best means of transport.

Brecon Beacons   H8
Powys. In the south of Powys these sweeping hills, now a National Park, rise to heights around 2,600 feet. A huge, unfenced sheepwalk, they provide grand riding and walking country, with Brecon town as a good centre.

Cadair Idris   F4
The name of this fine mountain means the chair or throne of Idris, a legendary Welsh king. It rises in regal splendour to a height of 2,927 feet, just south of Dolgellau. Glaciers left a deep, rock-bound hidden lake called Llyn Cau, 'lake of the cauldron', hidden on its south flank.

The Cambrian Mountains
Lie between Cader Idris and the Brecon Beacons – approximately 50 miles long by 10–12 miles wide. This is some of the most remote upland country of southern Wales. There are large tracts with no roads which cross it. It is inhabited by sheep and buzzards and it is always windy and beautiful – except where the dreaded conifers have been planted to blanket the hills. A popular drive across it is the mountain road from Rhayader to Devils Bridge. The steep (sometimes 1 in 3) and winding narrow road from Tregaron to Abergwesyn is also lovely but getting more filled with cars. These hills are best seen on foot – totally away from it all.

Clwyd Hills   H1
Clwyd. A long spine of hills running north-west parallel to the Dee Estuary and the Vale of Clwyd, and providing wide views

over both. The highest point, 1,820 feet, is Moel Fammau, the 'mother mountain', so named from the breast-like shape of its summit.

The Glyders   F1
This precipitous Snowdonian range runs inland from the Gwynedd coast, near Bangor, between the rugged Llanberis and Nant Ffrancon Passes. It is a famous ridge for skilled rock climbers though its highest point, Glyder Fawr at 3,279 feet, can be reached by stiff walking routes.

Moel Siabod   F2
The shapely cone of this isolated, though minor, mountain rises to 2,860 feet, and is constantly in view from most parts of central Snowdonia. An open sheep-walk, snow-capped for much of each winter, Moel Siabod is easily climbed by a ridge-track from either Capel Curig or Dolwyddelan.

Plynlimon   F5
Called in Welsh *Pumlimon*, from its five lumpy hilltops, this remote rounded hill range raises its sheep-grazed slopes to 2,466 feet, on the borders of Dyfed and Powys in mid-Wales. From the Eisteddfa Gurig summit on the Llangurig-Aberystwyth main road, A44, you can stroll to its far top, viewing on your way the sources of the Tarenig, Wye, Rheidol, Clywedog and mighty Severn rivers, and half the Welsh hilltops besides.

Preseli Mountains   C8
Dyfed. Inland from the little port of Fishguard, the strange Preseli Mountains stand as an irregular ridge, 1,760 feet high, with heather-clad rocky peaks tinged blue by the prevailing clouds blown off the Irish Sea. They are famous in Britain's archaeological history because the builders of Stonehenge quarried stone here, of peculiar bluish-grey rock, and transported them by land and waterways to the heart of the Wiltshire Downs.

Snowdon   E2
The highest and steepest mountain in England and Wales, 3,560 feet in altitude. Today Snowdon is easily ascended from Llanberis by a broad gently sloping track, and in summer even by its unique mountain railway. Away from the well-used paths, the cliffs should be left to skilled rock-climbers. Beware of sudden mists, and ice-bound rock surfaces in winter.

The Sugar Loaf   J8
This odd-shaped, aptly-named hill rises to 1,956 feet, north-west of the Gwent town of Abergavenny. There are good views from its summit over Gwent, Powys and Herefordshire.

Valleys

Conwy Valley   F1
Enfolded between the Snowdonian mountains and the Clwyd hills, the level Conwy Valley runs north from Betws-y-Coed's woodlands, past Llanrwst to the river's broad tide-washed estuary at Conwy town.

Glamorgan Coalfield   G9
Definitely *not* tourist country. The busy coalfields of 'the valleys' (including the famous Rhondda Valley) in Glamorgan and western Gwent are only likely to attract students of industry and social change. Mines, roads, and factories are crowded into every valley, thick with terraced houses, pubs and chapels.

Rhondda Valley   G9
Glamorgan. Cwm Rhondda, as the Welsh call this narrow, steep and winding dale, is typical of a score of mining and industrial valleys that run deep into the uplands of Glamorgan and Gwent.
In Victorian days men found abundant coal both beneath the valley bottom and in the very flanks of these same hills. Mines and steelworks sprang up, linked by a road and a railway. The later depression brought a sea of despair and despondency.

Severn Valley
Powys. This is in effect the Welsh share of the long valley of the Severn, which completes its course in England.

Snowdonia National Park   **E2**
This big conservation region includes a large part of Gwynedd. All the highest Welsh peaks of the Snowdon range come within it, as well as the surprisingly beautiful valleys of the Conwy, Glaslyn, Mawddach and Dyfi rivers, and the great Gwydyr Forest, centred on Betws-y-Coed.

Towy Valley   **D8**
Rural Wales at its best, the warm and fertile vale of the lower Towy sweeps down past Llandovery south-west to Carmarthen town, legendary seat of that powerful Celtic wizard, Merlin.

Lakes & bogs

Bala Lake   **G3**
Gwynedd. Llyn Tegid, or Bala Lake, is four miles long and half a mile wide. Its calm waters, which hold many trout and attract anglers, are surrounded by pastoral farms in a broad vale. A dozen swift hill streams feed it, and the lake discharges its overflow over a barrage to control floods at the start of the great River Dee.

Borth Bog   **F5**
Dyfed. Called Cors Fochno, meaning 'the mire', this remarkable marsh of rush, sedge, and salt-loving plants lies at sea level, in a triangle of land between the estuary of the River Dovey, the long sandspit where Borth faces the open sea, and the inland foothills of the Plynlimon range. Three miles long by one mile wide, Borth Bog is easily reached by the A487 Aberystwyth-Machynlleth road on the east, or the railway on the west. Since nobody can drain it, it remains a nature reserve, the haunt of rare marsh plants, nesting gulls and shelducks.

Clwyd Moors   **G2**
Clwyd. Between the Conwy Valley and the Vale of Clwyd, crossed by the high road A543 from Denbigh to Pentre Foelas, lies the expanse of wild moorland, strangely called in Welsh the Mynydd Hiraethog, or 'mountains of yearning'. Here stands the huge, ugly and highly productive national Forest of Clocaenog, largely of spruce trees, and the broad Alwen Reservoir that supplies water to Birkenhead.

Newborough Warren   **B2**
Gwynedd. At the south-western corner of Anglesey wind and tide have thrown up a sand-bank, called Aber Menai Point, which holds back the tides of the Menai Straits and fresh water flowing seaward from central Gwynedd. The resulting marshland has become the home of seabirds.
Rare plants include the yellow horned poppy and the shiny, blue-flowered sea holly. Now carefully preserved as a Nature Conservancy reserve, the Warren can be viewed from the track towards Llanddwyn Island; car park nearby.

Snowdonian Lakes   **F1**
Gwynedd. During the ice ages, great glaciers gouged out deep basins in the mountains of what is now Snowdonia National Park; these hollows filled with water when the last ice melted.
The loveliest are Llyn Gwynant and Llyn Dinas on the Betws-y-Coed to Beddgelert road, A498. Llyn Ogwen on the Bangor road, and Llyn Peris on the Caernarvon road, have stonier shores in wilder surroundings, while Llyn Llydaw stands below Snowdon's summit crags.

Trawsfynydd Lake   **F3**
Gwynedd. The name means 'beyond the mountains' – it is a huge man-made reservoir on the A487 road from Porthmadog to Dolgellau. Set high on bleak moors, it serves as a cooling tank for a nuclear power station, and a source of hydro-electric power.

Tregaron Bog   **F6**
Dyfed. Known in Welsh as Gors Goch Glan Teifi, or 'red bog of the Vale of Teifi', Tregaron Bog lies on a flat plain, 500 feet above sea level, beside the B4343 by-road north of Tregaron town. Here the River Teifi wanders through an impassable peat bog, two miles long by one mile across. The bog is called 'red' because of the orange-brown colour of its sedges, marsh grasses, and heather. Now preserved by the Nature Conservancy for its unique flora and fauna, and the fact that pollen grains preserved in the peat reveal the history of many thousands of years of vegetation of mid-Wales.

Rivers

Conwy   **F1**
Rising high on the Gwynedd moors, this river plunges over the rock-girt Conwy Falls near Betws-y-Coed, and then meanders over a flat flood plain past Llanrwst to Conwy town.

Dee   **G2**
The Welsh Dee begins as tributary streams of Llyn Tegid or Bala Lake, four miles long and nearly one mile wide, west of Bala town in Merioneth.
Flowing through a rocky cleft, beside the A5 London-Holyhead road from Corwen, past Llangollen to Ruabon, it then winds north over the flat Cheshire Plain to the walled frontier town of Chester.

Gwynedd Rivers   **F3**
The Mawddach follows a deep forest-clad valley south to Dolgellau, then turns west as a grand tree-lined estuary broadening towards the sea at Barmouth. Farther south it is matched by the even finer Dyfi (or Dovey) which runs through farmlands to Machynlleth, then follows a broad sandy estuary to Aberdyfi (Aberdovey).

Severn   **K10**
The Severn, so-named from the original Welsh Afon Hafren, is Britain's longest river. Rising high on Plynlimon Mountain, it runs for 220 miles to the sea below Gloucester. The upper course past Llanidloes and Newtown in Gwent runs through a long narrow forested gorge. Eight miles north-east of Newtown it enters a broad, well farmed valley and winds slowly north-west past Welshpool towards Shrewsbury, beyond the English border.

Towy   **F8**
Rising on remote uplands north of Llandovery it winds through a broad vale past Carmarthen town to its wide estuary, where coracle fishermen still net salmon from their quaint cockleshell craft.

Usk   **H8**
Powys and eastern Gwent hold the crystal-clear Usk, a salmon river with a perpetually lovely course from Brecon past Abergavenny and Usk town. The river ends at the Newport docks on the Bristol Channel.

Wye   **H7**
Rising from a little spring on Plynlimon, the Wye takes a tortuous course of 130 miles south towards the Bristol Channel. Wye's upper course past Llangurig and Builth Wells to the Herefordshire border at Hay is exceptionally beautiful. It ends its course in a magnificent limestone gorge between Tintern and Chepstow.

Ystwyth and Rheidol   **E5**
Dyfed holds the twin rivers Ystwyth and Rheidol, each with impressive gorges hidden amid oaks, woods and boggy moors; they unite at the tiny harbour of Aberystwyth.

Canals

The Llangollen Canal (west end) H2
Traverses mountainous country for part of the way. It has one of the best-known canal aqueducts in Britain – Telford's Pontcysyllte Aqueduct. Completed in 1805 this tremendous structure carries the canal across the valley of the river Dee in a narrow cast-iron trough supported on

eighteen brick pillars. It is over 1,000 feet long, and 127 feet high.

The Monmouthshire and Brecon Canal — H8

One of the most beautiful canals in the country, it runs for about 33 miles from Brecon to Pontypool, passing through the spectacular scenery of the Brecon Beacons National Park. The canal creeps along the sides of mountains, overhung by trees and itself overlooking the steep slopes of the Usk Valley. There are boats to hire at various points along the way, whilst its excellent towpath is ideal for walking.
Things to see: there are six locks on the canal, most of them grouped at Llangynidr. There is also a short tunnel by the road at Ashford, and a three-arched aqueduct over the Usk at Brynich. Picturesque bascule-type lift bridges may be seen at Talybont and elsewhere.

Archaeology

Bryn-Celli-Ddu — B2

Nr Menai Bridge, Gwynedd. A well preserved example of a stone-built circular-chambered cairn of Neolithic date. Unlike earthen barrows, these cairns had stone-built chambers and access passages, and must have been used over a period of time, as family or group graves. *Open 9.30–17.30 Mar, Apr & Oct. 9.30–19.00 May-Sep. 9.30–16.00 Nov-Feb. Closed Sun morning.*

Caer Gybi — A1

Holyhead, Gwynedd. The 4thC fort at Caer Gybi is unique in Roman Britain, a beach-head fortification for ship landings connected with fleet activity. *Open any reasonable time.*

Caerleon — J10

Nr Newport, Gwent. Roman Isca, one of the three permanent legionary fortresses of Britain, occupied by the II Augusta Legion. The barrack blocks in the western corner of the fortress are laid out in Prysg Field, long narrow buildings containing small rooms for the men with a verandah running along one side, and a larger block at the end with more spacious quarters for a centurion. Remains of interesting amphitheatre.
Open 9.30–17.30 daily Apr & 9.30–19.00 May-Sep. (9.30–17.30 Mar & Oct. 9.30–16.00 Nov-Feb. Closed Sun morning).

Caernarvon — E1

Gwynedd. Roman Segontium; strategically sited to cover the approaches to Anglesey, the fort at Caernarvon held a squadron of auxiliary soldiers. Approximately two-thirds of the fort is now visible. The site museum houses excavation finds. *Town walls open any reasonable time.*

Caerwent Roman Site and Walls — K10

Caerwent, Gwent. Roman Venta Silurum, the tribal capital of the Silures of south-east Wales. The single-arched north gate is well preserved, and the blocked south gate is also visible, but only fragments of the west and east gates survive.
The foundations of a courtyard house, and of a combined house and shop with a forge, are laid out in Pound Lane. The church porch has two inscribed stones. *Open any reasonable time.*

Carneddau Hengwm — E3

Nr Barmouth, Gwynedd. An unusual group of long mounds that have eluded precise interpretation, and whose date is still uncertain. They possibly belong to a local type of Neolithic chambered long barrow.

Din Lligwy Ancient Village — B1

Penrhos Lligwy, Gwynedd. The finest of the enclosed settlement sites characteristic of north-west Wales in the later Roman period, Din Lligwy was occupied during the 4thC. It consists of a polygonal walled enclosure containing rectangular buildings, with two circular huts about 22 feet across. *Open any reasonable time.*

Moel Hiraddug — H1

Dyserth, Clwyd. A large iron age hill fort with multiple bank and ditch defences, at the eastern end of a hill fort system running along the coast and down the Clwydian Range. Other large forts can be seen at Foel Fenlli (between Mold and Ruthin), Pen y Cloddiau, and Pen y Corddyn (Penmaenmawr), and smaller ones with a similar complex defensive system at Moel y Gaer (Ruthin), Moel y Gaer (near St Asaph), and Parc y Meirch, Dinorben (near Abergele).

Offa's Dyke

Stretching across Clwyd, Shropshire, Powys, Herefordshire and the Gwent-Gloucestershire border, the great bank and ditch earthwork was constructed by Offa King of Mercia in the late 8thC. It is not continuous, making use of water obstacles along the course of the middle Severn and the Lower Wye. The northern section is doubled on the eastern side by Wat's Dyke, crossing Clwyd and Shropshire.

St David's Head — A8

Nr St David's, Dyfed. Dyfed has a group of iron age forts built to defend coastal promontories. The best are those at St David's Head and at Castell Penpleidian, St David's, which have multiple defensive banks; others can be seen at Castell Heinif, St David's Head, and Nab Head, St Bride's, on St Anne's Head.

Tre'r Ceiri — D2

Nr Llanaelhaearn, Gwynedd. An iron age hill fort with a single defensive bank. Inside are numerous huts, suggesting permanent settlement rather than the usual temporary defensive use of hill forts. *Open any reasonable time.*

Tinkinswood Burial Chamber — H10

St Nicholas, S. Glamorgan. A Neolithic chambered long barrow, constructed of stone, with an access gallery. These cairns were probably intended as tombs for a group or family. *Open any reasonable time.*

Footpaths & ancient ways

Offa's Dyke Path — K10

From Sedbury Cliffs to Prestatyn the path covers the 168-mile length of Wales and Gwent. For 60 miles it coincides with the bank and ditch construction built by Offa King of Mercia in the 8thC.
Starting from the Severn Bridge the path continues beside the banks of the Wye, across the Gwent countryside dotted with tiny villages, to the eastern slopes of the Black Mountains, where the path climbs steeply along the ridge to Hay-on-Wye. Following the dyke from Kington to Knighton the uplands and valleys of the border country give way to the woodlands of Lymore and Leighton Parks, and beyond to the heights of Long Mountain.
North beyond Llanymynech there are views of Oswestry and the Shropshire Plain to the east. Across the River Dee the path follows the escarpment of the Clwydian Range leading to Prestatyn and the sea, with broad views of Snowdonia and the hills to the west.

The Pembrokeshire Coastal Path — C9

The first long distance footpath to be opened in Wales, it runs along the coast for 170 miles from Amroth in the south of Dyfed to St Dogmaels in the north.
The path meanders around bays and coves, and over cliff tops, with dunes, long stretches of beach and wild surf in view. On the Dale Peninsula the islands of Skokholm and Skomer are in sight, where migrants and breeding birds are protected on the nature reserve. Following the broad sweep of St Bride's Bay to St David's Head, the route passes Newgale Sands, with its pebble beach. Not far away is St David's, the birthplace of the patron saint of Wales. On to Strumble Head with its lighthouse and broad views along the coast. North of Fishguard the path climbs eastwards over Dinas Head to the seaside resort of Newport. Round Cemaes Head and St Dogmaels lies just beyond, on the River Teifi.

Regional sports

Canoeing   F1
The Dee at Llangollen is a favourite white water course for canoeists. Competitions are held there mainly in the autumn. There is lake canoeing at Mymbyr Lakes near Capel Curig and Llanberis Lakes. The rivers Usk and Wye in the south can provide interesting sport. Canoes can be hired on the beaches at Criccieth and Llanbedrog. Experienced canoeists can enjoy canoe surfing near Abersoch.

Caving   G9
In the Vale of Neath below the Craig-y-Llyn moors in Glamorgan there are waterfalls and caving holes with miles of underground passages and lakes, some open to the public.

Climbing and hill walking   H8
From the Brecon Beacons in the south, up the rocky spine of the Cambrian Mountains to Snowdonia in the north, Wales offers much to the walker and climber. Pen y Fan at 2,906 feet, the summit of the Brecon Beacons, is a bleak and imposing challenge to the mountaineer; but for a real challenge the empty vastness of Snowdonia takes some beating.
The chief centres in Snowdonia are rock faces at Llanberis Pass and Nant Ffrancon Pass. Plas y Brenin, the National Mountaineering Centre, is at Capel Curig. Mighty Snowdon at 3,560 feet dominates the area, while slightly further south the beautifully named Cadair Idris at 2,927 feet lies waiting for experienced climbers.

Coracle racing   C7
The coracle is a primitive boat made of animal skins stretched over a light wood framework. It is still used by fishermen on the River Teifi, and at Cilgerran in Dyfed every August there is a traditional race down the river.

Fishing   F1
Wales was made for the fisherman, with its excellent sea angling, game and coarse fishing.
Coarse Fishing. There is perch in Lake Trawsfynydd, bream in the lower Dee River, roach in Bala Lake, and pike in Lake Langorse in the Brecon Beacons. Sea and coarse fishing can be combined at Bosherston Lakes in Dyfed. Fish for tench in the lakes and, just over the sand dunes, in the sea for good bass, and rock fishing for tope.
Game Fishing. Particularly memorable along the rivers Usk, Wye and Severn. Further north from the River Towy at Ferryside to the River Dwryd of Gwynedd, sport is also good. There are plenty of hotels with their own private stretches of water open to residents and non-residents. Most mountain tarns and streams hold small but delicious brown trout.
Sea Fishing. At Lleiniog, Beaumaris, blow holes betray monster rag; there is crab in the weed at Port Dinorwic, and plentiful brown lug at Conwy Morfa. On the mid-Wales coast you will save yourself a lot of nugatory work by consulting the locals about bait. In the south at Milford Haven there's good lug, but you have to dig for it. Razor fish are plentiful at Kilpaison Angle.

Rugby Union   H10
Its a national sport. On the banks of the River Taff near the centre of Cardiff is Cardiff Arms Park, the home and capital of Welsh Rugby. There is nothing more thrilling when late in the second half, with Wales winning, the crowd breaks out spontaneously into the Welsh national anthem, and even if you aren't Welsh you will find your emotions fully engaged. This excess of emotion and enthusiasm resounds around the valleys of South Wales as the teams from Maesteg, Llanelli and other valleys battle it out on Saturday afternoons. If you get the opportunity, watch one of the valley games.

Surfing   E10
Apart from Cornwall, Wales is the only part of Britain offering all year round surfing. The M4 Motorway and the good main road through to Swansea have made the Gower Peninsula a surfing Mecca for Londoners.

One of the best beaches is Langland Bay, which is patrolled by a lifeguard. For holiday makers in the north, Gwynedd offers many good beaches. Try Whistling Sands (Porth Oer).

Festivals

Festivals
For information and tickets for festivals go to the local information centre or ticket agent.

International Music Eisteddfod   H2
Llangollen, Clwyd. 10,000 competitors converge on Llangollen every year from all over the world. A special event is the folk dancing and singing. Tremendously popular. *Early Jul.*

National Drama Festival   B2
Llangefni, Gwynedd. Devoted to presenting Welsh plays by Welsh authors in the Welsh language. An interesting experience – even if you can't understand the language. *Early Oct.*

Royal National Eisteddfod
Held alternately in north and south Wales in various centres every year. It is a celebration of Wales and the Welsh language with music, Pennillion singing and folk dancing. Special events include the crowning of the Bard ceremony, chairing of the Bard and a day of choral music. The bardic ceremonies date back to the Druids. *Early Aug.*

Fun things

Mari Lwyd Mummers   G10
Llangynwyd, Mid Glamorgan. Wales is surprisingly short of folklore traditions. There is of course the great National Eisteddfod, but the Mari Lwyd (Holy Mary) Mummers seem to be one of the few to survive. The mummers appear in fantastic dress, the leader wearing a horse's skull decorated with ribbons. They march round the town singing their traditional songs, stopping at certain houses where they are offered hospitality. The event takes place on the 31st December each year.

Narrow Gauge Railways
Railways came early to Wales, the Ffestiniog was opened in 1836 just eleven years after the Stockton and Darlington. Because of the hilly nature of the land most of the early railways were built to a narrow gauge of approximately two feet. The quaint steam locomotives with antique coaches running through glorious countryside make them tremendous fun. Wales Tourist Board publishes 'The Great Little Trains of Wales', free from High Street, Llandaff, Cardiff.

The Ffestiniog Railway   E2
Porthmadog, Gwynedd. The railway runs for ten miles up the renowned Vale of Ffestiniog to a temporary terminus at Dduallt on the shoulders of Moelwyn Mawr (2,527 feet). Once a small mineral railway, it nevertheless introduced many innovations which were later copied by the bigger standard gauge lines. First in the world to use articulated steam locomotives, still in use today, it pioneered the use of iron-framed coaches. The original pair dating from 1875 are still going strong. The round trip takes about two hours. *Open daily Mar–Nov. Weekends only Nov–Dec & Feb–Mar. Tel 2384.*

The Talyllyn Railway   E4
Tywyn, Gwynedd. This was the first railway in Britain to be saved from extinction by volunteers. The line climbs for six and a half miles up the side slope of the Fathew Valley to Dolgoch, with its three magnificent waterfalls in a wooded gorge. The round trip takes about two hours, unless you make a day of it and have a picnic lunch there. *Open daily Apr–Oct. Tel 71 0472.*

The Vale of Rheidol Railway **E5**
Aberystwyth, Dyfed. Runs twelve miles up
the valley to the famous Devil's Bridge (a trio
of bridges over the River Rheidol Falls).
The only British Rail steam-operated line
now left. The return trip takes two and a half
to three hours depending on the time of day.
Open daily late Apr–Oct. Also various days
throughout Apr. Tel Aberystwyth 2377.

Hotels

The following indicates the price range of a
single room per night:
£   inexpensive
££ medium priced
£££ expensive

Abergwesyn Powys **G7**
*Llwynderw Hotel, nr Llanwrtyd Wells. Tel
Llanwrtyd Wells 238.* Situated in the heart
of Wales, this is an excellent centre for
walkers. Good food. *££. No children
under 10.*

Aberystwyth Dyfed **E5**
Conrah Country Hotel. Tel 7941. Offers good
views and an attractive interior. *££.*

Caerleon Gwent **J10**
Priory Hotel, High St. Tel 421241. An old
building with a 15thC stained glass window,
a Regency dining room and a chandeliered
residents' lounge with Edwardian furniture.
££.

Cardiff S. Glamorgan **H10**
Royal Hotel, St Mary St. Tel 23321. A
'grand' hotel with a splendid staircase rising
from the foyer. *££.*

Cardigan Dyfed **C7**
Cliff Hotel, Gwbert-on Sea. Tel 3241.
Relaxing with splendid views; situated high
above Cardigan Bay. *£.*

Carmarthen Dyfed **F**
*Ivy Bush Royal Hotel, Spilman St.
Tel 5111.* This old but modernised and
extended coaching inn has a fine view over
the Carmarthen Valley. Good food. *££.*

Corwen Gwynedd **H2**
*Owain Glyndwr Hotel, The Square.
Tel 2115.* A former monastic hospice and
coaching house, this friendly inn offers
fishing, shooting and impromptu singing
among its amenities. *£.*

Llandrindod Wells Powys **H6**
Glen Usk Hotel. Tel 2085. A gabled hotel in
the centre of the town. Some bedrooms
overlook the pleasant gardens. *£. Closed
Jan–Apr.*

Llandudno Gwynedd North **E1**
*Bodysgallen Hall, on B5151 from Llandudno.
Tel Deganwy 83130.* A well-restored
Elizabethan-Jacobean building offering a
peaceful retreat in elegant surroundings. *££.
No children under 12, no dogs.*

Maenan Gwynedd **F1**
*Maenan Abbey Hotel, nr Llanrwst. Tel
Dolgarrog 247.* This 19thC granite building
stands on the site of a monastery destroyed
by Henry VIII. Rough shooting in over
300 acres and fishing available. *£.*

Monmouth Gwent **K9**
Beaufort Arms, Agincourt Sq. Tel 2411. An
old 18thC coaching inn with a Georgian
façade. Good base for touring Wye Valley. *£.*

Nantgwynant Gwynedd **E1**
Pen-y-Gwryd. Tel Llanberis 211. Situated in
the Snowdonia National Park, this is the
centre from which the 1953 Everest
climbers were trained. Simple comforts. *£.*

Penmaenpool Gwynedd **F3**
*George III Hotel, nr Dolgellau. Tel Dolgellau
422525.* A 300-year-old hotel with beamed
bar and lounge. Good centre for
pony-trekking. *£.*

Penrhyndeudraeth Gwynedd **E2**
Hotel Portmeirion. Tel 228. If
you were to allow yourself one more luxury
in life this is it. A carefree weekend in a
resplendent background of rich antiques.
You can also stay in one of the picturesquely
sited cottages which are annexes of the main
hotel. *£££. Closed Nov–Christmas &
Jan–Easter.*

Porthcawl Mid Glamorgan **F10**
Seabank Hotel, The Esplanade. Tel 2261. A
white sea-front hotel with a Spanish-style
bar and grill room. Swimming pool and
tennis. *££.*

Pumpsaint Dyfed **F7**
Dolaucothi Arms, nr Llanwrda. Tel 204. An
oak-beamed, white fronted coaching inn.
Simple but friendly. Private fishing. *£.*

Ruthin Clwyd **H1**
Ruthin Castle Hotel. Tel 2664. Built on the
ruins of a 13thC castle and set in 30 acres of
parkland. Mediaeval banquets are held six
nights a week. Log fires in some public
rooms. *££.*

Tenby Dyfed **C9**
*Royal Gate House Hotel, White Lion St.
Tel 2255.* A sea-front hotel overlooking the
beach and the bay. Popular basement grill.
££.

Usk Gwent **H8**
Three Salmons Hotel. Tel 2133. A well-
restored 17thC hotel which houses an
antique shop and offers good salmon and
trout fishing. *£.*

Regional food & drink

Laverbread
A popular delicacy made of edible seaweed.
An unattractive treat to the uninitiated!
Sold in local markets, often mixed with
oatmeal and served fried in butter or bacon
fat.

Soups
Leek soup, Cawl Cennin, is one of the
traditions of Wales. Like Welsh Cawl it is a
winter soup, the latter being akin to
Pot-au-Feu and becoming increasingly
available with the resurgence of interest in
Welsh food.

Welsh cakes
Called griddle scones, the Welsh version of
the scone, but cooked on a griddle pan rather
than baked.

Restaurants

£   inexpensive
££ medium priced
£££ expensive

Erbistock Clwyd **J2**
Boat Inn. Tel Overton-on-Dee 243. 16thC
inn. British food. Local produce. *LD. ££.
Book D.*

Llandewi Skirrid Gwent **J9**
Walnut Tree Inn. Tel Abergavenny 2797.
Pub with outstanding Italian food. Book
well ahead for restaurant, or eat the same
food in the bar.
LD. Closed Sun. ££. Book.

Newport Dyfed **C7**
Pantry Restaurant, Market St. Tel 420.
Outstanding cooking. Mainly French, some
English. *D. Closed Sun & Mon. ££. Book.*

Penarth S. Glamorgan **H10**
Caprice, The Esplanade. Tel 702424. This
seaside restaurant has a good selection of
English and international dishes. *LD.
Closed Sun. ££.*

Penrhyndeudraeth Gwynedd **E2**
Hotel Portmeirion. Tel 228. Hotel on the
estuary in Clough Williams-Ellis's
Italianate village. Anglo-French cooking
with a Welsh accent. *££. Book.*

Rhydwyn Gwynedd **A1**
*Lobster Pot, Church Bay, Holyhead. Tel
Llanfaethlu 241.* Busy little cafe. Local fish
and lobster. Steak and chips too. *LD. Closed
Sun. ££.*

Swansea W. Glamorgan **F10**
Drangway, 66 Wind St. Tel 461397. Real
Welsh traditional dishes served in a neat and
modern dining-room. Try the laverbread
(seaweed). *LD. Closed Sun & Mon. ££.*

The Midlands

Some people call this region the real England and in many ways it is her true heart. Birmingham forms the hub, England's second city, it embodies much of the industry and thrust that have transformed the Midlands. Full of car factories, hosiery works and all kinds of technology this area is prosperous.

The rebuilt centre of Birmingham has all the faults and merits of the 20th century writ large in reinforced concrete! Coventry's new cathedral is at the centre of a city that has risen out of the ashes of war time and rebuilt itself for the future. But it's not all industry, these great towns are set in some of the most beautiful countryside in England. Birmingham is a good centre for Shakespeare country and the gardens and trim cottages of Warwickshire. To the west are the glorious Welsh Marches, the weeping Malvern Hills (where the young Elgar distilled the essence of England into his music) and the fertile farms and forests of the Vale of Evesham. From busy Derby it is only moments to the Derbyshire Dales and in the east, Leicester's hinterland is the fields of Rutland where fox hunting is still the local passion.

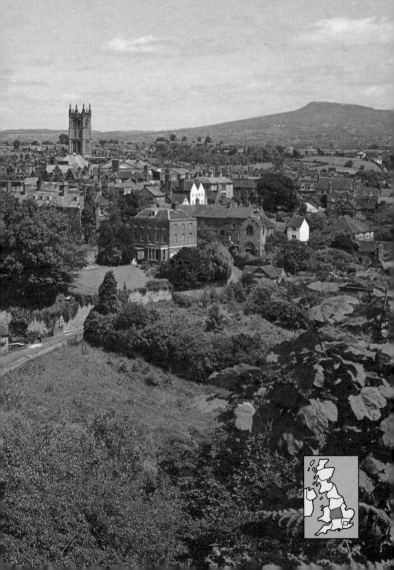

5

A B C D E

1
Formby
Ormskirk Burscough Standish Horwich Radcliffe Royton
Skelmersdale Wigan Farnworth Middleton Oldham
Crosby Maghull Kirkby Rainford Ashton-in- Leigh Failsworth Mossley
Bootle Knowsley Newton-le-Willows Makerfield Ashton-under-
Birkenhead St. Helen's Salford Manchester Lyne Glosso
Hoylake Upton Warrington Sale Stretford Stockport Marple Kinde
West Huyton Widnes Altrincham Cheadle 2088
Kirby Thurstaston Liverpool Allerton Hale Lymm High Legh Wilmslow Hazel Hayfield
Heswall Runcorn Stretton Gt. Budworth Alderley Grove New
Neston Bromborough Frodsham Edge Mills
2
Holywell Flint Ellesmere Northwich Knutsford Nether Bollington Whaley
Port Weaverham Alderley Bridge
Connah's Quay Rhydymwyn Davenham Macclesfield
Cilcain Mold Buckley Little Holmes Macclesfield
Llandyrnog Hawarden Chester Tarvin Budworth Middlewich Chapel Forest
3
Pontblyddyn Dodleston Tarporley Winsford Sandbach Congleton
Treuddyn Hope Aldford Church Mow
Caergwrle Burwardsley Tattenhall Minshull Crewe Cop Biddulph
Gresford Holt Bulkeley CHESHIRE Alsager Kidsgrove Leek
Coedpoeth Wrexham Nantwich Audlem Endon
1844 Malpas Bickley Aston Newcastle- Stoke-on-Trent
Llantysilio Bangor Moss Audlem under-Lyme Cellarhead Kingsley
Glyndyfrdwy Llangollen Ruabon Is Coed Whitchurch Whitmore STAFFS Cheadle Alton
Glyn Ceiriog Overton Adderley Standon Stone Hilderstone Uttoxeter
Chirk Penley Lightfield Market Sandon
4
Oswestry Knockin W. Felton Drayton Eccleshall Stafford Blithfield
Llanblodwel Kinnerley Myddle Hodnet Woodseaves Gnosall Haughton Rugeley Cannock
Nesscliffe Albrighton High Ercall Newport Church Eaton Chase Cannock
Melverley Middletown Shrewsbury Rodington Donnington Shifnal Penkridge Lichfield
Welshpool Meole Brace Westbury Wellington Telford Brewood Brownhills
5
Welshpool SALOP Dawley Codsall Walsall
Montgomery Minsterley Acton Burnell Much Buildwas Iron Bridge Wolverhampton Wednesbury
Church Wenlock Morville Sedgley West Bromwich
Bishop's Castle Stretton Hope Bridgnorth Claverley Dudley Warley
Clun Forest Lydbury Bowdler Ditton Billingsley Stourbridge Halesowen
Newcastle North Craven Winstanton Priors Kidderminster Bewdley
6
Bucknell Clun Culmington Bitterley Cleobury Hagley
Clungunford Ludlow Mortimer Clows Top Stourport Bromsgrove
Knighton Leintwardine Wigmore Orleton Tenbury on Severn Redditch
7
Presteigne Whitton Lingen Mortimer's Wells Astley Droitwich
New Radnor Norton Cross Wooferton Clifton upon Teme Witley Stoke Prior
Kington Shobdon Kingsland Leominster Wichenford Martley Worcester
8
Pembridge Monkland Hope Bromyard Spetchley
Eardisley King's under Dinmore Pershore
Whitney Staunton on Wye Pyon Bodenham Malvern WORCESTER
9
Bredwardine Credenhill Withington Great Evesham
Blakemere Wellington Ledbury Malvern Ashton
Dorstone Madley Hereford under Hill
Black Michaelchurch Vowchurch Mordiford Longdon Tewkesbury
Mountains Escley Abbey Dore Fownhope Much Eastnor
Longtown Kilpeck Marcle Bishop's
Talgarth Kings Caple Newent Cleeve Winchcombe
Llanthony St. Cleeve
Llangorse Weonards Peterstow Ross-on-Wye Hartpury Cloud Cheltenham
10
Sugar Pandy Grosmont Goodrich Staunton
Loaf Whitchurch Forest Huntley Gloucester
Abergavenny Monmouth Dean GLOUCS
Llanvihangel Mitcheldean Churchdown
Gobion Cinderford Longhope Paradise Winstone
Ebbw Coleford Newnham
Vale Blaenavon Hampton

5

A B C D E

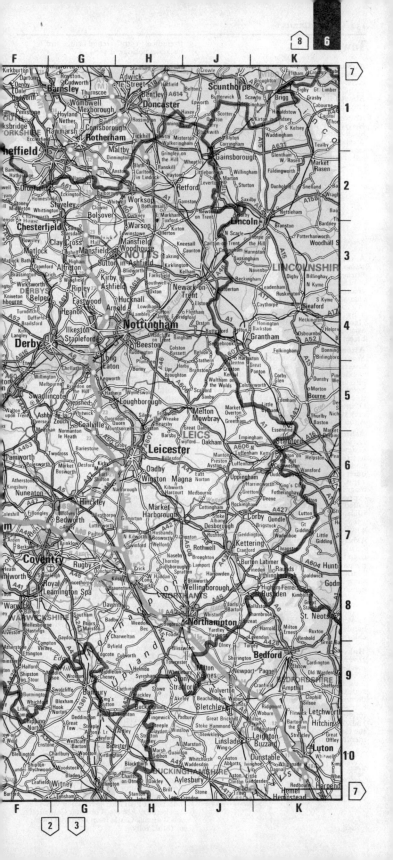

Towns

Abbots Bromley   E5
Staffs. Pop 1,100. A lyrical place of inns, old black-and-white cottages, a church with 14thC arcades, and an ancient butter-cross. Abbots Bromley is most famous for its ritualistic Horn Dance, held annually.

Abbots Morton   E8
Hereford & Worcs. Pop 100. A village of black-and-white houses with a whisper of Wagner in quiet corners. The 14thC church, surrounded by oaks and elms, stands on a hill at one end of the village street.

Abbots Morton, Worcestershire

Acton Burnell   B6
Salop. Pop 300. The village of Acton Burnell is as English as they come – a blend of black-and-white cottages and quiet Georgian houses blandly indifferent to the changing world about them. Tucked away in a corner of the village stands the ruin of one of the oldest fortified houses in England. Have a look at the 13thC church and the excavations of parts of Roman Watling Street and of a Roman bridge.

Alton   E4
Staffs. Pop 1,200. A stone-built village of towers, turrets and spires draped across the wooded slopes of the Churnet Valley. All hills and bends and close knit houses. At home on a Bavarian postcard as much as in this corner of Staffordshire Rhineland.
Of interest – remains of a Norman castle; grey stone lock-up in the village centre; Alton Towers.

Ashbourne   F4
Derby. Pop 5,500. EC Wed. MD Thur, Sat. Gateway to the Peak District, it's a light-hearted market town enveloped in an undulating eiderdown of green hills and quiet dales. The church is a 13thC and 14thC masterpiece, standing in a magnificent churchyard of yews and cypresses. With a 212-foot-high spire it is called 'The Pride of the Peak'. Of interest – Elizabethan grammar school founded in 1585; Green Man Hotel where Dr Johnson and Boswell stayed.

Ashby-de-la-Zouch   G5
Leics. Pop 8,900. EC Wed. MD Sat. Not far from the Leicestershire coal fields, it is a pleasant, small scale spa and market town. Market Street, where a market has been held since the early 13thC, is a long, wide and generous space. But the architectural heart is the parish church and the smouldering ruins of the 15thC castle, grouped together on the south side of the town.
Look for the Royal Hotel, built 1826 with a handsome small central hall with Doric columns.

Bakewell   F3
Derby. Pop 4,200. EC Thur. MD Mon. A market town set in a valley along the banks of the Wye, and surrounded by fat, wooded hills. It's a place of quiet streets, with cottages, gardens and gabled roofs, dominated by an impressive church with an octagonal central tower and spire. Of interest – late 17thC Market Hall; Town Hall, built 1709; Bath House, built 1697; the Georgian Rutland Arms Hotel, mentioned in Jane Austen's 'Pride and

Bakewell, Derbyshire

Prejudice'; 15thC arched bridge and packhorse bridge of 1664.

Belton   J6
Leics. Pop 300. EC Sat. A delightful hill top village grouped round the 14thC church. Of interest – 17thC Old Hall; Westbourne House of the Queen Anne period.

Betley   D4
Staffs. Pop 600. A half-hour's pleasure on a sunny day. Betley is a village of contentment with a wide street, half-timbered houses, and a very companionable 13thC church.

Bidford-on-Avon   E8
Warwick. Pop 2,500. EC Thur. It has a main street of salubrious 15thC and 16thC houses more on a par with a country town than a small village. This is Shakespearean villagescape in every creative, cobwebbed joint. The Falcon is a fine 16thC drunkard, tanked to the eyeballs.

Birmingham   E7
W. Midlands. Pop 1,000,000. EC Wed. MD Mon, Sat. A place of aspidistras and flyovers it is, in spirit, a frontier town, trouble-shooting its way from the industrial revolution to the electric seventies. Britain's second largest city, Birmingham is a two-gun Texan backslapping his way through company reports. It once tempered 16,000 sword blades for Cromwell's forces, and got its knuckles rapped by the Royalists for its pains. The new Bull Ring, a sort of shopping centre of subways, is an Aladdin's cave that misfired into endless emptiness. Still, they tried.
Of interest – 18thC cathedral church of St Philip with inspired Burne-Jones windows; Pugin designed red-brick Roman Catholic cathedral in 14thC Gothic style; Gas Street Basin – the junction of two canals with moorings for the traditional painted narrow boats.

Blyth   H2
Notts. Pop 1,130. EC Wed. An eloquent village of small scale delights. The parish church was developed from the 11thC priory. In the centre of the wide High Street is a 12thC stone building on an elm-shaded island. Once the Hospital of St John, it's now a school.

Bothamsall   H2
Notts. Pop 200. A pastoral picture, neat and quiet like a long lost water-colour. It is a small village on the slopes of a valley where the Meden and Maun flow together to become the River Idle.
Fine views to Sherwood Forest from the hill top. West of the village is the earthwork of a Norman castle.

Bredwardine   A9
Hereford & Worcs. Pop 200. A peaceful spot on the banks of the Wye with a backdrop of wooded hills. A mellow village with a long, curiously shaped Norman church.
Of interest – 18thC brick bridge; 18thC Red Lion Inn.

Bridgnorth   C6
Salop. Pop 7,600. EC Thur. MD Mon, Sat. An important town in the middle ages, it is spread across the top and at the foot of a sandstone ridge on the west bank of the Severn. It is really two towns, High Town and Low Town, threaded together by countless flights of steps and a railway. It has the hugger-mugger of mediaeval compactness with the exhilaration that you feel in only the best of hill towns as rooftop scrambles over rooftop.
Of note–the 17thC Town Hall; the church of St Mary Magdalene, designed by Thomas Telford; Cann Hall.

Broadway   E9
Hereford & Worcs. Pop 2,700. EC Thur. Involved, yet tranquil, like an epic poem. The epitome of the perfect Cotswold village, Broadway consists of a long grass fringed High Street which climbs a hill at one end. Notable are Abbot's Grange, from the 14thC; the 12thC church of timeless indecision; Fish Inn; spectacular views to Tewkesbury Abbey, Worcester Cathedral and Warwick Castle from Beacon Tower; an 18thC folly.

Buxton　　　　　　　　　　　　E2
Derby. Pop 20,300. EC Wed, MD Sat.
Centre of the Peak District, Buxton is an
18thC market town and spa riding a saddle
of land amongst the undulating hills of the
Derbyshire Dales. Roman watering place
and Pilgrimage centre of the middle ages, it
was here Mary Queen of Scots, as a
prisoner, was treated for rheumatism. The
town centre, built by the fifth Duke of
Devonshire around the mineral springs, was
conceived as a rival to Bath, but did not
really prosper until after the arrival of the
railway.
The town is old and new, Higher and Lower
Buxton. Originally centred around the
village green beyond The Slopes, Higher
Buxton is now a busy market square. In the
19thC the town centre moved down into the
valley below. This is Lower Buxton, with a
Crescent in the best Grand Design
tradition, with Pump Room and terraced
gardens.
Of note–the Devonshire Royal Hospital;
Solomon's Temple and St Anne's Well.

Chesterfield　　　　　　　　　　G2
*Derby. Pop 70,200. EC Wed. MD Mon, Fri,
Sat.* A con trick on a grand scale. Standing
in the Rother Valley among blustering hills,
it's fake Tudor from head to toe, with the
exception of some timid 20thC buildings and
the genuine Tudor bits in the market place
and Shambles. The best thing by far is All
Saints Church with its crooked spire 228 feet
high.

Cleobury Mortimer　　　　　　　C7
Salop. Pop 1,300. A quietly mannered place
minding its own business. It has a church
with a wooden spire complete with distinct
twist, a main street with pavements at
different levels, and a row of pollarded trees
and terraces of mostly Georgian houses.
Look at the Vicarage and the Manor House,
both early 18thC.

Collyweston　　　　　　　　　　K6
Northants. Pop 400. EC Wed. A big hearted
village of stone-built houses, limping up a
gentle hill. The roofs are all of Collyweston
tiles, the tiles still being manufactured in the
traditional way in the village. The Manor is
dated 1696, but there is an Elizabethan
dovecote and the remnants of an older house
to the west of the church.

Coventry　　　　　　　　　　　F7
*W. Midlands. Pop 335,000. EC Thur. MD
Wed, Fri, Sat.* Devastated during the last
war, the city has been feverishly rebuilding
ever since. It's run the whole gamut of
architectural and town planning theory from
car park roofed buildings to Golden-Egg-
Bar cathedral. But despite the odd excesses
it's still a pleasant matter-of-fact kind of
place hiding behind its apron strings.
Originally developed around a 7thC Anglo-
Saxon convent, it was the 11thC
Benedictine abbey that precipitated the
town's early growth. But few mediaeval
buildings remain. The most important is the
church of Holy Trinity.
Have a look at the Merchant Guild's Hall;
and St Mary's Hall, built in 1340, has a
splendid 15thC tapestry. The new cathedral
is a bit like a Mantovani string orchestra, but
nonetheless a heart-wrenching experience.
Also of interest–Bond's Hospital, built 1506;
and the University of Warwick.

Deene　　　　　　　　　　　　K6
Northants. Pop 100. A discreet limestone
village, tiny and unspoilt, playing hide and
seek among the trees. Have a look at Deene
Park, a beautiful house of pale Weldon
stone.

Derby　　　　　　　　　　　　G4
*Derby. Pop 219,000. EC Wed. MD Tue,
Thur-Sat.* Fought over by Romans, Saxons
and Danes, it was by the 12thC already a
busy trading centre. And by the beginning
of the 18thC England's first successful silk
mill was established here. The Market
Place, once the Grande Place of the
Midlands, is slowly coming alive again. On
the south is the Town Hall, built in 1841. On
the west side are some fine 18thC houses.
From the north side Irongate leads up to the
cathedral.
Of interest–19thC Westminster Bank House;
18thC Lloyds Bank; Friar Gate, a street with

some Georgian houses; 18thC St Mary's
Bridge with mediaeval chapel alongside.

Dudley　　　　　　　　　　　　D7
W. Midlands. A smack in the teeth for the
cosily comfortable. It is called the 'Capital of
the Black Country', with some justification,
as it was here in the 17thC that coal was first
used for smelting iron, and its vast ironworks
have prospered ever since. From the keep of
the Norman castle, the only important ruin
of its kind in Worcestershire, the panorama
extends over seven counties.

Eastwood　　　　　　　　　　　G4
Notts. Pop 11,000. EC Wed. The home of
D.H. Lawrence and the broad canvas of
impressions for his novel 'Sons and Lovers'.
A rural place of indiscriminate optimism
amidst sunken-eyed stone buildings in the
colliery area.

Edensor　　　　　　　　　　　F3
Derby. Pop 200. On the threshold of
Chatsworth it is a picturesque assortment of
gables, chimneys, turrets and roofs in a
free-for-all round a green and wayside edged
with lawn. Originally too close to
Chatsworth, the village was moved and the
present one planned and laid out by Joseph
Paxton in 1839.

Ellesmere　　　　　　　　　　B4
Salop. Pop 2,400. EC Thur. MD Tue. The
capital of Shropshire's Lake District, it is a
small market town set among nine meres.
Ellesmere is a handshake town of some
warmth which still has attractive old streets
and houses. In the centre of the town is the
Town Hall. Built in 1833, it is three bays
wide, ashlar-faced and originally had an
open ground floor.
Look at the timber-framed White Hart;
Fullwood House.

Empingham　　　　　　　　　　K6
Leics. Pop 600. A warm, sunny sort of
place, even in miserable weather. It's a large,
cinemascope-handsome village with a
splendid 13thC church.
Of interest – Prebendal House c1700; The
Wilderness.

Evesham　　　　　　　　　　　E9
*Hereford & Worcs. Pop 13,800. EC Wed.
MD Mon-Fri.* Pleasantly mannered market
place on the right bank of the Avon. Its air
of distinction and charm is set by the
tree-lined walks and lawns along the river.
Look at the 15thC Booth Hall, recently
restored; the 17thC Dresden House in the
High Street; the ruined Benedictine Abbey
founded 714; the two splendid parish
churches in the same churchyard, a sort of
Gilbert and George in ecclesiastical drag.

Evesham, bell tower.　　　*Evesham, Booth Hall.
Worcestershire*

Fotheringhay　　　　　　　　　K6
Northants. Pop 200. A leafy place with a
melancholy air like the end of a summer
evening. The road crosses the 18thC bridge
spanning the River Nene. The 12thC castle
where Mary Queen of Scots was beheaded
in 1587 is now a mound at the end of a
narrow lane. And on a hill opposite, the
tower of the church rises in stages like a
mediaeval space rocket. On the corners of
the first stage are four small turrets and
crowning them, in place of a spire, is a
superb octagonal lantern.

Fotheringhay

Great Malvern D9
Hereford & Worcs. Pop 29,000. EC Wed. A cheerfully elegant spa full of optimism like a carefree weekend.
Fashionable by the beginning of the 19thC, it was a rival to Buxton, Bath and Cheltenham. A hillside town of largely mid-Victorian buildings, it is dominated by the Norman priory church of SS Mary and Michael.
Great Malvern has four annexes – Malvern Link, which did not exist before 1846; Malvern Wells, a pleasant residential suburb; Malvern West, and Little Malvern, the smallest of the Malverns, with a gem of a church which is all that remains of another great priory founded in 1171.
Look at some of the ambitious buildings in Malvern College; Folly Arms Hotel, built 1810; the former Pump Room in Worcester Road, built 1819–23.

Hallaton J6
Leics. Pop 400. Amid some of the most attractive hill country east of Leicestershire, it is a rambling and handsome village. Of interest – Old Royal Oak; the church has a good broach-spire.

Hampton-in-Arden F7
W. Midlands. Pop 1,300. Supposedly the setting for Shakespeare's 'As You Like It', the village is a 16thC world of steep streets and rollicking timber-framed houses. The church has a late Norman nave as well as some extremely rare Calvary tiles, dating back to the Wars of the Roses.
Of interest – 16thC Moat House; 15thC packhorse bridge over the River Blythe.

Henley-in-Arden F8
Warwick. Pop 1,400. EC Thur. MD Mon, Wed, Sat. Once the stronghold of Plantagenet power, it's a whiskery old market town, nobly armed and bent-backed like a squint-eyed lecher.
Of interest – 15thC Guildhall; the White Swan; the Old George, the Blue Bell Inn, and the 15thC church.

Hereford B9
Hereford & Worcs. Pop 46,500. EC Thur. MD Wed. Edged on its south side by the River Wye, Hereford is a breezy place with a kindly twinkle. The 11thC cathedral has a massive central tower of red sandstone built in 1300. The 14thC church of All Saints is also of interest. In the centre of the town stands an attractive timber-framed house, Old House built in 1621. Nearby is Booth Hall, now a hotel.
Look in the City Museum and Art Gallery and see the bronze age burial.

Hereford

Hoar Cross E5
Staffs. A diminutive, but perky village which has for a church one of the most beautiful ever built in 19thC England.

Hoarwithy B10
Hereford & Worcs. Crossed by a loop in the Wye, it is a plump and pleasant village with an extraordinary Italianate church, built in the 19thC. Much of the detailing is straight out of early Roman basilicas.

Honington F9
Warwick. Pop 200. An agreeable village, wrapped snugly round a green. Visit Honington Hall, built in 1682; timber-framed Magpie House.

Ilam F4
Staffs. Pop 200. Ilam is a model village rebuilt with 19thC sensibility. Like a well constructed sentence, it is a well constructed concept.
Of interest – the 13thC church; Ilam Hall.

Ironbridge C6
Salop. EC Wed. MD Fri. The centre of the English iron industry in the 18thC, it is a little town ferreting its way on steep limestone slopes above a narrow gorge through which runs the River Severn. Ironbridge is a "knees-up-Mother-Brown" sort of place with lead weights. The bridge over the Severn, from which the town takes its name, was the first iron bridge constructed in England. Coalbrookdale is the site of the ironworks where iron was first successfully smelted with coke.

Ketton K6
Leics. Pop 1,100. An attractive giant of a village with a 13thC town-sized church. St Mary's has an exquisite spire which looms above the trees and sepia coloured slate roofs of the village.

King's Pyon B8
Hereford & Worcs. Pop 300. A tranquil village scene set in beautiful wooded country. The church slightly aloof as if there was a funny smell somewhere, stands on a hill overlooking the village. The church has a fine Norman doorway in the south; glorious black-and-white 14thC roofs over the nave and over the south transept.
Of interest – the 17thC timber-framed house the Butthouse.

Lambley H4
Notts. Pop 1,000. A handful of houses thrown in a deep sheltered vale with the Lambley Dumble running in between the lot. A nursery rhyme dream.
Have a look at the church, built in 1450 in a sort of club-room Perpendicular.

Lapworth F8
Warwick. A cheeky-eyed village of scattered houses linked by some invisible thread of companionship. The church has a small Norman north window.

Laxton H3
Notts. Pop 300. Registered as an ancient monument, the village is famous for preserving the old agricultural system of open-field farming. Saxon in origin, it consists of hedgeless, one-acre, co-operatively farmed strips. Large dignified late 15thC church.

Leamington Spa F8
Warwick. Pop 45,000. EC Mon, Thur. A fashionable spa in the late 18thC and early 19thC, it is a sedate place of Georgian, Regency and Victorian detachment. The Royal Pump Room was opened in 1814, but was rebuilt in 1925. The Royal prefix to the town name was granted by Queen Victoria in 1838.
Of interest – Lansdowne Crescent and Newbold Terrace; pleasant art gallery and museum.

Ledbury C9
Hereford & Worcs. Pop 3,600. EC Wed. MD Tue. The birthplace of John Masefield, the poet, Ledbury has a long main street with an angled market place dominated by a 17thC timber-framed Market House. It's a lovable place full of old fashioned comfort.
Of interest – 14thC St Katharine's Hospital; 16thC Ledbury Park; cobbled Church Lane; the Feathers Hotel; the mostly 14thC church with late Norman zigzag work above the west door.

Leek E3
Staffs. Pop 20,000. EC Thur. MD Wed. A settlement long before the Romans came, Leek is a poker-faced place standing at the southern end of some of the most impressive scenery in Staffordshire.
Of interest – remains of a 13thC abbey; the 14thC church; the Red Lion Inn, built 1626.

Leicester H6
Leics. Pop 284,000. EC Thur. MD Wed, Fri, Sat. An apparent desert of red-brick houses, ugly and featureless, yet at its heart one of England's historic cities. Long before the Romans established their township at Ratae by the River Soar, the Celts were here. And it was here that the largest Roman bath in England was found. Behind the 1690s facade of the castle is the original hall of the Norman castle, whilst St Mary de Caestro was the castle church, built 1107. In Guildhall Lane is the Guildhall begun in 1390, one of the most remarkable civic buildings in England.
Of interest – Chantray House, built 1511; the Grammar School, built 1573; the Jewry Wall; the cathedral church of St Martin; the Engineering Building, Leicester University.

Leominster B8
Hereford & Worcs. Pop 7,000. EC Thur. MD Fri. Wide Georgian thoroughfares of starched classicism make an invigorating

contrast to the overhung and gabled streets of mediaeval Leominster. Once a wool town, it is set among pasture land, hop gardens and orchards. Of note – the old timber-built Town Hall of 1633 enriched with elaborate carvings; the reddish stone priory of the 12thC; Berrington Hall, built in the 18thC three miles north of Leominster by the younger Henry Holland.

Lichfield E6

Staffs. Pop 23,000. EC Wed. MD Mon. From whatever direction you approach Lichfield it is dominated by the three spires of the red sandstone cathedral. Once inside the city, narrow streets huddle closely together in a breezy and convivial manner. The cobbled market square is an eloquent door-to-door salesman's kind of place, in contrast to the conservatively pleasant cathedral close. Strong associations with Dr Johnson, James Boswell and David Garrick.

Litchfield Cathedral.

Llanyblodwel A5

Salop. Pop 800. Within spitting distance of Wales and with a Welsh name to boot, it is wholly English in appearance – a fistful of cottages spread-eagled on the hillside above a swift-running river, a stone bridge, a 16thC black-and-white inn and, among the trees, one of the strangest churches in the country.

Ludlow B7

Salop. Pop 7,100. EC Thur. MD Mon, Fri, Sat. A town of huddled magnificence which grew in the shadow of a castle and of a large 12thC church. Wealthy from the cloth trade, Ludlow was planned on a hill with a discreet network of streets of varied scale and character. Its centre is delightfully tortuous, the narrow streets breathlessly alive.
Of note – Broad Street; Reader's House; the Rose and Crown; the Feathers Hotel.

Market Bosworth G6

Leics. Pop 1,300. A little town around a market place. Important during the middle ages, it's now a quiet place with some pleasant thatched cottages and a famous Hall. Built in the best Queen Anne manner, it is all red-brick and white stone. Market Bosworth is famous in English history for the battle fought here on the 22nd August 1485.

Market Drayton C4

Salop. Pop 7,000. EC Thur. MD Wed. A handsome grandfather of a town, famous as the birthplace of Clive of India. Its centre is the High Street, which is more like a market place. From here the main streets fan out with the church appearing only in odd glimpses.
Of interest – the Butter Market of 1824; the Star Hotel, dated 1669; the Crown Hotel.

Market Harborough H7

Leics. Pop 14,500. EC Wed. MD Tue, Sat. A market town created by Henry II, it is a good-to-be-alive kind of place. The parish church, a mixture of Decorated and Perpendicular, has a magnificent tower and spire which dominates the good-looking market place.
Of interest – the gabled grammar school, built 1613; the Three Swans.

Market Overton J5

Leics. Pop 400. With the remains of Roman earthworks and some remarkable Anglo-Saxon finds, Overton is a place knee deep in historical associations. Set on a high limestone plateau, it had a market as early as 1200. The church is almost wholly Decorated. On the village green are the stocks and whipping post. Have a look at Market Overton Hall, an early Georgian building.

The Matlocks F3

Derby. Pop 20,000. EC Thur. MD Tue, Fri. There are five Matlocks – Matlock Bath, Matlock Dale, Matlock Bridge, Matlock Town and Matlock Bank. They are a chain of small towns running north and south down the wooded Derwent Valley. This is a picture postcard of Switzerland tucked into a corner of England, with one crag, High Tor, rising 350 feet straight from the valley floor by Market Dale. Another side of the Dale is shut in by Masson, which rises 1,100 feet above sea level.
Matlock Bath was developed as a comfortable spa round warm springs. Matlock Bank is a place of indecision on a steep hill. Its church, built 1884, has stained glass by William Morris and Burne-Jones. Matlock Bridge has a fine 16thC four-arched bridge and pleasant riverside walks and gardens. Matlock Town, high above the river, is the oldest of the Matlocks. On the dominating hill top above stand the ruins of Riber Castle, built in the 19thC for a textile manufacturer.

Melton Mowbray J5

Leics. Pop 20,000. EC Thur. MD Tue, Sat. The hunting metropolis of early 19thC England, it is now a light-hearted and breezy market town on the River Weak. The church is one of the most impressive in the country, a stately encyclopaedia of Gothic styles. The town has also a fine open air market, characteristic of so many Midland towns. Melton Mowbray is also the home of pork-pies, Stilton cheeses and the Quorn Hunt.
Of interest – 15thC Anne of Cleves House; Swan Inn in the Market Place; Egerton Lodge.

Much Wenlock C6

Salop. Pop 2,500. EC Wed. MD Sat. A small market town with a village-scale High Street, some spacious Georgian brick houses and a 16thC Guildhall to charm the pants off anyone. Its most famous attraction is the ruined priory founded as a nunnery in 680. Have a look at the 15thC house near St Owen's Well which has an archway made of three pairs of oak boughs.

Newport D5

Salop. Pop 7,000. EC Thur. MD Fri, Sat. A wham-bam of a place – short, sharp and to the point. It's a small market town which is really one long High Street winding its way downhill to the canal. Half way down is a large town church plonked slap in the middle. Around this the street side-steps smartly in the best of ways.
Have a look at the Guildhall, dated 1615; the Royal Victoria Hotel c1830.

Northampton J8

Northants. Pop 126,500. EC Thur. MD Wed, Sat. A penny-arcade place without a memory. It was a Saxon town once burned by the Danes. The Normans built a great castle here on the site of the present railway station, and Thomas Becket was tried there before being exiled to France.
Hooked in an arm of the Nene, Northampton reached the peak of its prosperity in the 13thC and 14thC. A decline set in following the Wars of the Roses. The town revived again during the Civil War, but in 1675 a fire destroyed most of the city. Today it's largely a place of through-roads and indifferent buildings, relieved by some fine churches and spacious parks.
Of interest – Market Square, believed to be the largest in England; the Norman parish church of St Peter; the Holy Sepulchre, built in 1100, and one of the few round churches in England; the Italianate Manfield Warehouse.

Nottingham H4

Notts. Pop 295,000. EC Mon, Thur. MD Mon-Sat. A mud-in-your-eye kind of place, vigorous and with a laced drink. William the Conqueror built a castle here and it was nearby, some 600 years later, that Charles I raised his standard during the Civil War. The city's character was moulded most by the Industrial Revolution. It was here Hargreaves and Arkwright first set up a mill to spin cotton, and it was in 1811 that gross overcrowding and poverty brought unrest in the form of the Luddite riots. Modern planning has wrought its worst but,

despite failures like Maid Marian Way, the
city still has a kick to it. St Mary's is an
imposing Perpendicular church. The City
Museum and Art Gallery has good paintings
by Bonington and Sandby; Wallaton Hall is
a fine piece of Elizabethan Renaissance; the
mediaeval Goose Fair is three days of fun in
the first week of October; and modern
architecture has two notches to its credit –
the Boots factory and the Nottingham
Playhouse.

Oundle   K7
Northampton. Pop 3,700. EC Wed. MD Thur.
A refreshing leafy riverside town with stern
stone-built houses divided by inviting alleys
and narrow yards. A satisfying place of
almshouses, hospitable inns, a famous school,
and the romantic spire of St. Peters.

Overbury   E9
Hereford & Worcs. Pop 300. A village that
has taken good care of itself – grey-haired
and elegant in a red-faced way with an
occasional youthful twinkle. Greatly restored
church with Early English chancel and
Norman nave.

Pershore   E9
*Hereford & Worcs. Pop 5,200. EC Thur.
MD Mon, Fri.* A remarkably intact Georgian
town, as unbelievable as a win on the Pools.
Delightful and prosperous, it is set in the
middle of the fruit-growing district with the
Avon flowing away to the south of the town.
Many of the houses are of brick with stone
or stucco dressings, a number with Venetian
windows, bow windows, fanlights, pillared
porches and flights of steps.
The Benedictines built here what was
probably one of the greatest pre-Reformation
abbeys in the country. Destroyed at the
Dissolution, all that remains is the monastic
part of the church.
Look at the Three Tuns Inn; 14thC foot
bridge over the Avon; Perrott House.

Rockingham   J6
Northants. Pop 100. A leafy place of stone-
built houses striding briskly up a steep hill by
the River Welland. On a hill is the
Elizabethan castle standing on the site of a
former Norman castle. Interesting Jacobean
pulpit in the church.

Ross-on-Wye   C10
*Hereford & Worcs. Pop 6,500. EC Wed. MD
Thur, Sat.* A gentle jack-in-the-box sort of
place, with buildings popping up in
unexpected places, on a delightful wooded
cliff along a bend in the Wye. It is a modest
market town largely developed by one man,
John Kyrle, in the late 17thC. The Market
Place is dominated by the 17thC Market
Hall, a double-gabled businesslike sort of
building, like a mediaeval cash register. Fine
14thC church rich in monuments.

Ross-on-Wye

Rugby   G7
Warwick. Pop 59,000. EC Wed. MD Sat.
A fire in the belly sort of place of toil and
sweat under lead-grey skies. Developed
during the latter stages of England's
industrialization, it's a smouldering giant in
hob-nailed boots. Its main claim to fame is
Rugby School, made famous through
Thomas Hughes' 'Tom Brown's
Schooldays'.

Shipston-on-Stour   F9
Warwick. Pop 1,900. A once prosperous
sheep-market town with a wealth of
clean-faced Georgian houses. It is a stylish
place like a retired colonel with frayed cuffs.
Of interest – Horseshoes Inn in Church
Street; George Hotel in the High Street.

Shrewsbury   B5
*Salop. Pop 56,000. EC Thur. MD Tue, Wed,
Fri, Sat.* A mystical place of fine church
spires and an abundance of gentility, it is one
of the best preserved mediaeval towns in the
country. Formerly a Roman town, built,
following the departure of the Roman
Legions in the 5thC, on rising ground in a

loop of the Severn. When the Normans
arrived a castle was built, now in ruins.
Of interest – the Abbey Church of the Holy
Cross; the Norman Church of St Mary;
Clive House, the 18thC town house of Clive
of India; 16thC Old Market House;
Shrewsbury School; and Old Malting House
in the suburb of Ditherington, built in 1796
and the oldest surviving iron-framed
building in the world.

Stafford   D5
*Staffs. Pop 55,000. EC Wed. MD Tue, Fri,
Sat.* Built around a ford across the River Sow
it has a history going back 1,200 years. It was
mentioned in the Domesday Book, and by
the middle of the 13thC already had a busy
market. A mild-mannered place whose fame
rests on its being the birthplace of Izaak
Walton in 1593.
Look at the church of St Mary with its
unusual octagonal tower; the timbered High
House where Charles I and Prince Rupert
stayed in 1642 while recruiting; the 17thC
Noel Almshouses in Mill Street.

Stoney Middleton   F2
Derby. Pop 500. A place of lurking drama as
narrow streets and old houses rise tier on tier
on ledges of rock under steep hanging cliffs.
The church in the village square is
completely octagonal. It was built on to a
squat 15thC tower in 1759.

Stratford-Upon-Avon   F8
Warwick. Pop 19,500. EC Thur. MD Fri.
The birthplace of Shakespeare on the 23rd
April 1564, it has kept intact the cloth cap
character of a thriving Midland market town.
It was first a bronze age settlement and then
a Romano-British village. A monastery was
founded in Anglo-Saxon days, and in 1196
Richard I established it as a market centre.
The buildings are predominantly Elizabethan
and Jacobean, plus a good Georgian overlay.
A natural backcloth to Shakespeare, it was in
1769 that David Garrick, the actor,
organised the first Shakespeare celebrations.
Of interest – 15thC Clapton Bridge; Anne
Hathaway's Cottage; church of the Holy
Trinity; Harvard House; Royal Shakespeare
Theatre; the Canal Wharf on the
Birmingham Canal; Church Street and
Chapel Street.

Sudbury   F4
Derby. Pop 8,200. Another of Derbyshire's
model villages. Feudal in concept, it was
built in mellow red-brick around a wayside
green in the rich meadows of the Dove.
Sudbury Hall, begun in 1613, has a fine long
gallery and some exceptional carvings by
Grinling Gibbons.

Tenbury Wells   C8
*Hereford & Worcs. Pop 2,000. EC Thur. MD
Tue.* A disarming little market town full of
gentle bonhomie, situated on the banks of
the Teme in the midst of meadows, orchards
and hop gardens. In 1839 the Saline Springs
were discovered, a pump room erected, and
for a time the town enjoyed some popularity
as a spa.
The square tower of the church is late
Norman. Have a look at the 19thC Royal
Oak and the 17thC Cornwall House.

Tissington   F3
Derby. Pop 200. A sultry kind of place full of
smouldering warmth – a village ensemble
with triangular green, mellow stone houses,
with the church and Jacobean hall in the
background.

Tissington, Derbyshire

Uppingham   J6
Leics. Pop 2,000. EC Thur. MD Fri. An
18thC place of quiet streets and bow-fronted
shops, with a charming market place with
the church porch leading off it. It's a
sleepy-eyed town with the great public

school taking up a large part of the south-west corner.
Of interest – Tudor House c1600; the Manor House; The Hall, built 1612.

Waltham-on-the-Wolds J5
Leics. Pop 700. EC Tue. A decent sort of place like bread and butter teas. Formerly a market town in 19thC England, it is a large stone-built village standing high on the oolitic limestone. The church is handsome 14thC with a central tower.

Warwick F8
Warwick. Pop 18,000. EC Thur. MD Sat. Almost entirely rebuilt following a disastrous fire in 1694, Warwick stands on rising ground to the north of the River Avon. Perched eagle-eyed on a crag above the river is the mediaeval castle. Another dominant feature of this county town is the church of St Mary. Of Norman origin, it has an impressive 13thC crypt.
Of interest – 14thC Lord Leycester's Tudor House in West Street; 15thC Bridge End in Brome Place; Doll Museum in an Elizabethan house; late 14thC bridge across the Avon.

Whichford F9
Warwick. Pop 200. A serene gang of stone and thatched-roof houses in a jocular mood. Nothing too serious here, life's for having fun, so the buildings seem to say.
Of interest – 19thC village pumps; Norman church with a dog-toothed arch over the south doorway; remains of Norman castle.

Wigmore B8
Hereford & Worcs. Pop 300. A gentle giant of a village with the church at the top of the village street and a gang of hot-headed half-timbered houses jovially huffing and puffing at its feet. To the west of the church is the mound of the Norman castle.
Of interest – Wigmore Hall; the remains of the 12thC Wigmore Abbey.

Wolverhampton D6
W. Midlands. Pop 269,000. EC Thur. MD Wed, Sat. A jungle of a place with a sharp bite in odd corners. The most outstanding building is the church of St Peter which has all the grace of a small cathedral. St John's is almost a carbon copy of London's St Martin-in-the-Fields.
Of interest locally – Mosely Old Hall; Wightwick Manor; Chillington Hall.

Worcester D8
Hereford & Worcs. Pop 73,500. EC Thur. MD Mon, Sat. A sad-eyed city of long-forgotten summers. Repeatedly sacked by Romans, Danes, Saxons, Welsh and Roundheads, this ancient cathedral city was built on both sides of the Severn. The principal part of the city has grown over the centuries on the steeper eastern bank, more to avoid floods than the many marauding armies. A once fine Tudor town, robbed of its uniqueness by senseless redevelopments, but nonetheless rewarding for its leftover pleasantries. The whole place is dominated by the cathedral, with its magnificent 14thC tower. The 18thC Guildhall is one of the most gracious Queen Anne buildings in the county. Look at the 16thC King Charles House, New Street, and the 15thC guest house of the Franciscan friary in Friar Street

The Lost Villages of Leicestershire
Elmesthorpe is one of the best marked sites of a deserted mediaeval village in the county. It was already deserted in the late 15thC when Richard III stopped here on his way to the fatal battle of Bosworth. The nave of the church lies open to the sky. Forton, marked by earthworks, was deserted in the 16thC; in the Leicestershire uplands Frisby is another deserted village site nearly 600 feet up. The village of Noseby, set deep in hilly and wooded country, is now only a hall and private chapel. The village decayed when the Hazleriggs converted the open fields to pastures in the early 16thC. Prestwold village also disappeared, leaving only the big house and a church.

The Potteries
Staffs. The five towns of Arnold Bennett's novels, Tunstall, Burslem, Hanley, Fenton and Loughton. Amalgamated with Stoke-on-Trent when the present Stoke-on-Trent came into being. It's a

twilit coal-scarred land, made famous by the great names in pottery – Wedgwood, Minton, Spode, and Coalport. The clay kilns are curious bottle-shaped buildings.

Regional oddities

Well Dressing
Derby. A custom peculiar to this county. Probably pagan in origin, but later adapted by Christianity as an act of thanksgiving for plentiful water supplies. Of particular interest is the village of Tissington where, on Ascension Day, five wells are dressed with biblical pictures composed of flower petals, leaves and grasses. Other well dressing ceremonies at Eyan, Wirksworth, Buxton, Barlow and Youlgreave.

Famous people

Lord Byron (1788-1824) H3
Newstead Abbey, Notts. 4½ miles s of Mansfield off A60. Ancestral home of the Byrons from 1540, when it was converted into a house. When Lord Byron, the poet, inherited his title the abbey was crumbling away with neglect. For a while he was passionately involved in restoring the place. Stories abound of Byron and his friends, in monks' dresses hired from a masquerade warehouse, imbibing burgundy, claret and champagne from a 'skull-cup'. By 1818 he was forced to sell Newstead to pay his debts. Byron's favourite retriever, Boatswain, is buried close by. The skull-cup is on view. *Conducted tours 14.00, 15.00, 16.00 & 17.00 Apr–Sep. Closed Sun.*

Sir Edward Elgar (1857–1934) D8
Broadheath, Hereford & Worcs. 2 miles w of Worcester. This trim red-brick cottage is where the composer was born. His father was the organist at St George's Roman Catholic church and also owned a music shop. Elgar himself taught violin before he was able to devote his full time to composition. The cottage is now a museum, with a delightful jumble of Elgar relics to explore: scores, photographs, awards and medals, violin case, bow, desk, golf clubs and chemistry apparatus. *Open 13.30–18.30 Apr–Oct. 13.30–16.30 Nov–Mar. Closed Wed.*

Samuel Johnson (1709–84) E6
Birthplace, Bread Market St, Lichfield, Staffs. A childhood friend remembers the great Dr Johnson spending his holidays sauntering in the fields around Lichfield, and more engaged in talking to himself than to his companion. He was born in Bread Market Street above his father's bookshop. The house is now a museum stuffed with relics, pictures and a fine library. *Open 10.00–17.00 Tue–Sat & B. Hols Apr–Oct. 10.00–16.00 Tue–Sat Nov–Mar. 14.30–17.00 Sun Jun–Sep.*

D.H. Lawrence (1885–1930) G4
Eastwood, Notts. Lawrence was born at 8a Victoria Street, the fourth son of a miner, in this mining community. The surrounding farmland and collieries became the background for his early books, especially 'Sons and Lovers'.

Robin Hood (c1160–c1247) H3
Sherwood Forest, Notts. Some say he never even existed, but doubting Thomases aside, Robin and his Merry Men still haunt the greenwood in Sherwood Forest. In the part of the forest known as Birklands, the Duke's Drive leads to Robin Hood's Larder, the tree where Robin used to hang his venison after a day's hunting in the king's forest. Tradition has it that he married Maid Marian in Edwinstowe church, and he met King Richard in what is now the ruins of King John's Palace, once the royal hunting lodge of Sherwood Forest. Richard actually did stay there on his return from the Crusades. Robin Hood is said to be buried on the edge of Kirklees Park, near Huddersfield, Yorkshire, and a stone cross, and now a headstone, marks the spot.

In Clipstone, Nottinghamshire, is the Duke's Archway, otherwise known as the Duke's Folly. It stands just north of the village, was built 1842–44, and decorated with the figures of Richard I, Robin Hood, Little John, Friar Tuck, Allan-a-Dale and Maid Marian.

William Shakespeare (1564–1616)   F8
Stratford-upon-Avon, Warwick. Shakespeare *is* Stratford. From birth, marriage to death, there is a sacred spot marked somewhere to commemorate the event. There is the 'birth room' in Henley Street, furnished in the style of the period; King's New School where seven-year-old William learnt his Latin grammar; his wife Anne Hathaway's thatched farmhouse, complete with original furnishings; Hall's Croft, his son-in-law's home; Mary Arden's House, where his mother was born, and New Place, the largest house in the town, which Shakespeare bought in 1597, and where he died.
He is buried in Holy Trinity Church. On the wall on the north side of the chancel is Shakespeare's bust, executed soon after his death, and believed, by the intrepid few, to contain evidence that Shakespeare was really Christopher Marlowe.

Izaak Walton (1593–1683)   D5
Halfhead Farm, Shallowford, Staffs. 3½ miles sw of Stafford. Fisherman and author of 'The Compleat Angler, or the Contemplative Man's Recreation', Walton lived here from time to time during his retirement. The half-timbered cottage is preserved as a memorial to Walton, and there is a small museum. *Open 10.00–16.30 daily. Closed Tue.*

Cathedrals, abbeys & churches

All Saints   J7
Brixworth, Northants. A large, darkly brooding church built in the 7thC during that strange twilight age when Roman Britain was slowly crumbling. A comparatively sophisticated building utilising bricks and tiles from the many deserted villas around. Numerous Norman and mediaeval additions.

All Saints   J8
Earls Barton, Northants. The fortress-like tower of this church is perhaps the most famous Saxon tower in England. Rising in four stages, it's built of packed rubble, plastered and elaborately decorated with the typical Saxon pilaster strips. The corners are in long-and-short work.

Earls Barton
Northamptonshire

Ashbourne Church   F4
Ashbourne, Derby. Called 'the Cathedral of the Peak' it has a magnificent 212-foot-high spire. The earliest part of the church is the long east chancel with lancet windows. The nave arcade and the great windows in the transepts are Decorated. The tower and spire are 14thC.

Cheadle Church   E4
Cheadle, Staffs. One of Pugin's masterpieces. Built in 1864 it's a red stone Roman Catholic church full of explosive brilliance. The interior is rich and electric.

Derby Cathedral   G4
Derby. A deferential sort of building which has a 178-foot-high pinnacled tower, built during the reign of Henry VIII.
A cathedral since 1927, it was rebuilt by James Gibbs in the 18thC. It contains the elaborate tomb of Bess of Hardwick and a superb wrought-iron screen, the work of Robert Bakewell.

Hereford Cathedral   B9
Hereford, Hereford & Worcs. Begun in 1079 by the Norman Bishop Robert Losinga, it is notable for the superb Norman work in the great pillars of the nave arcade and choir.

Ashbourne Church.

Holy Trinity   B5
Meole Brace, Salop. Built 1867–8, it is a big red-faced church with a square tower. However, its chief glory is in its stained glass. Executed 1869–70 it was designed by William Morris and Burne-Jones. Perhaps their best work, rich like a technicolour dream.

Kilpeck Church   B9
Kilpeck, Hereford & Worcs. Architecturally one of the richest and best preserved Norman churches in Britain. The interior consists of a nave, chancel and apse, and a huge Norman font. The south doorway is a magnificent piece of carving.

Lichfield Cathedral   E6
Lichfield, Staffs. Built of red sandstone on sloping ground, it was begun in 1190. The nave, transepts, chapter house and west front are Early English. Forming the only triple group of spires in England, the graceful central and western spires are in the Decorated style.

Pershore Abbey   E9
Pershore, Hereford & Worcs. A 7thC abbey dumped in a meadow. All that survived the Reformation was the splendid tower, crossing, transepts and presbytery. The south transept has a Norman arcade of intersecting arches. The vaulted roof to the presbytery is the crowning glory of 14thC England.

St Bartholomew   E6
Wednesbury, Staffs. Dating from the 12thC, it's the most aloof and upright of Perpendicular churches in the Midlands. A leader among men.

St Chad's Roman Catholic Cathedral   E7
Birmingham, W. Midlands. A working-class piece of German brick Gothic. Sharp and austere, it was designed by Pugin in 1839 in the full flush of the Gothic revival.

St Chads, Birmingham.

St Martin Cathedral   H6
St Martin, Leics. Large and prosperous-looking, it was the parish church until 1927. Although on an ancient site, it has been restored so often that externally it's very much a Victorian job. The pier decoration of the interior remains unchanged.

St Mary Magdalene   D9
Croome d'Abitot, Hereford & Worcs. A clean, whistling 18thC Gothic fantasy, built as an eye catcher in Croome Park. The architect was Capability Brown whilst Robert Adam did the interiors. There is a fine tomb by Grinling Gibbons.

St Mary's   E5
Ingestre, Staffs. A miniature masterpiece,
built in 1676 to the designs of Sir Christopher
Wren. A delicate thing, fragilely balanced
like a spring blossom.

St Michael   D8
Great Witley, Hereford & Worcs. Self-
assured and unshowy it complements Witley
Court. A clean, classical concept, it has a
central west tower complete with cupola.
Faced with ashlar work, it was built in 1735.

Great Witley Church, Worcestershire

St Michael's Cathedral   F7
Coventry, W. Midlands. Designed by Basil
Spence, it was completed in 1962. Built on
to the north side of the old bombed cathedral
and joined to it by a porch, the great west
screen of clear glass enables the old
cathedral to be seen from inside the new.

Relatively simple exterior, with a rather rich
Mecca ballroom interior.

St Peter   B5
Melverley, Salop. A timber-framed church
in a wide meadow above the River Vyrnwy,
and one of only two in the county. Probably
built in the 15thC, it's more like a barn than
a church.

St Philip's Cathedral   E7
Birmingham, W. Midlands. Built originally as
a new church 1710–15. The architect was
Thomas Archer, and he gave the city a fiery
piece of warm European baroque.
Burne-Jones windows in the east and west
ends.

Dormston Church,   *Southwell Minster,*
Worcestershire   *Nottinghamshire*

St Nicholas   E8
Dormston, Hereford & Worcs. Something out
of a Bavarian fairy tale. Built in 1450, it has a
timber-framed west tower standing on a low
stone wall. The roof is steeply pitched.

St Nicholas   H6
Leicester, Leics. It is one of the best-known
Anglo-Saxon churches in England, probably
dated as early as the 7thC, with some
Norman and later work.

St Nicholas   J2
Littleborough, Notts. A miniature masterpiece. A tiny aisleless Norman church with
large areas of herring-bone masonry everywhere. It has a nave 24 feet long and a
thirteen foot chancel. A few Roman tiles
appear mixed up with the stonework.

Southwell Minster   H3
Southwell, Notts. A clean, sharp building,
proud and aloof, it dominates and dwarfs the
small town. Work began on the church in
1108. The facade, nave, towers and transept
are Norman, the whole composition robust
and lively. The choir was added in 1234.
The minster is unique in that it retains all
three of its Norman towers, two of them
complete with their pyramidal roofs.

Tideswell Church   F2
Tideswell, Derby. A 14thC embattled and
pinnacled church, one of the finest in the
county. Built in one period it consists of a
spacious nave with lofty aisles, huge
transepts with giant Decorated windows,
and a long chancel with four big flat-headed
windows. Interesting font, stone screen
behind the high altar, original roof,
Victorian stained glass.

Worcester Cathedral   D8
Worcester, Hereford & Worcs. A superb
sight, it sits on level ground on the banks of
the Severn. Although dating back to the late
7thC, the present building was begun in
1084. It has a Norman crypt, transepts, and a
circular chapter house which is the only one
in England. The choir is Early English. The
nave, cloisters and central tower, Decorated
and Perpendicular.

Castles & ruins

Acton Burnell Castle   B6
Acton Burnell, Salop. Almost intact, apart
from its roof. This is one of the oldest
fortified castles in England. Built for Robert
Burnell between 1284 and 1293. Of warm
red sandstone, it is a tall house with four
projecting angle towers. The ground floor
was an undercroft, the main rooms lying
above. *Open any reasonable time.*

Ashby de la Zouch Castle   G5
Ashby-de-la-Zouch, Leics. The thunderous
ruins of a formidable stronghold. Begun in
the 12thC it was developed extensively by
Lord Hastings from 1473 until his death.
During the Civil War it held out for over a
year against the Commonwealth troops, and
in 1648, by order of Parliament, it was
slighted. *Open 9.30–17.30 Mar, Apr & Oct,
9.30–19.00 May–Sep, 9.30–16.00 Nov–Feb.
Closed Sun morning.*

Bolsover Castle   G2
Bolsover, Derby. 6½ miles e of Chesterfield.
A curious affair, built in the 17thC at a time
when fortresses were no longer needed. It is
a fairy-tale castle of consciously romantic
taste, designed to catch the flavour of
yesteryear. It stands on a terrace of land
pontificating over the town below. *Open
9.30–17.30 Mar, Apr & Oct, 9.30–19.00
May–Sep, 9.30–16.00 Nov–Feb. Closed Sun
morning.*

Buildwas Abbey   C6
Buildwas, Salop. A Norman abbey in a
meadow beside the Severn. Reckoned to be
one of the three finest ruined abbeys in the
country, it was founded in 1135 by Roger de
Cinton, Bishop of Coventry and Lichfield.
*Open 9.30–17.30 Mar, Apr & Oct, 9.30–
19.00 May–Sep, 9.30–16.00 Nov–Feb.
Closed Sun morning.*

Goodrich Castle   C10
Goodrich, Hereford & Worcs. A brooding
ruin standing on a spur above the Wye. Built
in the 12thC and considerably enlarged in
the 13thC, it was the last Herefordshire
defence to hold out for Charles I. The walls
were finally breached by a locally made
cannon called Roaring Meg. *Open 9.30–17.30
Apr & 9.30–19.00 May–Sep (9.30–17.30
Mar & Oct & 9.30–16.00 Nov–Feb. Closed
Sun morning).*

Haughmond Abbey   C5
Haughmond Abbey, Salop. Founded 1135, it
was rebuilt 50 years later. After the
Dissolution it passed into private hands and
at times was used as a dwelling house. There
is an impressive grey stone front to the
abbot's lodging with its large bay window.

The 12thC chapter house has a finely carved Norman doorway. *Open 9.30–17.30 Mar, Apr & Oct, 9.30–19.00 May–Sep, 9.30–16.00 Nov–Feb. Closed Sun morning.*

Kenilworth Castle   F7
Kenilworth, Warwick. The grandest fortress ruin in England. It started as a wooden fortress in 1112. The keep, still standing, was built in 1162. Kenilworth was later developed by Plantagenet and finally Tudor monarchs. Following the Civil War, Cromwell ordered the castle to be dismantled. *Open 9.30–17.30 daily Apr & 9.30–19.00 May–Sep (9.30–17.30 Mar & Oct & 9.30–16.00 Nov–Feb. Closed Sun morning.)*

Kirby Hall   J6
Northants. 2 miles n of Weldon. A renaissance palace grafted on to an Elizabethan home, it is now a majestic ruin smelling of bats and the open sky. Begun in 1570, the hall was considerably altered and beautified in the mid-17thC by Inigo Jones. Deserted in the mid-18thC, it gradually fell into ruins. *Open daily. Closed Sun morning.*

Kirby Muxloe Castle   G6
Kirby Muxloe, Leics. A magnificent brick castle begun in 1480, but left incomplete when Lord Hastings for whom it was built was beheaded in 1483. It was intended to be a fortified stronghold complete with moat and gun posts at a time of near-anarchy in England. All that remains are the great gatehouse and the west tower. *Open 9.30–17.30 Mar, Apr & Oct, 9.30–19.00 May–Sep, 9.30–16.00 Nov–Feb. Closed Sun.*

Lilleshall Abbey   C5
Lilleshall, Salop. A sleeping group of roofless walls, rich and organic. It was a Norman abbey founded in 1148. Planned with aisleless nave crossing two transepts, two square-ended chapels and a longer square-ended chancel. *Open 9.30–17.30 Mar, Apr & Oct, 9.30–19.00 May–Sep, 9.30–16.00 Nov–Feb. Closed Sun morning.*

Stokesay Castle   B7
Craven Arms, Salop. **3** *mile s of Craven on A49.* A fortified house built in the late 13thC. It consists of two stone towers linked by a long, gabled banqueting hall. *Open daily Apr–Oct 10.00–16.30 Nov–Mar. Closed Tue.*

Sutton Scarsdale Hall   G3
Sutton Scarsdale, Derby. An early 18thC house on the grand scale. Now a baroque ruin amongst lush undergrowth.

Warwick Castle   F8
Warwick. A 14thC villain perched on a crag above the Avon, it's one of the few mediaeval castles in England still inhabited. The outstanding buildings are Caesar's Tower, the Gatehouse, and Guy's Tower. Good collection of armour; paintings by Van Dyck, Velasquez and Rubens. *Open daily 10.00–17.30 Mar–Oct. 11.00–16.00 Nov–Feb.*

Unusual buildings

Boots Factory   G4
Beeston, Notts. Built in two parts, it is the earlier which is the best. A milestone in British architecture, it is a giant glass shep, 550 feet long with a 30-foot cantilever over the unloading dock. Inside is the packing hall, open right to the top with galleries around like a huge department store. The interior was probably influenced by the design of the Larkin Building.

Boots Factory, Beeston, Nottinghamshire

Iron Bridge   C6
Ironbridge, Salop. A majestic, intricate construction, like winter foliage, this was the first iron bridge to be built. It was designed by Abraham Derby and cast in 1778 at his foundry in Coalbrookdale. Spanning the River Severn, it consists of semicircular arches with a web of connecting members. The major span is 100 feet long.

Leicester University,   H6
The Engineering Building
Leicester, Leics. By Stirling and Gowan, it was built between 1959 and 1963 on a small, restricted site. An aggressive building designed with the fun of a folly and the visual strength of 19thC dock buildings.

Longden-upon-Tern Aqueduct   B6
Longden-upon-Tern, Salop. A spectacular and unbelievable piece of reality. This is the first cast-iron aqueduct. Built in 1794 by Thomas Telford to carry the Shropshire Union Canal over the River Tern. It is a long, narrow iron duct raised on four arches.

New Ways   J8
Northampton, Northants. Built in 1926 by Peter Behrens. It has a symmetrical front, almost Egyptian in feeling, with a central window over an entrance canopy balanced by a window on each side. The rear elevation is true International Style with unbroken bands of windows, and, of course, a flat roof. One of the great buildings of 20thC British architecture.

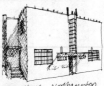

New Ways, Northampton

The Pastures   J6
North Luffenham, Leics. Built by C. F. Voysey in 1901. Simple and direct, with a cleanness of line associated more with the agricultural vernacular. A charming composition on three sides of a quadrangle with steeply pitched roofs, gables and small windows.

Houses & gardens

Alton Towers   E4
Staffs. 4½ miles e of Cheadle off B5032. Begun in 1814 by the Earl of Shrewsbury, this is a garden bordering on the fantastic, with an imitation Stonehenge, several ornate conservatories, colonnading, a decorative canal and statuary. The most memorable feature is the Chinese pagoda crowned with a fountain. All can be viewed by cable car. *Open 9.30–dusk daily, Apr–early Oct, gardens only.*

Belvoir Castle   J4
Leics. 7 miles wsw of Grantham off A607. Originally built in the 11thC, rebuilt in the 16thC, again in the 17thC and finally, in the 19thC. remodelled in the shape of a mediaeval castle. A spectacular and monumental ornament of towers, turrets and crenelations lying on a hill top. Inside are magnificent Gobelin tapestries and paintings by Van Dyck, Reynolds and Hogarth. It has one of the finest paintings by Holbein of Henry VIII. *Open 12.00–18.00 Wed, Thur & Sat (14.00–19.00 Sun, 11.00–19.00 B Hol Mon & Tue) Apr–Sep. 14.00–18.00 Sun Oct.*

Burford House   C8
Salop. 1 mile w of Tenbury Wells off A465. A most original selection of plants of decorative form and foliage (yuccas, ornamental grasses, lilies and hellebores) makes this garden interesting. The beautiful River Teme winds its way through the grounds, its water providing both a fountain in a formal pool and a stream garden with a good collection of bog plants. *Open 14.00–17.00 daily May–mid-Oct.*

Burghley House   **K6**

Cambs. 1 mile se of Stamford Lincs. A
great Elizabethan house, begun in 1552 by
Sir William Cecil, and built round a central
courtyard. From a distance it's a
magnificent mongrel of a building with a
forest of obelisks and pillared chimneys
crowned with miniature castles in the
roofscape. The great hall has a double
hammer-beam roof incorporating both
Gothic and Renaissance elements.
Interesting Roman staircase and fine carved
woodwork by Grinling Gibbons. Fine
furniture, tapestries and works of art. *Open
11.00–17.00 Tue–Thur, Sat & B.Hols
(14.00–17.00 Good Fri & Sun) Apr–Oct.*

Chatsworth House   **F3**

*Bakewell, Derby. ½ mile e of Edensor on
A623.* The seat of the Dukes of Devonshire,
set in the Derwent Valley near Bakewell.
Begun in 1687, it's more a palace than a
house: a complex giant of stone buildings
set against a wooded slope. The architects
were William Talman, Thomas Archer and
Sir Jeffry Wyatville. The magnificent state
rooms include works by Tijou, Verrio and
Laguerre, and paintings by Rembrandt
and Reynolds. The gardens are remodelled
by Paxton, with terraced water gardens and
lakes. *Open 11.30–16.00 Wed–Fri. 13.30–
17.00 Sat & Sun. 11.00–17.00 B. Hols
Apr–Oct.*

Compton Wynyates   **G9**

*Tysoe, Warwick. 10 miles w of Banbury off
B4035.* An unbelievably fine house lying in
a hollow of the hills. It's a brick-built
Tudor building with weathered wood and
mellow stone. Begun in 1480 on the site of an
old Norman house, it's an Alice in
Wonderland place with a garden full of
sculptured yews. *Open 14.00–17.30 Wed,
Sat, Easter & B.Hols Apr–Sep (also Sun
Jun–Aug).*

Coton Manor   **H7**

*Guilsborough, Northants. 10 miles n of
Northampton.* An enchanting old English
garden particularly noted for its wildfowl
tropical birds, and water gardens. *Open
14.00–18.00 Sun–Thur & B. Hols Apr–Oct.*

Eastnor Castle   **C9**

*Hereford & Worcs. 2 miles e of Ledbury on
A438.* With the Malvern Hills as a backcloth,
conifers both rare and exotic dominate the
skyline. A *pinus muricata*, the Bishop's pine
from California, *pinus montezumae*, a huge
Atlas cedar and the *abies venusta* fir
generally only seen growing in the Santa
Lucia mountains, are all here. There are also
noble pines from China, Japan and the Alps.
*Open 14.15–18.00 Sun & B. Hols May–Sep
& by special appointment.*

Easton Neston   **H9**

Easton Neston Park, Towcester, Northants.
An impeccably proportioned house of great
nobility sitting quietly like a stranded
whale. Built of local Helmdon stone, it was
designed by Nicholas Hawksmoor at the
beginning of the 18thC. The formal
parterre gardens, with their geometrically
curled and clipped golden yew hedges and
semicircular pool, although comparatively
recent, have an air of French 18thC charm.
Gardens open 1 day Jul.

Haddon Hall   **F3**

Derby. 2 miles se of Bakewell on A6. The
home of the Duke of Rutland, it's a grey
stone mediaeval manor house occupied and
adapted since the 12thC. It has a fine
banqueting hall and an athletic 100-foot-
long gallery.
A series of grey stone terraces forms the
backbone of the garden. The carved
balustrades and flights of steps provide
perfect support for clematis, honeysuckle,
tree peonies and the superb roses for which
Haddon Hall is justly famous. *Open 11.00–
18.00 Tue–Sat Apr–Sep & B.Hols. (14.00–
18.00 Sun.)*

Hanbury Hall   **D8**

*Hereford & Worcs. 2½ miles e of Droitwich on
B4090.* A palatial and complacent 18thC
house of red brick with stone dressings and a
central cupola. The interior decoration is by
Sir James Thornhill. *Open 14.00–18.00 Wed
& Sat Apr–Sep.*

Hardwick Hall   **G3**

*Derby. 2 miles s of Chesterfield-Mansfield
road (A617).* More glass than wall, it was
built by Smythson for Bess of Hardwick
between 1591 and 1597. Distinguished for
its symmetry, it's a brilliant Elizabethan
house. The Great Chamber is one of the
most beautiful rooms in Europe. *Open
13.00–17.30 Wed, Thur, Sat, Sun & B. Hols
Apr–Oct (12.00–18.00 Wed & Thur
May–Jul).*

Hardwick Hall.

Hodnet Hall   **C5**

*Salop. 12 miles ne of Shrewsbury, 5½ miles
sw of Market Drayton.* 60 acres of woodland
valley in which a stream plays the major
part, forming a series of lakes linked by
cascades and enhanced by bold groups of
astilbe, water iris, the giant-leaved gunnera
strongly scented azaleas, and some
magnificent forest trees. *Open 14.30–18.00
Mon–Fri (12.00–18.30 Sun & B. Hols)
Apr–Sep.*

Kedleston Hall   **F4**

Derby. 4½ miles nw of Derby. Grand design on
a grand scale. Begun in 1758 by Matthew
Brettingham who designed the north-east
pavilion. James Paine replaced him in 1761
and built the great north front – the grand
central block linked, in the Palladian
manner, to two smaller pavilions by curving
arcades. Robert Adam then designed the
domed south front and the superb
interiors. *Open 14.00–18.00 Sun & B.Hols
late Apr–Sep.*

Kedleston Hall, Derbyshire

Lea Rhododendron Gardens   **F3**

Derby. 5 miles se of Matlock off B6024. Set
in three acres of their natural woodland
habitat is an extensive collection of species
and hybrid rhododendrons and azaleas.
Open 9.00–20.00 late Mar–mid Jun.

Manor House   **G5**

Donington-Le-Heath, Leics. One of the most
important 13thC manor houses in England.
It was built in 1280 and slightly altered in
1600. The Hall is on the upper floor.
Open 14.00–18.00 Wed May–Sep.

Melbourne Hall   **G5**

Derby. 8 miles s of Derby on A514. Splendid
formal gardens by Wise, laid out in the
style of Andre Le Notre, landscape designer to
Louis XIV, and largely unaltered today.
The exquisite gilded wrought iron pergola
'The Birdcage' made by the 18thC
blacksmith Robert Bakewell is strategically
sited to form the focal point of one of the
many intersecting vistas. There are some
good pieces of sculpture including 'Four
Seasons' by Van Nost, a gift from Queen
Anne. *Open 11.00–18.00 late Jun–late Sep
(Closed Mon & Fri.) Open Sun & Wed
late Apr–late June.*

Packwood House   **F7**

Warwick. 2 miles e of Hockley Heath on A34.
A clean piece of domestic Tudor
architecture, built by a yeoman in 1560. It
has fine groups of chimneys and some
beautiful Jacobean panelling. It is famous
for the topiary yew garden planted about
1650 representing the Sermon on the
Mount–around the Christ are four
evangelists, twelve apostles, with the
multitude in the foreground. There is an
old furnace house used to warm the walls
where tender fruit trees once grew. Also a
charming Carolean formal garden. *Open
14.00–19.00 Wed–Sun Apr–Sep. Open
14.00–17.00 Wed, Sat & Sun Oct–Mar.*

Quenby Hall   H6
Leics. 8 miles e of Leicester. The most
important house in the Elizabethan-
Jacobean style in the county. It was built
1621–36 in brick with a stone trim, and
planned in an H. Interior almost intact.

Shugborough   E5
*Great Hawood, Staffs. 5½ miles se of
Stafford.* A slightly ham-fisted sort of place
full of dying grandeur. Begun in the 1690s,
it was extensively developed in the late
18thC. The principal rooms contain a
variety of interesting French and English
furniture, china, busts, tapestry and
paintings. *Open daily 10.30–17.30 Mar–Oct.
Closed Sun, Sun morning & Mon.*

Trentham Gardens   D4
Staffs, 3 miles from Stoke-on-Trent on A34.
In 600 acres of parkland, owned by the
Countess of Sutherland, work has begun to
create a national exhibition of gardening.
This includes a rock and peat-block
garden, a flower arranger's garden and
special ones for the blind, the W.I. and T.G.
There is an Italian garden with its formal
bedding displays and a splendid show of
spring bulbs. *Open 9.00–dusk daily.*

Wightwick Manor   D6
*W. Midlands. 3 miles w of Wolverhampton
(A454).* A many-gabled mediaeval affair like
a twilit afternoon full of Empire-building
passion. Designed by Edward Oald for
Theodore Mandor, industrialist and mayor
of Wolverhampton, it was begun in 1887.
Fine William Morris wallpapers and
materials as well as drawings and paintings
by Burne-Jones, Holman Hunt, Madox
Brown, Millais and Rossetti. *Open 14.30–
17.30 Thur, Sat & B.Hols (also 14.00–18.00
Wed May–Sep).*

Wollaton Hall   H4
Nottingham, Notts. 2½ miles w of city centre.
Built by Robert Smythson for Sir Francis
Willoughby 1580–88. It is one of the most
important Elizabethan houses in England,
distinguished from all the others by its
spectacular all-round symmetry and its
raised central hall. An extravagantly
crested and broken monster, sitting on a
raised mound in a billiard-smooth park; it
now houses the Natural History Museum.
*Open daily (Closed Sun morning) Oct–Mar.
10.00–19.00 daily (14.00–17.00 Sun)
Apr–Sep.*

Museums & galleries

Abington Museum   J8
Abington Park, Northampton, Northants.
This fine remodelled mediaeval manor
house preserves a reconstructed 18thC
street, collections of Chinese and English
porcelain and the uniforms, weapons and
medals of the Northamptonshire Regiment,
1741–1960. *Open daily. Closed Sun Oct–
Mar & Sun morning Apr–Sep.*

**The Avoncroft Museum of
Buildings**   E8
*Stoke Prior, nr Bromsgrove, Hereford &
Worcs.* An open-air museum with a good
selection of reconstructed old buildings,
some in the process of being restored. A
15thC timber-framed merchant's house, a
windmill, iron age dwellings, a nail and
chainmaker's workshops, and the 14thC
Guesten Hall Roof. *Open 11.00–18.00 Sat &
Sun & 14.00–17.00 Wed & Thur mid Mar–
Oct.*

**Birmingham City Museum
and Art Gallery**   E7
Congreve St, Birmingham, W. Midlands.
Special collections of the Pre-Raphaelites;
sculpture by Rodin and Henry Moore.
There are also departments of archaeology
and natural history with exhibits from
Nineveh, Ur, Mexico and Cyprus,
collections of British birds and gemstones.
Open daily Closed Sun morning.

**Derby Museum and
Art Gallery**   G4
Strand, Derby. Bonnie Prince Charlie
stopped in Derby during the 1745 rebellion
and a room in the museum commemorates
the occasion. Also collections of porcelain,

costumes, archaeology and paintings by
Joseph Wright of Derby. *Open daily.
Closed Sun.*

Doll Museum   F8
Oken's House, Castle St, Warwick. This
Elizabethan house holds a beautiful
collection of antique and period dolls, made
of china, metal, wax and wood; mechanical
and musical. *Open daily. Closed Sun
morning.*

**The Dyson Perrins Museum of
Worcester Porcelain**   D8
*The Royal Porcelain Works, Severn St,
Worcester, Hereford & Worcs.* The finest
collection of Old Worcester in the world, on
display in this converted Victorian school
house, also see china being made and
decorated. *Open Mon–Fri. Also Sat 10.00–
17.00 Apr–Sep.*

Jewry Wall Museum   H6
St Nicholas Circle, Leicester, Leics. Jewry
Wall is all that remains of Roman Ratae
Coritanorum, and the museum is devoted to
Roman relics. There's a fine mosaic
pavement. *Open 10.00–19.30 Mon–Sat.
14.00–17.30 Sun.*

**Museum of Childhood and
Costume**   E5
Blithfield Hall, nr Rugeley, Blithfield, Staffs.
There's a lovely exhibition of miniature and
toy theatres, two Victorian dolls' houses,
antique dolls and toys, embroidered
Georgian costumes, coronation robes and
uniforms. *Open 14.30–18.00 Wed, Thur, Sat
& Sun Easter–Sep & B. Hols.*

**Northampton Central Museum
and Art Gallery**   J8
Guildhall Rd, Northampton, Northants.
Queen Victoria's wedding shoes and the
ballet shoes of Nijinsky, Ulanova and
Fonteyn are part of the shoe-making
collection illustrating Northampton's local
industry. *Open daily (10.00–20.00 Thur &
Sat). Closed Sun.*

**Nottingham City Museum and
Art Gallery**   H4
The Castle, Nottingham, Notts. Built on the
site of a mediaeval castle, the present castle
was a 17thC residence adapted as a museum
in 1878. There are special collections of
paintings by Bonington and Sandby, lace
and embroideries, and also the museum of
the Sherwood Foresters Regiment. *Open
daily 8.00–dusk Mon–Fri, 9.00–dusk Sat &
Sun.*

**The Royal Shakespeare Theatre
Picture Gallery**   F8
*Royal Shakespeare Theatre, Stratford-
upon-Avon, Warwick.* Original costumes
and designs from RSC productions,
Shakespeare's gloves and a collection of
relics of famous actors, including David
Garrick and Ellen Terry, and some fine
portraits, from the 'Flower Portrait' of
Shakespeare to those of Irving, Kean,
Gielgud and Olivier. *Open daily Apr–Oct,
closed Sun morning, 10.00–16.00 Sat &
14.00–16.00 Sun only Nov–Mar.*

Wedgwood Museum   D4
Barlaston, Stoke-on-Trent, Staffs. A fine
collection of early Wedgwood ware including
experimental pieces. *Open 9.00–17.00 Mon–
Sat. Tel 2141.*

**Worcestershire County
Museum**   D7
*Hartlebury Castle, Hartlebury, nr
Kidderminster, Hereford & Worcs.* The north
wing of the Bishop's Palace houses this
museum of Worcester life. There are gypsy
caravans, horse-drawn carriages and a cider
mill on show. *Open daily Mon–Thur &
14.00–18.00 Sat & Sun.*

Zoos, aquaria & aviaries

Dudley Zoo   D7
Castle Hill, Dudley, W. Midlands. An open-
air zoo of enclosures without bars in a
natural setting surrounded by hills and dense
woods. The aquarium has been built in the
crypt beneath the ruined Dudley Castle
chapel. *Open daily.*

**Riber Castle Fauna Reserve and
Wildlife Park** F3
Derby. Off B6014 2 miles from Matlock.
The reserve has two sections, British and
European, and includes deer, otter, game
birds, lynx, wild boar and brown bears.
Open daily (10.00–19.00 Apr.–Oct)

Stapleford Lion Reserve J5
*Stapleford Park, Leics. On B676 5 miles from
Melton Mowbray.* A lesser Longleat, opened
in 1968 by Lord Gretton. 'Animal Land' is a
self-contained zoo in the park with a good
collection: tigers, lions, brown bears and
reptiles. *Open 10.00–18.30 daily Apr–Sep.*

Twycross Zoo Park F6
*Norton-Juxta-Twycross, nr Atherstone,
Leics.* A spacious zoo specialising in apes,
monkeys, orang-utans, lions, tigers,
kangaroos, crocodiles and elephants. *Open
daily (10.00–19.00 Apr–Oct).*

**The Wildfowl Trust and
The Waterfowl Gardens** K6
Peakirk, nr Peterborough, Cambs. This is
a small-scale Slimbridge and is
complementary to the Wildfowl Trust's
main collection there. Over 600 birds and
100 species of teal, mallard and geese. There
are ponds and rearing pens in the gardens.
*Open daily (9.30–16.30 Nov–Jan). Closed
Sun morning.*

Nature trails & reserves

Brockhampton Woodland Walk
*Hereford & Worcs. Park opposite Bringsty
Post Office, 2 minutes from start, e of
Bromyard off A44.* Typical oakwood birds,
including buzzard, raven and pied flycatcher.
Commoner waterfowl on the lake. 1–2 miles.
Guide at Post Office or at start.

Cannock Chase Forest Trail
*Staffs. Start 1½ miles from Ladyhill on
by-road s from Rugeley–Penkridge road.*
Pinewood and heathland birds. Guide,
from H.M.S.O.

Coombes Valley Nature Reserve
Staffs. On Apesford road s of Leek. An
RSPB Reserve in a wooded valley with a
rocky stream, the Coombes Brook.
Breeding birds include sparrowhawk,
kingfisher, dipper, wood warbler and pied
flycatcher. Access to main area by permit
only, details from RSPB, The Lodge,
Sandy, Beds. There is also a nature trail,
and a public footpath crosses part of the
reserve.

Earlswood Nature Reserve
Solihull, W. Midlands. A variety of oakwood
and lake species. Guide from the Museum
and Art Gallery, Congreve Street,
Birmingham.

Edale Nature Trail
*Edale, Derby. Start at the bridge over
Grindsbrook Stream.* In the Peak National
Park, there is a good selection of typical
species of a series of habitats–moorland,
stream and mixed woodland. 3 miles. Guide
at National Park Information Centre at
Edale, Castleton, Burton or Bakewell.

Hawksmoor Nature Reserve
Staffs. 1½ miles ne of Cheadle. Commoner
birds of moorland, forest and newly
afforested areas, seen in an interesting
gradation of habitats. There are three
nature trails, and a leaflet for these is
available from P.L. Wilson, The Spinney,
Greendale, Oakmoor.

Ilam Nature Walk
Staffs. 4½ miles nw of Ashbourne, at Ilam Hall.
Good woodland bird watching in Manifold
Valley. 1¼ miles, open mid Apr–October.
Staffordshire Nature Conservation Trust.
Leaflet from Ilam tea rooms and caravan
site.

Ravenshill Woodland Reserve
Hereford & Worcs. W of Worcester at Alfrick.
A varied woodland with nature trail.
Assorted warblers and woodcock among its
typical birds. Details from Hon Sec, High
Wood Alfrick, Worcester. *Open Sat & Sun.
Mon–Fri by arrangement.*

Bird watching

Blithfield Reservoir
Staffs. There is a causeway, *from which much
can be seen, north of Rugeley on B5013.* An
extremely good water for winter wildfowl,
with particularly large numbers of teal,
wigeon, pochard and tufted duck and many
grebes, goldeneye and goosander. Wader
passage is often very good, both in spring
and autumn, and migrant black terns and
little gulls are regular.

Clumber Park
*Notts. 2½ miles sw of Worksop and within ½
mile of the A1.* Clumber Park is accessible
from several points and easily explored. Its
parkland and woodland holds a rich variety
of breeding birds, including nightingale,
redstart, nightjar, and hawfinch, and is
equally rewarding in winter, when its large
lake has a good selection of wildfowl.

**Ellesmere and North Shropshire
Meres**
Salop. Nw of Shrewsbury. These meres are
variously notable for their wildfowl in
winter; regular species including wigeon,
goldeneye, goosander and cormorant;
breeding reed and sedge warblers, plus great
crested grebes on some of them; and a good
selection of autumn migrants–waders and
black terns among them.

Eye Brook Reservoir
*Leics. Good views can be had from public
roads from Caldecote on A6003; turn w to
Stoke Dry and the reservoir.* A notable area
for winter duck, including wigeon, pintail,
shoveler, and goosander and, with its
'natural' banks and margins, excellent for a
variety of waders in spring and autumn.
Black terns are regular on passage, and it is
a good place to see kingfishers.

Wyre Forest
*Hereford & Worcs. W of Kidderminster. The
area can be explored from Buttonoak on
B4194.* A good variety of woodland birds
may be found in this mainly deciduous
forest, including redstart, wood warbler,
pied flycatcher and tree pipit, while
kingfishers live along the Dowles Brook.

Brass rubbing

Brass Rubbing
The following is a short list of churches
that have brasses for rubbing. Permission
is almost invariably required.
Herefordshire & Worcs. Hereford Cathedral,
Fladbury, Kidderminster.
Leicestershire. Castle Donington, Little
Casterton, Stockerston, Wanlip.
Northamptonshire. Ashby St Ledgers,
Brampton-by-Dingley, Castle Ashby,
Charwelton, Cottestock, Easton Neston,
Greens Norton, Higham Ferrers, Lowick,
Newton-by-Geddington.
Shropshire. Acton Burnell, Adderley,
Edgmond, Harley, Tong.
Staffordshire. Audley, Horton, Norbury,
Okeover, Standon.
Warwickshire. Baginton, Merevale, Warwick
(St Mary), Wixford.
Worcestershire. Fladbury, Kidderminster.

Fossil hunting

Derbyshire
The best area for fossils is the carboniferous
limestone moorland of the Peak District –
the Dales to the north of Ashbourne and
around Matlock and Bakewell. The
limestone hills around Castleton contain
coral reefs with abundant fossils.

Herefordshire and Worcester
Much of the county is of old red sandstone
which for the most part is unfossiliferous,
but Silurian rocks, shales and limestones
with fossils occur around Woolhope and in
the Malvern Hills.
The most famous site is Dudley where
Upper Silurian limestones crowded with
fossils and fossil coral reefs may be seen at
the Wren's Nest.

Leicestershire
Although much of Leicestershire is made up of unfossiliferous red Triassic sandstones and the ancient rocks of Charnwood Forest, Rutland and the east of the county are of Lower and Middle Jurassic rocks. The Liassic rocks exposed at Barrow-on-Soar, in addition to normal ammonites, bivalves and gastropods, have in the past yielded many fossil lobsters. The Northampton ironstone can be collected in the large quarries around the steel works of Corby.

Northamptonshire
The best fossiliferous exposures are in the Middle Jurassic rocks; the Northampton Sands and ironstone have been extensively quarried over large areas around Kettering and Wellingborough. Other Middle Jurassic limestones may be seen in the districts around Irchester and Blisworth, and the highly fossiliferous Cornbrash beds around Thrapston and Islip.

Nottinghamshire
There are few fossiliferous areas as much of the county is covered by red Permian and Triassic desert sandstones.

Shropshire
The south of Shropshire is one of the classic geological areas where many of the Lower Palaeozoic beds have many fossils.
The main areas are for Ordovician rocks: the district around Shelve and Hope in the south-west, around Craven Arms and Church Stretton and to the east of Caer Caradoc Hill; for Silurian rocks the limestone ridges running south from Much Wenlock to Ludlow where the very fossiliferous Wenlock and Aymestry limestones occur, with shale in the valleys containing trilobites and graptolites.

Staffordshire
Permian and Triassic rocks cover much of the county with coal measures beneath. Only in the south fossils may be found in Silurian beds exposed to the north of Great Barr (the Barr Limestone). Around Leek in the north-west, the carboniferous limestone is fossiliferous.

Warwickshire
The Lower Lias is exposed in clay pits in the district around Rugby and at Wilmcote near Stratford-upon-Avon, and the Middle Lias Marlstone rock bed with its 'nests' of fossil brachiopods caps Edge Hill near Kineton where there are several old quarries.

Valleys & plains

Derbyshire Dales
The Derbyshire Peak District holds a fascinating series of dales, all tending southward. Derwentdale, the longest, runs from he heather moors west of Sheffield past Bamford and Chatsworth to Bakewell, Matlock and Derby. It carries the picturesque trunk road A6 from Rowsley south. Edale, near Hope, isolated in the folds of the hills below Kinder Scout, preserves a hill-farming pattern established in Norse settlement times. The Derbyshire Wye runs south from Buxton through Miller's Dale, a gorge in sheer limestone rocks, and on past Monsal Dale, fringed with its native ashwoods. Through Dovedale the River Dove takes a lonely isolated path deep in the hills, from Longnor, south of Buxton, to Ashbourne.

Herefordshire Plain
Hereford & Worcs. Most of Herefordshire forms one great plain, across which all roads lead to the county town and cathedral of Hereford, standing beside the broad River Wye. This is the home of the fat Hereford beef cattle, easily known by their red hides with a white stripe above; bulls are exported all over the world to improve local herds or breeds. Hops are grown here for beer, and small sour apples for strong cider.

Vale of Evesham
Hereford & Worcs. Around the town of Evesham, which stands beside the Avon in the south of Worcestershire, this vale extends as the most fertile tract in all England. A warm, sunny climate and light soil favour the growth of valuable fruit and vegetable crops, including strawberries and asparagus, and there are thriving orchards of plums and pears, cherries and apples.

Hills & mountains

Kinder Scout
Derby. Highest point of the Peak District, Kinder Scout forms a bleak moorland, 2,000 feet above sea level, covered by six-foot-deep peat bogs holding roots of prehistoric pine trees. This waste is crossed by the unfenced Snake Pass Road, A57, from Sheffield via Glossop to Manchester. Kinder Downfall, where a stream cascades over crags, gives wide views west over smoky industrial Lancashire. The 270-mile-long Pennine Way starts here.

Leicestershire Wolds
Leics. Between Leicester and Grantham these little-known wolds extend as rolling well-farmed pastures, based on their soft-grey Cotswold stone.

Malvern Hills
The steep-sided Malvern Hills raise their grassy slopes like true mountains above the Plain of Hereford and Worcestershire's broad vale. There are wide views stretching to seven counties.

Northamptonshire Uplands
In the heart of the Midlands, between Northampton and Rugby, these gentle grassy ridges form the source of many rivers.

North Staffordshire Uplands
Staffs. Off the beaten track, the uplands east of Stafford town, around Cheadle, attract all who appreciate rounded wooded hills, with pastures surrounding old stone-built farmsteads.

Peak District
Derby. Named after the mediaeval Peak Forest, and remotely from Norse *pikr*, pointed hill, the Peak District comprises all the North Derbyshire uplands. Brown sandstone rocks form high flat moors ending in dramatic cliffs called 'edges'. Elsewhere white limestone provides narrow gorges bounded by sheer cliffs, with underground caverns and huge quarries. A National Park, the Peak District makes grand walking and touring country, easily explored from centres like Buxton, Bakewell, Malvern and Ashbourne.

South Shropshire Uplands
Salop. The hills of south-west Shropshire provide magnificent walking and touring country. Each main ridge has well-wooded flanks, topped by pastures that are often common grazings; all have paths to their summits.

Forests

Arden Forest   F8
From the ancient royal Forest of Arden, in the lowlands of Warwickshire and Worcestershire, William Shakespeare drew his first-hand knowledge of woodland life, revealed in plays like 'As You Like It', and 'A Midsummer Night's Dream'.

Charnwood Forest   G5
Leics. A broken upland of ancient Pre-Cambrian rock, near the M1 motorway north-west of Leicester, Charnwood lends the Midlands a touch of highland scenery. Well wooded, it survives as fragments of a large mediaeval forest.

Clun Forest   A7
Salop. This remote hill region lies below the little village called Clun, on the Welsh Border in south-west Shropshire. It extends east through the great Mortimer Forest of

oaks and conifers towards Ludlow. Many of Clun's hidden winding valleys hold woods of oak, ash, birch and alder, surviving from the ancient forest.

Rockingham Forest   **J6**
Northants. The forest survives around Rockingham village as a fragment of a widespread mediaeval hunting ground.

Sherwood Forest   **H2**
Notts. North of Nottingham, between Mansfield and Worksop, the great mediaeval forest of Sherwood (the Shire Wood) still survives as a group of well-timbered private estates. These are also called 'The Dukeries' since at one time most were owned by sporting dukes. Here Robin Hood and his band of outlaws hid, traditionally robbing the rich to aid the poor. Great oaks still survive, especially in Clumber Park, a big National Trust property open to the public.

Rivers

The Avon
Warwick. Rising on the Midland plateau near Coventry, the Warwickshire Avon flows past Warwick Castle and Stratford-upon-Avon, Shakespeare's birthplace. It then runs through the warm, fertile and well cultivated Vale of Evesham to Tewkesbury where it joins the Severn.

The Derwent
Derby. The Derwent rises on the high Peak District moorlands west of Sheffield and flows through the scenic Derwent Valley Reservoirs, fringed with pine forests, to Bamford. It then follows a lovely wooded and steep-sided valley south through Bakewell and Derby, to join the Trent near Long Eaton.

The Nene
Northants. The River Nene is a sluggish waterway running north-eastwards from the Midland plateau through Northampton town to Peterborough city. It continues north-east as a slow canalised and navigable stream, almost at sea-level, to join the Wash.

The Severn
Leaving the Welsh border near Welshpool, the Severn winds east to Shrewsbury, which it almost encircles in a great loop. At Ironbridge it is crossed by the graceful arch of one of the world's earliest iron bridges. Then it turns south-east and passes the hill-top town of Bridgnorth, piercing the hills through the steep-sided Severn gorge. Turning south to enter Worcestershire, the Severn, now a slow, navigable stream, wanders over a broad flood plain to Worcester city. It leaves this region at Tewkesbury, flowing south through Gloucestershire to the sea.

The Soar
Leics. Cutting a deep, broad valley northwards through the Midland hills, the River Soar runs through Leicester city and Loughborough to join the Trent at Long Eaton.

The Trent
Starting as a trickle on the bleak Staffordshire moors near Leek, the Trent runs south-west through the bustling pottery town of Stoke-on-Trent, past Stafford and Lichfield, and then north-east through the brewery town of Burton-on-Trent. Skirting Derby, it then runs eastwards through the university city and industrial complex of Nottingham, where it becomes navigable. Thence it runs north, almost at sea-level, over a broad flat plain along Nottinghamshire's eastern border, to join the Humber near Goole. The Trent is now sadly polluted.

The Wye
Hereford & Worcs. The western old county of Hereford lies wholly in the lovely, well-farmed and well-wooded valley of the River Wye, or Plain of Hereford. This clear, salmon-rich stream flows from Plynlimon in the Welsh hills past Hereford city and cathedral. It leaves the county at Symond's Yat, through the dramatic gorge it has worn

through the limestone hills on its way to the Bristol Channel.

Canals

There is a large mileage of navigable canals in this section, for this area includes the whole of the intricate Midlands canal network. These canals were of course all built by individual canal companies, mostly in the late 18thC, and they provided the base for the whole of the present-day prosperity of the Midlands. The Birmingham area in particular is still a maze of waterways, most of them now decaying and forgotten, little used by boaters and undiscovered by walkers. There are plenty of contrasts. There is the winding rural course of the lovely but isolated Chesterfield Canal, the dead straight line of Telford's Shropshire Union Canal striking off from Wolverhampton towards Liverpool, the delightful course of the Grand Union Canal's Leicester section, twisting and turning through the gentle uplands of Leicestershire, and the business-like but daunting passage of the Grand Union main line through endless locks on its way to Birmingham.
Places to see:
Foxton Near Market Harborough, a busy canal junction with a flight of ten staircase locks and the remains of the ingenious 'inclined plane' that once replaced them.
Harecastle Near Kidsgrove, where two of the greatest canal tunnels ever built lie side by side, 3000 yards long.
Gas Street Basin Birmingham, one of the old-style canal communities, where there is always a collection of traditional narrowboats and their families – right in the heart of Birmingham.
Stourport-on-Severn A canal port with fascinating basins, locks and old warehouses.
Hatton Near Warwick, where the Grand Union Canal climbs a flight of 21 wide locks on its way up to Birmingham. Beside these locks can be seen the remains of the former narrow locks, which were replaced in the 1930s.
Braunston Near Rugby, a canal village complete with boatyards traditional and modern, canal pubs, a flight of six locks and a mile-long tunnel through the hills of Northamptonshire.
Stoke Bruerne A canal village with a fine Waterways Museum. Here is a fascinating collection of old canal photographs, machinery, signs and paintings. A must for anyone who passes through Northamptonshire.

Archaeology

Arbor Low Stone Circle   **F3**
Arbor Low, Middleton, Derby. The bronze age 'henge' monument at Arbor Low consists of a circular earth bank with a ditch on the inside, and two entrances at opposite ends. A complete stone circle of recumbent stones lies round the inner side of the ditch; as they obstruct the entrances, these may be a later feature. This type of monument apparently had a religious significance; the classic example of a henge site is Stonehenge.
Open 9.30–17.30 Mar, Apr & Oct, 9.30–19.00 May–Sep, 9.30–16.00 Nov–Feb.
Closed Sun morning.

Bredon Hill   **E9**
Nr Tewkesbury, Hereford & Worcs. Bredon Hill iron age hillfort, with its system of multiple bank and ditch defences, commanded a considerable area of surrounding countryside, and is a notable viewpoint. The hill also has an iron age cemetery site; finds are contained in a private museum at Overbury Court.

Creswell Crags   **G2**
Notts. Creswell Crags is one of the best preserved of the inhabited cave sites in Britain, and dates from the Upper Palaeolithic (later old stone age).

Great Casterton   **K6**
Leics. Great Casterton was one of the smaller towns of Roman Britain but like

larger cities, these were provided with wall and ditch defences during the 3rdC.

Leicester   H6
Leics. Roman Ratae Coritanorum, the tribal capital of the Coritani. The Jewry Wall, a stretch of walling that formed part of the city baths, is one of the most impressive Roman town monuments surviving in Britain. The foundations of the baths are visible in front of the wall, and are displayed in the grounds of the Jewry Wall Museum.

Letocetum Wall   E6
Staffs. **2** miles sw of Lichfield on A5. The Roman town of Letocetum probably originated as a trading settlement around a 1stC fort; later it was able to draw its custom from the nearby junction of two major Roman roads, Watling Street, on which it stands, and Ricknield Street. A large building that has been found on the site was probably a *mansio*, an official posting-station where lodgings and a change of horses would be available. The visible remains are those of the town bath building, and include plunge baths, hot rooms raised on tile columns above the heating pipes, and exercise rooms. The site museum houses excavation finds, including brooches and two military name-tags. *Open 9.30–17.30 Mar, Apr & Oct, 9.30–19.00 May–Sep, 9.30–16.00 Nov–Feb. Closed Sun morning.*

Melandra Castle   E1
Glossop, Derby. The Roman fort of Melandra is well situated on a hill overlooking the town. Parts of the rampart and ditch defences and foundations of the surrounding wall, including a small internal turret, can still be seen.

Midsummer Hill   D9
Nr Ledbury, Hereford & Worcs. One of the most impressive of the iron age hill forts in the county, Midsummer Hill has a system of multiple ditches and banks enclosing a large hilltop area. The county is rich in hill forts.

Nine Ladies Stone Circle   F3
Stanton Moor, Stanton, Derby. The Nine Ladies belongs to a type of bronze age monument peculiar to upland areas of Great Britain, and is characterised by having cremation burials inside the enclosure. It consists of a low bank with upright stones set in it in a circle. *Accessible any time.*

The Wrekin   C6
Nr Wellington, Salop. The large iron age hill fort on top of the Wrekin was probably the defensive centre of the Cornovii; in Roman times they were moved away from their fortified sites, and had their tribal capital at Wroxeter.

Wroxeter Roman City   B6
Wroxeter, Salop. Roman Viroconium Cornoviorum, the tribal capital of the Cornovii. Like many major Roman towns, Wroxeter was originally a military base, and was occupied by the XIV Gemina legion during the conquest of Wales in the 1stC. The town that developed around the fortress was later made the tribal capital, and grew into a large and wealthy city. The visible remains consist of a magnificent town bath building, arranged in the customary 'Turkish bath' system favoured by the Romans, with exercise halls, hot and cold plunge baths, dry and damp heat rooms, and a large swimming pool. The site museum houses a fine collection of Roman objects. *Open 9.30–17.30 Mar, Apr & Oct, 9.30–19.00 May–Sep, 9.30–16.00 Nov–Feb. Closed Sun morning.*

Footpaths & ancient ways

The Pennine Way
The 250-mile-long Pennine Way from Derbyshire to the borders of Scotland begins at Edale, a lonely Derbyshire village surrounded by the grey industrial Midlands. From here Kinder Scout looms down from the north – a magnificent sight. The first ascent of the Way is over

Grindsbrook, deceptively easy-going at first, but it gets tougher as you go with many streams crossing the route, and some rock-clambering to the 2,000-foot summit. The black peat-bogs stretch beyond for two miles. The path then crosses Black Ashop Moor, descending into the valley along the lower Snake Path. Featherbed Moss is another soggy patch to be tackled, and Bleaklow is a swampy wasteland not to be tackled on a misty day. Crowden will take you to the Cheshire border.

Regional sports

Angling
There are many excellent rivers flowing through the Midlands – the portion of England furthest from the sea. The Derbyshire Peak District rivers and streams such as the Wye, Lightwood, and Derwent have a national reputation among trout fishermen. Indeed the Wye is among the few rivers in the country where rainbow trout breed naturally. The lazy flowing River Trent, and the numerous canals in the Pottery district, provide first class coarse fishing. Most of the fishing is privately owned and carefully controlled. Further information from:
Trent Water Authority. Lucknow Ave, Nottingham. Tel 608161.
Severn River Authority. 64 Albert Rd North, Malvern, Hereford & Worcs. Tel 61511.

Cricket
The Midland Counties over the last hundred years have provided a solid base for English cricket, and produced many great players for England such as Mike Smith, Warwickshire's Captain, and Colin Milburn of Northamptonshire. It would be invidious to select a single club, so here are the current three best performers:
Warwickshire County Cricket Club The County Ground, Edgbaston, Birmingham. Tel 021-440 3521.
Worcestershire County Cricket The County Ground, New Road, Worcester. Tel 53607.
Leicestershire County Cricket The County Ground, Grace Road, Leicester. Tel 832 128

Football
There are many first class and good professional Association Football teams in the Midlands. At the age of 49, Stanley Matthews made football history when he was in the team that took Stoke City back into the First Division of the Football League in 1963. Other Midland clubs worth watching are the following, who are usually matched against the country's best. Look in the local papers for details: *Aston Villa, Birmingham City, Coventry City, Derby County, Leicester, Nottingham Forest, West Bromwich Albion & Wolverhampton Wanderers.*

Gliding
This is an increasingly popular sport in Britain, and the Midland skies are fortunate in not being over cluttered with commercial and military air space.
Burton and Derby Gliding Club. Church Broughton, Derby. Twelve miles e of Derby on A516. This is a gliding club which also offers cheap tuition under the aegis of the East Midland Region Sports Council, 26 Hunters Road, West Bridgford, Nottingham.

Motor Racing
Silverstone, near Towcester (pronounced Toaster), Northamptonshire, shares the distinction with Brands Hatch of staging the British Grand Prix for Formula 1 racing cars in the July of alternate years. Victory in the Grand Prix counts towards the world motor racing championship. Beside the Grand Prix the track is in regular use throughout the year. The circuit has been improved in recent years and is the fastest in Britain. Further information from the Booking Office Silverstone Circuit, Silverstone, nr Towcester. Tel Silverstone 857271.

Speedway
A specialised form of motor cycle racing on small enclosed cinder track circuits. Leicester's stadium has a meeting every Tuesday evening during the summer months. For further information see the local papers.

Festivals

Festivals
For information and tickets for festivals go to the local information centre or ticket agent.

Bromsgrove Festival
Bromsgrove, Worcs. A well rounded spring festival with something for everyone. A foreign theme is incorporated each year, and new musical works, drama, and music old and new, including classical and folk. *2 weeks in Apr.*

Ludlow Festival
Ludlow, Salop. The main event at Ludlow is the performance of one of Shakespeare's plays in the open-air theatre beside the castle walls. There are also concerts and exhibitions. *2 weeks in early Jul.*

Royal Shakespeare Theatre Season
Stratford-upon-Avon, Warwick. The first Shakespeare festival at Stratford was initiated by David Garrick, the 18thC actor-manager. The present theatre was opened in 1932, and from April to December every year Shakespeare's plays are performed by a glittering cast. Shakespeare's birthday celebrations on the 23rd April are a special event with bands, flag waving and a public luncheon given by the Shakespeare club.

Three Choirs Festival
Founded before 1719 the festival claims to be the oldest continuous music festival in Europe. It is held every year, in succession in the cathedral cities of Worcester Hereford and Gloucester. *Aug.*

Fun things

Billing Aquadrome   **J8**
Little Billing, Northants. 3 miles from Northampton off A45, 5 miles from M1 Motorway. The Aquadrome is an aquatic fun park set in beautiful countryside. Besides an old working water mill and milling museum, there is a lakeside marina, fishing, slides, and a miniature diesel railway. Space for caravans and campers at reasonable rates. For further details: Tel Northampton 890849.

Blue John Cavern and Mine   **F2**
Derby. ½ mile w of Castleton. Blue John is a translucent variety of the mineral fluorspar which is veined in red, blue, purple and yellow. It is so rare that it is found only here, and ornaments have been made from it since Roman times. Small vases made from Blue John can be bought at the mine and in Castleton. The caves are very beautiful with their coloured stalactites.

The Goose Fair   **H4**
Nottingham, Notts. The Fair is held on the first Thursday, Friday and Saturday in October at the Forest Recreation Ground by Gregory Boulevard. Sadly there are no more geese, though when the fair was granted its charter in 1284, when it was at its height of popularity, up to 20,000 geese met their fate there.

Hilton Valley Miniature Railway   **C6**
Hilton Valley, Salop. Off A454 9 miles from Wolverhampton, 4 miles from Bridgnorth. A mile of 7¼-inch gauge track runs through attractive scenery among trees and beside a trout stream. In addition to the four steam engines, this line is of interest for its comprehensive signalling system which is unusual on a model railway. *Open Sun afternoon & B.Hols mid Apr–Sep.*

Peak Cavern   **F2**
Castleton, Derby. Fascinating 60-foot-high cavern in the limestone. *Open daily mid Apr–mid Sep.*

Sarehole Mill   **E7**
Colebank Rd, Hall Green, Birmingham W. Midlands. Once used for working metal this water mill is now restored and houses a museum on milling. *Open 14.00–19.00 daily (11.00–19.00 Sat) Apr–Nov.*

Stapleford Park   **J5**
Leics. 4 miles e of Melton Mowbray off B676. An extensive and imaginative 10¼-inch gauge miniature railway runs from the car park to the Hall. At the Hall you can continue your steam-hauled journey in the Boat Train which connects with two scale models of the Shaw Saville liners – Northern Star and Southern Cross. *Open 14.30–18.30 Wed, Thur & Sun, Easter & B.Hols May–Sep.*

The Tramway Museum   **G3**
Matlock Rd, Crich, Derby. 5 miles se of Matlock. Created by a band of dedicated tramway enthusiasts it houses a good selection of trams which bring forth tears of pure nostalgia. Take your children for a ride on the mile of track and tell them what you got for a penny ticket when you were young. *Open 11.00–18.00 Sat Sun & B. Hols Apr–Oct & daily Tue–Thur Jun–Aug.*

Hotels

Hotels
The following indicates the price range of a single room per night:
£   inexpensive
££   medium priced
£££   expensive

Birmingham W. Midlands   **E7**
Albany Hotel, Smallbrook, Queensway. Tel 021-643 8171. Modern, open-plan. In the Bull Ring. No dogs. £££.

Brewardine Hereford & Worcs   **A9**
Red Lion Hotel. Tel Moccas 303. A 17thC red brick inn near the Wye. Good local fishing. £.

Broadway Hereford & Worcs.   **E9**
Lygon Arms, High St. Tel 2255. A 400-year-old hotel of great character. Some famous antiques. Good food. £££.

Castleton Derby   **F2**
Ye Olde Nag's Head, nr Sheffield. Tel Hope Valley 20248. A 17thC inn well placed for tours of the local caves. Large bar and well decorated restaurant. £.

Derby Derby   **G4**
Mackworth Hotel, Mackworth. Tel Kirk Langley 324. A red brick hotel on the Ashbourne Road with a friendly atmosphere and excellent restaurant. £.

Dovedale Derby.   **F3**
Izaak Walton Hotel, nr Ashbourne. Tel Thorpe Cloud 261. A converted 17thC stone farmhouse set in beautiful Dovedale. Splendid views. ££.

Droitwich Hereford & Worcs.   **D8**
Chateau Impney Hotel. Tel 4411. A chateau built in 1870 by a local millionaire for his French wife. Set in a 60-acre park. £££.

Great Malvern Hereford & Worcs   **D9**
Abbey Hotel, Abbey Rd. Tel 3325. Old established hotel with good views of the Severn Valley. ££.

Hereford Hereford & Worcs.   **B9**
Green Dragon Hotel, Broad St. Tel 2506. An interesting looking coaching inn with 18thC trimmings. ££.

Kenilworth Warwick.   **F7**
De Montford Hotel, The Square. Tel 55944. Modern. Well situated for touring and conferences. £.

Leamington Spa Warwick.   **F8**
Manor House Hotel, Avenue Rd. Tel 23251. 18thC; with one of the earliest recorded tennis courts. ££.

Leek Staffs. **E3**
*Three Horseshoes, Blackshaw Moor. Tel
Blackshaw 296.* A pleasant half-timbered inn
with good views of the Pennines. £.

Leicester Leics. **H6**
Grand Hotel, Granby St. Tel 56222. A
centrally situated hotel with a popular bar. £.

Loughborough Leics. **G5**
King's Head Hotel High St. Tel 214893. A
recently renovated town centre hotel. £.

Ludlow Salop. **B7**
Feathers Hotel, Corve St. Tel 2919. A fine
Tudor gabled hotel with a good period
interior. ££.

Malvern Hereford & Worcs. **D9**
Cottage in the Wood, Holywell Rd. Tel 3487.
A fine Georgian house with splendid gardens
and views of the Malvern Hills, the Severn
and the Evesham Vale. Good restaurant. £.

Market Harborough Leics. **H7**
Three Swans Hotel, High St. Tel 3247. A
15thC building which is being improved by
its owners. £.

Matlock Bath Derby. **F3**
New Bath Hotel, Derby Rd. Tel 3275. A
beautifully situated spa hotel. A good centre
for the Derbyshire Peak District. ££.

Melton Mowbray Leics. **J5**
George Hotel, High St. Tel 2112. A
comfortable inn patronised by Queen
Victoria before her accession. £.

Newport Salop. **D5**
*Royal Victoria Hotel, St Mary's St. Tel 071.
810831.* Patronised by Queen Victoria
before her accession. £.

Nottingham Notts. **H4**
Albany Hotel, St James's St. Tel 40131.
There is a mint bar here, to commemorate
the days when Nottingham minted its own
money. Good restaurant. £££.

Oundle Northants. **K7**
Talbot Hotel, New St. Tel 3621. This inn was
built in 1626 with the stones from the keep
of Fotheringhay Castle. ££.

Rothley Leics. **H5**
*Rothley Court Hotel, nr Loughborough. Tel
2618.* A very old hotel with many famous
patrons including Macaulay, who was born
here, Elizabeth I and Wilberforce. £.

Rowsley Derby. **F3**
*Peacock Hotel, nr Matlock. Tel Darley Dale
3518.* A good base for touring the Peak
District, built as the dower house to Haddon
Hall. Good trout fishing close by. £.

Rugby Warwick. **G7**
Three Horseshoes, Sheep St. Tel 4585. A
14thC coaching inn with beams and a
painting of the 'rugby' game. ££.

Shrewsbury Salop. **B5**
Lord Hill Hotel, Abbey Foregate. Tel 52601.
Named after the pioneer of the penny post. £.

Stafford Staffs. **D5**
Vine Hotel, Salter St. Tel 51071. This hotel
is reputedly the oldest in the town, and its
bars are popular with the local residents. £.

Stourbridge Hereford & Worcs. **D7**
Talbot Hotel, High St. Tel 4350. A 500-year-
old former coaching inn. Five bedrooms
have large canopied beds. £.

Stratford-upon-Avon Warwick. **F8**
Falcon Hotel, Chapel St. Tel 5777. An old
timber-fronted hotel in which a bar and a
lounge are panelled with oak from
Shakespeare's last home. ££.

Warwick Warwick. **F8**
Lord Leycester Hotel, Jury St. Tel 41481.
Once the home of the Earl of Leicester, the
hotel has a warm and pleasant atmosphere. £.

Wishaw Warwick. **F8**
*Belfry Hotel, Lichfield Rd nr Sutton
Coldfield. Tel Curdworth 70347.* A secluded
18thC mansion set in 49 acres. Some of the
bedrooms have four-posters. Gardens,
fishing and clay pigeon shooting. ££.

Wolverhampton W. Midlands. **D6**
Park Hall Hotel, Goldthorn Park. Tel 31121.
A Georgian house with views of both the
industrial Midlands and open countryside.
££.

Worcester Hereford & Worcs. **D8**
Giffard Hotel, High St. Tel 27155. Modern.
Named after Bishop Giffard, with views of
Worcester Cathedral. ££.

Regional food & drink

Bakewell Pudding
The original is still made by hand to a secret
recipe discovered by accident in 1860 at
'The Old Original Pudding Shop' in the
square at Bakewell.

Cheeses
Derby still provides the mild creamy cheese
and also the rarer Sage Derby. Buxton is the
place to buy your Stilton; at Dove Dairy in
Hartington. Other famous cheeses to buy in
their town of origin are Red Leicester and
Double Gloucester.

Melton Mowbray Pie
This famous pie can still be bought at
Melton Mowbray, freshly made from pork
and well seasoned.

Vale of Evesham
Roadside stalls sell delicious fresh fruit, and
particularly worth getting are the fresh
picked asparagus.

Restaurants

Restaurants
£ inexpensive
££ medium priced
£££ expensive

Armitage Staffs. **E5**
Old Farmhouse Restaurant. Tel 490353.
Friendly, family-run restaurant. English
cooking. Good value. Set menus. Cheerful
service. *LD. Closed Sat, Sun & Mon L. £L,
££D. Book.*

Birmingham W. Midlands. **E7**
Rajdoot, 12–22 Albert St. Tel 643 8805.
Very good Indian restaurant. Best curries in
the Midlands. *LD. Closed Sun. ££. Book.*

Broadway Hereford & Worcs. **E9**
Dormy House, Willersey Hill. Tel 2241.
Country hotel near the golf course. Well
planned menus. Mainly French and English.
D. ££. Book.

Bromyard Hereford & Worcs. **C8**
Hop Pole Hotel. Tel 2449. Old-fashioned
pub. English food. Generous helping. *LD.
££. Book.*

Cressage Salop. **C6**
Old Hall Hotel. Tel 298. Elizabethan house.
English cooking using fresh materials. Good
value. *LD. Closed Mon & Sun D. ££. Book.*

Dovedale Derby. **F3**
Izaak Walton Hotel. Tel Thorpe Cloud 261.
Restaurant in hotel overlooking entrance to
Dovedale. French, Italian, English. *LD. £L
££D. Book.*

Horton Northants. **J8**
French Partridge. Tel Northampton 870033.
Country-house restaurant. Outstanding
French cooking. *D. Closed Sun & Mon. ££.
Book.*

Nottingham Notts. **H4**
*Four Seasons Restaurant, Albany Hotel St
James's St. Tel 40131.* Mainly French. Not
cheap. *LD. £££. Book.*

Ross-on-Wye Hereford & Worcs. **C10**
Pengethly Hotel. Tel Harewood End 252.
Country-house hotel. Mainly English.
Outstanding wines. *LD. Closed Sun D. £££
£££D. Book.*

Stratford-upon-Avon Warwick. **F8**
Buccaneer, 11 Warwick Rd. Tel 2550. Hidden
down a back alley and decorated like a
smugglers' cave. Food, mainly French and
good. *D. Closed Mon & Feb. ££. Book.*

Wilmcote, Warwick **F8**
*Swan House Hotel. Tel Stratford-upon-Avon
67030.* Little Georgian hotel. Well planned
menus. French and English. *LD. ££. Book.*

East Anglia and the Fens

A character in Noel Coward's play 'Private Lives' once asked 'How was Norfolk?'. The reply was 'Flat'. This is however, a simplification because this region could more fairly be called boundless. After a drive through East Anglia it is the sky you remember, great rolling expanses of piling clouds that glide across these infinite, fertile acres.

The smoothness of the terrain only helps to emphasise the soaring Suffolk church towers and their dominance over the peaceful landscape. The fens of Cambridgeshire and Lincolnshire, now drained and dyked, remain wide and windswept, but nothing can match the moment when Ely Cathedral comes into view on its watery island like a glorious ship.

Lincolnshire has white stone churches, bulb fields, the stone elegance of Stamford and of course the great cathedral at Lincoln soaring over the roof-tops of the city. There's more to Cambridgeshire than its university city – the countryside has a rare remote quality for somewhere so near London and there are thatch and white-wash villages among the great elms.

Norfolk and Suffolk are arable, calm and full of unexpected villages with magnificent churches. This is Constable country, still full of great trees, flat fields and silent, reflecting pools. In parts of Norfolk you'll find the placid Broads and have that rare experience, the sight of a ship sailing slowly through the fields.

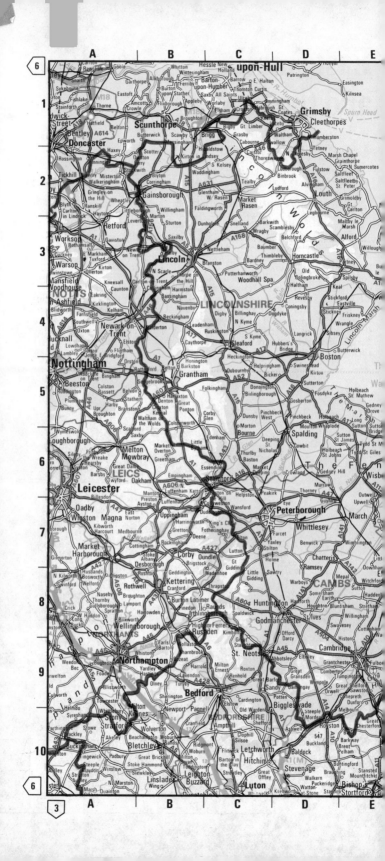

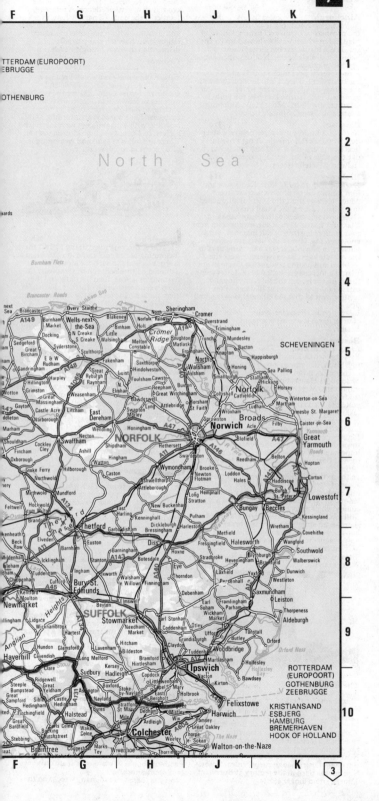

North Sea

SCHEVENINGEN

TTERDAM (EUROPOORT)
EBRUGGE

OTHENBURG

ROTTERDAM
(EUROPOORT)
GOTHENBURG
ZEEBRUGGE

KRISTIANSAND
ESBJERG
HAMBURG
BREMERHAVEN
HOOK OF HOLLAND

Cromer
Ridge

Norfolk
Broads

Norwich

Great
Yarmouth

Lowestoft

NORFOLK

SUFFOLK

Ipswich

Colchester

The coast

Aldeburgh K9
Suffolk. Pop 2,800. EC Wed. An offspring of the prosperous mediaeval fishing village of Slaughden which was swallowed up by the sea. It is a main street of elegant houses behind a shingle beach. Nothing spectacular, but full of character.
A prosperous port in the 16thC and a haven for smugglers, it went into hibernation with the silting up of the estuary waters. Spring came with the leisure boom in the 20thC. Of interest – 16thC Moot Hall; Aldeburgh Festival at Snape. Shingle beach.

Bawdsey J10
Suffolk. A huddle of houses behind a steep beach of dark red shingle. A paradise for beachcombers, it's a wild and lonely beach like the edge of the world, protected by a stalwart Martello tower.

Blakeney H4
Norfolk. Pop 705. EC Wed. Red-brick and flint houses climb down a narrow street which leads to the 15thC Guildhall, tucked in a hillside facing the small quay.
Overlooking a creek with sandy banks Blakeney has an aura of sun-swept calm in an ever endless horizon of salt marshes, sand and open sea. One of the most attractive villages in Norfolk, it was a thriving port in the middle ages. So prosperous were the woollen and fishing trades that German and Flemish merchants settled here. Later came the grain trade, but the tides continually carried the spit of land at Blakeney Point farther west so that the channel slowly silted up.
Lovely 15thC hammer-beam roof in the church nave. Remains of a 13thC Carmelite Friary.

Boston D4
Lincs. Pop 26,000. EC Thur. MD Wed, Sat. By 1204, when King John granted a charter to Boston, its fame as a port was second only to that of London. In the 13thC the North Sea and its Hanseatic League were important. Merchants grew rich in the wool trade with Flanders, and when the tower was added to the 14thC Boston church, they fashioned it in the style of those in Antwerp or Bruges. Known as the 'Stump,' it is a landmark for miles around.
Plagues, floods, and the turning of trade towards America, with the subsequent importance of western ports like Bristol, turned Boston into a depressed area by the 16thC.
In the 15thC Guildhall are the cells where some of the Pilgrim Fathers were imprisoned in 1607. By 1620 they finally landed in New England and founded a colony which they called Boston.
Still a busy commercial centre, it's full of sharp-eyed streets, ancient but breezy houses, and there are some exhilarating no-nonsense warehouses along the old quays. Magnificent views from the top of the 'Stump' of ships going down the River Witham to the sea.

Boston Stump

The Burnhams G5
Norfolk. The Domesday Book listed seven 'Burnhams by the Sea' of which two have disappeared. The five remaining, Burnham Deepdale, Burnham Norton, Burnham Market, Burnham Overy and Burnham Thorpe, are all small and unspoilt.
Burnham Deepdale has a church with an early round tower and an exceptionally fine Norman font. The 13thC church at Burnham Overy has an early central tower. Nelson was born in the rectory at Burnham Thorpe; it no longer exists.

Covehithe K8
Suffolk. The nicest place on the Suffolk coast, full of settled silence. A remote hamlet at the end of a narrow lane. Has a 17thC brick church built with a thatch roof and standing within the ruins of a much larger church which was partially dismantled in 1672. Shingle beach.

Cromer J5
Norfolk. Pop 5,300. EC Wed. A fishing village and small port which became a 'railway-age' resort, fashionable and exclusive, in the 19thC. Along the sea front a number of Edwardian hotels, spats and all, back on to narrow streets of fishermen's cottages. The church is an imposing 15thC building with a magnificent west tower, the highest in a county of high church towers. There are miles of sand and swimming is safe except in rough weather.

Cromer

Dunwich K8
Suffolk. A thriving town in the 12thC, the 'beginning of the end' came in 1326 when a storm blocked the harbour mouth and demolished three churches. Gradually the harbour defences, then the cliffs and the town were destroyed by further storms. By 1677 the sea had reached the market place. A melancholy spectre, at once both apprehensive and exciting, like butterflies in the stomach.
Ruins of a Franciscan Priory; a museum of town relics. Shingle beach.

Felixstowe J10
Suffolk. Pop 18,900. EC Wed. A Punch and Judy resort without pretensions, strung out along a gently curving bay. Today it's a booming container port where once the Romans built a castle. A priory was founded at the time of the Norman Conquest, King Edward III probably resided here in the 14thC, and Landguard Fort was built in the 17thC. But its real business, leisure, began with the arrival of the railway in 1877. Banks of red shingle with patches of sand at low tide are backed by a traffic-free promenade, neat lawns and flower beds. Good bathing.

Great Yarmouth K6
Norfolk. Pop 50,200. EC Thu. MD Wed, Sat. A long narrow town which was formerly a small fishermen's settlement on a sandbank. In the 14thC the town was enclosed on three sides by walls 23 feet high and 7 feet thick. Within the walls houses were packed tightly together in 145 streets known as 'rows'. Mostly damaged during the last war, traces of them can still be seen.
In the prosperous days of the East Anglian wool trade, Yarmouth was busy shipping first wool, and then woven cloth to the Low Countries which lay opposite her to the east. In the 19thC the wool trade moved north, and Yarmouth's shipping declined further when the growth of the railways deprived her of much of her coastal trade.
Running parallel to the harbour is the sea front, with its wide promenades, gardens and streets. It has all the trappings of a popular resort.
Of interest:–the 12thC parish church; the dungeons in the mediaeval Tolhouse; the 16thC Old Merchants House, now a museum; the Church of St George, built 1714. The sandy beach is excellent, and it is possible to swim at all times if care is taken.

Happisburgh J5
Norfolk. Dominated by the 110 foot high tower of the 15thC church, it's a village of hair-blown charm which stands on a rounded hillock of meadows set back from the sandy beach. For centuries its fortunes have been bound up with shipwrecks, and the formidable Happisburgh sands, littered with the bones of many ships, are only seven miles off-shore.
In 1904 there were so many wrecks on the

beach that they had to be blown up by Trinity House to clear them away.
The gaily painted lighthouse was built on the low hill south of the village in 1791. Swimming is reasonably safe.

Holkham Gap   G4
Norfolk. The Holkham 'Meals' which line the coast were once sandy islands like Scolt Head. Now they are part of the mainland and are covered with pine trees which provide attractive, sheltered picnic spots. The tide retreats over half a mile. Bathing is safe.

Ipswich   H9
Suffolk. Pop 122,800. EC (all day Mon), Wed. MD Tue. A dozen miles from the open sea this one-eyed ragamuffin of mediaeval charm is the county town of East Suffolk. At the head of the River Orwell, it's been a busy port for centuries. First developed by the Saxons, it was rapidly expanded by the Normans who realised its potential.
The town was the boyhood home of Cardinal Wolsey. Dickens stayed at the Great White House in Tavern Street, which formed a backdrop to the misadventures of Mr Pickwick.
A wealth of things to see: the Ancient House in Butter Market; Christchurch Mansion, a fine Tudor house and now a museum with furniture, fine panelling, model ships and dolls' houses; St Margaret's Church.

King's Lynn   F6
Norfolk. Pop 30,100. EC Wed. MD Tue, Sat. A place as sharp as a breeze, with the occasional straight-shouldered elegance of some classical buildings. The rivers flowing through Lincolnshire, Northamptonshire, Huntingdonshire and Cambridgeshire made Lynn the natural gateway to the Continent. Already a great port in the 14thC, her banks were lined with robust warehouses and her streets with the elegant houses of rich merchants. As her prosperity was based on the inland waterways, a decline set in with the growth of railways in the 19thC.
The town's heart is Tuesday Market-Place, a large sea-bright space. Ships still unload by numerous staithes and quays and by the famous 17thC Custom House, which is almost perfectly preserved. Of interest: the 15thC St George's Guildhall, once a theatre; the 12thC St Margaret's Church with Norman work in the south-west corner; the 17thC Duke's Head.

Cooston's House, King's Lynn

Lowestoft   K7
Suffolk. Pop 52,200. EC Thur. MD Fri. A dour place whose fortunes were made by the discovery of the Dogger Bank and other North Sea fishing grounds in the mid 19thC. The railway brought the rich London markets within easy reach, and put the Thames Estuary fishing ports out of business.
In an enviable position both on the sea coast, (wrapped efficiently round a fine harbour), and on the edge of the Broads, it is a town of salt-aired sincerity. Divided into two parts south and north of the piers and harbour. It's a courageous town much bombed during the war.
South of Claremont Pier, which forms the southern arm of the harbour, the beach is sandy and firm and safe for bathing.

Mablethorpe   E2
Lincs. Pop 6,200. EC Thur. The ideal family holiday resort with mile upon mile of gently sloping golden beaches. The town is protected from the sea by a terraced concrete promenade.
Tree stumps which appear on the sands at spring low tides are all that remain of a village and woodland swept away by the sea in 1289. Clean beach, particularly safe for children.

Overstrand   J5
Norfolk. Pop 1,000. This quiet half-pint of a village overlooks a sandy beach and the all-encroaching sea. In the year 1398 its church seems to have been washed away, for the lord of the manor gave half an acre for a new churchyard and the next year a patent was granted for the building of the present church of St Martin.
Sir Thomas Fowell Buxton of Northrepps Hall, fighter for the freedom of slaves, was buried here in 1845. Safe swimming.

Overy Staithe   G4
Norfolk. EC Wed. A pretty village with a harbour and the remains of a quay. One of the most attractive of the North Norfolk ports with a channel which twists between mud and sandbanks. Several footpaths lead across the marshes.

Burnham Overy Staithe

Sheringham   H4
Norfolk. Pop 4,700. Once a small fishing village with a reputation for lobsters (which it still has), Sheringham became a popular seaside resort with the advent of the railways. Neat and well planned, it lies along the cliff edge with Edwardian hotels and wind bleached houses overlooking the beach. Safe swimming.

Skegness   E3
Lincs. Pop 13,600. EC Thur. Six miles of unblemished beaches, safe for swimming and one of the best planned pleasure parks in Europe. No idle boast, for this place means business. It's a product of the railway age which, in 1863, linked it to the industrial towns of the midlands and provided millions with day excursions.
A Shangri-la in Walt Disney style, the town itself, with many tree-lined streets, is set back from the sea front.

Southwold   K8
Suffolk. Pop 2,000. EC Wed. MD Mon, Thur. Lying on a green knoll surrounded by marshes and with an aura of Edwardian elegance, crinoline, lace an' all, this gracious little town was rebuilt around wide greens after a devastating fire in the 17thC. A white lighthouse, topped with a golden weather vane, stands lookout over the rooftops. A battery of cannon, sent to Southwold by Charles I in 1745 for protection against privateers based at Dunkirk, glare out over the grass-topped cliffs above the sandy beach.
Have a look at 'Southwold Jack' the 15thC oak figure of a man-at-arms who strikes the bell of the church clock. St Edmund is one of the finest Perpendicular churches in England.
There is a small pier with good fishing and concrete terraces with bathing huts along the foot of the cliffs. Swimming from the beach is safe.

Southwold

Thorpeness   K9
Suffolk. A joke of escapist curios laid out this century by the dramatist and author Glencairn Stuart Ogilvie. Houses are built in a variety of styles, including Tudor, Jacobean and the tarred weather-boarded and mellow-brick styles of East Anglia. The water tower was disguised as a house and called the House in the Clouds. A windmill was brought from Aldingham, and in 1910 a 65-acre lake, three feet deep, was dug. The wide shingle beach is safe for bathing.

Walberswick   K8
Suffolk. Pop 500. EC Wed. A once-flourishing port, it has weathered into a quiet village of

mellow brick houses. Trapped neatly
between the River Blyth and a large area of
reed-filled-filled marshes, it offers the best
view of Southwold. The shore is sandy, and
there are lopsided holiday houses full of
jollity, leaping around the extensive sand
dunes. Safe bathing from an immense beach.

Wells-next-the-Sea   G4
Norfolk. Pop 2,400. EC Thur. MD Wed. A
port, delightfully old fashioned. Full of
memories like faded photographs, the town
consists of a number of narrow streets with
flint houses round the church and an
attractive green, the Buttlands, with trees
and Georgian houses. A street runs down to
a little used quay, dominated by a tall
granary.
From the western shore of the harbour a
narrow lane leads to an attractive beach
overlooked by pine trees and small huts.
Safe bathing.

Inland towns & villages

The Acres   G6
Norfolk. Pop 1,300. The most important of
the Acres, Castleacre, is a large village within
the outer bailey of the castle. A courteously
wide street with rows of cottages runs down
to the river. Southacre, one mile south across
the river, nestles among trees whilst
Westacre was once the site of a 12thC
Augustinian priory.
Nothing spectacular here, but all three
villages are full of gentle atmosphere.
Of interest:– the remains of a Clunaic
priory to the west of Castleacre; the 15thC
church of St James; the church of St George,
Southacre, and the priory gateway at
Westacre.

Aylsham   J5
Norfolk. Pop 2,600. EC Wed. MD Mon.
Small graceful town on the River Bure with
a handsome marketplace surrounded by
neat 18thC houses. To the north is the
church of St Michael, a juggle of decorated
and perpendicular.
Of interest:– Black Boy Inn, built in the
time of Queen Anne; the Knoll, the Manor
House and other fine houses; in the church
is a memorial in manicured Gothic to
Humphry Repton, the landscape gardener.

Bury St Edmunds   G8
*Suffolk. Pop 25,600. EC Thur. MD Wed,
Sat.* A cathedral town that grew up round
the 7thC Saxon monastery of
Beodericsworth. The burial place for a
martyred king, it was also the birth place of
Magna Carta.
Georgian in appearance and spaciousness,
the original plan, conceived by Abbot
Baldwin in the 11thC, was Roman in
concept. The town plan was later developed
on the mediaeval formula of a square form for
God and a square for man. The former –
just outside the Abbey – is known as Angel
Hill; the latter is the market place, still the
commercial heart of the town.
The remains of the 11thC Abbey Church
has Tudor, Georgian and Victorian houses
as infilling – grotesque in concept, splendid
in reality.
Of interest:– Angel Hotel where Mr
Pickwick stayed; Moyse's Hall, a rare 12thC
house; Cupola House built 1639; the Town
Hall, originally designed as a theatre by
Robert Adam in the 1770's.

Cambridge   E9
*Cambs. Pop 103,700. EC Thur. MD Mon,
Sat.* At the foot of a hill was a ford across
the River Cam, the junction of a network
of Roman roads with canals and rivers
just before the Fens. Of such great strategic
and commercial importance was this ford
that successive Roman developments
probably included the building of a bridge
hence the city name. Already an important
commercial centre by the time Peterhouse
College, the first of the university's
buildings. was established by Bishop Ely in
1284. Today much of the city's charm is in
small streets and passages like St Edwards
Passage and Botolph Lane. The collegiate

'The Backs' Cambridge

idea came into being in the 13thC to
replace the derelict lodgings the students
were forced to live in, grouped as they were
round the religious and lay teachers whose
ideas most appealed to them. The principal
accents are set by university and public
buildings. Many of the colleges are on the
main street which runs between the river
and Market Hill. Peaceful green lawns, the
Backs, run down from the colleges to the
river which is crossed by bridges and shaded
by willows.
Best mediaeval houses and cottages in the
city (two and three storied timber and
plaster houses, many with projecting upper
floors) are to be found in Northampton
Street and Magdalene Street. Little Rose
Inn, a 17thC inn, is probably the last to
have extensive stables. Enclosed stone
bridge over the River Cam at St Johns and
fine hammer-beam roof in the 16thC Hall.
See Wren's magnificent library for Trinity
College, with carvings by Grinling Gibbons,
and King's College Chapel with its fine
15thC fan-vaulted roof plus Rubens' 'The
Adoration of the Magi'. A cornucopia of
treasures in the Fitzwilliam Museum.

Castle Rising   F5
Norfolk. Pop 200. An important sea port
when King's Lynn was but a marsh, it's now
a small pretty village stranded on a beach of
grass green country from which the sea
receded long ago. There is an impressive
Norman castle standing behind Roman
earthworks. Approached through a ruined
gatehouse, it has a hall-keep with a great
stone staircase leading up to a fascinating
sequence of rooms, galleries and minor
staircases. Granted to the Duke of Norfolk
by Henry VIII in 1544.
Interesting 17thC brick almshouse.

Cavendish   G9
Suffolk. Pop 800. A warm assembly of
pinkly pleased thatched cottages cluster
round a sloping green and elegant 14thC
church in a fairy tale setting of countryside.
The characters from 'Lord of the Rings',
like Bilbo and Frodo, Sam and Tom
Bombadil seem more in place here than
20thC man.
Note the 16thC timber-framed farmhouse
of Nether Hall; the 19thC Cavendish Hall;
the 15thC flushwork panelling and
clerestory in the church.

Cavendish

Clare   F9
Suffolk. Pop 1,700. EC Wed. MD Mon.
A beautiful little town set in the heart of
Constable country. It's full to the brim with
half-timbered, tile hung houses, and some
discreetly Georgian. The wool church is a
magnificent monster to delight the eye
whilst the 15thC priest's house at the
churchyard corner has an exuberant
flourish of pargetting as fine as spring
blossom.
Of note:– the Swan Inn; an iron age fort;
Cliftons, with its splendid 17thC chimneys.

Debenham H8
Suffolk. Pop 900. EC Tue. A village of overhanging timbered houses, which catch fire slowly in the mind like a sunset. The first trickles of the River Deben run alongside the gently sloping main street. Look at Crow's Hall, built in 1508 and surrounded by a moat. It is the perfect example of an ancestral home. Interesting Galilee porch in the church of St Mary.

Diss H8
Norfolk. Pop 4,500. EC Tue. MD Fri. An invigorating hotch-potch of Tudor, Georgian and Victorian buildings built round a large lake, the Were. A small town of twisting streets with a sloping market square for a heart, dominated by the church at its head. The church, austere like a Lenten hymn, was built slap-bang up to the street with processional arches either side. John Skelton, Henry VIII's tutor, was rector here in the early 16thC.
Look at the Shambles; the former Dolphin Inn and Greyhound Inn; also mid-19thC Corn Exchange.

Downham Market F6
Norfolk. Pop 4,100. EC Wed. MD Fri.
A small congested market town all yellow and brown, brick and carrstone, which stands on a hill at the very edge of the Fens, twelve miles south of King's Lynn on the River Ouse. Higher still is the church, as perpendicular as rigor mortis, in a big churchyard of yews and weeping ashes reached by a steep lane.
Worth seeing:– Elizabethan-style work-house, built in 1836, and the neo-Gothic Clock Tower in cast iron (1878).

East Bergholt H10
Suffolk. Pop 2,000. An unspoilt village full of optimism, with grand houses and fine trees. Lying along a natural ridge above the River Stour, it has some enthusiastic half-timbering dating from the influx of Flemish weavers.
The church of St Mary is remarkable for its unfinished tower, begun in 1525. A 16thC timber-framed cage in the churchyard contains the church bells. Look at Flatford Mill and Willy Lott's cottage.

Edenham C6
Lincs. Pop 400. A village built to impress, like the best silver for Sunday dinners. The graceful cottages are built of crisp looking stone, and the large church, under an umbrella of cedars, contains the shaft of a mediaeval cross in the churchyard. Grimsthorpe Castle commands attention in a palatial park with a magnificent chestnut avenue and herds of fallow and red deer. Look at the collection of Brussels tapestries and paintings by Lawrence, Reynolds and Van Dyck in the castle.

Ely E8
Cambs. Pop 10,000. EC Tue. MD Thur.
A small town standing on a bluff above the River Ouse. Dominated by the cathedral, Ely is set in the flatness of the Fen landscape, of which it is the capital, Formerly an island, accessible only by boat or causeways until the Fens were drained in the 17th and 18thC, it was here that Hereward the Wake, 'The Last of the English', held out against William the Conqueror. A jumble of niceties, but best of all is Waterside: informal and humble, a street of 18thC cottages opening on to the Ouse. Here was the quay in the middle ages and later.
Worth seeing are the late Norman doorway in the Headmaster's House, King's School; the great south gate-house – all that remains of the 14thC Abbey; Bishop Alcock's Palace, and the chantry on the north side of Palace Green.

Euston G8
Suffolk. Pop 300. An affable street of half-timbered, thatch and tile-hung, flint and brick houses with a low ridge of downland behind. The church sits within the sleepy grounds of the Elizabethan Hall. The landscape around here was the setting for Robert Bloomfield's 18thC tale of rural life 'The Farmer's Boy'.
High quality carvings inside the church in Grinling Gibbons manner.

Folkingham C5
Lincs. Pop 500. A village of politely splendid houses wrapped round a large square on the edge of the Fens – an 18thC coaching halt which has its original atmosphere intact. Little effort needed here to stir the imagination.
Interesting church of St Andrew with an outstanding perpendicular tower.

Gainsborough B2
Lincs. Pop 17,400. EC Wed. MD Tue, Sat. A busy market town and industrial centre on the east bank of the Trent linked to Nottinghamshire on the opposite bank by a three-arched 18thC bridge. Still fun despite the apparent earnestness. Canute's father, King Sweyne, was murdered here in 1014 following a series of raids.
St Ogg's, in George Eliot's 'Mill on the Floss', was modelled on Gainsborough. There are some interesting 18thC ware-houses on the quayside; note also the Old Hall, c1500, one of the largest mediaeval houses in the county.

Grantchester E9
Cambs. Pop 500. Immortalised in the famous poem by Rupert Brooke. The place where he lived and wrote before the first world war, it's almost an integral part of Cambridge life and loved by generations of undergraduates and tutors. A tranquil little village empty of worries in timber, plaster and thatch. Interesting 15thC Manor Farm and 17thC Old Vicarage.

Helpston C6
Cambs. Pop 700. This is a fat and jolly stone-built village round a pleasant green. It was here that John Clare, the peasant poet, was born in 1793.
Look at the College House, complete with two buttresses, slit window and four centred archways; Helpston House with canted bay window, gables and dormers; 12thC Woodhall Manor.

Hemingford Grey D8
Cambs. Pop 1,500. A picture book village of timber, thatch and mellow brick cottages plucked from a Christmas calendar and set amongst trees by a curve of the Great Ouse. Little seems to have changed since a violent storm in 1741 nipped off the steeple top of St James' Church.
The 12thC moated stone-built Manor House is claimed to be the oldest inhabited house in England.

Hemingford Grey

Horncastle D3
Lincs. Pop 4,000. EC Wed. MD Thur, Sat. An engaging market town situated at the south west foot of the Wolds on the site of the Roman fort of Banovallum, traces of the Roman walls still being visible. The town buildings are straight-forward Georgian, grouped informally round a sloping market place. Horncastle was once famous for its annual horse-fairs, said to be the largest of their kind in the world.
Have a look at the Fighting Cocks Inn, which still has a cockpit in the yard and the interesting relics, in the church, of the Battle of Winceby fought in 1643 during the Civil War.

Houghton D8
Cambs. Pop 3,000. A tranquil riverside village as refreshing as a cold drink on a long summer's day. It's got the lot, pleasant tree shaded walks, picturesque cottages, a brown cobbled church and a village green complete with an elaborate Gothick-style cast iron pump.
Have a look at the massive timber watermill built on the River Ouse in the 17thC; also

the wall paintings of 1622 in the Three
Jolly Butchers Inn.

Huntingdon   D8
Cambs. Pop 17,200. EC Wed. MD Sat.
The twin towns of Huntingdon and
Godmanchester, now one borough, lie at the
intersection of three Roman roads. The
towns are separated by the 300-acre
meadow of Port Holme on one side of a
17thC raised causeway, and West Side
Common on the other. They are linked by
one of the finest mediaeval bridges in the
country.
Invaded by the Danes, Huntingdon then
endured the Normans, only to be nearly
wiped out by the plague in 1348. It sank
into oblivion except for a short period during
the Civil War when first Cromwell, and then
Charles I, made their headquarters here.
Both Cromwell and Samuel Pepys were
pupils at the Grammar School, built in 1565,
and now a museum of Cromwelliana.
Of interest:– the George, which still has two
sides of its 17thC courtyard intact, one with
an open gallery and external staircase; the
Falcon, with oriel windows and massive
doors, believed to have been the headquarters of Cromwell.

Kersey   G9
Suffolk. A twinkle in the mind's eye, it was
famous in the middle ages for cloth. The
village is a handful of weavers' cottages and
half-timbered houses running down hill to
a small stream. Across the ford the street
runs uphill again, this time to the 15thC
church of St Mary. There are carved
reminders of the Black Death in the north
aisle.
Priory Farm has the remains of an
Augustinian priory founded in the late
12thC.

Kimbolton   C8
Cambs. Pop 1,200. EC Wed. A beauty of a
place with a hustle of red roofs, a 13thC
church and a mediaeval castle where
Katherine of Aragon spent her last four
years. Set in the green valley of the River
Kim.
Look at the square gatehouse designed by
Robert Adam; St Andrew's 14thC tower
with a broach spire; the 19thC Moravian
church, the only one in the country.

Lavenham   G9
Suffolk. Pop 1,300. EC Wed. A cobwebbed
dream of perfect 15thC half-timbered
houses along irregular streets. Its prosperity
was founded in the mid-14thC when many
Flemish weavers settled here.
The 14th and 15thC church of SS Peter and
Paul is one of the finest of wool churches in
England. Look at the Old Wool Hall, built
1500; the 16thC Swan Hotel and Guildhall.
Some particularly fine pargetting work on
house facades.

The church at Lavenham

Lincoln   B3
Lincs. Pop 74,200. EC Wed. MD Fri, Sat.
The city is situated on the site of a former
Roman military garrison built in 48AD to
command the meeting of two great highways,
Ermine Street and Fosse Way. In 1068
William the Conqueror built an
impregnable castle here.
The historic centre climbs a limestone hill
200 feet high. On top towers a majestic
monster – the triple-towered cathedral built
in the 11thC. The third largest in England,
it stares out across the River Witham, a
preachy grin in its decorations, and a mass
of mediaeval buildings at its feet.
Of particular interest is the 12thC Jews
House and the House of Aaron the Jew; the

Roman town gate; the 16thC gateway with
the guildhall above it.

High Bridge, Lincoln

Little Gidding   C8
Cambs. A small church and a huddle of
buildings. It was here in 1625 that Nicholas
Ferrar, the son of a prosperous merchant
family, turned his back on worldly things
and founded a religious community. The
beliefs and practices of this community
inspired the last of T.S. Eliot's 'Four
Quartets' called 'Little Gidding'.
Charles I visited the community in search
of a hiding place from Cromwell's forces.

Long Melford   G9
Suffolk. Pop 2,900. EC Thur. Once a
mediaeval manufacturing town set in the
picturesque valley of the Stour, it is the
Rolls Royce of Suffolk towns. It has a gentle
mannered High Street, long and wide, lined
with dignified houses and charming shops.
At one end is an 18thC bridge, at the other,
the finest of Suffolk churches set behind the
grandest of all village greens.
Look at Melford Hall, the best of early
Elizabethan houses; the 15thC stained glass
in the church; the old Grammar School and
the half-timbered Bull Inn with its
galleried courtyard.

Long Melford

Nayland   G10
Suffolk. Pop 1,200. EC Wed, Sat. A gem in
most senses of the word, sitting comfortably
alongside the River Stour. Its 15th and
16thC houses congregate in a pleasantly
unassuming way, as the best of village
buildings do.
Look at White House and Queen's Head
Inn; also 15thC Alston Court.

Newmarket   F8
Suffolk. Pop 13,000. EC Wed. MD Tue, Sat.
Set magnificently on the splendid open
heathland which straddles the road from
London to Norwich, it is the centre of the
English horse racing world, and the home of
more studs than any other town in England.
The hunt-loving King James I started it
when he built a hunting lodge here after his
visit in 1605.
The High Street is an agreeable amalgam of
Georgian and Victorian buildings. A place
to wet your whistle in if ever there was one.
Of special interest are the Rutland Arms
Hotel with a red-brick front; the Georgian
Jockey Club; the mediaeval piscina in the
14thC church.

Norwich   J6
Norfolk. Pop 121,700. EC Thur. MD Sat.
The social capital, market and shopping
centre for Norfolk and a large part of
Suffolk. The industrial revolution which
gave the coup-de-grace to its handweavers
saw the birth of the city as one of the chief
shoe manufacturing towns in the country.
The city centre is enclosed on three sides by
the old city wall, the curve of the River
Wensum defining the fourth. Industry is
spread out along the river; civic buildings
around City Wall; the ecclesiastical area
centres on the cathedral with the shopping
centre dissecting the lot. Three major
landmarks dominate the centre – the

Norwich market

cathedral, an even-tempered masterpiece set in a low-lying hollow of land inside the curve of the river; the Norman castle, set high on a mound; and the City Hall, also set on high ground. The market place sits in the saddle of land, between the City Hall and the castle.
Originally the city was a series of villages, the Normans having developed the old Saxon centre in Tombland. Today its scale is still basically the same – narrow, intimate streets opening on to a series of plains, one of the biggest being St Andrew's Plain.

Peterborough   D7
Cambs. Pop 70,000. EC Mon, Thur. MD Wed, Sat. Crisply businesslike, it is a prosperous city and handsome market town, with the Market Place for its centre, dominated by the 17thC guildhall.
The Barnack stone built cathedral is one of the most complete and impressive Romanesque buildings in England. Its moment of real glory is in the unique west front, created when an ingenious screen wall was placed in front of the old Romanesque facade.
The best Georgian houses are in Priestgate; the Bull Hotel, Westgate, is an interesting 18thC building.

St Ives   D8
Cambs. Pop 8,400. EC Thur. MD Mon, Sat. Originally a village called Slepe on the north bank of the River Ouse, it was renamed in 1050 when a priory was built and dedicated to St Ivo, a Persian bishop whose remains were found in a nearby field.
St Ives is a leafy sunlit place with refreshing riverside views. It has a narrow six-arched bridge built in 1415 with a miniature bridge chapel, one of only three of its kind in England. Only a ruined wall remains of the priory.
Have a look at the Elizabethan manor house by the bridge with fine brick chimneys; the early 13thC, double piscina in All Saints Church.

St Neots   C8
Cambs. Pop 18,000. EC Tue. MD Thur. An ancient riverside market town which owes its origin to a priory founded in the 10thC by Benedictine monks. Its heart is the long and spacious Market Place which backs onto the river.
The beautiful church of St Mary's, one of the largest mediaeval churches in the country, is tucked away near the town centre in a large churchyard.
Look at the interior roof carvings of angels, birds and animals in the church; the 17thC Bridge Hotel and the Cross Keys Hotel.

Stamford   C6
Lincs. Pop 14,500. EC Thur. MD Fri, Sat. A quiet gray, sober town, built from the richly mellow local stone. Once the Danish capital of the Fens, it is one of Europe's finest mediaeval towns. An important wool centre in the 12thC, it had a university and seventeen churches of which only six remain. All but destroyed during the War of the Roses, it became socially desirable in the 18thC due to the close proximity of the Great North Road.
Of note:– All Saints' Place, the raison d'être of the town; the 17thC Barn Hill House; the ruined 7thC chapel of St Leonard's Priory; the golden choir of the church of St Mary.

Stilton   C7
Cambs. Pop 800. A mild mannered village on the edge of the Fens with a reputation for cheese it has never produced. It was really a half-way house in the business, for the famous cheeses made in Leicestershire were loaded on to coaches for London and the North at the 17thC Bell Inn.

Stoke-by-Nayland   H10
Suffolk. Pop 700. EC Sat. A village as alive as a breeze in a field of corn, but in its own quietly simple way. Another delicious slice of country fare in a countryside choc-a-bloc with such delights.
On the ridge rising up out of the Stour Valley stands the church, puritanically perpendicular, and proud of it.
Of interest is Giffords Hall, with an intriguing red-brick gatehouse on the south side; 17thC Thorington Hall; a yeoman farmhouse in Ox's Farm.

Stowmarket   H9
Suffolk. Pop 8,700. EC Tue. MD Thur, Sat. A small market town with a number of light industries. Despite a chequered history dating back to Saxon times few old buildings remain. In a sense it's a place without a memory, but friendly all the same.
It was a prosperous town in the early 19thC when the Gipping was made navigable to Stowmarket.
Of interest:– the half-timbered Vicarage of the 16thC; the Fox Hotel; the Butter Market; Abbot's Hall with its largely open air museum of rural life.

Swaffham   G6
Norfolk. Pop 4,300. EC Thur, MD Sat. A busy but beautiful 18thC market town of sturdy buildings, wrapped round a huge triangular market place with an elegant Palladian market cross. The church is a magnificent 15thC miracle with fine hammer-beam roof.
Some good fare in the Georgian buildings, including the School House and the Assembly Room.

Market Cross, Swaffham.

Thetford   G7
Norfolk. Pop 15,700. EC Wed. MD Tue, Sat. A quiet little market town by a river. In the Tudor period it was the cathedral city of East Anglia, with over twenty churches and four monasteries. The Dissolution brought a halt to all this splendour. Built, like so many mediaeval towns, within the outer defences of its castle, Thetford has winding streets of well-proportioned 18thC houses, with an element of surprise round each corner. Dormant until an attempt in 1820 to turn it into a full-blown spa, it then slipped serenely back into obscurity with the dignity of a Chelsea pensioner.
See the Old Gaol of 1816; St Mary's Church; the mediaeval Bell Hotel; the mid-18thC King's House built on the site of the hunting lodge of James I, and the remains of a Clunaic priory.

Wisbech   E6
Cambs. Pop 17,000. EC Wed. MD Sat. A Georgian market town and river port, at the centre of the rich agricultural Fenland. Wisbech prospered in the 18th and 19thC when river traffic made it an important trading centre in East Anglia. The chief glory is its front along the River Nene. At Wisbech the river forms a bend; on the bend is a bridge and around this, on either side of the river, the town has grown. On the south side, are the castle, church and market place, and across the bridge on the north side, the town hall and Corn Exchange. Along either side of the river are the quays and warehouses that represented the real business of the town. Beyond the bridge, where the vessels did not go, are the elegant houses of the rich merchants in two terraces, South Brink and North Brink, divided by the river.
Of particular interest:– Peckover House; Flint House and Nene Quay.

Wymondham H7
Norfolk. Pop 8,500. EC Wed. MD Fri.
A charming market town, rebuilt in 1615
after a fire had destroyed most of the town.
In the centre is the market place with its
beguiling market cross, and all around are
winding streets of 17th and 18thC jollity.
The most impressive building is the church
of SS Mary and Thomas of Canterbury with
two towers dominating the town. In its
churchyard, the remains of the abbey
founded in 1107.
Of interest:— Carick House, early 18thC
with fine plaster-work internally; Burfield
Hall, another 18thC house on a moated site;
mediaeval Gunvil's Hall with 17th and
18thC additions.

Regional oddities

Martello Towers
A pair of Martello Towers stand guard over
the mouth of the River Deben by
Woodbrige. Another four line the shingle
beach between Bawdsey and Shingle Street,
whilst south of Aldeburgh at Slaughden
Quay is the last of the Martello towers at this
end of the coast.

Cambridgeshire Mills
The post mill at Great Chishill was built in
1819. The fantail turns the mill on a central
post.
Burwell has two tower-mills. One was
working until recently but is now derelict; of
the other, bigger one, only the stump
survives. At Swaffham Prior there is another
tower-mill. Built 1875 it is preserved on a
mound originally made for a post-mill.
Nearby is a derelict smock-mill of the same
date.

post-mill, Great Chishill

Huntingdonshire Mills
At Eye there's an 80 foot high tower-mill, of
eight stories. It is now power driven, and
used for producing animal foods.

Neckving, 1877   Boston

Norfolk Mills
There is a straight-forward tower-mill on
the Yare, and a fine rust red brick tower-mill
with an elegant cap at Cley-next-the-Sea.
Just south of the village of Mundesley is a
smock-windmill complete with cap and
sails. Eleven miles north of Yarmouth is
Horsey Mill. It was built in 1912 as a
drainage mill on the site of an earlier mill.

Cley-next-the-Sea

Suffolk Mills
There is an elegant white painted post-mill
on Saxtead Green, dating from the 18thC: it
was rebuilt in 1854.

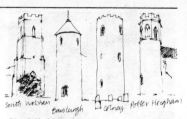

South Walsham   Bawburgh   Colney   Potter Heigham

Norfolk Churches
The Norfolk countryside is dominated by
churches that are isolated elements in a
completely flat and lonely landscape. Some
of the earliest of them are round, because it
was easier to build a tower of that shape with
the local pebbles. It wasn't until the 13thC
that stone from Barnack in
Northamptonshire became more readily
accessible.

Famous people

John Constable (1776-1837) H10
Flatford Mill, East Bergholt, Suffolk. Born
at East Bergholt, the second son of a
prosperous miller, Constable spent a year
working in his father's water mill at
Flatford when he was eighteen years old,
before setting out for London to try his luck
at painting. There are conflicting accounts of
how he spent his year as a miller. Some say
he was most likely to be found observing
nature, sketching in the fields and copying
drawings by Girtin.
This area of Suffolk was immortalised in
some of Constable's best pictures. The mill
is now a field study centre.

Flatford Mill

Oliver Cromwell (1599-1658) D8
Huntingdon, Cambs. Huntingdon is full of
associations with Cromwell. His family once
owned Hinchingbrooke House, now a
grammar school; the Protector was born in a
house in the High Street (the site is marked
by a plaque), and attended the grammar
school, now the Cromwell Museum. The
record of his birth and baptism is kept in the
church of All Saints in the High Street.

Sir Isaac Newton (1642-1727) B5
*Woolsthorpe Manor, Lincs. 7 miles from
Grantham.* English mathematician and
natural philosopher. He was born at
Woolsthorpe in 1642, educated at the
grammar school in Grantham, and at Trinity
College, Cambridge. When the plague came
to Cambridge he returned to the manor,
1665-66. It was in the garden that he
conceived the notion of gravitation as he
watched an apple fall from a tree. The room
in which Sir Isaac was born is on view. *Open
11.00-18.00 Mon, Wed, Fri & Sat Apr-Sat.*

Samuel Pepys (1633-1703) D8
Pepys's House, Brampton, Hunts. The home
of the Pepys family. A 15thC farmhouse.
Pepys is though to have been born in the
village.

Alfred, Lord Tennyson (1809-92) D3
Somersby House, Somersby, Lincs. The poet
laureate. Tennyson was the fourth of twelve
children. Born at Somersby, he spent the
first seven years of his life in this house; it
was then the rectory. 'Ode to Memory', one
of his early descriptive poems, describes the
rural charm of Somersby. There is a
memorial to Tennyson in the church.

Cathedrals, abbeys & churches

Burgh St Peter
K7

Burgh St Peter, Norfolk. A lanky 13thC–14thC building, thatched and with a crisp arch-braced roof. It has a splendid tower, like a giant toy – a series of brick squares piled one on top of another in diminishing size, the topmost one being of white brick.

Burgh St. Peter

Ely Cathedral
E8

Ely, Cambs. Begun in 1080 it has a rather abstracted and sleepy air. The best views are seen approaching across the fenland from the south or east – it's a silhouette standing out for miles above a flat, uniform and practically featureless landscape.
It has a Norman nave and transepts with a timber roof. The choir is remarkable for its carving. There's a unique central octagon 70 feet in diameter with rich wooden vault with octagonal lantern. Exceptional Lady Chapel and imposing west front.

Ely

Hales Church
J7

Hales, Norfolk. A 12thC thatched church with a round tower, arcaded apse and splendid doorways. Impressive, with a sort of small child's wide-eyed sincerity.

Hales

Knapton Church
J5

Knapton, Norfolk. It has one of the finest hammer-beam roofs in East Anglia, retaining much of its original colour. The 13thC font has a purbeck marble bowl and a charming cover of 1704.

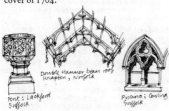

Font : Lackford Suffolk

Double Hammer beam roof, Knapton, Norfolk

Piscina : Cowling Suffolk

Lincoln Cathedral
B3

Lincoln. Rebuilt 1185–1280 on a steep hill dominating the town. Resembling Canterbury in general outline, but very English in treatment, it has double transepts, two western towers, and the highest central tower in England (271 feet high). The nave, transepts and choir are early English, the 'Angel Choir' Decorated. The unusual west front consists of a screen wall in front of the two western towers.

Lincoln Cathedral

Norwich Cathedral
J6

Norwich, Norfolk. An even-tempered masterpiece with a spire second only to that of Salisbury. It has a long, narrow Norman nave, built 1096–1145, with aisle-less transepts, and choir with apsidal chapels. The bold central spire, choir, clerestory, some windows on the south of the nave and the vaulting, are Perpendicular. The remains of the original Bishop's throne are behind the high altar.

Despite the additions it is, with the exception of Durham, one of the few English cathedrals to retain the appearance and characteristics of a great Anglo-Norman abbey church.

Peterborough Cathedral
D7

Peterborough, Cambs. Built 1117–90 it's a Norman cathedral with the finest interior after Durham. A squat, low lying building, it has a nave with a timber roof, probably the oldest in England. The grand western facade is a 158 feet high early English portico of three gigantic arches. A gable crowns each arch.

St Boltoph
D4

Boston, Lincs. A giant among English parish churches, begun in 1309 with a unified Decorated interior. Externally everything is overpowered by the 'Stump', a lofty tower in the style of Bruges, but more graceful. An audacious landmark with Decorated battlements and Perpendicular panelling around the doorway and on the main buttresses.

St Edmund
K8

Southwold, Suffolk. Impressive – with lofty aisle arcades and clerestories, and a high-pitched hammer-beam roof running the whole length of the nave and choir, it is one of the finest Perpendicular churches in England.

Look at the flushwork on the buttresses and at 'Southwold Jack', complete with church bell.

St Neots Church C8
St Neots, Cambs. A 15thC church with an elegant Perpendicular tower. Inside are wonderful interior roof carvings of angels birds and animals.

SS Peter and Paul G9
Lavenham, Suffolk. A massive square-buttressed tower of flint, 141 feet high, dwarfs the main body of the church. There is a superb porch with fine carvings and fan-vaulting.

Trunch Church J5
Trunch, Norfolk. The stiff-upper-lip variety of Perpendicular church with a lofty tower. There's a 14thC font with a magnificent canopy. It has six slender, delicately carved pillars supporting six flat and crested arches and a vault with a central pendant. The nave has an arch-braced hammer-beam roof with intricately traceried spandrels.

Castles & ruins

Castle Rising F5
Castle Rising, Norfolk. Built in 1150, the ruined castle stands within mighty earthworks rising to 120 feet. The finest stronghold of its time left in the country, only the shell of the keep remains. Queen Isabella, wife of the murdered Edward II, was banished here in 1330. *Open daily Apr–Sept (Open daily Mar & Oct & 9.30–16.00 Nov–Feb. Closed Sun morning).*

Tattershall Castle D3
Lincs. 3½ miles se of Woodhall Spa. A huge square fortified manor house built about 1440 by Ralph Cromwell, who had become Treasurer of England some years before, on the site of a mediaeval castle. The great 100 foot brick tower of this stronghold still stands. *Open 9.30–19.00 daily. Closed Sun morning.*

Freston Tower   Tattershall Castle

Thetford Priory G7
Thetford, Norfolk. One of the most extensive monastic remains in Norfolk, founded by monks from Lewes in 1103.
The oldest parts are the church and the west half of the chancel and the transepts, built 1114. The chancel as well as aisles ended in apses.

Unusual buildings

Cambridge University, Clare College E9
Cambridge, Cambs. Best seen from the river lawns of King's, it is a beautifully proportioned building in mellowed sandstone topped by balustrades and pierced by handsome windows. Built in 1638, it is more like a palace than a college. This is English Renaissance right out of the top drawer. *The colleges are open to the public on most days during daylight, but there are restrictions in term time.*

Clare College, Cambridge

Cambridge University, Faculty of History E9
Cambridge, Cambs. By James Stirling, 1964-8. Perhaps the most imaginative and creative of modern English buildings, it's a mammoth glass shed built like a greenhouse. It has an intriguing but elusive scale.

Cambridge University, King's College Chapel E9
Cambridge, Cambs. Full of fire, the chapel was the only completed mediaeval part of this college, founded 1441. In a mouth-watering site overlooking the banks of the River Cam this Perpendicular style building was completed 1515.

King's College, Cambridge

Cambridge University, St John's College E9
Cambridge, Cambs. An embalmed world of ordered calm. Founded in 1511, it has three magnificent red-brick courts and a fine gate-tower, complete with turrets and gilded heraldry. Inside the gate is the early 16thC First Court, with the college dining hall. The doorway at the far side leads to two further courts, the first of these being one of the finest in Cambridge, and then out across the river by the 19thC Bridge of Sighs to New Court.

Cambridge University, Trinity College E9
Cambridge, Cambs. Founded by Henry VIII in 1546 by amalgamating a number of earlier colleges and adding his own endowments. A diamond as big as the Ritz, it is the most spacious college in Cambridge. Its oldest buildings surround the two-acre Great Court, claimed to be the largest university court in the world.

Cambridge University, Trinity College Library E9
Cambridge, Cambs. A relatively sober classical building begun in 1676 to the design of Sir Christopher Wren. The fourth side to Nevile's Court, the library is on the first floor above a ground floor open to the court through a round-arched arcade. Some fine 17thC wood carvings by Grinling Gibbons.

East Anglia University J6
Norwich, Norfolk. An honest design by Denys Lasdun to accommodate 3,000 students.
It's essentially a compact squiggle of zigurats in a splendid site with a view of the river. Tortured and mannered, but hard to dismiss entirely.

Flatford Mill H10
East Bergholt, Suffolk. The mill of Constable's 'Hay Wain', it was built with the mill house in the 18thC and belonged to his father. Constable himself worked in the mill for about a year.

Freston Tower H10
Freston, Suffolk. One of the earliest of follies to be found. An elegant red-brick tower built on the banks of the Orwell. Ten foot by twelve in plan, it has six small rooms piled one on top of the other with increasingly larger pedimented windows.

The Guildhall G9
Lavenham, Suffolk. A shoulder-shrugging sort of building, friendly, but aloof. At one time a prison, workhouse and wool store. Through most of the 17thC it was used as the town hall, but originally it was a hall built in the 1520's for the Guild of Corpus Christi.
Little of the original panelling and carving

inside has survived, but the outside remains a good example of the rather ornate style of half-timbered buildings in fashion under Henry VIII.

Guildhall, Lavenham

Jew's House   **B3**
Lincoln, Lincs. As wealthy money lenders in 12thC England, Jews could afford to build their own houses. This is a modest stone built house, a symbol both of power and wealth. It was an impregnable little block house, strengthened for protection from the periodic anti-Jewish riots which occurred.

St Ives Bridge   **D8**
St Ives, Cambs. A 15thC bridge which crosses the Great Ouse at the market town of St Ives, it has a chapel in its centre bay. One of only three mediaeval bridge chapels surviving in England, it was converted into a house in the 19thC. An extra storey was added, but this was later removed.

chapel on the bridge, St. Ives

Triangular Bridge   **D6**
Crowland, Lincs. Almost an April Fool's joke – it's a triangular bridge at the meeting of four streets in the town. Originally it was built to cross the junction here of three streams of the River Welland. Late 14thC.

Yarmouth Pavilion   **K6**
Norfolk. Built like an elaborate but eccentric railway station, the Pavilion wiles away the time in an expressive rumba of curves which have danced themselves right out of a 30's musical. Delightfully vulgar, it's high altar art of the 20thC.

pavilion, Yarmouth.

Houses & gardens

Anglesey Abbey   **E9**
Cambs. ne of Cambridge on B1102 in Lode village. Begun by the late Lord Fairhaven in 1926, this 100 acre garden possesses all the grandeur of the 18thC with its superbly placed classical statuary framed by perfectly proportioned hedging and impressive trees. Noted particularly for the great avenues such as Emperor's Walk, flanked by the busts of a dozen Roman emperors, the large porphyry vase and the open temple with Corinthian columns which were created to mark the coronation in 1953. The main emphasis is on sculpture but look at the herbaceous border with its good clumps of *Dictamnus fraxinella* (Burning Bush), the dahlia bed, and the rose garden. *Open 14.00-18.00 Wed, Thur, Sat, Sun & B. Hols. Apr-Oct (12.00-1800 Sun late May-Sep).*

Belton House   **B5**
Lincs. 2½ miles ne of Grantham on A607. Unusual for Lincolnshire in that it is a garden set upon a limestone escarpment. The park surrounding the attractive 17thC house in the style of Wren contains some magnificent trees and flocks of black sheep and fallow deer.
The formal gardens near the house are worth seeing, as are the extensive rose gardens. Seek out the sundial depicting Father Time and Cupid, the Gothic ruin, the Bellmont Tower of 1750 and, with a cup of tea in mind, try the Orangery with its camellias. *Open 12.00-18.00 Tue-Thur, Sun & B. Hols Apr-Oct.*

Blickling Hall   **J5**
Aylsham, Norfolk. A fine Jacobean house built for Sir Henry Hobart by Robert Lymirge 1616-28. A symmetrical building of clean-cut charm, it is built of mellowed rose-red brick with many gables, chimneys, pinnacles and four corner turrets with lead caps. There is an elaborate Jacobean plaster-work ceiling in the Long Gallery, and a fine tapestry woven in St Petersburg in 1764 representing Peter the Great at the Battle of Postawa.
Open 14.00-18.00 daily Apr-mid Oct. Closed Fri. (Open 11.00-18.00 Sun late May-Sep)

Blickling Hall

Grimsthorpe Castle   **C6**
Edenham, Lincs. The earliest part, a bastion in the south-east corner, dates from the 13thC. The castle was considerably enlarged in 1540, and a north front was added by Sir John Vanbrugh in 1722. In scale with the rolling country of grass and corn it's a smouldering place of dark thunder.
The hall, arcaded in two tiers, is dramatically inventive.

Grimsthorpe Castle.

Harlaxton Manor   **B5**
Harlaxton, Lincs. Built in the 1830's. Designed by Anthony Salvin for George Gregory, it's sort of high church Victorian, with massive stone banded piers, rusticated stone niches, angular bay windows and a forest of oriental turrets and pinnacles. Smells of vampires. It is reached by an undulating drive which drops into a valley before climbing to this great house nestling in the hillside.
It's now the European Campus for the University of Stanford.

Heveningham Hall   **J8**
Heveningham, nr Halesworth, Suffolk. Designed by Sir Robert Taylor and built in 1777, it's a Palladian building with a pillared centre block rising from an arcaded basement with a pedimented wing on either side. James Wyatt decorated the interior of the house, and the grounds were laid out by Capability Brown. *Open 14.00-17.30 Wed, Thur, Sat, Sun & B Hols Apr-mid Oct (also Tue Jun-Aug).*

Heveningham Hall, Suffolk

Holkham Hall G5

Wells, Norfolk. A Palladian mansion built 1734–59 on reclaimed dunes and salt marshes on the edge of an artificial lake. Designed for Thomas Coke by William Kent, it consists of one central block connected to four lower oblong blocks. In a light grey brick the main building has a rusticated basement with small windows and a superb *piano nobile*. The overall length is 340 feet. There are four corner towers with pyramid roofs and a great central portico.

The interior is as lavish as the exterior is arid. A marble pillared and galleried entrance hall leads to a salon of dark velvet and gold with the Rubens painting of 'The Return from Egypt' as its dominant theme. With the full measure of 18thC magnificence, the interior was planned to give a long vista of connecting rooms.

The grounds of Holkham were laid out by Capability Brown in 1762. *Open 11.30–17.00 Thur & B Hols Jun–Sep (Mon & Thur Jul–Aug).*

Houghton Hall G5

Houghton, Norfolk. Designed for Sir Robert Walpole in the 1730's, it stands in a beautifully landscaped park. A simple statement, visibly expressed, in fine ashlar masonry, it is an oblong of nine by five bays, with a rusticated ground floor, a tall *piano nobile*, a lower second floor, and domed caps at each corner. The architects were Colin Campbell and Thomas Ripley, whilst William Kent handled much of the interior design.

There are rare Mostlake tapestries by Francis Poyntz; elaborate Renaissance jewellery and fine 18thC book bindings.

Ickworth G8

Bury St Edmunds, Suffolk. The eccentric Bishop of Deny with a taste for travel had the idea of building this unusual house to display his fine collection of paintings and sculpture. Begun in 1794 it was completed by his son in 1830. 700 feet long it consists of a large oval rotunda housing a central hall, with two curved corridors leading to the main rooms. It's a pop-eyed place standing in a park landscaped by Capability Brown.

Paintings include a Velasquez portrait of a son of Philip IV of Spain, and family portraits by Reynolds, Gainsborough and others. *Open 14.00–18.00 Wed, Thur, Sat, Sun & B Hols Apr-mid Oct.*

Kimbolton Castle C8

Kimbolton, Cambs. A mediaeval castle where Katherine of Aragon spent her last four years, it was re-modelled in the reign of William and Mary.

In 1707 part of the building collapsed and Vanbrugh was commissioned to rebuild it. It's a building with an inner courtyard, and battlemented mediaeval exterior. Robert Adam added the outer gate-house and the gateway in 1766. *Open 14.00–18.00 Thur & Sun late Jul–Aug & B Hols.*

Manor House B5

Boothby Pagnell, Lincs. Built in 1200 with its sole defence a moat, it is the most important Norman manor house in England. An austere rectangle with a vaulted ground floor, with a hall and solar above. Its massive walls are of oolite rubble with ashlar dressings.

Melton Hall H5

Melton Constable, Norfolk. Standing some distance away from the small village of Melton Constable the Hall, built 1670, is forlorn and neglected, overlooking a beautiful park and lake. The home of the Astleys, it was built to impress. A place of memories in the sky-filled Norfolk country-side. It has some ceilings with very fine plaster-work. Used as the setting for the film 'The Go-between'.

Moat Hall J9

Parham, Suffolk. This famous moated brick house of the Willoughbys is one of the most romantic sights of Suffolk. It's a small farmhouse with pantiles and Tudor chimney-stacks.

Oxburgh Hall F7

Norfolk. 7 miles SW of Swaffham. A fortified manor house, built in 1482 by Sir Edmund Bedinfeld. Built of brick, it sits squarely round a courtyard. The Great Tower, rising 80 feet straight from the edge of the moat, is impressive. A tenacious bulldog of a place as hard as a fist.

Displayed in the rooms are some panels of needle-work embroidered and signed by Mary Queen of Scots. Near the hall is a small chapel by Pugin 1835. *Open 14.00–18.00 Wed, Thur, Sat, Sun & B Hols Apr-mid Oct.*

Oxburgh Hall

Wenham Hall H10

Little Wenham, Suffolk. Best preserved of the 13thC English houses, and the earliest to be built in brick. The lower five feet of the walls are of rubble, the rest are of pink and pale yellow brick with stone buttresses. L-shaped in plan, the long side is occupied by a hall, the short side by a chapel. Both are on the first floor above a brick-vaulted undercroft.

Wimpole Hall D9

Wimpole, Cambs. Set in a park between two Roman roads, it is the most spectacular country mansion of Cambridgeshire. Its architecture is remarkably shy and domestic – a large red brick house of Palladian aspirations in a magnificent setting. Reached by a ceremonial avenue of trees 100 yards wide and two miles long. The hall was begun in 1640 with considerable alterations and additions in the early 18thC.

Artificial Ruins, Grounds of Wimpole Hall.

Museum & galleries

Abbot's Hall Museum of the Rural Life of East Anglia H9

Stowmarket, Suffolk. An open-air museum set in 34 acres. 17thC barn, watermill, 14thC farmhouse and smithy have been re-erected here. Also, a collection of farm implements, wagons and ploughs. *Open 14.00–17.00 daily Apr–Oct.*

Boston Museum D4

The Guildhall, South St, Boston, Lincs. The old Guildhall, 1450, contains a museum of local history and archaeology. Associations with the Pilgrim Fathers who set out from Boston in 1620. *Open 9.30–17.00 Mon–Fri. 9.30–12.00 Sat. (13.30–17.00 May–Sep).*

Bridewell Museum J6

Bridewell Alley, Norwich, Norfolk. Once a prison, dating from the 14thC, now a museum of rural crafts and industries. Weaving, leatherwork, fishing and agricultural equipment, clockmaking and a collection of early bicycles and tricycles. *Open 10.00–17.00 daily. Closed Sun.*

Cambridge and County Folk Museum E9

2–3 Castle St, Cambridge, Cambs. An interesting collection of local bygones dating from mediaeval times and kept in the former White Horse Inn (16thC). *Open 10.30–17.00 Tue–Sat. Closed Mon, & Sun morning.*

The Cromwell Museum D8

Market Sq, Huntingdon, Cambs. Once the grammar school where Cromwell and Samuel Pepys were educated, the museum displays a fine collection of Cromwelliana, including the Protector's death mask. *Open 11.00–17.00 Tue-Sat. Closed Mon, & Sun morning.*

East Anglia Transport Museum K7

Chapel Rd, Carlton Colville, Lowestoft,

Suffolk. For the transport fanatic, tram-cars
trolleybuses, cars and buses galore, a
miniature railway and an operating tramcar
service. *Open 11.00–17.30 Sun & B Hol
14.00–16.00 late-May–Sep.*

Fitzwilliam Museum E9
Trumpington St, Cambridge, Cambs.
World-famous collections of Egyptian,
Greek and Roman antiquities, coins and
medals, mediaeval manuscripts, paintings,
drawings, prints, ceramics, glass and armour.
Open daily. Closed Mon & Sun morning.

Gainsborough's House G10
Sudbury, Suffolk. Gainsborough was born
here in 1727. It's now a museum devoted to
his pictures, drawings and prints.
Exhibitions of contemporary work in the
modern art gallery. *Open 10.00–17.00 Mon–
Sat. Closed Sun morning.*

Gershom-Parkington Memorial
Clocks and Watches G8
8 Angel Hill, Bury St Edmunds, Suffolk.
A small but very special collection of clocks,
watches and time pieces from 500BC
onwards, kept in humming order.
Open 10.00–17.00 daily. Closed Sun.

Norwich Castle Museum J6
Norwich, Norfolk. The castle with its
Norman keep has been a museum since
1894. An iron age hoard of gold and coins
from Snettisham is on display. Also
Lowestoft porcelain, firearms, a small
aquarium. *Open daily. Closed Sun morning.*

The Scott Polar Research
Institute E9
Lensfield Rd, Cambridge, Cambs. Memorial
museum to Scott and his companions. Relics
of Arctic and Antarctic expeditions,
including some 400 water-colours and
sketches by Edward Wilson and examples of
Eskimo art. *Open 14.30–16.00 Mon–Sat.*

Strangers' Hall J6
Charing Cross, Norwich, Norfolk. A
merchant's house, once the centre for
immigrant weavers, then the assize judge's
lodging and now a museum. Rooms are
furnished in the style of different periods
from early Tudor to late Victorian. Cooking
equipment, dolls' houses and coach house
complete with the Lord Mayor's coach.
Open daily. Closed Sun.

Usher Gallery B3
Lindum Rd, Lincoln, Lincs. Fine collection
of watches, miniatures and porcelain; the
Peter de Wint collection of oils, water-
colours, drawings and portraits; relics and
first editions of Alfred, Lord Tennyson.
Open daily. Closed Sun morning.

Wisbech and Fenland Museum E6
Museum Square, Wisbech, Cambs. Fenland
and natural history, archaeology and
antiquarian collections are all here. 12,000
books and manuscripts, including the
original manuscript of Dickens' 'Great
Expectations'. *Open Tue–Sat & B Hols
(10.00–16.00 Oct–Mar).*

Botanical gardens

Bressingham Hall H8
Norfolk, 2½ miles w of Diss, on A1066.
Like a brilliant patchwork quilt thrown upon
the flat Norfolk fenland, Bressingham is
noted for its enormous collection of
herbaceous perennials to which this
remarkable garden is almost entirely
devoted. In island beds, there are over 5,000
species and varieties grouped in imaginative
and colourful settings, many of them
acquired by exchanges with botanic gardens
both in Britain and abroad. There are
interesting beds of alpines and dwarf
specimens and also a quantity of water and
bog plants. *Open 13.30–18.00 Thur, Sun &
B Hols May–late Sep.*

Cambridge University Botanic
Garden E9
Cambridge, Cambs. 1 mile from city centre,
Trumpington Rd. Although founded in 1761,
the recently completed and very large rock
garden is of particular interest as is the
range of greenhouses with their good plant
collections. There are some fine specimen
trees and shrubs. *Open daily 8.00–20.00.*

Zoos, aquaria & aviaries

Cromer Zoo J5
Cromer, Norfolk. Set in five acres and
overlooking the sea, this zoo has a good
range of animals: lions, leopards, bears
wallabies and monkeys, etc. *Open 10.00–
19.00 daily.*

Norfolk Wildlife Park and
Ornamental Pheasant Trust H6
*Great Witchingham, 12 miles nw of Norwich,
Norfolk.* Collection of European 'endangered
species bred in large natural enclosures in
the 50-acre parkland. Deer, wolverines, lynx,
ibex, mouflon, bears. Also, one of the largest
pheasant collections in the world. *Open
10.30–18.00 daily*

Thorney Wildlife Park E6
Thorney, 7 miles ne of Peterborough, Cambs.
Opened in 1969 and still growing, there are
large paddocks of elephants, giraffes, llamas
red kangaroos; cages of lions, tigers, Asiatic
black bear and various small mammals. *Open
daily mid Mar–Oct.*

Nature trails & reserves

East Wretham Heath Nature Trail
*Norfolk. n of Thetford, starting at the
Warden's Office, East Wretham.* 2 miles.
Breckland birds, also those of associated
meres and pines. *Open daily Mar–Sep.
Closed Thur.*

Havergate Island Nature Reserve
Suffolk. In River Ore s of Orford. Main
avocet breeding ground in England. Good
waders on passage and winter wildfowl.
Access strictly by permit only from R.S.P.B.,
The Lodge, Sandy, Beds.

Hickling Broad National Nature
Reserve
Norfolk. n of Potter Heigham. Outstanding
area for waterfowl, reedbed birds, passage
terns and waders. Easy access by boat. View
points south from Hickling village (north-
west corner) and, from the north, Hill
Common. Permits for the reserve area from
Norfolk National Trust, 4 The Close,
Norwich.

Holme Nature Reserve
Norfolk. ne of Hunstanton. Wildfowl,
waders and migrants. Details from The
Warden, The Firs, Holme, Hunstanton,
Norfolk. There is also a nature trail. For the
Holme Bird Observatory, details from
Warden, The Firs, Holme, Hunstanton,
Norfolk. *Reserve open May–Sep.*

Minsmere Nature Reserve
*Suffolk. On the coast nr Saxmundham, s of
Dunwich.* Outstanding nature reserve with
breeding bittern, marsh harrier, avocet,
tern, bearded tit, red-backed shrike, and over
90 others, plus many and varied migrants.
Public hides on the beach are always open,
but entry to the reserve is strictly by permit
only from R.S.P.B., The Lodge, Sandy,
Beds.

Ouse Washes Nature Reserve
Norfolk & Cambs. Public access along banks
and public hides at Purl's Bridge, Manea,
but otherwise limited access. Outstanding
area with immense numbers of winter
wildfowl, especially wigeon and Bewick's
swan. Breeding birds include garganey, ruff
and black-tailed godwit. Details from
Wildfowl Trust, Slimbridge, Glos.
(Welney northwards); R.S.P.B., The Lodge,
Sandy, Beds. (Welney to Welckes Dam);
and Cambridge and Isle of Ely National
Trust, 1 Brodeside, Cambridge.

Scolt Head Island National Nature
Reserve
Norfolk. Access by boat from Brancaster
Staithe on A149. Autumn and winter waders,
winter Brent geese and a very large colony
of common and sandwich terns. No
restrictions except at the ternery in summer
– but contact the Warden at Dial House,
Brancaster Staithe, King's Lynn, Norfolk.

Snettisham Nature Reserve
Snettisham, Norfolk. Outstanding for Wash

waders, some important roosts included, and good for assorted migrants and winter wildfowl, the last on flooded gravel pits. Public access along the beach only, and access restricted at the southern end. Contact the R.S.P.B. Warden at 18 Cockle Road, Snettisham, King's Lynn, Norfolk, or R.S.P.B., The Lodge, Sandy, Beds. for further details.

Wicken Fen Nature Trail
Cambs. 3 miles w of Soham, A1123 and A142. Wetland and reedbed birds. For full details apply to Warden, Lt Col C. E. Mitchell, Lode Lane, Wicken, Ely. *Closed Thur.*

Bird watching

Blyth Estuary
Suffolk. East of A12 and best seen from just north of Blythburgh and from the footpath starting near the White Hart Inn. Excellent for waders, especially black-tailed godwits in spring, waders on passage and winter wildfowl. Spotted redshanks are regular in winter and autumn.

Breydon Water
Norfolk. An exceptionally good area immediately behind Yarmouth. The recommended route is around the southern shore from the railway bridge to Burgh Castle. Brent and grey geese and large numbers of duck and waders occur in winter, plus hen harrier, merlin, short-eared owl, snow bunting and twite, while in spring and autumn the area is noted for a variety of migrant waders. Spoonbills are regular in spring.

Cley and Salthouse
Norfolk. Among the most famous bird watching areas in Britain, the reed marshes, grazing meadows, lagoons and shore are easily accessible from A149 between Cley and Salthouse via roads and the East Bank - but permits are required for entry to the areas off these access routes (Norfolk National Trust, 4 The Close, Norwich). Breeding marsh birds, include bearded tit and water rail, duck, especially wigeon, in large numbers, snow buntings and shore larks in winter, and an incredible variety of migrants of all kinds in spring and autumn, including many rarities.

Grafham Water
Cambs. 2 miles w of A1 at Buckden. A large reservoir much used for sailing and fishing, but nevertheless exceptionally good for winter duck and other water birds, and for migrant waders in autumn. It is accessible from three well-signposted public car parks and from the fishermen's car park near Grafham village, from which much of the water area can be seen.

Holbeach
Lincs. 8 miles n of Holbeach on A151. This area is best viewed from the sea wall between Fotheringham House and Holbeach St Matthew. While pinkfooted geese and various other wildfowl occur in winter, and short-eared owls are regulars, Holbeach is most interesting for the vast assemblages of waders from the Wash which roost in the area at high tide.

Brass rubbing

The following is a short list of churches that have brasses for rubbing. Permission is almost invariably required.
Cambridgeshire. Balsham, Burwell, Diddington, Ely Cathedral, Fulbourn, Hildersham, Horseheath, Offord D'Arcy, Sawtry, Trumpington, Westley Waterless, Wisbech, Wood Ditton.
D'Arcy, Sawtry.
Lincolnshire. Barton-upon-Humber (St Mary), Broughton, Gunby, Irnham, Linwood, Scrivelsby, Stamford (All Saints), Tattershall.
Norfolk. Aylsham, Elsing, Hunstanton, King's Lynn, Methwold, Narborough, Norwich (St George Colegate, St John

Maddermarket and St Lawrence), Reepham, Southacre, Upwell.
Suffolk. Acton, Barsham, Burgate, Ipswich (St Mary Tower), Letheringham, Long Melford, Mendlesham, Playford, Stoke-by-Nayland, Yoxford.

Fossil hunting

Visit the local museum. Its fossil collection usually states where individual fossils have been found. When visiting quarries always seek permission to enter if they look privately owned or worked. Be careful of falls of rock.

Aldeburgh Suffolk
Pliocene coralline crag with plentiful lamellibranchs, gastropods, bryozoa, forams and occasional fossil crabs and sea urchins in pits at Aldeburgh, Chillesford, Orford and Sudbourne.

Cromer Norfolk
The coast here is the youngest chalk found in England. At Trimingham rich cretaceous fauna and abundant yields of small oyster fossils. At West Runton mammal remains, plants, seeds and fruit can be found in the cliffs. The Pleistone gravels on the coast around Cromer have yielded many bones of vertebrates from the ice ages.

Ipswich Suffolk
Cretaceous belemites, sea urchins, corals, crinoids, etc, are found in exposures at Bramford Claydon and Sudbury.

Lincolnshire
Good Jurassic fossils in pits at Ancaster, Appleby, Bracebridge, Castle Bytham, Denton, Greetwell, Sleaford and Stickney. Chalk quarries also in the Lincolnshire wolds e.g. Caistor.

Peterborough Cambs.
The Jurassic clay is exposed in clay pits at Yaxley and at Warboys south of Peterborough. Yields abundant pyritized ammonites, gastropods, lamellibranchs and brachiopods.

Southwold Suffolk
Easton cliffs north of the town has fossil shells and the occasional bones of prehistoric animals. Look out also for semi-precious stones (cornelian and agates).

Forests

Aldewood
Nr Aldeburgh, Suffolk. The Forestry Commission's national Aldewood Forest near the Suffolk coast, draws its name from the River Alde nearby. Pines from Scotland and Corsica have been established on former sandy wastes and now provide shady walks, with car parks, picnic places, and views over estuaries towards the sea. Handy centres for visitors are Woodbridge, Aldeburgh, Dunwich and Southwold.

Thetford Chase   **G7**
Norfolk/Suffolk. England's largest lowland forest, Thetford Chase, has been farmed for timber since 1920 on 45,000 acres of the old Breckland, a sandy waste on the borders of Norfolk and Suffolk, near the towns of Thetford and Brandon. Pines are the only trees that thrive and can be used for timber and two kinds are grown, one from Scotland and the other from Corsica. They yield thousands of tons of softwood annually, used by local sawmills, as pit-props in distant coalfields, and for chipboard or paper pulp.
From the forest centre at Santon Downham, signposted footpaths lead along the banks of the Little Ouse, lined with poplars, and on through shady dells formed by stately pines or Douglas firs. Relics of past ages include the prehistoric Grimes Graves at Brandon, where stone age man quarried flints underground for tools and weapons. A Norman castle mound dominates Thetford, a market town fought over by Danes and Saxons, and given fresh life

to-day as a thriving 'new town'. The woods hold red and roe deer. Rare birds include crossbills that wrench pine seeds from cones, and the heath-loving stone curlew which probes below pebbles for insect food.

Hills

Cromer Ridge
Norfolk. East Anglia's only impressive upland, this ridge extends along the north coast of Norfolk from Holt, past Sheringham and Cromer, to Mundesley. It is a land of breezy heaths with sandy soils and the scattered pinewoods of Wensum Forest. Views to the broad North Sea give a sense of space. The highest point, 327 feet, is near East Beckham.

East Anglian Heights
Suffolk. A misleading name for the rolling countryside of central Suffolk, which is nowhere more than 420 feet above the sea. Between Sudbury and Bury St Edmunds. This watershed between the Wash and the Thames Estuary does however hold charming valleys and picturesque villages that merit search.

Gog Magog Hills
Cambs. 4 miles se Cambridge. Two low mounds, reaching a height of 234 feet, rising from the plain. Named after the legendary Celtic giant-gods who once defended London against prehistoric invaders. This is a favourite walk for Cambridge people, who otherwise never see a hill.

Kesteven Heights
Lincs. An upland ridge in the south of Lincolnshire, where the soft, fawn grey of limestone walls lends character to well-tended fields, prosperous villages and thriving market towns like Stamford and Grantham. Good hunting country with many woodlands, fine mansions and broad views over lowland plains to north, east and south.

Lincoln Edge
Lincs. From the famous cathedral set on its spine in the heart of Lincoln city, the Lincoln Edge runs due north for 25 miles to Scunthorpe, and also 25 miles south to Grantham. A limestone ridge, averaging 200 feet above sea level, its course is followed by a prehistoric trackway that became a Roman road, and finally a modern highway, A15. The Edge has few villages or houses; its slopes form pastures for settlements at its foot, on either hand. Grand views to the Wolds on the east, and westwards over the Trent Valley.

Lincolnshire Wolds
Lincs. These high chalk hills form a long spine that follows the line of Lincolnshire's northeast coast, about ten miles inland. Nowhere steep, they give a sense of spaciousness, thanks to their wide views over the coastal marshes towards the grey North Sea. The main road along the flanks of the Wolds runs from Skegness, an attractive seaside resort, through Louth, the principal market town, to Grimsby, a major fishing port on the Humber. The Wolds were settled between the 5th and 10thC, first by Anglians and later by Danish invaders, and have been farmed intensively ever since. Scattered woods near Wragby and Caistor, on the sandy eastern fringes. Highest point, 548 feet, is at Normanby-le-Wold, four miles south of Caistor.

Meadows & marshes

Blakeney Marshes
Norfolk. On the north coast, beside the villages of Blakeney and Cley-next-the-Sea. This marshland has developed where the little creeks are held back by the shingle spit called Scolt Head (now a nature reserve of the National Trust). Rare salt-marsh flowers grow along the muddy streams and many unusual birds nest and feed, or halt on seasonal migrations.

Broadland Marshes
Norfolk. The slow rivers and open broads of north east Norfolk are bordered by peaty fens of reeds and rushes, with occasional willows and alder trees. These remain haunts of rare waterfowl, including the bittern and the marsh harrier that nest in their midst; several have become nature reserves. They are the strongholds of the coypu, a huge water-rat introduced from South America for its fur, now running, and swimming, wild.

The Fens
A broad region of dead-flat country lying inland from the Wash, including much of Lincolnshire, Cambridgeshire, and part of Norfolk. Traversed by the lower courses of four great rivers, the Witham, the Welland, the Nene, and the Bedfordshire Ouse, the Fens were subject to seasonal floods and remained trackless marshes through the middle ages. Here Hereward the Wake—or the Watchful—the last Saxon leader to assert independence, defied William the Conqueror around 1070. Only fishermen, wildfowlers and reed-cutters frequented winding streams through alder and willow-tree swamps called 'carrs'.
From the 17thC onwards the Fens have been tamed by immense drainage schemes, planned originally by Dutch engineers. The upland rivers are confined within banks, the sea is kept back by dykes, the fields are drained by networks of ditches, and surface water is pumped uphill into higher carrier waterways.
The black humus-rich carr soil, thus safe-guarded, yields exceptionally heavy crops. View this vast treeless farmer's paradise from some hill-top town like March or Ely. Near Shippea 'Hill' six miles north-east of Ely, several square miles are actually below sea level.

The Spillway
Cambs. The Spillway, also called the 'Wash', is a unique watermeadow on the Isle of Ely, midway between the towns of Ely and March. To drain the fens and to cope with the floods of the Bedfordshire Ouse, engineers built two parallel drains, the Old Bedford River and the New Bedford River, for twenty miles north east between St Ives and Downham Market. When winter floods exceed their combined capacity, the Spillway carries the surplus. In summer it is grazed by herds of fat bullocks.

Wash Marshes
The shores of the Wash, from Skegness round past Boston and King's Lynn to Hunstanton, a total distance of 50 miles, are bordered by tidal marshes. On their inland side, high dykes protect fertile reclaimed land from flooding. A grim, grey, roadless region, difficult to visit, and popular only with fishermen and wild fowlers.

Rivers

Ouse and Cam
The Ouse begins half-way across England, near Banbury, and passes Bedford and Huntingdon on its way to King's Lynn, a seaport at the eastern corner of the Wash. The Cam, its main tributary (which rises near Royston), is broad enough to carry the university racing eights at Cambridge and flows on, almost at sea level, past Ely Cathedral to Downham Market. The Ouse drains a large area of west Norfolk and north west Suffolk. A huge new boundary drain keeps its eastern floodwaters clear of the Fens.

The Stour
Suffolk. The Stour, a typical Suffolk river, rises on the East Anglian Heights east of Cambridge, and wanders slowly eastwards in a shallow vale, passing a score of farmland villages and the little towns of Clare and Sudbury. Below Nayland its valley broadens out into the fertile Dedham Vale, beloved of Constable who painted its trees, mills, fields, and barges under striking cloud and sunlight. Beyond Manningtree it becomes a broad tidal estuary, forming a harbour for ferry steamers from Denmark

and Holland to Harwich port.

The Trent
For most of its lower course the great River Trent forms the boundary between Nottinghamshire and Lincolnshire, flowing between dykes through a level plain won for agriculture by draining the marshes. Newark, Retford and Gainsborough are market towns drawing prosperity from farms in this almost treeless vale. The Isle of Axholme, once isolated by fenland backwaters, is still surrounded by canals, and defended by dykes from the Humber tides to the north.

Witham, Welland & Nene
The River Witham rises near Grantham, runs north to Lincoln and there, surprisingly, breaks through the Lincoln Edge, to continue south west through the fens to Boston and the Wash. The Welland comes down from Leicestershire past Stamford and Spalding, crossing the fens to the western corner of the Wash. The larger Nene begins above Northampton, winds past Peterborough, and crosses the marshlands near Wisbech to the Wash's centre. All cross the dead-flat Fens within high floodbanks, and drainage water is pumped up to them from fields below.

East Anglia contains none of the familiar 18thC canals linked together as a waterway transport network. There are plenty of river navigations in this part of the world, most of which are still used by commercial seagoing craft. In Norfolk the River Yare still carries small freighters for 28 miles inland from Yarmouth to Norwich, and the rivers Great Ouse, Welland, Nene and Witham serve the ports of King's Lynn, Wisbech and Boston and then empty into the Wash. But the only canal as such is the disused *North Walsham & Dilham Canal* to the north of Norwich, which is partly a river navigation anyway. So the main 'canal interest' in East Anglia must be in the Fenland waterways. The Fens are an area of England which was once a swamp, of little use to man or beast. In the 17thC King James I invited Cornelius Vermuyden, the great Dutch engineer, to come over and drain the Fens and make them fit for cultivation. Vermuyden did a good job. He built a long sea wall, and constructed an intricate network of drainage canals and sluices, feeding the water into the rivers Great Ouse, Welland and Nene. In many cases, his earthworks left the drained land lower than the now-embanked rivers, so pumping engines were installed to pump the water out of the dykes into the rivers and so to the sea. Vermuyden's network still exists, little changed. His dykes and pumping stations are still a vital part of the finely balanced economy that is based on the richest soil in the country. And for boaters, the Fens present a unique yet unpredictable cruising network. The Fenland waterways are connected to the rest of the canal system via the River Nene and the Grand Union Canal.

Archaeology

Burgh Castle   H6
Nr Belton, Suffolk. Roman Gariannonum belongs to the series of 'Saxon Shore' forts constructed by the Romans in the late 3rdC around the south east coast. It is a narrow rectangle in shape, of which three walls survive to a height of fifteen feet – probably their full height apart from a parapet, since some of the five remaining bastions have a floor at this level, with a circular setting to hold a catapult turntable. One gate survives in the long east wall, and a postern in each of the short walls. The masonry, flint facing stones with tile courses, is amongst the finest in Roman Britain. *Open daily Mar, Apr & Oct. 9.30-16.00 Nov Feb. Closed Sun morning.*

Caistor St Edmunds   J6
Norfolk. The Roman Venta Icenorum was the tribal capital for the Iceni, whose queen, Boudicca (Boadicea), led a revolt against the Romans in 61 AD, during which London,

Colchester, and St Albans were razed. The town walls were probably built in the 3 dC, and are still standing; much of the town plan has been revealed by aerial photography. A major Saxon cemetery lay just outside the town. *Accessible with permission from the farm.*

Devil's Dyke   F8
Reaches to Ditton Green across Newmarket Heath, Cambs. Seven miles of linear earthworks with a massive embankment, cutting across the Icknield Way. Post-Roman in date, at least in part, and likely to have been constructed by early Saxon invaders as a defence against the Britons. The Dyke is best seen from the Swaffham Prior-Burwell road, which crosses it at right-angles.

Grimes Graves   G7
Nr Weeting, Norfolk. Before the discovery of metals, prehistoric man depended upon hard stone for manufacture of his tools and weapons, and in Britain flint was the best material for shaping fine, and often highly sophisticated, objects. Grimes Graves is the only ancient flint mine accessible to the public; it was in use from the later neolithic into the early bronze age, and supplied implements over a wide area. The mines consist of massive shafts sunk through chalk to the flint layer, with galleries fanning out to follow the deposits, and show as pits on the surface. There is a small display of finds at the site. *Open daily Apr & 9.30-19.00 May-Sep. (Open daily Mar & Oct & 9.30-16.00 Nov-Feb. Closed Sun morning.)*

Lincoln   B3
Lincs. Lindum Colonia, one of the major cities of Roman Britain, originated c50 as a timber-built fortress during the Roman conquest. It was occupied successively by the IX Hispana Legion and the II Adiutrix, and tombstones of soldiers of both legions have been found along the roads to the south. As the frontier was advanced northwards, Lincoln was abandoned as a military site and established as a settlement (*colonia*) for veteran soldiers. Later the town expanded southwards, towards the river, and the whole area was enclosed with stone walls, probably during the 2ndC. Two of the stone gateways survive in remarkably good condition: the Newport Arch in the North Wall, and, in Orchard Street, a gate inserted into the defences in the 4thC which contains much reused decorative stone. At East Bight is a section of wall and the heavy square foundation for a watertank where an aqueduct entered the city. The foundations of a corner tower, showing successive phases of timber fortress and stone town defences, is visible in Eastgate. Lincoln Museum houses a fine collection of Roman material, including tombstones and pottery from local kilns.

Sutton Hoo   J9
Nr Woodbridge, Suffolk. A fine group of Saxon barrows, Sutton Hoo includes the site of the famous ship-burial, which was probably a memorial to an East Anglian king, and is dated by coins to the mid-7thC. The superb treasure, which included a gilt-decorated helmet and objects of gold, silver, and enamel, is now in the British Museum; replicas of the finest pieces are in Ipswich Museum. *On private land, but visible from the public footpath.*

Footpaths & ancient ways

Icknield Way
A prehistoric trackway once stretching from the Wash to the Channel. The best sections of the way are west of Cambridge, but there are still a few traces of green way in East Anglia worth exploring.
Near Lackford by the River Lark there is a rough trackway for 3¾ miles through King's Forest to Weatherhill Heath, where it becomes the boundary of Elveden Park. Just two miles short of Thetford all trace is lost but there are signs of a causeway leading over arable land, from Weather Heath to Croxted Park.

Peddars Way

This is a prehistoric trackway running from what is now the High Street, Ixworth in Suffolk to the site of the Roman fort at Brancaster, which once guarded the entrance to the Wash. Castle Acre is the only village of any size that it touches.

The Romans improved the road, and for many miles it is a straight track across the countryside south of Brancaster. Parts of the Peddars Way are still green way, and there is much evidence of prehistoric occupation to intrigue the rambling Sherlock Holmes.

Via Devana

Built by the Romans, from Godmanchester, Huntingdonshire, to Cambridge, the Via Devana is a main road today. From Cambridge it becomes a trackway climbing over the Gogmagog Hills, across Wandlebury Camp, passing no villages and entering Suffolk at Withersfield, near Haverhill, where it disappears without trace.

Regional sports

Association Football

Norwich City, a professional team, were in the Third Division of the football league as recently as 1960, and since then spent sometime in the First Division. Nicknamed the 'Canaries', the team has its ground at Carrow Road, Norwich, Norfolk. Tel Norwich 23612.

The other top team of the area is Ipswich, who are usually a good match for any team in the country. The ground is at Portman Rd, Ipswich. Tel 57107.

Fishing

The main coarse fishing rivers are the Bure, Waveney, and Yare. They are particularly noted for their rudd and bream, but good pike, perch, roach, tench and gudgeon abound. On many of the Broads rudd will provide good sport on fly, though a long line must be cast. One of the chief joys of this area is the number of cosy country pubs from which a day's angling can be enjoyed.

Homersfield, Suffolk. On the River Waveney. Licences for fishing can be obtained from the landlord of the Black Swan Hotel.

Acle, Norfolk. Fishing on the River Bure at Acle is free to River Authority licence holders.

East Suffolk and Norfolk River Authority, 14 Albermarle Road, Norwich, Norfolk. Licences for the Bure, Waveney and Yare can be obtained for a trifling fee.

Flat Racing

Newmarket, Suffolk. A fine race course and the headquarters of horse racing in Britain since the 17thC. The home of the Jockey Club and the National Stud, it originally owed its pre-eminence to the interest shown by King James I (1603-25). Fixture cards can be obtained from the Jockey Club Office, High Street, Newmarket, Suffolk.

Motor Racing

There is a large motor racing circuit at Snetterton, Norfolk. This is one of the country's top fifteen circuits featuring a varied programme of important racing car and motor cycling events. More important events are regularly televised.

Sailing

The Norfolk and Suffolk Broads, large lakes interconnected by winding slow moving rivers, support many sailing clubs. If membership in a club is being contemplated it is worth choosing carefully. Many areas are densely shielded by trees giving flukey light winds. Oulton Broad at Lowestoft is a fine, large open lake on which a wide variety of dinghies and powerboats race.

The Waveney and Oulton Broad Yacht Club offer temporary membership for a month. The regatta is held in August. For details write to: the Hon. Secretary, H. D. Hannant, 29 The Avenue, Lowestoft, Suffolk.

For further information on other yacht clubs in the area write to Nigel Hacking, Secretary of the *Royal Yachting Association*, 5 Buckingham Gate, London SW1.

Festivals

For information and tickets for festivals go to the local information centre or ticket agent.

Aldeburgh Festival of the Arts

Aldeburgh, Suffolk. A small, intimate and world famous festival associated with Benjamin Britten. Traditionally first performances of new works are given, but early music is much in demand. Concerts, too, in the local parish churches. *Jun*.

Cambridge Festival

Cambridge. Cambs. Festival of music, representing the arts in both city and university. Events are held in the colleges, the Guildhall and Ely cathedral. *Late Jul*.

Hintlesham Festival

Hintlesham, Suffolk. A summer festival of the arts open to unknown and well established artists. The open-air stage is a main attraction and performances of classical opera are given on at least six nights during the festivities. *May–Jun*.

King's Lynn Festival

King's Lynn, Norfolk. Events centre around the 15thC Guildhall. Kathleen Ferrier, the Westminster Abbey Choir and the Hallé Orchestra have all performed here over the years. Music is the main attraction, but there are also exhibitions, historic films and talks. The annual flower show coincides with the first Sunday of the festival. *Late Jul*.

Fun things

Bressingham Steam Museum　　H8

Bressingham Hall, Norfolk. On the side of A1066, 4 miles w of Diss. There are three miles of rides on narrow gauge and miniature railways. This is probably the best private collection of steam and rail road locomotives in the country. For all those who find the combination of smoke and steam is irresistible.

Great Yarmouth Funfair　　K6

Great Yarmouth, Norfolk. The town possesses a large varied funfair, and the biggest of big dippers in Britain. For those with the nerves and stomach repeat rides are free. The fair is situated conveniently by the beach with good parking.

King's Lynn Fair　　F6

King's Lynn, Norfolk. Not a permanent fair, but included because of its antiquity. It has been held on the 14th February, Valentine's Day, since the early 11thC. Only the Plague in 1666 and two world wars temporarily stopped its appearance. It lasts for six days, and is one of the earliest fairs of the year, with a ceremonial opening by the mayor who, with his party, has the privilege of being first to ride on the roundabouts.

North Norfolk Railway Co.　　H4

Sheringham Station, Sheringham, Norfolk. An ideal visit for a wet summer's day as the exhibition is housed under cover and working steam train trips on some days. *Open daily Easter–mid Oct. afternoon Jul–Sep*.

Hotels

The following indicates the price range of a single room per night:
£　　inexpensive
££　　medium priced
£££　expensive.

Aldeburgh Suffolk　　K9

Brudenell Hotel, The Parade. Tel 2071. A well equipped red-brick hotel directly overlooking the sea. Games room. *££*.

Cambridge Cambs　　E9

University Arms Hotel, Regent St. Tel 51241. Well run. Blends traditional with modern. There is a fine Octagon room. *££*.

Cromer Norfolk   **J5**
Colne House Hotel, The Croft. Tel 2013.
A good family hotel with extensive grounds.
There are also ten self-catering bungalows £.

Felixstowe Suffolk   **J10**
Orwell Hotel, Hamilton Rd. Tel 5511.
Plain-fronted with well-restored interior.
Good amenities. ££.

Grantham Lincs   **B5**
Angel and Royal Hotel, High St. Tel 5816.
An old Trust House, well situated for the A1
Good restaurant. £.

Holt Norfolk   **H5**
Feather's Hotel, 6 Market Place. Tel 2318. A
17thC coaching inn close to the sea with a
cosy bar and friendly public rooms. £.

Horning Norfolk   **J6**
Petersfield House Hotel, nr Norwich. Tel 365.
A half-timbered country house with a neat
garden and private moorings on the Bure.
Hotel launch. ££.

Huntingdon Cambs   **D8**
Old Bridge Hotel, 1 High St. Tel 52681. This
pleasant country town hotel was famous in
the 19thC as the first Barclays Bank. £.

Ipswich Suffolk   **H9**
Belstead Brook Hotel, Belstead Rd. Tel 52380.
An attractive country house two miles from
the town centre. ££.

King's Lynn Norfolk   **F6**
*Duke's Head Hotel, Tuesday Market Place.
Tel 4996.* Georgian. Overlooks the Market
Square. The interior has been carefully
modernised. £££.

Lavenham Suffolk   **G9**
Swan, High St. Tel 477. Carefully renovated
with well-beamed public rooms. There is a
magnificent dining room which serves good
food. £££.

Lincoln Lincs   **B3**
White Hart Hotel. Tel 26222. In Bailgate
close to the Cathedral. The good atmosphere
of the public rooms is aided by fine antiques.
Well run. £££.

Long Melford Suffolk   **G9**
Bull Hotel, nr Sudbury. Tel 494. Another
well renovated 15thC timbered inn.
Bedrooms lead off the Weavers Gallery. ££.

Newmarket Suffolk   **F8**
Rutland Arms Hotel, High St. Tel 4251.
Constructed during the reign of Charles II,
it displays fine paintings and has spacious
bedrooms. New wing to the rear. £.

Norwich Norfolk   **J6**
Maid's Head Hotel, Tombland. Tel 28821.
Old and long established, well known for its
character and service. Offers traditional
and modern comfort. ££.

Stamford Lincs   **C6**
George Hotel, St Martins. Tel 2101.
Charles I and William II stayed here. A
beamed lounge combines historical interest
and modern comfort. £.

Thetford Norfolk   **G7**
Bell Hotel, King St. Tel 4455. A well-
preserved former Post House, with fine
Tudor murals and a cheerful atmosphere.
££.

Weybourne Norfolk   **H5**
Maltings Hotel, nr Holt. Tel 275. A 16thC
flintstone malting house in lovely countryside. Pleasantly decorated. No children
under 5. £.

Woodbridge Suffolk   **J9**
Seckford Hall Hotel. Tel 5678. A secluded
Tudor manor with splendid period rooms.
Individually styled bedrooms. ££.

Regional food & drink

Cambridge Sausage
A pork sausage flavoured with sage.

Felixstowe Tart
A shortbread tart filled with jam and topped
with meringue.

Frumenty Suffolk Style
Made of new crushed wheat, soaked in milk
and water overnight, and then boiled with
honey and cinnamon. The Frumenty is
traditional home cooking, eaten during the
twelve days of Christmas and a little put
outside for the fairies. Ely Frumenty is
similar to Suffolk Frumenty but distinctly
laced with rum.

Lincolnshire Potatoes
The flat Lincolnshire fenlands are perfect
for growing and producing the famous
Lincolnshire potato. The seed potatoes are
still much in demand all over the country.

Mustard
Norfolk is famous for the growing, milling
and blending of mustard, particularly in the
Norwich area.

Norfolk Apple Dumpling
This is a popular farmhouse dish. A whole
apple is stuffed with jam or sugar, covered
in a flaky pastry cover, baked and sprinkled
with castor sugar.

Norfolk Turkeys
Norfolk is noted for turkey breeding. Around
Christmas time it's a particularly busy place.

Suffolk Cheese
A very hard cheese, and as the saying goes
"hunger will break stone walls and anything
except a Suffolk cheese"

Yarmouth Bloaters
Bloaters are becoming increasingly rare:
uncleaned herrings are salted and smoked to
give a distinctly gamey flavour.

Restaurants

£   inexpensive
££   medium priced
£££   expensive

Brockdish, Norfolk   **J8**
Sheriff House, e of Diss. Tel Hoxne 316.
French. Eccentric. Order by telephone from
unpriced menu. *LD. Closed Wed. £££.
Book.*

Fressingfield Norfolk   **J8**
Fox and Goose, nr Diss. Tel 247. Excellent
French cooking served in charming oak-
beamed restaurant. Friendly service. *LD
Closed Tue, mid Apr & mid Oct. £££. Book.*

Grantham, Lincs   **B5**
*Angel and Royal Hotel, High St, on A1.
Tel 5816.* Trust House. Mainly English.
LD. £L, ££D. Book.

Grimsthorpe, Lincs   **C6**
*Black Horse Inn, 4 miles w of Bourne. Tel
Edenham 247.* Traditional 18thC inn.
Garden. Exclusively English. *LD. Closed
Sun. ££.*

Keyston Cambs   **C8**
*Pheasant Inn, 4 miles se of Thrapston.
Tel Bythorn 241.* Thatched pub on village
green. Fish and shellfish. Careful, individual
cooking. English and French. *LD. ££.
Book D.*

Melbourn, Cambs   **D9**
*Pink Geranium, off the A10. Tel Royston
60215.* Friendly cottage restaurant. English.
D. Closed Sun & Mon. ££. Book.

Norwich, Norfolk   **J6**
Marco's, 17 Pottergate. Tel 24044.
Distinctive Italian. Lunch good value. *LD.
Closed Sun & Mon. £L. ££D. Book D.*

Orford, Suffolk   **K9**
*Butley-Orford Oysterage, Market Square.
Tel 277.* Cafe-like surroundings. First-class
smoked fish and shellfish. Very popular.
Good value. *LD. Closed D Jan-Feb. ££.*

Trumpington, Cambs   **E9**
*Coach and Horses, 2 miles s of Cambridge.
Tel 2129.* Popular, welcoming pub on the
outskirts of Cambridge. Mainly English.
LD. Closed Sun. £L, ££D. Book.

Weybourne, Norfolk   **H5**
*Gasche's Swiss Restaurant, 3 miles ne of Holt.
Tel 220.* Unpretentious Swiss family
restaurant. Huge helpings. Popular. *LD.
Closed Mon L & Sun D. £L, ££D. Book.*

The Industrial North and the Moors

It was the Industrial Revolution that transformed this part of Britain, but it is not all 'dark satanic mills'. The best of the towns are rich and industrious and they have cleared up the worst excesses of industrial squalor. Some towns like Manchester and Bradford have been a little too eager to sweep away their past and you'd better go quickly to see the remaining Victorian splendours. This region is full of splendid towns and tough scenery; the Yorkshire Moors have a remote beauty that is rare in Britain. Lancashire can claim two of Europe's greatest cities: Manchester and Liverpool and both are vitally alive not just with football fans but music and glorious Victorian architecture.

York itself, from Roman times an important centre, is almost a perfect walled city at the heart of a region full of great houses and warm villages. The people of the industrial north are friendly and warmhearted with a rich sense of humour, the Beatles, Prime Ministers and comedians have come from here and when you come 'up north' you will find you are welcome.

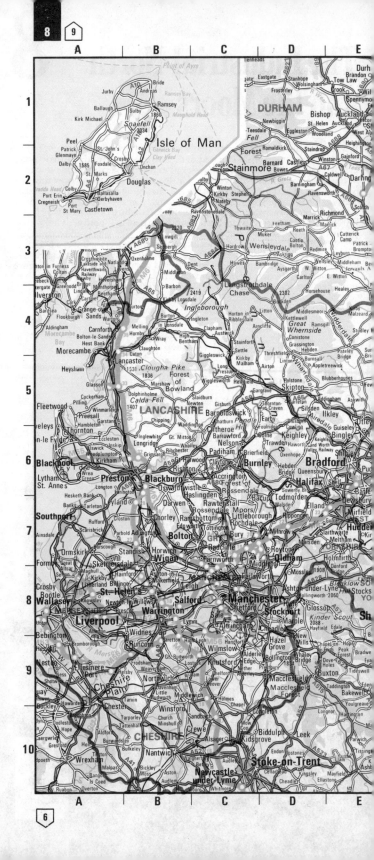

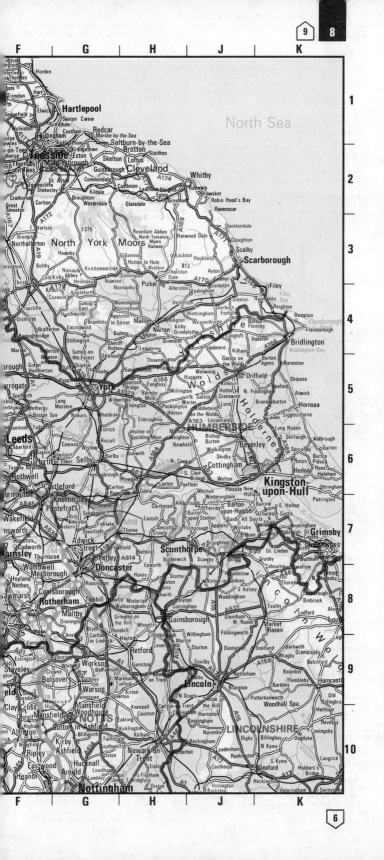

The coast

Blackpool   A6
Lancs. Pop 151,300. EC Wed. It was in 1887 when the Morning Post wrote 'Blackpool has discovered the lost art of entertaining . . . and offers more fun for less money than anywhere else!' It's still true today but on a much bigger scale. It is Britain's largest resort and the holiday season covers almost half the year, the political parties hold conferences there during October.
Everything is larger than life. The Prom is seven miles long, the tower is the nearest thing in England to the Eiffel Tower, and there are three piers. If it rains or the frantic pace of the Golden Mile gets too much for you there are nearly twenty theatres and top flight summer shows, including an epic ice show.
Two things remain unique to Blackpool, the first English monorail and the first electric tramway in the world. The beaches are sandy, patrolled by life guards and there are four swimming pools.

Blackpool

Bootle   A8
Mersey. Pop 74,200. Solid Mersey dockland softened a little by two indoor sea water pools – come to Bootle to see what a development area looks like. Masses of decanted offices from London including the new National Giro Centre and some twenty acres of new buildings. Sad that so much growth and development gives no indication at all of human imagination at work.

Bridlington   K4
Humber. Pop 26,700. EC Thur. MD Wed, Sat. Sheltered by Flamborough Head from the worst of the north-east gales, Bridlington is a popular beach resort with long stretches of level sand. The railway arrived in 1842 and changed the character of the town, originally planned for the rich families who built their elegant villas on the sea front. Piers, a harbour and every sort of holiday amusement are added attractions.
Bridlington is the model for Hardrascliffe in Winifred Holtby's powerful Yorkshire novel 'South Riding'.

Cleethorpes   K7
Humber. Pop 35,800. EC Thur. A hundred years ago it was a little fishing village. Now a large seaside town with a short season attracting over a million visitors a year, it's a a place you can read between the lines or take straight – a joke for some and paradise for others.
It has the largest open air swimming pool in Britain, a magnificent zoo and a 1,200-foot-long pier.
Good views of shipping on the Humber from the busy promenade. Three miles of sandy beach, safe for swimming.

Flamborough Head   K4
York. A majestic chalky place; the great headland is surrounded by coves and rock pools that can be explored at low tide. The ideal spot for scrambling among the rocks to look for cliff birds or investigate the seaweed-filled pools. Swimming is very dangerous.
The lighthouse on the headland is an important warning light for North Sea shipping; you can visit it during the afternoons.

Fleetwood   A5
Lancs. Pop 30,000. EC Wed. MD Tue, Fri. A rich young entrepreneur, Peter Hesketh Fleetwood, engaged the distinguished architect Decimus Burton to build a new town at Fleetwood in 1837. He achieved a great deal on the barren site and strict rules, even fines for not having thatched roofs covered with slate, made Fleetwood the beginnings of an elegant town.

Alas, the cash ran out and the completion of the railway over Shap made the proposed Glasgow-Fleetwood-London link unnecessary – so Fleetwood stands as an incomplete dream. It has gradually developed as a lesser Blackpool, and the fishing industry lands more than 40,000 tons a year from Arctic waters at the harbour. Wide sandy beaches.

Formby   A7
Mersey. Pop 23,500. The Mersey's Lancashire shore is now mostly dockland but Formby still has an unspoilt beach. Long stretches of high grassy dunes are an excellent vantage point to watch the Mersey shipping. Bathing is not safe.

Goxhill Haven   K6
Humber. Pop 1,200. Reached from a farmyard, it's a wild and lonely part of the Humber. A piece of muddy foreshore, with the cranes and the roofs of Hull visible on the opposite bank as well as spectacular views of river craft.

Grimsby   K7
Humber. Pop 95,700. EC Thur. MD Tue, Fri, Sat. An old world fishing port, not the most exotic of towns, but full of salty vigour; its name synonymous with trawlers and fishing. Little ships from North Sea ports sail into Grimsby, one of the oldest chartered towns in England. The Fish Dock, with nearly a mile of quays, is the largest fish market in the world. Sandy beaches towards Cleethorpes.

Hornsea   K8
Humber. Pop 7,000. Although this is a seaside resort and a very intimate and pleasant one, the main reason for a visit is the inland freshwater lake.
Hornsea Mere is the result of some long distant glacial action. Over two miles long, it is the home of water birds and large gatherings of swans. Take a rowing boat out for a watery wander among the reeds. The beach is sandy and there are amusements.

Hoylake   West A8
Mersey. Pop 32,200. This is a well tended rather swish little town, the opposite of Blackpool or New Brighton. Rather than disturb the retired residents you had better tiptoe across the bowling greens to the spacious sandy beach. Good golf links.

Hull   K6
Humber. Pop 282,900. EC Mon, Thur. MD Tue, Fri, Sat. Don't be put off by the industrial nature of this town, it is Britain's major deep-water fishing port and a visit to the fish dock when the trawlers come in from Iceland and beyond is fascinating. The docks extend for seven miles along the Humber and there are some recent additions – oil tanker jetties.
In the town itself there is a range of museums from William Wilberforce's birthplace to the Transport Museum. The university is worth a visit if only for its imaginative new Gulbenkian Theatre. One of England's finest modern poets, Philip Larkin, is librarian of Hull University. Nearest beach on river shore near Kilnsea.

St Andrews Dock, Hull.

Liverpool   A8
Mersey. Pop 574,600. EC Wed. The city of Liverpool is large, prosperous and in many ways outrageous. It has more of everything: more docks than anywhere but London; more cathedrals than most cities, and both of

Perhead, Liverpool

them modern; more successful football teams; it's produced more pop stars and comedians and has more dock and engineering strikes than anyone cares to count.

A city apart, it even has its own impossible accent. Liverpool grew very fast during the late 19th and early 20thC as Atlantic trade prospered and the wide Mersey accommodated more and more ships. There are nearly 40 miles of quay and a glance at only one dock, Albert Dock, is enough to show the quality of this early industrial architecture.

The town centre has an amazing series of Victorian civic buildings of a certain thrusting grandeur; St George's Hall is at the heart of this group. On the waterfront three commercial buildings are typical of the city's style and wealth – the Cunard building, the Royal Liver Friendly Society building, and the head offices of the Mersey Docks and Harbour Board.

Worth visiting for contrasts in style are the two cathedrals, one (Anglican) designed in the Gothic style in 1901, will be the largest religious building in the country when it is finished in 1975. The Roman Catholic cathedral is a white concrete, circular structure opened in 1967, with good stained glass by John Piper. The university and the Walker Art Gallery are both worth visiting. Sea and estuary too dangerous for swimming – go to Crosby for sandy beach.

Lytham St Anne's   A6
Lancs. Pop 42,100. EC Wed. A quiet merger brought two genteel resorts together in 1922, and despite the overpowering influence of nearby Blackpool they form a leafy retreat from seaside razmataz. Beaches sandy, backed by dunes, becoming muddy towards the River Ribble. Watch for sand yacht racing in the summer.

Morecambe   A4
Lancs. Pop 41,900. EC Wed. MD Tue.
A bustling, busy holiday town where the shrimps are the best to be found – try them in a screw of newspaper from the stalls on the seafront. There are new attractions every year; the latest are dolphins and expensive illuminations.

The beaches are muddy with some shingle in the northern part, but sandy as you approach Heysham. Swimming is safe here. Don't forget the Miss Great Britain bathing beauty contest held in August.

Morecambe Bay   A4
Lancs. At low tide there are 150 square miles of sand exposed in the bay, and they vanish with amazing rapidity as the sea comes in. Walkers trying to cross the bay should take great care and watch for red flags and listen for sirens that warn of the fast incoming tide. In the 19thC carriages hurtled across the sands to take travellers on the quickest route to the Lakes – sometimes they ended up taking a very long journey indeed. The possibility of a barrage across the bay is under discussion.

Southport   A7
Mersey. Pop 86,000. EC Tue, Sat. A genteel, Victorian town with no slums and lots of churches. Now a busy holiday spot because of its enormous sandy beaches, there is no shortage of things to do. The marine lake by the river has dinghy racing. There is golf, archery, trampolines, sailing, and a 'Rosebud' competition to find the sweetest little four-to-six-year-old!

Wallasey/New Brighton   A8
Mersey. Pop 94,500. EC Wed. A brash and busy seaside on the Wirral peninsula that has always attracted day visitors from the surrounding industrial areas. Lots of 'Kiss-me-Quick' and candy floss and all that goes with it. The beach is sandy with patches of mud and shingle; swim only where the beach is patrolled by lifeguards.

Withernsea   K6
York. Pop 6,000. Very small, quiet and simple, Withernsea is a family spot with two miles of clean, sandy beaches. The atmosphere is totally unsophisticated, yet you will get a friendly welcome, and if the sun shines a good day on the beach with the children. There is a miniature village, a lighthouse and a very well equipped caravan park. There really are bonny baby contests here during August.

Isle of Man

Reached by regular ferries from Liverpool, Heysham, Ardrossan, Belfast and Dublin. Flights from London, Liverpool, Manchester, Blackpool to Ronaldsway. One of the curious independent but not independent territories that float on Britain's fringes – under the rule of the Queen but not part of the United Kingdom. It has its own parliament that meets twice a week, a radio station, Manx money, and a special breed of cat with extra long back legs and no tail.

The scenery is a rich mixture with moors and mountains down the middle; streams run off the hills to the sea. The coast is mostly high cliffs except for the northern point where the swampy Curragh tails off into a flat sandy area. Unless you love motorbikes avoid the island during the roaring TT races.

Castletown *Pop 2,400. EC Thur.* The ancient capital of the island, dominated by Castle Rushen and thought to be site of a

Viking fort. The castle displays all the arms of the Lords of Man in the main halls, and a clock with only one hand given by Queen Elizabeth I. Good harbour and large sandy beaches on the bay towards **Langness Peninsula**.

Cregneish A tiny hamlet of white washed and thatched cottages; several of them form the Manx Folk Museum. You can see a spinning wheel maker's workshop, a smithy, and a weaver's shed.

Derbyhaven. Site of the first Derby horse race as long ago as 1627. Now a place to visit for the beach of fine sand; some rocks and lots of seaweed.

Douglas *Pop 19,300* Capital of the island; the long promenade curves along the edge of Douglas Bay where the beaches are wide and sandy. Horse trams, steam trains and the quaint Manx Electric Railway are only some of the unusual forms of transport that survive here.

A lively resort with good beaches and plenty of entertainment. The great indoor leisure centre, Summerland, was destroyed by fire in 1973 when 50 people died tragically.

Garwick Bay. A magical spot; leave the car at Baldrine and wander down the narrow path through the trees to this rocky cove. A lovely mixture of trees, sea, beach and foxgloves.

Glenmaye. A thickly wooded glen on the west side of the island; the stream rushes through woods to the sea. A small sandy beach amongst the rocks.

Jurby. On the island's rather weird northern plains – the cliffs here overlook miles of sand and shingle. Towards the Point of Ayre the cliffs turn into sand dunes. Don't miss the dazzling whitewashed church.

Laxey. A busy visitors' spot with a tiny harbour. Here the Snaefell Mountain Railway line starts, and you can see the giant water wheel, now over 100 years old. Sailing, sand and shingle beaches.

Peel. *Pop 2,700 EC Thur. MD Wed.*
A fishing port that is rightly famous for its juicy kippers. Harbour and beach are overtopped by castle and cathedral. Lots of sandy beaches. In summer the Vikings return to an annual festival.

Port Erin. *Pop 1,300 EC Thur.* At the end of the steam railway from Douglas. This resort is renowned for its fine bay with sandy beaches. Boat trips to the bird sanctuary on the Calf of Man; ideal conditions for underwater swimming.

Port St Mary. *Pop 1,400. EC Thur.* The rather gaunt row of Victorian guest houses belies the cheeriness of this sailing resort. The beaches are sheltered and sandy and there is a spectacular footpath to the Chasms, a series of romantic ravines. Sailing, swimming and golf.

Ramsey. *Pop 3,900. EC Thur. MD Mon.* Lies sheltered at the foot of the North Barrule mountain; the town clings around the harbour. Beaches either side of the harbour are sand and shingle. The mild climate encourages palm trees to flourish.

Inland towns

Appletreewick   **D5**
York. Pop 200. Lives up to its delightful name. Full of gabled 16thC cottages that were once proud houses called High Hall, Low Hall, etc. Thoughtful 16thC builders provided pigeon holes over the windows. The tiny church was originally two cottages.

Beverley   **J6**
Humber. Pop 17,100. EC Thur. MD Tue. An elegant market town that has kept a 15thC gateway and several fine Georgian houses. But you really come here for the minster which is one of the finest Gothic churches in Europe. It contains work from all periods – from the 14thC altar screen to Hawksmoor's great west door surrounded by the evangelists. Another church, St Mary's built around 1520 is overshadowed by the minster but should be seen.

Blackburn   **B6**
Lancs. Pop 101,700. EC Thur. MD Wed, Fri, Sat. A hilly mill town – the kind of place where you can see or sense the surrounding country from the centre of the town. Full of impressive mills, plain chapels and even a little cathedral converted from the parish church. The art gallery holds unexpected pleasures; apart from good English water-colours there are more than a thousand rare Japanese prints. Look out for the excellent and informative Textile Museum.

Bolton   **C7**
Gt Manchester. Pop 154,000. EC Wed. MD Tue, Thur, Sat. The distant moors and outlying stone cottages serve to redeem the otherwise industrial features of this Lancastrian city, the third largest town in the county. Close historical connections with the textile trade. Arkwright worked as a barber here and Samuel Crompton, the inventor of the spinning mule, spent his childhood at Hall-i'-th'-Wood, an attractive early Tudor half-timbered house on Tonge Moor, restored by Lord Leverhulme at the beginning of this century.

Bradford   **E6**
W. York. Pop 293,800. EC Wed. MD Mon-Sat. Solid Victorian prosperity created this town. It was developed by local builders and architects in a fairly undisciplined mixture of styles. There is a vigorous Gothic town hall, a Grecian courthouse, a Venetian Exchange with the interior a forest of polished pink granite columns.
Look for St Clement's in Barkerend Road, a 19thC church with a rare chancel roof by William Morris. Try and find the miniature Albert Memorial in Lister Park, and the monument to material wealth, Waterhouse's gabled red brick Prudential Assurance block. The city is a treasure trove of Victoriana – go soon before it's too late.

Chester   **A9**
Cheshire. Pop 62,700. EC Wed. MD Tue, Thur. An important centre on the River Dee for more than 2,000 years; there are lots of remains of Roman Chester to be seen in the Grosvenor Museum. The partly Roman and mediaeval walls still encircle the area of the fortified mediaeval town. The Rows is a unique and famous feature of the city – a two tier system of shopping built in the striking black-and-white timbering that belongs to this region. The Bridge Street Rows have been effectively extended by a well designed modern two-level system. Visit also the 12thC church of St Mary-on-the-Hill, the excellent zoo, and the riverside promenade – the Groves.

Chester

Great Ayton   **J8**
N. York. Pop 4,700. On the tiny River Leven was once the home of James Cook, the discoverer of Australia. A monument to him stands on the moor above the village. His cottage was taken down stone by stone and rebuilt in Australia.

Halifax   **D6**
W. York. Pop 88,600. EC Thur. MD Sat. A much under-rated town in a spectacular position on the River Calder. Hills rise on all sides, most of them so steep that moorland often looks into the windows of the houses. Roads, bridges and deep cuttings are mixed up with mills and tiny houses. Look at Barry's town hall; the 1775 Piece Hall – a large open cloth market; and the old farms and manirs that were incorporated into the city when it expanded so feverishly in the 19thC. See the folk museum at Shibden Hall.

Wainhouse's Tower, Halifax

Harrogate   **F5**
N. York. Pop 64,600 EC Wed, Sat. Sulphur and iron springs made this town into a successful spa. It still has the air of a restful recuperative sort of place. Full of fine gardens, particularly the Valley Gardens and the Harlow Car Gardens. The English passion for municipal gardening reaches its apogee in Harrogate. The happily haphazard scattering of spa and bath buildings among the buxom blooms is enough to effect a cure before you've tasted the waters.

Haworth   **D6**
W. York. A village full of gruff character. The steep main street is still cobbled and it's not impossible to imagine the Brontes' arrival up the hill at the Parsonage. The house is now run by The Bronte Society and the rooms where Charlotte and Emily wrote are arranged as they were then.
The village is surrounded by the Pennine Moors of 'Wuthering Heights' and some stiff climbs are possible to the houses and farms mentioned in the Bronte novels. A visit to the plain Georgian Parsonage set in the sombre beauty of the Pennines is a memorable experience.

Helmsley   **J9**
N. York. Pop 1,300. EC Wed. MD Thur. A good centre for outdoor pursuits; from here you can catch trout, ride horses or ponies, or just walk through the splendid scenery of the Hambleton Hills.

Huddersfield   **E7**
W. York. Pop 131,000. EC Wed. MD Mon. Growing fast from its original river valley position has meant that the town now

the castle castletown

clambers all over the hills, and it is an impressive sight among the smoky mills. Now worth seeing not just for its industrial grandeur but also for the large crop of 19thC churches (one, St John, by William Butterfield) and flat non-conformist chapels.

Knaresborough F5
N. York. Pop 11,900. EC Thur. MD Wed. Apart from possessing a most picturesque river gorge, the atmosphere of this town is designed to delight visitors. The terraces, rocky crags, caves and the celebrated Dropping Well are all fascinating to see. In the caves are suspended a varied selection of encrusted objects 'petrified' by the calcium-based water. Close by is Mother Shipton's Cave, the reputed birthplace of that famed priestess whose prophecies have now become history.

Knutsford C9
Cheshire. Pop 14,800. EC Wed. MD Fri, Sat. The olde-worlde charm of 19thC Knutsford inspired Mrs Gaskell to immortalise this town as 'Cranford'. Her tomb can be seen behind the Unitarian Chapel. The Royal George with its minstrel gallery is one of several buildings mentioned by her that still stand today. Nearby the 2,000 acres surrounding Tatton Park, the former seat of the Egerton family, is surely elegant economy run wild.

Lancaster A5
Lancs. Pop 50,600. EC Wed. A town you remember for its castle, its associations with John of Gaunt and the 18thC warehouse and Georgian merchant houses. It has a good silhouette of castle towers and the church of St Mary seen across the River Lune. Once a flourishing port that lost trade as the silt moved up the river; in 1787 Glasson Dock took over most of the trade. Now Lancaster has all the attractions of a comfortable, busy county town and the new university has helped to add some life but no architectural distinction.

Ashton Memorial, Lancaster

Leeds F6
W. York. Pop 500,200. EC Wed. MD Tue, Sat. Very big, fat and prosperous, Leeds was the national meeting point for the roads, railways and canals of the Industrial Revolution. Its massive columned Town Hall – with the eight-foot-high clock tower – is the high point of the city's centre Victorian splendour – a splendour based on coal, heavy industry and Yorkshire 'grit'. Today there is a traffic-free centre for easy shopping, an art gallery full of European masters, nearby at Temple Newsam a comprehensive collection of superb English painters, and in the City Museum a detailed working model of a coal mine. For cricket enthusiasts a visit to Headingley is essential, and theatregoers should try the new Leeds Playhouse.

Macclesfield D9
Cheshire. Pop 44,200. EC Wed. MD Tue, Fri, Sat. This mediaeval town, once famous as the centre of the silk industry, is now chiefly concerned with the modern textile industry, although several early mill buildings survive today. Two notable churches – the 13thC St Michael's and 18thC Christchurch. Look out for the remains of three mediaeval crosses in the pleasant West Park. Enjoy the charm of ancient Gawsworth Hall, once the home of Mary Fitton, thought to be the Dark Lady of Shakespeare's sonnets.

Malham, N. York.

Malham C4
N. York. Pop 100. A tiny village at the head of the River Aire, it is an agricultural community (mostly cattle and sheep) and dates back to before the 7th and 8thC. The village was once held by the two monasteries Fountains Abbey and Bolton Priory. The Pennine Way passes through here and there is a good Youth Hostel. Charles Kingsley is reputed to have planned his book 'The Water Babies' while on a visit to Malham Tarn House, and the fantastic Gordale Scar to the east of the village inspired the poet William Blake. The limestone above Malham Cove has been wrought by rain into sculptured shapes like Henry Moore's work.

Malpas A10
Cheshire. Pop 1,300. A small peaceful town set against a back-cloth of the Welsh mountains and the Wrekin. The parish Perpendicular church of St Oswald contains the Brereton family chapel amidst elaborate woodwork and good plasterwork.

Manchester C8
Gt. Manchester. Pop 530,500. EC Wed. MD Mon, Wed. Centre of the cotton industry and from the middle ages an important weaving centre. The arrival of the canals in the late 18thC brought raw cotton right into the city and spinning, weaving and the Industrial Revolution had arrived. Manchester grew and grew, helped by cheap labour and the ingenuity of inventors who improved the spinning and weaving processes. Its prosperity is reflected in its great Victorian buildings both commercial and public – particularly the Gothic revival Town Hall by Alfred Waterhouse. The city has a great public library, several good museums and galleries and a large university. Much of the central area, Piccadilly, has been rebuilt since the 1950s, but without distinction. Acres of slum housing have been cleared, but too many tower blocks have replaced them. A great city, well worth a visit.

Town Hall, Manchester

Nantwich B10
Cheshire. Pop 11,700. EC Wed. MD Thur, Sat. This attractive, friendly town was for many centuries a salt mining town ('wich' meaning salt town). Situated on the River Weaver, it houses several fine buildings worth seeing including the 14thC church of St Mary with its magnificent octagonal tower and Churche's Mansion, an outstanding example of half-timbered architecture. Good shopping centre.

Nether Alderley C9
Cheshire. Pop 600. This village near Macclesfield was the birthplace of Dean Stanley. The picturesque mediaeval church of St Mary contains striking monuments and the family pew. The machinery at the old water mill, east of the church, has been recently restored by the National Trust.

Pateley Bridge   E4
N. York. Known as the capital of Upper Nidderdale, a Dale region that has a stern, rugged grandeur. The mixture of thickly wooded slopes, rock-strewn glens and gorges make this exhilarating territory to explore on foot.
Once you've visited the fortnightly sheep and cattle fair in this little town take the road into Wharfedale. It climbs one of the longest and steepest hills in the county to the bleak, windy village of Greenho, the highest village in England.

York.

Pontefract   F7
N. York. Pop 31,300. There's not much left of the castle here but it has witnessed some stirring events: not just the Civil War sieges in the 1640s, but the tragic death of King Richard II. Now the castle guards the museum where the money manufactured during the Royalist occupation is on view. The peculiar art of licorice growing is still practiced in Pontefract; it dates back to the 13thC. Flat lozenges of juicy licorice, Pontefract cakes, are still made here. A most unusual hermitage (monk's or hermit's cell) can be seen in Southgate; it dates back to 1368 and had the rare convenience of an underground stream.

Prestbury Village   D9
Cheshire. Pop 2,200. One of Cheshire's oldest and prettiest villages, Prestbury on the River Bollin is now a popular spot for tourists. The Priest's House and the gay murals in the 18thC church of St Peter and separate 12thC chapel are particularly worth visiting.

Preston   B6
Lancs. Pop 94,800. EC Thur. MD Mon, Wed, Fri, Sat. This is cotton mills country. Arkwright was born here in 1732 and the first cotton mill started in 1777. A fast growing population meant that Preston didn't expand in a leisurely, beautiful way but it has benefited from the enlightened patronage of rich mill owners.
The Harris Library and Museum in Market Place is a spectacular Victorian classical pile full of good intentions. A good walk is a wander round the Fishergate area; plain, pleasing streets of brick houses with rich doorways. Visit Lancastrian Brigade Museum for good regimental relics.

Ripon   F4
N. York. Pop 12,600. EC Wed. MD Thur. The earliest records of this town date back to 888 when Alfred the Great granted its charter. Make a point of being in the ancient square around 21.00 when a strangely-clad figure executes the time-honoured tradition of hornblowing. It originated as a curfew in mediaeval times and has been performed ever since.

Runcorn   B8
Cheshire. Pop 42,700. EC Wed. MD Tue, Thur, Sat. One of the more recent new towns built around the older small settlement. Tightly planned around an express bus transport system, it is worth a visit to see how well a new community can function. There are some very pleasing housing areas and the enormous indoor town centre is an extremely pleasant place to shop in or stroll around.

Sheffield   F8
S. York. Pop 511,800. EC Thur. MD Mon, Tues, Wed, Fri. The centre of this prosperous town is largely new, no longer grimy, and now famous for its clean air. Still the centre of steel manufacture and justly renowned for good cutlery and plate.
Look out for the vast new terraces of Park Hill to the east of the centre, a giant vision of the future – already built! The university has masses of new buildings and you can shop in traffic-free centres. Of great interest is the new Crucible Theatre with its thrust stage and experimental productions.

York   G5
N. York. Pop 104,500. EC Wed. MD Thur, Sat. The city is where the North, East and West Ridings meet and it is the pride of Yorkshire. York still looks almost totally mediaeval, encircled by giant grey stone walls and dominated by the majestic Minster which was consecrated in 1472. Inside those soaring walls is some of the most amazing mediaeval coloured glass in the world. The whole structure of the Minster has recently been restored and cleaned.
A wander on the walls is an essential start to a visit to York, and then into the Shambles, a cluster of narrow streets full of houses that lean across the road to greet one another – these are the kind of streets where you can shake hands with the neighbour opposite. Visit the Castle Museum; the elegant Treasurer's House, and the Railway Museum with an amazing collection of old locomotives.

Regional oddities

Black-and-White Houses
Cheshire. Timber beams and whitewash are typical of the Cheshire region – these houses are the originals of all the by-pass Tudor that has spread all over the world. Among the finest are Moreton Old Hall, Woodford Old Hall, Adlington Hall and endless cottages in East Cheshire.

Brass Bands
The textile workers and colliery hands still let off steam in the traditional way, Famous works' bands compete regularly and reach dizzy heights of brassy musical splendour.

Choral singing
If you have never heard the 'Messiah' by Handel sung by the Huddersfield Choral Society, you haven't experienced true choral singing. No one else can make the hallelujahs ring out in the same way; Handel would love it.

Dialect
In Yorkshire and Lancashire dialects remain closer to their Anglo-Saxon roots than many other areas. It's a refreshing and important regional difference that must be maintained. It's not all 'Coronation Street' in this part of the world, but the dialects are symptoms of a strong community life.

Pot holes
There are hundreds of holes and caves under the Pennines and exploration can be a dangerous game. Gaping Gill is the largest and is rumoured to be big enough to take the whole of York Minster.

Famous people

Sir Richard Arkwright (1732-92)   C7
Bolton, Gt Manchester. The water-frame dubbed the 'Devil's bagpipes' by suspicious neighbours, was invented by Arkwright, who began his career as a successful barber and went on to revolutionise textile manufacture. The machine is on view at the local Textile Machinery Museum.

The Brontes   D6
Bronte Parsonage Museum Haworth W. York. Rev. Patrick Bronte brought his family to the parsonage in 1820. It was here that Charlotte, Emily and Anne wrote their novels and Branwell immortalised the neighbouring Black Bull Hotel.
The surrounding bleak moorlands of West Riding are alive with Bronte associations: a four-mile hike will take you to the site of 'Wuthering Heights' on Far Withens. Wycoller Hall, now a ruin, was probably the model for Ferndean Manor in 'Jane Eyre'. This stark Georgian parsonage now a museum, has a fine collection of Bronte manuscripts and relics. *Open 11.00–18.00 Apr-Dec; 11.00-17.00 Jan-Mar. Closed Sun morning.*

Samuel Crompton (1753-1827) **C7**
Bolton Hall-i'-th'-Wood, Gt Manchester. 300 yards n of Crompton Way By-pass. This half timbered manor house is where Crompton lived and invented the spinning-mule which combined the principles of Arkwright's water-frame and Hargreaves' jenny. The house is now a museum with 16thC furnishings and Crompton relics. *Open daily. Closed Thur & Sun morning.*

James Hargreaves (d. 1778) **B6**
Blackburn, Lancs. The inventor of the spinning-jenny was a Blackburn carpenter and weaver. His house and machinery were destroyed by a reactionary mob of spinners, so Hargreaves moved to Nottingham. Visit the local Lewis Textile Museum and see the jenny in action.

William Wilberforce (1759-1833) **J6**
Wilberforce House, 25 High St, Hull, Humber. Slave emancipator Wilberforce was born here, in this lovely Elizabethan mansion. The house is now a historical museum with Wilberforce relics and a collection relating to the abolition of the slave-trade. *Open daily (14.30–16.30 Sun).*

Cathedrals, abbeys and churches

All Hallows **A8**
Allerton, nr Liverpool, Mersey. A late Victorian sandstone church with a range of Burne-Jones windows that must be seen. The glass is vividly coloured tracery designs made by William Morris.

All Saints **H6**
Holme-upon-Spalding Moor, Humber. The battlemented 15thC tower on a hill in the Wolds acts as a landmark for miles around. The outside of the church is a mixture of all types of stones, indicating the complexity of the region's geology. The interior is delightfully unspoilt: a mixture of all the centuries from the 15th to the present.

Beverley Minster **J6**
Beverley, Humber. A magnificent Saxon church of cathedral size with Gothic restorations dating from the 13thC to 15thC.

Bradford Cathedral **E6**
Bradford, W. York. A large parish church dating chiefly from the 15thC is now the cathedral. Dedicated to St Peter, it was heavily restored in 1899.

Chester Cathedral **A9**
Chester, Cheshire. Originally a monastic foundation founded by an Earl of Chester in 1093, it became a cathedral during the reign of Henry VIII. It is a red sandstone building tucked into a corner of the city and still retains a fascinating range of monastic buildings. The cloister, chapter house, the infirmary, refectory and parlour are massive, albeit restored.
Inside the cathedral the choir is the highspot. Largely built in 1300 it contains remarkably carved stalls made around 1380. Each stall has a fine misericord illustrating fables and incidents from mediaeval bestiaries.

Liverpool Cathedral (Anglican) **A8**
Liverpool, Mersey. This massive building stands on a marvellous site that dominates the river and the city. The architect was chosen by competition and Giles Gilbert Scott was only 21 when his design was selected. The cathedral was started in 1904 and work is still going on, red sandstone being used in a completely traditional way. 1975 is supposed to be the finishing year, when the 600-foot-long nave will be complete. Liverpool must be the last of the

great Gothic revival cathedrals. It is impressive and right for the city.

Liverpool Cathedral by Gilbert Scott

Liverpool Cathedral (Roman) **A8**
Liverpool, Mersey. Dedicated to Christ the King, the circular building towers up to a spiky crown and at night the top part of the tower glows with brilliantly lit coloured glass. Again the building was the result of a competition held in 1959 when the original giant designs of Lutyens had to be abandoned. The plan is for a central altar lit by the dramatic lantern of John Piper's stained glass. Full of modern art the cathedral is in great contrast to the Anglican one – clearly you have to visit them both.

Cathedral of Christ the King, Liverpool (1962)

Manchester Cathedral **C8**
Manchester, Gt Manchester. The 15thC collegiate church of St Mary became a cathedral in 1848. It's a good perpendicular building with modern additions. Lovely ornate porch. The choir stalls are amongst the finest in the country: early 16thC with exquisitely carved canopies and crests, and charming carved animals and flowers.

Ripon Cathedral **F4**
Ripon, N. York. One of the oldest Christian buildings in Britain—the crypt is said to have been built in 670 for St Wilfrid. It is topped by a splendid Gothic nave of 1502 and an early English west front. The central tower was once crowned by a spire.

St Anne **A6**
Woodplumpton, Lancs. The long, low, warm coloured stone building is topped by a fish weather-vane. Three low aisles lead to the screen across the amazing width of the church.

St Helen **A8**
Sefton, nr Liverpool, Mersey. A late Perpendicular church that is worth seeing for the excellent woodcarving and monuments. The tombs of the Molyneux family are a great mediaeval series; look for the effigy in chain mail that has been there since 1296. Good brasses.

St Mary the Virgin **E4**
Studley Royal, N. York. A mid-Victorian dream church, standing in a lovely deer park – it was designed by W. Burges 1871-78. Full of rich colour, mosaic floors and stained glass. In a dome over the altar choirs of Angels sing a Te Deum. Well worth a visit.

St Michael **A9**
Shotwick, Cheshire. A strong tower dominates this very peaceful hamlet. Inside the church has twin naves and a rare three-decker pulpit. Two lovely 14thC glass windows.

St Oswald **C9**
Lower Peover, Cheshire. Go down a cobbled lane and you come to the inn, church and schoolroom. Behind the massive stone tower is a good example of a timber church. Inside all is dark oak, box pews and whitewash. Superb.

St Patrick   K7
Patrington, Humber. A 14thC church that is
often known as 'The Queen of Holderness'
because of the cruciform nature of the plan
dominated by a central spire. The church is
a consistent example of the Decorated style.

St Peter's   J7
Barton-upon-Humber, Humber. A fine 10thC
church with a Saxon tower and text book
nave to the west of it. Interesting 14thC
glass in the east window.

St Peter's   C10
Congleton, Cheshire. A 1742 town church;
inside the plain walls is a handsome
galleried interior complete with box pews.
Good 18thC glass and candelabra.

Sheffield Cathedral   F8
Sheffield, S. York. Formerly the parish
church of SS Peter and Paul, the present
building represents a virtual reconstruction
of the Perpendicular church. Much of the
work is modern and not particularly
distinguished. Some good Tudor monuments
in the Shrewsbury Chapel.

Wakefield Cathedral   F7
Wakefield, W. York. All Saints parish church
became the cathedral early this century. It is
large and plain and dates largely from the
14thC. The east end is modern and the
church is especially worth seeing for the
fine range of Jacobean fittings.

York Minster   G5
N. York. The cathedral church of St Peter is
one of the largest English cathedrals. The
present building is hard to grasp as one large
building because it is so surrounded by tiny
houses. In the north transept adjoining the
Chapter House are the famous 'Five Sisters',
five tall lancet windows of mediaeval stained
glass. Over the crossing is the largest central
tower in England, massive and simple.
In contrast the west front with its two
pinnacled towers is richly decorative. Inside
the Minster, the highest and broadest nave
in England is in fact somewhat dull. The
great glory of York is the glass. The steady
development of English glass painting can be
traced here through three centuries. The
earliest 13thC are the pale grisaille' of the
'Five Sisters' and the slightly later glass in
the Chapter House is similar.
In the aisles and nave are 14thC windows,
but the triumph is the amazing coloured sea
of glass that fills the east end. It was

York Minster, York.

completed by John Thornton of Coventry in
1405 and is one of Europe's finest windows,
with 117 yard-square panels telling the
Biblical story from the creation to the
Apocalypse.

Castles and ruins

Bowes Castle   D2
Nr Brough, Durham. A great three-storey-
high keep set up by Henry II to guard the
pass through the Pennines. It stands within
the limits of a former Roman fort. *Open
9.30–17.30 Mar, Apr & Oct, 9.30–19.00
May–Sep, 9.30–16.00 Nov–Feb. Closed Sun
morning.*

Fountains Abbey   E4
N. York. 4 miles sw of Ripon. A moving and
beautiful sight. The ruins of Fountains
Monastery show that this was one of the
mightiest monastic institutions in Europe.
Founded in 1132 by the Cistercians, many of
the outstanding features remain including
the long range of western buildings
impressively vaulted in 22 double bays.
During the 18thC the ruins were landscaped
with pools, waterfalls and lakes. *Open
9.30–16.00 daily Nov–Feb (Closed Sun
morning). 9.30–17.30 daily Mar, Apr & Oct.
9.30–19.00 daily May & Sep. 9.30–21.00
daily Jun–Aug.*

Fountains Abbey, York.

Jervaulx Abbey   E3
N. York, 4 miles nw of Masham. In 1156 the
Cistercians founded the abbey on what was
then a well wooded site. The church was of
vast length supported by 40 buttresses; now
little of any height remains.
There is nothing here as dramatic as
Rievaulx, but there are remains of many
fascinating monastic buildings, particularly
the high, long dormitory wall. The ruins are
privately owned and they haven't been
aggressively tidied up – instead they
emerge from a luxuriance of wild flowers.
Open daily.

Lancaster Castle   A5
Lancaster, Lancs. Dates from 1102 when the
Norman motte-and-bailey replaced the Saxon
fortifications on the hill overlooking the
River Lune. King John added a surrounding
wall with round towers and a great gateway.
John of Gaunt (son of Edward III) added
towers and feasting rooms and donated many
damp dungeons. Now used as a law court
there is little chance of prisoners leaping over
the 78-foot-high walls. *Open 10.30–18.30
daily May–Sep.*

Lancaster Castle. Lancs.

Spofforth Castle   F5
Spofforth, nr Wetherby, W. York. The castle
has belonged to one family, the Percys, for
600 years; rumoured to be the birthplace of
Harry Hotspur. Now a great shattered ruin,
it was badly knocked about in the Civil War.
*Open 9.30–17.30 Mar, Apr & Oct, 9.30–
19.00 May–Sep, 9.30–16.00 Nov–Feb.
Closed Sun morning.*

Unusual buildings

Abbeydale Industrial Hamlet   F9
*Abbeydale, S. York. Off A621 from Sheffield
to Bakewell.* This is a curiosity. A 200-year-

old steel and scythe works where the manufacture of a steel-edge tool can be traced from the raw material to the finished product. There is also an exhibition of industry in the Sheffield area.

The Ashton Memorial **A5**
Lancaster, Lancs. England's own Taj Mahal, built in 1907 to commemorate the life of a local merchant peer. A vast Portland stone edifice that is crowned by a high dome, you have to climb an elaborate staircase to reach it from Williamson Park.

Jodrell Bank Telescope **C9**
Jodrell Bank, Cheshire. One of the largest radio telescopes in the world. A great dish 250 feet in diameter supported by five lesser elliptic paraboloids – it tracked the first sputnik. They look like massive abstract sculptures and seem to be the tools of a race of men yet to be born. *Open 14.00-18.00 mid Apr-Oct. 14.00-17.00 weekends Nov–May.*

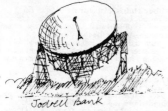
Jodrell Bank

Ilten Stonehenge **E4**
Nr Masham, N. York. William D. Sanby wanted to express his mystical leanings when he set about building a copy of Stonehenge on the moors. It is a very spooky spot and should be visited in the dark when the luminous lichens glow.

Ilten Stonehenge, Masham

Port Sunlight **A8**
Cheshire. Built in the early 20thC as a model town for the employees of Lever Brothers, soap manufacturers. Almost every known style of European architecture has been plundered to inspire the domestic and public buildings; the result is a fascinating *fin-de-siecle* village that is unique. The amazing variety of houses sits in a green setting – a curious mixture of sylvan vista and practical allotments. The whole place is dominated by the ever present soap works and the air of benevolent capitalism.

Quarry Bank Mill **C8**
Styal, nr Wilmslow, Cheshire. A well preserved cotton mill, designed in the simple Georgian Vernacular tradition in 1784. The mill is surrounded by a complete village of small cottages, all situated in lovely woodland.

Railway Viaduct **C8**
Stockport, Cheshire. A solid brick viaduct built about 1850. The railway threads its way between riverside warehouses and crosses the river on giant piers. The setting of the great structure is typical of the industrial revolution that created this cotton town in the 19thC.

Sisters Folly **A7**
Ormskirk, Lancs. In the 14thC two rich sisters agreed to build a church for the town, but they couldn't agree about giving it a spire or a tower. So they compromised and now the church has both. This must be the country's first folly.

Houses and gardens

Bramham Park **F6**
Boston Spa, W. York. 6 miles s of Wetherby. A friendly, lived-in stately home built for Lord Bingley in 1698 and still occupied by his descendants. Good pictures by Reynolds and Kneller. The park is delightfully laid out with great beech hedges, and vistas leading to temples or obelisks. *Open 14.00–18.00 Sun & B Hol Mon mid Apr-late Sep.*

Burton Agnes Hall **J5**
Burton Agnes, nr Bridlington, Humber. A comfortable, unspoilt Elizabethan (1598-1610) country house full of carved and panelled rooms. Inside a collection of paintings includes some unexpected French impressionists. *Open 13.45-17.00 daily May-mid Oct. Closed Sat.*

Burton Agnes House

Burton Constable Hall **K6**
Nr Hull, Humber. ½ mile n of Sproatley. Elizabethan red brick with stone trimmings. The house has very fine 18thC interiors. Good contents including rare mediaeval vestments in the chapel and don't miss the room decorated with murals of the Alice in Wonderland story. Lots of standard stately home attractions – vintage cars, zoo, aviaries and traction engine rallies. *Open 13.00–18.00 Sat & Sun mid Apr-Sep & Tue-Thur & B Hol Mon late May-Sep.*

Castle Howard **J10**
N. York. 6 miles w of Malton. A quite stupendous house, it is the most stately of them all. Designed by the wilful architectural genius Sir John Vanbrugh in 1700, the great facade is dominated by a superb dome. Beneath this is the great hall, one of the grandest rooms in England. Don't miss the grounds with the sublime temples and the circular mausoleum by Hawksmoor. *Open 13.00-17.00 daily mid Apr-Oct (11.30-17.30 B Hol Mon).*

Castle Howard

Harewood House **F5**
Leeds, W. York. At Harewood village 5 miles from A1 at Wetherby. One of the finest of Yorkshire's great houses and the home of Lord Harewood, it was designed by James Carr and Robert Adam. The interior is a series of exquisitely decorated rooms by Adam with fine plasterwork and painted ceilings. Much of the furniture and carved window swages are by Chippendale. There is a large collection of Sevres china and a solid line of family portraits. The park is mostly Capability Brown's work; a recent addition is the Harewood Bird Garden (q.v.). *Open 11.00–18.00 daily Apr-mid Oct.*

Harewood House, York.

Little Moreton Hall C10
Congleton, Cheshire. One of the finest examples of 16thC black-and-white half-timbered houses in the country, looking so much like a film set that you can't help but wonder if it's a fake. But it is the real thing. The timber frame is the structure and it has been carved at the gable ends. It is built around a courtyard. *Open 14.00–18.00 daily Mar-Oct. Closed Tue.*

Little Moreton Hall

Newby Hall F4
N. York. 4 miles se of Ripon. An elegant 18thC mansion with a good interior decorated by Robert Adam. The gardens lead down to a beautiful river and you can wander about freely among the old-fashioned roses or the enchanting sunken parterre garden of misty blues and greys. Don't miss the Gobelins tapestries or the miniature steam railway. *Open 14.00–18.00 Wed, Thur, Sat, Sun & B Hol Mon & Tue mid Apr-mid Oct.*

Newby Hall, Yorkshire

Rudding Park F5
N. York. 3 miles se of Harrogate. A lovely Regency house perfectly complimented by the simplicity of Repton's design for the park. Wide lawns with mature old trees lead to woodland glades and dappled walks which were skilfully incorporated into the overall plan at a later date. *Open 10.00-dusk daily late May-Sep.*

Speke Hall A8
Nr Liverpool, Mersey. A long, low, gabled, black-and-white timbered house which dates from Tudor days. The rooms are beautifully panelled and carved and full of attractive furniture. It is a refreshing place to visit, only seven miles from busy Liverpool. *Open 10.00–19.00 daily. Closed Sun morning.*

Studley Royal E4
N. York. 4 miles sw of Ripon. A supremely elegant garden of sweeping lawns, grand vistas and huge expanses of water. Throughout are well-placed classical ornamental buildings. The romantic ruins of the great Cistercian monastery add to the haunting, mysterious quality of this park. *Open 9.30-dusk daily. (Closed Sun morning Nov-Feb.)*

Tatton Park C9
Cheshire. 3½ miles n of Knutsford on Ashley Rd. 2,000 acres of park planned by Humphrey Repton of which the gardens cover 60, with a surprising variety of styles and periods dwelling together in apparent harmony. The fernery of 1856, with its jungly atmosphere and giant New Zealand tree ferns, is in contrast to the very English serenity of the mile-long lake, its calm ruffled only by the many waterfowl.
Perhaps the most delightful part is the Japanese garden, complete with Shinto temple upon a tiny island, and approached by an attractive bridge. There are authentic Japanese plants, stone lanterns and rock work. *Open 14.00–18.00 daily mid Apr-Oct. Closed Mon.*

Tatton Park, Cheshire

Victoria Park A7
Southport, Mersey. Although not strictly a garden, it is noteworthy for the outstanding collection of hardy perennials which flourish in a half-mile roadside stretch of herbaceous border on the edge of the park in Rotten Row. At its best in August. *Open daily.*

Museums and galleries

Abbey House Museum E6
Kirkstall, Leeds, W. York. Once the gatehouse of Kirkstall Abbey, and now a folk museum. Among the many exhibits are costumed dolls, musical instruments and three 'streets' of houses, shops and cottages that once stood in the Leeds area. *Open daily. Closed Sun morning.*

The Ashworth Museum C7
Turton Tower, Chapletown Rd, Turton, Lancs. A fine collection of weapons including blunderbuss, rapiers and flintlocks. Also brasses and the Timberbottom skulls. *Open 14.00-sunset Wed & Sat. Also 10.00-sunset Sun Apr-Oct.*

Bankfield Museum and Art Gallery D6
Akroyd Park, Halifax, W. York. A comprehensive collection of costume, fabric and textile machinery. The peasant work from the Balkans and Burma is a speciality. The Duke of Wellington's Regimental Museum is also here. *Open 11.00–17.00 Oct-Mar; 11.00–19.00 Apr-Sep. 14.30–17.00 Sun.*

Batley Art Gallery E6
Market Place, Batley, W. York. Contemporary paintings and drawings including the works of Max Ernst, Francis Bacon and Graham Sutherland. *Open 11.00–18.00 Mon, Wed & Thur; 11.00–20.00 Fri; 11.00–17.00 Sat.*

Blackburn Museum and Art Gallery B6
Library St, Blackburn, Lancs. Coins, English water-colours, mediaeval manuscripts and over 1,200 Japanese prints. There are also primitive weapons and African tribal costumes. *Open 9.30–20.00 Mon-Fri. 9.30–18.00 Sat.*

Bradford City Art Gallery and Museum E6
Cartwright Hall, Bradford, W. York. Collections relating to West Riding include natural history, Roman coins and electric tramcars once operating in the streets of Bradford. Also some fine paintings by Vasari, Gainsborough, Reynolds, Corot, Sickert and Sargent. *Open 10.00–17.00 Oct-Mar; 10.00–19.00 Apr & Sep; 10.00-20.00 May-Aug.*

City of Liverpool Museums A8
William Brown St, Liverpool, Mersey. Many fine treasures are gathered here. Greek, Roman and Egyptian antiquities, Anglo-Saxon jewellery, armour, Liverpool pottery, African masks and figures and horsedrawn and steam road vehicles. There is also an aquarium and planetarium. *Open daily. Closed Sun morning.*

Grosvenor Museum A9
Grosvenor St, Chester, Cheshire. Archaeological exhibits come from the Roman legionary fortress of Deva. Many inscriptions and sculptured stones, instruments of torture, mediaeval pottery and Anglo-Saxon coins. *Open daily, closed Sun morning.*

Manx Village Folk Museum A2
Cregneish, IOM. A typical Manx village with thatched houses including a furnished crofter-fisherman's cottage, weaver's shed, smithy and turner's shop. *Open 10.00–17.00 Mon-Sat mid May-end Sep.*

Manx Museum, Douglas, I.O.M.

Town Docks Museum　　　　**J6**
Queen Victoria Sq, Hull, Humber. Shipping
and the fisheries of Hull are represented
here. A good display of 'Whales and
Whaling' shows Hull's importance in the
days when Britain took thousands of whales
from the sea around Greenland. *Open
10.00–17.30. Closed Sun morning. Mid
May-end Sep.*

Nautical Museum　　　　**A2**
Bridge St, Castletown, IOM. Housed in a
200-year-old boat-house, there are models
of deep sea vessels, local fishing boats and a
reconstructed sailmaker's workshop. Star
attraction is the 'Peggy' a schooner-rigged
armed yacht. *Open Mon-Sat mid May-end
Sep.*

Pilkington Glass Museum　　　　**A8**
Prescot Rd, St Helens, Mersey. Glass-making
through the ages is illustrated here. An
exquisite collection including an ancient
Egyptian god-figure. *Open 10.00–17.00
Mon-Fri (10.00–21.00 Wed Mar-Oct);
14.00–16.30 Sat & Sun.*

Royal Pump Room Museum　　　　**F5**
Harrogate, N. York. Opposite Valley
Gardens. Local history, Yorkshire china,
toys, costumes and Victoriana are housed in
the Pump Room. The old sulphur well is
here too. *Open 11.00–19.00 Mon-Sat May-
Sep. Closed Sun morning Oct-Apr.*

Sheffield City Museum　　　　**F8**
Weston Park, Sheffield, S. York. The
world's largest collection of cutlery
appropriately resides here. Some date from
the stone age. Also Old Sheffield Plate. *Open
daily Sep-May (10.00–20.00 Jun-Aug).
Closed Sun morning.*

Temple Newsam　　　　**F6**
Temple Newsam, W. York. A magnificent
treasure house full of English paintings and
silver; the birthplace of Lord Darnley.
During the reign of Elizabeth I it was a
centre of English and Scottish intrigue. Now
owned by Leeds Corporation and well
maintained. *Open 10.30–18.15 daily but
10.30–20.30 Wed May-Sep.*

Tonge Moor Textile　　　　**C7**
Machinery Museum
Tonge Moor Rd, Bolton, Gt Manchester. A
superb collection of textile machinery
including Crompton's mule, Hargreave's
jenny and Arkwright's water frame. *Open
daily 10.00–17.00 Mon, Tue, Thur, Fri &
Sat. Closed Wed & Sun.*

Wakefield City Art Gallery　　　　**F7**
Wentworth Terrace, Wakefield, W. York. A
fine collection of 20thC art including works
by Henry Moore, Barbara Hepworth,
Sickert, Sutherland and Alan Davie. *Open
daily 12.30–17.00. Closed Sun morning.*

West Park Museum　　　　**D9**
and Art Gallery
Prestbury Rd, Macclesfield, Cheshire.
Egyptian antiquities, Victorian paintings and
a stuffed giant panda. *Open daily. Closed Sun
morning.*

Whitworth Art Gallery　　　　**C8**
Oxford Rd, Manchester, Gt Manchester. Fine
collections of water-colours, prints and
textiles. Turner and the Pre-Raphaelites are
well represented. Coptic and Peruvian cloths
Spanish and Italian embroideries. *Open
10.00–17.00 Mon-Wed, Fri & Sat.
10.00–21.00 Thur.*

York Castle Museum　　　　**G5**
Tower St, N. York. One of the most
important folk museums in the country.
Kirkgate, with its cobbled street of original
Victorian shop fronts, lamp-posts, cabs and
stage coach is fantastic, and very popular.
Also the Edwardian Half Moon Court
with a gaslighted pub and a gipsy caravan.
*Open 9.30–18.30 daily Apr-Sep. 9.30–17.00
daily Oct-Mar.*

Botanical gardens

Churchtown Botanic Garden　　　　**A7**
Mersey. n of Southport. Of greatest interest
here is the Victorian fernery with a good
collection grown amidst moss, water and
rock. Outside is a pretty rose garden and a
colourful display of carpet bedding with
summer annuals. *Open 10.00–18.00. Closed
Sun morning.*

Harlow Car　　　　**E5**
*N. York. 1½ miles from Harrogate on Otley
Rd.* The Wisely of the north, being the show
gardens and trials area of the Northern
Horticultural Society. Formed in 1948 to
illustrate the type of gardening and planting
that could be possible in the colder more
difficult northern climate.
Apart from a splendid heather garden, there
are some fine specimen azaleas and
rhododendrons in a woodland setting which
follow the drifts of daffodils and narcissi
which have now naturalised. There are good
herbaceous plants, interesting trial beds and
greenhouses, a water garden and a splendid
rose garden. *Open 9.00–sunset daily.*

Liverpool University　　　　**A9**
Botanic Gardens
Ness, Wirral, Cheshire. The gardens were
started by Arthur Kilpin Bulley at the turn
of the century. The heather garden is said to
be one of the best in Britain. Also rose
gardens with demonstration beds tracing the
development of the rose from the Chinese to
the present hybrids. *Open 9.00–Sunset daily.*

Zoos, aquaria, and aviaries

Belle Vue Leisure Park　　　　**C8**
Belle Vue, Manchester, Gt Manchester.
Beginning as the first successful privately-
owned zoo in Britain, it continues as an
innovator first in Europe to exhibit in the
open-air and without bars, and first to breed
alligators and cobras in captivity.

Chester Zoo　　　　**A9**
Upton-by-Chester, Cheshire. Outsize
describes this excellent zoo: 333 acres of
land, a 30-foot waterfall in the Tropical
House which houses 200 free-flying birds of
85 species. Also apes, crocodiles and
nocturnal animals. Probably second only to
London Zoo in size and variety. To see it all,
take a conducted tour on a canal waterbus.
Look for the rare pigmy hippo, mountain
gorilla, and both black and white rhinos.
Open 9.00–dusk daily.

Cleethorpes Leisure Park　　　　**K7**
Humberston, Humber. Built on 17 acres of
reclaimed marshland, Cleethorpes boasts
one of the largest walk-through aviaries in
Britain; dolphin pool with views above and
underwater; children's farm. Some animals
are moved to Yorkshire in the winter. *Open
9.00–18.30 daily.*

Curraghs Wildlife Park　　　　**A1**
Isle of Man. 1 mile e of Ballaugh Bridge. This
is a bird and botanical sanctuary within a
designated nature reserve and wildlife park.
Many birds to be seen in the walk-through
aviary and wading birds' aviary. Also sea
lions and penguins and a Noah's Ark for the
children. *Open 10.00–18.00 May-Sep,*

Harewood Bird Garden F6
Harewood House, Leeds, W. York. This new
bird garden (1970) offers flamingos
wandering by the lake, penguins seen
underwater through a glass-sided pool, and a
tropical house with birds at liberty. Included
are snowy owls, lorikeets, weavers,
ornamental pheasants. An added attraction is
Harewood House, designed by Adam with a
park laid out by Capability Brown. *Open
11.00–18.00 May-Sep. 11.00–17.00 Oct-Apr*

**Marineland Oceanarium and
Aquarium** A4
Morecambe, Lancs. Guaranteed-professional
performances from the sea lions, dolphins,
seals, penguins and chimpanzees who dive,
toot and drink tea to order. In the aquarium
see the origin of your turtle soup (green
turtle), your tortoiseshell comb (hawksbill
turtle) and the fish for your chips (marine
life from Morecambe Bay). *Open 10.00–19.30
May-Oct. 10.00-16.30 Nov-Apr.*

Port Erin Aquarium A2
Port Erin, IOM. Local fishes and
invertebrates at the Marine Biological
Station (a teaching and research department
of the University of Liverpool). *Open daily
(Closed Sun morning) May-Sep.*

'Winged World' A4
*Morecambe & Heysham, Lancs. Nr Heysham
Head Entertainment Centre.* The tropics
transplanted in Britain. See scarlet ibis,
spoonbills, toucans, fruit pigeons, many
flying free in this conservatory-aviary
landscaped with banana palms. In the
children's zoo prosaic lambs rub shoulders
with white-eared marmosets bred in
'Winged World'. Don't miss the flying fruit
bats flying. *Open 10.00-dusk daily.*

Nature trails & reserves

Eaves Wood Nature Trail A4
Silverdale, Lancs. N of Lancaster. Start
from Woodland Hotel or Waterslack. 1½
miles. Natural and managed woodland, with
interesting flora on limestone pavement.
Guide from National Trust, 27 Springbank,
Silverdale; Waterslack Farm; local post
office; National Trust and National Park
Information Centres.

Hornsea Mere Nature Reserve K5
Hornsea Mere, Humber. Large numbers and
varieties of winter wildfowl; excellent for
assorted migrants. Limited access via public
footpath on the south side; otherwise by
permit from RSPB Warden, The Bungalow,
Kirkholme Point, Hornsea, York.

Leighton Moss Nature Reserve A4
*Leighton Moss, Lancs. Nr Silverdale, reached
via Yealands from A6 n of Carnforth.* A large
reedbed with open water. Details from
RSPB, The Lodge, Sandy, Beds.

Malham Tarn Nature Reserve C4
*Malham Tarn, N. York. N of Aire-Ribble gap
nr A65.* The Field Centre is an excellent
base for exploring surrounding moorland/fell
country. For further details: The Field
Studies Council, 9 Devereux Court, Strand,
London. Accommodation available.

Spurn Nature Reserve West K7
*Spurn, Humber. E from Hull on A1033, right
in Partington on B1445 to Easington, thence
on minor roads to Kilnsea and Spurn.* Well
known for a wide selection of migrants in
spring and autumn, but also good for winter
wildfowl and waders. Public footpath, but
main area by permit only. Details from the
Warden, Spurn Bird Observatory, Kilnsea,
via Patrington, Hull, Humber.
Accommodation available.

Tatton Park Nature Trail C9
*Cheshire. From Knutsford via A50 and
A5034.* Start within the Park. 1½ miles.
Birds of mixed woodland and a mere which
is well known for winter wildfowl, breeding
great crested grebes and black tern on
passage. Further details from County Hall,
Chester or Manager, Tatton Park, Knutsford.

Bird watching

Bempton Cliffs K4
*Humber. Turn left in Flamborough to Bempton
village; a small road leads to the cliffs.* While
much of the area is an RSPB reserve, access
is unrestricted along the clifftop public
footpath. Huge numbers of seabirds breed
in a spectacular colony, with tens of
thousands of kittiwakes and a large
population of guillemots and razorbills.
Puffins, fulmars and herring gulls are also
present, and the small gannet colony (the
only one on the mainland of Britain) is a
particularly noteworthy feature. Permits
are not required.

Dee Estuary West A8
Hilbre, Cheshire. An estuary noted for very
large numbers of passage and winter waders,
a variety of other passage birds and numerous
winter wildfowl. The best area is around
West Kirby and Hilbre, with the islands of
Hilbre, Little Hilbre and Little Eye; the
Marine Lake at West Kirby is also worth a
look.
The islands are accessible on foot from West
Kirby, which you should leave at least three
hours before high tide, the best route being
from Little Eye north to the main island.
Permits are required for the main island
from Hoylake UDC, Hoylake, Wirral,
Cheshire.

Derwent Floods H6
*Derwent Valley, Humber. 6 miles ne of Selby
via A19 n from Selby.* Turn onto A163 to
Bubwith 1 mile past Barlby. Work n from
Bubwith and left onto B1228. This and other
minor roads in the area cover the best spots.
Visit in February and March when the floods
bring duck, often in spectacular numbers. It
is regularly used by a sizeable flock of
Bewick's swans.

Flamborough K4
*Humber. E from Bridlington via B1255 and
B1259.* Has breeding kittiwakes and is a very
good vantage point for seeing passing
seabirds – including spring and autumn
migrants.

Morecambe Bay A4
*Lancs. The best viewing areas are from
Heysham to Morecambe and Hest Bank,
most of which is beside A5105.* This immense
inter-tidal area holds the largest
concentrations of winter passage waders in
Britain, and the numbers of oyster-catchers,
knot and dunlin, for example, are often
spectacular. Also quite good for wildfowl,
notably sea duck and sawbills. There are
good shore walks at Lower Heysham (minor
roads from Heysham) and Hest Bank (cross
the railway north of the station).

Southport A7
Mersey. A very good area, easily accessible
from the town itself, for waders and winter
wildfowl. The Southport Marine Lake is
good for sea duck; Hesketh Park Lake has
various roosting duck. The whole shore is
good for waders – the pier is one place to
look at. Several thousand pink-footed geese
roost out on the sands and feed at nearby
Martin Mere and the mosses between
Southport and Scarisbrick, and Lydiate and
Hightown.

Brass rubbing

The following is a short list of churches that
have brasses for rubbing. Permission is
almost invariably required.
Cheshire. Macclesfield, Wilmslow
Lancashire. Childwall, Manchester
Cathedral, Ormskirk, Sefton, Winwick.
Yorkshire. Allerton Mauleverer,
Brandesburton, Cottingham, Cowthorpe,
Harpham, Ripley, Topcliffe, Wensley,
York Minster.

Fossils

Visit the local museum. Its fossil collection usually states where individual fossils have been found. When visiting quarries always seek permission to enter if they look privately owned or worked. Be careful of falls of rock.

Cheshire
But for a small area of lower lias on the Shropshire border, Cheshire is almost entirely made of Triassic sandstones and marls laid down in desert conditions. Almost completely unfossiliferous but for rare fossilised reptile footprints and bones found in large-scale quarrying operations. In addition much of the area is covered by glacial drift in which it is sometimes possible to find small shells of recent aspect.

Lancashire
Lancashire proper is mainly carboniferous with a strip of unfossiliferous Triassic sandstone in the west. The eastern uplands – Bowland Fells and the west side of the Pennines – are largely millstone grit with few fossils, but for the carboniferous limestone hills around Clitheroe and Ribblesdale which contain many fossils: corals, bryozoans, brachiopods, algal reefs, bivalves and gastropods. The lower land to the west around Manchester is of coal measures poorly exposed and with few fossils. Plant remains and rare shells may turn up in coal workings and tips.

Yorkshire
East Riding. The area is largely made up of Cretaceous and Jurassic rocks. The chalk forms the upland areas, the Wolds, where small quarries are scattered around, and reaches the sea in the cliffs around Flamborough Head to the north. A ridge of chalk runs south to the Humber with some large quarries towards the southern end, and middle and upper Jurassic limestones are exposed in places to the west of it as in South Cave, with ammonites, belemnites, sea-urchins, occasionally fish and reptiles, bivalves and gastropods.

West Riding. Largely carboniferous rocks – in the west the Dales of lower carboniferous limestones, in the east the upper carboniferous coal measures of the Yorkshire coalfield. It is a feature of carboniferous limestone that it forms areas of thin soil cover, so that exposures of the rock are numerous. The best known areas are around Malham and Ingleton and the valleys of Wharfedale, Wensleydale and Swaledale.

South from this area the Pennines consist of the upper carboniferous millstone grit series which though largely unfossiliferous does contain a few goniatites and bivalve shells. The coal measures form a belt of strata running from Leeds south to Sheffield and a few fossils, eg plants, may be found. Lower Palaeozoic rocks with a few fossils (trilobites and graptolites) are found in the Howgill Fells on the Lancashire border and small areas around Ingleton.

Forests

Macclesfield Forest   D9
Cheshire. Though little remains wooded today, Cheshire's eastern hill country around the silk-weaving town of Macclesfield was formerly a royal forest and hunting ground. A profusion of grassy hills rises steeply from rippling streams – the Dean, the Bollin and the Dane – that wander west to the Cheshire plain, past attractive black-and-white half-timbered farmhouses. Good walking country. If you motor expect fierce gradients on narrow, winding by-roads.

Forest of Rossendale   C6
Lancs. This, with the neighbouring Forest of Trawden, comprises the hill country of east Lancashire, north of Manchester. Once a mediaeval hunting ground, it saw the growth of the Lancashire textile industry using first wool, then cotton, from a cottage industry based on local sheep with water

power, to a coal-based technology with world-wide export trade. Breezy moorlands still separate bustling manufacturing towns like Bury, Burnley and Blackburn.

Trough of Bowland   B5
Lancs. The Trough or Forest of Bowland holds the course of the River Hodder, a tributary of the Ribble, which winds down past Clitheroe towards Preston. Surrounded by high falls, the Trough holds stone-built farmsteads in tree-clad folds of green pastures. Its restful, harmonious scenery merits a leisurely tour. Whalley, near Blackburn, has an old church and abbey ruins, for Bowland was once a Cistercian sheep-walk.

Hills and mountains

Calder Fell and Clougha Pike   B5
Lancs. On either side of Wyersdale, source of the River Wyre, these bold hills stand out above Lancashire's northern coastal plain, just south of the county town of Lancaster. Inland their closely-grazed sheep walks rise to Ward's Stone (1,856 feet) and Sykes' Fell (1,707 feet), high points of the Bowland hill range. 'Pike', from Norse *pikr*, means a pointed hill; 'fell' is Norse for mountain.

Langstrothdale Chase   C4
N. York. A wilderness of high fells amid the headwaters of the west-flowing rivers Lune and Ribble, and several Yorkshire Dale streams, Langstrothdale once formed a mediaeval chase or hunting territory. Roads are few, but the hills and dales, largely open pastures, can be explored from the tiny stone-built towns of Sedbergh, Hawes, Askrigg and Leyburn on the north, Pateley Bridge, Grassington and Settle to the south, and Ingleton on the west. The highest hills, all around 2,300 feet high, are Great Shunner Fell, Ingleborough, Pen y Ghent, Buckden Pike and Great Whernside.

Pendle Hill   C6
Lancs. Lancashire's central hill, Pendle, raises its odd, wedge-shaped form to a height of 1,851 feet above the Ribble Valley, between Clitheroe and Burnley. The name embodies the old Celtic word of *pen* for headland or hilltop. Its broad slopes, often hidden in mists, formed the mediaeval forest of Pendle, wild country indeed until the industrial towns of Nelson and Colne grew up on the south-east. To the west and north all is unspoilt farmland rising to high far fells.

Rivington Pike   B7
Lancs. Above the village of Rivington, midway between Bolton and Chorley, the Pike rises to 1,498 feet as a western outlier of the Pennines, with views over the whole South Lancashire plain. Rivington reservoirs at its foot send water gathered from the high Belmont moorlands to Liverpool.

Moors and dales

Cheshire Plain
Cheshire. Most of Cheshire forms a broad plain, a few hundred feet above sea level,

with a clay soil over sandstone. It is all well farmed, with year-round green pastures and a pond in every field. Little rivers meander through wooded clefts, and good roads make exploration easy.

The Fylde
Lancs. This flat coastal plain between the Lune at Lancaster and the Ribble at Preston is well farmed with dairy cattle, pigs and poultry, though otherwise featureless. The Fylde coast is now a fifteen-mile-long promenade from Blackpool to the Fleetwood fishing harbour, but its broad sandy beach, washed every tide, survives and it's usually sunny. The main river, the Wyre, flows from Wyersdale near Garstang to Fleetwood.

South Lancashire Plain
Industry has made a killing of this whole 40-mile-wide stretch between Liverpool on the coast, Manchester below the Pennines, Warrington on the Mersey, and Preston on the Ribble. Every kind of highway, motorway, canal and railway criss-crosses it, carrying heavy burdens of steel, textiles, chemicals, coal and oil from port or mine to factory and back.

Vale of York
Running through the heart of Yorkshire, from Darlington on the Tees in the north to Doncaster on the Don in the south, the Vale of York forms a level plain with a warm sunny climate, ideal for prosperous farming. The walled city of York, with its tall Minster towers, rises in the centre, and at intervals good roads run through prosperous market towns like Selby, Wetherby, Ripon, and Thirsk, each with its bridge across a river, and a historic church.

Yorkshire Dales and Pennine Moors
All the east of Yorkshire, along the high Pennine Chain, is dales country. The rural regions north of the industrial West Riding, from Skipton and Ilkley north to County Durham, comprise the Yorkshire Dales National Park. A typical dale is bounded at its head, and down both sides, by fells or moorlands, around 2,000 feet above sea level. These open, unfenced treeless areas of heather and many species of grasses are grazed by neighbouring farmers, who hold ancient rights to pasture sheep, cattle and ponies 'in common'. The sheltered dale bottom holds a string of pastures and meadows, bounded by stout dry-stone walls, with stone-built barns and farmsteads at regular intervals, and grey stone villages, each with its church, set a few miles apart. A tree-lined river flowing over occasional waterfalls courses down the dale, giving it its name, and is followed by a winding by-road. Until recently every steading housed an independent farmer, possibly a descendant of Scandinavian settlers who gave this region its wealth of harsh-sounding Norse place names. Today, with fewer men needed for the land, many houses have become holiday or retirement homes for wealthy people from northern industrial cities. But the peaceful Dales scenery is safeguarded, preserving magnificent country for leisurely wanderings by car or afoot.
Outstanding northern dales include Swaledale, Wensleydale, Nidderdale and Wharfedale.

Yorkshire Wolds
Humber. In the old East Riding of Yorkshire, between the busy commercial port of Hull and the seaside resort of Scarborough, the Wolds rise as a broad whale-back of chalk, 40 miles long, ten miles across and from 400 to 800 feet high. This is all well farmed

pastoral country. The underlying chalk is dramatically exposed in the sheer cliffs of Flamborough Head.

Rivers

Derwent
N. York. The Yorkshire Derwent rises high on the North Yorkshire Moors north of Scarborough, within sight of the North Sea. Leaving the hills through a lovely wooded valley near Hackness, it turns inland to wind through the whole Vale of Pickering to York.

Lune and Ribble
Lancs. In north-west Lancashire the River Lune gives its name to the city of Lancaster, the Lune *castra* or Roman fort, and hence to the whole county. It rises high on breezy uplands in Westmorland, and flows south to this small industrial seaport.
The Ribble, beginning farther east, takes a parallel course south past the beautiful, though nowadays little-wooded, ancient forest – or Trough – of Bowland, through Clitheroe to Preston. Below this big industrial town and minor port it broadens into a wide, muddy estuary.

Mersey
The Mersey, from the Norse *myr sjo*, or marshy lake, draws its name from its broad, muddy, tidal estuary between Liverpool and Widnes (the wide *ness* or headland). It is fed by several small Pennine rivers, including the Goyt, the Etherow, the Tame and the Irwell, each with an industrialised valley. Near Warrington it is canalised as part of the Manchester Ship Canal. At Liverpool, where it is crossed by ferry boats and tunnels, its tidal waters, carrying chemical effluents, are unspeakably foul. Dangerous sandbanks fringe its final seaward outlet. Most of Cheshire is drained by small Mersey tributaries, notably the Weaver, winding over its pleasing plain.

Ouse and Humber
Several of Yorkshire's major rivers converge and unite at or near the cathedral city and county town of York to become the Ouse, a broad, winding navigable river. It has carried in turn the ships of Anglian and Danish settlers and the war-galleys of invading Norsemen. Below Goole the Ouse broadens out into the broad tidal estuary called the Humber, flowing east past the port of Hull to the North Sea at Spurn Head.

Yorkshire Dales Rivers
N. York. From the 2,000-foot-high Pennine Chain, which forms a classical water-parting, the Yorkshire Dales rivers run eastwards towards the North Sea. Every major river rises on high, misty rain-soaked and peaty moorland, and after a rapid descent, often over waterfalls, through picturesque, well-farmed uplands used for stock-raising, takes a winding course over a lowland flood plain.
Reservoirs are frequent in the uplands, to meet the region's immense water demands for industry and domestic use. The lower reaches of the south Dales rivers serve as outlets for industrial waste as well as sewage, and some are horribly polluted. From north to south the succession of Dales rivers run: the Swale and Ure from Wensleydale; the Nidd from Nidderdale and the Wharfe, all coming within the Yorkshire Dales National Park. Then in the industrialised south of the county you will find the Aire, the Calder and the Don.

Swaledale, York.

Canals

The canals and navigable rivers in this area range from the wide and heavily used industrial waterways of South Yorkshire to the beautiful meandering course of tiny rural canals like the upper Peak Forest Canal and the Trent and Mersey Canal. The geography of all these waterways is of course much affected by the Pennine Hills, the great ridge that runs north to south all the way from Scotland to Derbyshire. The Pennines have effectively divided Lancashire from Yorkshire since the ice age, and it was only when three canals – the Rochdale Canal, the Leeds and Liverpool Canal, and the Huddersfield Narrow Canal – were built to cross these great hills that effective communication and trade was opened up between the two regions.

The Aire and Calder Navigation   F6

This waterway, which runs from Leeds to Goole, with branches to Selby and Wakefield, is of interest as the only really busy trading canal in this country. It is based on the River Aire, which has been at least partly navigable for many centuries. The countryside it passes through shows considerable signs of long-established mining activities, and is nowadays mostly unattractive. But the navigation is fascinating for the coal barges, oil tankers and miscellaneous trading craft that plough constantly up and down. Much of the traffic is coal from the collieries of South Yorkshire to Goole for onward shipment in large sea-going freighters – often in trains of little compartment boats hauled by a tug. At Goole the compartment boats are lifted right out of the water by tall gantries and turned upside down, spilling their cargo into the holds of the waiting ships. This unusual but efficient technique was evolved at the beginning of this century, and has been very much the basis of the Aire and Calder's continued prosperity to this day.
Things to see: Goole Docks; the big locks at Ferrybridge, Castleford and Pollington; and the interesting waterway 'crossroads' at Castleford. There is also a shipbuilding yard at Knottingley.

The Leeds and Liverpool Canal D5

This is the only one of the three trans-Pennine canals that is still open to navigation, and it is very handsome indeed. On the Lancashire side, it leaves the scruffy outskirts of Liverpool and enters the little valley of the River Douglas. At Wigan it climbs up a great flight of 21 locks to look down on to the town. From here onwards it assumes an industrial guise, passing through many manufacturing towns of east Lancashire before reaching a long tunnel on the summit level. Some very fine scenery leads into Yorkshire, where the canal enters the valley of the River Aire. The upper part of Airedale is rural and of great scenic interest (the Yorkshire Dales are nearby) but at Keighley the industrial towns begin, and lead inevitably to the vast manufacturing conurbation of Leeds.

Liverpool–Leeds canal at Parbold

Archaeology

Blackstone Edge   D7
Nr. Littleborough, Lancs. The finest example of a paved Roman road in Britain. The surface is made up of small blocks with occasional transverse ribs. The road lies in a deep cutting through the peat, and in parts the natural rock has been used for the road surface.

Bleasdale Circle   B5
Nr Garstang, Lancs. A bronze age 'henge' monument consisting of a stone circle constructed around a burial side. Excavation has shown that the whole monument was surrounded by a timber palisade. *Accessible with permission from the farm.*

Castle Hill   E7
Almondbury, nr Huddersfield, W. York. One of the major hill forts of the Brigantes, the iron age people of the Pennines area, with multiple earth bank and ditch defences. Its ancient name was Camulodunum, 'Fortress of Camulos', after a Celtic war-god. Its fine strategic position led to later use as the site of a mediaeval castle, and a Victorian tower now stands on the hill. *Accessible any time.*

Chester   A9
Cheshire. Roman Deva, one of the three fortresses that were occupied virtually throughout the Roman period. The permanent garrison was the XX Valeria Victrix legion, whose symbol of a boar can be seen stamped on tiles in the Grosvenor Museum. The mediaeval city walls were built on the line of the fortress walls, and Roman work survives on the north side, and on part of the east side near the cathedral; the south-east corner tower foundations can be seen in Newgate. The amphitheatre, which was probably used as a parade-ground as well as for games, is now open to the public, and the nearby Hypogeum is laid out as a garden with Roman pillars.
The Grosvenor Museum had models of Roman Chester and a collection of Roman objects, including carved stones, stamped water-pipes, and lead ingots from the Flintshire mines. *Amphitheatre open any reasonable time.*

Danes' Graves   J5
Nr Driffield, Humber. East Yorkshire is the richest area for burial mounds of known iron age date, and the group at Danes' Graves contains a large number of small barrows. Some of the excavated burials have produced dismantled chariots buried in the grave.

The Devil's Arrows   F4
Boroughbridge, N. York. An important group of standing stones, probably dating from the bronze age. The stone shafts are set up in line, and the deep vertical ribbing is due to the weathering of the hard millstone grit.

Isle of Man   A2
From the 8th to the 11thC most of Britain suffered to some degree from the Viking invasions, and the Isle of Man was one of the areas completely taken over and settled. Vowlan Fort is typical of the small promontory forts of this date, with a strong landward defence of earth bank and ditch; there is just room inside for one of the characteristic Viking 'longhouses'. It may belong to the initial raiding period, as it guards a landing-place and commands wide views of the sea. The Braidd probably represents a more permanent settlement site, and contains large round and long buildings. Tynwald Hill was the assembly place for the Tynwald, the Manx parliament, during the Viking period.

Ribchester   B6
Lancs. Roman Bremetennacum, a fort site occupied by a squadron of Sarmatian cavalry from the area of modern Romania. The foundations of two granaries are visible, with small internal columns to raise the floor level and so prevent rodents from reaching the grain. The porch of the White Bull is supported on two Roman columns, and various pieces of Roman stonework can be seen re-used in the church walls. Ribchester Museum contains Roman finds. *Granaries and museum open 14.00–17.30 Mon–Sat May–Aug. Closed Fri. 14.00–17.00 Mon–Thur & Sat Sep–Nov & Feb–Apr. 14.00–17.00 Sat Dec–Jan for parties by arrangement only*

Thornborough Circles   E4
Nr Ripon, N. York. A major bronze age 'henge' monument consisting of three concentric earthen circles, approximately 550 feet across overall. It has two opposed entrances, and a ditch on each side of the earthwork. An earlier feature is the 'cursus', a pair of parallel banks with external ditches of which little now remains. As commonly occurs with henge monuments several burial mounds were constructed nearby. *Accessible any time.*

York   G5

N. York. The Roman fortress of Eboracum was established in 71; its permanent garrison from the turn of the 1stC until the end of the Roman period was the VI Victrix Legion. Like Chester, most of the fortress is buried under the mediaeval city, but the 'multangular' tower at the south-west corner, with the foundation of its interior walls, and a section of wall beside it, are basically Roman and can be seen in the museum gardens. There was also a large civilian town south of the fortress, and York was the capital of northern Britain from the 3rdC; the emperors Septimius Severus and Constantine both stayed there.

The Yorkshire Museum has a large collection of Roman material including inscriptions, a sculptured head of Constantine, and objects carved from Yorkshire jet.

Footpaths & ancient ways

The Pennine Way   C4

From Derbyshire to the Scottish border the Pennine Way winds along the backbone of England. At Crowden the route enters Cheshire, then leads north-west to Wessenden Head Moor, past the reservoirs, across White Moss and Black Moss, and beyond to where the Roman road climbs over Blackstone Edge and on to Broadhead Drain, the eastern side of Edge End Moor, Heptonstall Moor, Keighley Moor, Cowling, Lothersdale and Thornton. At Thornton stop by Market Street and see the house where the Brontes were born. The track across Fountains Fell was once used by packhorses carrying coal. Pen-y-ghent, famous for its purple mountain saxifrage in April, and Ingleborough are in the heart of pot-holing country. Descending Dodd Fell towards Hawes there are magnificent views across the smooth, green dales of Wensleydale.

The Wolds Way   J6

The gently rolling hill country of the East Riding offers a pleasant stretch of path for 67 miles from the Humber to the North Sea, from North Ferriby to Filey Brigg through cultivated land. The southern half of the Way starts at Thixendale, and the surrounding area has some of the broadest views along the Way, with Garrowby Hill rising to 807 feet, the highest point of the Wolds.

A special feature of the area is the lost villages such as Cleaving which were abandoned with the advent of intensive sheep farming in the 15th-16thC. The Green Dragon pub in Welton village is another high spot on the Way: tradition has it that highwayman Dick Turpin was arrested here in 1739, and thence transported to the York assizes.

Regional sport

Cricket and cricketers

It is in Lancashire and Yorkshire that the cricket battles become serious, and the Wars of the Roses live again on the turf.

Yorkshire County Cricket Club. Headingley Cricket Ground, St Michael's Lane, Leeds. Tel 52865.

Lancashire County Cricket Club. Old Trafford Ground, Manchester. Tel 061-872 0261.

Fell walking   D4

The Yorkshire Dales offer some of the best opportunities in the country for fell-walking as there is an excellent network of footpaths and bridleways. This is a tough occupation calling for boots and strong legs; full details from any National Park Information Centre.

Football

The crowded lengths of Merseyside have become a northern football capital over the years. The best known team in the area, or perhaps even in Britain, is Manchester United. The club team was rebuilt by Sir Matt Busby after the disastrous air crash in

1958 which killed eight players and nearly Busby as well. In one of the most remarkable comebacks in history the 'United' team went from strength to strength in the 1960s when they won the European Cup. Liverpool have now taken over to become the country's top team in the 1970s.

Everton Football Club Goodison Park, Liverpool. Tel 051-521 2020

Liverpool Football Club Anfield Rd, Liverpool. Tel 051-263 2361

Manchester City Football Club Maine Rd, Moss Side, Manchester. Tel 061-226 1191/2

Manchester United Football Club Old Trafford, Manchester Tel 061-872 1661/2.

Pigeon racing

Competitive racing of pigeons is a widespread sport, but particularly so in the industrial areas of Northern England. Many races are in excess of 400 miles and starting points on the continent, such as for the classic Avranche Race, are by no means uncommon.

A good bird can win over £2,000 in a lifetime. In Britain the sport is organised by local federations, many of whom now own huge lorries to carry and release pigeons, something done by obliging railway porters in days gone by.

Pot holing

Also known as 'caving' – lots of opportunities in Yorkshire and Lancashire for underground ramblings. As long as the rules are followed accidents can be avoided and only relatively mild adventures result. Strictly for those with subterranean tastes and under experienced guidance. For information about clubs etc. write to: The Hon. Secretary, Council of Northern Caving Clubs, 6 Monkroyd Avenue, Barnoldswick, via Colne, Lancs.

Rugby League

There are two varieties of rugby played in Britain, Rugby Union and Rugby League. Rugby League is a game developed from Rugby Union, which used to be played by the clubs in the Northern Rugby League. There are only thirteen men to a team, as opposed to fifteen in Rugby Union. Most of the players in Rugby League are professionals to some degree, but many of them also have other jobs during the week. The game is confined principally to Yorkshire and Lancashire where many of the smaller industrial towns have their own teams. Best known of the 70 teams comprising the league are Batley, Bradford, Halifax, Oldham and Rochdale.

Festivals

Festivals

For information and tickets for festivals go to the local information centre or ticket agent.

Bolton Festival of Music   C7

Bolton, Lancs. The festival lures many visitors to this industrial area. The orchestras and soloists are the best in the country. The biennial festival is devoted to individual composers such as Mozart and Brahms. *Mid Sep.*

Chester Festival   A9

Chester, Cheshire. The main event in this major arts festival every three years is the Chester Mystery Plays. Written by a local monk in 1375, they are now presented in the very latest theatrical genre. *Late Jun.*

Harrogate Festival of Arts and Sciences   F5

Harrogate, N. York. Music, poetry and drama events mingle here with scientific lectures and exhibitions. Audience and artist can also get together in the writers' conference, poets' meeting and art exhibitions. *Early Aug.*

Harrogate International Youth Festival   F5

Harrogate, N. York. In a famous 19thC spa, this festival presents classical works of all nations with a few modern composers. A chance to hear music by talented young people from all parts of the world. The high musical standards and informal atmosphere make it a very popular event. *April.*

York Mystery Plays and
Festival of the Arts G5
York. Every third year the 14thC York cycle of miracle plays are faithfully re-created in Paris. Staged dramatically in the abbey garden or on wagons around the city in mediaeval style, the plays describe man from creation to the last judgment. The arts festival is another major attraction with some excellent performers.

Fun things

Blackpool Tower A6
Blackpool, Lancs. Britain's answer to Mr Eiffel's little steel confection in Paris. Believe it or not there is a zoo on the top floor housing a lion, tiger, bear, dingo and hyena. At the bottom is an aquarium which houses amongst other things a red-tail shark. The tower is by the sea front; look up and you can't miss it.

Chester Canal Boats A9
Chester, Cheshire. Do you hanker for the tranquil days before the internal combustion engine was invented? Then a trip in a horse-drawn canal boat might appeal to you. Return trips from Cow Lane Bridge, Frodsham Street to Backford. *14.30 Wed, Fri-Sun July-Sep. Sat & Sun. Apr-Jun. Tel 21519.*

High Corn Mill D5
Chapel Hill, Skipton, N. York. An 18thC four-storey mill which had been restored to its probable appearance, but some Victorian machinery is being added. Milling has been carried out here since the 12thC. There is a wealth of operating machinery: a working water wheel, a turbine of 1912, and a winnowing machine which took a prize in the great exhibition of 1884. *Open 12.00–18.00 Sun & B Hols.*

Keighley and Worth Valley
Light Railway D6
Haworth, N. Yorks. 10 miles nw of Bradford. A standard gauge railway running five miles up the Worth Valley from Keighley to Oxenhope. The railway starred in the film 'The Railway Children'. Look at the collection of engines and coaches at Haworth Station. *The trains run at weekends. Museum open 10.30–dusk daily. Tel 43629.*

Mere Brow Leisure Centre A7
Nr Tarleton, Lancs. 10 miles sw of Preston on A565. This place really caters for the family picnic outing with a specially laid out picnic park, Easter hovercraft racing and boating. *Open 9.00–20.00 daily May–Sep.*

North Yorkshire Moors
Railway H3
Pickering, N. York. 7 miles sw of Whitby off A169. At Goathland Station is an interesting collection of locomotives and coaches from the steam age. The preservation society have purchased the six miles of ex-LNER track from Grosmont to Pickering and are running trains. *Daily Easter–mid Oct. Tel 72508.*

Pateley Bridge Flax Mill E4
Pateley Bridge, N. York. 12 miles sw of Ripon off B6265, nr Foster Beck. At the Watermill Inn there is a mid-17thC flax mill with a high-breast water wheel. At 36 feet in diameter and some 30 tons in weight it is the largest in Britain after the Manx monster at Laxey. Temperance travellers will be pleased to note that the mill is open outside licensing hours.

National Railway Museum G5
Leeman Rd, York. No one could pass up the opportunity of seeing such a superb collection of steam locomotives. North-eastern England was the cradle of the railways and here you can see a complete panorama of British railway history. *Open 10.00–18.00 daily. Closed Sun morning.*

Stump Cross Caverns D4
N. York. Between Plately Bridge & Grassington on B6265. The best place in the country to see stalactites and stalagmites, but here you will have to like your caves floodlit in technicolour. The mystery of these caves has gone but they are easier to visit than most potholes – you won't need a torch. *Open daily Apr–Oct. Sat & Sun Nov–Mar.*

Hotels

£   inexpensive
££   medium priced
£££   expensive

Alderley Edge Cheshire C9
Edge Hotel, Macclesfield Rd. Tel 3033. A Victorian house which has now been extended. Good views across the Cheshire plain. ££.

Bingley W. York. D6
Bankfield Hotel, Bradford Rd. Tel 7123. This mansion is set in woodland with views of the River Aire. ££.

Birtle Gt. Manchester. C7
Normandie Hotel, Elbut Lane. Tel 061-764 3869. A former country house set on a hill above the industrial area. Friendly atmosphere and good food. No dogs. ££.

Blackpool Lancs. A6
Imperial Hotel, North Promenade. Tel 23971. Popular with political parties, this 100-year-old building also had Charles Dickens among its guests. Good for family holidays with many baby-listening facilities. £££.

Bolton Abbey N. York. D5
Devonshire Arms Hotel, nr Skipton. Tel 265. Also offers guests fishing in the River Wharfe. No dogs. ££.

Boroughbridge N. York. F4
Three Arrows Hotel, Horsefair. Tel 2245. A recently renovated mansion set in 26 acres of parkland near the A1. Pleasant garden and swimming pool. £.

Bradford W. York. E6
Baron Hotel, Highfield Rd. Tel 611914. New and full of interesting design features. Luxury bedrooms with circular baths. ££.

Bromley Cross Gt Manchester. C7
Last Drop Hotel, nr Bolton. Tel Bolton 591131. Began life as a stone barn 250 years ago. It now houses an interesting collection of 19thC and early 20thC relics. ££.

Bucklow Hill Cheshire. C9
Swan Hotel, nr Knutsford. Tel 830295. Motel-style bedrooms in modern block built-on to old monestry. £.

Burnley Lancs. C6
Rosehill House Hotel, Rosehill Avenue. Tel 27116. Formerly the home of a cotton baron; there are large public rooms. £.

Chester Cheshire A9
Ye Olde King's Head, Lower Bridge St. Tel 24855. A splendid old inn which once housed Charles I. £.

Clayton-le-Moors Lancs. C6
Dunkenhaigh Hotel, nr Accrington. Tel Accrington 34333. An early 19thC country house set in parkland. ££.

Clitheroe Lancs. C6
Roefield Hotel, Edisford Bridge. Tel 22010. An elegant Georgian house with woodlands, fishing in the River Ribble and riding. Good English food. ££.

Douglas Isle of Man
Palace Hotel and Casino, Central Promenade. Tel 4521. Modern and lively with pleasant public rooms and a swimming pool. £.

Grimsby Humber K7
Humber Royal Hotel, Littlecoates Rd. Tel 50295. A well designed modern hotel. The neighbouring golf course is visible from the public rooms. ££.

Halifax W. York. D6
Cavalier Country Club, Holmfield. Tel 44270. Used as a meeting place for Cromwell's generals when it was Holdsworth House. Splendid beams in the first floor rooms. ££.

Harrogate N. York. F5
Hotel Majestic, Ripon Rd. Tel 68972. Victorian. Dates from Harrogate's fame as a spa. Pleasant grounds. £££.

Huddersfield W. York. E7
George Hotel, St George's Square. Tel 25444. A traditional hotel with Edwardian grace. ££.

Hull Humber. J6
Royal Station Hotel, Ferensway. Tel 25087. A dignified city-centre hotel with Victorian

decor. Pleasant grill room. £.

Knutsford Cheshire   **C9**
Royal George Hotel, 60 King St. Tel 4151.
A truly historic hotel where George II,
Queen Victoria (before her accession) and
Louis Napoleon have stayed. ££.

Leeds W. York.   **F6**
Hotel Metropole, King St. Tel 450841.
Situated near the station. There is a vast
lounge and dining room. ££.

Liverpool Mersey.   **A8**
*Adelphi Hotel, Ranelagh Place. Tel
051 709 7200.* A city-centre hotel which has
undergone alterations. The lounge has a
water garden and the basement a sports club
and discotheque. Good restaurant. ££.

Manchester Gt. Manchester.   **C8**
*Hotel Piccadilly, Piccadily Plaza.
Tel 061 236 8414.* Modern. Towers above
the city centre and offers comfort to the jet
age traveller. £££.

Monk Fryston N. York.   **G6**
*Monk Fryston Hall Hotel, nr Leeds. Tel South
Milford 682369.* An 18thC manor with
country house atmosphere. Good plain
cooking. £.

Puddington Cheshire.   **A9**
*Craxton Wood Hotel, Parkgate Rd.
Tel 051 339 4717.* A former club situated
between Chester and Liverpool. Well run
restaurant. ££.

Ripon N. York.   **F4**
Spa Hotel, Park St. Tel 2172. An Edwardian
hotel with a collection of racing photographs
and prints. ££.

St. Michael's-on-Wyre Lancs.   **A6**
*Rivermeade Country House, Hotel nr Preston.
Tel 267.* On the river: friendly and informal
atmosphere. Good restaurant. £.

Sheffield S. York.   **F8**
*Hallam Tower Hotel, Manchester Rd,
Broomhill. Tel 686031.* Set in its own grounds
on the outskirts of the city. £££.

Threshfield N. York.   **D4**
*Wilson Arms Hotel, Station Rd. Tel
Grassington 752666.* Situated in the
Yorkshire Dales National Park this is ideal
for weekends. Local fishing. Good food. ££.

York N. York   **G5**
Royal Station Hotel, Station Rd. Tel 53681.
A large Victorian hotel with fine panelled
public rooms. Good service and pleasant
ornamental gardens. ££.

Regional foods

Cakes
Eccles and Chorley cakes are the best known
of this region – both being a spicy currant
mixture enclosed in pastry.
Fig or fag pie and simnel cake are
traditional Mothering Sunday offerings.
Parkin is made for the 5th November.

Cheese
Lancashire is a crumbly white cheese. When
young it has a mild and creamy flavour which
lends itself to toasting. Most of the cheese is
consumed locally and is popular as part of a
ploughman's lunch.
Wensleydale is produced in the Dales of
Yorkshire. This white cheese has a unique
lingering flavour and is sweet and velvety in
texture. Blue cheese is available but much
rarer.
Cheshire the oldest of English cheeses is
made in three colours – red, white and
blue – the latter happening rarely and
purely by accident.

Isle of Man
The island is noted for its scallops and
lobster – scallops are known as 'tanrogan'
locally. The Manx kipper is traditionally
smoked, and it is illegal to dye them as they
often are elsewhere. Available by post, and
in most hotels, restaurants and shops.
Home bred Manx lamb is also famous;
usually roasted and served with new
potatoes and mint sauce.

Lancashire hot pot
This traditional dish comes from Burnley
and was devised when oysters were
plentiful. Oysters also feature in Scouse – the
Liverpool version of their lamb, potato,
onion and kidney stew. Pickled red cabbage
and spice vinegar are the accompaniments.

Morecambe Bay shrimps
The charming Lancashire seaside resort of
Morecambe is well known for its seafood
and especially the local pink shrimps.

Sweets
Both Harrogate Toffee and Pontefract cakes
have been made for many years in the region
to traditional and well tested recipes.
Blackpool Rock is the delight of many a
schoolboy.

Yorkshire pudding
Surely one of Britain's best known dishes,
which is traditionally eaten with roast beef.
The pudding should be light and well risen
and in Yorkshire it is often served before the
meat with a little gravy – to help make the
meat go further!

Restaurants

£   inexpensive
££   medium priced
£££   expensive

Wild Boar Motor Lodge. Tel Bunbury 260309.
Mainly French; some English. Emphasis on
good quality raw materials. Set lunch is
good value. LD. £L, £££D. Book.

Birtle Gt Manchester.   **C7**
*Normandie Restaurant, Elbut Lane.
Tel 061 764 3869.* Outstanding French food.
Magnificent wines. D. *Closed Sun.* ££. Book.

Bradford W. Yorks.   **E6**
Cottage, 869 Thornton Rd, Tel 832752. A
formal restaurant in a cottage on the
outskirts of the city. Mainly English cooking.
LD. *Closed Tues & Sat L.* ££. Book.

Dodworth S. York.   **F7**
Brooklands Restaurant. Tel Barnsley 6364.
Converted transport cafe opposite slag
heap. Hearty British food. Good value.
Friendly service. LD. *Closed Sun & Mon.*
£L. ££D. Book.

Ilkley W. York.   **E5**
Box Tree Cottage, Church St. Tel 2983. Tiny
17thC cottage. Outstanding cooking. Mainly
French. D. *Closed Mon & Sun.* £££. Book.

Kildwick W. York.   **D6**
*Kildwick Hall, nr Keighley, Tel Cross Hills
32244.* Views over the beautiful garden from
this elegant Jacobean hall. English and
French cooking. D. *Closed Tues (L served
Sun).*

Liverpool Mersey.   **A8**
*Adelphi Hotel, French Restaurant, Ranelagh
Place. Tel 051 709 7200.* Traditional hotel.
Authentic French cooking. Outstanding
wines. LD. *Closed Sun.* £££. Book D.

Lower Peover Cheshire.   **C9**
Bells of Peover. Tel 2269. 13thC pub. Plain
British cooking. Set meals are good value.
LD. £L. ££D. *Closed Mon L.* Book.

Manchester Gt. Manchester.   **C8**
*Midland Hotel, French Restaurant, Peter
Square. Tel 061 236 3333.* Traditional hotel.
Outstanding wines. French and English
cooking. D. *Closed Sun.* £££. L Fri only.
Book.

Nantwich Cheshire   **B10**
Churche's Mansion, Hospital St. Tel 65933.
Elizabethan mansion. Mainly English. Set
meals offer fair choice. LD. *Closed Sun SD.*
£L. ££D. Book

Thornton-le-Fylde Lancs.   **A5**
River House, Skippool Creek. Tel 883307.
Yachting hotel. Good, straightforward
cooking. Fresh local materials. LD. *Closed
Mon.* £L, ££D. Book.

Northumbria and the Lakes

The Lake District and England's most northerly counties are two contrasting regions both hilly, the lakes have a green mellowness while Northumbria is high and remote. Cumbria takes in the last northern thrust of the Pennines that leads to the fells and pikes of the Lakes. The coast on the west alternates between the wild and the industrial from coal mining under the sea to the cool power of Britain's first atomic plant at Calder Hall. Wordsworth and the lakeland poets have said almost all that can be said about the green glories of the Lake District. The neighbouring large towns have tapped the almost inexhaustible water supply and the weekend invasion of small boats and water skiers means you have to travel a bit further off the beaten track to find the peace that delighted the poets.

County Durham still has a grey, gaunt, silent quality best seen in the high fells of Weardale and Upper Teesdale where blue gentians can be found in remote hollows. You cannot fail to be impressed by the rugged splendours of the east coast and along the silver spine of Hadrian's Wall you may yet hear the clang of the Roman centurions patrolling the farthest reaches of their civilisation.

A B C D E

1

Forth Carlops
Braehead West Linton Leadburn Heriot Oxton Westruther Polwarth Swinton Whits
Carnwath Dolphinton Romannobridge Eddleston Fountainhall Lauder Greenlaw Leitholm Cornhill
Newbigging Neidpath Peebles Stow Gordon Eccles Coldstream Twe
Libberton Biggar Skirling Castle Innerleithen Galashiels Earlston Stichill Birgham Sprouston Carham
Broughton Stobo Walkerburn Clovenfords Melrose St. Boswell's Kelso
Drumelzier Traquair Selkirk Eildon Roxburgh Maxton Kilham

BORDERS Yarrow Eildon Hills Linton Yetholm
Broad Law Ettrickbridge Ashkirk Ancrum Crailing Morebattle Th
Cappercleuch End Ettrick Forest Denholm Bedrule Jedburgh Oxnam Hownam 268
2756 Hawick Kirkton

2

Abington Crawford Ramseycleuch Hott Hill Bonchester Eckford

Moffat Davington Teviothead Kielder Alwinton Harbott
Beattock 1996 Newcastleton Kielder Forest Rochester Redesdale
St. Ann's Holm Kirkstile Falstone NO
Parkgate Templand Corrie Common Langholm Greenhaugh
Lochmaben Lockerbie Canonbie Bellingham Redesmouth Birtle
Tinwald Bankshill Eaglesfield Rowanburn Chipchase Castle Simonburn
Collin Ecclefechan Kirtlebridge Longtown Gilsland Greenhead Newbrough Henshaw
Mouswald Smithfield Walton Haltwhistle Haydon Bridge Hexh
Bankend Brampton Lambley Whitfield Catton Allendale
Bowness-on-Solway Low Row
Solway Plain Carlisle Castle Carrock Slaggyford Knarsdale Alston Carr Shield
Silloth Kirkbride Drumburgh Wetheral Cumwhitton Leadgate Nenthead
Beckfoot Dulton Thursby Dalston Ainstable High Kirkoswald Garrigill Westgate
Mawbray Waverton Rosley Hesket Lazonby Glassonby St. John's
Allonby Westnewton Sebergham Melmerby Great Salkeld Chapel
Maryport Aspatria Torpenhow Caldbeck Inglewood Forest Plumpton Wall Langwathby Cross Fell 2930 The High Force
Flimby Dearham Bothel Uldale Bassenthwaite Skelton Penrith
Clifton Brigham Cockermouth Skiddaw 3053 Pennruddock A66 Eden
ington Broughton High Lorton Threlkeld Greystoke Lowther Dufton Middleton-in-Tees
moresby Braithwaite Keswick Dockray Pooley Bridge Askham Hackthorpe Murton Mickle Fe
Arlecdon Lamplugh Lowéswater Buttermere Grange Ullswater Gt. Strickland Hilton Lune Fore
Cleator Moor Frizington Kirkland Derwent Rosthwaite Patterdale Bolton Crosby Appleby Brough Stainm
Bees Egremont Haile Calder Bridge Borrowdale Helvellyn 3118 Shap Ravensworth Warcop Soulby Winton

8 Beckermet Gosforth **Lake District** Grasmere Orton Kirkby Stephen
Boot Sca Fell Pikes 3210 Ambleside A685 Tebay Ravenstonedale Nateby
Seascale Skelwith Troutbeck Thwaite
Drigg Old Man Bridge Hawkshead Staveley Gayrigg Lowgill 2220 Hardrow
Ravenglass Ravenglass and Eskdale Railway 2635 Windermere Sedbergh Dent Hawes

9 1881 Coniston Bowness Ferry Kendal Oxenholme Middleton Barbon Langstroth Chase
Bootle Broughton in Furness Colton Crosthwaite Natland 2419 Ingleborough
1969 Grizebeck Haverthwaite Railway Levens Kirkby Lonsdale Horton in Ribblesdale
Whitbeck Silecroft Kirksanton Soutergate Greenodd Lindale Heversham Milnthorpe Burton Clapham Austwick
Askam in Furness Ulverston Cartmel Grange-over-Sands Melling Ingleton Stainf
Dalton-in-Furness Bardsea Flookburgh Burton in Lonsdale Austwick Settle
Barrow-in-Furness Aldingham Bolton-le-Sands Wray Clapham Kirkby Malham
Vickerstown Morecambe Bay Hest Bank Hornby High Bentham Giggleswick Hellifield
Isle of Walney Heysham Morecambe Carnforth Claughton Wigglesworth
Hilpsford Point Lancaster Caton Clougha Pike 1836 Forest of Bowland Long Preston
1531 Marshaw Dolphinholme
Glasson

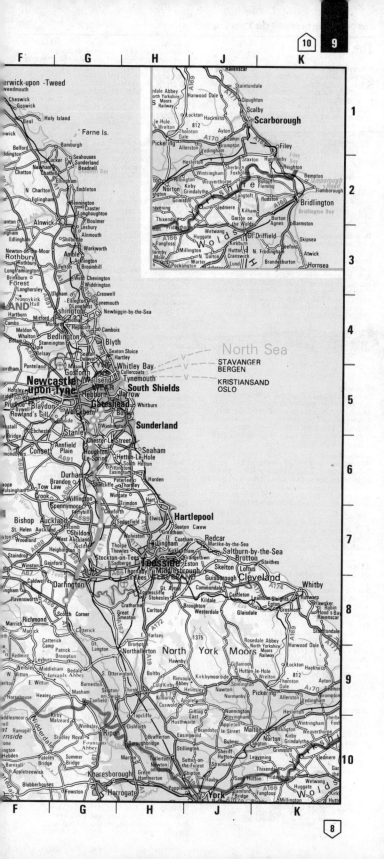

The coast

Alnmouth G3
Northumberland. Pop 700. EC Wed. A boisterous undulation of red-roofed houses beside the estuary of the River Aln. The port for Alnwick in the 12thC, it was also an important grain-port.
A quiet resort with a good sandy beach.

Alnmouth

Beadnell G2
Northumberland. Pop 600. Suburban oddities entwined in a tight-fisted way round a small harbour on the end of Beadnell Bay. Of interest – the disused 18thC lime kilns; Beadnell Towers.
Wide sandy beaches; safe swimming.

Berwick-upon-Tweed F1
Northumberland. Pop 11,600. EC Thur. MD Wed, Sat. A weather-beaten place crouching behind an encircling town wall. Once an important Elizabethan port, and now a busy market centre, it was for centuries a bone of contention along the Scottish-English border. Of interest – the 18thC town hall; the remarkable town defences; the 18thC barracks; the castle; the three bridges; quay walls. Sandy beach.

Berwick-on-Tweed

Craster G2
Northumberland. Pop 500. A diminutive fishing village washed in round a tiny harbour. A poetic memorial, built by the Craster family in 1906 for a brother who died in far off Tibet. Of interest – Craster Towers; the gaunt ruins of Dunstanburgh Castle. Sandy beach.

Cullercoats H5
Northumberland. Stuck on the end of Tynemouth it still manages to retain an air of independence. It is a conspiratorial huddle of houses spread-eagled on a cliff top. Of interest – 18thC church of St George, built with 13thC fervour. Fine sandy beach.

Drigg A8
Cumbria. Pop 600. Unruly houses lead to high dunes which curve down to a broad sandy beach. Of interest – the late Georgian Carlton Hall; the church of St Peter. Sandy beach.

Filey East K9
N. York. Pop 5,300. EC Wed. A shirt-sleeves-and-braces resort hell-bent on family fun. The six miles of sandy beaches are safe for swimming and sheltered enough for those who just want to play about with bucket and spade. Good donkey rides.

Hartlepool H7
Cleveland. Pop 96,900. EC Wed. Complete with charters from King John, Elizabeth I and Victoria, plus two 12thC churches, it's an outrageously indulgent town. Much is modern and mean but there's still a wry smile in odd corners. Long sandy beaches.

Holy Island F1
Northumberland. Pop 200. A lyrical place. It was the cradle of Christianity in England during that twilit period following the Roman exodus. There is a refreshing dirt-smudged village, a 16thC castle built on a knoll, the haggard ruins of the 11thC priory, and a farm or two. Swimming is safe.

Holy Island

Jarrow H5
Durham. Part of the teeming industrial Tyneside, it was the scene of intense poverty in 1933 following the closing of the shipyards. The desperate hunger march which followed was a forlorn kick in the crotch of an apathetic and complacent Britain.
Have a look at St Paul's church and the remains of the monastery in which the Venerable Bede spent his life in the 8thC.

Maryport A6
Cumbria. Pop 11,600. EC Wed. Once a busy port until the docks silted up, it is now a quiet holiday resort and small industrial town. The Romans built a fort here. Have a look at the Roman altars and relics in the local museum. Good sandy beaches.

Millom B9
Cumbria. Pop 7,100. EC Wed. MD Mon. Tucked into a corner of the Duddon Estuary is this bright and animated little stone-built town silhouetted by Black Combe Mountain. Of interest – the 14thC castle; the late Norman church of Holy Trinity.
A good centre for fell walking. Marshy shore and low tide mud flats.

Newbiggin-by-the-Sea G4
Northumberland. Pop 10,700. EC Wed. Huddled in a horseshoe of sand is an indiscriminate cluster of cottages. A stone breakwater provides harbour for a handful of brightly coloured cobbles. Look at the 13thC church of St Bartholomew.
White sandy beach; good swimming.

Ravenglass A8
Cumbria. EC Sat. An endearing fishing village of cottages wedged between shingle foreshore and a steep wooded ridge of land behind. Of interest – the Eskdale Miniature Railway; the four-acre Roman fort; the Methodist chapel built in 1848.

Redcar J7
Durham. Not a very beautiful town to look at but the place to go for sand and sea. There are three miles of sandy beaches and good facilities for children to the east of the town. The neighbouring towns of Coatham to the north and Marske and Saltburn to the south have turned this stretch of coast into a playground for the workers of Teesside. Beaches are sandy, patrolled by lifeguards, and safe for swimming. Some mackerel fishing, and fresh crab and lobster for sale on Redcar's beaches.

Robin Hood's Bay K8
N. York. Yorkshire's most picturesque fishing village. A jocular mob of buildings tumbles round a tight maze of steep streets. The bay itself is a curve of rocky cliffs that overlook a foreshore scattered with large boulders. Rocky beaches.

Robin Hood's Bay

St. Bees A8
Cumbria. Pop 1,200. EC Wed. A sympathetic and silent village which grew up round a 7thC priory and a Norman abbey of the 12thC.
A broad shingle bank reinforces the sandy beach.

Scarborough East K9
N. York. Pop 44,400. EC Wed. MD Thur. Electric and elegant. The discovery of medicinal springs in 1620 started the town off as a spa to be visited by people of fashion, and the invention of the bathing machine added the attractions of sea water to the 'cure'. The natural beauty of Scarborough's two great bays has ensured the town's continuing success as a resort. Jammed between the two is the ruined castle, standing on an imposing headland.
Of interest – The Crescent (1832) which puts Scarborough on a par with Bath and Edinburgh; the Mere, a sheltered lake. Beaches are sandy in both bays, and there

are two good heated outdoor pools for those too timid to brave the North Sea.

Seascale   A8
Cumbria. Pop 2,000. Pleasant uncommercialised place along a gentle sea shore. Of interest – St Cuthbert's church built in 1890; 18thC Seascale Hall; Windscale and Calder Hall atomic stations.

Silecroft   A9
Cumbria. An ordinary village leads to a spectacular stretch of sandy beach, open-ended to the sky.

Silloth   A6
Cumbria. Pop 2,700. EC Wed. Broad, practical streets of simple yet dignified terraced houses make up this mid-Victorian holiday resort.
Separated from the sea by an expansive green and a wave of pine trees. There are exhilarating views to the Scottish coastline. Pleasant sandy beach.

South Shields   H5
Tyne & Wear. Pop 96,900. EC Wed. MD Mon, Sat. A popular seaside resort and busy port stranded at the southern shore of the Tyne Estuary. It was here that the world's first lifeboat service began. Of interest – Roman fort at the north end of Baring Street; the museum with the prototype model of the first lifeboat designed in 1790 by William Wouldhave.
Mile-long pier sheltering a sandy beach. Safe bathing.

Staithes   K7
N. York. A tough little village that hasn't changed much since the days when Captain Cook explored it as a boy. There are steep streets with abrupt changes of level as the village tries to adjust to its precipitous site. Swimming is safe only from a few sheltered sandy patches among the rocks when the tide is in.

Sunderland   H5
Tyne & Wear. Pop 214,800. Having wisely chosen to throw in its lot with Cromwell during the Civil War, Sunderland then benefited from a judicious takeover of the coal trade from Royalist Newcastle.
Able to trace its origins back to the 7thC, the town has also been a busy shipbuilding centre since the 14thC. Of interest – the stuffed walrus in the museum, said to have inspired Lewis Carroll's 'The Walrus and the Carpenter'; the football team; the new civic centre.
Wide beaches with safe bathing.

Tynemouth   H5
Tyne & Wear. Pop 67,000. EC Wed. At its best a bright and bracing place terracing the cliff tops to the north of the river mouth. This was the fashionable part in the early 19thC when Tynemouth was a popular watering place. Of interest – ruins of the 11thC priory; the 14thC castle ruins; the terrace houses in Dawson Square, Bath Terrace and Allendale Place.
Magnificent sea front, particularly Long Sands.

Tynemouth Priory

Warkworth   G3
Northumberland. Pop 1,200. EC Thur. Dominated by its 12thC castle, an alive little town above a loop of the Coquet. Of interest – the 14thC fortified bridge complete with tower; the 18thC Bridge End House; the Norman church of St Laurence. Sandy beach one mile away.

Whitby   K8
W. York. Pop 12,700. EC Wed. MD Sat. One of the best towns on the east coast. This is the spot where Captain Cook started his sailing life in coal ships.
Climb up from the busy harbour and nearly 200 steps later you will be at St Mary's church, one of the least spoilt and most fascinating churches in the country. The ruined abbey on the hill was the scene of the great Synod of Whitby in 664.
Sandy bathing beaches to the west of the harbour.

Whitby, York

Whitehaven   A7
Cumbria. Pop 26,700. EC Wed. MD Thur, Sat. A conspicuous and charming place of well cut streets running down to a busy harbour. Inspired by Christopher Wren's plans for rebuilding London after the Great Fire. Its port rivalled Liverpool and Bristol in the 18thC. Of interest – St James's church built 1752-53; the 17thC Town Hall; the old quay of 1687; the 18thC Whitehaven Hospital.

Whitley Bay   H5
Tyne & Wear. Pop 37,800. EC Wed. A busy and bracing place. In the centre of the town is an exotic cabbage-white fun-palace. Sandy beaches provide safe bathing.

Workington   A7
Cumbria. Pop 28,400. EC Thur. MD Wed, Sat. An industrial town grovelling through parks and playing fields on the site of what was once an enormous Roman town and fort. Workington is a town that prospered on the exploitation of coal. Of interest – the delightful Portland Square; St John, Washington Street; 14thC Workington Hall. A mud and sand beach.

Inland towns and villages

Alnwick   G3
Northumberland. Pop 7,100. EC Wed. MD Sat. An undulating and leafy market town full of poker-faced buildings and narrow mediaeval streets, hidden in the shadow of an enormous 12thC castle. Of particular interest is the Hotspur Gate (1450); 15thC church of St Michael; the Lion Bridge, built in 1773 by John Adam; the 18thC town hall.

Alston   D6
Cumbria. Pop 2,100. The highest market town in England. A sharp-tongued but friendly place which slides down a steep hill. From Market Place you can see the bleak heads of the Pennine hills peeping above the rooftops. Alston was once an important mining town until the early 19thC. Look at the 19thC town hall; 18thC Friends' Meeting House; Randalholm Hall.

Ambleside   C8
Cumbria. Pop 2,600. EC Thur. MD Wed. Quiet and unassuming, this grey-slated little town has a literary pedigree as long as your arm with its memories of the Wordsworths, the Coleridges, Ruskin and others. Of interest – the church of St Mary (1850-54); the curious Bridge House; 19thC Rothay Holme.

Bridge House, Ambleside

Appleby   D7
Cumbria. Pop 2,000. EC Thur. MD Sat. This poker-faced place divided by the broad River Eden is the county town. The main street has a touch of Georgian gentility. Look at the 12thC castle; the church of St Lawrence; the 16thC moot hall.

Aysgarth F9
N. York. Pop 200. In the centre of some of the loveliest country in Yorkshire. Stand on the single-span Elizabethan bridge and watch the foaming River Ure plunge over three cataracts. Of interest – St Andrew's church, with good Victorian glass.

Bampton C7
Cumbria. Pop 400. EC Sat. A gentle rustic village, quietly meditating in open-landscape. Pleasant Georgian church.

Barrow-in-Furness B10
Cumbria. Pop 64,000. EC Thur. MD Wed, Fri, Sat. An uncompromising place as hard as nails, famous as an industrial and shipbuilding town. It was here that the monks of Furness Abbey smelted iron with wood in the early 13thC.
The present town developed in the mid 19thC when the local iron field was first exploited. Of interest – the 19thC church of St James; the town hall; Abbey House built 1913-14 by Lutyens.

Bellingham F4
Northumberland. Pop 1,200. A small-scale market town full of plain and simple fare jostled by rollicking hills.

Belsay F4
Northumberland. Pop 500. One of those imperious gestures by which a whole village was bodily uprooted from in front of the drawing room windows of Belsay Hall and neatly rebuilt in a less intrusive part of an estate. This one happened in the 1830s, and the result was an attractive arcade of sandstone shops in the Italianate style. Have a look at the 19thC Belsay Hall; also the ruins of 14thC Belsay Castle.

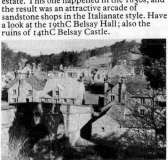

Blanchland. Northumberland

Blanchland F6
Northumberland. Pop 200. EC Tue. A gentle and dignified village in a narrow leafy valley of the Derwent with wild moorland above. Look at Blanchland Abbey, founded in 1165.

Bolton D7
Cumbria. Pop 300. A ruddy-faced village, standing on the west bank of the River Eden. The north and south doorways of the church of All Saints are Norman. Look at the ruins of Bewlay Castle.

Bothal G4
Northumberland. A leafy, sleepy hamlet full of long lost summers. There is an interesting 14thC miniature castle of the tower house type. The little 13thC church has an unusual triple bell tower.

Bowness-on-Windermere C8
Cumbria. Pop 3,500. EC Thur. A wistful place full of the forgotten summers of Victorian England's heyday. Italianate villas and barge-boarded and gabled boarding houses are built out across the waters of Windermere. Of interest – Belle Isle; 19thC Storrs Hall; Broadleys, Voysey's masterpiece built in 1898.

Brampton C5
Cumbria. Pop 4,000. EC Thur. MD Wed. A handsome half-pint of a town wrapped round a hearty market place. Of interest – 19thC church of St Martin with fine stained glass designed by Morris and Burne-Jones. Moot Hall built 1817; Four Gables, a house designed in 1876 by Philip Webb.

Buttermere B6
Cumbria. Pop 255. Like a small fiery featherweight this village is a diminutive tough battling away between two expanses of water. An ideal centre for the Cumbrian Mountains.

Bywell F5
Northumberland. An enchanting derelict in a secluded bend of the Tyne. Every sign of a once lively town has gone. All that remains is a forlorn castle, two wistful parish churches, a vicarage, a farm, a mansion and a mediaeval cross. Bywell Castle is a particularly well preserved tower house of the 15thC.

Carlisle C5
Cumbria. Pop 71,500. EC Thur. MD Wed, Sat. An invigorating hotch-potch full of outspoken chauvinism. Since Roman times, Carlisle has been a key defence and trading centre standing near the western end of Hadrian's Wall. Warred over by the Picts, sacked by the Vikings, and conquered by the Normans it then became a perpetual bottleneck for the border wars between England and Scotland.
The small sandstone cathedral was begun in 1130. Of interest – the castle founded in 1092; the 15thC Tithe Barn; the Citadel built by Sir Robert Smirke in 1807; the 18thC town hall.

Carlisle, Assize Courts

Cockermouth A7
Cumbria. Pop 6,400. EC Thur. MD Mon. A sharply etched market town with an optimistic air. Mary Queen of Scots held court here; Fletcher Christian, leader of the mutiny on the Bounty, and Wordsworth were sons of the town. Of interest – the 13thC castle; church of All Saints; Wordsworth House.

Coniston B8
Cumbria. Pop 1,100. EC Thur. The climbing centre for Coniston Fells. A weather-beaten village as tough as old boots.

Corbridge F5
Northumberland. Pop 2,900. EC Thur. A Tyneside town full of sombre stone-built houses. It wallows over its glorious, if stormy past. It was here Ethelred, King of Northumbria, was slain in 796 and King Ragnal the Dane defeated the English and Scots in 918. Have a look at the Roman camp of Corstopitum; the Saxon church of St Andrew.

Corbridge

Coxwold H9
N. York. Pop 200. A beautiful North Riding village. Particularly interesting is Shandy Hall, a humble brick house where Laurence Sterne lived and wrote 'Tristram Shandy' in 1769. One mile south is Newburgh Priory whose former owners rode to battle in the Light Brigade at Balaclava.

Coxwold, N. York

Crosby Ravensworth D7
Cumbria. Pop 500. Wrapped in antiquity sits this sharp-fisted village. St Lawrence church, enveloped in splendid trees, is invigorating.

Darlington G7
Durham. Pop 85,900. EC Wed. MD Mon, Sat. A blunt and uninhibited place. An energetic little town which grew from a humble Anglo-Saxon settlement, via a lively market and textile town, to being the play-pen of British Rail – until the locomotive engineering shops were closed in 1966. St Cuthbert's with its needle-sharp spire is a fine Early English church.

Durham G6
Durham. Pop 29,500. EC Wed. MD Sat. An ecstatic place, dominated by its cathedral, monastery and castle, the old city struggles over a rocky peninsula wrapped in a loop of the Wear. Founded in 875, the present cathedral was begun in 1093. Of interest – Durham University; some 18thC corners in South Street and Old Elvet Street; the Gulbenkian Museum of Oriental Art; the 13thC monastic ruins of Finchale Priory two miles to the north-east.

Edmondbyers F6
Durham. Pop 200. Crisp as an icicle, the village stands high in the moors. Have a look at the 12thC church; also the giant reservoir built on the River Derwent.

Elsdon E4
Northumberland. Pop 200. A solitary moorland village. A handful of mainly 18thC houses squashed in round a large triangular green. The 14thC church of St Cuthbert has an interesting bell-cote. Look at the remains of St Cuthbert's 11thC motte-and-bailey castle; the stone circles on Catcleugh Hill; the 14thC tower house to the north of the church.

Elsdon, vicar's pele

Pele tower Corbridge

Etal E1
Northumberland. An enchanting piece of village vernacular with a sprinkling of stone and white-washed houses with the occasional thatched roofing. Of interest – the ruins of Etal Castle; the 19thC church of St Mary; the 18thC Etal Manor.

Gainford G7
Durham. Pop 1,100. An unfussy place full of warmth and tranquillity. A mainly stone-built village crowded round a large green and down tight-knit streets. The accent is predominantly Georgian. Of interest – the 13thC church with fine Jacobean font cover.

Gateshead G5
Tyne & Wear. Pop 91,200. EC Wed. A severely practical place devoid of pleasantries in a businessman's world, linked to Newcastle-upon-Tyne by five bridges. A fire in 1854 destroyed most of its past. Here Daniel Defoe is said to have written 'Robinson Crusoe'.

Gilsland D5
Northumberland. EC Wed. When the chalybeate springs were discovered in the 19thC this gentle little village flourished briefly as a spa. It was here Sir Walter Scott met his wife. Have a look at the ambitious Spa Hotel, built 1865; the ruins of Triermain Castle, built in the 14thC.

Grasmere B8
Cumbria. Pop 1,000. EC Thur. A surprising place, jammed between towering crags and broad lake. There is nothing much here but atmosphere, and that's not easily sneezed at. To the south is a handful of houses, Town End. Here, in Dove Cottage, Wordsworth lived with his sister.

Guisborough J7
Cleveland. Pop 14,900. A discreet town

beneath the Cleveland Hills. The long main street is tree-lined and full of unpretentious small houses. Of interest – the dovecote, a rare monastic survivor in the priory ruins; the gargantuan chestnut tree in the priory gardens.

Haydon Bridge E5
Northumberland. A gruff stone-built village straddling the broad South Tyne. Standing alone on a hillside to the north is the old church where the mediaeval village lay. Of interest – the 14thC Langley Castle; the ruined 17thC tower of Staward Pele; the 18thC church.

Haydon Bridge

Heighington G7
Durham. Pop 2,400. A handful of houses thrown together in an endearing tangle round a spacious green. St Michael's is a fine Norman church.

Hesket Newmarket B6
Cumbria. A fine village with a handsome wide high street complete with a rambling green and some elegant 18thC houses. Of interest – 17thC Hesket Hall.

Hesket Newmarket

Heversham C9
Cumbria. Pop 700. An alert and sensitive village spread-eagled on a hill top. The church of St Peter has a delightfully pompous Victorian church tower built in the Early English style. Look at the 14thC Heversham Hall; early 19thC Plum Tree Hall.

Hexham E5
Northumberland. Pop 9,800. EC Thur. MD Tue. A romantic town spread over a hill top. It's been a tempestuous place ravaged by the Danes and pillaged half a dozen times by the Scots. The abbey, founded in 673, makes Hexham important. Have a look at the colonnaded 18thC market building; the Moot Hall, built in 1415; the nine-arched bridge built in 1785.

Hutton-le-Hole J9
N. York. Pop 200. A moorland village with a stream that runs through the centre; a kind of rugged Cotswold scene. The grass verges and village green are kept closely cropped by sheep that roam freely. Do visit the Ryedale Folk Museum.

Kendal C9
Cumbria. Pop 21,700. EC Thur. MD Sat. A grey-faced but breezy town riding a ridge of high ground along a curve in the River Kent. The largest town in the county, Kendal was an important weaving centre in the middle ages. Of interest – the prosperous Perpendicular church of Holy Trinity; the 19thC Friends Meeting House; the earthworks of the 12thC castle; Abbot Hall, built in 1759; Little Holme built by Voysey in 1908.

Keswick B7
Cumbria. Pop 5,200. EC Wed. MD Sat. Within a short distance of Derwentwater, a poetically allusive place of twisting narrow streets. The main street has an unexpected fillip – an early 19thC town hall astride an island site. Charles Lamb came here for holidays whilst Coleridge lived at Greta Hall. Of interest – the Royal Oak Hotel; the three islands on Derwentwater; Salvin's church of St John Evangelist built in 1838; the local museum.

Kirkby Lonsdale D9
Cumbria. Pop 1,500. EC Wed. MD Thur. Dark grey buildings jammed round a market square. As you wander through the town the fells squint round silent corners or pop up above the rooftops. Hidden behind Market Street is the church of St Mary with some rich Norman trappings. Of interest – the motte-and-bailey castle; the mid 19thC Market House; 16thC Abbots Hall.

Kirkby Stephen E8
Cumbria. Pop 1,600. EC Thur. MD Mon.
A sprightly old market town nestling down
amongst the moors. Of interest – the church
of St Stephen with an elegant Perpendicular
west tower; 16thC Wharton Hall.

Kirkwhelpington F4
Northumberland. Pop 200. Well heeled stone
cottages stand gawping round a churchyard
in a rolling sea of farmland.

Lowther Village and New Town C7
Cumbria. Lowther village, a miniature 18thC
masterpiece, consists of two well-mannered
closes of properly proportioned houses.
Not far away is Lowther New Town full of
hipped-roof rusticity. Built in the late 17thC
as a replacement for the old village. Of
interest – the remains of Lowther Castle,
rebuilt by Smirke in 1806; Hackthorpe
Hall, a fine Jacobean house.

Morpeth G4
*Northumberland. Pop 14,100. EC Thur. MD
Wed.* A dog-eared place with only modest
signs of antiquity, and yet it's as old as the
hills. Trapped in a U-bend of the River
Wansbeck it has an unassuming market
place; the town hall rebuilt in 1870, but
originally designed by Sir John Vanbrugh
in 1714; a 15thC clock tower; the ruins of a
12thC Cistercian monastery, Newminster
Abbey.

Newcastle-upon-Tyne G5
*Tyne & Wear. Pop 212,400. EC Wed. MD
Tue, Thur, Sat.* Dreary streets and drab
houses break out into a flourishing hotch-
potch of culture and comfort at the centre o
one of Britain's most important cities. A
dignified and exuberant place. Of interest –
the church of All Saints, built in 1786; the
cathedral; the 17thC guildhall; Central
Station; High Level Bridge, built in 1849 by
Robert Stephenson; the university; the
Theatre Royal.

Newcastle-upon-Tyne

Norham E1
Northumberland. Pop 600. One of the largest
villages in the county, plump and plain like a
grey-haired blue stocking. Eagle-eyed above
it all stands the 12thC castle on high rocks
overshadowing the river.

Orton D8
Cumbria. Pop 600. A place full of earthy
honesty. Have a look at Orton Hall, an
affable Georgian gesture; the 13thC church
of All Saints.

Patterdale C7
Cumbria. Pop 700. EC Wed, Sat. A tranquil
little village hemmed in by Ullswater and
heady mountain peaks. The ordinary
becomes extraordinary against such a
powerful backdrop. Look at Patterdale Hall;
the prehistoric settlement south of Brothers
Water.

Penrith C7
Cumbria. Pop 11,300. EC Wed. MD Tue. An
historic town. Occupied by the Celts in 500
BC, and later by the Romans who built a
road through it. The castle is a compact
square. Look at the Mitre Hotel, 1669, and
the Crown Hotel, 1794; the castle; the
three-acre Roman fort five miles along the
Penrith-Carlisle road.

Peterlee H6
Durham. Pop 21,800. EC Wed. A distinctive
but self-conscious new town built to
accommodate 30,000 people.

Richmond E3
N. York. Pop 7,200. EC Wed. MD Sat. This
is the one after which all the other
Richmonds are named. A beautiful town with
a busy cobbled market place and masses of
fascinating buildings. Do not fail to see the

Richmond

theatre built in 1788 and completely restored
in 1962 – it is one of the oldest theatres still
in use.
There is a strong masculine profile to
Richmond, and it is still the garrison town
for Catterick Camp, and regimental
headquarters of the famous Green Howards.

Rosthwaite B7
Cumbria. EC Wed. A sprinkling of houses
amongst peaks and fells. Everything sharp,
bright and crisp.

Rothbury F3
Northumberland. Pop 1,800. EC Wed. An
attractively situated hillside town in the heart
of Coquetdale and in the shadow of wooded
hills. Of interest – Whitton, a 14thC tower
house; Norman Shaw's mansion, Cragside,
built in 1870.

Rothbury

Sedgefield G7
Durham. Pop 5,300. Half asleep round a
more than comfortable green is this pleasant
small-scale market-town. The 13thC church
has an alert and sharp-faced nave.

Simonburn E5
Northumberland. Pop 200. Whitewashed
cottages gather about a square green. Of
interest – the 13thC ruined castle.

Stamfordham F5
Northumberland. Pop 1,200. A lean and
lanky village green trapped by rows of 18thC
houses. Of interest – the little market
building; the 13thC church.

Stanhope F6
Durham. Pop 5,100. 700 feet up, with the
fells all around, Stanhope is a handsome
little Weardale town memorable for its lime
trees. There is a mediaeval church, some
18thC houses and a castle built in 1798.

Tebay D8
Cumbria. Pop 700. A railway village of
apparent rock-faced indifference until you
get to know it. Look at the church of St
James, built by the sweat of railway workers
and their companies in 1880. Nor far away
is the site of a motte-and-bailey castle.

Temple Sowerby D7
Cumbria. Pop 300. EC Thur. Discreetly,
this small scale village awakens your every
sense to the pleasanter things in life. Of
interest – the church of St James; Temple
Sowerby Manor.

Thirsk H9
N. York. Pop 2,900. EC Wed. MD Mon. It
was in this busy market town with its ancient
cross that Thomas Lord was born in 1755.
He went on to found the cricket ground,
Lord's, in London.
The town was once an important posting
station on the stage coach routes; nowadays
visited for the panoramic views of the Vale
of York, and for an excellent horse racing
course. Growing in importance as a gliding
centre.

Thorton Dale, York

Thorton Dale K9
N. York. Pop 1,200. EC Wed. Largely
unscathed by the visitors attracted to 'the
prettiest village in Yorkshire'; all its scenic
charms remain. Good centre to hire a nag
and go riding over the dales.

Troutbeck C8
Cumbria. EC Thur. An alert handful of
houses thrown casually along a spectacular
and wild valley. There is some fine stained
glass by Burne-Jones and Morris in Jesus
Chapel; Town End is a fine yeoman
farmhouse built in 1626.

Wark-on-Tyne E4
Northumberland. Pop 700. EC Thur. An
invigorating group of pleasantries snuggling
round a central green. Look at Chipchase
Castle; the early 19thC church of St
Michael.

Whittingham F3
Northumberland. Pop 400. This demure little
place straddles the River Aln. Of interest –
Callaly Castle; Eslington Hall; Whittingham
Tower.

Windermere C8
Cumbria. Pop 8,000. EC Thur. Formerly a
small lakeside village, it was popular during
the railway age, and has been a holiday
centre ever since. Of interest – the 19thC
church of St Mary; the splendid Gothic
priory; 17thC Rayrigg Hall.

Wooler F2
Northumberland. Pop 2,000. EC Thur.
Frequently raided during the middle ages;
now mainly a 19thC market town clambering
eagerly up a hillside to its church tower.

Regional oddities

Fortified houses and churches
Perpetual raids from marauding Scots
created problems for those outside the
castle walls. From the 13th to the 16thC
many houses and churches were fortified.
Church towers often provided refuge with
access to an upper floor being by ladder only.
Marks on the door pillars of Elsdon Church,
Northumberland, are said to have been made
by parishioners sharpening their swords
when called from prayer to battle.
The most distinctive feature of the area is
the tower house. Called pele-towers, after
the Latin *palus*, meaning stockade, they
consisted of a barricaded ground floor for
cattle; people took refuge on the first floor.
The floor itself was vaulted as a precaution
against fire. Living quarters were later added
to many of the towers. Good examples at
Corbridge, Doddington, Aydon Castle,
Cresswell, Dacre and Grasstoke.

The Lake poets B7
Grasmere and Keswick, Cumbria.
Wordsworth's arrival at Dove Cottage
precipitated an avalanche of poets on the
Lake District. Coleridge and his family
settled at Great Hall, Keswick, in 1800.
Robert Southey arrived in 1803 (he and his
family are buried in the churchyard in
Keswick), and Hartley Coleridge came later
and is now buried in the same churchyard.

The White Horse, Kilburn, York.

The White Horse H9
Kilburn, N. York. A giant horse cut into the
turf of the Hambleton Hills, it is really big;
over 300 feet long. You can see it clearly
from a distance of twenty miles and twenty
people can picnic quite comfortably on the
grass eye.

Famous people

Dr Thomas Arnold (1795-1842) C8
Foxhowe, Ambleside, Cumbria. The renowned
headmaster of Rugby spent his summers at
Foxhowe with his family.

Thomas Bewick (1753-1828) F5
*Cherryburn House, Ovingham,
Northumberland.* Noted for his illustrations
to 'Gay's Fables', 'Select Fables', and the
famous 'British Birds' this superb wood
engraver was born at Cherryburn, and is
buried in the churchyard at Ovingham.

Lancelot 'Capability' Brown
(1715-83) F4
Kirkharle, Northumberland. The landscape
gardener and architect was born in
Kirkharle. His debut as a landscape
gardener was at Kirkharle Park, which is
now a farm.

James Cook (1728-79) H7
*Stewarts Park, Marton, Middlesbrough,
Cleveland.* This small museum is dedicated
to the great circumnavigator who was born in
Marton. He spent his childhood in Great
Ayton where he attended the local village
school. A granite obelisk now marks the spot
on nearby Easby Moor where his cottage
once stood – since transported to Melbourne,
Australia. *Museum open daily. Closed Sun &
Mon.*

Harriet Martineau (1802-76) C8
*The Knoll, Clappersgate, Ambleside,
Cumbria.* The much loved literary lioness
built The Knoll, where she spent the last 30
years of her life. She entertained many of the
leading literary figures of her day, and among
those who visited Ambleside were Charlotte
Brontë, Emerson, George Eliot and
Wordsworth.

Beatrix Potter (1866-1943) C8
Hill Top, Near Sawrey, Cumbria. Beatrix
Potter lived in this 17thC house. While she
was busy creating her Peter Rabbit books a
parade of small animals inhabited the house,
from mice to rabbits and pigs. When she
married and went to live on a neighbouring
farm her writing virtually ceased. *Open
11.00-17.30 daily mid Apr-Oct. Closed Sun
morning.*

John Ruskin (1819-1900) B8
Brantwood, Coniston, Cumbria. Ruskin lived
here from 1871 until his death. The house is
now owned by the Council of Nature, and
relics and paintings are on show. A fine
collection of related manuscripts, drawings
and photographs at the Ruskin Museum
near the church. *Brantwood open 10.00-17.0
Sun-Fri, Mar-Oct. Nov-Feb by appointment.*

Laurence Sterne (1713-68) H9
Shandy Hall, Coxwold, N. York. Sterne
wrote part of 'Tristram Shandy' and 'A
Sentimental Journey' here. The 15thC hall
was renamed in his honour, and is now a
museum. Sterne is buried in the churchyard
nearby. *Open 14.00-18.00 Wed Jun-Sep.*

Sir Hugh Walpole (1884-1941) B7
Brackenburn, Keswick, Cumbria. The New
Zealand writer lived here for many years.
The surrounding country was the
background for many of his novels,
particularly the ever popular and gloomy
'Herries' series. He is buried in the
churchyard of St John's in Keswick.

William Wordsworth (1770-1850) B8
*Dove Cottage, Town End, Grasmere,
Cumbria.* Most of the poet laureate's life was
centred round the Lake District. He was
born in Cockermouth and grew up there and
in Hawkshead and Penrith.
In 1799 he moved to Dove Cottage with his
sister Dorothy. His most productive years
were spent here, living with Dorothy, with
Coleridge as a constant companion, and in
1802 with his wife Mary Hutchinson. He is
buried in the churchyard. *Open 9.30-17.30
daily May-Nov. 10.00-16.15 Oct-Apr.
Closed Sun May-Nov.*

Cathedrals, abbeys & churches

All Saints G5
Newcastle-upon-Tyne, Tyne & Wear. Proud and expressive, like a trumpet voluntary. Built by David Stephenson in 1786, it towers above the quayside. Some extravagant woodwork inside.

Brinkburn Priory F3
Brinkburn, Northumberland. The Augustinian priory was founded about 1135 in a secluded loop of the Coquet, and was a roofless ruin until restored in 1858. A cavern of a building, it is one of the most dignified and elegant Gothic churches in Northumberland.

Carlisle Cathedral, Cumbria.

Carlisle Cathedral C5
Carlisle, Cumbria. Originally part of an Augustinian abbey, it became a cathedral in 1133. Only two bays of the Norman nave are left. Have a look at the magnificent 14thC east end.

Durham Cathedral, Durham.

Durham Cathedral G6
Durham. Begun in 1096 this is the most impressively situated of all the English cathedrals as it soars above the wooded cliffs of the River Wear. The Norman nave is the most spectacular in Europe.

Gibside Chapel G5
Gibside, Tyne & Wear. Standing in grounds landscaped by Capability Brown is this late 18thC chapel dressed in the most impeccable of classical garments.

Pittington Church G6
Pittington, Durham. An alert and sensitive church. Originally Anglo-Saxon, it has a fine 12thC north arcade, composed of six round arches with bold zigzag carving. Pleasant Norman font.

Priory Church E5
Hexham, Northumberland. Extremes jammed up against each other in the most unpredictable of ways – brilliant in one part, dull in another. Founded in 673, the building today consists of a patchwork of early 13thC and late 19thC pieces.

St Andrew's F4
Bolam, Northumberland. A mildly mannered church with a late Saxon tower, tall and unbuttressed. Predominantly Norman interior.

St James A7
Whitehaven, Cumbria. Built 1752-53 it stands on a hill. Nothing special outside, but the inside is a glowing Georgian interior, as magnificent as anything in the county.

St John's F2
Edlingham, Northumberland. A fierce little church with half a mind to swap roles with some fortified castle. The Norman porch has a tunnel vault.

church, Escomb

St John's G7
Escomb, Durham. An Anglo-Saxon church as sharp as the north wind. Probably built in the 7thC, it's the most complete example of its kind. Have a look at the striking round-headed chancel arch; the pre-Norman carved stone cross behind the altar.

St Martin's C5
Brampton, Cumbria. The only church by Philip Webb. Built 1874-78 it's a jittery and jumpy masterpiece, like a nervous prima donna. A strange and imaginative building, with vibrant stained glass by William Morris and Burne-Jones.

Brampton church.

St Mary's F7
Staindrop, Durham. An enviable little masterpiece of Anglo-Saxon descent. The west tower, aisles and arcades are Norman. In the 14thC the south aisle and porch were added. The only pre-Reformation screen in the country is here.

St Michael's B6
Torpenhow, Cumbria. An unpretentious little masterpiece built in 1170. The interior is warm and friendly. Bell cote and battlements are 17thC.

St Laurence G3
Warkworth, Northumberland. An imposing and forceful monolith. A fairly complete Norman church unique in Northumberland. St Laurence has one of the few vaulted chancels of 12thC England.

St Nicholas Cathedral G5
Newcastle-upon-Tyne, Tyne & Wear. Outside it's an affable 14th and 15thC parish church made a cathedral in 1882. The joyous and distinguished 'crown spire' was built in 1435. The interior is something special – alert and sensitive.

SS Andrew and Peter F5
Bywell, Northumberland. Two unlikely miracles – St Andrew's, called the White Church because it belonged to the White Canons of Blanchland, has a fabulous Saxon tower; St Peter's, called the Black Church because it belonged to the Benedictine monks of Durham, is pleasantly 13thC with some invigorating 11thC leftovers.

SS Mary and Bega A8
St Bees, Cumbria. Originally part of a 12thC Benedictine priory, an expressive and memorable building. The doorway is an exotic Norman masterpiece complete with figure work and zigzag ornamentation.

Castles and ruins

Alnwick Castle   G3
Alnwick, Northumberland. An explosive
powerhouse which began life as a wooden
motte-and-bailey. In 1157 a stone shell-keep
was built. The Percys purchased the castle in
1309, and by the middle of the 14thC it had
assumed its present form.
Considerably restored in the late 18thC and
early 19thC. The barbican is the best in the
country. Many splendidly furnished rooms
and a magnificent grand staircase. *Open
13.00–17.00 daily May-late Sep. Closed Fri.*

Bamburgh Castle   G1
Bamburgh, Northumberland. A lion of a
castle, standing confidently on its own on a
precipitous outcrop of the Whin Sill. An
enormous spectacle over a quarter of a mile
long and covering eight and a half acres. It
consists of a 12thC keep and three baileys.
Derelict throughout much of the 18thC, it
was drastically restored in the late 19thC.
Open 14.00–20.00 daily mid Apr-Sep.

Barnard Castle   F7
Barnard Castle, Durham. A violent and
agitated skeleton glowering down from a cliff
above the Tees. Built in 1150. Of interest –
the 14thC Round Tower, said to have
inspired Sir Walter Scott when he was
writing 'Rokeby'. *Open 9.30–17.30 Mar, Arp
& Oct, 9.30–19.00 May-Sep, 9.30–16.00
Nov-Feb. Closed Sun morning.*

Belsay Castle   F4
Belsay, Northumberland. An aggressive
muscle bound thug thrown together in the
mid-14thC. It's a single tower castle, with a
later house added in 1614.

Bowes Castle   F8
Bowes, Durham. On A66 to Brough. A
massive keep, built for Henry II in 1171.
Made of sandstone including some re-used
Roman materials, it was meant to guard the
Yorkshire approach to Stainmore Pass over
the Pennines. *Open 9.30–17.30 Mar, Apr &
Oct, 9.30–19.00 May-Sep, 9.30–16.00
Nov-Feb. Closed Sun morning.*

Brough Castle   E7
Brough, Cumbria. A majestic ruin, like an
aging eccentric. Begun in the late 11thC it is
perched in a dominant position above a steep
bank of the Swindale Beck. *Open 9.30–17.30
Mar, Apr & Oct, 9.30–19.00 May-Sep,
9.30–16.00 Nov-Feb. Closed Sun morning.*

Brougham Castle   C7
Penrith, Cumbria. Begun in the 12thC, it's an
impressive and explosive giant. Built on the
banks of the River Eamont, the castle is
largely late 13thC. Of interest – outer and
inner gatehouses; the keep. *Open 9.30–17.30
Mar, Apr & Oct, 9.30–19.00 May-Sep,
9.30–16.00 Nov-Feb. Closed Sun morning.*

Calder Abbey   A8
Calder Bridge, Cumbria. Founded in 1135 by
William de Meschines for the order of
Savigny, all that remains are the ruins of the
cloister, the nave and church aisles. Part of
the monastic buildings are tucked inside a
late Georgian house. *Open 10.00–16.00 Fri.*

Carlisle Abbey   C5
Carlisle, Cumbria. Standing on the highest
point along the Eden it guarded the west end
of the border in case of a Scottish attack. The
existing keep was built in the 12thC. Of
interest – Tile Tower; Queen Mary's
Tower; the museum. *Open 9.30–17.30 daily
Apr & 9.30–19.00 May-Sep. (9.30–17.30
Mar & Oct. 9.30–16.00 Nov-Feb. Closed Sun
morning.)*

Dunstanburgh Castle   G2
Northumberland. 2 miles e of Embleton. A
forlorn skeleton clutching the coastal cliffs.
It was a great 14thC fortress. Below was the

Dunstanburgh Castle

harbour, now blocked, which once sheltered
Henry VIII's navy. *Open 9.30–17.30 Mar,
Apr & Oct, 9.30–19.00 May-Sep, 9.30–16.00
Nov-Feb. Closed Sun morning.*

Egglestone Abbey, York

Egglestone Abbey   F7
Durham. N of Richmond. Situated close to
the River Tees, the abbey was built for the
Premonstratensian canons in 1196. Now just
a very romantic ruin set in woods and water.
Turner painted the ruins. Visit by
moonlight. *Open 9.30–17.30 Mar, Apr &
Oct, 9.30–19.00 May-Sep, 9.30–16.00 Nov-
Feb. Closed Sun morning.*

Finchale Priory   G6
Durham. 4 miles n of Durham. Trapped in a
bend of the Wear are the wistful ruins of this
priory. A stone chapel was built in the 12thC
on the site of a hut where St Godric lived as a
hermit. This was later extensively enlarged
by Durham Priory in the 13thC. *Open
9.30–17.30 daily Apr & 9.30–19.00 May-
Sep. (9.30–17.30 Mar & Oct. 9.30–16.00
Nov-Feb. Closed Sun morning.)*

Haughton Castle.

Haughton Castle   E5
Humshaugh, Northumberland. Begun in the
late 13thC, this finely proportioned
tower-house was heavily restored and
altered in the late 19thC. The setting is
spectacular.

Lanercost Priory   C5
Brampton, Cumbria. A tranquil ruin tucked
into a secluded corner along the River
Irthing. The priory was founded in 1144 by
Robert de Vaux for the Augustinian canons.
The church is exceptionally well preserved.
*Open 9.30–17.30 Mar, Apr & Oct, 9.30–
19.00 May-Sep, 9.30–16.00 Nov-Feb. Closed
Sun morning.*

Langley Castle   E5
Haydon Bridge, Northumberland. Built like a
knuckleduster, it's a battlemented 14thC
tower house ready to strike. Restored by the
historian Cadwallader Brown, at the end of
the last century. Now an entertainment centre
with banquets and dances. *Open all year.*

Lindisfarne Priory   F1
Holy Island, Northumberland. Founded by
the Benedictines in the 11thC it's a
weather-beaten dark red ruin as sharp as
broken glass. Much of the original detailing
was copied from Durham Cathedral. Have a
look in the museum. *Open daily Apr &
9.30–19.00 May-Sep. (9.30–17.30 Mar &
Oct. 9.30–16.00 Nov-Feb, Closed Sun
morning.)*

Middleham Castle   F9
Leyburn, N.York. On A6108 to Ripon. Built
to guard the road from Richmond to Skipton,
it is a rectangular Norman keep of 1170, and
one of the largest in England: 105 by 78 feet.
Ruins of the chapel and gatehouse also
remain. *Open 9.30–17.30 Mar, Apr & Oct,
9.30–19.30 May-Sep, 9.30–16.00 Nov-Feb.
Closed Sun morning.*

Naworth Castle   D5
Cumbria, Ne of Brampton. Freshened up by
Salvin after a disastrous fire in 1844, it is
wrapped round a central courtyard. Built on
an impressive site it was begun in 1335.
Extensive alterations and additions were
made in the 16thC. Of interest – the great
hall; Lord William Howard's Tower; fine
tapestries. *Private.*

Norham Castle

Norham Castle   E1
Norham, Northumberland. Planted
menacingly on high rocks above the River
Tweed are the remains of a once powerful
border stronghold. It was built in 1160 by
Bishop Pudsey of Durham. *Open 9.30-
17.30 Mar, Apr & Oct, 9.30-19.00 May-
Sep, 9.30-16.00 Nov-Feb. Closed Sun
morning.*

Richmond Castle   G8
Richmond, N. York. A huge, almost square
keep built by the Normans to dominate
Swaledale. Long walls of 11thC masonry run
for 150 yards along the river-side. Visit the
barbican, Robin Hood's Tower and
St Nicholas's Chapel. *Open 9.30-17.30 daily •
Apr & 9.30-19.00 May-Sep. (9.30-17.30
Mar & Oct. 9.30-16.00 Nov-Feb. Closed Sun
morning.)*

Rievaulx Abbey, York.

Rievaulx Abbey   J9
N. York. 2½ miles nw of Helmsley. Must be
seen first from the Rievaulx Terraces.
The Cistercians founded the monastery on
the banks of the Rye in 1131. The choir and
presbytery have good stone ribbed vaults,
arcading and moulded capitals. The
140-foot-square cloister is surprisingly
complete. *Open 9.30-17.30 daily Apr &
9.30-19.00 May-Sep. (9.30-17.30 Mar &
Oct. 9.30-16.00 Nov-Feb. Closed Sun
morning.)*

Scarborough Castle   East K9
Scarborough, N. York. This is the castle
that Edward II gave to his favourite, Piers
Gaveston. Situated on a headland it surveys
a narrow neck of land that links it to the
mainland. Today it remains a mass of 13thC
walls and dykes – it looks pretty frightening,
even the Germans had a go at it from the sea
in 1914. *Open 9.30-17.30 daily Apr &
9.30-19.00 May-Sep. (9.30-17.30 Mar &
Oct. 9.30-16.00 Nov-Feb. Closed Sun
morning.)*

Shap Abbey   D7
Shap, Cumbria. Founded in the late 12thC. A
thin wistful skeleton buried in a valley of the
River Lowther. Very little remains except
memories. *Open 9.30-17.30 Mar, Apr &
Oct, 9.30-19.00 May-Sep, 9.30-16.00
Nov-Feb. Closed Sun morning.*

Sizergh Castle   C9
Cumbria. 3 miles s of Kendal on A6. Since
1239 owned by the Strickland family. A
14thC pele-tower, perhaps one of the most
memorable houses of its type in
the area. There is a wealth of early
Elizabethan woodwork and some fine
chimney pieces. *Open 14.00-17.45 Wed &
Sun Apr-Sep, also Thu Jul & Aug.*

Warkworth Castle   G3
Warkworth, Northumberland. A domineering
bully sneering at all and sundry from the top
of a high hill. Building was begun in the
12thC, and the great keep was added in the
late 14thC. *Open 9.30-17.30 daily Apr &
9.30-19.00 May-Sep. (9.30-17.30 Mar &
Oct. 9.30-16.00 Nov-Feb. Closed Sun
morning.)*

Warkworth Castle

Unusual buildings

Calder Hall and Windscale   A8
Calder Bridge, Cumbria. Calder Hall, which
was opened in 1956, was the first full-scale
nuclear power station in the world. It
consists of two giant cooling towers and
three reactor buildings built like elephantine
car batteries. Windscale, opened in 1951, is a
plant producing plutonium.

The Devil's
Bridge   D9
*Kirkby Lonsdale,
Cumbria.* Spanning
the River Lune, an
elegant stone bridge
built with three
acrobatically round
arches. Probably
15thC.

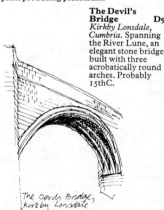

The Devils Bridge,
Kirkby Lonsdale

Dunelm House,
Durham University   G6
Durham. Seen at its best across the River
Wear. An alert and cheeky building skipping
along the edges of a sloping bank. Designed
by Architects Co-Partnership in 1964, it is
the university staff house and student club.
The elegant and slender footbridge is by
Ove Arup.

Scarborough Castle, York.

Fylingdales Early Warning Station, York.

Fylingdales Early Warning Station　　　　　**K8**
Fylingdales, N. York. At vast expense, and some cost to the beauty of Fylingdales Moor, we have seven minutes warning before the nuclear holocaust.

Penshaw Monument　　　　　**G5**
Penshaw, Tyne & Wear. A smut grey Doric temple shivering in the northern light. Built in 1844 as a memorial to John George Lambton, first Earl of Durham and first High Commissioner to Canada. This roofless edifice is more at home in Paestum than on Penshaw Hill.

Raby Castle Folly　　　　　**F7**
Staindrop, Durham. Standing on a hill behind the castle, about 25 feet high with a long castellated facade with pairs of tapering stone towers on either side of an arch. Gothic windows have been painted on the brick between the towers. The whole thing's ludicrous but jolly.

Sharp's Folly　　　　　**F3**
Whitton, Northumberland. Used as an observatory and prospect tower it's a plain round tower, 30 feet high. Built in 1720 and designed to relieve unemployment among stone masons in Archdeacon Thomas Sharp's parish.

Berwick-on-Tweed

Town Hall　　　　　**F1**
Berwick-upon-Tweed, Northumberland. Built 1754-60 this contrary little monster stands bold as brass in the most prominent part of the main square, Marygate. It is a severe somewhat Wagnerian orphan with a giant portico of Tuscan columns up a high flight of stairs. The top floor was once the town gaol. Above is a socking great belfry.

Twizell Bridge

Twizel Bridge　　　　　**E1**
Twizel Bridge, Northumberland. A beautifully shaped 15thC stone bridge slung in a single 90-foot span across the wooded glen of the Till.

Union Bridge　　　　　**E1**
Horncliffe, Northumberland. Built in 1820 by Sir Samuel Brown. The first suspension bridge to be built in England, over 140 yards in length. It's an elegant chain structure suspended between the wooded banks of the Tweed.

union bridge

Houses and gardens

Acorn Bank　　　　　**D7**
Temple Sowerby, Cumbria. Set against a red sandstone house, the herb garden is of special interest here. There is also a delightful walled herbaceous garden and lots of bulbs in spring. *Open daily mid Apr-late Oct.*

Askham Hall　　　　　**C7**
Lowther, Cumbria. A 14thC tower house with Elizabethan wings spread round an oblong courtyard. Fine 17thC staircase.

Askham Hall

Aydon Castle　　　　　**F5**
Corbridge, Northumberland. Aydon Castle is a fortified manor house built in the early 14thC. It glares out above the Cor Burn from a steep and densely wooded slope. It consists of an outer bailey to the north, an inner bailey with square walls, and a hall along the south side.

Belsay Hall　　　　　**F4**
Belsay, Northumberland. A lovely honey-coloured stone house built 1810-17. Created by the owner, Sir Charles Monck, following studies undertaken during his honeymoon in Athens. Raised on a podium like a Greek temple the front facade is punctuated by giant Doric columns; the others by Doric pilasters.

Belsay

Chesters　　　　　**E5**
Chollerford, Northumberland. The house was built originally in 1771, and considerably enlarged and altered by Norman Shaw in 1891 with the best of his cosmetic art. The result was a dextrous interpretation of the picturesque and romantic English 18thC.

Chillingham Castle　　　　　**F2**
Northumberland. 6½ miles se of Wooler. Now falling into decorous decay this mediaeval castle was built in 1344 and drastically updated by Wyatville in 1828. The result is an involved but sensitive masterpiece set in a gargantuan park of lyrical beauty. *Open 10.00-17.00 weekdays Apr-Oct. (Closed Tue, Sat & Sun.)*

Chillingham Castle

Chipchase Castle　　　　　**E4**
Chipchase, Northumberland. One of those tricks that nature is usually best at. A large mid-14thC tower crossed with a Jacobean mansion and Georgian additions – and hey presto, an elegant rough house.

Chipchase Castle

Cragside

Cragside F3
Rothbury, Northumberland. A heady and romantic Wagnerian giant set against a theatrical back-drop. In real life the mansion is a turreted and bay-windowed Tudor myth created by Norman Shaw for the first Lord Armstrong in 1870. Some lush William Morris glass in the library. *Grounds only open 10.00-20.00 daily mid Apr-late Sep.*

Hutton-in-the-Forest C6
Cumbria. E of Skelton. Originally a 14thC pele-tower. The exuberant bits of Jacobean and Baroque were added with some panache during the 17thC. The whole thing's an elaborate juggling trick not to be taken too seriously. Later additions date from the 19thC. *Gardens open all year. House by appointment only.*

Levens Hall C9
Levens, Cumbria. A richly evocative Elizabethan house consisting of pele-tower and an attached hall. Of interest – the grand staircase; plasterwork ceiling in the drawing room.
The topiary garden is one of England's most famous. Laid out in 1689 by Beaumont, there are fantastic forms cut in yew and box including 'Maids of Honour', 'Coach and Horses', as well as birds and other incredible shapes. *Open daily Apr-mid Sep. (House closed Mon, Fri & Sat.)*

Lowther Castle C7
Lowther, Cumbria. A gaunt and garrulous shell of a once spectacular house. Begun in 1806; the architect was Smirke, fresh from Greece and Italy. *Open 10.00-17.00 July & Aug.*

Lowther Castle

Middleton Hall D9
Middleton, Cumbria. An unobtrusive manor house built round a courtyard in the 15thC.

Moresby Hall A7
Moresby, Cumbria. 2 miles nne of Whitehaven. An elaborately rusticated building all dark and brooding. Built 1690-1700.

Muncaster Castle A8
Ravenglass, Cumbria. An elaborate and sumptuous building standing in magnificent landscape. Completely reconstructed by Anthony Salvin in 1862, the original castle was built in the 13thC. Splendid collection of furniture; some beautiful chimney pieces. A lush 300-acre garden. *Open 13.00-18.00 Tues, Wed, Thur, Sun & B. Hols mid Apr-Oct.*

Nunnykirk Hall F4
Netherwitton, Northumberland. Built in 1825, it is one of the finest of all Dobson's early houses. There is an elaborate Ionic porte cochere on the entrance side.

Nunnykirk

Raby Castle Gardens F7
Staindrop, Durham. Nw of Darlington. A ten-acre sheltered garden famous for sweet peas. There are also large walled formal gardens, majestic trees, clipped yews and a good collection of fruit trees. Herds of deer wander at will through the 270-acre park. *Open 14.00-17.00 daily Aug. Wed, Sat & Sun Jun, Jul & Sep.*

Rydal Mount C8
Ambleside, Cumbria. Wordsworth's home for over 37 years, the very interesting garden with its two long terraces was designed by the great man himself. Many unusual trees and shrubs. See also Dora's Field (1½ miles north-west of Ambleside), one and a half acres of daffodils planted by the poet for his daughter. *Open daily Mar-Jan.*

Seaton Delaval Hall G4
Northumberland. ½ mile from coast at Seaton Sluice. Begun in 1720 it is one of the best of Vanbrugh's great houses. A haunting and magnificent place of sombre grey stone. A square symmetrical Palladian plan with a touch of Piranesi creeping in at dusty corners. *Open 14.00-18.00 Wed, Sun & B. Hols May-Sep.*

Seaton Delaval

Wallington Hall F4
Cambo, Northumberland. 12 miles w of Morpeth on B6342. A late 17thC mansion built in a lush park. In 1855, on the advice of Ruskin, a breath of fresh air crept in. The courtyard was roofed in and given an Italianate arcade. For the mural paintings he suggested William Bell Scott, a follower of the Pre-Raphaelites. The whole effect is electric.
The gardens, half-a-mile away from the house, were laid out by Capability Brown in 1766. The conservatory has a superb collection of fuchsias. *Open 14.00-18.00 Mon, Wed, Thur, Sat & Sun Apr-late Sep. 14.00-17.00 Sat & Sun Oct.*

Washington Old Hall G5
Washington, Durham. The home of George Washington's ancestors, it's an early 17thC manor house. An awkward rather cottagey sort of place built on a grand scale. *Open 10.00-18.00 daily. Closed Fri.*

Museums & galleries

Abbot Hall Museum C9
Kendal, Cumbria. Lakeland life and industry are represented here. Costume, printing, weaving and local industries. *Open 10.30-17.30 Mon-Fri. 14.00-17.00 Sat & Sun.*

Berwick-upon-Tweed Museum and Art Gallery F1
Marygate, Berwick-upon-Tweed, Northumberland. Paintings presented to the gallery by Sir William Burrell include Degas' 'Russian Dancer'. Also a 16thC wall-painting and small collections of silver, bronze, brass and ceramics. *Open 14.00-17.00 Mon-Sat Jun-Sep.*

The Bowes Museum F7
Barnard Castle, Durham. A magnificent collection of Spanish paintings including some by El Greco and Goya; period settings of English and French furniture of the 17th and 18thC; porcelain; glass, jewellery and metalwork. *Open 9.30-17.30 Mar, Apr & Oct, 9.30-19.00 May-Sep, 9.30-16.00 Nov-Feb. Closed Sun morning.*

Carlisle Museum and Art Gallery C5
Tullie House, Castle St, Carlisle, Cumbria. This handsome Jacobean mansion contains the city's art gallery, library and museum with finds from Hadrian's Wall. Pre-Raphaelite paintings, sculptured stones, a bird display and porcelain. *Open 9.00-20.00 Apr-Sep. 9.00-17.00 Oct-Mar. 14.30-17.00 Sun only Jun-Aug.*

The Clayton Collection E5
Hadrian's Wall, nr Chollerford, Chesters, Northumberland. Finds from Hadrian's Wall

including sculpture, coins, pottery, Roman inscriptions, weapons and tools. *Open 9.00-17.00 (14.00-16.30 Sun) Mar-Apr. 9.00-17.30 (14.00-17.00 Sun) May-Sep. 9.30-16.00 (14.00-16.00 Sun) Oct-Feb.*

Darlington Museum G7
Tubwell Row, Darlington, Durham. Early railway material and models (the Stockton and Darlington Railway was the first locomotive passenger line). Also local history and machinery. *Open 10.00-18.00 daily. Closed Thur afternoon & Sun.*

Fitz Park Museum and Art Gallery B7
Station Rd, Keswick, Cumbria. Original manuscripts of Wordsworth, Walpole and Southey, who is buried in nearby Crosthwaite Church. *Open daily Apr-Oct (10.00-19.00 Jul & Aug). Closed Sun.*

The Grace Darling Museum G1
Bamburgh, Northumberland. The little museum commemorates Grace and her father William Darling who rescued nine survivors from the wrecked SS Forfarshire. Relics on display include the original 'Grace Darling bonnet', cradle, shawls and trinkets. *Open 11.00-19.00 Mon-Sat mid Apr-mid Oct or by arrangement.*

Gulbenkian Museum of Oriental Art G6
Elvet Hall, Durham, Durham. A beautiful collection of Chinese carved jade, pottery, porcelain, ivories and textiles, Tibetan art, Indian sculpture and Japanese and Egyptian antiquities. *Open daily. Closed Sun morning.*

Hancock Museum G5
University of Newcastle-upon-Tyne, Barras Bridge, Newcastle-upon-Tyne, Tyne & Wear. Stuffed animals and birds and ethnological specimens – some probably brought back by Captain Cook from Africa and the South Sea Islands. Egyptian mummy cases, fossils and a freshwater fish aquarium. *Open 10.00-17.00 Mon-Sat. 14.00-17.00 Sun mid Apr-Sep.*

Laing Art Gallery and Museum G5
Higham Place, Newcastle-upon-Tyne, Tyne & Wear. British paintings and water-colours from the 17th century to the present. Also Greek and Egyptian antiquities, costumes and textiles. *Open 10.00-18.00 Mon, Wed, Fri & Sat. 10.00-20.00 Tue & Thur. 14.30-17.30 Sun.*

Newcastle-upon-Tyne Museum of Science and Engineering G5
Exhibition Park, Great North Rd, Newcastle-upon-Tyne, Tyne & Wear. Mining and engineering of the north-east are represented here. Also shipbuilding; and there's George Stephenson's locomotive built for Killingworth Colliery in 1830. *Open 10.00-18.00 Mon-Sat. 14.00-17.00 Sun.*

Preston Hall Museum H7
Preston Park, Eaglescliffe, Stockton-on-Tees, Cleveland. Antiquities and industrial equipment. The Spence arms and armour collection and archaeology and natural history, toys and local pottery. *Open daily. Closed Sun.*

Ryedale Folk Museum J9
Hutton-le-Hole, N. York. Illustrating life in an agricultural community over the past 400 years. Many tools, appliances, furniture, a mediaeval glass kiln and a blacksmith's shop. *Open 16.00-18.00 daily (except Tue Apr & May) mid Apr-Sep. 11.00-18.00 daily mid Jul-Aug.*

South Shields Roman Fort and Museums H5
Baring St, South Shields, Tyne & Wear. Memorial stones, the South Shields Roman sword, stamped roof tiles, lead seals and enamels. *Open 10.00-19.30 Mon-Sat. 11.00-17.30 Sun May-Sep. 10.00-16.00 Mon-Fri. Sat 10.00-12.00 Oct-Apr.*

Whitby Literary and Philosophical Society Museum K8
Pannett Park, Whitby, York. A fine collection of fossils and flint weapons, relics of Roman occupation, and of Captain Cook who sailed to Tahiti from Whitby. *Open daily May-Sep (Closed Sun morning). 9.00-17.00 Mon-Fri.*

14.00-17.00 Sun. 10.30-13.00 Mon-Fri Oct-Apr. Closed Wed morning. 14.00-16.00 Sun Oct-Apr.

Wordsworth Museum B8
Grasmere, Cumbria. Wordsworth manuscripts and first editions are preserved here, near Dove Cottage where the poet once lived. *Open 9.30-17.30 daily May-Nov. 10.00-16.15 Oct-Apr. Closed Sun.*

Zoos, aquaria and aviaries

Chillingham Wild Cattle Herd G3
Chillingham Park, Alnwick, Northumberland. Believed to be descendants of the Arorochs (*bos primigenius*), these cattle have lived in the park for 700 years. Still living wild, they are the only cattle of their kind uncrossed with domestic breeds, and are completely self-sufficient save for winter hay feeding. *Open 10.00-17.00 daily mid Apr-Oct. Closed Tue.*

Flamingo Park K10
Kirby Misperton, Malton, N. York. Super-progressive zoo and walk-through safari park exhibiting over 1,100 animals in natural surroundings. The spacious 360 acres include performing dolphins and a jungle cruise, sea lions and crocodiles. Also a tropical house and children's farm. *Open 10.00-dusk daily*

Lowther Wildlife Park C7
Hackthorpe, Penrith, Cumbria. Animals and birds live free in the 130 acres of the Earl of Lonsdale's estate. Of interest: Old English longhorns and Highland cattle, the Lowther herd of red deer, fallow and sika. Also sheep. monkeys and waterfowl on a five-acre lake. *Open 10.00-17.00 Apr-Oct.*

Stanley Zoo G5
Harperley Hall, Tantobie, Newcastle-upon-Tyne, Tyne & Wear. A small zoo on the banks of an old mill stream. Tropical house, aquarium, reptile house and a good selection of animals. *Open 10.00-19.00 May-Sep.*

Nature trails and reserves

Farne Islands Nature Reserve G1
Northumberland. One of Britain's outstanding bird 'meccas', famous for many breeding birds and access is by boat from Seahouses. There is an excellent nature trail on Inner Farne.

Friars Crag Nature Trail B7
Cumbria. Start at the car park, Friars Crag, Keswick. 1½ miles. Lake edge and woodland birds and plants at Keswick-on-Derwentwater. Historical interest and superb scenery. Guide and information from either of the two National Park Information Centres in Keswick.

Lindisfarne National Nature Reserve F1
Northumberland. This magnificent coastal reserve includes Holy Island, and much of the adjacent coast, particularly Goswick Sands, Fenham Flats, Skate Road, and Budle Bay. The whole area is notable for migrants in season, and Holy Island for bird and marine flora-watching.
Holy Island is accessible from Beal (off A1) and the Causeway at low tide, while roads off the A1 to Fenham and Fenham Lowmoor lead to Fenham Flats. Skate Road is reached from the A1 via Elwick and Ross, and Budle Bay from the A1 via Warren Mill.

Ravenscar Geology Trail K8
N. York. 8 miles se of Whitby. Start from road junction nr Raven Hall Hotel. Impressive cliff scenery and of considerable geological interest. Noted for fossils. Guide available at local shops and cafes.

Ravenglass Nature Reserve A8
Cumbria. Ravenglass and Drigg Dunes are best known for birds and particularly for the largest British breeding colony of black-headed gulls, shore and dune wild life and vegetation. Much of the estuary area can be seen from A595 at Ravenglass. Visits to the reserve are by permit only – details from Cumberland County Council, The Courts, Carlisle.

Tarn Hows Nature Trail   **B8**
*Nr Hawkshead, Cumbria. Reached nia
Hawkshead-Coniston Rd (B5285).* 1¾ miles.
Mixed woodlands with good botanical
interest and outstanding scenery. Guide
from all National Trust and National Park
Information Centres.

Walney Nature Reserve   **B10**
*Walney, Cumbria. Access by bridge from
Barrow-in-Furness.* Large numbers of birds
and shore vegetation of special interest.
Details from 82 Plymouth St, Walney
Island, Barrow-in-Furness. *By permit only.*

Bird watching

Bamburgh/Seahouses   **G1**
*Northumberland. Accessible from B1340. For
Bamburgh, leave A1 s of Belford on B1342 or
B1341.* This stretch of coast with the Farnes
offshore is excellent for sea duck, divers and
grebes in winter, for a variety of passage
migrants in autumn and for seabirds during
the breeding season. 'Bird watching' can be
very worthwhile, especially from Islestone
(Stag Rocks).

Cresswell Ponds   **G3**
Northumberland. 1 mile n of Cresswell. Noted
for a wide variety of migrants in season,
including waders of many kinds, while the
foreshore is also a good wader haunt. Sea
duck are good offshore in winter. The ponds
are on private land but can be seen well from
the road, as can the sea and the shore.

The Lake District   **C8**
The fells around Scafell, Borrowdale, the
Gramere area and Easedale can all be
recommended. A long walk away from the
roads produces the best results.
Breeding birds include buzzard, peregrine,
common sandpiper, ring ouzel, redstart,
wood warbler, pied flycatcher, dipper and
raven – and the lucky observer may glimpse
the area's latest addition, the golden eagle.

Marsden Rocks   **H5**
Durham. S from South Shields on A183. A
footpath leads along the cliff top to this
interesting area. 'Sea watching' can be good
in autumn and winter while in summer
Marsden Rock itself, a high offshore stack,
has breeding fulmars, cormorants, shags and
kittiwakes.

St Bees Head   **A7**
*Cumbria. Footpath after leaving Sandwith,
right off B5345 1½ miles s of Whitehaven.* An
important seabird colony is situated here,
with breeding fulmar, guillemot, black
guillemot, razorbill and puffin, as well as
nesting ravens. A public footpath along the
cliff tops allows good views of the birds and
in due course details of an RSPB reserve on
the headwill be available.

Teesmouth   **H7**
Durham. In spite of being virtually
surrounded by industry of all kinds, and the
proximity of a very large urban complex,
Teesmouth is famous for its birds. The
'marshes' north of the Tees, parts of which
are visible from the Seaton Carew road and
its offshoots, contain many pools and fleets,
often good for wildfowl and waders, while
Greatham Creek (crossed by the Seaton
Carew road) is also worth a look. Seal Sands
are being rapidly reclaimed, but are still
noted for waders and duck. Sea watching
from South Gare breakwater can often be
very rewarding.
For the visitor this is a difficult area,
especially as access arrangements may
change frequently. Prior enquiries are
therefore recommended. Contact the
Secretary, Teesmouth Bird Club.

Brass rubbing

The following is a short list of churches that
have brasses for rubbing. Permission is
almost invariably required.
Cumbria. Carlisle Cathedral, Edenhall, Great
Musgrave.

Durham. Auckland (St Andrew), Sedgefield.
Tyne & Wear. Newcastle-upon-Tyne.

Fossils

Visit the local museum. Its fossil collection
usually states where individual fossils have
been found. When visiting quarries always
seek permission to enter if they look
privately owned or worked. Be careful of
falls of rock.

Cumbria
In the Lake District the rocks are mainly
Silurian – shales, mudstones and some
coarser rocks – with fossils in places. The best
areas are around Kentmere where the
Stockdale and Skelgill shales contain
graptolites and the Brathay flags contain a
shelly fauna of trilobites and brachiopods.
Most of the east of the county is of
carboniferous limestones containing corals,
bryozoans, brachiopods, crinoids, algal reefs
etc., to be seen in the areas around Tebay,
Ravenstonedale, Kirkby Stephen and the
escarpment to the east of Appleby to the
Yorkshire border at Stainmore.
The Ordovician Skiddaw slates, which occur
in a broad band in the north of the Lake
District, especially around Skiddaw
Mountain, have a few fossils – mainly
graptolites – but these are not common. The
Coniston Limestone Group with shelly
fossils – brachiopods and trilobites – of
Upper Ordovician age crops out on the hills
near Millom.
Around Whitehaven on the coast tip-heaps
from mining may give a few fossils such as
plants. The carboniferous limestone,
containing corals, algal reefs and
brachiopods, is exposed in two main
outcrops: around the northern and eastern
edges of the Lake District massif – from
Cockermouth round to the west of Penrith
on the western side of the Vale of Eden; to
the east of the Eden forming part of Alston
Block of the Pennines. Exposures are
common everywhere especially on the
escarpment on the east side of the Eden
Valley, at Melmerby Fell, Renwick Fell and
around Alston itself.

Durham
The coal measures outcrop in the west has
been extensively mined for coal, with few
fossils but rare plants and thin bands
containing small shells. Many of the mines
are on the magnesian limestone area,
extracting the coal beneath, so tip-heaps of
waste material of coal measures may be found
there.
Around Barnard Castle and Brough the
carboniferous limestones crop out with
plenty of fossils – corals, crinoids and
brachiopods.

Northumberland
Except for a patch of Devonian (old red
sandstone), mainly lavas with sands and no
fossils; in the Cheviot Hills, Northumberland
is mostly carboniferous. The east and most
of the coast is coal measures of the coalfield
with fossils occurring rarely. The coast is all
coal measures between the mouths of the
Tyne and the Aln. Further west and north is
the millstone grit series and the limestones of
the carboniferous which may be seen in the
valleys of the Tyne and Lyne and in
Liddesdale, Redesdale, Tweedsdale and
Berwick-upon-Tweed with the normal
coral-algal reefs brachiopods, crinoids and
bivalves fauna to be found as well as their
locally-developed coal beds.

Yorkshire
North Riding. Main collecting areas are in
the Jurassic rocks which are best exposed in
the cliffs of the coast: the Liassic rocks are
famous for fossils in the line of cliffs and the
foreshore from Redcar in the north to
Whitby and Robin Hood's Bay in the south;
upper Jurassic beds may be seen around
Scarborough and inland around Hackness.
The middle Jurassic is largely unfossiliferous
except for a few limestone beds, as at East
Ayton.
The middle lias in the escarpment to the
south of Guisborough was formerly worked
for iron ore and the tips and old workings

contain iron-stained fossils. Upper Jurassic corallian beds may be collected in scattered small exposures in the west of the Vale of Pickering to the west of Malton. Scarborough and Whitby Museums have collections of local fossils.

Forests

Grizedale Forest   B9
Cumbria. In the Furness region of Cumbria, between Coniston Water and Windermere, the national forest of Grizedale has been established over twelve square miles of wild fell-sides. It is centred on Satterthwaite, where pastures and oak-woods lie by a stone-built village.

Kielder Forest   D4
One of the largest man-made forests in Europe, Kielder fills the whole upper dale of the North Tyne River, between Bellingham and the Scottish Border.

Lune Forest   E7
N. York. Named after the minor River Lune, a tributary of the Tees, this wild mediaeval hunting territory lies at the extreme north of Yorkshire's North Riding. Between Middleton-in-Teesdale and Brough. Rugged Mickle Fell, a limestone, crag-girt ridge in the heart of trackless moorland, is the highest point in Yorkshire, 2,561 feet. Best viewed from the B6277 Middleton to Alston road.

Redesdale   D3
The forest is a vast dark artificially planted thickness of conifers – dull and uninteresting and swarming with flies by the millions in summer. It's a quick growing commercial crop and without any of the attraction that a mixed natural forest has.

Moors & plains

The Cheviots   E2
Form a 50-mile-long high-level sheep pasturage between the Northumbrian plain and Scotland's Tweed Valley.
The heights are totally natural with vast areas of moorland and deep bog. The Pennine Way follows the boundary between Scotland and England along the crest. Magnificent views.

The Lake District's mountains
900 square miles of some of the wildest, highest and most attractive mountains in Great Britain. Make sure you buy locally the little guide books by A. Wainwright, a local writer who put into them a whole lifetime of love and accurate observation – they are not only the best for hill walking but a joy to look through. There are three principal groups of mountains. North of Keswick are the Skiddaw Slates and include Skiddaw itself and the Saddleback. The central massif consists of the Borrowdale Slates, rugged high peaks that provide the most dramatic climbing. This includes the famous Great Gable, Scafell Pike, the Langdale Pikes, and Helvellyn with a host of smaller mountains between 2,000-3,000 feet in height. Around Windermere Lake and Coniston Water are the Bannisdale Slates, rounded wooded hills below 1,000 feet and lovely country it is.
All the major mountains above are around 3,000 feet with Scafell the highest at 3,210 feet. This area is totally unspoilt and forms the most marvellous walking and climbing country. There are many paths and established routes through cols or to the tops of mountains. Never walk alone high up and acquire some elementary knowledge at least of survival as the weather can change to mist or snow without warning. Even in early spring near Arctic conditions can exist above 2,000 feet with blinding blizzards and sub-zero temperatures. However in bright weather nothing can equal the beauty of this unspoilt region.

North York Moors   J8
N. York. This splendid National Park in the North Riding of Yorkshire, extends over 600 square miles from a rugged cliff-bound coastline between Middlesborough and Scarborough towards Northallerton and Thirsk in the Vale of York. The central and northern moors are broad expanses of heather, over 1,200 feet above sea level. They rise on their north-western border to the steep-sided Cleveland Hills, whose western slopes carry extensive forests of pine and larch.
The southern half of the moors has a score of well-proportioned stone-built villages, each with its open, sheep-grazed green. The Cistercian Rievaulx Abbey stands as a magnificent ruin in a dale north of Helmsley.

Northumberland's coastal plain   G3
For 80 miles from the industrial city of Newcastle-upon-Tyne to the border stronghold of Berwick-on-Tweed, the coast of Northumberland holds a level plain of pastoral farms. Castles at Bamburgh on the sea-cliffs and at the market towns of Alnwick and Morpeth show how this fertile countryside was defended during its troubled past.

The Pennines
This northern part of the Pennine range has two formidable peaks: Mickle Fell (2,591 feet) and Cross Fell (2,930 feet) the highest point of the Pennines – a wild boggy summit but with fine views to the Lake District. The rest of the range is high fells and moors and superb walking country.

Solway Plain   C5
From the castle and cathedral of Carlisle you look out over a spacious plain stretching down to the broad Solway Firth. Across this level, well-farmed expanse five great rivers wind their way to the tide-washed sandbanks of the estuary.

Rivers and lakes

The Lakes
Most of the valleys of the Lake District, which fan out like the spokes of a wheel from Scafell and Great Gable, are delightful, cradling clear streams and splendid lakes. The whole area is still working farmland as well as being a National Park, and this adds to its charm.
Notable lakes are ten and a half miles long Windermere, small and lovely Rydal Water, Grasmere, Haweswater under High Street, Ullswater, Thirlmere, serene Derwentwater with its islands, Bassenthwaite, quiet Buttermere, Ennerdale and the awesome Westwater, deep and black. In addition there are a total of 463 mountain tarns.

The Tees   F7
The Tees starts as a moorland stream in a national nature reserve, then tumbles over magnificent High Force waterfall. From its beautiful dale around Barnard Castle it flows through Darlington and the modern industrial complex of Teeside and Middlesbrough.

The Tyne   G5
The North Tyne starts at Deadwater on the Scottish border, and flows through forests and hill farms to Hexham, where it meets the South Tyne from the Cumberland Fells. At Newcastle-upon-Tyne the combined stream becomes a busy, industrial river lined with shipyards and wharves to Tynemouth on the coast. Impressive bridges cross it at Newcastle, with a tunnel lower down.

The Wear   G6
Starting on high bleak moorlands, the Wear flows down a lovely dale to Durham, encircling the castle and cathedral in a great loop.

Archaeology

Hadrian's Wall   D5
Bowness-on-Solway, Cumbria to *Wallsend-on-Tyne, Northumberland.* The

Hadrian's Wall, Northumberland

great Roman frontier work of Hadrian's Wall was originally built during the 120s, after a visit by the Emperor Hadrian to Britain. The Hadrian's Wall system is composed of several types of defensive works, of which the Wall itself is only one part.

The Ditch. To the north the Wall was defended by a ditch some 27 feet wide, which was separated from it by an open strip, a *berm*, twenty feet wide.

The Wall. Originally built partly of turf, it was later reconstructed in stone throughout its length.

The best preserved sections are in the centre, particularly at Walltown Crags and Sewingshields.

The Vallum. To the south of the Wall was a second ditch, twenty feet wide and crossed by causeways to the forts and milecastles. A good example of a causeway can be seen at Benwell.

The Military Way. Between the Wall and the Vallum ran a road linking the various stations, used primarily for supplies and couriers.

Milecastles. Small forts built every mile along the length of the Wall. Well-preserved milecastles can be seen at Winshields, Poltross Burn, Harrow's Scar, and Cawfields.

Turrets. Two were built between each pair of milecastles. Good examples are at Denton Hall, Brunton, Piper Sike, Leahill, and Banks East.

Forts. Seventeen forts were placed at strategic points along the Wall. The size varies from under two acres for a force of 500 infantry to almost nine and a half acres for a cavalry force of 1,000. The best preserved are at Chesters (which includes a bath-house), Housesteads, Chesterholm, Great Chesters and Birdoswald.

Supply Bases. In addition to the defensive works, large supply depots had to be constructed to maintain the garrisons. Corbridge was originally a fort south of the Wall, but was later converted into a depot, with massive granaries and workshops. South Shields also held granaries, and was probably the fleet base at which goods were unloaded. Some sites have a museum, and there are collections at the Tullie House Museum, Carlisle, and the Museum of Antiquities, Newcastle-upon-Tyne. The Newcastle Museum also has a fine series of models of the Wall, and a reconstruction of the Carrawburgh Mithraeum.

Hardknott Castle   **A8**
Eskdale, Cumbria. Mediobogdum, one of the most spectacularly sited Roman forts in Britain. The granaries, headquarters building, commandant's house, and much of the defensive wall are preserved, and a simple bath-house can be seen outside. Uphill from the fort an area was flattened to form a parade-ground. *Open any reasonable time.*

Long Meg and Her Daughters   **D6**
Long Meg, Cumbria. A large bronze age stone circle, over 50 feet in diameter. Like henge monuments, these circles probably had religious and burial significance.

Scamridge Dykes   **K9**
On moorland between Pickering and Scarborough, N. York. The finest of the complex series of boundary banks, probably of iron age date, characteristic of the Yorkshire Wolds and the North York Moors. Built to prevent the wandering or theft of livestock.

Scarborough Signal Station   East K9
Scarborough, N. York. The best preserved of the series of Roman signal stations built along the Yorkshire coast in the 4thC. Their function was to look out to sea for raiders

and, by signalling along the coast, to inform fortified fleet bases when necessary. The signal tower is square, massively built, and probably stood about 100 feet high.

Yeavering Bell   **E2**
Northumberland. An impressive iron age hill fort with single bank defences. Shallow depressions on the interior show the situations of circular huts. Excavations at the foot of the hill revealed the timber halls of a royal residence belonging to the Saxon king Edwin of Northumbria. but these are not now visible on the surface.

Footpaths & ancient ways

The Cleveland Way   **J7**
Cleveland. A U-shaped path skirting the borders of the North York Moors and the coast from Saltburn-by-the-Sea to Gristhorpe. For 100 miles this long-distances path crosses moorland with spectacular view over the Vale of York.

Start at the old market town of Helmsley at the foot of the Cleveland Hills and take the old drove road along Whitestone Cliff to Osmotherley. Climb now to Swinestyle Hill and beyond are the moors. At Saltburn the Way follows the coast past Staithes, Sandsend, Whitby, Ravenscar, Scarborough, and comes to an end near Gristhorpe.

Lyke Wake Walk   **K8**
This is a 40-mile-long moorland walk across the North Yorkshire Moors from Scarth Wood Moor, near Osmotherley, to Wyke Point at Ravenscar. Start from Scarth Wood Moor and continue to Scarth Nick where the scarp stares down over the Cleveland Plain. From here to the sea the Walk is across miles of bog and heather, over Coalmire to Botton Head, the highest point of the North Yorkshire Moors, to Shunner Howe, with sweeping views almost to the sea.

From Hamer continue to Simon Howe where the bogs are murky and difficult to cross, and on to Ravenscar and Wyke Point, a short distance beyond.

The Pennine Way   **D6**
From Wensleydale, north across Durham, Cumbria and Northumberland, the Pennines and the Cheviots, the Way comes to an end at Kirk Yetholm, on the Scottish border. From Great Shunner Fell, rising to 2,340 feet, the Way descends into Thwaite. Tan Hill boasts the highest licensed inn in England at 1,730 feet. Cross Stainmore Gap to Teesdale, past the magnificent waterfall at High Force, crashing down from a 72-foot-high cliff. Climb again to Cross Fell (2930 feet), the highest point in the Pennines; below is Alston, the highest market town in England. North of Hadrian's Wall are the moors and Forestry Commission plantations near Redesdale, and at Chew Green, the Roman camps. Descend Halterburn Valley, and the end of the Way is in sight at Kirk Yetholm.

The Wolds Way   **K10**
The northern stretch of the Way begins at Filey Brigg on the Yorkshire coast, and continues to Thixendale.

Leave the steep cliff on Filey Brigg, and take the road to Muston village via cinder track and hedgerow. On from Fordon to Ganton, with the Vale of Pickering and the glowering Wold escarpment in view, and on to Settrington, the loveliest village along the route.

Wharram Percy is the most famous of the 'lost villages', abandoned around 1500 and has been excavated for several years. Just beyond, Raisthrope is another deserted site, and half a mile away is Thixendale.

Regional sport

Angling
Northern England with its miles of coastline to the east and west, its deeply incised interior, and abundance of lakes gives the angler a wide choice of fishing areas and catches. On the east coast there are salmon

and trout in the River Coquet at Warkworth, Felton, Rothbury, and Acklington, and there is coarse fishing on the Rivers Wansbeck and Blyth. Other rivers to fish are the Tees, the North and South Tynes, and the famous River Tweed.
In the west the Cumbrian lakes offer superb coarse fishing. There is also excellent sea fishing along the coast, enhanced by its remoteness from major industrial outpourings.

Climbing
Nearly all the valleys of the Lake District provide good rock climbing, but Great Langdale and Wasdale are the principal centres. From Wasdale rises England's highest mountain, Scafell Pike (3,210 feet); at Langdale is the famous Gimmer Crag with climbs all rated more than 'very difficult',
Because of the extensive use made of the rocks in this region many of the important foot and toe holds are becoming more polished each year, As a result nails are inadvisable on the more popular Lake District rock climbs, except in the gullies.

Fell running   B8
Normally the race is started from an arena and the runners race to the top of the nearest fell and back.
The honour of winning these races is highly prized by the shepherds and young farm lads who have the physique and stamina for this testing sport. Fell running can be seen at Ambleside, Patterdale, Beetham, Grasmere, and other places in Lakeland.
A more arduous adaptation is the marathon fell running of conquering as many peaks over 2000 feet as possible in 24 hours. For example E. Beard in 1963 managed 56 mountains in 23½ hours!

Hound trailing   B8
The circuits are some eight to ten miles in length. A trail is laid by two men who set out from the furthest point on the course and take two different routes to the start point, by dragging along the ground a large old sock impregnated with aniseed and other delectable canine olfactory stimulants.
There are fixtures throughout the summer, but the biggest events take place at Coniston, Torver, Ulverston, Cartmel, Rusland, and Armathwaite. Dates vary, so look out for placards.

Wrestling   C8
Cumbria. One of the traditional sports of north-west England. The wrestlers stand facing each other with their hands locked across their opponent's back. The aim is to throw your opponent to the ground.
During the summer wrestling can be seen at Ambleside, Patterdale, Beetham, Grasmere and other places. Look out for placards, as dates vary from year to year.

Festivals

For information and tickets for festivals go to the local information centre or ticket agent.

Durham Music Festival   G6
Durham. Thoroughly modern music, 20thC only, with at least one famous orchestra performing each year. Durham Castle provides the great hall for concerts and cheap overnight accommodation. Mid Oct.

Hexham Abbey Festival   E5
Hexham, Northumberland. Hexham's abbey, an artistic haven in the middle ages, inspired this modern festival to promote the arts. Many of the concerts, poetry readings and exhibitions are held within its walls; very popular are the unaccompanied motets by candlelight. Late Sep.

The Lake District Festival   C8
Cumbria. This festival provides a rare opportunity for the Lake District to hear artists of international standing. Concerts are given in the parish churches of Ambleside, Windermere, in Kendal Town Hall and at Cartmel Priory; opera is performed in the 16thC Levens Hall and Wordsworth poetry readings in Grasmere church. Early May.

Richmondshire Festival   G8
Richmond, York. The main event is a production in the only remaining classical Georgian playhouse in England. Built in 1788 and now restored with sunken pit and narrow forestage, it is normally a museum. Late May.

Fun things

Hardrow Force   E9
N. York. 1½ miles n of Hawes. A detour from the Pennine Way in the Yorkshire Dales brings you to England's highest (above-ground) waterfall – it drops a spectacular 96 feet.

Lake Side and Haverthwaite Railway   C8
Ambleside, Cumbria. Join one of the lakeland steamers at Ambleside for a trip from the northern extremity of Lake Windermere to Lake Side at the southern end. At Lake Side disembark and join the railway for a seven mile return journey by steam-hauled train through magnificent countryside.
For information Tel Newby Bridge 594.

North of England Open Air Museum   G6
Beamish, Durham. Off A693 from Stanley 3 miles from A1M. Beamish Hall and its surrounding 200 acres was designed to show the social and industrial history of the region. 1973 saw the opening of an operational electric tramway. There is also a collection of early vehicles and machinery which is steamed irregularly. Open 10.00–17.00 daily late May–Sep. 10.00–16.00 Oct–May. Closed Mon except B. Hols.

The Ravenglass and Eskdale Railway   A8
Ravenglass, Cumbria. Starts adjacent to the British Rail station. This is probably the most scenic miniature railway in the country. It climbs from the ancient port of Ravenglass up two beautiful valleys. Open throughout the year, but the winter service is thin. Tel Ravenglass 226.

Ryhope Engines Museum   H6
Ryhope, nr Sunderland, Tyne & Wear. This is possibly the finest single industrial monument in north-east England, and is a distinctive example of the industrial architecture of mid-Victorian times. The huge engines are now in full running order again. Open 11.00–18.00 Sat & B. Hols. (14.00–18.00 Sun) Apr–Sep.

Hotels

The following indicates the price range of a single room per night:
£   inexpensive
££   medium priced
£££ expensive

Alston Cumbria.   D6
Hillcrest Hotel. Tel 251. A stone inn with fine views of the Pennines and the South Tyne, in England's highest market town. £.

Ambleside Cumbria.   C8
Rothay Manor, Rothay Bridge. Tel 2331. Pleasantly situated on the outskirts of this attractive Lake District town. Personal service. ££.

Armathwaite Cumbria.   C6
Red Lion Hotel, nr Carlisle. Tel 204. A former coaching house which is now a well situated fishing hotel. £.

Askham Cumbria.   C7
Queen's Head, nr Penrith. Tel Hackthorpe 225. A pleasant inn near the Lowther Wild Life Park. £.

Barrowdale Cumbria.   B7
Lodore Swiss Hotel, near Keswick. Tel 285. Excellent for families; three miles from Keswick, Views of the lake, fells and falls are splendid. Closed Nov–Feb. £££.

Bassenthwaite Lake Cumbria.   B7
Pheasant Inn, nr Cockermouth. Tel 234. At the north end of the lake, this pleasant inn offers good English food. £.

Belford Northumberland.   F1
Blue Bell Hotel. Tel 203. Holy Island and the Farne Island bird sanctuary are nearby. £.

Berwick-upon-Tweed F1
Northumberland.
Castle Hotel, Castlegate. Tel 6471. A popular
local hotel, especially on market day. Fishing
is available. £.

Blanchland Northumberland. F6
Lord Crewe Arms Hotel, nr Consett. Tel 251.
Historically this was the abbot's guest house,
and has in its time housed Henry VIII and
both protagonists in the Civil War. £.

Bowness-on-Windermere C8
Cumbria.
Old England Hotel. Tel Windermere 2444.
Summer barbecue meals by the swimming
pool are among the many attractions. ££.

Braithwaite Cumbria. B7
Coledale Inn. Tel 272. Once a pencil mill, the
inn has fine views of the Derwent Valley and
Skiddaw, and a pleasant garden. £.

Cornhill-on-Tweed E1
Northumberland.
Tillmouth Park Hotel. Tel Coldstream 2255.
Offers fishing on both the Tweed and the
Till. Pleasant garden and country house
atmosphere. £.

Durham G6
Royal County Hotel, Old Elvet. Tel 66821.
Well situated and recently renovated. ££.

Eskdale Cumbria. A8
Bower House Inn, Holmrook. Tel 244. Good
for climbers and walkers; pleasant fell views
£.

Gateshead Tyne & Wear. G5
Five Bridges Hotel, High West. Tel 71105.
A very modern seven-storey hotel which
reflects its industrial environment. ££.

Grasmere Cumbria. B8
Swan Hotel. Tel 551. A pleasant inn,
featured in Wordsworth's poetry.
Comfortable and relaxing. ££.

Kirkby Stephen Cumbria. E8
King's Arms Hotel, Main St. Tel 378. A fine
Georgian hotel. The lounge has an Adam
ceiling and an adjoining 18thC powder
room. £.

Morpeth Northumberland. G4
Queen's Head Hotel, Bridge St. Tel 2083.
Once a stopping place on the Great North
Road; a popular local hostelry. £.

Newcastle-upon-Tyne G5
Tyne & Wear
Royal Turk's Head Hotel, Grey St. Tel 26111.
Pleasantly situated with the Theatre Royal
opposite; comfortable and elegant. ££.

Otterburn Northumberland. E4
Percy Arms Hotel. Tel 261. Popular with
motorists to and from Scotland. Amenities
include pony trekking and shooting. £.

Piercebridge Durham. G7
George Inn, nr Darlington. Tel 576. A
much-haunted 17thC inn with a
bow-windowed restaurant. Local fishing and
riding. £.

Rosthwaite Cumbria. B7
Scafell Hotel. Tel Barrowdale 208. This little
hotel set in the centre of the Lake District is
an ideal one for climbers and walkers. £.

Stockton-on-Tees Cleveland. H7
Queen's Hotel, Bishopton Lane. Tel 65772.
Well situated near the station. ££.

Threlkeld Cumbria. B7
White Horse, Scales, nr Keswick. Tel 241. Set
back from the A66; 17thC beamed bar.
Splendid views. £.

Ullswater Cumbria. C7
Leeming House Hotel, Watermillock. Tel
Pooley Bridge 444. A fine Georgian country
house set in many fine acres beside Lake
Ullswater. *No dogs or small children.* ££.

Wark Northumberland. E4
Battlesteads Hotel, nr Hexham. Tel 209.
Beautifully situated in a valley near to
Newcastle. Comfortable rooms and a
pleasant garden. £.

Windermere Cumbria. C8
Langdale Chase Hotel. Tel Ambleside 2201.
Built in 1891; many fine details including
carved fireplaces. Many amenities. ££.

Regional food

Cumberland sausage B7
An expensive pork and herb sausage which
is mostly meat. Local butchers have their
own recipes.

Fish G2
Salmon are caught from the Leven and
Solway Firth in the west and the Tweed in
the east. Local fish include char from Lake
Windermere and Flookburgh flooks, flat fish
which are driven into the nets – this process
marks the dorsal side with three-inch
diamonds. Fine kippers are prepared at
Craster, a delightful Northumbrian seaside
village.

Northumbrian beer
This was one of the first areas in Britain to
brew beer. 'Newcastle Brown' is said by beer
connoisseurs to be the strongest beer
produced in quantity in this country.

Singin' Hinny
This traditional Northumberland rich
currant scone is baked on a griddle and sings
whilst it cooks. Hinny is a local term of
endearment.

Restaurants

£   inexpensive
££ medium priced
£££ expensive

Alston Cumbria. D6
Lowbyer Manor. Tel 230. Comfortable,
family-run hotel. Mainly English food. LD.
££. Book.

Ambleside Cumbria. C8
Rothay Manor, Rothay Bridge. Tel 2331. A
country-house hotel on the Langdale Road.
Well planned set menus, English and French
LD. Closed L. Mon. ££. Book.

Blanchland Northumberland. F6
Lord Crewe Arms. Tel 251. In a peaceful
village. Straightforward English cooking.
LD. ££L, £££D. Book.

Brompton-by-Sawdon N. York. K9
Brompton Forge Restaurant. Tel Snainton
409. Small family-run inn. British cooking.
LD. Closed Sun D Mon, L Tue & Sat. £L,
££D.

Carlisle Cumbria. C5
Below stairs, Crown & Mitre, English St.
Tel 25491. Situated in a modernised cellar.
Good steaks and grills. LD. Closed Sat L &
Sun Nov-Mar. ££.

Newcastle-upon-Tyne Tyne & Wear G5
Dante's, 1-3 Market St. Tel 22816. Small
and popular, serving a wide selection of
international meals. LD. Closed Sun. £.

Moulin Rouge, 27 Sandhill. Tel 20377.
Situated under Tyne Bridge, serves good
French dishes. LD. Closed Sun. ££. Book.

Ovington Northumberland. F5
Highlander Inn. Tel Prudhoe 32016. 17thC
inn. Authentic French cooking. LD Closed
Sun. ££. Book.

Ullswater Cumbria. C7
Sharrow Bay Hotel. Tel Pooley Bridge 301.
Very comfortable country house hotel.
Elaborate set meals. Individual cooking.
LD. ££L, £££D. Book.

Underbarrow Cumbria. C9
Tullythwaite House. Tel Crosthwaite 397.
Friendly Farmhouse restaurant in a remote
village. Mainly English. Good high teas.
Unlicensed. L (Sun only) D. Closed Sun D.
££. Book.

Windermere Cumbria. C8
Miller Howe Hotel. Tel 2536. Well-run
country house hotel with spectacular views
from the dining room. Set meals. Inspired
cooking. L (Sun only) D. ££L, £££D.
Book.

Scottish Lowlands and Border Country

The Lowlands are the turning point where Scotland breaks away gradually from its neighbouring English counties and firmly establishes itself with the two great cities of Glasgow and Edinburgh. The sparkling Tweed river enlivens the centre of the Lowlands, skirting the romantic, ruined abbeys of Melrose and Dryburgh. The hills are gentle and often wooded and the true Scottish woollens come from Peebles, Hawick and Galashiels. To the west things flatten out a bit to accommodate that great Scottish sport on the golf links of Ayr; it's unlikely you'll ever see smoother greens than those at Turnberry.

Glasgow has more delights along the Clyde where the shipyards slowly slip away as you sail to the remoter islands. Edinburgh stands proud on its crags and has one of the most stirring silhouettes of any city in Europe. The castle is full of poignant reminders of Scotland's independent history and from the ramparts you can see the great road and rail bridges sweeping over the Forth to the Highlands.

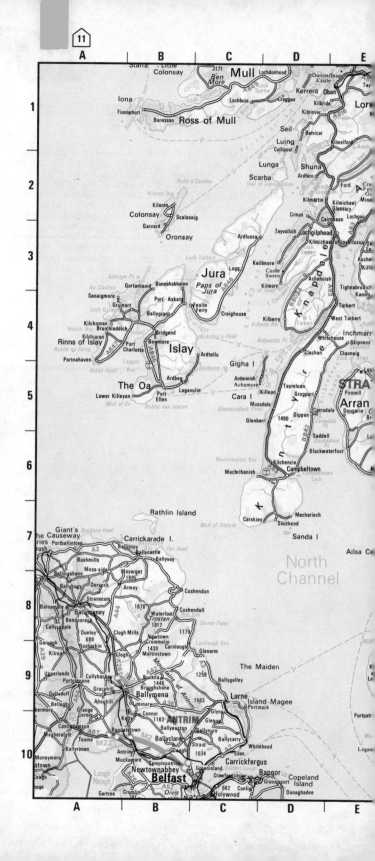

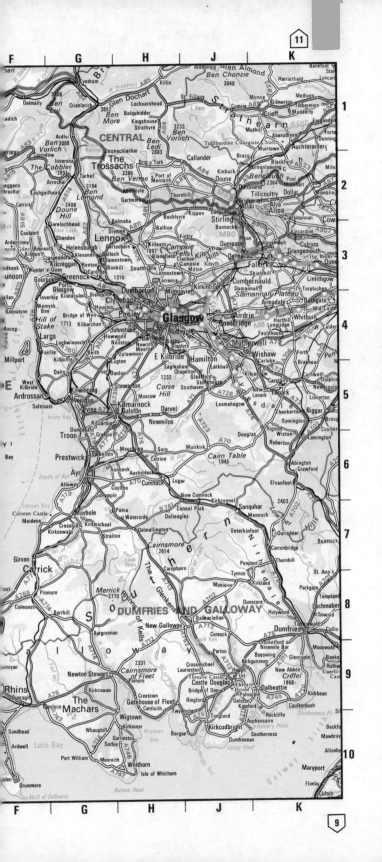

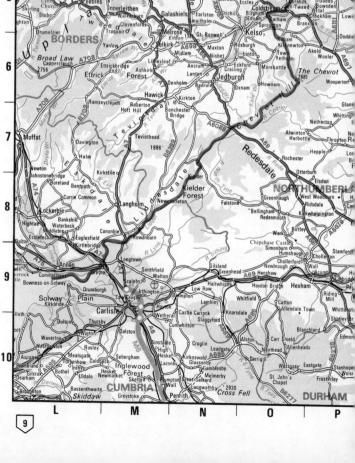

The coast

Aberdour Fife L3
Fife. EC Wed. The shore of Aberdour is untainted by the industrial and urban pollution for which many parts of the Forth are notorious. 12thC St Fillan's church is worth a visit; also Aberdour Castle. The silver sands are backed by trees and an attractive old town.

Ailsa Craig Dumfries & Galloway E7
Ayr. Set ten miles off the Ayrshire coast, at the mouth of the Firth of Clyde, this remarkable rock rises from the waves in the shape of an onion – in fact a well-known strain of onion is named after it! It carries a powerful lighthouse, nicknamed 'Paddy's Milestone', after the thousands of Irish immigrants who sailed this way to reach prosperous Clydeside.

Annan Dumfries & Galloway L9
Dumfries. Pop 6,100. EC Wed. MD Fri. This Victorian red stone town stands on the eastern shore of the Annan Estuary. Still a fishing and boating port, the poor beach hardly makes it the seaside. Of interest: Georgina Moat House, now a museum, and Annan Academy where Thomas Carlyle taught.

Ayr. Strathclyde G6
Ayr. Pop 47,900. EC Wed. MD Tue. The centre of the Robert Burns 'Industry' and country. The cottage where Burns was born in 1759 is at Alloway, two miles south. Also of interest, 13thC Brig o'Ayr, the Auld Kirk, and Loudoun Hall. An attractive resort with two miles of safe sandy beaches and fishing harbour.

Bass Rock Lothian N3
East Lothian. Set two miles offshore from North Berwick, at the mouth of the Firth of Forth, this sheer rock carries a lighthouse to warn navigators, and a dense colony of nesting gannets that dive from a great height to grab fish.

Burntisland Fife L3
Fife. One of the ghost ports of the Forth, yet in recent memory it was a flourishing place sending coal to southern England, and before that the terminus of the Firth of Forth rail ferry, the first in the world. Yet not all is decay. Outstanding is the Kirk, built in 1592 as a copy of the old North Church in Amsterdam, and in very recent times the first steps towards the renaissance of the town centre have been undertaken. Surprisingly there is an outdoor Olympic-size heated sea-water swimming pool, and all the trappings of the seaside, including a small sandy beach to the west of the deserted docks.

Cairn Ryan Dumf. & Gall. F9
Wigtown. EC Wed. This town of whitewashed cottages on the shore of Loch Ryan was an important wartime port, and parts of the Mulberry Harbour used in the Normandy landings were assembled here. Sadly the wartime mess has not been cleaned up too well. East of the harbour is the unusual Dutch style Lochryan House (1701).

Campbeltown

Campbeltown Strathclyde D6
Argyll. Pop. 6,000. EC Wed. The capital of Kintyre, and possibly the site of Dalriada the capital of the ancient Kingdom of Strathclyde. An attractive seaside holiday town which seems to have avoided the more vulgar excesses of its southern competitors. Of interest: the fine Celtic cross at the quay-head. Davaar Island has a painted crucifixion scene in the cave. Shingle beach.

Connel Ferry Strathclyde E1
Argyll. Pop 200. EC Wed. Delightfully situated on the south side of Loch Etive. Two notable features are the Falls of Lora, and the cantilever road and rail bridge which spans the loch.

Cowal Strathclyde F3
Argyll. The Cowal Peninsula lies in south Argyll, between Loch Long and Loch Fyne. Four other sea-ways run deep into its forested hills, namely Loch Goil, the Holy Loch, Loch Striven, and the Kyles of Bute. Most of its magnificent scenery can be explored along coastal roads, though many steep loch-sides are roadless, and indeed pathless, for stretches of many miles. Dunoon, the only town, is usually approached by car ferry from Gourock on the Clyde. Shingle beaches, often weedy, but safe for bathing.

Cramond, Midlothian.

Cramond Fife L3
Midlothian. Right at the mouth of the River Almond, this large village is held back from the riverside by a long terrace of whitewashed houses which border the quay. Almost a suburb of Edinburgh it's a favourite place for an evening walk along the causeway to Cramond Island if the tide is right, or to watch the sailing boats and shipping in the Forth. Unsafe for bathing.

Creetown Dumfries & Galloway H9
Kirkcudbright. Pop 900. EC Thur. A welcoming little place identified as the Portanferry in Scott's novel 'Guy Mannering'. The well displayed rock and gem museum is the best of its type in Britain. Four miles south is Carsluith Castle, a roofless 16thC tower; a little further south are a few safe sandy beaches.

Crinan Strathclyde D2
Argyll. An enclosed harbour nestles at the foot of the cliffs forming the western basin of the Crinan Canal. Locks lead west to the sea and eastwards for eight and a half miles to the sheer beauty of Ardrishaig on Loch Fyne. What a delightful spot this is, with puffers, as the small coasters are known, moving slowly through the canal with the cruising yachts and the Loch Fyne herring fleet.

Culross Fife K3
Fife. Pop 500. Steeped in history, this once busy port and royal burgh, retains much of its past. Thanks to the Scottish National Trust its many 16th and 17thC houses, exhibiting the characteristic crowstepped gables and red tiled roofs, are in good heart. See: St Mungo's Chapel, Culross Palace, Dunimarle Castle.

Dirleton Lothian M3
East Lothian. This village has everything. Set around a wide green and 17thC church. It also has one of the loveliest ruined castles in Scotland. Attractive walks down to the beach.

Dumbarton Strathclyde H4
Dunbarton. Pop 25,000. EC Wed. Dumbarton grew up round an ancient stronghold dominating the town from its 240-foot rock. Little is left of any mediaeval buildings but 17th and 18thC fortifications are still visible. Today it makes its living from ship-building (the Cutty Sark was built here) and the blending and bottling of whisky.

Dumbarton Rock Strathclyde H4
Dunbarton. A landmark to every traveller by road, rail, or ship down the Clyde, the rock that protects Dumbarton Harbour was originally a plug of molten basalt at the heart of an ancient volcano. Its twin summits have earned it the sailor's nickname of 'The Maiden's Breasts'. Castles have crowned the rock since the 5thC; the latest 17thC fortifications are now a museum.

Dunbar Lothian   **N3**
East Lothian. Pop 4,600. EC Wed. A narrow
steep-sided gash in the cliffs form the
dramatic gateway to Dunbar's harbour.
Around the harbour is a picturesque
collection of old warehouses, and further
inland the old Burgh with its quaint town
house of 1620. South of Dunbar are the
White Sands; good bathing.

Dunbar

Dunoon Strathclyde   **F3**
Argyll. Pop 9,000. EC Wed. A holiday town
on the Firth of Clyde with two fine bays with
safe swimming, and ruins of a castle. Mary
Campbell, Burns's sweetheart 'Highland
Mary' was born here. There is a statue of her
on Castle Hill.
The town has always been popular with
Glaswegians as the Clyde ferries call here
regularly. In August however bursting point
is reached with the Cowal Games, the largest
of all 'Highland Gatherings' with its
spectacular 'march of a thousand pipers'.

Eyemouth Borders   **P4**
Berwick. Pop 2,500. EC Thur. A busy fishing
town with cobbled streets, narrow 'pends' or
archways leading to small courtyards. To the
east of the harbour is Gunsgreen. Now a
boarding house, the Georgian Gunsgreen
House became a centre of smuggling in the
18thC because of its many secret passages. A
popular seaside centre with good sandy
beaches.

Garlieston Dumfries & Galloway   **H10**
Wigtown. Once one of the many little
thriving Solway ports, the small harbour is
now used by boating and fishing enthusiasts.
Approximately one mile to the north-east is
the ruin of Eggerness Castle, and three miles
south are the remains of Cruggleston Castle,
with nearby a 12thC church in the
Romanesque style used as a potato store.
The beach is mud and shingle.

Girvan Strathclyde   **F7**
Ayr. Pop 2,700. EC Wed. With a foot in the
industrial camp as well as one in the tourist,
Girvan is managing well. Terraces of red and
grey stone houses flank wide roads leading
down to the harbour which bustles with
activity. There is a good beach and plenty of
the traditional amenities.

Glenluce Dumfries & Galloway   **F9**
Wigtown. EC Wed. The 12thC abbey ruins,
north of the village, hold much of interest
including an almost intact chapter house of
1470. The village itself faces a wide expanse
of saltings, mud and shingle. Unfortunately
the sands to the west are occupied by a firing
range.

Helensburgh Strathclyde   **G3**
Dunbarton. Pop 14,000. EC Wed. A superior
suburb of Glasgow, it has also become a
popular seaside town. Laid out in the 18thC
on a rectangular grid that still survives. John
Logie Baird the television pioneer was a
native of the town.

Kippford Dumf. & Gall.   **J9**
Kirkcudbright. Stone houses built on a
hillside overlook a pebble beach and rough
Firth. Although the Firth dries out at low
water the harbour is a safe anchorage, which
probably accounts for its popularity with old
smugglers. Ten miles along the coast to the
east is the village of Kirkbean where the
pirate John Paul Jones was born.

Kirkcudbright Dumf. & Gall.   **J10**
Kirkcudbright. Pop 2,500. EC Thur. A
gorgeous 18thC souvenir lying on the River
Dee with a picturesque little harbour
dominated by McLellan's Castle built in
1583. The 17thC Tolbooth in which John
Paul Jones, pirate and founder of the U.S.
Navy, was imprisoned still stands.
Visit the Hornel Museum in 18thC
Broughton House, home of the artist, the late
E. A. Hornel. The town has a flourishing
artists' colony. Sandy beaches.

Largs Strathclyde   **F4**
Ayr. Pop 9,800. EC Wed. Wimpy bars in
little seaside houses and a large seafront
amusement arcade rather spoil this old
fashioned Victorian resort. Even so the two
mile long 'prom' has superb views of Ailsa
Craig, and the town itself is hemmed in by
green hills. Shingle beach, but very safe
bathing.

Limekilns Fife   **K3**
Fife. On the flat levels bordering the Forth,
the unremarkable houses of this little village
stand up like tombstones. Even so the place
has a charm quite apart from the relief of
getting away from the sprawl of the nearby
dockyard. The Ship Inn was mentioned in
Stevenson's novel 'Kidnapped'.

Musselburgh Lothian   **M4**
Midlothian. Sometimes called 'Honest Toun'
(whether by its inhabitants or the
surrounding villages is not known!). A
fishing and manufacturing town at the
mouth of the River Esk. The 16thC
Tolbooth, and the bridge which rests on
Roman foundations, are well worth seeing.
Above the town Inveresk has some good
Georgian houses. Sand and shingle beach.
Sea is polluted and unfit for bathing.

North Berwick

North Berwick Lothian   **N3**
East Lothian. Pop 4,400. EC Thur. The
harbour is a delight, and bustles with sailing
craft and inshore fishermen's boats. Small
shops and restaurants abound in the busy,
narrow, sheltered High Street, and behind
it all the Napoleonic period tower on the
613-foot North Berwick Law still maintains
a watchful eye. By the tower is an archway
formed from the jawbones of a whale.
Either side of the harbour are good bathing
beaches.

Oban Strathclyde   **E1**
Argyll. Pop 6,900. EC Thur. MD Tue. An
old fashioned Victorian seaside town, but in
the nicest way. The chief glory of the place
is in its setting, overlooking the Firth of
Lorn. Ferries leave here for Mull and other
islands. 'McCaig's Folly', overlooking the
town, is an unfinished replica of the
coloseum in Rome built by a banker John
Stuart McCaig in 1890 as a memorial to his
family.
See also the Free Church in Rockfield by
Augustus Pugin, and St Columba's Roman
Catholic Cathedral by Sir Giles Scott.
Shingle and rock shore.

Portpatrick Dumf. & Gall.   **E9**
Wigtown. Pop 1,100. EC Wed. Until about
1860 this used to be one of the main ports for
Ireland, but its harbour was too badly
exposed to winter gales, and the service was
transferred to Stranraer. Set at the foot of
low cliffs, terraces of brightly painted
cottages make a brave sight from seaward.
No beach, but good sailing facilities.

Port William Dumf. & Gall.   **G10**
Wigtown. EC Wed. A small fishing village
built along a pebble beach at the foot of low
hills. The tiny harbour dries out at low
water. Of interest: the remains of Chapel
Finian five miles north-west, a small chapel
or oratory dating from the 10th or 11thC in a
contemporary Irish style.

St Abb's Borders   **O4**
Berwick. Picturesque little fishing harbour,
with sands. The lighthouse on St Abb's
Head is above 400-foot cliffs amongst the
highest in Scotland.

St Andrews Fife   **M1**
Fife. Pop 11,600. EC Thur. This old grey
town, besides being famous for golf, is the
home of the oldest university in Scotland
founded in 1412. The university
incorporates a 17thC library where the
Scottish parliament met in 1645.
Worth a visit: the castle; the remains of St
Rule's church and the University College

Chapel. Attractive harbour, and all the seaside trappings except a decent safe beach.

Southerness Dumf. & Gall. K9
Kirkcudbright. The Solway Firth has few safe places to swim. At Southerness Point there are safe sandy beaches, with a few rocks. The hamlet is clustered around a lighthouse which fell into disuse with the decline of the little Solway ports. Sadly caravansville and bungaland is erupting to the north.

Lighthouse, Southerness-on-Solway

Stranraer Dumf. & Gall. F9
Wigtown. Pop 9,900. EC Wed. MD Fri. Scotland's port for Ireland, and very busy too, but in the older part of the town there is peace in the narrow attractive winding streets. A market town with a fine 16thC castle which was doing its job repressing the peasantry well into the 19thC, though latterly as the town goal!
At Coreswall Point there are magnificent views to Ireland, Arran, and the Mull of Kintyre. Good sandy bathing beaches near the harbour.

Whithorn H10
& Isle of Whithorn Dumf. & Gall.
Wigtown. Pop 1,000. Whithorn, another of the quiet little dignified towns of this area, with a broad main street. It has secured its niche in history as the place where Christianity first came to Scotland. The 12th-15thC priory of St Ninian is approached through a delightful 17thC archway or 'pend' which contains a museum of 5th and 7thC carved stones.
The Isle of Whithorn, three miles south-east, is no longer an island but ruins of a 13thC chapel mark the spot where St Ninian landed in 395.

Wigtown Dumfries & Galloway G9
Wigtown. Pop 1,100. EC Wed. An elegant village with a wide main street fringed with stone houses and a Victorian French Gothic town hall.
The church dates from 1853, built close to the ruins of a very much older foundation. In the churchyard there is a stone commemorating the Wigtown Martyrs of 1685, two women Covenanters who were tied to stakes in the estuary and left to drown for their beliefs.

Islands

Arran Strathclyde E5
An attractive and unspoilt island of nearly 200 square miles in the Firth of Clyde. Mountainous, particularly in the north where Goat Fell gives marvellous views. Coasts of rock and sand.

Islay Strathclyde B4
Argyll. When the Lord made time, he made plenty of it, and life on Islay moves at a gentle tempo. The delightfully named Port Ellen is an attractive little town with a sandy safe beach at Kilnaughton Bay. Whisky drinkers will want to make the pilgrimage to nearby Glen Laphroaig.
In the north steep, thickly wooded slopes plunge down to the picturesque hamlet of Port Askaig where the ferries for Jura and the mainland berth. Kilarrow church at Bowmore is circular, it is said, so that the devil would have no corners in which to hide.

Keills, Jura

Jura, Colonsay and C3
Oronsay Strathclyde
Argyll. Jura is a lonely sparsely populated island with one road and only one real village. It is dominated by the Paps of Jura, three peaks over 2,000 feet high. In the north the road peters out at Killchianaig, but the energetic may feel like the eight mile walk

up the track to the very northern tip where the whirlpool of Corryvreckan can be seen and heard.
The small islands of Colonsay and Oronsay lie eight miles to the west. They are separated by a narrow strait which can be crossed on foot at low water. Colonsay House at Kiloran has sub-tropical gardens; Oronsay has the remains of a 14thC priory.

Inland towns & villages

Abbey St Bathans Borders O4
Berwick. A pleasant little village in the Lammermuir Hills, on the Whitadder Water. The church incorporates part of an important 12thC abbey. On Cockburn Law nearby is Edin's Hall Broch (defensive tower) one of the very few iron age brochs in lowland Scotland.

Bannockburn Central J3
Stirling. A small mining village today, but in 1314 it was the site of one of the classic battles of history. Robert the Bruce with a lightly equipped army of 5,500 soundly defeated the forces of King Edward II of England numbering some 20,000.
The effects of this cunningly conceived and bravely fought battle were to last for 200 years until the Battle of Flodden in 1513 when the English not only got their revenge, but killed the unfortunate Scots King James IV.

Blantyre Strathclyde J4
Lanark. A small industrial town which gave its name to Blantyre in Rhodesia. David Livingstone, the great missionary-explorer of Africa, was born in 1813 in a cottage in Shuttle Row. Relics of his journeys and displays of his life's work can be seen in this national memorial.

Broughton Borders L5
Peebles. Pop 1,100. EC Wed. Small Tweeddale village noted for its colourful gardens. The restored vault in the ruined church is thought to be the cell of 7thC St Llolan. Numerous hill forts on the surrounding hills.

Castle Douglas, Kirkcudbright.

Castle Douglas Dumf. & Gall. J9
Kirkcudbright. Pop 3,300. EC Thur. MD Mon, Tue, Thur. A modern town regarded as the commercial capital of Kirkcudbrightshire. It is, however, a well built place and fortunate in having Carlingwark Loch and on its shores a civic park.
On an outlet in the River Dee, west of the town, is the ruined 14thC Threave Castle. It belonged to the Black Douglases and over the castle doorway projects the 'gallows knob' from which the Douglases hanged their enemies. Replaced in 1640 by Threave House which has stupendous gardens.

Ceres Fife M2
Fife. A cottage place with a mediaeval humped-back bridge. The church above the village contains the fine tombs of the Earls of Crawford. The fat, happy, bibulous old gentleman seen carved into a 16thC wall was the last provost of Ceres, 1578.

Clackmannan Central   **K3**
Clackmannan. The ancient county town of Scotland's smallest, but perhaps not least, county. In the picturesque square are the Tolbooth with its 17thC bell tower, the old town cross, and the mysterious stone of Mannan, of unknown antiquity. The old Clackmannan Tower on King's Seat Hill is worth a visit.

Coldstream Borders   **O5**
Berwick. A well built small town in a delightful setting on the Tweed. Once a refuge for eloping couples. The bridge across the Tweed here was built by Smeaton, designer of the first successful Eddystone Lighthouse. Contrary to tradition the Coldstream Guards were not raised here, but this was the place where their depot was originally set up in 1659.

Cumbernauld Strathclyde   **J3**
Dunbarton. Pop 38,300. EC Wed. A completely new town started in the 1950s to house Glasgow's overspill. Cumbernauld New Town is an outstanding example of community architecture. The buildings are grouped together to form neighbourhoods in a variety of layouts safely away from main roads.

Dalkeith Lothian   **L4**
Midlothian. Pop 9,500. EC Wed. An industrial and market town whose centre has recently been well restored and rebuilt. One mile south are the remains of the 12thC Newbattle Abbey, now an educational college.

Dollar Central   **K2**
Clackmannan. Pop 2,300. EC Tue, Thur, Sat. Sometimes referred to as the 'classic burgh', it is a small well built town famous for its academy designed by William Playfair and founded in 1818.
About a mile to the north is 15thC Castle Campbell, or Castle Gloom as it used to be called. It has a wonderful setting over deep gorges and superb views.

Dumfries Dumfries & Galloway   **K8**
Dumfries. Pop 29,400. EC Thur. MD Wed. A compact mass of mature buildings through which the River Nith cuts a swathe. The river is crossed by no less than five bridges of which the oldest goes back to the 13thC. The Globe Inn was one of Burns's favourites, and he and his family are buried in a mausoleum in St Michael's churchyard. See also the picturesque Mid Steeple of 1707 and the old town hall.

Dumfries

Dunfermline Fife   **K3**
Fife. Pop 53,400. EC Wed. Long ago Dunfermline was capital of Scotland, now it is a flourishing textile town. It has that dark grey look that so many other Scottish towns possess, but once one comes to terms with the place, and its traffic, its charm is yielded up.
Dunfermline Abbey was founded in 1072; its foundations lie beneath the present nave which is Norman.

Duns Borders   **O4**
Berwick. Pop 1,800. EC Wed. Pleasing little Duns is the county and market town. In the burgh chambers is a small museum commemorating the former world racing driver Jim Clark, killed in 1966, who was a native of Duns.

East Linton Lothian   **N3**
East Lothian. Pop 900. EC Wed. A 14thC bridge town in origin, although the buildings in the main street are 18thC.
The town had a single street plan, widening into two triangular places, one handsomely decorated with a bronze fountain. The

scene from the 14thC bridge over the river is particularly lovely and much admired by Scottish artists of the 19thC.

Ecclefechan Dumf. & Gall.   **L8**
Dumfries. EC Thur. A large quiet village of distinctive character with a burn flowing through its centre. Thomas Carlyle's birthplace, the 'Arched House', is a good example of its period (1790).

Edinburgh Lothian   **L3**
Midlothian. Pop 453,400. 'Auld Reekie' is not one city but two. Both are equally beautiful, but so very different. The old city grew up around the castle and its rock, but was constrained by the Flodden Wall built during the panic after Scotland's defeat by the English at Flodden in 1513.
Not feeling safe to build outside the walls, the citizens built upwards. The 'lands' or tenements, sometimes up to fourteen storeys high, crowded all estates together in a warren of wynds, closes and courts. The steep winding streets and high buildings made old Edinburgh unique in Europe. Of interest in the Old Town: Edinburgh Castle, containing the Scottish Crown Jewels; the Royal Mile, the road from the castle to Holyrood Palace; Holyrood Palace, originally an abbey but substantially rebuilt in 1671; John Knox House; and of course St Giles Cathedral with its open steeple. The new Georgian city lies to the north of the gorge now occupied by Waverley Station. Building the new town started in earnest when the Acts of Union of Scotland and England removed the danger of invasion. The centre of Edinburgh owes much to the inspiration shown in only completing one side of Princes Street, and leaving the opposite side open as a public garden. But it is behind this street where the real glories of the new town reveal themselves: streets laid out to a grid iron pattern, austere cool squares, grand terraces, and just occasionally a really sumptuous facade. Charlotte Square designed by Robert Adams is quite outstanding. Heriot Row is on a more comfortably domestic scale; and Moray Place (almost a circus) should not be missed.

St Giles Cathedral, Edinburgh

Ednam Borders   **O5**
Roxburgh. A small village with unusual literary connections. The birthplace (1790) of James Thomson who wrote 'Rule Britannia', and Henry Lyte who wrote 'Abide with Me' and other popular hymns.

Falkirk Central   **K3**
Stirling. Pop 37,600. EC Wed. MD Tue. An industrial town in sight of the Highlands on the River Carron. To the east and west of the town are sections of the Roman Antonine Wall which once stretched from the Forth to the Clyde. The parish church has a tower (1734) by William Adam, and in the churchyard are monuments to the dead of the two battles of Falkirk, 1298 and 1746. Callendar House south-east of the town centre has been evolving for 400 years. In the nearby town on Carron were made the carronades which were the first guns fired by HMS Victory at Trafalgar.

Falkland Fife   **L2**
Fife. A small town of picturesque old houses and cobbled streets. The 16thC Falkland Palace was a favourite residence of Scottish kings. The Royal Tennis Court, dating from 1539, is the oldest in Scotland.

Fintry Central   **H3**
Stirling. Pop 2,000. EC Wed. A tiny village on the Endrick Water with the Fintry Hills to the north and the extensive Campsie Fells to the south. Three miles east, the Loup of Fintry is a fine waterfall.

Galashiels Borders   **M5**
Selkirk. Pop 12,600. EC Wed. A modern town with a few old gems, notably the mercat cross (1695), Old Gala House with 17thC ceiling paintings, and an impressive war memorial comprising a fine statue of a

mounted border 'Riever' or mosstrooper. The 'Braw Lads' Gathering', a mounted procession in June, shouldn't be missed.

Gifford Lothian **N4**
East Lothian. A delightfully planned 18thC village with a 17thC church and an old mercat cross.

Glasgow Strathclyde **H4**
Lanark. Pop 816,300. Poor black old Glasgow suffered from the growing pains of 19thC industrialism to an extent possibly unequalled elsewhere in Britain. Glasgow's slums, and the Gorbals in particular, were notorious for their misery and hard sub-culture. Thank goodness their complete clearance is in sight. Britain's third most populous city also produced some of the most significant buildings of the late 19thC; the National Commercial Bank in Gordon Street; the Egyptian Halls in Union Street, and most important of all, Charles Rennie Mackintosh's School of Art. Built in 1897, the school was probably the first truly 20thC building in Britain.
In contrast Glasgow has the only complete mediaeval cathedral on the Scottish mainland, and a large number of imaginatively laid out parks. Also of interest: Glasgow's oldest domestic building, Provand's Lordship (1470); Kelvingrove Park Gallery and Museum: the Necropolis and George Square with the City Chambers. Glasgow's underground railway is an interesting contrast for Londoners.

Gordon Borders **N5**
Berwick. Once associated with the 'Gay Gordons' who moved to Aberdeenshire in the 14thC. The nearby turreted Greenknowe Tower dates from 1581 and retains its 'yett' (a sort of iron gateway).

Gretna Green Dumf. & Gall. **M9**
Dumfries. Pop 1,900. Until 1856 it was possible in Scotland to contract a binding marriage by making a solemn statement before witnesses. Since then the law has been tightened up but it is still possible to get married in Scotland without parental consent. Gretna Green was ideally situated for this 'trade'. The Toll Inn for instance performed no less than 1,300 of these marriages in six years, and well over 1,000 were joined in wedlock in front of the anvil in the village smithy.

Haddington Lothian **N3**
East Lothian. Pop 6,500. EC Thur. MD Fri. The folk of Haddington are justly proud of their town, and the council have spared no efforts to preserve the many historical and architectural gems. The town's three main streets, divided from each other by William Adam's town house, make perhaps the finest centre in Scotland for good 18thC and early 19thC houses. See also St Mary's church, the classical Carlyle House and Haddington House.

haddington town hall

Hawick Borders **M6**
Roxburgh. Pop 16,300. EC Tue. Pronounced Hoyck. Home of the knitted twinset, this Victorian town has suffered and triumphed through the centuries in bloody tit-for-tat raids with the English. The common riding celebration, held in early June for centuries, commemorates principally the victory over the English at nearby Hornshole in 1514. Reputed to have the oldest livestock market in Britain.

Innerleithen Borders **M5**
Peebles. Pop 2,200. EC Tue. A small tweed manufacturing town where Leithen Water joins the River Tweed. See Traquair House, the oldest continuously inhabited house in Scotland, and St Ronan's Games and Cleikum Ceremony in July.

Inveraray, Argyll.

Inveraray Strathclyde **F2**
Argyll. Pop 400. EC Wed (winter). A beautiful whitewalled royal burgh near the head of Loch Fyne. Mainly 18thC, two and three storey houses run along beside the harbour, linked by archways. Inveraray Castle, the seat of the Dukes of Argyll, is beside the River Aray. Designed in 1743 it contains a collection of paintings, furniture, tapestries and Scottish weapons. See also the preserved village of Auchindrain five miles to the west.

Jedburgh Borders **N6**
Roxburgh. Pop 4,000. EC Thur. An ancient royal burgh and county town. Mary Queen of Scots' House, a charming example of a 16thC dwelling house, is now a museum. See also the castle, built as a county jail in 1823, which replaces an earlier structure destroyed in 1409 by order of the Scots parliament as the English were getting more use out of it than the Scots! The substantial ruins of Jedburgh Abbey are well worth visiting.

Kelso Borders **O5**
Roxburgh. Pop 5,000. EC Wed. MD Fri. What a romantically beautiful place this is, with a wide market square, gracious buildings and floral displays. The 12thC abbey was the greatest in the borders until destroyed by the Earl of Hertford in 1545, and now only a small part remains. The fine five-arched bridge was built by Rennie and was the model for the old London Bridge. Of interest: Floors Castle, one mile north-west; Ednam House, now a hotel, with preserved Italian ceilings.

Kinross Tayside **L2**
Kinross. Pop 3,000. EC Thur. The small county town of Kinross-shire is a popular base for fishermen on nearby Loch Leven. The 17thC Tolbooth has fine decorations by Robert Adam, and the town cross still has attached the old jougs or iron collar for wrongdoers.

Kirkliston Lothian **L3**
West Lothian. Now by-passed by the M9 motorway, peace has returned to this centuries old village noted for its 12thC church. Two miles west are the remains of Niddry Castle where Mary Queen of Scots stayed in 1568.

Kirkoswald Strathclyde **G7**
Ayr. A small farming village lying some four miles west of Maybole. Noted for its Robert Burns associations through 'Souter Johnnie' and 'Tam o'Shanter'. Nearby is the great Robert Adam mansion of Culzean Castle.

Langholm Dumfries & Galloway **M8**
Dumfries. Pop 2,300. EC Wed. The chief town of Eskdale, its good stone houses and woollen mills sit well by the river.

Linlithgow Lothian **K3**
West Lothian. Pop 5,700. EC Wed. On viewing the roofless remains of Linlithgow Palace it is not hard to imagine why it was a favourite Royal Palace. It stands on a knoll overlooking Linlithgow Loch, and huddled by its side is the village which is still a royal burgh.

Lockerbie Dumfries & Galloway **L8**
Dumfries. Pop 3,000. EC Tue. MD Thur. A quiet redstone town in Annandale where in 1593 the last great border feuds ended in a bloody battle between the Johnstones and the Maxwells. There were few Maxwells left.

Lockerbie

Melrose Borders **N5**
Roxburgh. Pop 2,200. EC Thur. Another town which grew up beside a 7thC monastery. The existing monastery ruins date however mainly from the 15thC, although there is evidence to suppose Robert the Bruce's heart is buried in the abbey. The market cross dates from 1642.
Don't miss Sir Walter Scott's house 'Abbotsford'; Darnick Tower; and two miles west, Dryburgh Abbey where Field Marshall Haig and Scott are buried.

Moffat Dumfries & Galloway **L7**
Dumfries. Pop 2,000. EC Wed. The leader of 'The Few', Air Chief Marshal Lord Dowding was born here, and John MacAdam the roadmaker is buried here. Set in gorgeous hills, its wide square with Colvin's ram fountain and pleasant shops make this a good stop-over place. In the middle years of the last century this was a fashionable spa. Of interest: Moffat House (1727) now a hotel; The Grey Mare's Tail, a 200-foot waterfall to the north-east.

Moscow Strathclyde **H5**
Ayr. The name is authentic and it even sits on the Volga, a local burn. A small hamlet some five miles north of Glaston on the Glasgow road.

New Abbey Dumfries & Galloway **K9**
Kirkcudbright. EC Thur. This village is overlooked by the red sandstone ruins of the Cistercian abbey founded in 1273 by Devorguilla, mother of the King, John Balliol. When her husband, also John Balliol, died she kept his embalmed heart in a silver-and-ivory casket by her side for 21 years until her death. She and the casket were buried beside Balliol in front of the abbey altar. Since then the church has been called 'Sweetheart Abbey'.

New Lanark Strathclyde **K5**
Lanark. A late 18thC 'new' cotton spinning town founded by the philanthropist David Dale as an experiment in community living. Dale's son-in-law Robert Owen has been allocated most of the praise by history for this scheme which he extended to include improved factory management and education. An attractive place: the old mill is a real gem.

Peebles Borders **L5**
Peebles. Pop 5,900. EC Wed. MD Fri. An old pleasant county town in an outstanding setting with connections with the explorer Mungo Park and John Buchan. The tower of old St Andrew church is 13thC as are the remains of Cross Kirk.
Of interest: Neidpath Castle, just west of the town; it played a part in the Civil War.

Romanno Bridge Borders **L5**
Peebles. A tiny village in the Lyne Water. Three miles south are the ruins of Drochil Castle, left unfinished in 1581 after its owner, Regent Morton, had been executed.

Ruthwell Dumfries & Galloway **L9**
Dumfries. In a specially constructed apse the church holds the beautiful 8thC Ruthwell Cross, one of the most notable carved stone crosses in Europe. Dr Henry Duncan, founder of the savings bank movement, was minister here and in a still standing cottage the first savings bank was opened in 1810.

Selkirk Borders **M6**
Selkirk. Pop 5,700. EC Thur, Sat. A town which made its contribution to the years of border bloodshed, but now concentrates on its tweedmills on the banks of the River Ettrick.
Sir Walter Scott was Sheriff of the county for 33 years; his statue stands in the triangular market place. Nearby is a statue of Mungo Park, the African explorer born in 1771. Of interest: The 'Common Riding Ceremony' with 250-300 horsemen; the Ironmongery and Countryside Museum in 17thC Halliwell's Close.

Skirling Borders **K5**
Peebles. A delightful village with a green. Curious ironwork at Skirling House.

Stirling Central **J3**
Stirling. Pop 29,800. EC Wed. MD Thur. A well mannered university town of substance. Stirling Castle, high on its rock, has dominated much of Scottish history just as it dominates the town today. It went from fortress to royal palace, to barracks, and is now one of Stirling's most interesting show places.
Fine houses in Stirling include Mar's Work, built in 1570 though never completed; Argyll's Lodging, built in 1630; the 16th-17thC Darnley's House reconstructed in 1957; and Cowane's Hospital built in 1639. The town holds a well known spring festival.

Stirling Castle

Stobo Borders **L5**
Peebles. Another pretty village in the Tweed Valley. The tower, nave and chancel of Stobo church are Norman. A barrel-vaulted porch protects a 13thC doorway. Across the river is Dawyck House where Carl von Linne (Linneus), the great Swedish naturalist, visited his pupil Sir James Nasmyth, who introduced many species of trees, including the larch, into Scotland.

Stow Borders **M5**
Midlothian. Pop 1,400. EC Thur. A charming little village on the Edinburgh-Galashiels road, with a fine packhorse bridge of 1655.

Regional oddities

Model fish boats
Many of the more old fashioned fishmongers in this region have model trawlers on display in their shops. A thoughtful reminder of the men who still have to hunt the fish, and the dangers they still have to face even in this technological age.

Northfield Doo'cots Lothian **N3**
Preston, East Lothian. Beehive shaped stone doo'cots or dovecotes like the one at Northfield House held anything from 600 to 1,000 brace of pigeon, bred all the year round to provide fresh young 'squab' which were a delicacy in mediaeval times when all meat had to be salted to last the winter. There are 62 doo'cots remaining in East Lothian, and many more over the rest of the lowlands.

Doo'cot, East Lothian

Famous people

Robert Burns (1759–96) **K8**
Burns' House, Burns' St, Dumfries & Galloway. Scotland's most famous bard, author of 'Auld Lang Syne' and many other verses. Written in dialect, much of his work is difficult for the Anglo-Saxon to understand. Many places of pilgrimage have been preserved, including his birthplace at Burns' Cottage, Alloway, near Ayr, which is now a museum. The Bachelors Club, a debating society founded by Burns and his friends, used to meet in a little 17thC house at Tarbolton in Ayrshire which is now maintained by the National Trust for Scotland. From 1791 until his death Burns lived in Dumfries, and his house in Burns' Street has been turned into a museum. *Open 10.00–19.00 Apr–Sep (closed Sun morning), 10.00–17.00 Oct–Mar (closed Sun).*

John Knox (1505–72) **L4**
John Knox House, High St, Edinburgh, Lothian. Knox led the Protestant Reformation in Scotland. He was one of the many crosses that the devout Catholic Queen Mary had to shoulder.
Knox's house in Edinburgh was occupied by him from 1561 to 1572. The house itself, built in 1490, is one of the most picturesque of the historic dwellings of Edinburgh and has the sole remaining example of the once commonplace timber galleries. It contains a Knox museum. *Open 10.00–17.00 daily. Closed Sun.*

John Knox's House, Edinburgh.

Mary Queen of Scots (1542–87) **L4**
Queen of Scotland at six days old, at sixteen years she married the Dauphin, at seventeen years she was Queen of France and at eighteen widow. Mary returned to Scotland in 1561 to begin her tragic tumultuous six year reign. Mary is associated with many places in Scotland, principally Holyrood House. But she was imprisoned twice in Loch Leven Castle near Kinross; Falkland Palace was her place of relaxation; and she spent her honeymoon with the Earl of Bothwell at Borthwick Castle in Midlothian. At Craigmillar Castle, three miles south of Edinburgh on the old Dalkeith Road, stayed many of Mary's French entourage and the district is still known as Little France.

Sir Walter Scott (1771–1832) **N5**
Abbotsford House, Borders. 3 miles W of Melrose. An ordinary house set in an extraordinary landscape which helped to shape much of Anglo Scottish history. Scott's genius and romanticism gave him the vision to set the border story down on paper in his study at Abbotsford which was been preserved as he left it. *Open 10.00–17.00 daily mid Mar–late Oct. Closed Sun morning.*

Cathedrals, abbeys & churches

Ceres Church Fife **M2**
Ceres, Fife. In the late 18thC oblong hall churches with handsome galleries for the excess congregation appeared. Here the gallery is supported on cool white Grecian columns above which runs a simple plaster frieze. The irreverent may be assailed by doubts that they may have really come to the theatre.

Dalmeny Church Lothian **L3**
Dalmeny, nr Edinburgh, Midlothian. One of the finest specimens of a 12thC Romanesque church in Britain. The ribbing vaulting is exceptionally fine.

Dunfermline Abbey Church Fife **L3**
Dunfermline, Fife. This massive and soulful Norman church is built on the remains of a Benedictine abbey founded by Queen Margaret. Notice the carved columns of the nave with that peculiarly Norman zig-zag pattern and topped off with bold cushion capitals. Before the high altar lies buried Robert the Bruce, his grave being marked by a modern brass.

Dunsdeer church.

Durisdeer Church Dumf. & Gall. **K7**
Dumfries. An elegant late 17thC church, built by the Duke of Queensberry and still containing its original box pews. In the north wing is the elaborate, but very beautiful, black and white marble monument to the second Duke and Duchess of Queensberry.

Glasgow Cathedral Strathclyde **H4**
Glasgow, Larnark. A perfect example of pre-Reformation Gothic architecture by an unknown architect. The cathedral is without doubt the most noteworthy building in Glasgow. The fan vaulting in the crypt over the tomb of St Mungo is particularly fine. Good modern stained glass.

Lyne Church Borders **L5**
Lyne, Peebles. A small church built in 1645 to meet the simple needs of Reformed worship. Like the new religion it's compact without frills and sturdy. The church contains the original barrel-shaped pulpit and canopied pews which are now rarely seen in buildings of this period.

Melrose Abbey Borders **N5**
Melrose, Roxburgh. There were buildings here in the distant past, but nothing to compare with the simple delicate grandeur of the 15thC abbey, much of which survives today. The window tracery of the south transept is formed into curvilinear and flamelike forms, and the great east window is of a very high order. One of Scotland's great religious houses: what a pity it was so ravaged in 1544.

Melrose Abbey

St Giles High Kirk Lothian **L4**
Edinburgh, Midlothian. St Giles has suffered from a succession of enthusiastic over restorations and alterations through the years. But its square central tower (c1495) still raises unspoiled the famous 'Crown of St Giles' while the interior has been restored to dignity and beauty.
It was in this church that the first blow against Episcopalianism was struck – literally! Miss Jeanny Geddes in 1637 was so incensed at hearing Laud's Book of Common Prayer read out, that she threw her stool at the unfortunate Dean of Edinburgh.

St Monance Church Fife **N2**
Between Elie and Crail, Fife. The old kirk of St Monance has been a place of worship for 600 years. It is built so close to the sea that in stormy weather spray is flung right to the church door. Interesting octagonal steeple incorporating belfry windows. The interior is lit by beautiful decorated windows.

St. Monance

Castles and ruins

Caerlaverock Castle Dumf. & Gall. **K9**
Dumfries. 7 miles sse of Dumfries. Fierce, large and impressive this old sandstone pile has been dominating people since 1290. The castle is triangular in plan, an unusual design,

with round towers at the angles. *Open 9.30-16.00 Oct-Mar, 9.30-19.00 Apr-Sep, Closed Sun morning.*

Castlesweerock Castle

Castle Sween Strathclyde **D3**
Knapdale, Argyll. 8 miles sw of Lochgilphead.
This is the earliest stone castle in Scotland. The broad flat buttresses and the round arched entrance are characteristic of Norman work. There are no windows, and all the living quarters were built of wood with the courtyard being partially roofed in. *Open any reasonable time.*

Dirleton Castle Lothian **M3**
Dirleton, East Lothian. The castle of warm red and grey stone is set on a rock outcrop overlooking a rich arable plain. It dates partly from the 13thC but there is a three-storey Renaissance portion still standing. *Open 9.30-19.00 Apr-Sep. 9.30-16.30 Oct-Mar. Closed Sun morning.*

Dunstaffnage Castle Strathclyde **E1**
Argyll. 3 miles nne of Oban. A 13thC castle of enclosure, but with a few frills in the way of extra flanking towers. It was burnt down in 1685, but partially restored and lived in until 1810 when it was again burnt down. It is said that the Stone of Destiny, or Stone of Scone, was kept there until removed to Scone.

Edinburgh Castle Lothian **L4**
Edinburgh, Midlothian. On dark misty evenings this old fortress takes up an ethereal look when viewed from Princes Street. There has been a strong point atop Castle Rock since at least the 7thC, and the little Norman St Margaret Chapel (1076) within the existing castle precincts is the oldest building in Edinburgh in regular use. Most of the rest of the structure dates from the 16thC. You won't miss the great gun fired every day at 13.00 as a time check. *Open daily. Closed Sun morning.*

Edinburgh Castle, Midlothian.

Neidpath Castle Borders **L5**
Nr Peebles. Set on a bluff overlooking the River Tweed, this castle was once a stronghold of the Frasers, but eventually came into the hands of the Dukes of Queensberry. The walls of the oldest part are eleven foot thick, but even that didn't prevent Cromwell's artillery smashing it into submission during the Civil War.

Tantallon Castle

Tantallon Castle Lothian **N3**
East Lothian. 3 miles e of North Berwick.
Perched precariously on the edge of the cliff above the Firth of Forth and opposite the Bass Rock, the ruins of Tantallon are so substantial as to make one believe they have beaten time as well as old foes. The frontal curtain wall and imposing central gatehouse date from the 14thC. *Open 9.30-19.00 Oct-Mar, 9.30-19.00 Apr-Sep. Closed Sun morning.*

Threave Castle Dumf. & Gall. **J9**
Kirkcudbright. 1½ miles w of Castle Douglas.
The 14thC home of the Black Douglases, so called for their merciless pillaging of the countryside. The castle looks hard and pitiless as it rises out of the waters of the River Dee, and in the old days this was enhanced by the Douglas habit of hanging their enemies from a gallows knob over the main entrance. *Open 9.30-19.00 daily Apr-Sep. Closed Thur & Sun morning.*

Unusual buildings

The Forth Bridges **L3**
The great rail bridge built 1893-90 was the wonder of its age. Designed by Sir John Fowler and Sir Benjamin Baker it is of steel construction on the cantilever principle. Over a mile long it cost over £3,000,000, a phenomenal figure at the time.

Forth Rail Bridge

By contrast the Road Suspension Bridge, opened in 1964, seems to soar effortlessly over the water with a spectacular centre span of 3,300 feet. Even so the two bridges set each other off.

Forth Road Bridge

Nuffield Transplantation Surgery Unit Lothian **L4**
Edinburgh, Midlothian. The recently built unit is part of the Western General Hospital in Edinburgh. A reinforced concrete structure designed for a specific medical purpose. In meeting its special requirements (filtered ventilation, and windows guarded against direct rays of the sun), a building of impressive architectural merit has been created.
Proof that concrete buildings need not be monolithic slabs. Curved and flat surfaces, light and shade, and a strong outline combine to make this a most satisfying structure.

The Watchtower Fife **L2**
Kinross. At one end of the spacious Kinross Park is an old churchyard with a squat watch tower. It was erected to guard against the 'Resurrectionists' who illegally exhumed bodies and sold them for anatomical research, notably in Edinburgh. There are several other examples of such care for the departed 'loved one' dotted round the region.

The Watchtower, Kinross

Houses and gardens

Achamore Strathclyde **D5**
Isle of Gigha, Argyll. ¼ mile from Ardminish by ferry from mainland. With the climatic benefit of the Gulf Stream this outstanding garden, built up by Col Sir Brian Horlick, boasts tender and exotic plants. Shrubs from the Himalayas, Andes and Caucasus flourish here. *Open 10.00-Sunset daily Apr-Sep.*

The Binns Lothian **K3**
Nr Linlithgow, West Lothian. The historic home of the Dalyells, among them General Tom Dalyell who raised the Royal Scots Greys there in 1681. Fine plaster ceilings put in between 1612 and 1630. *Open 14.00-17.30 daily mid Apr-Sep. Closed Fri.*

Brodick Castle Strathclyde **E5**
Isle of Arran. A large baronial mansion dating

back in parts to the 14thC though the major part was designed by Gillespie Graham in 1845. There is a magnificent collection of treasures including paintings by Clouet, Watteau, and Turner. Also silver, china and other objets d'art. Lovely gardens. *Open 13.00–17.00 daily (14.00–17.00 Sun) mid Apr-Sep.*

Culross Palace Fife **K3**
Culross, Fife. An attractive late 16thC town mansion built around an open yard by Sir George Bruce. Many of the panelled rooms are painted all over with religious scenes. *Open 9.30–19.00 (14.00–19.00 Sun) Apr-Sep 9.30–16.00 (14.00–16.00 Sun) Oct-Mar.*

Culzean Castle Strathclyde **G7**
Maybole, Ayr. Pronounced Culeen. One of the finest Adam houses in Scotland, built in 1777 for the 10th Earl of Cassilis in mock Gothic style, incorporating the tower of an earlier Kennedy stronghold. Fine plaster ceilings, oval staircase and a round drawing room with its own circular carpet. *Open 10.00–18.00 daily Mar-Oct.*

Culzean Castle, Ayrshire

Falkland Palace Fife **L2**
Falkland, Fife. Owned by The Queen, Falkland was the hunting palace of the Stuart Kings from the mid 15thC until the death of King James II in 1625. The south wing, the only one in tolerable preservation, presents an elegant ornamental facade with attractive mullioned windows. See: the 17thC Flemish tapestries; the old Royal Tennis Court. *Open 10.00–18.00 daily (closed Sun morning) late Mar-mid Oct.*

Glenarn Strathclyde **G3**
Rhu, Dumbarton. A wonderful springtime garden with magnolias, daffodils, primulas and rhododendrons. *Open 14.00–21.00 daily Mar-late Aug.*

Hopetoun House Lothian **L3**
South Queensferry, West Lothian. Massive and spreading, this large house commanding the Firth of Forth was built by Sir William Bruce for the 1st Earl of Hopetoun. In 1721 William Adam began the work of enlargement, eventually completed in 1751. The interior is magnificent with woodcarving and plasterwork. *Open 13.30–17.30 Sat-Wed May-mid Sep.*

Inveraray Castle Strathclyde **F2**
Inveraray, Argyll. Grey, massive and square relieved only by a round tower at each corner. It could be ugly, but somehow Roger Morris, who designed the house in 1746, just gets away with it. Inside the great hall, armoury, state rooms, tapestries and portraits are very well worth inspection. *Open daily. Closed Sun morning & Fri Apr-late June.*

Inveraray Castle, Argyll

Kellie Castle Fife **N2**
Nr Pittenweem, Fife. It now consists of two 16thC towers united by a 17thC range. Good plaster work and painted panelling. A fine example of the domestic architecture of the lowland counties of Scotland. *Open 14.00–18.00 Wed-Sun Apr-Sep.*

Kinross House Tayside **L2**
Loch Leven, Kinross. A grand 17thC garden with a superb formal parterre, statuary and topiary. The herbaceous borders are lovely. *Open Wed, Sat & Sun May-Sep.*

Lauriston Castle Lothian **L3**
Davidson's Mains, Edinburgh, Midlothian. Built around a turreted and corbelled 16thC tower it is now a country mansion of great charm, standing in grounds overlooking the Firth of Forth. Fine furniture, Flemish tapestries and Blue John ware. *Open 11.00–*

17.00 daily (closed Fri) Apr-Oct. 14.00–17.00 Sat & Sun Nov-Mar.*

Mellerstain Borders **N5**
Gordon, Berwick. One of the most attractive mansions in Scotland and another joint effort by the Adam family. William built the wings in 1725 and Robert the main block 40 years later. The interior decorations and ceiling by Robert are very fine. Old master paintings and antique furniture on view. *Open 14.00–17.30 daily May-late Sep. Closed Sat.*

Palace of Holyrood House, Midlothian.

Palace of Holyrood House Lothian **L3**
Edinburgh, Midlothian. The Queen's official residence in Scotland. The palace originated as a guest house of the abbey of Holyrood, now a picturesque ruin. As seen today the palace is mainly the work of King Charles II who began rebuilding in 1671. The portraits of 111 Scottish Kings were knocked off in two years by a hack artist, one James de Witt, completing in 1684. *Open daily. Closed Sun morning & when Royal Family in residence.*

Traquair House Borders **M5**
Innerleithen, Peebles. Dating back to the 10thC, Traquair is one of the oldest inhabited homes in Scotland, although most of it was rebuilt in the 17thC. A gaunt grey place with little turrets and small windows. The house contains silver, glass, tapestries and embroideries from the 13thC and relics of Mary Queen of Scots. Beer is brewed to a 200-year-old recipe and sold to visitors. *Open 13.30–17.30 daily May-late Sep & B. Hols. Closed Fri.*

Winton House Lothian **M4**
Pencaitland, East Lothian. A fine Renaissance mansion built by George Seton, 3rd Earl of Winton, in 1620 and enlarged in 1800. Interesting carved twisted stone chimneys, and good plaster ceiling said to have been decorated for the visit of King Charles I in 1633.
Terraced gardens, fine trees and lawns give the house a lovely setting. *Open to parties only or others very specially interested at any time. Tel 222.*

Museums and galleries

Broughton House Dumf. & Gall. **J10**
Kirkcudbright. A collection of the books and paintings of E. A. Hornel. *Open 11.00–16.00 Mon-Fri Apr-Sep. 14.00–16.00 Tue & Thur Oct-Mar.*

Fire Engine Museum Lothian **L4**
McDonald Rd, Edinburgh, Midlothian. Covers the history of fire fighting. Edinburgh had the first municipal brigade in the world. *Open daily. Closed Sun.*

Gladstone Court Museum Strathclyde **K5**
Biggar, Lanark. Recreation of a 19thC shopping street. *Open daily May-Oct. Closed Wed afternoon & Sun morning.*

Glasgow Art Gallery Strathclyde H4
Kelvingrove, Glasgow, Lanark. One of the
best municipal collections. Superb Flemish,
Dutch and French paintings, drawing and
prints. Also ceramics, silver, costumes and
armour. *Open daily. Closed Sun morning.*

Halliwell's House Borders M6
Selkirk. Fascinating ironmongery and
countryside museum. *Open daily. Closed
Sun.*

Hunterian Museum Strathclyde H4
*University of Glasgow, Gilmorehill, Glasgow,
Lanark.* Manuscripts, early printed books
and Roman pieces. *Open daily. Closed Sat
afternoon & Sun.*

Museum of Childhood Lothian L4
*Hyndford's Close, High St, Edinburgh,
Midlothian.* Unique collection of toys, books,
costumes and dolls. *Open daily. Closed Sun.*

Museum of Transport Strathclyde H4
Albert Drive, Glasgow, Lanark. A fine
collection of trams, cars, horse-drawn
carriages, six steam locos and bicycles. *Open
daily. Closed Sun morning.*

National Gallery of Scotland Lothian L4
Mound, Edinburgh, Midlothian. Opened in
1859. A very fine exhibition of paintings
from the Renaissance to the 20thC including
a good collection of Scottish painting, some
superb Constables and Rembrandts and one
El Greco. *Open daily. Closed Sun morning.*

Provand's Lordship Strathclyde H4
High St, Glasgow, Lanark. Glasgow's oldest
house and now a museum of 17th-18thC
furniture and household articles. *Open
10.00–17.00 daily Apr–Sep. 11.00–16.00 Oct–
Mar. Closed Sun.*

Queen Mary's House Borders N6
Jedburgh, Roxburgh. Mary stayed here in
1566. Her bedroom, thimblecase and watch
are among interesting memorabilia. *Open
daily Apr–Sep. Closed Sun morning.*

Royal Scottish Museum Lothian L4
Chambers St, Edinburgh, Midlothian.
Britain's largest comprehensive display in
one building. Four main departments –
technology, geology, natural history, art and
archaeology. *Open daily. Closed Sun
morning.*

The Scottish Fisheries N2
Museum Fife
Anstruther, Fife. Everything to do with
fishing, ancient and modern, including an
aquarium. *Open 10.00–18.00 daily. (Closed
Sun morning) Apr–Oct. 14.30–16.30 daily
Nov–Mar*

Scottish National L4
Portrait Gallery Lothian
Queen St, Edinburgh, Midlothian. Collection
of famous Scots from 16thC to the present.
Also National Museum of Antiquities with
bits and pieces from the past. *Open daily.
Closed Sun morning.*

Souter Johnnie's Cottage Strathclyde G7
Kirkoswald, Ayr. The home of John
Davidson, the prototype of Souter Johnnie
in Burns's 'Tam o'Shanter'. Burns relics.
*Open 14.30–20.00 daily Apr–Sep. Closed Sat
& Sun.*

Botanical gardens

Benmore Younger F3
Botanic Garden Strathclyde
Argyll. 7 miles nw of Dunoon. A garden given
by the late Sir Harry Younger in public
trust. Some rare and beautiful plants, shrubs
and trees. There is also a good pinetum and a
fine avenue of sequoias. *Open daily Apr–Sep.*

Crarae Forest Garden Strathclyde E2
Argyll. 11 miles s of Invararay. A 33-acre
forest garden set in a Highland glen
containing a splendid selection of conifers,
eucalyptus and shrubs. *Open daily.*

Royal Botanic Garden Lothian L4
Inverleith Row, Edinburgh, Midlothian.
Started in 1670, there are some superb
collections, notably hardy plants and shrubs
from western China, rock plants and alpines.
The modern palmhouse with its suspended
glass roof houses some fine tropical and
sub-tropical specimens. There are

experimental gardens, conservatories and a
charming woodland garden. *Open 9.00–dusk
Mon–Sat (11.00–dusk Sun) Feb–Oct.*

Glasgow Botanic H4
Gardens Strathclyde
Great Western Rd, Glasgow, Lanark.
Established in 1817, the garden's 42 acres
are crammed with interest, including the
famed Kibble Palace glasshouse with its
fabulous tree ferns and exotic plants. *Open
7.00–dusk daily.*

Kilmun Arboretum Strathclyde F3
Nr Holy Loch, Dunoon, Argyll. Established
by the Forestry Commission in 1930, there is
a large collection of conifers and hardwoods
grouped in specimen plots. Look out for the
fine plantings of eucalyptus. 180 acres with
three marked routes and woodland walks.
Open daily.

Logan Botanic Garden Dumf. & Gall.F10
Nr Ardwell, Wigtown. A sub-tropical
paradise. Huge cabbage palms reflect in
lily ponds; the odd stunted shapes of the
Australian tree ferns provide an exotic
background for the fabulous rhododendrons
for which Logan is also famous. *Open daily
Apr–late Sep. No animals.*

Threave House Dumf. & Gall. J9
Castle Douglas, Kirkcudbright. A 1,300 acre
estate used by the National Trust as a
gardening school. There are peat, rock and
water gardens including a wildfowl refuge,
and in spring great drifts of daffodils. *Open
daily.*

Zoos, aquaria and aviaries

Glasgow Zoo Strathclyde H4
Calderpark, Uddingston, Glasgow. Set in
parkland, this zoo includes lions, lemurs,
chinchillas and reptiles in its collection.
*Open 9.30–19.00 Apr–Oct. 9.30–17.00 Nov–
Mar.*

Edinburgh Zoo Lothian L4
*Corstorphine Hill, Murrayfield, Edinburgh,
Midlothian.* Set in 80 acres of natural
landscape. Famous for its penguins,
children's farm with small scale buildings
and implements, and chimpanzees' teaparty.
*Open 9.30–19.00 Apr–Oct (12.00–19.00 Sun).
9.30–sunset Nov–Mar.*

Nature trails and reserves

Aberlady Bay Lothian M3
East Lothian. Excellent area for wildfowl
and waders, marine biology and botany.
Access from car-park beside A198 just
outside Aberlady village.

Ae Forest Dumf. & Gall. K8
Dumfries. Start at Forest Office at Ae
village, 2½ miles off Ae Bridge on A701. 3½
mile forest walk with forest and wildlife
interest and good scenery. Information from
the Conservator, Greystone Park, 55
Moffat Rd, Dumfries.

Barns Ness Lothian O3
East Lothian. Off A1 se of Dunbar. ½ mile.
Geological interest and good for coastal
birds and migrants in season. Marine biology
and botanical interest. Guide from
information centres at North Berwick and
Dunbar.

Enterkine Wood Strathclyde G6
Ayr. Scottish Wildlife Trust reserve at
Annbank, entrance from road between B744
and B730. Birds, plants and mammals of
mixed woodland and stream. Details from
Wildlife Trust, 19 Highfield Ave, Prestwick.

Inverinan Strathclyde E1
Argyll. At Loch Awe off B845. Wildlife of
managed forest. Forest Centre. 5 walks of
1¼–5 miles. Booklet from Forestry
Commission, 21 India St, Glasgow.

Loch Lomond National Nature
Reserve Central G3
Dunbarton/Stirling. Via A809 from

Glasgow, B837 to Drymen and then to Balmaha. Woodland scenery, birds and botany. Archaeological interest. Details from Nature Conservancy, 12 Hope Terrace, Edinburgh, Midlothian.

South Bute Strathclyde
Bute. Three-hour walk. Seashore and hill. Plants and coastal birds. Guide from Bute Museum, Rothesay.

Bird watching

Ayr and Doonfoot Strathclyde   **G6**
Ayr. The sea front at Ayr south to the mouth of the Doon generally produces good birds of passage and in winter a selection of waders and duck may be found. Fulmars, gannets and kittiwakes are seen offshore in summer, while glaucous gulls are regular in winter, especially in Ayr harbour itself.

Bass Rock Lothian   **N3**
East Lothian. Superb seabird island off North Berwick with a huge gannet colony, shags, fulmars and auks. Local boatmen run regular sailings around the Bass in summer and these give superb views of most of the birds. Details are posted at North Berwick Harbour.

Carsethorn and   **K9**
Southerness Dumfries & Galloway
Kirkcudbright. The Solway Firth is quite superb for its numbers and variety of wildfowl and waders in autumn and winter. Carsethorn, reached via the minor road from A710 at Kirkbean, is particularly good for scaup, pintail and huge knot flocks, while Southerness, also easily accessible from A710, has sea duck and purple sandpipers and often grey geese on the fields inland.

Edinburgh Lothian   **L3**
Midlothian. The birdwatcher visiting Edinburgh will find the Forth coast from Seafield (Leith) east to Portobello and Joppa good for waders and winter sea duck and grebes – the duck often in astonishing numbers (scaup and goldeneye especially). In the city itself, Holyrood Park is well worth a visit and Duddingston Loch has a good selection of birds and an impressive winter flock of pochard.

Islay Strathclyde   **B4**
Argyll. A superb island for birds at any season, with a variety of habitats. Golden eagle, peregrine and hen harrier may well be encountered, while eiders, mergansers and black guillemots are certainties. Choughs are found on the Mull of Oa. In winter, look at Loch Indaal for divers and sea duck and barnacle and grey geese. Leaflet from the Islay Tourist Office at Bowmore.

Kilconquhar Loch and Elie Fife Fife **M2**
Fife. Off the A917 n of Elie. Good for assorted wildfowl and famous for its August passage of little gulls. Can be viewed from the footpath beside the church. Elie itself is an excellent spot for winter divers and sea duck, shearwaters and skuas.

Kintyre Strathclyde   **D5**
Argyll. The whole of this long peninsula is splendid birding country at any season. Two particularly good areas are the Mull of Kintyre in summer (easily found via signpost from Southend) – good for hen harrier, golden eagle, peregrine and seabirds – and, in winter, the area around Rhunahaorine Point – Greenland whitefronted and grey lag geese, great northern divers, grebes and sea duck; this second area lies opposite Gigha and alongside A83 to Campbeltown.

Fossil hunting

Visit the local museum. Its fossil collection usually states where individual fossils have been found. When visiting quarries always seek permission to enter if they look privately owned or worked. Be careful of falls of rock.

Lower Palaeozoic rocks, Ordovician and Silurian, with fossils may be seen around Girvan, Ayrshire, where there are corals, brachiopods, trilobites, molluscs and crinoids with graptolites in thin bands. Further east at Moffat, Dumfriesshire, Ordovician and Silurian shales have common graptolites. Graptolites and trilobites may also be collected around Barr, Ayrshire. Devonian rocks around Cupar in Fifeshire have yielded fish-remains as have lower carboniferous cementstones in Berwickshire, together with arthropods (insects, etc.), plants and molluscs. Coal measures with plants and molluscs occur in the areas of Sanquhar, Canonbie and Thornhill in Dumfriesshire and in the coalfields of the central valley of Scotland.

Hills and Mountains

Arthur's Seat Lothian   **L4**
Edinburgh, Midlothian. This 800-foot rounded hill, springing up in the grassy King's Park, is the remains of an old volcano. Columns of hard basalt rock are revealed in its sheer inland cliffs nearby, the Salisbury Crags and Samson's Ribs. A motor-drive climbs its flanks, and the easy walk to its summit cairn gives splendid views over the city.

Ben Lomond Central   **G2**
Stirling. The shapely cone of Ben Lomond, 3,192 feet, and the southernmost Highland mountain, rises gracefully above Loch Lomond's eastern shore.
Tremendous views, far into the Highlands or east across Scotland to the Forth, reward the climber. Ben Lomond means 'the beacon mountain'.

Campsie Fells Central   **H3**
Stirling. Set centrally in the Lowlands, between Dumbarton on the Clyde and Stirling on the Forth, the Campsies are a grim grey mass of basalt rocks and thin sheep pastures, continually seen but seldom visited. They hold the huge Carron Valley reservoir, surrounded by the sprucewoods of Carron Valley Forest.

The Cobbler Strathclyde   **G2**
Argyll. A quaint mountain this, towering over Arrochar. Its twin summits earn it the Gaelic name of An Goblaich – the 'forked one'. Once English tourists arrived, somebody saw a resemblance to a cobbler bent over his last, and everyone has imagined this ever since. You can climb both forks, but it's risky.

Dunbartonshire   **G2**
Highlands Strathclyde
Little-known, the Dunbartonshire highlands form a broken range of rounded peaks holding deep glens, between Loch Lomond and Loch Long. North of Tarbet, where there is a narrow lowland gap, they get grimly mountainous.
Between Ben Vane and Ben Vorlich, both craggy 3,000-foot peaks, lies grey, cold Loch Sloy, a high level hydroelectric power reservoir that feeds a power-house on Loch Lomond-side.

Eildon Hills Borders   **N6**
Roxburgh. According to legend these shapely hills, soaring above Melrose where the plain of the Tweed first meets the western uplands, were cleft into three by a wizard, to settle a dispute with the devil. Geologists, more practically minded, insist that they are relics of three extinct volcanoes. Either way, they look miraculous.

The Lothians Lothian   **L4**
The Lothians comprise the southern shores of the Firth of Forth, for 50 miles from Falkirk east to Dunbar. Throughout this good farming country, easily reached by boat before roads were built, great estates developed from the middle ages, and their pattern persists today. West Lothian centred on the abbey and palace of Linlithgow and has become disfigured by industrial developments, including the red shale heaps which are relics of a defunct oil mining enterprise. Midlothian is nowadays

largely hidden by the spread of Edinburgh.
East Lothian, centred on Haddington,
remains unspoilt, its sunny farms and hills
a perpetual delight.

Moorfoots and Lammermuirs M4
This twin hill range runs halfway across
Scotland south of Edinburgh, dividing the
fertile Lothian lands along the Firth of Forth
from the equally rich Tweed Valley county
of the borders.
Vast 1,500-foot-high sheep walks, they give
sweeping views from their broad summits,
which are crossed by excellent roads. Soutra
Hill commands a splendid prospect over the
Forth to the Highlands.

Ochil Hills Tayside K2
Stirling to Kinross. Often mistaken for the
Highlands themselves, this dramatic range
can be seen from everywhere in the central
Lowlands. Built up of hard brown basalt
rocks, they rise sheer from the level
Clackmannan plain, for twenty miles east of
Stirling, tapering down in height towards
Kinross. The highest point is Ben Cleuch,
2,363 feet.

Pentland Hills Lothian L4
Midlothian. Uncrossed by any road, the
1,500 foot Pentland range stretches for
twenty miles south-west of Edinburgh. Its
grassy slopes, which serve as sheep pastures
and water catchments for reservoirs, are
crossed by fascinating hill tracks. At the
northern end, close to Edinburgh, there is a
popular artificial ski-slope. Highest point,
Scald Law near Penicuik, 1,898 feet.

Countryside

Dumfriesshire Dumf. & Gall. K8
The county is made up of three broad
sunny dales, all facing southwards towards
the Solway Firth. Its northern boundaries
lie high on the sheepwalks of the rolling
Lowther Hills, but the southern lowland is
rich farming country, broken by forests and
the parklands of great mansions. Nithsdale,
on the west, runs down past Drumlanrig
Castle, historic seat of the Duke of
Buccleuch, to Dumfries, the bustling
county town.
Annandale runs south past Lockerbie to the
English border at Gretna Green. Eskdale,
the narrowest, comes down through
Langholm with its lovely riverside
woodlands. The highest point is Hart Fell,
2,651 feet, which rises close to the Devil's
Beef Tub Pass, so named after cattle-raiders,
which lies six miles north of Moffat.

Fife Peninsula Fife L2
This hilly peninsula between the Firth of
Forth and the Firth of Tay was the
historical cradle of the Scottish Kingdom
where authority and religion flourished, safe
from attack from northern Highlander or
southern English invader. Easily reached
today by the Forth and Tay road and rail
bridges, its landscape bespeaks centuries of
care. Every fertile acre is fully tilled, or
grazed by thriving cattle, and the lower
slopes carry plantations of larch or pine.
Scattered at random, small steep basalt
hills, relics of old volcanoes, rise to rounded
moorland summits, hiding little lochs
within their folds. The rock-girt, stormy
coast holds a string of tiny fishing harbours
such as Crail, Pittenweem and Anstruther.
The highest point is West Lomond, a steep
bell-shaped hill, 1,712 feet in altitude,
south-west of Auchtermuchty.

Galloway Dumf. & Gall. G8
South-west Scotland's Highland province.
Its heart is the lonely 'Range of the Awful
Hand', so called from its shape when viewed
from the north. Now embodied in the
Galloway Forest Park, this is a roadless
region of 2,500 foot granite hills, broken by
peat bogs and studded with clear, cold lochs.
The Merrick, 2,764 feet and the highest
point of southern Scotland, is so called from
Gaelic *tiu meurig*, the finger or highest
knuckle of the 'hand'. Glen Trool, the glen
of the 'winding loch', namely Loch Trool,
runs far into these hills which have all the
wild rocky character of the Highlands.

Galloway Highlands.

Kintyre Strathclyde D5
Argyll. This 50-mile-long, narrow peninsula,
only eight miles across, runs due south from
mainland Argyll to end in a bold bluff
called the Mull of Kintyre, only fifteen miles
from Benmore Head on the coast of
Northern Ireland.
Kintyre itself is a pleasing blend of small
stock-raising farms, heather moors on low
hills, and young spruce forests planted by
the Forrestry Commission. Its only main
road, A83 from Lochgilphead, runs first
down lovely Loch Fyne on the eastern
shore, to Tarbert, a picturesque fishing
harbour.
Crossing the narrow isthmus to West Loch
Tarbert, with the west coast islands of Islay
and Jura in view, there follow ten miles of
open Atlantic coast, pounded by great
waves blown in from distant America.

Lanarkshire Strathclyde K5
This fine expanse of the upper dale of the
Clyde, 800 feet above sea level, deserves
exploration from centres such as Biggar or
Lanark town. The exposed, conical summit
of windy Tinto Hill, 2,335 feet, dominates
the scene, with larger ranges of the southern
uplands, all grassy sheepwalks, rolling
away on every hand. On the level valley
floor a pattern of shelterbelts and small
woods around mansion houses protects the
upland farms from the worst snowy weather.

Lorn Strathclyde
Argyll. Lorn is the romantically beautiful
hinterland of Oban, between the Firth of
Lorn on the western seaboard and Inveraray
on Loch Fyne, a parallel arm of the sea.
From Oban the winding west coast road
follows a succession of sandy bays south
between rocky headlands to Lochgilphead.
Loch Fyne's coast road, A83, north to
Inveraray, runs through forests yet gives
grand views across the water. The
north-westerly return route, back to Oban,
runs by the tree-clad shores of Loch Awe, an
inland freshwater loch 30 miles long, with
the gaunt ruins of Kilchurn Castle at its
head. After following the Oban railway
through the Pass of Brander, it runs by Loch
Etive and the Falls of Lora, where the
seawater falls eastward or westward,
according to the run of the tides.

Mull of Galloway Dumf. & Gall. F10
Wigtown. Shaped like a hammerhead, the
Mull's peninsula stands out west of the
Galloway mainland, coming within twenty
miles of Northern Ireland. The Mull itself
is a headland of steep cliffs, topped by a
lighthouse, and is the most southerly point
of all Scotland. Around it sea currents flow
ceaselessly – it is the spot 'where seven tides
meet'.

Rivers and lochs

Clyde H4
The Clyde, whose course has been the
cradle of Scotland's industrial growth, starts
as a moorland stream in the grassy Lowther
Hills of northern Dumfries-shire, near the
A74 Glasgow–Carlisle main road. One
tributary runs from Queensberry Hill, 2,285
feet within sight of the Solway Firth.

Flowing north past Lanark, and the industrial coalfield towns of Hamilton and Motherwell, the growing Clyde winds through the heart of the commercial and manufacturing capital of Glasgow. Here it becomes tidal and navigable, and wharves and shipyards line its banks towards Dumbarton. There it broadens out to become the Firth of Clyde, a broad arm of the sea running first west to Gourock, then south towards the open Atlantic.

home of Sir Walter Scott, and Melrose with its romantic ruined abbey. Crossed by bridges at Kelso and Coldstream, where it becomes the English border, the Tweed next glides through a rich agricultural landscape, with tall broadleaved trees, to Berwick-upon-Tweed. Flowing below the high railway viaduct and the old stone arch bridge. it gains the North Sea over a sandy bar at the mouth of Berwick Harbour,

Canals

The Crinan Canal
This is a short canal, only 8½ miles long, which was constructed to cut off the long journey round the peninsula of the Mull of Kintyre. It passes through a very beautiful landscape of wooded mountains. There are plenty of locks.
Things to see: the terminal basins at Ardrishaig and Crinan, and the locks halfway between them.

Forth Bridge

Forth   J3
The great river rises very near Scotland's west coast, in Loch Chon, above Loch Ard. One tributary, the Dubh Water, starts on Ben Lomond, only four miles from the western sea. Falling quickly almost to sea level, the Forth wanders east, over a flat peaty wilderness called Flanders Moss, to Stirling.
East of Stirling the Forth broadens out into its long tidal estuary, the Firth of Forth, which carries cargo ships to Grangemouth on the south side, and warships to Rosyth on the north shore. At the Queensferry Narrows, named after a historic ferryboat crossing, it is spanned by two bridges, each over a mile long.

The Crinan Canal

The Forth and Clyde Canal
This waterway cuts across the Lowlands of Scotland, from Bowling Basin on the north bank of the Clyde through Glasgow, Kirkintilloch, Kilsyth, Bonnybridge and Falkirk to Grangemouth Docks on the Forth. It is sad and neglected, and some sections have been filled in so through navigation can never be restored. But the canal is excellent for walking along, and it sports one or two elegant and very substantial aqueducts.
The waterway is easily accessible by road—and a passenger railway is never far away. The best lengths to explore are the basin at Bowling, the attractive wooded section around Kilsyth, a short tunnel near Bonnybridge and the remains of a flight of locks on the outskirts of Falkirk.

Loch Lomond, Stirling & Dumbarton.

Loch Lomond Central Strathclyde G3
Stirling & Dumbarton. The largest fresh-water lake in Britain. At its southern end, near Dumbarton, the loch is like an inland sea, bordered by level fields and studded by tree-clad islands. In the north its narrow upper reaches are shut in between the 3,000-foot peaks of Ben Lomond and Ben Vorlich. Here is a true Highland glen, with torrents, crags and pinewoods.
The best beaches are around Rowardennan, and holiday centres are at Balloch, Balmaha, Luss and Tarbet. 22 miles long by five miles at its broadest point, Loch Lomond is tapped as a water supply. What's left flows down the short River Leven to the Clyde at Dumbarton.

Tweed   L6
Springing from Tweed's Well on Hart Fell, near the Devil's Beef Tub in the heart of the southern uplands, this fine unspoilt river runs north towards Peebles, then east through a steep valley that carries fifteen miles of thriving pine, larch, and spruce forests.
Near Galashiels the dale of the Tweed widens; the river flows on past Abbotsford,

Archæology

Antonine Wall Lothian   K3
Old Kilpatrick, Dunbarton, to Bridgeness, West Lothian. Shortly after the completion of Hadrian's Wall a change of policy under the emperor Antoninus Pius led to the reconquest of the Lowlands, and in 142-43 a new frontier work was constructed between the Clyde and Forth.
During the 150s, and finally by about 180 it was abandoned in favour of Hadrian's Wall.
The Ditch This ran in front of the Wall, separated from it by a berm twenty feet wide, and measures 40 feet wide and twelve feet deep. Well-preserved sections can be seen at Callendar Park, Watling Lodge, Seabegs Wood, Rough Castle, Croy Hill and Westerwood.
The Wall Built of turf layers, the Wall probably stood some nine feet high, with a wooden parapet above. The turf was laid on a stone foundation some fourteen feet wide, and this can be seen in New Kilpatrick Cemetery and Roman Park, Bearsden. The Wall itself has not survived well, but a good section is visible at Rough Castle.

Forts Thirteen forts are known along the Wall, usually attached to its back, and there may have been eighteen in all, at roughly two-mile intervals. Three fortlets have been found. Only one fort survives well, at Rough Castle; one acre in size, it includes a headquarters building, granary, officers' quarters, and has an annexe with a bath-house. The outlines of other forts can be traced at Castlecary, Westerwood, and Bar Hill.

Military Way A service road running behind the Wall; the Way passed through the Wall forts. The forces building the Wall erected sculptured slabs recording their work, and most of these, with altars, tombstones, and models of the Wall, can be seen in the University of Glasgow Hunterian Museum; a smaller group of finds is housed in the National Museum of Antiquities, Edinburgh.

Ballochroy Strathclyde   **D5**
Mull of Kintyre, Argyll. The group of antiquities at Ballochroy probably dates from the bronze age, and includes three standing stones and a stone burial cist.

Burnswark Dumfries & Galloway   **L8**
Birrenswark, Dumfries. The iron age hillfort at Burnswark was one of the centres of the Selgovae, and, like the famous site at Masada in Israel, stormed by the Romans from a series of siegecamps placed halfway up the hill.
The siegecamps are distinguished by the large round artillery emplacements on the side facing the fort; the interior of the fort has produced quantities of lead bolts, and the defences were destroyed, the tumble spreading down the hill.
The nearby fort at Birrens, Blatobulgium, was built as an advance post for Hadrian's Wall, and continued in use as part of the Lowland garrison while the Antonine Wall was occupied.

Cairnholy Dumfries & Galloway   **H9**
Kirkcudbright. A group of Neolithic chambered cairns, with horn-like projections at the ends, which are peculiar to Scotland.

Dun Mor Vaul Strathclyde   **A7**
Isle of Tiree, Argyll. The iron age broch is built on the edge of the seashore, and its recent excavation has provided much information about the inhabitants of these defensive towers. It was apparently used only in times of danger, when the local inhabitants sheltered there.
Towards the end of the 2ndC it became the home of the chief local family.

Edin's Hall Broch Borders   **O4**
Edin's Hall, Berwick. The defensive towers of iron age Scotland are rare in the Lowlands where, as in England, the usual defensive structure was a hillfort. The broch at Edin's Hall was short-lived, and belongs to the period after the first Roman withdrawal from Scotland at the end of the 1stC. *Open any reasonable time.*

Eildon Hill North Hillfort Borders   **N6**
Eildon Hill North, Roxburgh. The large iron age hillfort was one of the centres of the Selgovae, and was destroyed by the Romans in 79. A signal-station was placed on the hill, in connection with the nearby fort of Trimontium (Newstead).

Ruthwell Cross Dumf. & Gall.   **L9**
Ruthwell Church, Ruthwell. Dumfries. 9 miles se of Dumfries. The cross at Ruthwell is one of the finest examples of Anglian sculpture, and a major European dark age monument. It was carved towards the end of the 7thC and its good state of preservation suggests that it stood inside a church. *Open any reasonable time.*

Traprain Law Lothian   **N3**
Dunpender, East Lothian. The large iron age hillfort at Traprain Law was a major tribal centre (oppidum) for the Votadini, who occupied the eastern Lowlands. Excavations have produced numerous huts, and evidence for a settled population throughout the Roman period, suggesting that the Votadini enjoyed friendly relations with the Romans. The fort continued in use during the dark ages, and a fine treasure of silver vessels was buried here during the early 5thC, probably raided from Britain or Gaul; it is now in the Museum of Antiquities, Edinburgh.

Wemyss Fife   **M2**
Fife. In addition to carving free-standing stones, the dark age Picts cut their symbols and animal representations on the walls of caves, as here at Wemyss.

Whithorn Dumfries & Galloway   **H10**
Wigtown. St Ninian probably came to Whithorn as bishop in the early 5thC and built the stone church known as Candida Casa; there is now a museum, containing crosses and tombstones. The saint later withdrew to a cave, probably that on the shore at Physgill, where later dark age gravestones have been found.

Woden Law Hillfort Borders   **O7**
Woden Law, Roxburgh. A large iron age hillfort with multiple bank and ditch defences. Woden Law was a centre for the Selgovae, and was abandoned after the Roman conquest. The line of Roman siegeworks on the hill probably represents manoeuvres, as the hillfort was unoccupied when they were built.

Footpaths

Antonine Wall   **K3**
Built 20 years after Hadrian's Wall, this earth wall stretched for 36 miles between the Firth of Forth and the Firth of Clyde.

Dere Street   **N6**
This great Roman military road was driven through the Cheviot massif towards a crossing with the Tweed near Melrose, and thence through Lauderdale to Inveresk, near Edinburgh on the Firth of Forth. The line of this Roman road remains well defined in certain sections. The Roxburgh County Council have signposted the section from the county boundary to Bonjedward, and have plans to do more.

Regional sports

Curling   **L4**
There are rinks at Kelso, Edinburgh (Haymarket), Falkirk, Glasgow, Kirkcaldy, Lockerbie, and Stranraer. (*See also Section 11.*)

Fishing   **K9**
At Glencaple on the River Nith in Dumfriesshire traditional fishing methods still live on: local fishermen operate their stake nets for flounders, and even more of a Solway speciality, catch salmon by use of a 'haaf' net. The haaf netters stand in a line chest deep in water, facing the current, holding a fourteen-foot spar to which is attached a net. The bottom of the net is held up so that it forms a series of open pockets. When a salmon snags the net the fisherman throws net and fish over the spar, stuns it with a mallet and deposits it in his creel. A most profitable sport, but licences are hard to come by.
Apart from the esoteric this area offers superb sport. In the rivers Dee and Tweed and their tributaries on the east coast is excellent sea fishing, and the largest fresh water lake in Britain, Loch Lomond, offers varied sport.

Football   **H4**
Football in Scotland means Celtic and Rangers. The teams have dominated Scottish football for years and are fierce rivals. This rivalry finds its counterpart in the equally fierce partisanship of their supporters. Celtic was formed by Irish Catholics living in the east end of Glasgow, and religious differences being what they are, the other big team in Glasgow, the Rangers, attracted a large Protestant following. The result is that when the two teams play tickets are like gold dust. Celtic play at Parkhead, and Rangers at Ibrox Park.

Golf
M1

St Andrews, Fifeshire, is famous the world over as the home of the Royal and Ancient Golf Club, the ruling body of world golf. The game and its development is uniquely Scots. Fife probably has more golf courses per head of population than any other part of the world.

Golf in Scotland is also cheap. There are four courses in St Andrews: Old, New, Eden and Jubilee. Other seaside Fifeshire courses are Crail, Elie and Earlsferry, Scotscraig at Tayport, Leven, Kinghorn and Aberdour.

Inland there are excellent courses at Canmore, Glenrothes, Ladybank, Pitreavie, and Kirkcaldy and the testing hill courses like St Michael's and Cupar. There are hundreds of other first class courses, mainly south of the Highlands. The Scottish Tourist Board publishes a brochure detailing over 300 golf courses which welcome visitors (23 Ravelston Terrace, Edinburgh).

Sailing
F5

The Clyde is the Scottish answer to the Solent. Clyde Week has an international reputation, and deservedly. If the rather dodgy Scots west coast weather is ignored, this is probably one of the finest places in the world to sail. Large areas of semi-sheltered waters, exceptional scenery, and the close proximity of other outstanding sailing areas make this the *sans pareil* of sailing.

Sub aqua
O4

Berwick. Reliable, above average visibility has made the coast between St Abb's and Eyemouth in Berwickshire a popular area for skindivers and diving clubs. The clear waters enable wrecks and the Cathedral Rock to be seen to advantage. At the Scoutscroft Diving Centre, Coldingham, air is readily available at 3,500 psi.

Festivals

Edinburgh Festival Lothian
L4

Edinburgh, Midlothian. Started in 1947, it's a grand festival of film, opera, music, drama,

art and military pageant. 'Beating the Retreat' on Castle esplanade, Wednesday and Saturday evenings. *Mid Aug–Sep.*

Stirling Festival Central
J3

Stirling. Begun in 1959; Albert Hall is the centre of activity for this festival of concerts and recitals. The concert of popular Scottish music is a main attraction. *Mid May.*

Fun things

Camera Obscura Lothian
L4

Outlook Tower, Castle Hill, Edinburgh, Midlothian. A Victorian toy for projecting onto a screen in a darkened room a panorama of the countryside surrounding the building in which it is housed.

This fine specimen has been operating since 1892 and is described in a fifteen minute tour by a guide. It belongs to Edinburgh University's Divinity Faculty. *Open daily (12.00–18.00 Sun) Jun–Sep.*

Cruachan Power Station Strathclyde
F1

Nr the Pass of Brander, Argyll. 7 miles w of Dalmally. An underground power station which takes water from a reservoir high up the side of Ben Cruachan and turns it into electricity at peak periods, and when the grid is lightly loaded takes water from Loch Awe and returns it to the reservoir.

During the summer the Scottish Hydro Electric Board run a minibus service down to the underground galleries from the car park. *Open 10.00–18.00 daily.*

Grants Distillery Strathclyde
F7

Girvan, Ayr. This is a far cry from the whitewashed black-roofed little distilleries of the Highalnds. Automated and among the most modern distilleries in Europe producing both grain and lowland malt whisky. *Guided tours 10.00–17.00 daily. Closed Sat & Sun.*

Lochty Private Railway Fife
M2

Fife. 6 miles nw of Anstruther on B940 Cupar Crail road. On Sundays a steam train with an observation car and a restored LNER streamlined pacific (similar to Mallard which holds the world's speed record for a steam engine) puffs up and down the line between Lochty and Knightsward. *Open Sun afternoon Jun–Sep.*

Myreton Motor Museum Lothian
M3

Nr Aberlady, E Lothian. On A198 Edinburgh-North Berwick road 1 mile e of Luffness House. The largest motor museum in Scotland with a constantly changing exhibition including over twenty motor cycles, twenty bicycles, and the Bullnose Morris used by 'Doctor Finlay' when compiling his well known television 'Casebook' came from here.

There is a branch of the museum at Castle Park, Dunbar. *Open daily. Closed Mon–Fri, Nov–Mar.*

Prestongrange Historical Site Lothian
M4

Midlothian. 2½ miles e of Musselburgh between A1 and A198. One of the few remaining working Cornish beam engines. Until about fifteen years ago it was still giving yeoman service all over Britain. This specimen was built in 1874 for the New Battle Abbey colliery and ceased pumping in 1955. For details Tel 661-2718 or Haddington 4161.

Preston Mill Lothian
N3

East Linton, E Lothian. 5 miles w of Dunbar off A1. A rather rough building with great charm. This is the only working water mill left on the River Tyne and is the oldest working grain mill in Scotland. Dates from the 18thC. *Open 10.00–19.30 Apr–Sep. 10.00–16.30 Oct–Mar. Closed Sun morning.*

Scottish Railway Preservation Society Central
K3

Wallace St, Falkirk, Stirling. A collection of locomotives, coaches and waggons dating from 1875 to 1953; also items of railwayana. Locomotives are occasionally steamed. *Open 11.00–18.00 Sat.*

Hotels

Arduaine Strathclyde
D2

Loch Melfort Motor Inn, by Oban. Tel Kilmelford 233. Secluded with excellent views; sailing is offered to guests. £.

Bridge of Allan Central **J2**
Royal Hotel, Henderson St. Tel 2284.
Convenient with a pleasant garden and
restaurant. *££*.

Castle Douglas Dumfries & Galloway **J9**
Douglas Arms Hotel, King St. Tel 2231.
Porcelain is displayed in this former
coaching inn. Pleasant garden. *££*.

Drymen Strathclyde **H3**
Buchanan Arms Hotel. Tel 588. Well-
situated for touring the Trossachs and
Loch Lomond. *££*.

East Kilbride Strathclyde **J4**
Bruce Hotel. Cornwall St. Tel 29771. A
modern town centre hotel in this 'new'
town. Good food. *££*.

Edinburgh Lothian **L4**
*Caledonian Hotel. Princes St. Tel 031-225
2433.* A fine looking hotel with many
amenities and an elegant restaurant.
£££.

Fintry Strathclyde **H3**
Clachan Hotel, nr Glasgow. Tel 237. A truly
Scottish inn set in a valley in the Fintry
Hills. Popular with locals. *£*.

Gatehouse
of Fleet Dumfries & Galloway **H9**
Calley Hotel. Tel 341. This country house
hotel is set in fine grounds with many
amenities both indoors and out. *££*.

Glasgow Strathclyde **H4**
Central Hotel. Gordon St. Tel 041-221 9680.
Dignified and useful to business men. Good
service and restaurant. *££*.

Gullane Lothian **M3**
Greywalls. Tel 842144. This country house
was designed by Lutyens and its gardens
were laid out by Gertrude Jekyll. *££*.

Loch Lomond Central **G3**
*Lomond Castle Hotel. Arden by Alexandria.
Tel Arden 247.* A Victorian home which has
been converted to a hotel. Fine grounds, a
private jetty and a pleasant garden. *££*.

Oban Strathclyde **E1**
Caledonian Hotel, Station Square. Tel 3133.
This gable-fronted hotel has sea views.
Public rooms are comfortable. *££*.

Peebles Borders **L5**
Peebles Hotel Hydro. Tel 20602. This grand
hotel is splendidly situated in the Lowlands.
Many amenities. *££*.

Rockcliffe Dumfries & Galloway **K9**
Baron's Craig Hotel, nr Dalbeattie. Tel 225.
A 19thC hotel with fine rhododendrons in
the spacious garden. Good views of Solway
Firth. *££*.

St Andrews Fife **M1**
Old Course Hotel. Tel 4371. A modern hotel
built on the site of railway sheds. Well-
situated for golf and beaches with views of
the course. *£££*.

Troon Strathclyde **G6**
Marine Hotel. Tel 314444. Conveniently
situated for Prestwick Airport. Fine views
of Arran. Good restaurant. *££*.

Turnberry Strathclyde **F7**
Turnberry Hotel. Tel 202. A fine Edwardian
hotel which offers guests numerous
amenities including two golf courses.
Good restaurant. *£££*.

Uphall Lothian **K4**
*Houston House, Millers Bridge. Tel Broxburn
853831.* A house typical of 16thC domestic
architecture with a good restaurant. *££*.

Regional food and drink

Black bun
This Edinburgh bun is a loaf-shaped rich
fruit cake encased in pastry.

Butterscotch
A delicious concoction of butter, brown
sugar, lemon juice and ground ginger.

Haggis
This traditional Scottish dish arrives at the
table to the skirl of bagpipes. Made of
sheep's stomach stuffed with oatmeal, suet,
liver, hearts, onion and spices. It is served on
Burns' Night and sometimes Hogmanay.

Kippers
Very fine kippers come from Scotland's east
coast, Eyemouth being one of the centres.

Mussel brose
This is traditionally made from mussels
which originate from Musselburgh where
there is a famous mussel bed at the mouth of
the River Esk.

Salmon
This universally favourite fish is at its best
in Scotland. The Tay and the Tweed are the
best known salmon rivers.

Scottish Dunlop
This cheese is very similar to cheddar in
flavour, but it is moister and eaten whilst
young.

Selkirk bannock
This is a yeasted loaf shaped in a round.
Very popular in the Lowlands, with local
bakeries having their own recipes.

Whisky
There are two distinct types – malt which is
made by the traditional pot still method and
grain whisky which is made in the coffee
still patented in 1831.
Most whisky is a blend of both types and any
well known brand will be made up of
between fifteen and 40 different whiskies.
Malts are classified in four groups:
Highland, Lowland, Islay and Cambeltown,
all of which are to be found in this region.

Restaurants

Arduaine Strathclyde **D2**
Loch Melfort Hotel. Tel Kilmelford 233.
House with cedarwood extension.
Breathtaking views towards Jura. Plain food;
good-value. *LD. £L. ££D. Closed
Nov-Easter.*

Bonchester Bridge Lothian **N7**
Wolfelee Hotel. Tel 202. Hotel in Scottish
baronial style. Good, honest cooking; fresh
local produce. *LD. Closed Sun D. ££. Book.*

Cupar Fife **M1**
Timothy's, 43 Bonnygate. Tel 2830. Little
restaurant serving Danish open sandwiches
and salads. Good value. *LD. Closed Sun.
£. Book.*

Edinburgh Lothian **L4**
Le Caveau, 13b Dundas St. Tel 031-556 5707.
Wine cellar/restaurant. French food and
wines. *LD. Closed Sun. £. Book D.*

*Henderson's Salad Table, 94 Hanover St. Tel
031-225 3400.* Self service vegetarian.
Queues. Open late. Good value. *LD.
Closed Sun. £.*

*Restaurant Denzler, 80 Queen St. Tel
031-226 5467.* Smart restaurant; Swiss food.
Good value. *LD. Closed Sun. £L, ££D. Book.*

Glasgow Strathclyde **H4**
*Central Hotel, Malmaison Restaurant,
Gordon St. Tel 041 221 9680.* Traditional
hotel. Outstanding classic French cooking.
LD. Closed Sat L & Sun. £££. Book D.

*Ubiquitous Chip, Ashton Lane, off Byres
Rd. Tel 041 334 5007.* Simply furnished
restaurant. Some unusual Scottish dishes.
Unlicensed. LD. £. Closed Sun.

Gullane Lothian **M3**
La Potiniere, Main St. Tel 843214. Converted
shop. Outstanding French-provincial
cooking. *L & Sat D. Closed Wed. £. Book.*

Isle of
Whithorn Dumfries & Galloway **H10**
Queens Arms, Main St. Tel 369. Hotel
serving straight-forward food. *LD. £. Book.*

Peebles Borders **L5**
*Cringletie House, 3 miles n on A703. Tel
Eddleston 233.* Quiet restaurant in huge
country house set in 28 acres. Original
cooking. *LD. Closed Nov-Mar. ££.*

Uphall Lothian **K4**
*Houstoun House, nr Livingston. Tel Broxburn
853831.* 16thC house with modern additions,
twenty minutes from Edinburgh. Set menus.
No choice. Often outstanding cooking. *LD.
££. Book.*

Wester Howgate Lothian **L4**
Old Howgate Inn. Tel Penicuik 74244.
Family-run restaurant. Soups, open
sandwiches, wines. They sell delicatessen
and kitchen equipment, too. *LD. Closed Sun.
££. Book.*

Scottish Highlands and Islands

II

The Highlands are remote and richly beautiful. Skye and the Western highlands are almost separated from the great mass of the mountains and glens by the great gash across the map of Loch Ness and Caledonian canal. Fort William guards one end of the Great Glen overshadowed by the usually snow covered summit of Ben Nevis. Fort Augustus, hard and forbidding, is the key to Loch Ness which stretches (monster permitting) the distance to Inverness – a town full of gun shops and all the gear you need to go deer stalking. Royal Deeside, Balmoral and Blair Atholl are centres that are still redolent of a Victorian escape fantasy – you can almost see the Monarch of the Glen striding through the heather.

Towards Aviemore and Cairngorms there are more contemporary pursuits, Highland nostalgia is replaced by brisk ski-ing and all the air conditioned pleasures. You need stamina, good maps and stout shoes to explore the glens, crags, and islands – and a dram of malt whisky to ward off the nip in the air.

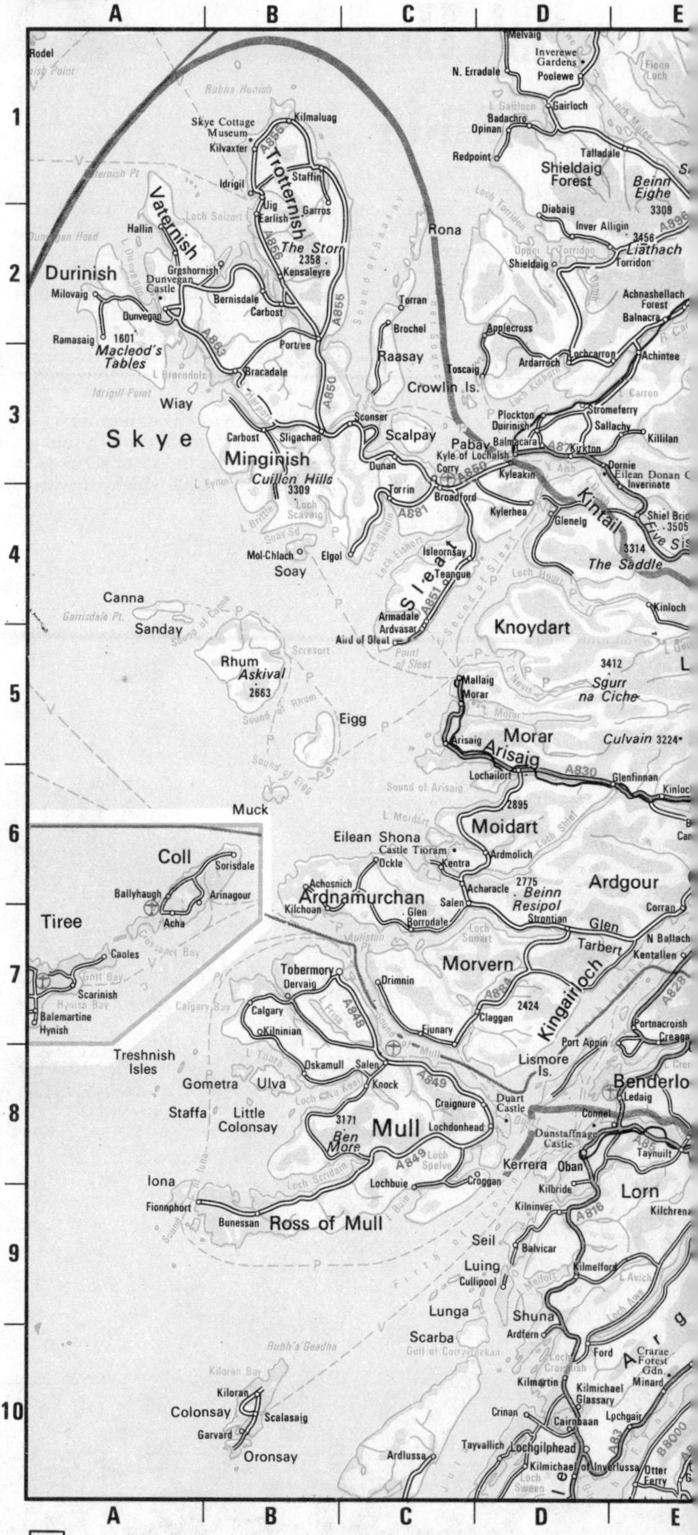

A · B · C · D · E

Rodel
nish Point
Inverewe Gardens
Melvaig
N. Erradale
Poolewe

1

Skye Cottage Museum
Kilmaluag
Kilvaxter
Idrigil
Staffin
Aig
Earlish
Garros
Badachro
Opinan
Gairloch
Talladale
Shieldaig Forest
Redpoint
Beinn Eighe 3309

Durinish
Vaternish Pt.
Loch Snizort
Trotternish
The Storr 2358
Kensaleyre
Diabaig
Inver Alligin
Liathach 3456
Torridon
Shieldaig
Achnashellach Forest
Balnacra
Beinn

2

Milovaig
Greshornish
Dunvegan Castle
Bernisdale
Carbost
Torran
Brochel
Applecross
Ardarroch
Lochcarron
Achintee
Dunvegan
Ramasaig
1601 Macleod's Tables
Hallin
Portree
Bracadale
Raasay
Toscaig
Carron
Stromeferry
Sallachy
Killilan

3

Idrigil Point
Wiay
Carbost
Sligachan
Sconser
Scalpay
Crowlin Is.
Plockton
Duirinish
Balmacara
Kyle of Lochalsh
Kirkton
Dornie
Eilean Donan C
Invernate
Shiel Bri

S k y e
Minginish
Cuillen Hills 3309
Dunan
Torrin
Pabay
Corry
Broadford
Kyleakin
Kintail
Eve Sis 3505

4

Mol-Chlach
Elgol
Soay
Isleornsay
Teangue
Kylerhea
Glenelg
The Saddle 3314

Canna
Sanday
Armadale
Ardvasar
Aird of Sleat
Knoydart
Kinloch
L

5

Rhum
Askival 2663
Eigg
Mallaig
Morar
Arisaig
Sgurr na Ciche 3412
Culvain 3224

Muck
Morar
Arisaig
Lochailort
Glenfinnan
Kinloc

6

Coll
Sorisdale
Eilean Shona
Castle Tioram
Ockle
Kentra
Ardmolich
Moidart
2895
Beinn Resipol 2775
Ardgour
Can

Ballyhaugh
Arinagour
Acha
Achosnich
Kilchoan
Ardnamurchan
Glen Borrodale
Salen
Acharacle
Strontian
Glen
Tarbert
Corran
N Ballach
Kentallen

7

Tiree
Caoles
Scarinish
Balemartine
Hynish
Tobermory
Dervaig
Drimnin
Morvern
Claggan 2424
Kingairloch
Port Appin
Portnacroish
Creag

Treshnish Isles
Calgary
Kilninian
Fiunary
Lismore Is.
Benderlo
Ledaig

8

Gometra
Ulva
Dskamull
Salen
Knock
Craignure
Duart Castle
Connel
Taynuilt

Staffa
Little Colonsay
Ben More 3171
Mull
Lochdonhead
Danstaffnage Castle
Kerrera
Oban
Lorn

Iona
Fionnphort
Lochbuie
Croggan
Kilbride
Kilninver
Kilchrena

9

Bunessan
Ross of Mull
Seil
Balvicar
Luing
Cullipool
Kilmelford
L Avich

Lunga
Shuna
Ardfern
A

10

Colonsay
Scalasaig
Garvard
Oronsay
Scarba
Ford
Crarae Forest Gdn.
Minard
Kilmartin
Kilmichael Glassary
Lochgair
Cairnbaan
Crinan
Ardlussa
Tayvallich
Lochgilphead
Kilmichael of Inverlussa
Otter Ferry

A · B · C · D · E

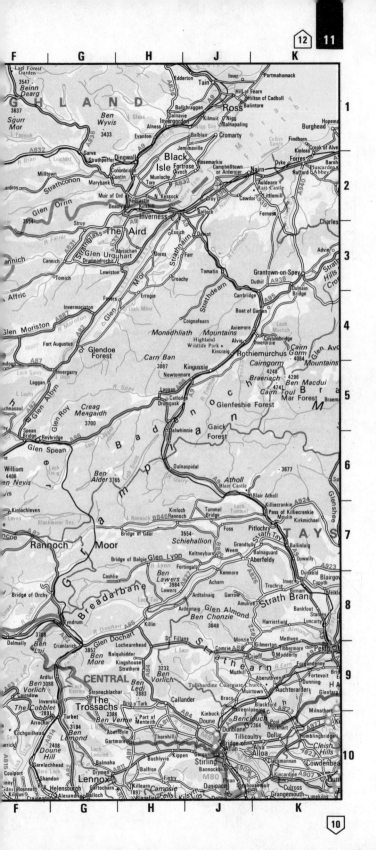

L M N O P

1

Lossiemouth
Duffus
Kingston
Spey Bay
Garmouth
Urquhart
Portgordon
Buckie
Findochty
Portknockie
Cullen
Portsoy
Banff
Macduff
Pennan
Longmanhill New Aberdour
Troup Hd.
Rosehearty
Sandhaven
Kinnirds Head
Fraserburgh
Inverallochy
St. Combs

Elgin
Lhanbryde
Longmorn
Fochabers
Fordyce
Cornhill
A98
New Pitsligo
Strichen
New Leeds
A981
Rathen
Mensie
Crimond

Dallas
Birnie Kirk
Rothes
Mulben
Keith
Aberchirder
New Byth
Delgatie Castle
Turriff
Cuminestown
Old Deer
Buchan
A950
Fetterangus
Mintlaw
Burnhaven
Boddam

2

Archiestown
town of Aberlour
Craigellachie
A920
Dufftown
Huntly
Milltown
Knock
New Deer
Auchnagatt
Clola
Longside
Stuartfield

Belleshiglach
2755
Ben Rinnes
Bridgend
Leith Hall
Kennethmont
Kirkton of Culsalmond
Fyvie
Rothienorman
Haddo House
Methlick
Tarves
A920
Ellon
Hatton

3

Tomnavoulin
Cabrach
Rhynie
Clatt
Leslie
Auchleven
Insch
Oyne
Oldmeldrum
Formartine
Collieston
Newburgh

Ladder Hills
Lumsden
Mossat
Tullynessle
Inverurie
Kintore
Hatton of Fintray
Newmachar
Balmedie
Belhelvie
KIRKV
LERW

Tomintoul
Kildrummy
Kildrummy Castle
Strathdon
Alford
A944
Towie
Craigievar Castle
Sauchen
Kemnay
A96
Dyce
Stoneywood
Bridge of Don

4

Cock Bridge
Migvie
GRAMPIAN
Lumphanan
Blackburn
Bucksburn
Aberdeen
Girdle Ness

Morven
2857
Logie Coldstone
Tarland
Kincardine O'Neil
Torphins
Cullerlie
Echt
Peterculter
Cults
Cove Bay

Crathie
Urdie Dinnet
Aboyne
Deeside
Crathes Castle
Portlethen
Downies

5

emar
Ballater
Banchory
Kirkton of Durris
Newtonhill
Muchalls

S
3789
Lochnagar
R Dee
A957

3502
Glas Maol
Braedownie
Glen Tarfside Esk
Fettercairn
Howe of the Mearns
Arbuthnott
Inverbervie
Stonehaven
Dunottar Castle
Roadside of Kinneff

6

ittal of Glenshee
Glen Clova
Clova
R North Esk
Edzell
Luthermuir
Laurencekirk
Gourdon
Johnshaven

Forter
Folda
Kirkton of Menmuir
Inchbare
Marykirk
Hillside
St. Cyrus

Blacklunans
Cortachy
Fern
Brechin
A935
Montrose
Scurdie Ness

7

IDE
Bridge of Cally
Kirkton of Kingoldrum
Tannadice
Bridge of Dun
Farnel
Ferryden

Alyth
Rattray
A926
Kirriemuir
Forfar
Aberlemno
Rescobie
Guthrie
Lunan Bay

Meigle
Glamis
Inverarity
Friockheim
Inverkeilor

wrie
Coupar Angus
Newtyle
1492 Balgray
A929
Carmyllie
Auchmithie
St. Vigean's Museum

8

Cargill
Burrelton
Muirhead
Fowlis
Liff
Muirdrum
East Haven
Arbroath

Guildtown
Balbeggie
Inchture
Dundee
Barry
Carnoustie

New Scone
Kinfauns
Errol
Wormit
Monifieth
Broughty Ferry
Buddon Ness

Cates
Glencarse
Newport-on-Tay
Tayport

Inchcape
or
Bell Rock

9

Newburgh
Abernethy
Luthrie
Kilmany
Leuchars
St Andrews Bay

ghtermuchty
Strathkinness
A91
St. Andrews

e of
Cupar
Pitscottie
Ceres
Peat Inn
Dunino
Boarhills
Kingsbarns
Fife Ness

Falkland
Lomond Hills
1713
Ladybank
Kirkton of Largo
Kellie Castle
Crail
Kilrenny
Anstruther

Leslie
A911
Markinch
Leven
Largo Ward
St. Monance
Pittenweem

Glenrothes
Methil
Buckhaven
Elie
Earlsferry
Isle of May

10

Lochgelly
Kirkcaldy
Bass Rock
North Berwick

Auchtertool
Kinghorn
Burntisland
Dirleton
Gullane
Tantallon Castle

fermline
Aberdour
Firth of Forth
Whitekirk

Inverkeithing

L M N O P

The coast

Aberdeen Grampian **O4**
Aberdeen. Pop 180,000. EC Wed. MD Fri.
The Granite City is a place of many parts: an oil boom town, the third largest fishing port in Britain, a major holiday resort with thirteen miles of sands, a stately university city, and a repository of much of Scotland's past. The city can be divided into three areas: the old city on the north bank of the Dee, the equally ancient new city joined together by the 16thC Bridge of Dee (the scene of another military triumph by Montrose), and finally to the north-west is the new post-war city.

Aberdeen

Union Street, the broad central thoroughfare, is a fine example of the local use of granite. The church of St Nicholas nearby is divided by a 12th and 13thC transept and contains many old treasures. In the summer a 48-bell carillon is rung daily. St Machar is the only ancient granite cathedral in Britain. For the morbid, Aberdeen's municipal buildings incorporate the tower and spire of the old Tolbooth which was the scene of public executions until 1857. Also of interest: Provost Skene's House (16thC); King's and Marischal University colleges; the City Cross in Castle Street, and the Auld Brig o'Don.

Arbroath Tayside **N8**
Angus. Pop 22,600. EC Wed. Gaily coloured fishing boats crowd the harbour, landing the haddock which is turned into the local delicacy, Arbroath Smokies. Inland is a bustling pleasant work-a-day town with some fine old buildings. On the north side of the town is the restored and enlarged Hospitalfield and, more historically significant, the remains of Arbroath Abbey. The Declaration of Arbroath was signed in 1320 in the abbey and was Scotland's formal statement of independence after Robert the Bruce's victory at Bannockburn. The large circular window in the abbey's south transept used to be illuminated as a guide to ships at sea. There are sandy beaches to the east and west of the harbour with good bathing.

Arisaig Highland **C5**
Inverness. Pop 700. On the Road to the Isles where it first meets the open sea, this clachan provides exceptional views of the Inner Hebrides. When the weather is right the islands of Rhum and Eigg seem to float on the seas like gigantic prehistoric monsters. Sandy beach.

Auchmithie village

Auchmithie Tayside **N7**
Angus. The 'Mussel Crag' of Scott's 'The Antiquary' is picturesquely placed high above its harbour. Boats can be hired here to visit the many caves in the neighbourhood connected with 18thC smugglers. Rock and shingle beach.

Banff Grampian
Banff. Pop 3,700. EC Wed. An ancient royal burgh and port standing on the mouth of the River Deveron, and linked to the town of Macduff on the opposite bank by a handsome seven-arched bridge designed by Smeaton. Banff still retains some attractive 17th and 18thC burghers' houses around High Shore; the old cemetery is reputed to be the resting place of some 40,000 old Banffers.

Banff.

One famous old Banffer who does not lie there is James Macpherson who, on route to the gallows in 1701, now marked by the Biggar Fountain in Low Street, insisted on playing defiant music all the way on his fiddle. Of interest: Mercat Cross and the town house with its 17thC steeple. Sand and shingle beach.

Broughty Ferry Tayside **M8**
Angus. Pop 12,500. EC Wed. Dundee's seaside, and once a ferry terminal for the Tay road ferries which were replaced by the new Tay Bridge in 1966. The whaling museum is well worth a visit. A fine sandy beach. Bathing is safe close inshore, but avoid the mouth of Dighty Water.

Buckie Grampian **M1**
Banff. Pop 7,900. EC Wed. The largest town in Banffshire and the busiest fishing port on the Moray Firth. Buckie, through no fault of its own, has developed into a long straggling town, as Buckpool, Gordonsburgh, Ianstown, Portessie and Strathlene spread blindly into each other.
The Tayside the town on cliffs above the port is dominated by the tall spires of St Peter's Roman Catholic Church (1857). Almost a cathedral, it is a reminder that Banffshire remained a stronghold of popery despite John Knox and the Reformation. Rock, shingle and sandy beach.

Carnoustie Tayside **M8**
Angus. Pop 7,400. EC Tue. Two championship golf courses and children's playground are right by the beach. Lovely golden sands which at low tide contain gorgeous warm pools.

Cruden Bay Grampian **P3**
Aberdeen. Pop 2,000. EC Thur. Good swimming, good golf, and the dramatic ruins of Slains Castle make this a satisfying all round place. A couple of miles to the north is Bullers of Buchan, a spectacular amphitheatre 200 feet deep and 50 feet across, into which the sea flows through a natural arch. Doctor Johnson and Boswell nervously walked round this cauldron by a path which can still be used today. Several miles of sand and dunes.

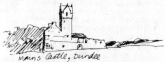
Mains Castle, Dundee

Dundee Tayside **M8**
Angus. Pop 182,000. EC Wed. MD Tue. Whaling has gone, but the docks, jam and jute remain to keep Dundee prosperous. Fought over for centuries, Dundee is an earnest university city which is modernising rapidly, served from the south by two fine long bridges. The railway bridge replaces one that was blown down in a gale whilst a train was crossing it in 1879. The road bridge, opened in 1966, is over one and a half miles long, and Britain's longest road bridge over a river. The highest point of the city, Dundee Law (571 feet), is the remains of a volcanic plug. From the top is a splendid vista of the city and the coast from Buddon Ness right up to the Firth of Tay. Worth a visit is the fascinating Golf Museum

and the Barrack Street Shipping and Industrial Museum. There is a splendid riverside park.

Pitsligo Castle

Fraserburgh Grampian   **P1**
Aberdeen. Pop 10,600. EC Wed. MD Wed.
A holiday and fishing town with an attractive and busy harbour founded in 1546 by Sir Alexander Fraser. The northernmost part of the town is on Kinnaird's Head which is surmounted by a lighthouse. Near it is the Wine Tower, the origin and use of which is unknown. The only entrance is on an upper storey. Sandy beach.

Inverbervie Grampian   **O6**
Kincardine. Pop 900. Strikingly situated on the south bank of the Bervie Gorge where the river forces its way to the sea. Hercules Linton, the designer of the Cutty Sark and an Inverbervie man, is honoured by a memorial here. The nearby town of Gourdon is worth seeing to watch the women baiting the hand fishing lines for their fishermen husbands – up to 1,200 hooks per line. Beyond the river mouth is a shingle bar of brilliantly hued pebbles. The beach is also shingle.

Inverness.

Inverness Highland   **H2**
Inverness. Pop 36,600. EC Wed. MD Tues, Fri. The so called capital of the Highlands is managing to expand gracefully. Cromwell occupied Inverness, and a clock tower remains from the star-shaped fort he built by the river. Other old buildings are Queen Mary's House, Abertarff House (early 17thC), Dunbar's Hospital (1668) and the old High Church of 1722. Most of the buildings in the town centre are sternly Victorian. A town of quiet decent dignity which avoids being sombre on account of the friendliness and vitality of its people. Inverness is still a port of medium importance and possesses its own fishing fleet which regularly passes through the Caledonian Canal to fish off the west coast. Five miles south-east of Inverness is Culloden Moor. A cairn marks the site of the Highlanders' last stand in 1746. Fast currents make it dangerous for bathing. Muddy sand.

Kinlochmoidart Highland   **D6**
Inverness. A small crofting hamlet at the head of Loch Moidart, famous for its visit by Bonnie Prince Charlie on his way to raise the standard at Glenfinnan. The support of Moidart is commemorated by seven beech trees planted in a meadow nearby, and called the Seven Men of Moidart. The seven men are also remembered in a Highland Reel of the same name. See Castle Tioram set on an island further down the loch.

Lossiemouth Grampian   **L1**
Moray. Pop 5,700. EC Thur. A prosperous fishing port where initiative and enterprise has paid off. The administrative side of money-making is handled in the twin town of Branderburgh perched on the cliffs above the port. A holiday resort with good beaches and swimming, but avoid bathing near the mouth of the River Lossie.

Mallaig Highland   **C5**
Inverness. Pop 900. EC Wed. A full stop in all senses. It is the end of the road and railway to the Isles. To the west Skye is served by a ferry service to Armadale, and to the north and east is the roadless emptiness of Knoydart.
Apart from the ferry Mallaig supports itself from fishing, a kipper factory, and lobster tanks. A nondescript village quite overpowered by the grandeur of the surrounding country. Rock and shingle beach.

Montrose Tayside   **N7**
Angus. Pop 10,000. EC Wed. MD Wed, Fri. A town that never got itself involved with history. This pleasing place is still put to bed at 22.00 every night by 'Big Peter', the curfew bell rung from the 22-foot steeple of the old kirk in the High Street.
Originally built out of warm rose-coloured stone (nothing to do with the name, which comes from the Gaelic) to meet the needs of outlying gentlemen farmers, Montrose has now become a holiday resort. Four miles of sandy beaches, sailing in Montrose Basin, and the usual seaside activities keep Montrose popular.

Morar, Inverness.

Morar Highland   **C5**
Inverness. EC Thur. The village sits on a narrow neck of land between the deepest lake in Britain, Loch Morar (1,080 feet deep), and the Atlantic. The road and railway compete for space to cross the gorge containing the falls of the River Morar. The blinding white singing sands of Morar set off the superlative landscape of this area.

Nairn Highland   **J2**
Nairn. Pop 5,900. EC Wed. A popular and still developing holiday centre. Like all good resorts it claims to have a monopoly of fine weather, though to be fair all the Moray coast is noted for its warm and dry summer climate. Facilities include a heated indoor sea-water swimming pool, children's paddling pool and playground, and in fact all the trappings of a well equipped resort. Five miles to the south-west lies Cawdor Castle, a name well known to those who take their Shakespeare. In the High Street see the old cross, the post office and Town House of 1818. There are excellent sandy beaches, and a picturesque river mouth harbour much used by pleasure craft and some fishing boats.

Peterhead Grampian   **P2**
Aberdeen. Pop 14,200. EC Wed. A snug harbour hiding behind two breakwaters built with the help of convict labour. The stark and dangerous way of life of the fisherfolk is echoed in the spare and economic buildings of the town, relieved only by the warmth of red granite. The Town House by John Baxter at the end of Broad Street is worth a visit. There is a bathing beach on the southern half of the bay.

Stonehaven Grampian   **O5**
Kincardine. Pop 4,800. EC Wed. A cheeky, cheerful town nestling in the mouth of a sheltered valley formed by two rivers. It still has its fishing fleet, but Stonehaven today is known as a sailing centre. The harbour is attractive with an interesting 17thC Tolbooth used now as a museum on the

Stonehaven

quay. You shouldn't miss Dunnottar Castle. Bathing is off a shingle beach, or in comfort from the town's open air heated pool.

Dunnottar Castle, Kincardine

The Islands

Coll Strathclyde   **A6**
Argyll. Pop 200. Both this island and Tiree get the full force of the Atlantic. A low rocky island divided into farms. Miles of beach and shell sand dunes on the western side.

Eigg Highland   **B5**
Inverness. Six miles long, dramatic and mysterious, this small island is well worth visiting. Its most attractive feature is An Sgurr – 1,280 feet of twisted columns and walls of pitch-stone lava. Contains remnants of old hazel scrub and is rich in many species of mosses. Many sea birds.

Eigg and Rhum, Inverness.

Iona Strathclyde   **A8**
Argyll. St Columba landed here from Ireland in 563 with twelve followers. A man not only of great piety, but evidently also of great energy as these thirteen men managed to start a movement which brought Christianity ultimately to all Scotland. St Oran's cemetery is the oldest in Scotland. St Mary's Abbey, where St Columba is buried, dates from the 13thC.

Muck Highland   **B6**
Inverness. Only two miles long this low island is very attractive with some sandy beaches. The cliffs are full of sea birds of all sorts. No ferry service.

Mull Strathclyde   **C8**
Argyll. A mountainous island with two peaks over 3,000 feet and at Gribun there are 1,000 foot high cliffs. The north of Mull is green with bracken and trees in sheltered areas. A bus service covers the island and there are many hotels. There is salmon and trout fishing and a 15,000 acre deer forest. Mull is surrounded by many smaller islands – all attractive and all can be visited by boat. Several sandy bays and beaches.

Dervaig   **B7**
An attractive little village at the end of a long narrow sea loch. During the summer months a professional theatre operates in a

converted barn near the church. Beaches of sand and shingle.

Tobermory Strathclyde   **C7**
Pop 600. EC Wed. A sweet, but not sticky, little town of colour-washed buildings arranged in neatly planned streets round Tobermory Bay.
In 1588 the 'Duque di Florencia', a remnant of the Spanish Armada, sank in Tobermory Bay with an alleged three million gold dubloons on board. In spite of intensive searches this treasure still remains drowned.

Raasay Highland   **C3**
Inverness. A rocky, hilly and very pleasant island which has decreased in population from 600 to 200 over the last 100 years. This was helped by the disastrous potato famine in the last century but the main cause was the infamous 'Clearances'.

Rhum Highland   **B5**
Inverness. Once known as the 'forbidden island' it is still open to day visitors only who are very welcome. Overnight stays are by permission in advance from the Nature Conservancy who own the island. It is used as a huge open air laboratory for Scotland's environmental and ecological problems.

Kyleakin, Skye.

Skye Highland   **B3**
Inverness. Still heavily crofted despite its depopulation over the years, this is a magnificent mountainous island with its Cuillin Hills (over 3,000 feet) and its fantastic Old Man of Storr. There are many sea lochs in the north. The people are hospitable, dignified, respect the Sabbath, and mostly speak the Gaelic.

Kyleakin. Highland   **D3**
EC Wed. One of the two modern gateways to Skye. Here the visitor will first see the island's characteristic whitewashed stone terraced cottages. Overlooking the town and the modern invaders are the remains of the 14thC Castle Maol, a small but important Highland strongpoint used to control the strait between Skye and the mainland. The '-akin' part of Kyleakin is said to come from the 13thC King Hakon of Norway who sailed by on his unsuccessful way to invade Scotland.

Portree. Highland   **B2**
Pop 2,000. EC Wed. Portree, or in English 'King's Haven' is the capital of Skye. A pleasing little place with a harbour delineated by whitewashed stone terraced houses. The town rises to the north and culminates in an attractive main square. An excellent touring centre for Skye and there are steamer trips from here to nearby Raasay Island.

Uig. Highland   **B1**
Pop 2,000. Like so many Highland villages Uig refuses to be pinned down by the cartographer's dots on a map, and is a picturesque conglomeration of crofts and cottages scattered over a hillside to the north of a harbour. From here motor car ferries leave for the Outer Hebrides.

Tiree Strathclyde   **A7**
Argyll. A low island of sand, the major part being only 25 feet high and mostly arable crofts. With Coll the islands are marvellous for birds of all sort

Inland towns & villages

General Wade's bridge, Aberfeldy

Aberfeldy Tayside   J7
Perth. Pop 1,600. EC Wed. A peaceful market town set in delightful countryside. The Wade Bridge over the Tay is a little masterpiece, showing very obviously the assistance of William Adam in the design.

Aberfoyle Central   H10
Perth. Pop 2,100. EC Wed. Really two villages, old and new. The area was used in two of Sir Walter Scott's works 'Rob Roy' and the 'Lady of the Lake'. The surrounding scenery without being grand is broken and romantic.

Abernethy Tayside   L9
Perth. Once a town, now a village, it has a circular refuge tower for the preservation of the local clergy, one of only two in Scotland. The tower is 74 feet high with an entrance door six feet from the ground, and is built of hewn square stones.

Aboyne Grampian   M5
Aberdeen. Pop 2,300. EC Thur. MD Mon. A neat and, for Scotland, unusually geometric village arranged around a large flat green surrounded by distant hills. It has its moment of glory every September with the very popular Highland Gathering held on the green.

Alford Grampian   M4
Aberdeen. Pop 1,800. EC Wed. MD Tue. A pleasant little market town on the south bank of the River Don in the centre of the Howe of Alford. Alford came briefly to the notice of history when the Royalist Marquess of Montrose engulfed the Covenanting army of General Baillie in 1645.
Four miles to the south is Craigievar Castle, an extravaganza of turrets, gables and conical roofs built in 1626. Inside is a superb Renaissance ceiling.

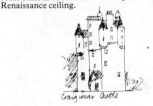

Craigievar Castle

Ardgour Highland   E6
Argyll. The large white lighthouse guards the entrance to the narrows at the foot of Loch Linnhe. From Ardgour is a ferry service to the main Fort William road, and the frenzy of the main road underlines the tranquillity of this little village. The church was built to a design produced by Telford for the government's Highland church building programme in the 1820s and 30s.

Aviemore Highland   K4
Inverness. Pop 700. EC Wed. Until the mid 1960s Aviemore was a pleasant sleepy little village which had grown up round a railway station. With the advent of commercially organised skiing, change came with a vengeance.
The Aviemore Centre, a complex of hotels and indoor and outdoor sporting facilities was designed to combat the Scottish weather's assaults on the skiing season. Now the centre offers all the year round holidays. An environmental triumph.

Ballater Grampian   L5
Aberdeen. Pop 1,100. EC Thur. Ballater has done well out of its neighbours, the Queen at Balmoral and the Queen Mother at Birkhall just down the road. But it would be uncharitable to dismiss the place. A busy resort surrounded by beautiful wooded hills. The torrents of the River Dee give the place an individual charm.

Balquhidder Central   H9
Perth. Pronounced 'Balwhidder'. The final resting place of Rob Roy (died 1734), his wife, and two of his five sons is near the remains of the old chapel. The village is set in a glen called the Braes of Balquhidder which opens out on to Loch Voil. This beautiful spot is perhaps too popular for its own good.

Banchory Grampian   N5
Aberdeen. Pop 2,400. EC Thur. Another attractive and expanding Deeside holiday village in a sylvan setting. Nearby the River Feugh joins the Dee. The Brig of Feugh half a mile upstream has an observation platform to watch the salmon leaping the rapids.

Blair Castle, Perthshire

Blair Atholl Tayside   J6
Perth. Pop 1,400. EC Wed. A dignified village dominated by the fantasy Blair Castle, seat of the Duke of Atholl, and swamped by a main road.

Blairgowrie Tayside   L7
Perth. Pop 5,600. EC Thur. A small town set in a sea of raspberry farms which produce half the total crop of Scotland. The road to Perth passes a magnificent beech hedge planted in 1746 in the grounds of Meikeour House. Now over 85 feet high, it borders the road for 580 yards. The 19thC Brig O'Blair over the swift running River Ericht links Blairgowrie to Rattray. About two miles north the river runs through a gorge with 200-foot-high cliffs.

Braemar Grampian   L5
Aberdeen. Pop 1,000. EC Thur. Dominated by the massive Cairn Toul (4,241 feet) this Deeside village is world famous for its Royal Highland Gathering, held in September and normally attended by the Queen and Royal Family. Braemar Castle is worth a visit; still surviving are inscriptions made by the bored 18thC soldiery.

Brechin Tayside   N7
Angus. Pop 6,600. EC Wed. An ancient historical town with precipitous streets. The cathedral is mainly 13thC but suffered from a disasterous early 19thC restoration. Fortunately much has been put right and the choir is a pleasing and delicate example of lancet work.

Callander Central   H9
Perth. Pop 1,800. EC Wed. Just south of the Pass of Leny this spacious well laid out Regency town is sometimes called the Gateway to the Highlands. When the heather is out the skyline above Callander goes a delicate mauve which sets off this happy little town to perfection.

Comrie Tayside   H8
Perth. Pop 1,800. EC Wed. A quiet holiday resort on the River Earn popular with walkers. A particularly good walk is up Glen Lednock to the Devil's Cauldron where the River Lednock rushes down a narrow channel and through a hole in the rock. Comrie is one of the few places in Britain still shaken (but very gently) by earth tremors.

Coylumbridge Highland   K4
Inverness. A bed-and-breakfast village on the approaches to Cairngorm ski slopes and a good base for hill walkers with routes to Lairig Ghru and Braeriach.

Crieff Tayside   J9
Perth. Pop 5,600. EC Wed. MD Tue. Despite almost total annihilation in the two Jacobite rebellions, this attractive country town seems to have won back against history and to be at peace with itself. Look at Crieff Cross, a 10thC carved slab not to be confused with the market cross in front of the 17thC Tolbooth. Drummond Castle two miles south is worth a visit.

Dunkeld

Dunkeld Tayside **K8**
Perth. Pop 1,100. EC Thur. A large but delightful village with the 600-year-old remains of a once great cathedral. The National Trust for Scotland has been very active restoring the little 18thC houses to the south of the main street. Pause to admire Telford's fine bridge over the Tay.

Elgin

Elgin Grampian **L1**
Moray. Pop 16,400. EC Wed. MD Fri. A compact busy little shopping town built to a cruciform plan. Approaching the town across the Laich of Moray the western towers of the ruined cathedral are seen reaching up to the sky.
The cathedral was first mentioned in 1190, and what remains gives a sketchy portrait of what was once one of the finest churches in Scotland. Notice the old arcaded houses in the High Street, and the fine early 19thC church of St Giles designed by Archibald Simpson. See also Thunderton House and the mediaeval church of the Greyfriars Monastery in Abbey Street.

Fettercairn Grampian **N6**
Kincardine. Pop 1,600. An attractive village with a triumphal arch of Rhenish-Gothic design built to commemorate a visit of Queen Victoria and Prince Albert. The village is also custodian of the shaft of Kincardine's town cross on which the bearing marks of the Scots ell (37 inches) are marked.

Fettercairn, Kincardine.

Forfar Tayside **M7**
Angus. Pop 10,500. EC Thur. MD Mon, Fri. The county town of Angus keeps itself busy milling jute. There seems to be some doubt about the town's antecedents, as Cromwell's merry men burnt the town records in 1651, and the town was not re-incorporated until 1665.
The town hall was designed by William Playfair (1789-1857) and houses some portraits by Romney, Raeburn and Thorwaldsen. It also houses the 'Forfar Bridle' – a collar with a prong used in mediaeval days to gag those about to be executed. About one mile to the east are the remains of Restenneth Priory, mainly 12thC with a 15thC spire.

Forres Grampian **K2**
Moray. Pop 5,600. EC Wed. King Duncan, murdered by Macbeth, held court in Forres. Today an obelisk to a Crimean war hero marks the spot where the royal castle stood at the west end of the High Street.
There is little pretension in this neat little burgh, except perhaps for the market cross (1844) modelled on the Scott memorial at Edinburgh. The town museum has a famous collection of local fossils, and at the eastern end of the town, a few hundred yards along the Kinloss road, is the Sweno Stone, a thin shaft of sandstone 23 feet high, carved with figures of warriors, animals and knots, and is thought to commemorate the final defeat of the Danes in 1014.

Fort Augustus Highland **G4**
Inverness. Pop 900. EC Wed. This village is situated on the land separating Loch Oich and Loch Ness, and originally grew up round a fort built by General Wade in 1730. The fort has now gone and in its place is a Benedictine abbey and school.
The school and tower were designed by the inventor of the Hansom cab, Joseph Hansom. The cloisters and other parts were designed by Peter Pugin. On the south side of the school runs Wade's Road over the Corrieyarrick Pass which was used by Bonnie Prince Charlie's army on its march to Edinburgh.

Fortingall village

Fortingall Tayside **J7**
Perth. Unusual for Scotland, a village of thatched cottages. It has an ancient yew tree in the churchyard which is thought to be over 2,000 years old. At the west end of the village is Glenlyon House, formerly the home of Captain Robert Campbell who led the Glencoe massacre.

Fort William Highland **F6**
Inverness. Pop 4,200. EC Wed. Originally an important outpost guarding the southern end of the strategically important Great Glen. Named after William III who ordered the building and garrisoning of a stone fort in 1690. Now an important tourist centre. The old town consists of a high street of typical West Highland buildings nestling at the foot of Ben Nevis, and straggles out to absorb nearby villages on the banks of Loch Linnhe to Oban. See the West Highland Museum with important relics of the Jacobite rebellions of 1715 and 1745.

Fowlis Easter Tayside **L8**
Angus. A village noted for the fine restored 15thC church of St Marnan. See the preserved screen door, four fine

Fort William, Inverness.

pre-Reformation paintings, sculptured font, and most unusual for Scotland, a tabernacle with an annunciation. Note the iron collars or jougs beside the south-west door for wrong-doers.

Glamis Tayside   M7
Angus. Pop 1,000. A picturesque village given a bogus connection with Macbeth by Shakespeare. The castle, which was almost completely rebuilt in the 17thC has a fine collection of armour, furnishings and paintings. In contrast, the Angus Folk Museum focuses on the life of the peasantry. The village jougs (stocks) are near the churchyard gates.

Glamis village

Glenfinnan Highland   E6
Inverness. A clachan at the head of Loch Shiel. There is a tower surmounted by a statue of a kilted Highlander marking the spot where Bonnie Prince Charlie raised his standard on the 19th August 1745. The little Roman Catholic chapel has an intriguing bell mounted outside in a frame on the ground.

Grantown-on-Spey Highland   K3
Moray. Pop 1,700. EC Thur. From Georgian times a holiday town with a pleasant spacious atmosphere. In the winter 'apres ski' life is well catered for, and in the summer fishing and golf keep the tills chattering happily. The parish church contains a fine black oak pulpit and some old panelling.

Huntly Grampian   M3
Aberdeen. Pop 4,100. EC Thur. MD. Wed. Cupped in the hills of Strathbogie, Huntly is laid out like a formal garden. Unfortunately roads wide enough for the 18thC find modern traffic giving them thrombosis. Not to be missed is the fine Huntly Castle which evokes the whole of Scots castle development from Norman times to the 17thC.

Inverurie Grampian   N3
Aberdeen. Pop 5,400. EC Wed. MD Fri. An innocuous little town on the banks of the River Don, characterised by wide open streets bordered by granite houses. Until recently the home of a minor railway works. In the churchyard of the ruined Kinkell Church two miles south is the inscribed Pictish 'Brandsbutt Stone'. The church itself contains a fine sacrament house. See also The Bass, a 50-foot-high mound which was probably an important motte and bailey stronghold.

Keith Grampian   M2
Banff. Pop 4,200. EC Wed. MD Tue. A neat country town still benefitting from its planned re-building at the hands of the Earl of Findlater in 1750. Keith's oldest building is the Milton Tower (1480); its ruins stand near a new distillery.
The Roman Catholic church of SS Peter and Paul has its pediment embellished by two enormous figures of its patron saints; look at the altarpiece presented by Charles X of France.
If you're morbidly inclined, cross the Auld Brig O'Keith (1609) to Fife Keith. Near the churchyard there is the Gaun Pot or pool in which witches were drowned.

Kenmore Tayside   J7
Perth. Pop 700. EC Thur. A pretty little model village at the eastern end of Loch Tay. The church (1760) is by William Baker. Don't miss the village inn where Burns wrote about his pleasure in the view from the bridge, over the fire place in the inn parlour.

Killin Central   H8
Perth. Pop 1,300. EC Wed. The village is sheltered by the towering 4,000 foot mass of Ben Lawers – on whose slopes grow a remarkable variety of rare Alpine plants. In the grounds of nearby Kinnell House is a

Killin, Perth.

well preserved prehistoric circle of standing stones. See also St Fillan's eight healing stones at the tweed mill near Bridge of Dochart.

Kincardine Grampian   N6
Kincardine. Once a straggling village which took its name from mighty Kincardine Castle and gave it to a county. Now only the county remains. The castle and village, with the exception of the disused kirkyard of the vanished St Catherine's Chapel, have all disappeared.

Kingussie Highland   J5
Inverness. Pop 1,000. EC Wed. A long, low straggle of a place, rich in historical associations. One time stronghold of the Comyns and Wolf of Badenoch. There is an interesting Highland Folk Museum.

Northmuir, Kirriemuir

Kirriemuir Tayside   M7
Angus. Pop 4,100. EC Thur. A bijou town of red houses with narrow streets. J. M. Barrie was born at No.9 Brechin Road. In a pavilion behind the cemetery (in which Barrie is buried) is a camera obscura. See the gardens of Logie House about one mile south.

Laurencekirk Grampian   N6
Kincardine. Pop 1,400. EC Wed. MD Mon, alt Sat. In the rich heartlands of the Howe of Mearns it is hard to imagine how this burgh with its one-and-a-half miles of main street was planned. The town owes its inspiration and original economy to Lord Gardenstone who encouraged hand loom weaving and the making of snuff boxes.

Lochearnhead Central   H8
Perth. EC Wed. A hamlet of solid substance at the western end of Loch Earn, which has become a centre for aquatic sports, notably water skiing.

Milton of Clova Tayside   L6
Angus. A lonely hamlet overlooked by the very attenuated ruins of Clova Castle. Glen Clova is one of the loveliest of Angus glens and the road which finishes at Clova follows the course of the River South Esk. On the banks of the South Esk grow many rare plants and ferns.

Newtonmore Highland   J5
Inverness. EC Wed. This Speyside summer holiday resort doubles in the winter as a skiing centre. There is good fishing, golfing and tennis. The tennis courts, with typical Scots economy, convert into curling rinks in the winter. Of interest is the Clan Macpherson Museum which includes the famous 'Black Chanter' and 'Green Banner' both used as lucky talismans by the Macphersons in war.

The Old Perth Bridge

Perth Tayside   **K9**
Perth. Pop 43,000. EC Wed. MD Mon, Fri.
Nicknamed the 'Fair City' this ancient and
important city has suffered over the years
from the 19thC city councils' willingness to
pull down its heritage. Even so it remains
a good looking, well laid out place, with
plenty of green open spaces. It was for many
years the capital of Scotland.
Of interest: the mediaeval St John's Kirk
with its fine collection of silver; the
Salutation Hotel (1699) at which Prince
Charles Edward Stuart stayed in 1745; and
the museum in the 'Fair Maid's' House.
Smeaton's Perth Bridge (1771) is well
complemented by the Queen's Bridge (1960).

Pitlochry Tayside   **K7**
Perth. Pop 2,000. EC Thur. A famous
holiday resort set in beautiful countryside,
it is also the home of the Pitlochry Festival
Theatre. Across the River Tunnel at the
entrance to the mausoleum of Dunfallandy
House is one of the finest examples of a
Pictish sculpted stone in Scotland. ·

Port of Menteith Central   **H10**
Perth. A quiet holiday resort on the north
side of the Lake of Menteith. Boats may be
hired here to visit the 13thC ruins of the
priory on Inchmahome Island. Mary Queen
of Scots stayed in the priory as a young girl.

Scone Tayside   **K9**
Perth. Famous in Scottish history, Scone
(pronounced 'scoon') was a seat of
government in Pictish times; the home of the
Stone of Destiny until its removal by
Edward I to Westminster Abbey in 1296.

Turiff Grampian   **N2**
Aberdeen. Pop 3,100. EC Wed. A busy little
place, the centre of a prosperous agricultural
district. The old church belonged to the
Knights Templar, but only the choir and the
double belfry remain.

Regional oddities

Section 12 contains many entries under this
heading that apply equally to this section. To
avoid repeating the same information it is
suggested that you refer to the following
entries in section 12 – burghs, clans, crofters,
hydro-electricity, peat, the Sabbath, etc.

Pass of Killiecrankie Tayside   **K7**
Perth. EC Thur. The site of a furious
bloody battle in 1689 when the Jacobite
Highlanders' army under the redoubtable
'Bonnie Dundee' routed William III's army
under General Mackay. Sadly Dundee
perished in the moment of victory.
A steep footpath descends to the narrow
opening of the gorge known as Soldier's
Leap, after a formidable jump made by a
fleeing redcoat. In the village the National
Trust maintains an information centre.

Spean Bridge Highland   **F6**
Inverness. EC Thur. The bridge is one of
1,200 that the great Scots engineer Thomas
Telford built in his native country. The
village church, built in 1812, is one of the
older ecclesiastical structures in this part of
the world. Glen Spean extends eastward
giving access to Roy Bridge and the parallel
roads of Glen Roy which are scars left by an
ice age lake which once filled Glen Roy.

The Scottish language

Throughout much of the Highlands, which
are covered by this section and section 12,
the people's first language is Gaelic. It is a
soft lilting tongue derived from old Irish,
which fits well with the quiet friendly nature
of the Highlanders. The Anglo-Saxon may
well be confused by the way place names are
pronounced as opposed to how they are
spelt. 'Ch' for instance either sounds like
someone gently clearing the back of his
throat as in 'loch' or as the letter 'h' in
'Acharacle'. The letter 'B' is frequently
sounded as a 'V' so that 'Beag' (meaning
little) sounds like 'Veck'. Below are a few of
the more common Gaelic root words found
in place names:

aber	mouth or confluence of a river
ben, beann, beinn	mountain
caolas	a strait or firth
car	bend or winding
coire, corrie	hollow
dubh, dhu	black, dark
dun	hillfort
eilean	island
inch, innis	island
inver, inbhir	mouth of a river
mor, more	great, extensive
ross	peninsula, forest
ru, rhu, row, rudna	point
strath	broad valley
tobar	well
uamh	cave
uig	nook, sheltered bay

Famous people

J. M. Barrie (1860-1937)   **M7**
9 Brechin Rd, Kirriemuir, Tayside. The
birthplace of the creator of Peter Pan is now
a Barrie Museum, and it was the inspiration
of many of his other writings. In particular
Kirriemuir was the model for his town of
Thrums. *Open daily Apr-Oct. Closed Sun
morning. By appointment Nov-Mar.
Tel Kirriemuir 2646.*

Bonnie Prince Charlie (1720-88) **E6**
Glenfinnan, Highland. Loch nan Uamh
beside the Fort William-Mallaig road was
where Bonnie Prince Charlie landed in 1745
in his attempt to win back the English
throne. The cave where he spent his first
night is clearly marked from the road down a
small footpath where it is possible to follow
Charles's first few days' journeyings.
Follow the road back to Lochailort and
turn right to Kinlochmoidart where there is
a row of six (originally seven) beech trees
called the Seven Men of Moidart, to
commemorate the Prince's most faithful
companions. On an island in Loch Moidart
stands the remains of Castle Tioram (visible
from the road) which was destroyed in the
abortive rebellion of 1715, and was
originally Clanranald's home. Charles then
went on to Glenfinnan at the head of Loch
Shiel where he set up his standard on the
19th August 1745. The place is marked by a
tower surmounted by a statue of a kilted
Highlander.

HM Queen Elizabeth II (1926-) **L5**
Balmoral Castle, nr Ballater, Grampian.
Whenever possible the Royal Family have
always gone to Balmoral in the summer.
This is not a state residence but belongs to
the Queen personally, an inheritance of
Queen Victoria's enthusiasm for all things
Highland.
The house was designed by William Smith
of Aberdeen with a great deal of consultation
with Prince Albert, the Prince Consort. A
magnificent baronial mansion. *Grounds open
daily May-Jul. Closed Sun & when Royal
Family is in residence.*

James Ramsay MacDonald
(1866-1937)   **L1**
Lossiemouth, Highland. Ramsay Mac' was
Britain's first Labour Prime Minister. He
was born in a little backroom at No 1,
Gregory Place, Lossiemouth in 1886. The
cottage was originally thatched, and is now
marked by a stone plaque; his first school
was a little Free Church General Assembly
School which is still teaching.

St. Columba (543-615)   **A8**
Island of Iona, Mull. Iona was the home and
headquarters of St Columba, who set out
from here in 563 to convert Scotland to
Christianity. The island is more than a

collection of old ruins, it's a living religious experience that one can share with countless thousands of others from times gone by. St Columba's original mud and wattle chapel disappeared centuries ago, but the Norman cathedral magnificently remains as a testament to faith, and its restoration by the Iona community a continuance of the same. Nearby is St Oran's Chapel, the oldest building on the island, said to occupy the site of St Columba's original chapel. The chapel cemetery is the oldest Christian burial place in Scotland and contains the graves of 50 kings. Among the monarchs buried at Iona is Macbeth who was preceded there by Duncan I, killed in 1040 by Macbeth.

Robert William Thomson
(1822-1873) **O5**
Stonehaven, Grampian. A bronze plaque on the side of a house sited at the southern end of the Market Square is all that marks the site of the great inventor's birthplace. Robert Thomson best known for creating the first resilient tyres, both solid and pneumatic, when only aged 23, is less remembered for giving us the first fountain pen, rotary engine, drydock, road steamers, sugar machinery and the donkey-engine type of travelling crane.

Cathedrals, abbeys & churches

Bellie Parish Kirk Grampian **L2**
Fochabers, Moray. John Baxter's splendid little classical church (1798) with pillared portico and spire mirrors the time's sophistication in thought and faith.

Birnie Kirk Grampian **L2**
Moray. Built on a site hallowed since early Celtic times, this is one of the few surviving Norman churches in Scotland still used for worship. Inside is the Ronnel Bell, said to have been made in Rome of silver and copper, but probably of Celtic origin. A gentle reminder of simplicity of faith and daily life.

Dunblane Cathedral Central **J10**
Perth. A beautiful 13thC Gothic building with a Norman tower incorporated in the south wall of the nave. The west front is pure early English.

Grandtully Church Tayside **K7**
Perth. Pronounced Grantly. Outside a plain little 16thC church, but inside the arched ceiling is extravagantly ornamented with painted wooden medallions depicting subjects from the Bible.

Pluscarden Abbey Grampian **L2**
Moray. 7 miles ssw of Elgin. This 13thC Cistercian abbey is an intriguing cross between the Romanesque and early English styles. Used as a secular building for 400 years it was taken over in 1948 by the Benedictine order at Prinknash Abbey in Gloucestershire. A happy, hopeful rebirth which sadly so many of Scotland's fine old ecclesiastical buildings cannot share.

Pluscarden Abbey, Moray.

St Machar's Cathedral Tayside **O4**
Aberdeen. As blunt and as uncompromising as the religious beliefs of many of the worshippers here through the centuries. The only ancient granite cathedral in Britain, the main body of the work was executed 1424-40, although earlier work was incorporated.
The twin spires were added in 1552. The west front contains an original seven-light window and a round-arched doorway. The nave has a good clerestory. See also the charter room and the restored ceiling.

St Serfs Tayside **K9**
Dunning, Perth. Dominated by its massive, seemingly square and simple Norman tower, which is in fact cunningly tapered. The light from the small windows gives a subdued effect to the nave, and one's gaze is drawn into the chancel and beyond to the altar glittering with candles.

Tullibardine Collegiate Cathedral Tayside **K9**
Perth. A simple 15thC place of worship, and one of the very few of its kind in Scotland still unaltered. It has a remarkable open roof and heraldic decorations. The gables have typical Scots crow-stepping.

Castles and ruins

Dunnottar Castle Grampian **O5**
Stonehaven, Aberdeen. A breathtaking island stronghold with a savage history matched by the wild beauty of its position. The important parts of the remains are a 14thC keep and 16thC entrance works. At one stage the Crown Jewels of Scotland were kept here.
Of interest is the Convenanters' memorial which commemorates a Scottish version of the Black Hole of Calcutta when 122 men and 45 women were herded into one dungeon where many died.

Dunvegan Castle Highland **A2**
Dunvegan, Skye, Inverness. Probably the oldest continuously inhabited castle in Scotland. A massive, square, uncompromising building with very few exterior frills. Parts of the building are said to date back to the 9thC, but the main body of work was executed between the 15th and 19thC. The moat is now bridged.
The castle is the seat of Clan MacLeod and is full of many of the clan's historical relics such as the 'fairy flag' and the 12thC chief Rory More's two-handed sword and drinking horn. *Open 14.00-17.00 daily Mar-mid Oct. Closed Sun.*

Duart Castle

Duart Castle Strathclyde **D8**
Duart Point, Isle of Mull, Argyll. A dark, brooding, sinister building on a rocky eminence, or a fairy tale castle of enchantment, it all depends on the weather. Duart was commenced about 1250, extended in 1633, ruined in 1691 and restored in 1911. The Tobermory Galleon prisoners were held in the dungeon. *Open 10.30-18.00 Mon-Fri May-Sep. Also Sun afternoon Jul & Aug.*

Huntly Castle Grampian **M3**
Huntly, Aberdeen. Sometimes called Strathbogie Castle, this ancient pile represents a veritable pot-pourri of different ideas and periods. The earliest part of the castle is the Norman motte or earthmound; there is a mediaeval keep with enormously thick walls, but perhaps pride of place goes to the Renaissance works by the first Marquess of Huntly between 1597 and 1602. Notice the delicately angular first floor windows, the carvings round the entrance to the north-east tower, and finally the richly

featured fireplaces. *Open 9.30-16.00 Oct-Mar, 9.30-19.00 Apr-Sep. Closed Sun morning.*

Kildrummy Castle Grampian   M4
Nr Mossat, Aberdeen. This is the best example of a 13thC stone courtyard castle in Scotland, and still possesses a complete layout of domestic buildings. Powerful and massive it is hard to believe that it was captured by Edward I who cruelly put to death here Robert the Bruce's youngest brother. *Open any reasonable time.*

Rait Castle Highland   J2
Nairn, 3½ miles s of Nairn. A remarkably complete 13thC castle, notable for its round tower and remains of Gothic traceried windows. The scene of a bloody massacre in 1424 when the Mackintoshs attacked the Comyns.

Unusual buildings

Baxter's Lower   M8
Dens Jute Mills Tayside
Dundee, Angus. Designed by Peter Carmichael in 1866, these mills are an excellent example of the architect-engineer's work. The name architect-engineer was given to the pioneers in the field of structural engineering who created works of artistic merit. It was the functional aspect of these which has had such a profound appeal to the architects of the 20thC.

Bell Rock Lighthouse Tayside   N8
Angus. The oldest sea swept lighthouse in Britain, it is everyone's idea of where the lighthouse keeper stands his lonely vigil. Built 1807-11, the tower was made of inter-locking granite blocks to the same design as Smeaton Tower on the Eddystone Rock.

Brechin Round Tower Tayside   N7
Brechin, Angus. Built nearly a thousand years ago, it is one of two remaining round towers in Scotland. 87 feet high, fifteen feet in diameter at the base, twelve and a half feet at the top, and surmounted by a 14thC conical roof. Some six feet from the ground is a narrow round-headed doorway through which frightened clerics used to squeeze themselves to safety in times of danger.

Spey Bridge Grampian   L2
Craigellachie, Banff. Designed and built in 1815 by the engineer, Thomas Telford. The castellated pair of stone turrets guarding the bridge at both ends are an interesting concession to the taste of the time, though of greater significance is the use of prefabricated cast iron in its construction.

Houses & gardens

Balmoral Castle Grampian   L5
Nr Ballater, Aberdeen. A well-forested park on the River Dee which compliments the baronial style of this famous royal summer residence. *Grounds open daily May-Jul. Closed Sun and when Royal Family is in residence.*

Balmoral Castle

Blair Castle Tayside   J6
Blair Atholl. Perth. A large whitewashed mansion of various dates in the Scots' Disneyland/baronial style. Situated in wooded grounds approached through an avenue of lime trees. Originally built in 1269, this imposing structure was restored in 1869 by David Bryce. The castle has a lovely tapestry room, Jacobite relics and a fine collection of armour. *Open daily May-mid Oct. Closed Sun morning.*

Branklyn Gardens Tayside   L8
Perth. 12 miles e of Perth. A two-acre garden crammed with goodies. Created by Mr and Mrs John Renton and bequeathed to the Scottish National Trust, it has a particularly fine collection of alpines, clematis and roses and old fruit trees beneath which can be found a wide selection of herbaceous plants such as bearded iris, lilies and the heavenly blue meconopsis. *Open daily Mar-late Oct. Closed Sun morning.*

Craigievar Castle Grampian   M4
Nr Lumphanan, Aberdeen. One of the finest tower houses in Scotland, completed in 1626 and has remained unaltered and continuously inhabited. The building with its turrets and high pitched roofs was built by William Forbes. The fine hall has a magnificent Renaissance ceiling with pendants and retains its screens and a huge fireplace. Over the fireplace is the family motto, 'Do not waken sleeping dogs'. *Open 14.00-19.00 Wed, Thur & Sun May-Sep. Also Sat Jul & Aug.*

Crathes Castle Grampian   N5
Nr Banchory, Kincardine. Crathes dates from the late 16thC and is one of the finest Jacobean castles in Scotland. It contains some remarkable paintings (1599) of the Muses, the Virtues, and the Nine Worthies, and an oak panelled ceiling unique in Scotland.
The lovely garden dates from 1702 when the east wing was added. *Open 11.00-18.00 daily May-Sep. Wed, Sat & Sun afternoon April & Oct.*

Cullen House Grampian   M1
Cullen, Banff. The castellated house, home of the Earl of Seafield, contains portraits by George Jamesone and R. Waitt, old weapons and fine painted ceilings.
Also of interest are the library and the Monks' Passage – a relic of the days when the oldest part of the house was a monastic school. *Open 15.00-18.00 Tue-Fri Jun-Sep.*

Delgatie Castle Grampian   N2
Delgatie, Aberdeen. The seat of Clan Hay. Rebuilt by the Hays 1315-16 on earlier foundations. Painted and groined ceilings (1570). Mary Queen of Scots stayed here in 1562. There is an interesting museum on armour and weapons. *Open 14.30-19.00 Wed & Sun Jul & Aug.*

Doune Park Gardens Central   J10
Perth. 12 miles w of Doune. Laid out in the 19thC, it is divided into five distinct areas: the walled garden with herbaceous plants and roses, glens with azaleas, rhododendrons and shrubs, a pinetum and parkland with spring bulbs. *Open daily Apr-Oct.*

Drummond Castle Tayside   J9
Perth. 3 miles s of Crieff. A magnificent garden in the form of St Andrew's Cross dominates the scene from the terrace. Note the interesting sundial dated 1630 at the centre of the cross. *Open 14.00-16.00 Wed & Sat Apr-Aug.*

Glamis Castle Tayside   M7
Glamis, Angus. What a complicated confection this place is, with its clusters of turrets, bartizans, and extinguisher roofs. The castle owes its pleasant aspect to the remodelling by the 1st Earl of Strathmore, 1675-87, but portions of the high square tower, fifteen feet thick, are much older. The drawing room has a fine cradle-vaulted ceiling. *Open 14.00-17.30 Sun-Thu. May-Sep.*

Blair Atholl, Perth.

Haddo House Grampian   **O3**
Nr Ellon, Aberdeen. Built in 1732 to the
design of William Adam and greatly altered
inside by the first Marquess of Aberdeen in
1880. It contains interesting paintings and a
private chapel by G. E. Street. *Open 14.30-
17.00 Wed & Sun Jun-Sep.*

Haddo House

Leith Hall Grampian   **M3**
Nr Kennethmont, Aberdeen. The home of the
Leith family since 1650. It contains a
fascinating collection of family treasures
recalling associations with the Jacobites.
*Open 11.00-18.00 daily May-Sep. Closed Sun
morning.*

Leith Hall, Kirdanshire

Pitmedden Grampian   **O3**
Nr Udny, Aberdeen. 14 miles n of Aberdeen.
A formal garden originally planned by
Alexander Seton in 1675, it was neglected
until reconstructed by the Scottish National
Trust using surviving yews and Seton's
pavilions as a guide line. There are four
parterre gardens edged with miles of box
hedging and planted with 30,000 annuals
grown in the glasshouses here. *Open daily.*

Provost Ross's House Grampian **O4**
Shiprow, Aberdeen. Built in 1593, it takes its
name from Provost John Ross of Arnage
who owned it as a town house in the 17thC.
As an excellent example of early domestic
town architecture it was restored in 1954 by
the National Trust for Scotland. *Open
14.30-16.30 Mon & Fri.*

Provost Skene's House Grampian **O4**
Guestrow, Aberdeen. The home of a 17thC
provost or mayor of Aberdeen has been
restored as a museum. The Duke of
Cumberland stayed there in 1746 before
marching to Culloden where he defeated
Prince Charles Stuart. *Open 10.00-17.00
daily. Closed Sun.*

Scone Palace Tayside   **K8**
Scone, Perth. The present castellated
mansion is the early 19thC successor to a
Renaissance house and a mediaeval abbey.
The latter was the home of the Stone of
Destiny until 1296 when Edward I of
England removed it to Westminster Abbey.
There is a fine collection of French furniture,
china, ivories and 16thC needlework,
including bed hangings worked by Mary
Queen of Scots. *Open daily mid Apr-Oct.
Closed Sun morning.*

Museums & galleries

Abbot's House Tayside   **N8**
Arbroath, Angus. A folk museum with
Robert Bruce associations. *Open 10.00-16.30
Oct-Mar, 9.30-19.00 Apr-Sep. Closed Sun
morning.*

**Aberdeen Art Gallery
& Museums** Grampian   **O4**
Schoolhill, Aberdeen. Good collection of
Scottish art; painting and sculpture,
water-colours and prints. Marine exhibits.
Open daily. Closed Sun morning.

Broughty Castle   **M8**
and Museum Tayside
Broughty Ferry, Angus. Local history,
including whaling and armoury. Also
Scottish Tartan Society Information Centre.
*Open daily. Closed Fri & Sun (except Sun
afternoon Jun-Sep).*

Doune Park   **J10**
Motor Museum Central
Doune, Perth. A fine collection of historic
cars including many sports models collected
by Lord Doune. *Open daily Apr-Oct.*

**Dundee City Museum
and Art Gallery** Tayside   **M8**
Albert Square, Dundee, Angus. Local history
and archaeology; well documented. *Open
daily. Closed Sun.*

Glennfidditch   **L3**
Distillery Grampian
Dufftown, Banff. A museum attached to a
whisky distillery showing the history of
'Scotch'. *Open 10.00-17.00 Mon-Fri.*

St Vigeans Museum Tayside   **N8**
Nr Arbroath. Angus. A cottage museum with
a fascinating assortment of early Christian
and mediaeval sculptured stones. *Open
9.30-19.00 Apr-Sep. 9.30-16.00 Oct-Mar.
Closed Sun.*

Skye Cottage Museum Highland **A2**
Kilmuir, Isle of Skye. Highland crafts and
furniture in a restored island house. *Open
daily Apr-Sep. Closed Sun.*

Spalding Golf Museum Tayside **M8**
Camperdown House, Dundee, Angus. Devoted
to that most Scottish of games, with exhibits
dating back to 1680. *Open 9.00-18.00 daily.
Closed Sun.*

West Highland   **F6**
Museum Highland
Fort William, Inverness. Smacks of the
Jacobites and Bonnie Prince Charlie. *Open
9.30-21.00 Jun-Aug. 9.30-17.00 Sep-May.
Closed Sun.*

Zoos and aviaries

Aberdeen Zoo Grampian   **O4**
Hazlehead Park, Aberdeen. A modern zoo
with an emphasis on educational studies and
native Scottish animals. The Exhibition
House is especially interesting. *Open 10.00-
20.30 Apr-Oct. 10.00-dusk Nov-Mar.*

Camperdown   **M8**
Children's Zoo Tayside
Camperdown Park, Dundee, Angus. A
ten-acre zoo with wallabies, monkies, goats,
rabbits and donkeys. Also waterfowl
including flamingoes. *Open daily.*

Highland   **J4**
Wild Life Park Highland
Kincraig, Inverness. Wild animal compound–
bears, wolves, reindeer. *Open daily.*

Scotland's African   **J10**
Safari Park Central
Blair Drummond Castle, Perth. Lions,
giraffes, elephants, zebras and eland roam
free. Monkey jungle. Performing dolphins,
sealions; boat service to Chimpanzee Island. Als
cheetah reserve. *Open 10.00-dusk daily Mar-Oc*

Nature trails and reserves

Achlean Nature Trail Highland **J4**
Achlean, Inverness. Rich variety of birds on
lower Cairngorms slopes; heather moorland.
2 miles long. Also red deer and observation
tower. Guide and details from Achlean
Croft at the end of the road down
Cairngorms' side of Glen Feshie – enter the
glen from B970 near Feshiebridge.

Ben Lawers Nature Trail Tayside **H8**
Perth. Start at car park, turning left 5 miles n
of Killin on A827. Outstanding flora, but also
good for mountain birds including buzzard
and raven. 1½-2 miles. Leaflet from National
Trust for Scotland Centre at car park.

**Cairngorms National Nature
Reserve** Highland   **K4**
Cairn Gorm, Inverness. Highest mountain
massif in Britain with arctic/alpine plants
and a fine variety of breeding birds. Easy
access to high tops via Cairn Gorm
chairlift above Glen More (Speyside), and
other good areas are above Glen Feshie at
Allt Ruaidh and Achlean (Carn Ban Mor).
Details from Nature Conservancy, 12 Hope
Terrace, Edinburgh. *Tel 031 447 4784.*

Landmark Highland   **K3**
Carrbridge, Inverness. Off A9 at Carrbridge
on Aviemore-Inverness road. A free nature
trail with Speyside forest species forms part
of this unique centre. Excellent exhibition on
Highland history, wildlife, etc. Car park and
restaurant. *Open Jun-Oct.*

Loch An Eilean Highland   **K4**
*Inverness. Left from B970 after leaving s from
Rothiemurchus.* Picturesque Speyside loch
with typical forest birds and historic castle–
originally used by Wolf of Badenoch, but by
Ospreys in the 19thC. 2½ miles. Guide from

Cairngorms in winter.

information centre on north side of the car park. *Open Easter-Mid Oct*

Loch of the Lowes
Nature Reserve Tayside   **K8**
Perth. Leave Dunkeld on A923, fork right after about 1½ miles onto minor road which runs s of the loch. Scottish Wildlife Trust reserve with breeding ospreys and waterfowl, including great crested grebes, and woodland birds. Observation post and visitor centre open to the public.

Queen Elizabeth Forest Park
Nature Trail Central   **H10**
Perth. Off A821 2 miles s of Aberfoyle. Starts at Cobleland caravan site. Birds and plants of plantation and natural woodland. 5 routes, 1½–8 miles. Guide from Forestry Commission, 6 Queen's Gate, Aberdeen.

Queen's Forest   **K4**
Nature Trail Highland
Glenmore, Inverness. Start at campsite at Loch Morlich. Superb scenery and birds of Speyside forest and lower Cairngorms slopes. Guide is available from Camp Warden.

Bird watching

Flanders Moss Central   **H10**
Perth. S of Lake of Menteith. Good for black and red grouse, for the grey geese and often also for hen harriers. The disused railway line from Buchlyvie provides excellent viewing of part of this large area, and other access points are via B835, Buchlyvie to A81, and from B822 south of Thornhill.

Fowlsheugh Grampian   **O6**
Kincardine. Crawton s from Stonehaven on A92; turn left after about 3½ miles. An important stretch of seabird cliffs, with breeding fulmars, razorbills, guillemots and kittiwakes. Excellent views can be had from many points along the clifftop footpath north from Crawton.

Lake of Menteith Central   **H10**
Perth. Good for winter wildfowl, including whooper swans and, in the evenings, roosting pink-footed geese. It is overlooked by B8034 from Arnprior to Port of Menteith, but access via the Big Wood (enter from the minor road south of the lake) is better as it brings a chance of black grouse, capercaillie and woodcock, among many woodland species.

Spey Bay Grampian   **L1**
Moray. Where the Spey meets the sea there is an excellent area for breeding common and Arctic terns, winter wildfowl and waders and a good selection of migrants in season. There are good viewing points at Spey Bay village on the eastern side, while to the west the river can be reached from Garmouth and Kingston (from B9015 from Mosstodloch, west of Fochabers).

Speyside Highland   **K4**
Inverness. The valley of the Spey, a huge area lying between the Monadhliaths to the west and the Grampians to the east, has long been a Mecca for bird watchers. There are dozens of good spots, and virtually everything may be found by exploring from the roads and numerous footpaths. Good general areas include Rothiemurchus and Abernethy Forests, Loch Morlich and Glen

More, and Glen Feshie. Parts of the marshes below Loch Insh can be seen from B970; the RSPB have a new reserve here. Birds of the rivers and lochs include goosander, osprey, common sandpiper and dipper, while forest specialities include capercaillie, crested tit (virtually confined to Speyside as a British bird), crossbill and siskin. Buzzards and sparrowhawks are not uncommon, and both golden eagle and peregrine may be seen around the fringes of the mountain massifs.

Troup Head Grampian   **O1**
Banff. 10 miles e of Banff. Walk north to the large gully and via its left bank to the cliffs: a large seabird colony with breeding fulmars, kittiwakes, razorbills, guillemots and puffins, and with cliff-nesting house martins.

Ythan Estuary Grampian   **P3**
Aberdeen. 13 miles n of Aberdeen. A long, rather narrow estuary, excellent for migrants of all kinds, in autumn especially, and famous for its eiders at all seasons. Waders and duck are abundant in winter, sea duck included, and both grey lag and pink-footed geese occur in good numbers. The adjacent Sands of Forvie National Nature Reserve has large breeding colonies of terns (common, Arctic, Sandwich and little). Much of the area can be covered from the A975 north from Newburgh.

Fossil hunting

Visit the local museum. Its fossil collection usually states where individual fossils have been found. When visiting quarries always seek permission to enter if they look privately owned or worked. Be careful of falls of rock.

Mostly unfossiliferous rocks in this area, but small outcrops of Jurassic beds occur in Skye, at Broadfoot and Loch Staffin and on the island of Raasay and locally in Mull, in which are ammonites, belemnites, gastropods and bivalves. Also on Mull is some cretaceous chalk with fossil echinoids, belemnites, sponges, bivalves and some ammonites.

Forests

The ancient 'Wood of Caledon'
Only small portions of this magnificent old forest are left – the largest is in the basin between the Cairngorms and Aviemore and consists of the Abernethy, Glenmore and Rothiemurchus forests (where the native Scottish wild cats prowl at night). Mostly pine with some oak and birch. Good examples of this old forest in the Forest of Mar in the valley of the Dee. Many forests of old pines occur in the Inverness glens. Areas also exist precariously at Crannock Wood as it reaches the Moor of Rannoch in Argyll.

Birch forests
Natural birch forests occur in many places below 2,000 feet. Craigellachie in Moray has one of the most mature and extensive.

Oak forests
The remnants of the ancient oak forests still exist in Argyll and extend up the Great Glen. Also in the Trossacks in the Tay Valley and along the shores of Lochs Earn, Rannoch and Tay. They are normally below 700 feet.

Mountains

Approximately three-quarters of this area is mountains and is very wild and inaccessible. The main mountain groups are the Monadhliath Mountains, the Cairngorms and the Grampians. Don't venture off the beaten track alone; weather conditions can change suddenly and be very severe; tell someone where you are going and have some knowledge at least of how to survive.

Ardgour   **E6**
Inverness and Argyll. Reached by car ferry

across the Corran Narrows south of Fort William. This is the short-cut to mountainous Ardgour, whose peaks, particularly Sgurr na h'Eanchainne, 2,597 feet, afford superb scenery when viewed from Ballachulish.

Atholl J6
The Central Perthshire highlands form the ancient dukedom of Atholl, and much land is still owned by the present Duke of Atholl, who has his seat at Blair Atholl Castle. It is a richly-wooded country. Great forests of larch, spruce and pine, all skilfully tended by foresters, clothe its hillsides between the heather moors above and the flat fertile fields of the low straths. From the north the River Garry flows down over rocky cascades through the narrow Pass of Killiecrankie to join the Tummel.

Ben Lawers H8
Rising steeply above Loch Tay, and the A827 road from Aberfeldy to Killin, Ben Lawers comes just short of the 4,000 foot level. Rare alpine plants, including saxifrages and mountain rhododendrons, survive here, and the upper slopes have been declared a national nature reserve.

Bennachie Grampian N3
Aberdeen. 5 miles w of Inverurie, nr the A979.
Named from the Gaelic *beinn a' ciche*, or peak of the pap, from its shapely silhouette, this fine isolated summit is called in Scots 'The Mither Tap', for the same reason. It rises to 1,733 feet. Last outpost of the Grampians, it commands wide views over the broad plain of Buchan towards the North Sea.

Ben Nevis, Inverness.

Ben Nevis Highland F6
Inverness. The highest mountain in Britain, the 'mountain of snows' towers up majestically within a mile of the west coast town of Fort William. In shape it is half a plum pudding with the steep face to the north-west. In summer it's a gruelling climb, five miles of pack-pony track. Winter climbing, under snow and ice, and the crags of the north face, test the hardiest mountaineers.
On the rare clear days the views from Ben Nevis' 4,406-foot summit extend over all the Highland peaks, and far out to sea over the Hebrides.

Cairngorm Mountains.

Cairngorm Mountains K4
Scotland's largest group of high mountains, the granite Cairngorms stand as a 30-mile-broad, 4,000-foot-high range between Aviemore and Braemar. No roads cross them, and a drive round involves 140 miles! The northern group, including Ben Macdhui (Britain's second highest

mountain at 4,296 feet) and the Cairn Gorm are separated from the southern group of Braeriach and Cairn Toul by the deep defile of the Lairig Ghru, or 'gloomy pass'. The Cairngorms give the toughest walking in Britain as well as severe mountaineering. Near Aviemore are Scotland's finest skiing grounds.

Lochaber F6
The wild hill country around Fort William, east of Loch Linnhe. Ascend the lower Nevis Glen and a steep rocky path climbs above waterfalls to the charming seclusion of the upper glen, hidden amid the peaks. Grim Loch Leven is an arm of the sea trapped within the mountains. Glen Roy is crofting country and is famous for its 'parallel roads', gravel beds high on the hillside that mark the shores of an ice age glacier-dammed lake.

Monadhliath Mountains J4
The Gaelic name, 'the grey mountains', aptly describes this huge, dull, 50-mile range between Loch Ness and Speyside. Good deer stalking and salmon fishing, but lacking any other attractions.

Sidlaw Hills L8
A stately range of basalt hills, running up the eastern side of Perthshire and Angus for 40 miles from Perth to Montrose, the Sidlaws shield Dundee from northern blasts. Rich arable farms are carried surprisingly high up their flanks, then give way to heather-clad moorlands. The highest point is Auchterhouse Hill, 1,492 feet.

Strathspey K4
Known also as Speyside and Badenoch, this upland strath, here 800 feet above sea level, has frosty, snowy winters, fine for skiing, and dry, sunny summers. Birchwoods and pine forests clothe the lower clopes up to 2,000 feet, and beyond the high Cairngorm range soars steeply to over 4,000 feet, rimmed with snowfields even in June. Top-spots include the Aviemore Visitor Centre and Glen More Forest Park.

The Trossachs G9
An attractive mountain group centred on Loch Katrine (the setting for Scott's 'Lady of the Lake'). Ben Ledi (2,873 feet) is the highest point. Classical Scottish scenery of woods, rugged mountains and lakes.

Glens

Angus Glens M7
From the fertile plain of Strathmore several long glens run north from old stone foot-hill market towns, to the heart of the Grampian mountain mass. North of Blairgowrie the main Braemar road, A93, winds up Glen Shee to its highest level at Cairnwell, 2,000 feet. These uplands are always deep in snow each winter, but snowploughs maintain a clearway to the Glen Shee skiing slopes. Glen Clova and Glen Doll, north of Kirriemuir, end at a magnificent amphitheatre of crags, below the slopes of Dreish, 3,105 feet and Glas Maol, 3,504 feet. North of Edzell, Glen Esk winds through sheep pastures and pinewoods to remote Loch Lee, hemmed in by the eagle-haunted deer-stalking hills of Mount Keen, 3,077 feet, and Muckle Cairn 2,699 feet.

Buchan P2
Aberdeen. Though little visited, this 'cold shoulder of Scotland' has a most attractive countryside. Its undulating raised plain, well-farmed for grain and fat cattle, is broken at intervals by the deep glens of winding rivers like the Deveron, lined with ash trees, oaks and alders. Stray ranges of hills are topped by pinewoods, and the rugged coast has staggering sandstone cliffs.

Glen Affric F4
The exotic name of this long glen is derived from Gaelic *Glean Affaraich*, meaning the 'glen where the oats are grown'. It runs inland from Beauly just west of Inverness for nearly 40 miles. The road that winds up Loch Beneveian's north shore gives wide views over natural woods of Scots pine and birch, managed by the Forestry Commission. The southern road from

Cannich leads to the Guisachan pinewoods and the Plodda Falls, the northern one through sprucewoods to remote Loch Mullardoch, where anglers seek trout and deer-stalkers range the mountainsides.

Glen Coe   F7

Argyll. 'Just the place for a massacre!' – has been the comment of more than one tourist descending the gloomy Pass of Glencoe on a stormy day, for the towering hills shut in the high road from Tyndrum to Fort William where it drops from the Highland plateau towards Ballachulish and Loch Leven on the coast. Inevitably memories of that dread day, the 13th February 1692, linger here where 40 Macdonalds were slain because of the tardiness of their chief MacIan in declaring allegiance to King William III. But on a clear day the majesty of Glen Coe's peaks, now protected as a National Trust property, impress every beholder. North of the road stands the 'notched ridge' of Aonach Eagach, which ends on the west in the shapely Pap of Glencoe, 2,403 feet. The southern buttresses are called, in the Gaelic, the 'shepherds of Etive', after the great sea loch on their southern flanks. The eastern, lesser one, is Buchaille Etive Beag, 3,129 feet, and the western higher one is Buchaille Etive Mor, with a summit buttress called Stob Dearg, the 'red post', of 3,345 feet.

The Great Glen   H3

Glen More, or the Great Glen, cuts straight as a knife through the central Highlands, from Fort William on the west coast for 60 miles north-east to Inverness on the east coast. A string of lochs in deep narrow basins are set between steep-sided mountains that rise past forested foothills to high moors and remote rocky summits.

Strathmore   O5

The 'great valley' runs for 50 miles north-east of Perth towards Stonehaven. Sheltered by the Grampians on the north and the Sidlaws to the south, its warm rich red-brown sandstone soils yield heavy crops of grain, raspberries and nowadays flower bulbs, grown under the world's thriftiest farming conditions.

Rivers & lochs

Deeside and River Dee   O4

Running inland from Aberdeen for 70 miles, the level strath over which the river wanders carries thriving crops and herds of sleek beef cattle. Foothills as far as the eye can see are clothed in woods of the native Caledonian pines, with the snow-tipped Grampain peaks in the distance.

Lochs Linnhe, Leven, Eil and Lochy   F6

Every visitor to Fort William is sure to pass along the shores of one or all of these lochs, narrow waters set deep amid high hill ranges. Loch Linnhe is a 30-mile long tidal inlet of the sea. Near Corran the deep and dismal Loch Leven runs fourteen miles east; Loch Eil, also salt water, extends nine miles west from Fort William; Loch Lochy is a ten-mile-long freshwater loch, fringed with the Forestry Commission's thriving conifer forests.

Loch Ness   H3

Longest loch in Scotland, Loch Ness lies in a deep trench of the hills between Inverness and Fort Augustus, 22 miles long and one mile wide. Mystery surrounds the Loch Ness Monster, a legendary dinosaur-like beast said to show itself occasionally above the surface.

Spey   G5

The great River Spey rises in the very heart of the Highlands, in remote hills above Loch Spey. A turbulent river, subject to sudden spates, it often floods its higher valley, called Upper Strathspey, around Kingussie and Aviemore. Below Grantown-on-Spey it cuts through a scenic, forested gorge, rushing steadily north-east to gain the North Sea at the sandy bar of Speymouth, near Fochabers.

Loch Ness.

Strath Earn   J9

Loch Earn, the headwater of this lovely salmon river, extends from Lochearnhead to St Fillans. Below the loch, the Earn winds through a wooded glen past the charming towns of Comrie and Crieff. Then it leaves the hills for its broad fertile strath, below the breezy hills of Gleneagles and Auchterarder, to join the larger River Tay near Bridge of Earn township.

River Tay   H8

Loch Tay, fed by the River Dochart from Crianlarich, is the starting point of this great Perthshire river. From Aberfeldy to Dunkeld the Tay winds through steep wooded hills, then crosses fertile Strathmore to Perth, the ancient bridgehead, where it becomes navigable by coastal craft. Slowly its estuary broadens out towards the handsome, industrial city and port of Dundee.

Canals

The Caledonian Canal

This very fine waterway, the greatest in Scotland, is rare in at least two respects. Firstly it was commissioned by the Government, mainly to afford to ships that would have sailed round Cape Wrath protection from both the weather and any potential aggressors: the French were on the warpath at the time. (The canal is still much used by coastal fishing vessels.) Secondly the Caledonian Canal is only a true canal for about a third of its 60-odd miles in length. The rest of the way the navigable channel follows the several deep lochs that stretch along the Great Glen: lochs Lochy, Oich and Ness. (The latter is about 24 miles long.) There are 29 locks on the canal itself, which climbs up from either end to a summit level at Laggan. The great cutting here is the main engineering feature of the canal. Many of the locks are in 'staircase' formation (the best places are at Muirtown, Banavie and Fort Augustus). Indeed one of the best things about this waterway from the tourist's point of view is that good roads follow the canal virtually from end to end.

The 'Scot II', which in winter functions as the canal's official icebreaker and tug, runs daily trips (except Sunday) along the canal every summer. The boat leaves the top of Muirtown Locks, passes through

Caledonian Canal.

Dochgarroch Lock and then cruises down Loch Ness to Castle Urquhart and back.

Archaeology

An Sgurr Highland **B5**
Eigg, Inverness. The iron age fort at An Sgurr, with bank and ditch defences, occupies one of the most spectacular fort-sites in Scotland.

Ardoch Roman Fort **K8**
Ardoch, Perth. The defences of the Roman fort are among the most impressive of their kind in Britain. Originally a fort of five and a quarter acres with triple ditches, it was shortened at the north end during the later 2ndC. Two more ditches were added on the north and east sides, making five in all; these would have held attackers within the range of missiles thrown from the fort.

Clava Cairns Highland **J3**
Clava, Culloden Moor, Inverness. The group of Neolithic cairns on Culloden Moor belongs to a type of monument confined to this area of north-east Scotland. The burial cairns are roughly circular, with a passage for access to the central chamber, and are supported round the edge by a kerb of heavy slabs; around each cairn is a ring of free-standing upright stones. The associated ring cairns lack the passage, and now consist of an open ring with retaining kerb; they also have a surrounding stone circle.

Dun Bhuirg and Dun Nan Ceard Strathclyde **A8**
Iona, Argyll. Dun Bhuirg and Dun Nan Ceard are iron age duns, small sub-circular forts with a thick surrounding wall of drystone masonry. The single entrance passages were apparently defended with timber bars set in sockets.

Dyce Sculptured Stones Grampian **O4**
Dyce, Aberdeen. Two pagan Pictish symbol-stones are preserved in the old parish church. *Open any reasonable time.*

Finavon Tayside **M7**
Nr Forfar, Angus. Finavon is a classic example of a 'vitrified' fort, a type of iron age hillfort apparently peculiar to Scotland. These were originally defended with a stone wall, braced with timber beams, and timber buildings probably stood against the back of the wall.
In a subsequent fire, presumably during a siege, the buildings and bracing timbers caught fire; the stone was fused (vitrified) by the heat, and the complete length of wall collapsed.

Glenelg Brochs Highland **D4**
Glenelg, Inverness. 10 miles s of Kyle of Lochalsh. This well-preserved group of monuments illustrates two types of iron age defensive structures peculiar to Scotland. Dun Grugaig is a *dun*, a small fort, usually less than 60 feet across, which could be round, oval or D-shaped in plan. They had thick drystone walls, sometimes with an inner stair up to the parapet, and an entrance passage defended by timber barriers.
Dun Telve, and Dun Troddan are *brochs*, defensive towers dating from the late iron age. The base is a massive masonry ring on which stands a hollow wall built of two concentric drystone shells; these are bonded at intervals by continuous rows of slabs, forming galleries inside the wall connected by winding stone stairways. The entrance passage was defended by guard cells and a wooden barrier. *Open any reasonable time.*

Inehtuthil Tayside **K8**
Caputh, Perth. The Roman legionary fortress (Pinnata Castra) was built during the Scottish campaigns of the 80s, and guarded the main exit from the Highlands down the Tay. The rampart and ditch of the rectangular fortress, and those of the nearby stores compound, can still be seen; excavation has shown that the fortress was never completed.
A short distance to the north is the contemporary Cleaven Dyke, a Roman boundary earthwork with a watch-tower.

Loanhead of Daviot Grampian **N3**
Daviot, Aberdeen. The bronze age site is of a type called a 'recumbent' stone circle and is peculiar to this part of Scotland. The irregular circle of uprights increases in height up to two large stones which flank a massive flat block. In the centre is a low ring cairn, a circle of stones with a kerb of upright slabs. *Open any reasonable time.*

Maiden Stone Grampian **N3**
Nr Inverurie, Aberdeen. The Maiden Stone is a fine example of the standing stones carved during the dark ages, and shows early Christian influence. One side has an elaborately carved Celtic cross, the other has symbols used by the native pagan Picts. *Open any reasonable time.*

Pitcur Earth-house Tayside **L8**
Pitcur, Angus. The iron age 'earth-houses' of Scotland, of which Pitcur is a typical example, belong to the class of monuments known elsewhere as fogous or souterrains, and are usually attached to domestic or defensive settlements.
Most earth-houses are smaller than Pitcur which, at 190 feet long, is the largest known. They consist of a narrow underground gallery, curved in plan, entered by descending a flight of stairs and a narrow 'creep'. Others in the county are at Ardestie, Carlungie, and Tealing.

Raedykes Roman Camp Grampian **O5**
Raedykes,Kincardine. The Roman camp at Raedykes covers some 120 acres, and probably belongs to the campaign conducted in Scotland by the emperor Septimus Severus during the early 3rdC. Such camps were essentially temporary, and accommodation would have been in leather tents.
Raedykes is unusual in its irregular outline, which follows the natural contours. It has a single bank and ditch defence, and probably had six entrances, of which five survive; there are simple breaks in the bank with a short bank placed in front to provide defensible cover.

Rubh'an Dunain Highland **B4**
Skye, Inverness. The iron age dun at Rubh'an Dunain is of the type known as 'galleried' from the method of building the defensive wall. The overall plan follows the sub-circular form of a standard dun, but the drystone wall is built in two concentric shells, with the hollow between spanned by horizontal slabs.
There is also a chambered Neolithic cairn on the site, built of drystone masonry.

Footpaths and ancient ways

Glenuig Path Highland **C6**
Inverness. The hamlet of Glenuig, situated on a tiny bay between Loch Moidart and Loch Ailort, has only recently been given a road. Until then everything came by sea, or via a six mile path to the nearest road at Kinlochmoidart. The coffins of the dead had to be carried out along this path and at the top of the pass between the two villages, where the corteges halted for a rest, cairns were erected. The old path, which can still be used. It also extends through Glenuig to Inverailort seven miles to the north.

Regional sports

Canoeing **C6**
This area offers unrivalled variety and opportunity. The fast flowing rivers such as the Tay and Spey are a test for the experts. The chain of fresh-water locks linked by the Caledonian Canal between Fort William and Inverness offer great scope for canoe camping.
The west coast between Ardnamurchan and Mallaig offers a unique chance to view marine wildlife, and just north of here the canoe is the only real alternative to foot for exploring the remote area of Knoydart.

Climbing and hillwalking   F6

The magnificent desolation of the Highlands provides exhilarating climbing and walking. Britain's highest mountain, Ben Nevis (4,406 feet) offers a challenge both to the hillwalker who toils up one of the several well known paths, and to the climber who insists on fighting his way up the precipitous north face.

The saw-toothed Cuillin Mountains on the Island of Skye are the steepest and rockiest in Britain and there are only a few summits which can be reached without rock climbing or at least a good deal of scrambling. The Cairngorm Mountains offer good climbing, with the added attraction of the recognised climbing bases of Aviemore and Kingussie.

For the man on foot the western and central Highlands offer unparalleled freedom. Don't forget that in summer the weather is very unstable: in a matter of an hour brilliant sunshine can change to a thick wet driving Scottish mist.

Curling   H2

Played all over Scotland for at least 350 years, and in essence rather like bowls on ice. The curling stones look like old fashioned earthenware bedwarmers and are made from polished granite with handles let into the top. The object of the game is to slide the curling stone down the ice so that it stops inside the tee; the team with the most stones at the centre of the tee is the winner. There are curling rinks at Aviemore, Aberdeen, Inverness and Dundee.

Highland Games   K7

The Games are staged in various parts of Scotland each year, mainly in August and September. Their origin is obscure but they have a history going back to the 11thC. More than a Pictish athletics meeting, beside the traditional Highland sports there are bag-pipe and dancing competitions. The nice thing about these events is that they are still run and entered in by the locals, although no one minds if the visitor wants to enter a competition. However, beware of offering to toss the caber. The largest of the cabers at the Braemar Gathering is over nineteen feet long and weighs 120 lbs. It is claimed that this has been tossed successfully less than five times. Other traditional sports are throwing the heavy hammer and putting the stone. See the games at Portree in Skye, Crieff, Glenfinnan, Pitlochry, Braemar and Aboyne.

Shinty   J5

If skiing is the new sport of the Highlands, shinty is very much the traditional game; described as the fastest game played on foot in the world. Like the related game of hurley they play in Ireland, it is graceful and thrilling, a species of hockey unshackled. There is no rule on how high the stick can be raised to strike the ball. The game is played all the way up the Great Glen, in Skye, along the course of the River Spey, and in other parts of the Highlands. Shinty is primarily a winter sport and skiing visitors can see the game played at Kingussie, near Aviemore, at the Dell Ground.

Skiing   K4

It is only in the last fifteen years that the magnificent potential for skiing in Scotland has been discovered and exploited. There are now three very modern skiing centres, two in the Cairngorms at Aviemore and Glenshee, and the third in Glencoe near Fort William. They all possess chair lifts, ski tows and schools and in fact everything one has come to expect from the longer established Swiss resorts. Indeed Scots skiing, when conditions are right, is every bit as good as Switzerland. The only real drawback is the unpredictable weather. The official season is Dec-May.

Festivals

For information and tickets for festivals go to the local information centre or ticket agent.

Montrose Festival   Tayside   N7

Montrose, Angus. Concerts, art exhibitions and drama are presented at this festival, founded in 1963. A military pipe and drum band is usually on hand. *Sep.*

Pitlochry Festival Theatre   K7

Tayside
Pitlochry, Perth. Started as a theatre festival under canvas. The spirit is still maintained, although there are many new additions. *Apr-Sep.*

Fun things

Flambeaux Procession   J9

At Comrie in Perthshire one of the most exciting Hogmanay or New Year's Eve celebrations takes place. Townspeople in fancy dress, led by pipers and torchbearers march to the main square. There the costumes are judged and prizes given. Dancing, singing and general merry making follow, and all revels come to an end when the torches have burnt out.

Glenfiddich Whisky Distillery   N2

Grampian. On A941 n of Dufftown. There are hundreds of whisky distilleries in the Highlands. They can be recognised by the pagoda-shaped tops of the kiln houses where the barley is dried before malting. For security reasons not all that many throw their doors open to visitors. However the Glenfiddich Distillery gives guided tours. There is also a bar and a Scotch Whisky Museum. *Open 10.00-17.00 Mon-Fri.*

Pearl hunting   F6

In summer the Lower Spey is the centre of a pearl fishing industry. Fishermen scoop up mussels from the river bed and about one in 100 contains a fully formed pearl. The mussel is found in great quantities in the river estuaries on both the east and west coasts, where you can find your own pearls. All you need is a sharp knife and a bit of persistence. You can always take the mussels home and boil them in water and white wine – delicious.

Pitlochry Dam
and Power Station   K7

The North of Scotland Hydro-Electric Board has a display of their activities and provides tours of the power station during daylight hours. But perhaps more fascinating is the large fish ladder which is fitted with an observation chamber so that the passage of some 5,000 salmon a year can be viewed.

Hotels

The following indicates the price range of a single room per night:
£   inexpensive
££   medium priced
£££   expensive

Aberdeen   Grampian   O4

Station Hotel, Guild St. Tel 27214. A fine granite building which houses an efficient and well-run hotel. *££.*

Aberfeldy   Dumfries & Galloway   J7

Breadalbane Arms Hotel. Tel 364. In a delightful village by the river. A lively bar; sometimes there are ceilidhs. *£.*

Aberfoyle   Dumfries & Galloway   H10

Forest Hills Hotel, Lochard Rd. Tel Lochard 277. Close to Loch Ard. Sailing, riding and rough shooting are among the amenities. *£.*

Auchterarder Tayside **K9**
Gleneagles Hotel. Tel 2231. Splendid and
spacious. Ideal for golfers; it has numerous
other amenities too. Excellent food. £££.

Aviemore Highland **K4**
Strathspey Hotel, Aviemore Centre. Tel 681.
A stylish hotel set in the new winter sports
centre. There is a resident ski instructor;
ideal for children. £££.

Banchory Grampian **N5**
Raemoir House Hotel, Raemoir Rd. Tel 2622.
An 18thC mansion set in many acres. Rough
shooting and fishing are available to guests.
£££.

Comrie Tayside **J9**
Royal Hotel, Melville Square. Tel 200. A
former coaching house in the village square.
Pleasant and informal restaurant. £.

Craignure Strathclyde **D8**
Isle of Mull Hotel, Isle of Mull. Tel 351. A
peaceful hotel which offers salmon, trout and
sea fishing to its guests. Good for families.
££.

Dundee Tayside **M8**
Angus Hotel, 101 Marketgate. Tel 26874. Set
in the city centre; modern and comfortable
with efficient service and fine views. ££.

Dunkeld Tayside **K8**
Dunkeld House Hotel. Tel 243. A fine house
set in parkland beside the River Tay.
Amenities include fishing. ££.

Fochabers Grampian **L2**
Gordon Arms Hotel. Tel 508. A former
coaching inn; pleasant public rooms. £.

Fort William Highland **F6**
Inverlochy Castle. Tel 2177. A fine
Victorian-Gothic castle near Ben Nevis.
Splendid grounds and many rural amenities.
Excellent food but very expensive. £££.

Kildrummy Grampian **M4**
Kildrummy Castle Hotel, nr Alford. Tel 288.
A typical Victorian-Gothic castle with fine
views and pleasing public rooms. £.

Lochboisdale Western Isles West **A6**
Lochboisdale Hotel, S Uist. Tel 332. A
comfortable family hotel with excellent
views. Lots of fish. £.

Lochearnhead Central **H9**
Lochearnhead Hotel. Tel 237. Splendidly
situated at the head of the loch; many
sporting facilities and fine views. £.

Nairn Highland **J2**
Golf View Hotel, Sea Bank Rd. Tel 52301.
Overlooks the golf course and beaches.
Amenities include tennis and sauna. ££.

Netherley Grampian **O5**
*Netherley House Hotel, nr Stonehaven. Tel
Newtonhill 765.* A fine Georgian house.
Fishing and shooting available to guests. £.

Perth Tayside **K9**
Royal George Hotel, Tay St. Tel 24455. An
attractive hotel by the River Tay. Friendly
with good plain food. ££.

Pitlochry Tayside **K7**
*Pitlochry Hydro Hotel, Knockard Rd. Tel
2666.* A 19thC hotel on a hill above the town
with its own golf course. ££.

Portree Highland **B2**
Coolins Hills Hotel, Isle of Skye. Tel 3. A
country house hotel with good views of the
harbour. Pleasant garden. ££.

Rothes-on-Spey Grampian **L2**
Rothes Glen Hotel. Tel 254. A Victorian style
hotel built by the architect of Balmoral.
Pleasant period dining room. ££.

Regional food and drink

Refer also to some of the entries in the next
section (No. 12) which are also common to
this area.

Aberdeen sausage
The home of the Aberdeen Angus – famous
for steaks – this granite city has also given us
Aberdeen sausage. A mixture of minced
beef, bacon, oatmeal and spices which have
been boiled in a greased cloth.

Arbroath smokies
These are smoked haddock which have been
salted before smoking in the 'Arbroath
Smoke Barrel.'

Cock-a-leekie soup
This is a very rich clear soup, more akin to
a stew of chicken and leeks. Stewed prunes
are sometimes added.

Crowdie
This example of one of the many local cream
cheeses is made of fresh milk which is
soured. The curd is mixed with double
cream and salt and served with oatcakes and
butter.

Cullen skink
This local soup is based on smoked haddock,
preferably from Findon, which is thickened
with mashed potato.

Dundee cake and marmalade
Keillers of Dundee first made orange
marmalade commercially in the late 18thC.
The cake is a rich fruit mixture, whose top
is decorated with almonds.

Finnon haddie
Findon is the home of this fine smoked
haddock. It is ideal poached and also in
kedgeree.

Grouse
Shooting of grouse begins on the 'glorious
twelfth' of August and the birds will be on
the table of many restaurants that night. For
best results the bird should be 'hung' for
about a week.

Whisky
There are many distilleries in the area
around the Dufftown, Craigellachie and
Rothes – that of the major Highland Malts,
the Glenlivets and Glenfiddich.
Many of the distilleries are open to
visitors.
Read also the entry on whisky in the next
section (No. 12).

Restaurants

£   inexpensive
££   medium priced
£££   expensive

Alyth Tayside **L7**
Lands of Loyal Hotel. Tel 2481. Comfortable
country house. Straightforward cooking.
Some traditional Scottish dishes. LD. £L,
££D. Book. *Closed Feb*

Dundee Tayside **M8**
Le Mirage, 2 Constitution Rd. Tel 27072. A
good continental restaurant with music and
dancing on most nights. LD. *Closed Sun.* £.

Fort William Highland **F6**
Inverlochy Castle. Tel 2177. Scottish
baronial mansion. French and British
cooking. Not cheap. L (residents only), D.
£££. Book.

Nairn Highland **J2**
Clifton Hotel. Tel 3119. Well-kept hotel.
French and British cooking. Good value, L
(mainly residents), D. £L, ££D. Book.

Old Meldrum Grampian **O3**
Meldrum House. Tel 294. Country house
hotel. Cooking mainly British. Good value.
LD. ££. Book.

Perth Tayside **K9**
Timothy's, 24 St John St. Tel 26641.
Restaurant serving Danish open
sandwiches and salads. Good value. LD.
Closed Sun. £. Book.

Skeabost Bridge Highland **B2**
Skeabost House Hotel, Skye. Tel 202. Hotel
by a loch. Fairly traditional cooking. Set
meals. LD. £. Book D.

Weem Tayside **J7**
Ailean Chraggan Hotel. Tel Aberfeldy 346.
Comfortable family hotel. Straightforward
cooking. Set meals. LD. £L, ££D. Book.

Northern Scotland

This is the remotest part of the British Isles, a land full of the secret signs of vanished races. Frequently invaded by the Norsemen and the Vikings who have left their silent stone tombs and remnants of their culture in the Gaelic language. The distant islands, the Orkneys, Shetlands and far Hebrides depend on the sea and the sparse landscape for their livelihood and they are peopled by the friendliest folk you could hope to meet.

The lands of Sutherland and Caithness are less hilly than most of the Highlands, and much of the agricultural land is reclaimed peat bog. Here you find the shaggy horned Highland cattle and watch for wandering sheep in the path of your car on the narrow quiet roads. Fishing is the other main occupation, mostly white fish but there are good lobsters in the Thurso markets. You can't escape the sea on the hundred miles of coastline, and in a good summer you can wander and swim from the deserted white sandy beaches on the west coast with only the seals for company.

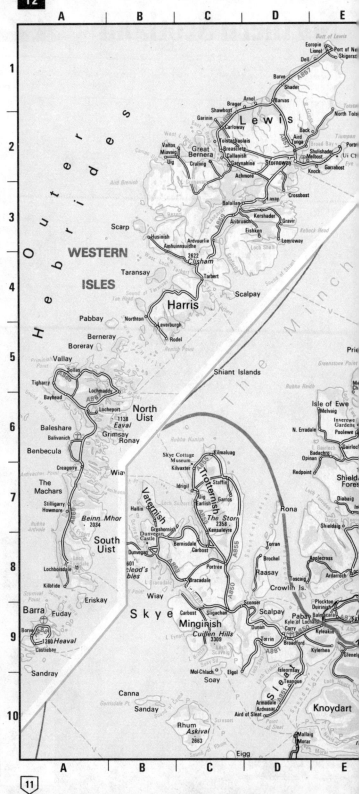

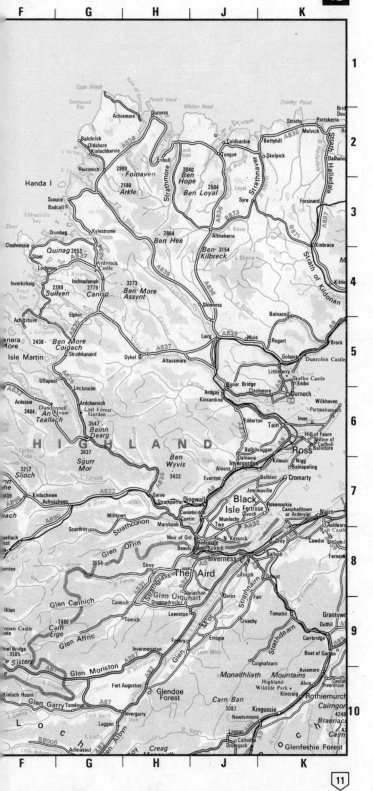

F   G   H   J   K

1

2

3

4

5

6

7

8

9

10

F   G   H   J   K

Cape Wrath
Sandwood
Bay
Faraid Head
Whiten Head
Strathy Point
Bridge
Dou
Achiemore
Durness
Strathy
Portskerra
Balchrick
Oldshore
Kinlochbervie
Coldbackie
Bettyhill
Melvich
R B73
Rhiconich
Friboll
Tongue
Skelpick
Dalhalv
Handa I
2980
Foinaven
3040
Ben
Hope
2504
Ben Loyal
Syre
Forsinard
2580
Arkle
Scourie
Badcall
Ben Hee
Altnaharra
Kinbrace
M
Eddrachillis
Bay
Clashnessie
Drumbeg
Kylestrome
2864
Ben 3154
Kilbreck
En Choire
Kildo
Stoer
Quinag 2653
Ardvreck
Castle
Lochinver
L Assynt
Inchnadamph
3273
Ben More
Assynt
Shinness
Strath of Kildonan
Inverkirkaig
2399
Suilven
2779
Canisp
Balnacoil
Achiltibuie
Elphin
Laird
Muie
Rogart
Brora
nera
More
2438
Ben More
Coigach
Strathkanaird
Oykel Br
Altassmore
Golspie
Dunrobin Castle
Isle Martin
Bonar Bridge
Littleferry
Skelbo Castle
Embo
Ullapool
Leckmelm
Ardgay
Clashmore
Dornoch
Ardessie
Dundonnell
House
Ardcharnich
Lael Forest
Garden
Kincardine
Wilkhaven
3484
An
Teallach
3547
Beinn
Dearg
Edderton
Tain
Inver
Portmahomack
H I G H L A N D
3637
Sgurr
Mor
Ben
Wyvis
Ballchraggan
Hill of Fearn
Milton of
Cadboll
Balintore
3217
Slioch
3433
Dalnavie
Alness
Kilmuir
Nigg
Balnapaling
Ross
Kinlochewe
Achnasheen
A832
Garve
Strathpeffer
Dingwall
Evanton
Invergordon
Nigg Bay
Cromarty
Scardroy
Milltown
Strathconon
Cononbridge
Black
Isle
Rosemarkie
Nairn
Contin
Fortrose
Avoch
Campbelltown
or Ardersier
Muir of Ord
Marybank
Munlochy
Tore
Auldearn
East Castle
Beauly
Redcastle
Kirkhill
N Kessock
Cawdor
Clemlie
Struy
Inverness
Balloch
Ferness
The Aird
Essich
Daviot
Glen Orrin
Glen Urquhart
Dores
Farr
Carn
Eige
Cannich
Lewiston
Abriachan
Drumnadrochit
Strathnairn
Tomatin
Grantown
Glen Cannich
Tomich
Croachy
Duthil
Glen Affric
Invermoriston
Foyers
Errogie
Carrbridge
Boat of Garten
Glen Moriston
R Moriston
Loch Mhor
Coignafearn
Aviemore
Glen Garry
Tomdoun
Fort Augustus
Glendoe
Forest
Monadhliath
Mountains
Highland
Wildlife Park
Alvie
Inverdruie
Rothiemurch
Invergarry
Laggan
Carn Ban
3087
Kingussie
Kincraig
Cairngo
Cairngor
4248
Braeriac
Achnasaul
Catlodge
Drumgask
Laggan
Glenfeshie Forest

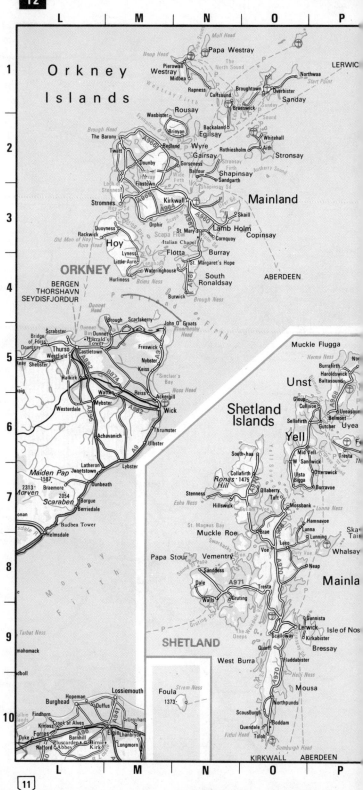

L M N O P

1

Orkney

Islands

Mull Head

Noup Head Papa Westray LERWIC
Pierowall *The North Sound* Northwaa *Start Point*
Westray Midbea
Rapness Broughtown Overbister
Westray Firth Calfsound Sanday
Wasbister Rousay Braeswick *Sanday*
Brough Head Backaland *Sound*
The Barony Brinyan Egilsay Whitehall
Bedland Wyre Rothiesholm Aith Stronsay
Twatt Gairsay *Stronsay*
Dounby Gorseness *Firth* Shapinsay
Finstown Balfour Sandgarth
Stromness *Wide* Mainland
Firth
Kirkwall *Deer Sd*
Skaill
Orphir St. Mary's Lamb Holm Copinsay
Rackwick Quoyness *Scapa* Cornquoy
Hoy Italian Chapel Burray
Lyness Flotta
ORKNEY Little Ayres St. Margaret's Hope
Wateringhouse South ABERDEEN
BERGEN Hurliness *Brims Ness* Ronaldsay
THORSHAVN
SEYDISFJORDUR Burwick *Brough Ness*
Dunnet
Head
Brough Scarfskerry Muckle Flugga
Dunnet John O'Groats
Bay Dunnet *Duncansby Head* *Herma Ness* Nor
Scrabster Harrald's Burrafirth
Bridge Tower Freswick Haroldswick
of Forss Thurso Baltasound
Dounreay Castletown Nybster Unst
Westfield Keiss Gloup
Shebster Cullivoe *A968*
Halkirk *Sinclair's* Sellafirth Uyeasour
Bay Belmont
Watten *Noss Head* Gutcher Uyea
Westerdale Mybster Reiss Shetland Yell Fe
Ackergill Islands Mid Yell
Wick W Sandwick Tresta
Achavanich South-haa Ulsta Otterswick
Thrumster Bigga Burravoe
Ulbster Collafirth
Ronas Ollaberry
Maiden Pap Latheron *Hill* 1475 Taft
1587 Janetstown Stenness Mossbank
2313 Braemore Lybster Hillswick *Lunna Ness*
Morven 2054 Dunbeath *Esha Ness* Hamnavoe Ska
Scaraben Borgue Brae Lunna Tai
Berriedale *St. Magnus Bay* Laxo
Badbea Tower Muckle Roe Whalsay
Helmsdale Papa Stour Vementry Voe
Swarbacks Neap
Moray Sandness *Min*
Tarbat Ness *Sound St Papa* Dale A971 Tresta Mainla
Firth Walls Gruting Gunnista
mahomack *Greting Voe* *The* Scalloway Lerwick Isle of Nos
dboll *Deeps* Kirkabister
SHETLAND Quarff Bressay
Lossiemouth West Burra Fladdabister *Helli Ness*
Hopeman *Stram Ness*
Burghead Duffus Foula Mousa
Findhorn Urquhart 1373
Kinloss Crook of Alves Scousburgh Northpunds
Dyke Forres Elgin Lhanbryde Poddam
Barnhill Birnie Quendale Tolob
Rafford Pluscarden Abbey Kirk Longmorn *Sumburgh Head*
KIRKWALL ABERDEEN

L M N O P

The coast

Applecross Highland   D8
Ross & Cromarty. Pop 600. On a good day
it is an exhilarating experience to follow the
hairpin bends of the 'Pass of the Cattle' – the
steepest road in Britain – which leads to the
remote hamlet of Applecross. The views
from the top of the pass (2,054 feet above sea
level) are predictably magnificent. The only
other way to reach Applecross is by ferry
from the Kyle of Lochalsh. Red sand bay,
with cliffs to north and south.

The Road to Applecross.

Avoch Highland   J7
Ross & Cromarty. Pop 1,100. A colourful,
thriving fishing village. Tradition has it that
the inhabitants are descendants of a wreck of
the Spanish Armada; certainly many of them
are darker in colour and speak with a softer
accent than the other inhabitants of the
Black Isle.
The beach is sandy with a shingle-backing.
Strong currents make bathing unsafe.

The Black Isle Highland   J7
Ross & Cromarty. The Black Isle is
mysteriously named as it is not an island but
a green fertile peninsula with a ridge of
forested land crowning the patchwork of
undulating fields: in the summer roses bloom
in profusion. Tradition maintains that it owes
this name to its mild climate – which never
allows the landscape to become white with
settled snow.
Though most resorts have sandy-
backed beaches, and between Rosemarkie
and Cromarty there are steep cliffs and
rocky bays, the coastline is mainly fringed
with muddy saltings – the haunt of wading
birds. Ornithologists will find this a
particularly rewarding area.

Brora Highland   K5
Sutherland. Pop 1,000. EC Wed. With its
beach, golf course and excellent fishing
river Brora is a predictably popular resort.
Rather more unexpected is the fact that it
also has a coal mine (which has been worked
since the 16thC) and owes its development
as much to industry as to tourism. There is a
tweed mill, a distillery and a brickmaking
plant. Of interest – the tiny, decayed
harbour and the Victoria Jubilee drinking
fountain. Long sandy beach.

Castletown Highland   L5
Caithness. It is unusual to pass through
woodland in windswept Caithness, but trees
shade the road leading into Castletown. This
small village grew up in the early 1820's to
house the people who worked in the
Castlehill flagstone quarries. In Victorian
times Caithness flag was exported all over
the world – and the streets of many well-
known cities were paved with it – but with
the advent of concrete the quarries and the
harbour fell into disuse.
Dunnet Bay with its two mile stretch of
shell strewn sand lies just to the north of the
village.

Cromarty Highland   K7
Ross & Cromarty. Pop 500. EC Wed. The
scent of roses mingled with the tang of the
sea wafts through the labyrinth of narrow
streets. With the eclipse of its harbour
Cromarty seemed doomed and its buildings
began to decay. In recent years however the
National Trust for Scotland, aided by the
local Development Council have arrested
this threat and the place has been restored
so thoughtfully that in the rebuilding of the
fabric of the buildings, the bewitching
atmosphere of an 18thC fishing village has
been captured. Muddy, shingle-scattered
sandy beaches. Bathing safe except after
heavy rains, which produce strong currents.

Dingwall Highland   J7
*Ross & Cromarty. Pop 4,200. EC Thur.
MD Wed.* A bustling workaday town watched
over by 'Fighting Mac's Tower' – built in
the 19thC to the memory of the able General
Sir Hector Macdonald.
The mudflats and saltings of the Conon
Estuary make bathing unsuitable.

Dornoch Highland   K6
Sutherland. Pop 800. EC Thur. Dornoch
with its mellow sandstone buildings set
round the former cathedral is the nicest town
in northern Scotland. It has three other
claims to fame: the best sunshine record in
northern Scotland, the third oldest golf
course in the world, and it burnt the last
witch in Scotland. Make time to take the
gentle walk up Ben Struie: the view is
excellent.
Sandy beaches curve away from either side
of the town. Beware of the ebbing tides at
Dornoch Point.

Dunnet Bay Highland   L5
Caithness. A great sweep of firm white sand,
almost too large for comfort, but providing
excellent conditions for sand-yacht racing.
Try to catch the moment when the setting
sun fills the gap between the headlands
turning the sand to silver, and enjoy
collecting the sea 'gold' – the rich treasure
of shells washed in by the Atlantic rollers.

Cliffs, Dunnet Head.

Fortrose Highland   K7
Ross & Cromarty. Pop 1,100. Most of the
buildings of this demurely attractive village
are perched decorously on the plateau above
Chanonry Point, encircling the ruins of
Fortrose Cathedral. Near the harbour some
of this discipline is lost and the houses spill
colourfully down the grassy slopes towards
the golf course and the sand and shingle
beach.

Gairloch Highland   E6
Ross & Cromarty. Pop 1,800. EC Wed. A
village built round a small harbour, with
magnificent views to the south of Ben
Alligan (3,232 feet) and Baeishven (2,869
feet). The large fleet of trawlers have to wait
their turn in the loch outside the little
harbour before unloading their catch at the
quay. An immense eight-mile sweep of
white sand stretches westwards from the
village.

Helmsdale Highland   L8
Sutherland. EC Wed. A small fishing port at
the mouth of the lovely Strath of Kildonan,
famous for its lobsters which are flown to
France from Wick. Visitors are welcome at
the lobster sheds.
To the north the bay is wild and rocky, but a
stretch of shingle leads to a sandy beach on
the south side.

Invergordon Highland   J7
Ross & Cromarty. Pop 2,200. EC Wed. The
gleaming towers and orange roofs of this
outpost of industry look splendid when
viewed from the northern shores of the
Black Isle. The natural harbour is one of the
deepest and most sheltered of the British
Isles; it was used as a seaplane and naval
base during both world wars, and in more
recent years has attracted the development
of a whisky distillery and aluminium
smelter. There are beaches of silty, pebbled
sand.

John O'Groats Highland   M5
Caithness. The tourist's goal: the north
eastern tip of the county, with enjoyable
views over the tide race of the Pentland Firth
towards the Orkneys. Steeped in the legend
of the Dutchman John de Groot, a local
ferryman who gave his name to the place.
The beach has rocks, shingle and white
sand. Safe bathing close inshore on an
incoming tide.

John o' Groats

Kyle of Lochalsh Highland E9
Ross & Cromarty. Water-flanked mountains glower down from all sides on this one-horse town, whose few facilities include a large and famous hotel, a terminal railway station complete with steam-powered crane, and a ferry service to Mallaig (round the back of Loch Alsh), Skye (just across the water), and the Applecross Peninsula. The rocky headlands and strong tidal races are not suitable for swimming.

Lochinver Highland F4
Ross & Cromarty. The village is small but memorable, chiefly on account of the charm of its harbour with its colourful fleet. Even more memorable is the surrounding wild landscape dominated stolid dome of Mt Suliven 'the sugar loaf mountain'.

Rosemarkie Highland K7
Ross & Cromarty. EC Thur. Chanonry Point, a grassy promontory which has been made into an excellent golf course separates this village from Fortrose. Rosemarkie is a quiet continuation of its twin. The A832 climbs steeply out of the village offering a superb view across the voraciously swirling currents of the Moray Firth to the 18thC Fort George Its sandy beach gives way to rocky bays backed by cliffs to the north.

Sandwood Bay Highland G2
Kinlochbervie, Sutherland. Flat golden sands, immense and beautiful, are the rewards for a four-mile walk from where the road at Kinlochbervie ends. Strong tides; unsafe for bathing.

Sutherland's North Coast H2
The main road A836/A838 that strikes west from Thurso in Caithness to follow Sutherland's north coast towards Cape Wrath runs through a countryside of dramatic beauty. Usually it traverses bare unfenced moorland a mile or so inland from the sea, and the few small crofting villages scattered along the coast are only distantly seen amid their green fields. Occasionally, as at Melvich and Durness, it touches on lonely beaches of white sand where you can swim in the clear caressing waters of the warm Gulf Stream. Elsewhere it winds around two deep cliff-bound inlets of the Atlantic, called the Kyles of Tongue and Loch Eriboll. To the south three grey-brown bold mountains soar to the clouds, namely Ben Loyal, 2,304 feet, Ben Hope, 3,040 feet and Ben Spionnaidh, 2,837 feet. For 80 miles there is no town, but wayside hotels provide refreshment for deer stalkers, bird watchers, salmon fishers, and those who come simply to watch the waves pound on the craggy shores. People sometimes wonder how this far northern county came to be called 'Sutherland'. The Vikings came from the north, and settled first in the Orkneys and Caithness; then they moved south into this, to them, the 'southern land'.

Thurso Highland L5
Caithness. Pop 9,100. Thurso is the most northerly town on the British mainland. It originated as a Viking settlement, hence its name which is derived from the Norse

Thurso, Caithness

'Thor's-a' – literally 'river of the god of Thor' The river, which is rich in salmon and trout, flows gently through the town and out into Thurso Bay. The ruins of the 17thC castle, ancestral home of the earls of Sinclair, stand sentinel over the small harbour at the river's mouth. Several 17th and 18thC fishermen's cottages can be found near the harbour. The enlightened Sir John Sinclair initiated the buildings of the 19thC part of the town where the broad streets are lined with some handsome neo-classical houses Over the two decades since the decision to site the nuclear power station at Dounreay, ten miles west of Thurso, the population has tripled. The expansion of the town has been thoughtfully planned; use of local flagstone and slates has ensured that the old and the new buildings blend together perfectly. Note the attractive way in which the stepped profiles of the houses climb round the sloping green by Riverside Walk. Comparison between Wick and Thurso is inevitable and, on the whole, Thurso comes out the best: it is the more attractive of the two and although in the 18thC Wick was known as the 'boom town of the north', today Thurso has indisputably won that title. Of interest: the 'other' castle of Thurso – dating from 1832; the ruins of St Peter's church, some of which date from the 13thC; Meadow Well, a former source of the local water supply and the town museum housing locally-collected geological and botanical specimens. Sandy beach backed with pebbles. Safe bathing away from the river.

Ullapool

Ullapool Highland G5
Ross & Cromarty. Pop 1,500. EC Tue. Unlike many of the villages created by the British Fisheries Society in the late 18th and early 19thC, Ullapool continues to draw a large income from its fisheries. The guaranteed excellence of the catch has also provided the basis of much of the tourist industry. For years men have loaded their wives, nets and rods into the car and headed for this village. Most sea-fishing widows enjoy their bereavement – what better solace than the magnificent scenery of this corner of Western Ross. Passengers for the first steamer of the day to Stornoway (Isle of Lewis) will find their early rise well rewarded if they drive into the town from the north. This route leads through the Inverpolly Nature Reserve, and it is quite likely that a glimpse will be caught of a marten, or perhaps a wild cat stalking a heron. Worth making time for: a boat trip from the harbour to see the birds of the Summer Isles.

Wick Highland M6
Caithness. Pop 7,600. EC Wed. MD Thur. If you drive into Wick on a wet day, doubtless feeling rather bored by the surrounding featureless countryside, you will probably agree entirely with Robert Louis Stevenson's description of it as 'the bleakest of God's towns on the baldest of God's bays', but gradually your feelings will mellow, as did those of Stevenson. Drive round to South Head and gaze down at the harbour with its three basins – always the scene of some activity: trawlers setting out to sea, men repairing nets, small boys dodging perilously under the wheels of the lorries collecting wooden boxes of fish. As the road climbs up to South Head it passes the sturdily handsome terraces of Pulteneytown, a model fishing village laid out by Thomas Telford during the boom of the herring industry in the early 19thC. During the heyday of this industry vast sums were spent on the harbour without conspicuous success – it can still be entered by large boats only at high tide. With the mysterious disappearance of herring from

the eastern coastal waters of Scotland Wick's prosperity declined. But today it is the market centre of the rich farmland of the region – tucked down a side street you will discover the delightfully old-fahsioned auctions rooms. Of interest: the modern glassworks (visitors warmly welcomed); the parish church (said to have the widest roof span in Scotland); the Andrew Carnegie library and museum; ruins of Gringoe and Sinclair castles which lie together three miles north-east of the town and Wick Castle (the Old Man Wick) some one and a half miles south-east.

Islands

The Outer Hebrides Western Isles
The name is taken from the Norse *haf bred eyr* – 'islands on the edge of the ocean'. The climate reflects this, being moderated by the Gulf Stream but lashed with Atlantic gales that batter the western shoreline.
The winter nights are long and the living is hard for the majority of the people who are tenants of absent landowners, with crofters' rights. They are a friendly, courteous and intelligent people and look 'foreign'. In fact they still speak a soft Scots Gaelic. Their economy is based on small farms, fishing, home weaving and tourism, and the impression given is that of a peasant community.
Power comes from peat (cut on the islands), coal and hydro-electricity. Roads are sufficient, but narrow and winding.
A visit here will stir your soul, and remind you of some of the basic values missing from town life.
There are many safe, sandy beaches, but enquire locally before swimming.

Barra   A9
The central island of the remotest group of the Outer Hebrides; the steamer from Oban takes a day to reach Barra. The most amusing way to arrive is by 'Heron' – the BEA aircraft which land on the firm Cockle Sands at Traigh Mhor, the only area flat enough to use as an airstrip in the whole of the rocky island. Flights have to be timed carefully as the 'runway' is covered by the tide twice a day. Barra is known as 'the Garden of the Hebrides' – over 1,000 species of wild flowers can be found here.
The beaches are superb – miles of empty sand.

Barra

Harris   C4
The southern part of the 'Long Isle', where grey gneiss creates a 'moonscape' of bare rocks and craters filled with peaty water, softened only by large water lilies growing in profusion in the pools. Crofting villages shelter behind rugged headlands and in tiny bays the fishing, particularly for lobsters, remains profitable.
Harris tweed is dyed and handwoven here in the cottages to the traditional colours and patterns, and exported throughout the world. There are several long, sandy beaches.

St. Clements, Rodel, Harris

Leverburgh **(B5)** *EC Thur*. Once called Obbe, the present name of this village dates from the 1920s and is a tribute to Lord Leverhulme's vastly expensive failure to improve the economy of the Long Island. Forced into selling Lewis, he determined to develop a fishing station at Leverburgh. Remnants of its brief excursion into the 20thC can easily be identified: for example, the wooden 'Swedish' style houses. The only good feature of the harbour that remains is its view across the Sound of Harris.

Tarbert **(C4)** *EC Thur*. Tarbert is strategically placed on the isthmus connecting the peninsula of South Harris with the rest of Long Island; cars and coaches automatically pass through the town while car ferries regularly make the two hour trip to Skye. The seething activity of the place is heightened because it is the centre of Harris's tweed industry. Viewed from the south-west the village is striking, with lines of houses radiating along the banks of its twin lochs.
There are some excellent beaches to the south-west: take the A859 out of Tarbert – you will have to drive for about ten miles – but the wide choice of sandy bays will be ample reward.

Lewis
The northern part of the 'Long Isle', an exciting landscape of peaty-moorlands with menacing outcrops of grey rock and sheer cliffs forming sandy bays and numerous lochs.
Over the years the crofters have improved the pastures, now rich with wild flowers, and have cultivated oats and potatoes. The traditional 'black houses' of stone and thatch are being replaced with modern buildings, standing open to the winds. There are few trees.

stornoway harbour

Stornoway **(D2)** *Pop 5200. EC Wed*. The only town in the Hebrides: it is more bright and breezy than beautiful, but always surprising. A community of Pakistani shopkeepers speak Gaelic, overlooked by the turreted Lewis Castle. The Harris tweed industry is centred here. The town has two harbours, sheltered and accessible in all tides and weathers. Of interest are the Nicholson Institute and St Peter's church. Excellent sandy beaches, with safe bathing.

Valtos **(C2)** *Isle of Lewis*. The scattered houses of this tiny crofting township conform to the usual rather dismal architectural standard of the Long Island, but the beach is superb. Heaped high with orange and brown limpets, razor shells, tiny pink delicacies and sea-worn stones of an agreeably portable size, it's a beachcomber's paradise. Those with an insatiable lust for shells should also visit Reef, the next bay along.

Uig Bay **(B2)** Tucked away on the south-west of Lewis lie Uig Sands – a vast expanse of white velvet bordered by sweet smelling clover meadows. A haven in the strangely menacing 'lunar' landscape of this corner of the island. Beware of the area of quicksands at the western edge.

St Kilda   West A4
This group of tiny rocky islands, the westernmost of all Britain, lies 110 miles west of the northern Scottish mainland. These were inhabited until 1930, when the last group of Gaelic-speaking crofters was evacuated. Now belonging to the National Trust for Scotland, St Kilda has only temporary visitors today, usually naturalists on study tours run by the Nature Conservancy. Its cliffs, up to 1,396 feet high, are the tallest in Britain, the wildest, and most dangerous. Wild sheep, left by the last crofters, survive and maintain their numbers, and thousands of sea birds nest.

North and South Uist and
Benbecula   **A6**

These southern Hebridean islands form a long, broken chain, running for 35 miles south of the larger 'long island' of Lewis and Harris. They average eight miles wide, but their coasts are deeply indented everywhere by sea lochs. Inland lie wastes of rock and peat, broken by a maze of countless freshwater lochs, with rocky peaks springing steeply from the wilderness. Down the west coast, however, there is fertile land beside the *machair* (see Regional oddities) a long sandy beach washed by the fierce Atlantic waves. Here stands a string of crofting villages along the single main road, A865. The three main islands of North Uist, Benbecula and South Uist are now linked by causeways. A ferry from Uig in Skye carries cars to Lochmaddy in North Uist, and other ferries link Lochboisdale in South Uist with Oban and Mallaig on the mainland. Most visitors come to fish, watch birds, or get-away-from-it-all, for the islands have no attractions save their wild scenery and clear air. There are miles of safe, sandy beaches, but beware of the tidal currents that flow swiftly through the channels between the islands.

Orkney   **M3**

Many of the islands of Orkney cluster around the 'Mainland' (the largest island – Orcadians refer to the Scottish Mainland as 'The Sooth'). They are low lying, with a few gentle hills. The exception is Hoy, mountainous with grandiose coastal scenery including the 'Old man of Hoy', a tempting vertical carrot to intrepid mountaineers. Surprisingly, Orkney is not a fishing community: beef cattle and hens are the mainsprings of the economy, both heavily mechanised.

The Orkneys and the Shetlands were appropriated from Scandinavia in 1528 and the Norse flavour is very evident. Communications with the mainland are good, and there is a well-run internal air system. There are many stretches of sandy beach where bathing is safe close inshore.

Stromness **(M3)** *Pop 1,600. EC Thur.* Excellent harbour with daily steamers to the mainland (Scrabster). Many of the houses back on to the water front and have their own stone piers.

Scapaflow **(N3)** Was the scene of intense activity in both world wars, but now only thistles invade this submarine base.

Shetland   **O8**

Fingers of the sea (voes) thrust their way deep into the land, and from the air the islands of the Shetland group look like the pieces of a jigsaw which has been abandoned because no one could quite sort out the blue bits from the green and brown ones, and there are no 'straight edges' to help. There are nearly 100 islands of which Mainland is the largest, but the best known is the Fair Isle – its knitting patterns are world famous. Shetland only became part of Britain at the end of the 15thC when their ruler, Christian I of Denmark, having 'pawned' the group was unable to produce the money to redeem his pledge. The culture remains basically Scandinavian and all the place names and the local dialect (Shorn) have Norse origins.

The islands lie on the same line of latitude as the tip of Greenland and Siberia, and experience the same long summer daylight hours and the interminably long winter nights. They do not have to undergo the rigours of the Arctic climate because their shores are washed by the Gulf Stream, but the low moorland landscape is frequently lashed by fierce gales. Predictably the land is treeless and not notably fertile, though it is being improved and the peat bogs are slowly being reclaimed. There are some crofters who rear the hardy Shetland breed of sheep and the famous ponies, but the islands lie in the midst of some of the best fishing grounds in the world, and most of the men look to the sea for their living. Few places are more than a mile away from the sea: it is without doubt the most dominating feature of the Shetlanders' lives. People eager to escape from the urban antheap and to revel in the seascapes, to fish, to sail and to observe the bird life, are visiting the islands in increasing numbers: a boon to the tourist industry but a self-destroying process. Access by air and by ferry from Aberdeen and Leith. Swimming is only safe from bays, which provide protection from strong currents.

Lerwick **(O9)** *Mainland. Pop 6,300.* The capital of Shetland, and the home of more than half the population. A maze of narrow paved streets twists down to the waterfront. Although one might expect the inhabitants of such a remote town to have an insular approach to life, in fact more than 50% of the population have visited most of the major ports of the world. For centuries the port has been the meeting place of sea-faring folk: the Viking warriors used to meet here between raids; in the 17thC the Dutch were frequently in the harbour (the houses which overhang the waters of the harbour are a testimony to the fact that their visits were not altogether confined to fish trading: the arrangement was ideal for secret landing of contraband) and today trawlers from all over the world, not to mention the international oil men, maintain the cosmopolitan tradition.

Lerwick harbour.

Inland towns

Lairg Highland   **J5**
Sutherland. Pop 1,100. EC Wed. Though probably the largest of Sutherland's inland villages, Lairg is little more than a hamlet clustered around the eastern shores of the Little Loch – a reservoir created by the damming of the head of Loch Shin and the narrows of the River Shin. It lies at the junction of the roads leading north and west and is basically a touring centre, with a market. The 'Great Plough', a monument found about three miles north of the village, commemorates the large scale land reclamation instigated by the Duke of Sutherland in the 1870s.

Lairg, Sutherland.

Fair Isle, Shetlands

Strathpeffer Highland   **H7**
Ross & Cromarty. Pop 1,100. EC Thur. A prosperous town basking luxuriantly in the shelter of the encircling hills. From the 1770s until after World War I

Strathpeffer was a fashionable spa; members of the Royal Family came to take the waters of the nearby chalybeate and sulphur springs. Today it has become a popular touring centre, famous for its smoked salmon. With its abundant trees and shrubs and its chalet-type architecture the town seems like a cross between Bournemouth and a Swiss mountain resort. The continental atmosphere is reinforced in the evenings, when the shops stay open late and visitors saunter round the square.

Strathpeffer

Regional oddities

Black houses Western Isles
Outer Hebrides. The landscape of parts of the Outer Hebrides is dotted with these long, low drystone buildings. They probably owe their name to the fact that there was no chimney to allow the escape of smoke from the central peat fire. Other traditional features include a roof thatched with heather weighted down with boulders and a byre leading off the living quarters. Very few people still live in these houses, and they are either used as stores or else allowed to gently disintegrate. The Black Houses at Arnol (fourteen miles south of Stornoway, Isle of Lewis) and near Eochdar (Isle of S. Uist) may be visited – they have been converted into museums.

Black Houses, Berneray, Outer Hebrides

Brochs
A triumph of drystone walling, these bell-shaped towers are found only in the north of Scotland, the Outer Hebrides, Orkney and Shetland. It is thought that they were built by the Picts as defensive structures during the 1st and 2ndC. Typical features include a central courtyard, a low-roofed entrance passage and a spiral staircase built within the outer and inner walls to allow access to the upper galleries. In all there are over 500 brochs in the far north of Scotland and its islands; the best preserved examples are at Mousa and Clickhuinin (both on Shetland) and Carloway (Lewis).

The Broch, Carloway, Lewis

Burghs
Burghs were originally created in Scotland by King David (1124–53) in order to confirm and define rights of trading, and thereby strengthen them by the process of monopoly. A rampart or wall was set up as protection for the privileged traders, and sometimes a royal castle as well. The burgh and its men – burgesses – were partly self-governing, and in return for the advantages gained for a town being created a burgh, burgesses paid customs duties on important exports, and a rent. Some burghs were called royal, either because they were the King's own burghs or because they contributed to royal funds. A royal burgh had privileges which included the right to trade abroad, whereas the lesser burghs were confined to the home market only. 51 lesser burghs were founded between

1450 and 1516, each of which had its own privileged area with the monopoly on buying and selling and craftwork.
By the 1830s, town government in Scotland was undergoing complete reform and in 1833 the Burgh Reform Acts were passed because the form, scale, nature and powers of burghs were completely unsuited to the needs of the new age.

Clans
The word clan originates from the Gaelic 'clann' meaning children, leading to the modern term family. The clan system was at its peak during the 16thC and the order of family precedence was strictly observed.
Theoretically a clan is headed by the chief or father of the family, followed by his immediate family who would inherit land and lease it out on long-term 'tacks' to middlemen or 'tacksmen', who in turn leased it out to their tenants. Thus a clan was built up under the protection of its chief who was held responsible for the conduct and welfare of his clansmen.
The clan system started to die in the 18thC and was abruptly supressed by the English after the 1745 rebellion. They believed that the clan system with its fierce internal loyalties lay at the root of the Highland disturbances. However the old loyalties could not be totally destroyed, and something of the clan spirit has survived right through to the modern day, aided by the efforts of clan societies who acquire land and property, establish museums and, above all, maintain the famous clan spirit.

Crofters
Originally the land in the North of Scotland and the Western Isles was considered to be the property of the local clan; exceptions occurred in the Orkney and Shetland Isles, where sturdy Vikings admitted no over-lordship save that of Almighty God! But gradually ownership passed to the great lairds and noblemen, and the common people had to be content to remain as tenants, paying a minimal rent.
By the late 18thC, sheep farmers from the Scottish Borders were offering substantial annual cash rents for Highland grazing land, and from one glen and island after another the clansfolk were driven out and their homes destroyed. Those who remained were offered 'crofts', small farms along the coast, where they could raise some crops and keep a few livestock, fish the seas, or start cottage industries like knitting and weaving. Later legislation, around 1880 and 1950, gave the crofters firm tenure of their limited lands. Though they rarely own either ground or house, they and their families cannot again be evicted.
This explains the pattern of landscape that visitors encounter in Scotland's north and west, where expanses of open, uninhabited country lead suddenly to settlements of neighbouring small farms. Many crofts have vanished, and are perpetuated only by the ruins of stone cottages. But many still survive, for today's crofter holds tenaciously to his ancient birthright. Also in recent years many crofts have been taken over by Englishmen, some are used merely as holiday homes, but some of the new owners have adopted this way of life permanently. It is still an open question as to whether these newcomers will revitalise the system or hasten its disintegration.

Daylight hours
Caithness is almost 9° of latitude nearer the Arctic than Cornwall; this has a radical effect on the length of daylight hours. During May and June the day never seems to end – it is often light enough to read till midnight. Conversely in winter the days are extremely short: on the 21st December, the sun only appears for five hours, 52 minutes. However the interminable hours of darkness are sometimes brightened by displays of the aurora borealis – the northern lights.

Gaelic
Gaelic is one of the oldest languages in Europe; by the end of the 11thC it had spread across most of Scotland, and in the Highlands it was spoken as the first and often the only language. However its use has slowly disappeared over the years since the end of the 18thC and the decline of clanship.

Street names in the Outer Hebrides are sometimes bilingual, as in Stornoway on Lewis, and Gaelic songs are still sung in the 'ceilidhs' (pronounced 'kayli'), the informal gatherings for singing and story-telling that are very much part of the self-contained way of life of the Highlander.

Today there are 75,000 Gaelic-speaking people in Scotland, of which about 900 speak no English. For those interested in increasing these figures, there is an Association in Scotland called 'An Commun Gaidhealach' which is dedicated to the furtherance of Gaelic throughout the Highlands. See also previous section (No. 11).

Hydro-electricity

The North of Scotland Hydro-Electric Board was established by an Act of Parliament in 1943, in order to provide electricity supplies in the under-populated areas by developing water-power resources. The development of hydro-electricity has brought many important changes to life in the Highlands and Islands.

Hydro-electric schemes have to be approved by the Secretary of State for Scotland and laid before Parliament. The Board must 'have regard to the desirability of preserving the beauty of the scenery and any object of architectural or historic interest, and of avoiding as far as possible injuries to fisheries and to the stock of fish'; to this end there are Amenity and Fisheries Committees to advise the Board, and in fact a lot of research has been undertaken with regard to fisheries.

The Hydro-Electric Board is unique in that it does not merely produce and supply electricity: it is also involved in the economic and social improvement of North Scotland, a duty which includes research into raw materials and agricultural experiments, thereby encouraging new industry in the north.

An example of the extent of the Board's work may be seen at the Conon Valley development, which took fifteen years to complete, involving seven generating stations, seven main dams, 20 miles of tunnels, fifteen miles of aqueducts, a main-line railway station, two miles of track and 30 miles of roads. There are small hydro-electric schemes on various islands, such as those at Ullapool, Gairloch, Gisla (Lewis), and Chliostair (Harris), and the Board has diesel-engined power stations on the islands without water-power resources, as at Kirkwall, Lerwick and Stornoway.

In order to supply electricity to the islands, over 50 miles of submarine cables have been laid: a fact which helps to illustrate the immense problems involved in the distribution of electricity in such remote areas.

Lack of inland towns and villages

Even the most cursory inspection of a map of the Northern Highlands and Islands will reveal the fact that while the coast is lined with towns and villages, inland they are a rare feature. Those which do exist tend to be sited at the intersection of major routes. A partial explanation of this phenomenon lies in the native Celtic dislike of living cheek by jowl with his neighbour. (This is not to say that the people are anti-social; the feeling of community within each rural parish is extremely strong.) This is reinforced by the economic impracticability of living on top of one another in farming areas where the soil is poor: some members of the community would have to travel long distances to reach their land.

The Highland Clearances of the 18th and 19thC were the main underlying cause of the lack of inland towns. After the 1745 rebellion the English broke down the clan system extremely efficiently and the lairds no longer felt under the obligation of kinship to care for their tenants. When it was realised that the best returns from the infertile moorlands and mountainsides were derived by the development of extensive sheep farming or sporting estates, the tenants were ruthlessly evicted. Some were murdered, thousands sailed to the colonies, others were driven to the coast. Of course, there were humane men who did their best to help the victims to their feet again. For example, Sir John Sinclair tried to exploit the resources of the sea. Many of the rivers which drained to the east coast had carved natural harbours where they met the sea; the eastern coastal waters were rich in herring – all seemed set for the fishing boom. Unfortunately many of these harbours also had natural disadvantages: they were either often blocked by rock and sand, washed down when the rivers were in spate, or they were not tidal and, worst of all, the shoals of herring mysteriously disappeared from the eastern coastal waters. Hence the many decayed harbours found along the east coast, as at Dunbeath, Janetstown, Lybster, and Staxigoe.

Lighthouses

There are many lighthouses on the wind-swept headlands of the north coast of Scotland: the seas are stormy and difficult, and the coastline is notoriously rocky. It is worth making a detour to some of the many headlands for the views on clear days are magnificent, and many different birds may be seen nesting on the cliffs.

Many of the lighthouses in Scotland are situated in remote areas, and some keepers are glad to see visitors and may often be prevailed upon to show people round at reasonable hours; some have a considerable knowledge of the local wildlife. The most northerly lighthouse in the British Isles is at *Muckle Flagga*, Shetland, situated on a rock one mile north-west of the entrance to the Barrafirth. In fine weather, a boat may be hired at Barrafirth, to view the lighthouse and the stacks of Hermaness – the promontory west of the firth which is now a sea-bird sanctuary.

The lighthouse at the Butt of Lewis is situated at the northernmost point of the Outer Hebrides: 100 feet high, it is surrounded by impressive cliffs and rock pinnacles – the haunt of seafowl.

The *Flannan Islands*, or 'Seven Hunters' off Lewis are famous for the mysterious disappearance in 1900 of three lighthouse keepers. The lighthouse is now automatic and, on climbing up the circular stairs to the balcony, one is either stunned by the view or knocked sideways by the wind.

The windows of the lighthouse at *Dunnet Head* are said to have been broken, on occasion, by stones hurled from the sea 346 feet below; nonetheless the views across the Pentland Firth to Orkney are worth the visit. Another lighthouse that should be visited for the views is at *Scalpay Glass Island*, off Harris. The lighthouse stands sentinel over the Minch at the south-east end of the island, with views across to Skye, Lewis, Harris, the Uists and the mainland.

The lighthouse at *Duncansby Head* – the north-east promontory of Scotland – commands a fine view of Orkney, the Pentland Skerries and the headlands of the east coast. To the north, at the entrance to the Pentland Firth, the Boars of Duncansby may be seen: a reef whose name suggests the fierceness of the sea. To the south are the three Stacks of Duncansby – towering pinnacles of rock rising from the sea – and home of a myriad of seagulls.

Machair

Large areas of grass abutting the white shell-sand of the beaches of the Outer Hebrides on which a wide variety of wild flowers flourish. Many rare species can be found but the soft scent of clover which drifts through the air in summer is the best feature of the machair lands.

North Sea oil

Geographically, Scotland is very well placed to take advantage of North Sea developments. Caithness being the most northerly mainland county in Scotland is ideally situated in proximity to the North Sea oilfields. Tanks may be seen at Scrabster, and they form a landmark on the farms in the county.

One important benefit arises from the North Sea developments, they have opened up wide-ranging opportunities for industry and services in Scotland, thereby stopping the drift of population; there are prospects of some 8,000 jobs in Scotland for new projects, and the possibility of many more in the future.

However, it is sad to see Scotland's magnificent coastline being affected by these developments, as at Dunnet Bay where the proposed building of a storage tank would ruin the effect of the dramatic cliffs and long sandy beach.

Peat

Ten per cent of the land surface of Scotland is covered with peat: a composite of soil mingled with half decayed vegetable material – the remains of reeds, sedges, moss or heath. It varies in consistency from being highly fibrous to a shapeless black substance, depending on age and the type of vegetation. It is still forming in the Island of Lewis, but is receding in other parts of the Highlands. In 1949 the Scottish Peat Commission was set up to investigate the possible exploitation of peat in Scotland, which led to a survey of peat bogs in the Highlands and Islands, and research into the use of peat in the generation of electricity. An unsuccessful attempt to generate electricity from a closed cycle peat-burning turbine was made in 1959 at the Attnabreac Bog in Caithness. Peat has been used as a fuel in Scotland throughout her history: it burns with a subdued heat but has the advantage of being almost smokeless, and it is still widely used as a domestic fuel in the Outer Hebrides. Its various uses were first exploited in 1844 by Sir James Matheson who, having bought the Island of Lewis, attempted to extract paraffin wax. Peat was also being used at that time for salt evaporation, fish and meat curing, lime burning, charcoal making and metal working. Nowadays, however, it is used mainly for whisky distillation, fish curing and domestic fuel; evidence of the last may be seen piled high beside the Highland cottages, providing a long-familiar landmark.

The Sabbath

Still very much a day of rest in the Highlands and Islands of Scotland, particularly in the Outer Hebrides where religion plays an important part in the lives of the people. The inhabitants of Lewis, Harris and North Uist are Protestant, and lay a great emphasis on the Sabbath observance.

At Stornoway, on Lewis, a six day week is observed on public transport: this includes the ferries, which is worth bearing in mind in order to avoid being stranded on the island over the weekend. Licensed premises and other amenities are also closed on Sunday. One of the many objections raised to the exploitation of the North Sea oil fields off the coasts is that the men will work a 24 hour, seven day week.

Shielings

During the summer months the livestock were taken to graze the higher pastures; this ensured that the unfenced fields of crops around the townships were able to ripen without risk of being eaten or trampled upon. The crofters built themselves temporary huts, usually with drystone walls and heather-thatched roofs. The ruined remains of these shielings (*Gaelic 'hut'*) are dotted around the landscape of the far north of Scotland and its islands. The aptly named beehive huts at Kinloch, Isle of Lewis are a striking version of the shielings. The crofters enjoyed the respite from their daily chores and the idyllic weeks of the summer were eagerly anticipated and have been fondly recorded in folk songs and poems.

Tartan

Traditionally the wearing of a tartan kilt is the distinguishing mark of the Highlander. The custom dates back to the 13thC when the Highlanders wore brightly coloured clothes of checked material known as 'breacan'. In 1747 the English Government forbade the wearing of Highland dress as part of their successful efforts to crush the rebellious spirit of the Highlanders by destroying the clan tradition. Inevitably when the Act was repealed in 1782 there were few who could recall the expertise required to weave and dye the tartans. However, the demand for clan tartans was revived in 1822 by George II who wore a kilt at Holyrood, and it has continued up to the present day. There are now over 250 tartans.

Tweed

The Outer Hebrides is the only place in the world where genuine Harris Tweed is made. The tweed was originally woven by the islanders for their own use but the Dunmores of Amhuinnsuidhe Castle in Harris realised its potential and helped to create a demand for the cloth, and today it is the Harris Tweed industry which supports the islanders 'cottage industry'.

In 1909 the Harris Tweed Association was set up to protect the industry from imitators of their unique product, and a 'Genuine Harris Tweed' label now means it was made from pure virgin Scottish wool, spun and dyed in the Outer Hebrides and hand woven by islanders in their homes in Lewis, Harris, Uist and Barra.

The process involved in producing a piece of cloth bearing this famous label is complicated and slow: raw Scottish wool is shipped to Stornoway in bales; it is then taken to the mills for dyeing, blending, carding, spinning and hand warping. Lorries take the spun yarn to the crofters and return later for the woven tweed, which is left lying at the roadside for collection: a familiar sight, and sure proof of its durability.

This 'cottage industry' today employs 1,200 self-employed weavers who contract to work for various mills, and over 1,000 mill-workers.

Seven million yards of tweed are woven a year, in over 5,000 different colours and designs.

Weaving Harris tweed

Famous people

J. M. Barrie (1860-1937)   B4
Loch Voshimid, 8 miles nw of Ardhasaig Bridge on the Island of Harris. The island on this loch is reputed to have provided inspiration for Barrie's novel 'Mary Rose'. He wrote much of it at Amhuinnsuidhe Castle, on the coast beside of West Loch Tarbert. The castle, a magnificent structure, was built by the Earl of Dunmore in the 19thC (not open to the public). There is a river beside the castle where the salmon leap several feet over a sheer rockfall into the upper waters, and the hills to the north of the castle are rich in red deer: a setting which Barrie must have enjoyed while writing his famous novel.

Bonnie Prince Charlie (1720-88)   D2
The legend of Bonnie Prince Charlie began when he reached Scotland in 1745 in an attempt to win the English throne for his father, the son of the deposed James II. He soon had the support of over 2,000 Highland clansmen who helped him to his first victory, at the Battle of Prestonpans. By December his army of loyal Highlanders had grown to 5,000, but they were defeated again George II at Derby, and the prince retreated again to Scotland. He gained another victory at Falkirk, but his Highland army was finally outnumbered and overthrown at Culloden Moor in 1746 by an army headed by the Duke of Cumberland – King George's son. In the months that followed he was pursued mercilessly by Cumberland, but was never betrayed by his loyal supporters in spite of a considerable price on his head.
The Highlands and Islands played a major part in the legend of Bonnie Prince Charlie; he set foot on Scottish soil for the first time in July 1745, on the island of Eriskay in the Outer Hebrides. In 1746 he was on the mainland, and spent a day in Kintail eluding the redcoats. He hid in a forester's hut between the mountains Hekla and Ben More on South Uist from May to June 1746, and in the same year he landed at Ardvourlie Bay on the island of Lewis, from whence he was forced to walk twenty miles back to Arnish. 'Prince Charlie's Cairn and Loch' is a monument on Arnish Moor, near Arnish Lighthouse at Stornoway, which records the fact that he spent some time there while on the run after his defeat at Culloden.
In June 1746 he set sail from Creagorry on the island of Benbecula with Flora MacDonald, famed for taking the fugitive prince 'over the sea to Skye'. He finally left Scotland for France in September 1746, but his legend lives on in the Scottish Highlands and Islands.

HM Queen Elizabeth the Queen Mother (1900-   )   M5
Castle of Mey, off A838, nr village of East Mey. In 1953 Queen Elizabeth the Queen Mother purchased the Castle of Mey for use as a summer home. Originally called Barrogill Castle, it was built in 1568 by the 5th Earl of Caithness, and remained in the family for over 350 years. *There are special day openings of the castle in aid of charity during Jul and Aug, and the grounds are open to the public on certain days: enquire locally for dates.*

Famous travellers
People have always hankered to travel to the Highlands and Islands, attracted by the remoteness, the scenery and the different way of life of this part of the British Isles. Many travellers through the centuries have written down their impressions, but none more expressively than Johnson and Boswell, as may be seen in Johnson's 'Journey to the Western Isles of Scotland' and Boswell's 'Journal of a Tour to the Hebrides': written as a result of their trip to explore the Highlands and Islands in 1773. Queen Victoria visited Loch Maree in Ross and Cromarty in 1887: an event which is commemorated by a stone with an inscription in Gaelic. The same year Anthony Trollope visited St Kilda – the lonely group of islands west of North Uist in the Outer Hebrides. Keats, on sailing home from Cromarty after his visit to Scotland, was 'heartily sickened of accursed oatcakes', but otherwise appeared to have enjoyed his visit.

Flora MacDonald (1722-90)   C8
Fionnghal MacDonald met Bonnie Prince Charlie in 1746 at her brother's shieling of Alisary (at Milton, 18 miles from Carnan, in South Uist), where it was suggested that the safest way of escape from the Duke of Cumberland and his army would be for Flora to disguise the prince as her maid: 'one Betty Burke, an Irish girl and a good spinster'. Although reluctant to partake in such a dangerous adventure, she eventually agreed to the plan, and set to sewing a suitable dress for her 'servant'. Charles wanted to wear a pistol under his petticoat, but Flora said if he were searched the pistol would give him away, to which he replied: 'Indeed, Miss, if we shall happen with any that will go so narrowly to work in searching me as what you mean, they will certainly discover me at any rate'.
They finally left for Skye on the 18th June and arrived safetly the next day, when Flora took leave of Prince Charles, having risked her life for 'her king', never to see him again.

Robert Louis Stevenson (1850-94)   M6
There is a plaque over the Customs House at Wick in Caithness recording the months the author spent there. His father, David Stevenson, designed and built a breakwater as part of a scheme to improve the harbour, but a storm washed it away (the remains can still be seen near the lifeboat shed).
RLS was employed to improve the harbour in 1868 but found the work unsuited to his health.
In retaliation to the townsfolks' scornful words about his father's workmanship, the author of 'Treasure Island' described the town as the 'bleakest of God's towns on the baldest of God's bays'.

Thomas Telford (1757-1834)   M6
In 1803, as engineer to the Society of British Fisheries, Telford was asked to produce a report examining the possible ways in which the communications system could be improved to enable the Highlands and Islands to be opened up to economic expansion. The Government acted on his suggestions and he was put in charge of a vast civil engineering project which took over eighteen years to complete and led to the construction of over 1,000 bridges, 920 miles of roads, the improvement of 280 miles of military roads and numerous harbour modernisation schemes.
In 1815, at a cost of £9,600, he built The Mound; a 1,000-yard-long embankment carrying his road from Wick across the head of Loch Fleet, thereby reclaiming the marshy valley of the River Fleet. Finally, in 1824 he designed a number of churches and manses in the Highlands which were built at the Government's instigation. Telford's churches can still be found on Lewis, Harris, North Uist, Quarff (in the Shetlands) and North Ronaldshay (in Orkney). Telford's brilliant engineering skills enabled a social revolution to take place in the previously inaccessible Highlands and Islands of Scotland. In terms of historical importance and sheer magnitude, this work must represent the greatest achievement of his extremely successful career.

Cathedrals, abbeys & churches

Dornoch Cathedral Highland   K6
Dornoch, Sutherland. Begun in 1224 by Bishop Gilbert de Moravia, the cathedral is on the probable site of a Celtic foundation. It was badly damaged in 1570 and subsequently neglected. The nave was rebuilt in 1835-37 for the Duchess of Sutherland, and further restoration work took place in 1924 when, happily, some of the 13thC stonework was revealed.
Sixteen Earls of Sutherland are said to lie in the cathedral; at the west end there is a statue by Chantrey of the 1st Duke of Sutherland. In the cathedral graveyard, and closely resembling a tombstone, is a

'Plaiden Ell': this was used for measuring cloth at fairs and markets.

Fortrose Cathedral Highland **K7**
Fortrose, Ross & Cromarty. Founded by David I of Scotland in the 12thC, the remaining fragments of this cathedral stand in a superb green close surrounded by yew trees; a perfect foil for the deep red tones of the sandstone. Cromwell is said to have used many of its stones to build Inverness Castle.

Old St Peter's Highland **L5**
Thurso, Caithness. Founded in the 13thC by Gilbert Murray, Bishop of Caithness, the church was in use until 1832 but is now roofless, after a fire. The nave and transept are 16th and 17thC, and the churchyard has a tombstone possibly dating from the 14thC.

Old St. Peter's Church, Thurso

St Clements Western Isles **B5**
Rodel, Isle of Harris. A stolidly handsome piece of 16thC architecture looking composedly out to sea; its intrinsic beauty is heightened by the loveliness of its setting. Effective use has been made of natural stone, with black crystals glowering in the northern transept.
There are strong stylistic connections with Iona Cathedral, notably the use of Celtic carving – as seen for example in the tower. (Freely accessible to the visitor who is prepared to scale a few ladders.) The tombstones are great fun; they too display a free use of Celtic motifs, in some cases the iconography has clearly not been drawn from Christian sources!

Probably built in 1528 to house the tomb of the 8th chief of MacLeod, which is set into the south side of the choir, the church was restored in 1873.
The key has to be fetched from Rodel Hotel; this however permits a glimpse of a superb relic of a by-gone era.

Tomb, St Clements

The Cathedral of St Magnus **N3**
Kirkwall, Mainland, Orkney. Dedicated in 1137 to the memory of his saintly uncle by Earl Rognavald, then ruler of Orkney, this impressive sandstone building represents the zenith of the Norse civilization in Orkney. It is the only cathedral, apart from the one in Glasgow, to have survived without structural damage from the pre-Reformation period.

Ui Chapel **E2**
Eye Peninsula, Lewis. The roofless and neglected 14thC chapel of St Columba at Ui, or Eye, was the traditional burial place for the chiefs of the Clan MacLeod. It contains an armed effigy of Roderick MacLeod, and a memorial to his daughter Margaret MacFingone (died 1503), mother of the last abbot of Iona. Some of the Seaforth Mackenzies are also buried here.

Castles & ruins

Ardvreck Castle Highland **G4**
Loch Assynt, Sutherland. On n bank of Loch Assynt, off A894. A ruin of three storeys, built about 1591 by the MacLeods of Assynt. It was here that the Marquess of Montrose was captured and confined after his defeat at the Battle of Carbisdale.

Badbea Tower Highland **L7**
Badbea, Caithness. 3 miles sw of Berriedale off A9. A small tower near the cliffs, built

from the stones of a cottage belonging to John Sutherland, one of the early 19thC lay religious leaders. It is the only remaining part of a village inhabited by crofters who were driven off their lands in nearby Ousdale. The tower was used for shelter, and it is said that the children and cattle had to be tethered to prevent them hurtling down the steep cliff.

Earls Palace, Kirkwall

Bishop's Palace and Earl Patrick's Palace **N3**
Kirkwall, Orkney. The ruined Bishop's Palace, south of Kirkwall Cathedral, was founded in the 13thC and altered by Bishop Reid in the 16thC. King Hakon of Norway died here in 1263 after his ill-fated Scottish invasion. To the east is the ruined Earl's Palace, built 1600–07 for Earl Patrick Stewart and described as 'the finest relic of domestic Renaissance architecture in Scotland'. Both ruins are scheduled Ancient Monuments. *Open daily.*

Carbisdale Castle Highland **J5**
Ardgay, Ross & Cromarty. 3½ miles nw of Bonar Bridge off A9. A turreted mansion resembling a Rhine Schloss, built in the 1900s by a former Dowager Duchess of Sutherland. It is now a youth hostel.

Dunrobin Castle Highland **K5**
Golspie, Sutherland. On a natural terrace near the sea, the castle originally consisted of a keep built by Robert, 2nd Earl of Sutherland, in 1275 and called Dun Robin after him. It was enlarged in 1844–48 by Sir Charles Barry, and altered by Sir Robert Lorimer in 1921 after a fire. The castle has been used as a school since 1965. *Open 11.00–18.00 daily May–mid Sep. Closed Sun morning.*

Dunrobin Castle

Eileean Donan Castle Highland **E9**
Dornie, Ross & Cromarty. Built in 1609 on a superb site overlooking Loch Duich, the castle was blown up in 1719 by an English warship, but was restored 1912–32. For generations a stronghold held by the MacRaes, it serves as a war memorial to the clan. Relics of the Jacobites and Dr Johnson may be seen inside. But the exterior is more deserving of a visit; the castle's best feature is its magnificent siting. *Open 10.00–18.00 daily.*

Fort Charlotte   O9
Lerwick, Shetland. Begun in 1665 to protect the Sound of Bressay against the Dutch, the massive fort was burned by them in 1673. It was rebuilt in 1781, and garrisoned during the Napoleonic War. *Open daily.*

Castles Girningoe and Sinclair Highland   M6
Caithness. 3 miles ne of Wick off A9. Spectacularly situated together on a rocky ledge above the sea at Sinclair's Bay, the two castles appear at first glance as one ruin. Sinclair, built in the 17thC, is now a complete ruin but the remains of Girningoe, dating from the 15thC, include the dungeon where the 4th Earl of Caithness murdered his son the Master of Caithness after six years' imprisonment between 1570 and 1576. Both castles were deserted and in ruins by the end of the 17thC.

Castle Sinclair, Caithness

Harold's Tower Highland   L5
Thurso, Caithness. 1½ miles ne of Thurso off A836. Harold, Earl of Caithness was buried here after the Battle of Clairdon, 1196. The tower was built over his grave in the early 18thC by Sir John Sinclair, the agriculturist (1754–1835) as a family burial place.

Italian Chapel   N3
Lamb Holm, Orkney. 6½ miles s of Kirkwall. An attractive chapel built in a Nissen hut by homesick Italian prisoners of war in 1943. The concrete structure, completely transformed with beautiful decorations and intricate wrought-iron work, is an impressive monument to Italian workmanship.

Kisimul Castle, Barra

Kisimul Castle Western Isles   A9
Castlebay, Barra, Outer Hebrides. The castle dates from 1030 and apart from the 200 years leading up to 1938, it has always been inhabited by the Macneils of Barra. The family has a reputation for eccentricity and independence: this is illustrated by their alleged rejection of Noah's offer of a place in the Ark because 'the Macneil had a boat of his own'. *Open Sun May–Sep.*

Castle of Old Wick Highland   M6
Caithness. 1 mile se of Wick, ¼ mile e of A9. Known as 'The Old Man of Wick', standing on a narrow spine of rock projecting into the sea, the remaining ruined tower was besieged and taken by the Master of Caithness in 1569. The castle, the oldest in Caithness, dates from the 12thC. *Open daily except when nearby rifle range is in use.*

Scalloway Castle Western Isles   O9
Scalloway, Mainland, Shetland. The castle was built in the 16thC by the wicked Stewart Earls. Legend has it that warriors' blood and maiden's hair were used as cement. Its ruins may be visited. *Open any reasonable time.*

Skelbo Castle Highland   K5
Loch Fleet, Sutherland. 3½ miles n of Dornoch off A9. The ruined keep and walls dating from the 14thC command fine views of Loch Fleet from the grassy hillock on which they stand. The castle itself is not open to the public.

Thurso Castle Highland   L5
Thurso, Caithness. The ruins of the 17thC castle, rebuilt in 1872, overlook the harbour. The original castle of 1660 was said to be close enough to the sea to fish from the windows. *Not open to the public.*

Unusual buildings

Dounreay Nuclear Reactor Highland   L5
Dounreay, Caithness. 10 miles w of Thurso on A836. This remarkable installation can be seen for miles, perched on the clifftops looking like a giant golf ball waiting to be teed off into the Atlantic. Fortunately it is restrained by the maze of cables and pylons that lead off inland. The world's first 'fast-breeder reactor', it is a prototype nuclear power station that 'breeds' as much fuel as it uses in the production of electricity. *Open 9.00–16.00 daily May–Sep. Closed Sun.*

Strathpeffer Pump Room Highland   H7
Strathpeffer, Ross & Cromarty. The present pump room was built in 1909. With its green and white tiles it has a chilly atmosphere – and a remarkable resemblance to a dairy. Any hopes of achieving a return to the elegance of the 18thC as you gently sip the waters are shattered at the self-service counter where you may unceremoniously help yourself to a 9p bottle of sulphur water. However, a stroll across the svelte lawns waiting outside should restore your poise.

Bonar Bridge, Sutherland

Telford's bridges   J6
The engineer Thomas Telford (1757–1834) spent eighteen years in the Highlands on a government programme of improving communications in the region. Apart from the great Caledonian Canal, most of his work involved the construction of roads and bridges, and Wick Bridge, Helmsdale Bridge, Bonar Bridge and a host of minor bridges were all Telford's, as well as the great Craigellachie Bridge further south. Most of his bridges still stand intact, but inevitably some are succumbing to today's heavy road traffic and are being replaced. Telford's arched and typically castellated Bonar Bridge has recently gained a worthy neighbour in the delicate modern structure that now stands beside it.

Whalebone arches   D2
A novel feature of the far north of Scotland and its isles. The arch at Bragar, Isle of Lewis, was clearly erected in a spirit of triumph: the harpoon which killed the mammal still dangles from it. Another of these arches is found leading into a field beside the A9 about a mile north of Latheron, Caithness. It was made from the remains of a whale washed ashore in 1869.
Note: basking whales can sometimes be seen off the northern coasts, and during the 19thC the Shetlanders made an abortive attempt to establish a whaling industry.

whale bone arch, Bragar

Houses & gardens

Many people open their gardens to the public once or twice a year; it is impossible to give details here, but do make a point of enquiring locally as they are well worth seeing. For details write to Scotland's Garden Scheme, 26 Castle Terrace, Edinburgh.

Dundonnell House Highland   **G6**
Ross & Cromarty. 10 miles nw of Braemore. Superb private gardens only occasionally open to the public, with rare and oriental shrubs. There are also aviaries of exotic birds.

Dunrobin Castle Highland   **K5**
Nr Golspie, Sutherland. With lovely views over the Moray Firth, this is a formal garden laid out in the best 17thC French manner. *Open 11.00-18.00 daily May-mid Sep. Closed Sat & Sun morning.*

Fairburn Highland   **H7**
Ross & Cromarty. 6 miles nw of Muir of Ord. An attractive garden with azaleas, rhododendrons and specimen trees. *Open 14.00-19.00 Thur & Sat May.*

Inverewe Gardens, Ross & Cromarty

Inverewe Gardens Highland   **E6**
Poolewe, Ross & Cromarty. A garden of enormous interest, started in 1862 by Osgood Mackenzie on an exposed, barren site. He planted Corsican pines as windbreaks, gradually adding eucalyptus, Monterey pines, Chinese and Himalayan rhododendrons, azaleas and camellias. The garden is informally laid out; the 'Bambooselem' section is devoted to bamboos and a wonderful collection of hydrangeas. There are also many lilies, spring bulbs and alpines. *Open daily.*

Lael Forest Garden Highland   **G6**
Ardcharnich, Ross & Cromarty. 4 miles se of Ullapool. The garden on the edge of Inverlael Forest contains some 150 different shrubs and trees. There is an explanatory Forestry Commission leaflet available. *Open daily.*

Langwell Highland   **L7**
Berriedale, Caithness. A splendid garden which well illustrates what can be achieved in exposed areas. *Open various days Aug & Sep.*

'900 Roses' Rose Garden Highland**K6**
Tain, Ross & Cromarty. The garden was laid out to celebrate the 900th anniversary of the Burgh of Tain receiving its royal charter.

Rovie Lodge Gardens Highland   **K5**
Rogart, Sutherland. 8 miles nw of Golspie. The house is situated in the valley of Strath Fleet with wonderful lawns sloping down to Torbreck Burn. There are some fine herbaceous borders and heaths, and a water garden. *Open 14.00-18.00 daily mid Jul-Sep.*

Museums & galleries

Carnegie Museum Highland   **M6**
Wick, Caithness. Generously endowed by the American Andrew Carnegie, the museum contains collections of local antiquities and natural history specimens. *Open daily. Closed Sun.*

Cottage Museum Western Isles   **A7**
South Uist, nr Bualdubh Eochair, Outer Hebrides. On Eochair to Ardvaicher road w of A865. This little museum has only recently been opened and displays old husbandry utensils, local costumes and other items of interest. *Open daily.*

Croft Museum   **N9**
Voe, Dunrossness, Shetland. A croft house which has been restored as a museum. *Open daily. Closed Mon.*

Hugh Miller's Cottage Highland   **K7**
Cromarty, Ross & Cromarty. The birthplace of this eminent 18thC writer, naturalist, theologian and geologist. Now a museum, its exhibits include his collection of geological specimens. The fossils are particularly worth seeing. The cottage has been furnished with early 18thC furniture by the National Trust for Scotland. *Open daily Apr – Oct. Closed Sun except Sun afternoon Jun – Sep only.*

Shawbost Museum W. Isles   **C2**
Shawbost, Isle of Lewis. A folk museum set up by the local school children in a disused church. It is now under the aegis of the National Trust for Scotland. The exhibits reflect many aspects of the islanders' life centring round the traditional activities of fishing, crofting and weaving. Well worth a brief visit.

Shetland County Museum   **O9**
Lerwick, Mainland, Shetland. Housed above a library containing a special 'Shetland Room', the museum contains a variety of interesting relics depicting Shetland's past. *Open daily. Closed Sun.*

Stromness Museum   **M3**
Alfred St, Stromness, Mainland, Orkney. Good botanical and ornithological collection; also display of boats and model ships, and an exhibition of traditional agricultural tools. *Open 11.00-17.00 daily. Closed Thur afternoon and Sun.*

Tankerness House Museum   **N3**
Broad St, Kirkwall, Mainland, Orkney. A 16thC farm house with a collection of pre-historic and historic relics of Orkney; also occasional travelling exhibitions and art shows. *Open 11.00-17.30 daily.*

Thurso Museum Highland   **L5**
The Town Hall, Thurso, Caithness. Local geological, zoological and botanical exhibits. Houses a collection of fossils, plants and mosses gathered by Robert Dick (1181–66), a Thurso baker with a flair for natural history. *Open daily. Closed Thurs afternoon and Sun.*

Nature trails & reserves

Beinn Eighe National Nature Reserve Highland   **F7**
Ross & Cromarty. W of Kinlochewe via A832. An outstanding Highland reserve with fine mountain plants, native pine forest, golden eagles. Nature trail at Glas Leitire, otherwise enquiries to the Warden at the reserve or to Nature Conservancy, 12 Hope Terrace, Edinburgh.

Dale of Cottasgarth and Birsay Moor   **M2**
Orkney. Two almost adjacent RSPB reserves on the mainland with typical moorland. Parts are visible from the minor road joining A986 and A966 but no regular access at present: consult RSPB representative, Easter Sower, Orphir, Orkney, for further details.

Glas Leitire Nature Trail Highland **F7**
Ross & Cromarty. Part of Beinn Eighe National Nature Reserve. 1 mile. Pine forest

on Loch Shore with associated wildlife.
Fine scenery. Start from car park/picnic site
(clearly signposted) on A832, where guide is
available.

Slattadale Nature Trail Highland **E7**
*Ross & Cromarty. On Gairloch-Kinlochewe
road, A832.* Forest trail along Loch Maree.
Fine scenery and good all-round wildlife
interest. 1–5 miles. Guide from Forestry
Commission, 21 Church St, Inverness.

Torridon Nature Trail Highland **E7**
Ross & Cromarty. Superb mountain
scenery with deer, feral goats, golden eagle,
peregrine and interesting upland plants.
Information centre and car park. Self guided
walks – full details at the Information Centre,
Torridon; or from National Trust for
Scotland, 5 Charlotte Square, Edinburgh.

Bird watching

Dornoch Firth Highland **K6**
Ross & Cromarty. The large area of this
firth is exceptionally good for autumn
waders and grey geese, whooper swans and
other wildfowl in winter – but a summer
visit is likely to be equally rewarding. The
A9 provides good access to Tarbae Ness, via
B9165 south of Tain (seabirds, sea duck);
Edderton Sands and Ferry Point, north from
A9 from about three miles west of Tain
(waders and wildfowl); Skibo Inlet, south
from A9 at Clashmore and right to
Ferrytown (wildfowl); and Cuthill and
Dornoch Sands via the road from Clashmore
across Cuthill Links.

Dunnet Head Highland **L5**
*Caithness. Via B855 from Dunnet on the
A836.* As well as being the most northerly
point on the British mainland, Dunnet Head
boasts a lighthouse, superb cliffs and a large,
mixed seabird colony where puffins are a
particularly noteworthy attraction. It is also
a good area for great and Arctic skuas and
twite, and red-throated divers can usually
be seen along the B855.

Fair Isle Western Islands South **O10**
Shetland. This island, famed for its migration
studies, is one place all serious bird watchers
visit sooner or later. Accommodation is
available at Fair Isle Bird Observatory.
Enquiries to: The Warden, Fair Isle Bird
Observatory, Fair Isle, Shetland.

Kyle of Tongue, Sutherland

Kyle of Tongue Highland **J2**
Sutherland. W of Tongue. Much of this area
can be seen from the A838; it is within easy
reach of the Loch Loyal. The tidal estuary is
good for waders at passage times while most
seabirds, including skuas, black guillemots
and Arctic terns occur offshore. The minor
roads to Talmine on the west and Skerray
on the east give good access to the coast
nearby. Storm petrels nest on Eilean nam
Ron opposite Skerray and wintering
barnacle geese (visible from the mainland)
linger there well into spring.

Loch Loyal Highland **J3**
Sutherland. An area of spectacular loch and
mountain scenery crossed by the A836 from
Altnaharra to Tongue, which can be covered
from the road but is best explored on foot.
The massif of Ben Loyal is good for
mountain birds, including golden eagle,
raven and ring ouzel, and possibly peregrine,
while the low-lying ground at the south east
and north east ends of Loch Loyal itself is

good for breeding birds such as red-throated
diver and greenshank. Both black-throated
diver and grey lag goose are worth looking
out for in this area.

Orkney and Shetland
It is difficult to do justice to these two island
groups but both are exceptionally rich in
seabirds and some of our most northerly
breeding species are famous for their
migration. Visitors should contact the
RSPB representatives for advice and help at
Easter Sower, Orphir, Orkney or Redfirth,
Mid Yell, Shetland.

Summer Isles Highland **F5**
Ross & Cromarty. These delightful islands
at the mouth of Loch Broom are regularly
visited by boats from Ullapool and
Achiltibuie; anyone holidaying in this area
should not miss them. Breeding birds likely
to be seen include grey lag goose, red-
throated diver, Arctic tern, black guillemot
and buzzard. Storm petrels breed on at least
one island and wintering barnacle geese may
still be about in April.

Fossil hunting

Visit the local museum. Its fossil collection
usually states where individual fossils have
been found. When visiting quarries always
seek permission to enter if they look
privately owned or worked. Be careful of
falls of rock.
Mainly unfossiliferous highly-altered rocks.
The Cambrian Durness limestone of
Durness, Sutherland has yielded some
trilobites. Devonian rocks contain few fossils
but there are fish-bands in the rocks of
Thurso, and Caithness in general, and
around Dingwall and on the Black Isle in
Ross & Cromarty. Around Brora,
Sutherland, are Upper Jurassic beds with
ammonites, belemnites and bivalves,
together with a coal-bed, and Lower Jurassic
(lias) occurs at Applecross, Ross & Cromarty
on the west coast.

Forests

Birch and oak forests
Remains of these ancient forests can be
found in various parts notably at Letterewe
in Western Ross and the northern edges of
the Great Glen.

Deer forests
Of the two million acres of deer forest
(nearly all over 2,000 feet) in the Highlands
most is unfit for grazing. The red deer is a
thriving animal and needs to be kept in
check. The largest area of deer forest in
Scotland is that north and west of the great
Glen where it is possible to walk through 100
miles of continuous forest.

Mountains

Arkle and Foinaven Highland **G3**
Sutherland. Away to the north of Laxford
Bridge the twin hills of Arkle, 2,580 feet,
and Foinaven, 2,980 feet, extend their
terrific ranges of white Torridonian
sandstone crags. As the last major range of
the Highlands here in the far northwest they
create a vivid sense of space and isolation.

Ben Loyal, Sutherland

Ben Wyvis Highland   **H7**
Ross & Cromarty. Ben Wyvis raises its vast
bulk to a height of 3,423 feet, just north of
the town of Dingwall. Its gracefully curving
slopes, a landmark from all directions, are
rimmed at the summit with snow-wreaths
for most of the year, and there are proposals
to start a skiing ground on the rarely seen
northern side where deep snow fields linger.
Easily climbed in summer from Strathpeffer.
The western slopes of Ben Wyvis carry the
huge 7,000-acre Torrachilty Forest of the
Forestry Commission, and here there are
car parks and splendid waterfalls where in
June and July leaping salmon can be seen.

Coigach Highland   **F5**
Ross & Cromarty and Sutherland. In the far
north-western corner of Ross and Cromarty,
peaks of the pinkish white Torridonian
sandstone tower up from the Highland
plateau in fantastic shapes. From north to
south the tally of outlandish names runs:
Quinag (highest at 2,652 feet), Canisp,
Sulven, Cul Mor and Cul Beag, Stac Polly
and Ben More Coigach. All can be seen in
clear weather from the main road north
A835, then A837, and their ascent involves a
tough scramble amongst a wilderness of
rock and peat.

Ben Eighe, Ross & Cromarty

Kintail Highland   **F9**
Ross & Cromarty. This is the wild high
mountain county where the Scottish
mainland faces Skye across the Kyle of
Lochalsh and the Sound of Sleat. Here two
broad sea-lochs, Loch Carron and Loch
Duich, run deep into the hills, their slopes
clad in waving forests of pine, spruce and
larch trees. The Five Sisters of Kintail, steep
peaks set in a rhythmic pattern, tower over
Glen Shiel. They now belong to the Scottish
National Trust; highest is Sgurr Fhuaran, at
3,505 feet. For the finest views take the
tricky Mam Ratagan by-road due west from
Shiel Bridge.

**Maiden Pap, Morven
and Scaraben** Highland   **L7**
Caithness. This shapely trio of peaks springs
up from the broad tableland of southern
Caithness, providing landmarks visible from
the whole county. Indeed in clear weather
they can be plainly seen from Morayshire
away to the south, across the 40 mile
expanse of the Moray Firth. Morven, the
'great mountain' is the westernmost and
highest at 2,818 feet, has the comely shape its name suggests.
Scaraben, literally the 'scarred mountain',
2,054 feet altitude, has a long jagged skyline.
All three lie in Langwell Forest, wild and
rocky deer-stalking country with scattered
birch woods.

Rivers & lochs

Dornoch Firth Highland   **K6**
Sutherland. This long narrow arm of the sea
runs inland for a total of fifteen miles,
though mostly less than one mile wide. At
Bonar Bridge it is crossed by the main road
and becomes the Kyle of Sutherland. Both
sides of Dornoch Firth are heavily wooded,
and there are fine views across it, especially
from Struie Hill.

Corrieshalloch Gorge Highland   **G6**
Ross & Cromarty. Eleven miles south-east
of Ullapool you will find this stupendous
gorge close to the oddly named Braemore
Junction on the A835 road towards Inverness.
First take the A832 road towards Gairloch
for half a mile to see, from the car park, the
breathtaking view over the Lael larchwoods
towards Loch Broom in its deep glen. Then
walk back to the entrance to the gorge, which
belongs to the Scottish National Trust and
is clearly signposted. A good path leads
down through the larches to a slender
suspension bridge (only six people at one
time) slung over the deep cleft in the rocks
where the Falls of Measach swirl and tumble
in their wild cascades. A viewpoint a 100
yards lower down the gorge gives an even
better view of this tree-hung defile, which
incidentally taxes the photographer's skill
to its utmost.

Cromarty.

Cromarty Firth Highland   **K7**
Ross & Cromarty. This remarkable long inlet
of the sea has a narrow cliff-bound entrance
between two headlands called the Sutors of
Cromarty. It broadens out to the muddy
tidal sandbanks called the Sands of Nigg,
then runs south-west like an estuary, scarcely
a mile wide, to Dingwall and Beauly; total
length eighteen miles.

Helmsdale Highland   **K3**
The Helmsdale River, near the borders of
Caithness and Sutherland springs from
Loch nan Clar, one of several trout-rich
waters in an inland, upland region of peaty
moors, diversified by steep, isolated and
rock-girt peaks. It flows south-eastwards,
quickly dropping into a fifteen-mile-long,
narrow vale called the Strath of Kildonan.
Many unfortunate conifer plantations have
been made along this lovely curving hollow
amid the hills.

Loch Broom Highland   **F5**
Ross & Cromarty. This broad arm of the sea,
ten miles long by half-a-mile wide, runs
deeply inland in a south-easterly direction
from the open west coast of Ross and
Cromarty. All along its shores crofting
settlements lie as green oases, often high up
the slopes.
Following the loch shore south towards
Inverness you find the flat fields of Lael – a
Norse word meaning 'low country'. Little
Loch Broom, eight miles long, near Inverewe
is a parallel sea-loch of wilder aspect, with
steeper slopes and more remote crofts. Above
it on the south towers An Teallach, 3,480
feet high and usually stormswept.

Loch Maree Highland   **F7**
Ross & Cromarty. Loch Maree lies beside
the A832 Dingwall-Gairloch main road.
Twelve miles long by one to two miles wide,
it runs from Kinlochewe straight north-west
to its outlet, down the River Ewe to the sea
at Poolewe. On its northern shore, Slioch, a
tremendous wedge-shaped mountain of bare
blue-grey rock, rises to a height of 3,217 feet.
On the south is the Nature Conservancy's
large national reserve of Beinn Eighe, which
preserves native Caledonian Scots pine
woods and their associated plant and
animal life.

Loch Shin Highland   **H4**
Sutherland. Fifteen miles long, though only
half-a-mile across, this upland freshwater
loch runs north-west through the heart of
Sutherland. Shin Forest, a vast 75,000 acres

lies a little to the east. South of Lairg the River Shin, which drains the loch, plunges amid forests through the deep Achany Glen with impressive waterfalls where salmon leap, to reach the sea near Bonar Bridge.

Loch Torridon Hig   E7
Ross & Cromarty. A fine sea loch, twelve miles long by two miles wide, running deeply south-east into the wild coast of western Ross. Around it stand the gaunt, bare, rocky hills of the ancient Torridonian sandstone. Beinn Eighe, 3,309 feet, to the east has a dazzling white summit of white quartzite rock; it is now part of a large nature reserve. A fascinating singletrack road from Kinlochewe-Dingwall-Gairloch main road leads to the seashore crofting villages of Torridon and Shieldaig, both with hotels. To the south lies the even hillier Applecross Peninsula with a tricky hairpin-bend road climbing across bare Beinn Bhan to Applecross village.

Moray Firth   K7
Deep-sea fishermen regard the Moray Firth as the great bight of the North Sea between the coasts of Moray on the south and Sutherland to the north, 30 miles across. This narrows to a wedge-shaped bay, still ten miles across, north of Nairn, which forms a foreground to the grandest distant prospects in Northern Scotland. From the south you gaze across the Moray Firth to the far Sutherland and Caithness highlands. From the shores of Ross and Cromarty to the north you get an equally immense view towards the Cairngorms in the central Grampian highlands. Nearer to Inverness the great firth narrows to the straits then broadens out into an inner Moray Firth, still two miles across by ten miles long, with steep, though sheltered, shores often wooded. Running west again, beyond the Kessock Narrows, the tidal waters become the Beauly Firth fringed by broad mudbanks where shelducks breed each spring.

Strath Naver Highland   J3
Sutherland. Loch Naver, five miles long by half a mile wide, lies in the wilderness of northern Sutherland, close to the road north from Lairg. Above it towers Ben Klibreck, 3,154 feet high. The by-road that follows the loch's shores runs on for a dozen miles down Strath Naver, once a densely-peopled, well-farmed glen, but deserted since the 'clearances'.

Strath Oykell Highland   G4
Sutherland and Ross & Cromarty. The River Oykell rises high on Ben More Assynt, a great mountain, 3,273 feet high in western Sutherland. In its 30 mile course east to reach the sea near Bonar Bridge it flows through a broad, almost uninhabited, strath past huge forests and isolated sheep farms. The main road, from Bonar Bridge to Lochinver on the west coast, gives a fine impression of this lonely yet lovely countryside.

Archæology

Callanish Stones Highland   C2
Isle of Lewis, Ross & Cromarty. Callanish is one of the major British antiquities of the bronze age. The great circles of free-standing stone uprights are undoubtedly religious, and associated with the group of burial cairns which forms part of the monument. The stone avenue, built of large stones (megaliths) and running a considerable distance, is an accessory to the religious function of the site. *Open any reasonable time.*

Callanish Stones, Lewis.

Camster Cairns Highland   M6
Camster, Caithness. A fine group of Neolithic long cairns, with narrow stone-built chambers and projections at each end resembling horns.

Clickhimin Broch Western Isles   O9
Nr Lerwick, Shetland. This site began as a stone-built courtyard house, and was later fortified with a ring wall along the edge of the island. This was commanded from a strong blockhouse, which also provided housing; other shelter was provided by penthouses inside the perimeter wall. A rise in the water level made change necessary, and a late iron age broch was constructed, with characteristic galleried wall. *Open any reasonable time.*

Dun Carloway Broch Highland   C2
Isle of Lewis, Ross & Cromarty. The broch at Dun Carloway is one of the finest of these iron age defensive towers, and survives to a height of over twenty feet. *Open any reasonable time.*

Dwarfie Stane   M3
Hoy, Orkneys. A monument unique in Britain. The only Neolithic tomb to be cut into rock rather than built free-standing. *Open any reasonable time.*

Holm of Papa Chambered Cairn N1
Westray, Orkneys. A fine group of Neolithic long chambered cairns, including one with a corridor-like chamber with mural cells, and another of the 'stalled' type where the long chamber is divided into cells with upright slabs.

Jarlshof, Shetland.

Jarlshof Western Isles   O10
Sumburgh, Shetland. During the bronze age the site at Jarlshof was occupied by settlers living in courtyard houses but, as elsewhere in the north of Scotland, the need for shelter against the strong winds, and the availability of good building stone, led to the development in the iron age of a dwelling known as a 'wheelhouse'.
This is a round structure, between 20 and 35 feet across with a thick outer wall, probably roofed by a corbelled vault. A number of radial walls ran from the outer wall in plan like the spokes of a wheel but stopping short of the centre; this formed eight or so compartments, roofed by slabs or corbelling. The central area was some ten feet across, and may have been left open. Some wheelhouses have a passage or 'aisle' inside the outer wall, and others have connecting doorways between the radial walls. A fine broch tower, with the characteristic galleried wall, is probably the latest iron age structure on the site. The dark age settlement that followed was succeeded by a Viking settlement, with Scandinavian longhouses and smaller attendant structures. *Open 9.30-17.00 Mar, Oct-Mar, 9.30-19.00 Apr-Sep. Closed Sun morning.*

Knowe of Yarso Chambered Cairn   N2
Rousay, Orkneys. The cairn at Knowe of Yarso is of a type peculiar to the Orkneys. A Neolithic long cairn, it contains a long chamber divided by opposed pairs of upright slabs into several lateral cells. Others of this 'stalled' type can be seen on Rousay, at Blackhammer, Knowe of Rowiegar, and Mid Howe (which also has an iron age broch). *Open any reasonable time.*

Langwell Wag Highland   L7
Langwell, Caithness. The type of monument found at Langwell, known as a wag, is of a type apparently unique to Caithness, and is a variation of the 'wheelhouse' type of iron age dwelling. The basic house is a strongly built circular hut, to which has been added a

stone-built oval chamber about twice as large, with its floor excavated below ground level. This contains an arrangement of stalls built from large slabs of stone, and was perhaps also roofed with slabs. Wags have been interpreted as shelters to protect cattle from wolves.

Maes Howe Chambered Cairn   M3
Orkney Mainland. Maes Howe is the most important monument of its type in Britain, a Neolithic round cairn with a corbelled roof built from the local laminated stone; the roof survives intact. The cairn is abnormally large, and has links with the great cairns found in Ireland. It also has the unique feature of a surrounding ditch 35 feet wide. *Open 9.30–17.30 Mar, Apr & Oct, 9.30– 19.00 May-Sep, 9.30–16.00 Nov-Feb. Closed Sun morning.*

Mousa Broch   Western Isles   O10
Island of Mousa, Shetlands. In addition to being the best-preserved, the iron age broch on Mousa is also the smallest (some 51 feet in diameter) and the best built, and must be among the latest examples of the type. It is the usual tower, built as a double shell of drystone masonry on a solid foundation, linked with slabs to form a gallery within the wall; the gallery is lit from the interior. *Open any reasonable time.*

Skara Brae prehistoric village   M2
Orkney Mainland. The superb Neolithic settlement at Skara Brae was exposed by a storm in 1851. The huts are closely grouped, roughly rectangular in shape with rounded corners; the groups are linked by paved causeways.
The huts are set into the ground, and built from the local stone which splits naturally into long slabs. They contain unique features in drystone masonry, including box-beds made of stone planks, and tanks, probably to hold shellfish. *Open 9.30–17.30 Mar, Apr & Oct, 9.30–19.00 May-Sept, 9.30–16.00 Nov-Feb. Closed Sun morning.*

Skelpick   Highland   J2
Sutherland. A group of Neolithic cairns; Skelpick illustrates the variety of forms found in this part of Scotland. It includes plain round cairns, and round and long horned cairns, in which the ends of the cairn are extended to form horn-like projections. Another group of chambered round cairns with horn extensions can be seen at Spinningdale.

Stenness Stone Circles   M3
Orkney Mainland. A major late Neolithic or bronze age henge monument, Stenness has a surrounding earthwork with interior ditch, and two opposed entrances. In addition, there are the stone circles, the Ring of Stenness, the Ring of Bookan, and the Ring of Brodgar. The whole would have formed an important religious site. Associated is a group of burial cairns. *Open any reasonable time.*

Taversoe Tuick Chambered Cairn   O2
Taversoe Tuick, Rousay, Orkneys. A rare type of cairn belonging to the Neolithic period, with two chambers built one on top of the other and provided with separate entrances. The remains of another can be seen at Huntersquoy on Eday. *Open any reasonable time.*

Vementry   Western Islands   N8
Shetland. A Neolithic 'heeled' cairn, a type peculiar to Scotland, in which a chambered cairn is placed on a stone-built platform in the shape of a heel. The chamber is cross-shaped, with its entrance sited at the concave part of the heel to give the effect of a forecourt.

Regional sports

Note that many of the sports mentioned in the previous section (No. 11) also apply to this part of Scotland.

Climbing and hill walking   F5
The northern highlands include some of the finest mountains in Scotland, and even the lower peaks do not lack for character. There

are three outstanding mountains above Loch Torridon: Beinn Alligin (3,232 feet), Liathach (3,456 feet) and Beinn Eighe (3,309 feet). Stac Polly (2,009 feet) to the north of Ullapool is easily climbed from the roadside between Drumrunie Lodge and Achiltibuie, but watch out on the soft sandstone.

Fishing   H7
The north of Scotland offers little coarse fishing, but with salmon and trout fishing costing so little, who's fussed about variety. A salmon permit for Loch Achonachie near Strathpeffer will cost a small amount per day or per week. The islands tend only to offer trout, though there is salmon to be fished on Lewis, Harris and North Uist.
Sea fishing round Orkney and Shetland is in some respects the finest in Europe. The European Record Skate (226½ lbs) was a fish taken in Shetland. In 1971 the European Sea Angling Championships were held out of Scrabster, Caithness, when 25,000 lbs of fish were caught.

Golf   M6
Obviously the further north one goes the fewer golf courses there are, but as this is Scotland there are still a lot. Charges are all very low; the courses at Wick and Stornoway are good and not expensive other courses include Tain, Muir of Ord, Thurso, Kirkwall and Golspie.

Ullapool, Ross & Cromarty

Pony trekking   G5
There are riding establishments all over Scotland, licensed by local authorities who offer this means of exploring wild country. The ground is often rough and the treks lead across moors and mountains, along forest paths, through burns and rivers. Try the Ullapool Pony Trekking Centre, Ullapool, Ross & Cromarty (Tel 2488), and the Tower Farm Trekking Centre, Urray, Muir of Ord (Tel 273). *June-Sep.*

Stalking   F5
The season for stalking red deer begins on the 1st July, although in practice stalking seldom starts much before the beginning of September, when the stags' antlers are in prime condition, and ends on the 20th October. This is an expensive sport, rates per day or per week, and this is excluding accommodation charges. The following hotels offer stalking (some also offer grouse, pheasant and rough shooting): Summer Isles Hotel, Achiltibuie, Ross & Cromarty; Lochdhu Hotel, Altnabreac, Caithness; Forsinard Hotel, Forsinard, Sutherland.

Fun things

Cheese Factory   K6
Highland Fine Cheeses, Tain, Ross & Cromarty. With the depopulation of the Highlands the art of making traditional cheeses was almost lost. Fortunately their manufacture has now been taken up commercially. See the making of Highland cheeses from start to finish, with free tasters afterwards. *Open 10.00–16–30 daily.*

Click Mill   M2
Orkney. Ne of Dounby off B9057. Old machinery is always interesting, but perhaps this rare example of a very old horizontal water wheel of Norse design is more interesting than most, and still in working order. *Open daily.*

Tweed Weaving K5
Dickson's The Tartan Flag, Benarty, Brora, Sutherland. Left of main road n from Brora.
See the looms and ancilliary equipment; warping and weaving methods demonstrated. The manufacture of woollen cloth is one of the few industries in this part of Scotland. *Open 9.00–21.00 Mon-Sat. Sun by request.*

Up Helly Aa O9
Lerwick, Sheltand Islands. This picturesque ceremony, the climax of which is the burning of a Norse galley, dates back to Viking times when the bodies of dead chieftains were sent to Valhalla in a blazing ship. A 30-foot model of a Viking ship is paraded through the town, accompanied by up to 300 Guisers bearing torches.
After dark the galley leads a huge procession down to the sea. The band plays 'The Norsemen's Home' as torches are flung into the galley which then sinks in a mass of flames. Sadly the citizens of Lerwick feel that they can only afford this lavish destruction once a year on the last Tuesday in January.

Hotels

The following indicates the price range of a single room per night:
£   inexpensive
££   medium priced
£££ expensive

Dornoch Highland K6
Royal Golf Hotel, Castle St. Tel 283. Ideal fishing and golfing. Views of the adjacent golf course. £.

Gairloch Highlands E6
Gairloch Hotel. Tel 2002. A modernised Victorian hotel. Good service and amenities. £. *Closed Nov-Mar.*

Garve Highland H7
Strathgarve Lodge Hotel. Tel 204. An elegant relaxing atmosphere, with fine views. ££.

Kinlochbervie Highland G2
Garbet Hotel, off A838. Tel 275. A fishing hotel which will cook a resident's catch. Good Scottish food. £.

Kyle of Lochalsh Highland E9
Lochalsh Hotel. Tel 4202. Good hotel to use as a touring centre. There are fine views of Skye, and the public rooms are pleasant. ££.

Lairg Highland J5
Sutherland Arms Hotel. Tel 2291. Comfortable and convenient. ££.

Muir of Ord Highland J8
Ord Arms Hotel. Tel 286. Set on the A9, this inn is comfortable and friendly. Pleasant garden. £.

Stornoway Highland D2
Caledonian Hotel, South Beach. Tel 2411. On the harbour front; pleasant and friendly local atmosphere. £.

Talladale Highland E7
Loch Maree Hotel, by Achnasheen. Tel Gairloch 2200. An unabashed fishing hotel, once patronised by Queen Victoria. ££.

Tongue Highland J2
Tongue Hotel. Tel 206. Built as a Victorian shooting-fishing lodge. Skilfully renovated. Good use of local produce in the restaurant. ££.

Ullapool Highland G5
Royal Hotel. Tel 2181. A modern white-fronted hotel with views of Loch Broom. Fishing is available to guests on the rivers Kanaird and Polly. ££.

Regional food & drink

Guga
This young gannet is a local delicacy caught with long poles hung over the steep cliffs to the nests. The birds are prepared by salting.

Lobsters and crab
Mostly exported from the catching area, but local delicacies such as Parton Bree – a crab soup thickened with cream – are still available.

Mutton hams
A leg of mutton is cured and smoked over a peat and wood fire to produce this local delicacy. Beef, pork, duck and goose are also similarly cured.

Scones and oatcakes
The girdle is a popular cooking utensil here as in Wales and Ireland, and such fine things as oatcakes and Scottish dropscones are produced on it.

Shortbread
One of the true delicacies of the Scottish kitchen, this is traditionally baked in a round flattish mould.

Trout
Though caught and sold throughout Scotland, trout is best when just caught. It is often cooked in tossed oatmeal.

Highland whisky
The word whisky is derived from the Gaelic 'uisge-beatha', 'water of life'. The main ingredients – fresh mountain air, pure burn water, locally grown barley and aromatic peat are all, happily, provided free by nature. There are three main types of Scotch whisky: malt, grain and blended. Malt whisky is made from a watery extract of malted barley, the peat fire over which it is dried providing the smoky flavour for which all genuine Highland whisky is famous. It takes up to fifteen years in oak casks to mature properly, although it may legally be sold after only three years. Grain whisky is usually made from imported maize, but rye and oats can also be used. It is lighter in colour and chemically purer than malt whisky, but the flavour is less distinctive. Today it is used for blending with malt whiskies and not usually drunk as whisky. Blended whisky is a mixture of matured and grain whiskies, combining the best properties of both.
Many happy hours may be spent touring those distilleries open to the public in order to select a favourite brand of Highland whisky. Bear in mind, however, the old Highland saying: 'There are two things a Highlander likes naked and one is whisky'.

Restaurants

£   inexpensive
££   medium priced
£££ expensive

Achiltibuie Highland F5
Summer Isles Hotel. Tel 232. Family-run hotel. Fresh, home-grown produce. Cooking fairly elaborate. D. ££. *Book.*

Contin Highland H7
Craigdarroch Hotel. Tel Strathpeffer 265. Hotel with well-chosen set menus. Mainly residential. Good, straightforward cooking. Good value. LD. £L, ££D. *Book*

Dornoch Highland K6
Burghfield House. Tel 212. Beautifully situated country house with fine views. Good home cooking. LD. *Closed Oct-Mar.* ££.

Garve Highland H7
Inchbae Lodge. Tel Aultguish 269. Converted shooting lodge. Serve yourself from the central table in the dining-room. Imaginative cooking. Good value. LD. £L, ££D. *Book.*

Kyle of Lochalsh Highland E9
Lochalsh Hotel, Ferry Rd. Tel Kyle 4202. Good range of well-cooked dishes. ££.

Tongue Highland J2
Tongue Hotel. Tel 206. Pleasant hotel. Imaginative use of local materials. Good value. LD. £. *Book.*

Northern Ireland

Northern Ireland is a self-governing province of the United Kingdom. After the wars of Queen Elizabeth I most of the land in the north was confiscated in 1610 by King James I and redistributed, to soldiers and settlers from England and Scotland. Of these the largest number were the Scots who built towns, villages, roads and churches and established agriculture and industry; the native Irish having been a pastoral race living mainly by livestock and having few durable settlements. The transformation of Northern Ireland, during the 17thC, was called the Plantation of Ulster.

Today about two thirds of the population are of Scottish stock and staunch Protestants. The landscape is beautiful and full of rare things like the Mountains of Mourne and the Giant's Causeway. There are masses of good golf courses, excellent spots for fishing and walking and outside a few localities, you can forget the Irish troubles. The people are warm and welcoming and you won't lack good conversation in this part of Ireland.

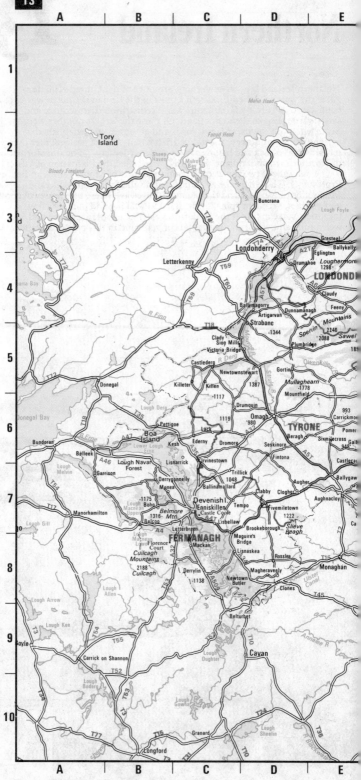

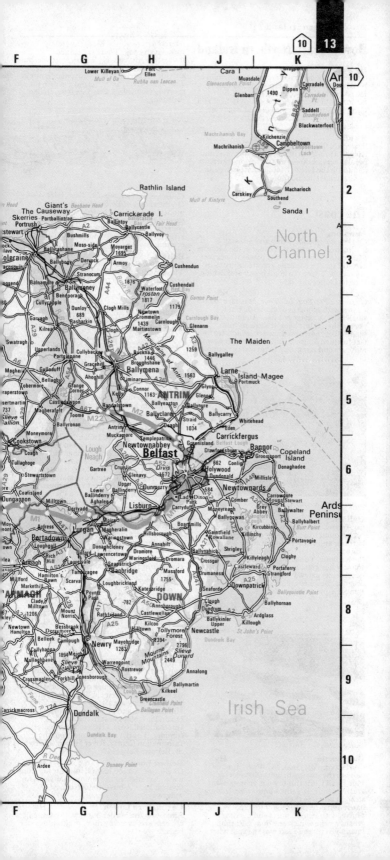

How to reach Northern Ireland

By Sea
There are six main sea routes from Britain to Northern Ireland: Liverpool to Belfast; Heysham to Belfast; Preston to Belfast; Stranrossan to Larne; Ardrossan to Belfast and Campbeltown (Scotland) to Red Bay (Co Antrim). Good sea ferries operate on all these routes.

By air
There are flights to Belfast's Aldergrove Airport from both of London's airports, and regular services from all the regional airports including the Isle of Man. Belfast is also on several transatlantic routes.

The coast

Annalong   J9
Co Down. Pop 600. A tiny and attractive fishing port that lies at the foot of the Mourne Mountains. One of the few places where you can still see the Mourne granite industry in operation. There is a good beach and fishing trips in Dundrum Bay.

Ardglass   K8
Co Down. Pop 800. EC Thur. It is rare to find a town with more than one castle but this small fishing village has five. An important port in the middle ages its citizens built themselves these small castles, which are in fact fortified houses. Jordans Castle is now a museum and Ardglass Castle was revamped in the Gothic style in 1789.

Ballintoy, Co Antrim.

Ballintoy   G3
Co Antrim. Dazzling white cliffs are the background to a genuinely picturesque harbour and village. Rough stone cottages cling to the corkscrew road that goes down to the harbour. You can't fail to notice the weirdly designed house that overlooks the beaches, its gateways guarded by bronze dragons. Beaches are small and sandy with some chequerboard rocks.

Ballycastle, Co Antrim.

Ballycastle   H3
Co Antrim. Pop 3,000. EC Wed. Situated close to the soaring heights (600 feet) of the Fair Head Cliffs this town is an important seaside resort. It's just a long street leading straight down to the sea. The disused harbour has been turned into a sports centre, with tennis courts and bowling greens on the wide stone quays. Rathlin Island just off the coast was the spot where

Marconi transmitted his first wireless message in 1905. There is a ruined monastery, Bunamargy Friary, that was built for the Franciscans around 1500. Look out also for the pretty 18thC Protestant church. This area is Northern Ireland's centre for sporting sea fishing. Good sand beach one mile long.

Bangor, Co. Down.

Bangor   J6
Co Down. Pop 26,900. EC Thur. MD Wed. On the shores of Belfast Lough this is a modest and popular seaside town. There are several rocky caves and some good golf courses. During the summer season you can visit the Little Theatre for an entertaining evening.

Belfast   J6
Co Antrim. Pop 420,000. EC Wed or Sat. The capital city of Northern Ireland has grown from a small trading post to a modern industrial city. During the 18thC it developed the linen industry and was surrounded by fields. Now it still produces textiles and has large ship building yards, notably Harland and Wolff where the Titanic was built.

Stormont, Belfast.

Belfast is a political town and partisan feelings run high as the recent troubles have shown. Way back in 1791 Wolf Tone formed the Irish republican movement in the city, his United Irishmen were determined to end British domination of Ireland. The history of British influence lingers on in the shape of William of Orange whose image on a white horse is still painted on the sides of Protestant houses. His colour orange is the talisman of all Protestant groups. Queen Victoria's ghost is present in the more substantial form of statues and the predominance of Victorian buildings. Don't miss the Victorian offices for the Gas Board in Ormeau Road by John Lanyon, or the Belfast memorial to Prince Albert which Queen Victoria described as 'one of the most graceful monumental erections in the kingdom'. Next to Albert is an excellent Custom House built in 1857 in the style of Italian Palazzo.

Belfast City Hall.

There is a cathedral to see, St Anne's; a university, Queen's red brick neo-Tudor colleges hemmed in by newer buildings; and the Parliament in a huge neo-classical pile six miles from the city at Stormont. All around the city are attractive parks; Cave Hill has a zoo and pre-historic remains while Dixon Park plays host to the only International Rose Trials in Britain every summer. Tourist information from the Information Centre, River House, 48 High St, Belfast. Tel 31221.

Belfast Lough   J6
Co Antrim. A good natural inlet for big ships which has enabled the famous shipyards to flourish here. A busy, industrialised waterway.

Carlingford Lough   H9
Almost on the border but now the smugglers are being replaced by more profitable oyster beds.

Carrick-a-Rede H3
Co Antrim. 5 miles w of Ballycastle. A spot for
dare devils to try their luck – a rocky island is
separated from the cliffs by an 80 foot
chasm: the only link is a swinging rope
bridge. It's an unnerving experience to cross
the bridge. Once you've reached the island
don't forget you have to make the same dizzy
journey back.

Carrickfergus J5
Co Antrim. Pop 10,900. EC Wed, Sat.
Famous for its firm square castle but it is a
pleasant town in itself. The town hall, 1779,
has an attractive facade and has been the
scene of political trials. The church of St
Nicholas began its life in 1185 but was
rebuilt for Protestant use in 1614; look for
some good early 20thC windows. Much of
the town wall survives including the north
gate and a corner bastion.
A short journey to the north-east is
Ballyhill, where you will find Dalway's
Bawn, one of the best preserved Plantation
towers; it dates from 1609.

Coleraine F3
Co Londonderry. Pop 12,000. EC Tue. A very
handsome harbour town, now the home of a
new university. Founded as a Plantation
town in 1613 it has the typical central
'diamond' plan. Linen and whiskey are made
here and you should see the salmon leap,
called the Cutts.

Cushendall H3
Co Antrim. Pop 620. EC Tue. The tall
sandstone curfew tower is a landmark of the
Glens of Antrim and this little town is an
ideal centre. Behind the town is the little
rounded Tiveragh – it is the home of several
fairies. Each glen has a safe and sandy beach;
the one at Cushendall is very good for
bathing, boating and fishing.

Cushendun H3
Co Antrim. Pop 150. EC Tue. A lovely
village looked after by the National Trust. A
bit Cornish with some coy little houses
designed by Clough Williams-Ellis of
Portmeirion fame. From the village to the
west stretches the beautiful Glendun. John
Masefield, the poet, found this area so
glorious he often stayed here. Long stretch
of sandy beach.

Devenish Isle C7
Lower Lough Erne, Co Fermanagh. Come
here for an experience you can only have in
Ireland – the atmosphere of exquisite Celtic
melancholy. The whole island is a mass of
ruins among the bracken. It is hard to
imagine the richly endowed monastery in its
glory. Only the thick, shattered and roofless
walls give a notion of its strength. Now only
cattle wander along the nave under the
watchful eye of the round tower.

Donaghadee K6
Co Down. Pop 3,300. EC Thur. A seaside
resort that stands at the head of the Ards,
which run south between the sea and
Strangford Lough. Once a busy
cross-channel port until the big ships left it
for Belfast. Now the harbour is a marina for
yachts. Bird sanctuary on the off-shore
Copeland Islands. Good sandy beach.

Fair Head H3
Nr Ballycastle, Co Antrim. Cliffs 600 feet
high look across to Scotland, only fourteen
miles away. The atmosphere here is really
out of this world. On the cliff top are two
dark lakes, one has a prehistoric fortified
island said to be the haunt of underwater
horsemen. Golden eagles nest here and you
can enjoy a rare geophysical experience
looking at the curvature of the earth along
the rim of the distant Atlantic.

Giant's Causeway G2
Co Antrim. A rare and famous series of cliffs
that resulted from gigantic outpourings of
volcanic basalt in remote tertiary times. The
rock cooled as a lower layer of thousands of
regular hexagonal columns and an upper
layer of slim uneven prisms that resemble a
crazy architect's fantasy. The whole of this
amazing piece of coast belongs to the
National Trust – take the North Antrim
Cliff Path, an eleven mile right of way from
the Causeway to Ballintoy.

Glenarm J4
Co Antrim. Pop 600. EC Wed. The first
village you come to as you approach the
Glens of Antrim from Larne; a quaint place
with narrow streets of gaily painted houses.
In Altmore Street is the entrance to the
forest where there are well planned walks by
the side of the river and waterfalls. Sandy
bay with safe swimming and sea fishing from
the rocks.

Holywood J6
Co Down. Pop 8,000. EC Wed. The centre of
Irish golf on the shore of Belfast Lough and
a good spot for a country holiday. In the
High Street is a permanent maypole, used for
the occasional jig. Don't miss an outing to
the delightful Ballymenoch Park.

Larne J5
Co Antrim. Pop 16,500. EC Thur. Irish
terminal for the ferry that brings passengers
from Preston or Stranraer. Not a resort but a
good spot for a game of golf on either of the
two good courses. On a strip of land to the
south of the town (the Curran) great
quantities of mesolithic flints have been
found. Good sand beach and heated pool.

Island Magee J5
Co Antrim. A narrow peninsula, well wooded
and once a breeding ground for goshawks.
Now a lovely spot for a walk by the sea,
especially along The Gobbins. The cliffs are
the well known haunt of witches: a black
magic cult operated here until the 1960s.

Newcastle J8
Co Down. Pop 4,300. EC Thur. This is where
the mountains of Mourne sweep down to the
sea. Close by are Tollymore and
Castlewellan Forest Parks; they offer
camping caravan sites and an excellent
arboretum. The beach is three miles of
excellent sand, and is backed by the Royal
County Down championship golf course.

Newcastle, Co Down

Portaferry K7
Co Down. Pop 1,400. EC Thur. A tiny and
picturesque village on the east side of the
narrow entrance to Strangford Lough. There
is a 16thC castle; an 18thC mansion,
Portaferry House, worth the few miles' trip.
Not a swimming resort but excellent
fishing. Rumour has it that skate of over
180 lbs have been caught.

Portrush F3
Co Antrim. Pop 4,300. EC Wed. A mile long
promontory that juts into the Atlantic, it has
excellent long sandy beaches and the famous
Royal Portrush Golf Course. Justifiably one
of Ulster's most popular seaside resorts,
good sailing, perfect swimming, bowling,
tennis and putting.

Portstewart F3
Co Londonderry. Pop 4,000. EC Thur. Neat
little seaside resort with a good harbour and
two golf courses – but you really come here
for the two miles of beautiful sandy beach.
Thackeray used to visit here back in the
1840s.

Rathlin Island H2
Co Antrim. A beautiful high island with
buzzards breeding in the great cliffs. It was
here in a cave that Robert the Bruce was
inspired by the determined spider and he
returned to become King of Scotland. The
Earl of Essex, Elizabeth I's favourite,

Giant's Causeway

carried out a spectacular massacre in 1573 of all the 600 inhabitants and refugees on the island during the Desmond Rebellion. Now a peaceful spot and a glorious sanctuary for wild birdlife.

Rostrever   H9
Co Down. Pop 1,400. EC Wed. A spot that has the blandest climate in Northern Ireland due to its sheltered site on the Carlingford Lough. As a peaceful centre for mountain walking, pony trekking and bathing it's hard to beat. Good little beach.

Strangford Lough   K7
Co Down. One of the loveliest wild life sanctuaries in the British Isles. A good spot to see geese migrating, herons and all kinds of waders. On the islands seals can often be seen.

Inland towns and villages

Antrim   H5
Co Antrim. A town where the economy is based on linen. Modest and pleasant with one outstanding thing to see – the round tower. The tower is a survivor of an early monastery; it is in perfect condition, only the conical roof being restored. The castle is ruined.

Armagh

Armagh   F7
Co Armagh. Pop 10,000. EC Wed. Ecclesiastical capital of Ireland with two cathedrals and homes of the two archbishops. Traditionally visited by St Patrick, this is where he built his first church; on its site now stands the Church of Ireland cathedral. The Catholic cathedral now stands on its own hill. It is 19thC with a jolly interior full of modern Italian angels. The town is full of fine Georgian houses: look at the Mall, Charlemont Place and Beresford Place. One of the most attractive towns in Ireland.

Castlewellan   H8
Co Down. A tiny, elegant town laid out around two squares well planted with good trees. The 18thC market house is a fine example. In a park nearby is a good arboretum around a Victorian-mediaeval castle.

Cookstown   F6
Co Tyrone. Pop 5,000. EC Wed. Laid out by a Planter called Cook in 1609, the main feature is the 40-yard-wide High Street that runs for a mile as an elegant promenade. Now it is largely an agriculture centre. Visit the Drum Manor Forest Park close by with its unique butterfly garden.

Downpatrick   J8
Co Down. Pop 4,300. EC Thur. Among some pleasant hills the town is reputed to be the burial place of St Patrick – a stone in the cathedral grounds marked 'Patric' was set up in 1900. A shrine to the saint existed in the early monastery and nearby at Saul, where the saint arrived in Ireland, is a giant hilltop statue of him.

Dungannon   F7
Co Tyrone. An O'Neill stronghold until the end of the 16thC, now a simple little town, distinguished only by a great coaching inn sadly in need of repair.

Enniskillen   C7
Co Fermanagh. A Protestant stronghold that has been fought over and defended many times. Loyal troops served King William at the Battle of the Boyne and two Inniskilling regiments were subsequently created from men in the town. Look out for the column on Fort Hill from which there are fine views. On a hill to the west is Portora Royal School, founded in 1626, where Oscar Wilde and Samuel Beckett were educated.

Enniskillen, Co Fermanagh

Hillsborough   H7
Co Down. Pop 800. EC Sat. Another Plantation town founded in 1650 by one Sir Arthur Hill. When Northern Ireland had a Governor General he lived in Hillsborough Castle, a large mainly 19thC house. The fort has an elegant 18thC Gothic gatehouse and the church at the end of an avenue is well worth seeing.

Hillsborough, Co Down.

Killyleagh   J7
Co Down. Pop 2,200. EC Thur. A delightfully unspoilt village with its own romantic castle looming over the village and the lough. The castle is solid with pinnacle roofs on each tower and a great walled park. Real feudal splendour.

Limavady   E3
Co Londonderry. A lovely little Georgian town, moved away from the castle by an early Planter because it spoilt his view. Thackeray came here and fell in love with a maid at the inn, though he was only there for ten minutes. A mile or so to the east is Drenagh, a cool classical house of 1830.

Lisburn   H7
Co Antrim. Pop 21,500. EC Wed. MD Tue. A trim town round a triangular market place. In the centre is a statue of one Sir John Nicholson who was killed in a storming party in Delhi, India. Nice little Church of Ireland cathedral in typical 1625 'Planter's Gothic'.

Londonderry   D4
Co Londonderry. Pop 53,000. EC Thur. The second city of Ulster stands four square on the River Foyle inside its firm ancient walls. Usually called Derry except by British officials. It has two cathedrals, Roman Catholic and Protestant, and in the southern part of the city are good Georgian houses. A quiet town that still remembers its great sieges and its past. Close by are the mountains and coast of County Donegal.

Lurgan   G7
Co Armagh. Pop 20,700. EC Wed. MD Thur. A busy industrious centre of the linen industry; good damask is still made here. Like many small Ulster towns, shades of the Plantation days still linger – here the demesne of the original settlers has become a public park.

Newry   G8
Co Down. Pop 12,200. EC Wed. MD Thur, Sat. A plain town set in pretty hilly country and alongside the River Newry and the canal. The town is also on the border with the Republic and is frequently fought over. Some interesting Georgian houses remain in Trevor Hill and Upper Water Street but the town is no architectural masterpiece.

Town Hall, Newry

Omagh D6

Co Tyrone. Pop 8,000. EC Wed. County town of Tyrone. Good classical court-house and regimental museum of the Royal Inniskillin Fusiliers. Now a centre for the Gortin Glen Forest Park, beautiful moorland rich in waterfalls. Good fishing.

Omagh, Co. Tyrone

Portadown G7

Co Armagh. Pop 18.000. EC Thur. Famous above all for roses grown here by the McGredy's. (The mayor's chain of office is made of gold medals won in rose competitions.) The town is to be linked to Lurgan as a new city called Craigavon.

Strabane D5

Co Tyrone. Pop 8,800. EC Thur. MD Tue, Thur. A busy, small town that is worth a visit only for its associations. In the Main Street is the bow-fronted Gray's Printing Works – John Dunlap (1747-1812) left here after an apprenticeship to found America's first daily paper, 'The Pennsylvania Packet'. He was also the first printer of the Declaration of Independence. Another employee was the grandfather of President Woodrow Wilson.

Regional oddities

History
You need a sense of history to understand Northern Ireland and its people. The whole island has had a long history of spasmodic anarchy. Settlers from England moved in to a relatively rich land and developed loyalties to local chiefs, and conflict with the English crown has often been the result. In Tudor times the English Crown saw that Ireland could become of potential value to an enemy and the result was a more ruthless colonisation. The native Irish and the Gaelic nobility were practically wiped out, and James I allocated most of the best lands in the north to Scottish settlers. Many of these settlers resented the laws which helped British farming and industry at the expense of Irish progress – and a republican tradition developed in the north and spread southwards. Resentment against England grew in the 17thC particularly after Cromwell's vicious suppression in 1649. In 1782 the colony was given a measure of Home Rule but the rising of 1798 and the example of the French Revolution caused all power to return to London. Absentee landlords became a commonplace thing in the 19thC and the Irish workers suffered greatly from neglect and (after the potato blight) famine, and the population fell from eight and a half million in the mid 19thC to four and a half million in 1901. A gradual extension of Home Rule early this century was not enough. Because the English had broken so many promises, the Irish seized power by force between 1916 and 1921. The counties of Northern Ireland were the exception. Staunch Protestants disliked Popery more than they disliked the British, and so the six counties remained part of the United Kingdom. They had to use force to do so and the result has been a very precarious union that hovers on the edge of total tragedy to this day.

Contrasts
Because of a troubled history of colonisation you will notice great contrasts in the Irish scene. There are magnificent Anglo-Irish houses – homes of the rich landlord, and small cottages for the tenantry. There is more of a gap between rich and poor than in some 20thC countries, and this may be one of the reasons behind the present troubles. Poverty has led in the past to massive emigration particularly to the United States and England.

Ballad singing
Many pubs have traditional musicians and ballad singers. A good and popular one is the Cross Keys Inn at Portlenone, County Antrim. The seaside resort of Warrenpoint is noted for these singing pubs.

Belleek ware, Co. Fermanagh

Belleek Pottery A6
Belleek, Co Fermanagh. This small village produced porcelain in the 19thC, from the local feldspar, that was superbly designed. Highly glazed, intricate pieces often resembling basket work are much prized. Tours of the factory are full of interest but the 20thC products are hardly collectors' items.

Celtic Crosses
Often to be seen just outside the villages of the north, these great high stone crosses are links with the early Christian settlements of the 9th and 10thC. Usually sandstone with intricate carved decoration of scenes from the Bible. Two of the finest crosses are at Donaghmore, County Tyrone, and the Arboe Cross east of the village of Coagh, County Tyrone, on the west shore of Lough Neagh.

Fairies
It is not just the poets who knew that Ireland is the last stronghold of the fairies, many visitors come especially to find them – and they always do. A good spot to tiptoe after a few is in the glens of Antrim. Usually fairly easy to recognize, they stand about two feet high and are, of course, dressed in green. Sometimes also known as the wee folk.

Irish Tweed
Splendidly made hand woven tweeds are produced in Ulster. They are usually thornproof and ideal for sporting wear. All kinds of tweed can be purchased in the larger shops in Belfast, some made in Ulster at Rostrevor and Hillsborough, County Down, and at Cushendall in the Glens of Antrim.

Linen
Northern Ireland is one of the world's centres for the manufacture of damask linen. Flax grows well in the Irish climate and the industry has flourished since the 17thC when Huguenot weavers arrived from France. You can see the traditional methods of linen manufacture at the Ulster Folk Museum at Cultra, County Down. Look towards the future at the world's most advanced textile laboratory at the Linen Research Institute at Lambery, County Antrim.

Monkey puzzle trees (Chili pine)
You can't fail to notice that Ulstermen

actually like these strange trees. Many front gardens have a male and female pair of these dark green prickly trees.

Peat
Perhaps more commonly cut and dried for fuel in the west of Ireland, peat is still used in Ulster. On the road to Ballymoney in County Antrim you cross one of the largest peat bogs in Northern Ireland. The Garry Bog is covered with mounds of peat that look like little houses, they are in fact carefully built stacks designed to allow the peat blocks to dry. Watch out for the curiously shaped spades that the cutters use.

Pegged and round thatching
To be seen all along the north and west coasts of Ireland – the straw thatch is secured by a complete network of ropes fastened to the walls below the eaves. The roofs are often rounded to withstand gales.
An older method of securing the ropes is to weight them with small boulders. The ropes are now usually made of sisal but they were once made of the tough fibres of bog-fir roots. Cottages like these are to be seen around the border with County Donegal.

The potato
Once the staple food of the whole country, when the crops were blighted in the 1840s a great famine spread causing great distress and suffering. Ireland is still the best place to buy seed potatoes and to eat potatoes served the simple way – boiled in their skins and served with butter as a separate course.

The pub
Traditional Irish pubs can be found all over the province of Ulster. Although now rather dangerous places to frequent in Belfast they are safe in the rural areas, and you can be assured of a warm welcome, good stout and excellent conversation.

Stone figures
Boa Island, Lower Lough Erne, Co Fermanagh. On both the islands of Lustymore and Boa the visitor will find stone idols. They have triangular shaped heads set on torsos with crude arms crossed on their breasts. Some of them are two faced, like Janus, and gaze out of the ferns. Thought to be 7thC they represent some enigmatic pagan cult.

The Irish Language

Early in the 19thC the Irish language was spoken by over half the population of the whole of Ireland. But by the end of the 19thC the language was almost dead, spoken only in outlying regions and by the Gaelic League. When the country was split the Republic of Ireland adopted Irish as the first official language in 1937, and now it is taught in the Republic's schools and is being generally revived. In the North, English is the first language and there are only remnants of Gaelic Irish left. Nonetheless it can add interest to a visit to Northern Ireland as any language is part of a nation's history. It is a difficult language to learn as it is inflected with complicated verbs. Interestingly there are no words for 'yes' and 'no' which perhaps explains why the Irish answer is usually 'I will' or 'I will not.'

Famous people

John Dunlap (1747-1812)   **D5**
Grays Printing Press, Main St, Strabane, Co Tyrone. Said to be the house where Dunlap learnt his trade before going on to found the first American daily paper, 'The Pennsylvania Packet,' and to print the American Declaration of Independence.
Open daily Apr-Sep. Closed Thur & Sun.

Woodrow Wilson (1856-1924)   **D5**
Wilson House, Dergat, Co Tyrone. Traditional farmhouse home of the ancestors of American President Wilson.
Open 14.00-18.00 daily Apr-Sep. Closed Tue

Cathedrals, abbeys & churches

The Catholic Church   **F7**
Moy, Co Tyrone. This church is a later addition to this curious Italianate village. It has a typical pedimented facade and a rectangular plan which has been embellished with Gothic trappings. It is full of early 19thC conceits, narrow lancets, battlements and an amusing pinnacled bell-cote.

Down Cathedral   **J8**
Downpatrick, Co Down. On the site of St Patrick's first stone church after he landed from Strangford Lough nearby in 432. The tomb of the patron saint of Ireland is in the cathedral churchyard. The cathedral was destroyed three times in Irish wars and rebuilt.

Dungiven Priory   **E4**
Dungiven, Co Londonderry. On the outskirts of Dungiven, the ruins of an Augustinian priory church, founded 1100 by the O'Cahans, chieftains of the Derry region. Fine canopied altar-tomb, with figure believed to be Cooey-na-Gall, the 14thC O'Cahan chieftain, in Irish armour though the tomb is in mediaeval English style.

First (Unitarian) Presbyterian Church   **H6**
Crumlin, Co Antrim. An 1835 rubble and basalt church with a brick tower that is sturdy and unusual. The shape is octagonal, while inside a horseshoe gallery dominates; yellow pine pews remain. Very pretty Gothick organ.

Old Cathedral of St Patrick   **F7**
Armagh, Co Armagh. (Church of Ireland.) Stands on the hilltop where St Patrick erected a church in 445. It is probably the oldest church in Ireland, still in use and contains many fine marble monuments and sculptures and the colours of famous Irish regiments.

Our Lady of Bethlehem Abbey   **G5**
Portglenone, Co Antrim. Begun in 1962 by Patrick Murray, a modern Cistercian monastery built of concrete and brick around a cloister. It has a certain impressive austerity.

Parish Church   **H7**
Hillsborough, Co Down. The town is built in the Classical style, whilst this church is in the 18thC Gothic mode. Planned like a Greek cross with towers at the end of each transept balancing the great western spire. The interior is full of elegant 18thC plaster work including false vaults.

St Anne's Cathedral   **J6**
Belfast, Co Antrim. Begun in 1899 and still not finished as the variety of its styles shows. Sir Thomas Drew designed it in Romanesque style and it is a heavy pretentious edifice. The floor of the nave contains stones from every part of Ireland. In the west portals a 1914-18 war memorial with figures of Sacrifice, Victory and Peace by Charles Nicholson. In the baptistry are mosaics by Gertrude Stein.

St Columb's Cathedral   **D4**
Londonderry, Co Londonderry. The square tower and tall, graceful late Georgian spire make this church more like a London parish church of the 16thC than a cathedral. The general style is a pure Gothic of great simplicity which has come to be called 'Planter's Gothic'. Look out for the Tomkins and Elvin memorial commemorating the first Planters and John Elvin who became mayor and lived to be 102.

St Patrick's Catholic Cathedral   **F7**
Armagh, Co Armagh. It stands on a hill facing the old cathedral. A stately building with two exquisite spires, the foundation stone was laid on St Patrick's Day 1840; it was dedicated and opened in 1873, building having been delayed by the Great Famine.

Castles and ruins

Antrim Round Tower   H5
Antrim, Co Antrim. These towers were built during the 9th to 12thC by monks as look-outs and refuges for treasures following the Viking invasions. All traces of the ancient monastic foundations were removed in the 19thC.

Belfast Castle   J6
Belfast, Co Antrim. A full-blooded Victorian castle built in 1870 by a Belfast firm of architects. Standing high above the city the castle looks like a misplaced Balmoral. In fact it is a curious mixture of Scottish baronial and French Renaissance.
In the grounds a mortuary chapel contains a marble group of the Earl of Belfast dying on a sofa and mourned by his mother. It is life size and sums up the Victorian way of death.

Carrickfergus Castle   J5
Carrickfergus, Co Antrim. A fine example of a large Norman stronghold. Begun in 1180 by John de Courcy, first Anglo-Norman invader of Ulster. It stands on a rocky headland and its keep and outer and inner courts are impressive remains of this enormous fortress. Attacked frequently from the seige of King John in 1210 to the late 18thC. The cannons along the outer walls date from the 19thC when the castle was still an armoury.

Castle Carra   H3
Cushendun, Co Antrim. The keep of Castle Carra has all the essential qualities of a romantic ruin. Remote, ivy clad chunks of masonry are scattered on the slopes of the north-east coast, and they have the required associations with a legendary hero – Sean the Proud. Here is true picturesque desolation.

Devenish Abbey   C7
Co Fermanagh. On Devenish Island, Lower Lough Erne, you will find one of the most remarkable groups of ecclesiastical buildings in Ireland. On the site of a 6thC monastery there is a round tower, 81 feet high of the 9th-10thC, perfectly preserved; the ruins of St Molaise's church and house (12thC) and St Mary's Abbey (15thC).

Dundrum Castle   J8
Dundrum, Co Down. Striking remains of a Norman castle, built in 1177 by John de Courcy. It was beseiged and taken in 1210 by King John and bombarded by Cromwellian troops in 1652. The tall keep affords magnificent views of mountains and sea.

Dunluce Castle, Co Antrim

Dunluce Castle   F3
Portrush, Co Antrim. Picturesque turreted ruin on a steep, sea tunnelled crag, three miles east of Giant's Causeway. Probably built about 1300 by Norman Richard de Burgo. Vacated after the kitchen and servants fell into the sea in 1639. The cave below penetrates right through the crag from the land to sea.

Greencastle   J8
Greencastle, Co Down. Substantial ruined royal castle at the south-east point of Northern Ireland. Completed in 1261 at the same time as Carlingford Castle on the opposite shore to control Carlingford Lough; it was abandoned after bombardment by Cromwell's army 1652. The best example in County Down of 13thC military architecture, comparable in plan and size with great Norman towers in England, and firmly illustrating the Anglo-Norman's determination to command Irish sea accesses.

Grey Abbey, Co Down.

Grey Abbey   K7
Greyabbey, Co Down. The ruins on the shore of Strangford Lough of a Cistercian abbey founded in 1193 by Alfreca, wife of John de Courcy. Extensive and well-maintained remains give an excellent idea of an important early English style abbey.

Inch Abbey   J8
Downpatrick, Co Down. Well maintained, beautifully sited ruins of a Cistercian abbey on the bank of the River Quoile. Established in 1180 by John de Courcy in atonement for his destruction of the abbey at Brenagh which had resisted his advance into Ulster. Fragments remain of the nave and transepts, tower and presbytery, cloister, chapter house and bakery.

Kilclief Castle   K8
Nr Strangford, Co Down. Perhaps the earliest datable tower-house in Ireland, on the seashore two miles south of Strangford, and a possible model for many similar ones throughout Ulster. Built in the early 15thC as the residence of a Bishop of Down (later unfrocked for living with a married woman in the castle).

Maguire's Castle   C7
Enniskillen, Co Fermanagh. Guards the island town of Enniskillen on the narrows linking Upper and Lower Lough Erne. Home of the two world famous regiments, the Inniskillin Dragoon Guards and the Royal Inniskillin Fusiliers. Their history, from the Seige of Derry by way of Waterloo to World War II, is commemorated in the new museum behind the picturesque, turreted water gate. The castle is the former stronghold of the chieftains of Fermanagh.

Monea Castle, Co Fermanagh.

Monea Castle   B7
Monea, Co Fermanagh. A ruined Plantation castle near the west side of Lower Lough Erne showing marked Scottish influence. It was the governor of Enniskillen's residence in the late 17thC.

Navan Fort   F7
Co Armagh. Two miles west of Armagh lie these early iron age remains. Traditionally the residence of the kings of Ulster for six centuries. It is often referred to in Irish heroic tales, which date Queen Macha at around 300 BC, and it is mentioned in Ptolemy's 'Geography'. There are finds of many periods from Navan Fort in the museums of Belfast and Dublin.

Struell Wells   J8

Downpatrick, Co Down. The site is associated with St Patrick who is reputed to have come here to bathe from his nearby church at Saul, thus extending Christian auspices to the pagan Irish reverence for holy wells. Drinking Well and Eye Well are still visited for cures on midsummer night. Water still flows through the men's and women's bath houses (17thC).

Tullaghoge Fort   F6

Tullaghoge, nr Cookstown, Co Tyrone. A hilltop ring fort. Interesting as the site of the inaugurations of the O'Neills, kings of Ulster, by sub-chieftains from the 11thC onward. The inauguration stone was smashed in 1602 on the orders of Queen Elizabeth's Lord Deputy Mountjoy. The kings were not crowned, but the chieftains placed a shoe on the O'Neill's foot.

Unusual buildings

Ballycopeland Windmill   K6

Millisle, Co Down. An 18thC corn grinding mill with good machinery, kept in working order.

Belfast City Hall   J6

Belfast, Co Antrim. A very sumptuous Edwardian Baroque building of 1906 that dominates Donegall Square. Inside it is a classic of the icing-sugar school, slightly improved by some recent murals. The copper covered dome is visible for miles.

Bishop Gate and the City Wall   D4

Londonderry, Co Londonderry. This gate was built in 1789 and takes the form of a triumphal arch to commemorate the epic siege of 1688–89. It is an austere design by Aaron Baker carved with laurels and martial trophies by Edward Smyth.
The city walls were built by the first Protestant settlers from England who clearly felt the need of complete protection from the native Irish. You can walk along the great stone walls and see the four massive bastions. The city has now spread far beyond its walls.

Crown Liquor Saloon   J6

Belfast, Co Antrim. Just opposite the Great Northern Station is this most magnificent, lavish Victorian pub. It is full of polished mahogany, brass and mirrors, and has remained unspoilt. A glass of stout in this sombre, beautiful temple is a delicious experience.

The Mall   F7

Armagh, Co Armagh. A well preserved terrace terminating in a classical courthouse, all designed by Francis Johnston in 1809. This is a lighter version of the famous Dublin terraces, with particularly fine fanlights each shaped like a sunflower cut in half.

Mussenden Temple, Co. Londonderry

Mussenden Temple   F3

Downhill, Co Londonderry. Built on the cliffs by the megalomaniac fourth Earl of Bristol, who was Bishop of Derry from 1768. He built himself Downhill (now ruined) as his home, to be about the size of Blenheim. This circular temple with its untopped dome was his library where he sat alone long into the night. *Open 14.00–1   daily Apr–Sep. Closed Tue.*

The Round Tower   C7

Devenish Isle, Lower Lough Erne, Co Fermanagh. The best preserved and best built round tower in Ireland. Once part of the monastery of St Molaise it is remarkable for its fine cut ashlar masonry and a rare decorated frieze below the cap.

At each point of the compass on the frieze is a carved head, each with a luxuriant moustache. The perfection of the tower is enhanced by the surrounding ruins.

Round Tower, Devenish Isle, Lough Erne, Co. Fermanagh.

St Columb's Wells   D4

Londonderry, Co Londonderry. During the middle years of the 19thC Londonderry became a great centre for those fleeing from potato famine. Large numbers of Catholic workers from the south came to work in the shirt factories of Londonderry, and they built this maze of small scale streets next to the sober Georgian area of the Protestants. The houses are one-storeyed and resemble the country cottages the emigrants had left behind. Now the cottages are brightly painted with Gaelic script over some of the shops.

The 'Saint's Tomb'   E4

Bovevagh, Dungiven, Co Londonderry. A tiny stone oratory on a wooded slope above the River Roe, said to date from the 11thC. It is a rare form of dry stone construction – the side walls projecting strangely beyond the gables. A curious ecclesiastical remnant that retains a lot of mystery.

Houses & gardens

Ardress House   G7

Nr Portadown, Co Armagh. A mid 17thC manor that was extended to create the present house by the architect George Ensor who married the heiress to the estate. He employed the craftsman Michael Stapleton to carry out the stucco work. The decoration bears his distinctive mark – a vigorous almost rococo style using natural forms and classical detail. The rooms have recently been completely restored using Stapleton's drawings which have survived. *Open 14.00–18.00 Apr–late Sep. Closed Tue.*

Castlecoole, Co. Fermanagh

Castlecoole   C7

Co Fermanagh. Se of Enniskillen. James Wyatt designed this great house for Lord Belmore in the 18thC and it remains exactly as it was – designed and made all at one time. The composition is traditional, a central block flanked by collonades with small terminal pavilions, and it relates perfectly to its setting among the great trees. The house was built of Portland stone shipped from England at fantastic cost.
Inside the rooms are a triumph of restrained classical decoration, particularly the salon with its black, grey and white plasterwork. The furniture, doors, bookcases and shutters were made on the spot and all the accounts survive. *Open 14.00–18.00 daily Apr–late Sep. Closed Tue.*

Castle Upton   H6

Templepatrick, Co Antrim. A fine house by Robert Adam who also designed the Upton Mausoleum (1783). This has a main front in the shape of a triumphal arch with sombre funerary urns. *Open daily.*

Castle Ward   K7

Co Down. 7 miles ne of Downpatrick. A splendid estate on the shores of Strangford Lough with an unusual house designed in a mixture of Classical and Gothick in the 18thC. Look out for the amazing collection of buildings surrounding this house. There is a Victorian laundry, an 18thC summer-house and two 15thC castles. The garden temple is an amazing replica of Palladio's Redentore. The whole park should be seen on a slightly misty day when it is just like a painting by Claude. *Open daily.*

Derrymore House
G8
Nr Newry, Co Armagh. A very rare survivor of the small, thatched country houses which were popular with the Irish yeomanry during the 18thC. Probably built for a member of parliament in 1776. By tradition the house was often visited by Lord Castlereagh, and the Act of Union 1880 was drawn up in the Treaty Room.

Florence Court
C7
Co Fermanagh. 7 miles sw of Enniskillen. A wild garden with a notable rhododendron glen. The original Irish yews were discovered wild here in 1780, from which all other cultivated Irish yews descend: used widely in topiary. *Open 14.00–18.00 daily Apr–late Sep. Closed Tue.*

Lady Dixon Park
J6
Malone, Belfast, Co Antrim. The scene throughout the summer of the greatest International Rose Trials in the British Isles, when about 20,000 roses of all kinds form an extensive display.

Mount Stewart
J6
Co Down. 5 miles se of Newtownards. Planned by Edith, Lady Londonderry in 1921, there is much to be seen in the 78 acres. Formal layouts such as the sunken Spanish garden, the Tin-N'An Oge and Italian gardens are surrounded by woodland. Tender plants and shrubs abound: eucalyptus, palms, bamboos, mimosa trees, lapagerias. See the shamrock garden, laid out in the shape of that most Irish of plants. The Red Hand of Ulster is planted at its centre. Topiary is superb with hunting scenes and Irish harps. The charming 18thC 'Temple of the Winds' should not be missed. *Open 14.00–18.00 daily Apr–late Sep. Closed Tue.*

Rowallane
J7
Nr Saintfield, Co Down. 11 miles se of Belfast. Renowned for rare and beautiful plants, its 50 acre were planned in 1903 by Hugh Armytage-Moore from rocky farmland. There are the famous Rowallane primulas, viburnams and hypericums here as well as *celmisias, rogersias* and many Asiatic magnolias. *Open 9.00–18.00 daily. Closed Sat & Sun morning. Fine evenings 19.00–21.00 May–Jun.*

Springhill
F6
Nr Moneymore, Co Londonderry. A late 17thC house; once fortified it was exactly the kind of stronghold needed by settlers supporting Cromwell. Today the fortifications have gone, but the low outbuildings for the servants remain with the laundry, turf shed and brew house. This is a lovely plain Plantation house of the kind only found in Ireland, reputedly occupied by two arguing ghosts. There is a costume museum. *Open 14.00–18.00 daily Apr–late Sep. Closed Tues.*

Museums and galleries

Armagh County Museum
F7
Armagh, Co. Armagh. Collections of archaeology, folk material, local history, natural history and paintings by Irish artists. *Open daily. Closed Sun.*

Arthur House
G4
Cullybackey, nr Ahoghill, Co Antrim. An old farmhouse, and the traditional home of the grandfather of American President Arthur. *Open 14.00–18.00 daily Apr–Sep. Closed Tue.*

The Arts Council Gallery
J6
Bedford St, Belfast, Co Antrim. Specialises in exhibitions of painting and sculpture by modern Irish artists. Tel 44222.

The Planetarium
F7
Armagh, Co Armagh. The only Planetarium in Britain outside London, and it has a permanent display of astronomical instruments. It adjoins the Observatory that has been in use since 1789. *Exhibition open 14.00–17.00 daily. Planetarium public showing Sat afternoon. Closed Sun.*

The Transport Museum
J6
Witham St, Belfast, Co Antrim. This contains a collection of ancient vehicles including Belfast trams that covers over 200 years of transport history. *Open daily (10.00–20.00 Wed.) Closed Sun.*

Ulster Folk Museum
J6
Cultra Manor, Belfast, Co Antrim. The traditional life of Northern Ireland can be sampled at the Ulster Folk Museum, in the house and 136-acre grounds of Cultra Manor. A water-powered spade mill continues to make spades and other agricultural and domestic implements by the traditional methods; even the workmen are descendants of the original family. A weaver produces damask linen to be spread on a bleach green which is defended by a traditional stone sentry tower. Two centuries ago the sentry was entitled to shoot anyone attempting to steal the linen. A scutch mill shows the original process of turning the flax into linen fibre. Griddle baking and rural cookery are demonstrated in the traditionally furnished cottages. Some of the cottages retain their floors of beaten earth. *Open 11.00–19.00 daily (11.00–21.00 Tue & Wed) Apr–Oct. 11.00–17.00 Nov–Mar.*

Ulster Museum
J6
Botanic Gardens, Belfast, Co Antrim. Departments of antiquities, art, botany and zoology, geology and technology. It also has a cafe, a cinema and a shop. The antiquities department has good exhibits of life in Ireland since the arrival of the first human beings in 6,000 BC. The outstanding treasure is priceless jewellery recently recovered by divers from the wreck of a galleon from the Spanish Armada at the Giant's Causeway. Part of the museum is housed in an exciting new building. *Open 11.00–18.00 Mon, & Fri. 14.30–17.30 Sun.*

Wellbrook Beetling Mill
F6
Cookstown, Co Tyrone. 3 miles sw on Omagh road B4. A water-powered mill operated from 1765 to 1961. Fully restored and now a museum. *Open daily Apr–Sep. Closed Tue.*

Botanical gardens

Botanic Gardens
J6
Belfast, Co Antrim. Founded in 1829, the outstanding feature here is the remarkable cast iron Palm House by Richard Turner and Charles Lanyon, which precedes Kew's by several years. *Open daily 8.00–sunset.*

Zoos, aquaria and aviaries

Belfast Zoological Gardens
J6
Bellevue, Newtownabbey, Co Antrim. During watime bombing most animals here were destroyed for humane reasons. Now enlarged to thirteen acres, its enclosures are mostly open-air, merging with the wooded Cave Hill. Aquarium, monkey house, bird and reptile collections. Llamas, lions and wolves bred here. *Open 10.00–17.00 daily May–Oct. 10.00–17.00 Sat & Sun Nov–Feb.*

Causeway Coast Lion Park
G3
Nr Benvarden, Co Antrim. 6 miles e of Coleraine. One of the newest safari parks in the UK. A visit here makes you feel you could be in Kenya as you drive close to the free roaming lions in the 62 acres of woods. There are also elephants, baboons, ostriches and chinchillas and a shop selling African masks. *Open daily Jun–Sep. Sat & Sun only mid Apr–Jun.*

Tropical Bird Gardens
G4
Coleraine, Co Londonderry. 1 mile s of Ballymoney road A20. Flamingoes, bantams, ducks, pheasants and lots of rare birds in attractive gardens. *Open daily mid Apr–Sep.*

Nature trails and reserves

Castle Caldwell Nature Reserve
B6
Co Fermanagh. Mixed commercial woodland

and Lough Erne shore, woodland birds and wildfowl. Nature trail and displays. No permit required. Five miles east of Belleek, signposted from the main Belleek, Kesh road.

Castle Ward Nature Trail K8
Co Down. Start at Stable Yard car park, 1½ miles w of Strangford on A25. Woodland and Strangford Lough wildlife. 1 mile. Display and self guiding panels.

Downhill Glen Nature Trail F3
Co Londonderry. Start from Bishop's Gate public car park, 1 mile w of Castlerock on A2. General natural history and geology. Self guiding panels.

Giant's Causeway Nature Trail G2
Co Antrim. Off B146, 9 miles e of Portrush. Coastal birds and superb geology. 3 miles. Guide from National Trust, Malone House, Barnett Demesne, Belfast.

Portglenone Nature Reserve G5
Co Antrim. ¾ mile s of Portglenone. Mainly commercial woodland, with arboretum and typical woodland birds. Nature trail. No permit necessary. Signposted on main Portglenone/Ballymena road.

Shane's Castle Nature Reserve G5
Co Antrim. Woodland birds and wildfowl on adjacent Lough Neagh, RSPB reserve with nature trail and miniature railway. Access from main Antrim-Randalstown road. *Open Summer weekends & B Hols.*

Whitepark Bay Nature Trail G3
Co Antrim. 1½ miles w of Ballintoy on A2 w of Ballycastle. Botany, geology and coastal birds. Guide from National Trust.

Bird watching

The 300 miles of coatline of Northern Ireland and the islands, five sea loughs, the abundance of freshwater, woodland, moor and mountain offer a unique opportunity of seeing more species than in any other single area of the UK. The lack of industrial pollution and fewer large mechanical farms has meant more hedgerow, clean water and more birds.
The following is a list of good places for watching birds.

Copeland Islands K6
Off Donaghadee. Good observatory. For details write to Mr. C. S. Bailey, 17 Hillside Drive, Belfast, Co Antrim.

Garron Plateau H4
Co Antrim. For 30 miles you can walk without seeing any sign of human habitation. A good area for lovely golden plover.

Green Island H9
Carlingford Lough, Co Down. A nature reserve under the control of the RSPB, there is a hide from which four species of tern can be watched. Permits from RSPB.

Lough Erne C7
Co Fermanagh. Both parts of the lough are rich in birdlife, particularly attractive heronries.

Lough Neagh G6
Good bird watching of all kinds, especially where there are beds of tall reeds.

North Antrim Cliffs H3
Co Antrim. This is the best area to see buzzards.

Randalstown Nature Reserve G5
Co Antrim. Two hides run by RSPB give excellent views of water fowl.

Rathlin Island H2
Co Antrim. Good for sea birds, especially off the west and north cliffs; eider duck rest all over the island.

Rostrevor Forest Nature Reserve H9
Co. Tyrone. Woodland birdlife, especially good for jays.

Sheep Island G2
Nr Ballintoy, Co Antrim. Extensive colonies of razorbill and kittiwake gulls on this island.

Sperrin Mountains E5
Co Tyrone and Co Londonderry. This mountainous region is a haunt of the peregrine falcon, raven and golden plover.

Strangford Lough K7
Co Down. A number of wild life refuges and hides at several sites around the lough. Tern, ringed plover, oyster catchers, redshanks, lapwings, snipes, grey lag geese and mute swans are only some of the species. Visitors wanting to discover the best places to visit on the lough should contact the National Trust Warden. Tel Killinchy 516.

Fossil hunting

Visit the local museum. Its fossil collection usually states where individual fossils have been found. When visiting quarries always seek permission to enter if they look privately owned or worked. Be careful of falls of rock.
Much of the land is covered by basalt, which makes up the Giant's Causeway, but other, sedimentary rocks occur in places.
Upper Ordovician and Silurian rocks with trilobites and brachiopods outcrop around Pomeroy, and there are Silurian graptolites on the foreshore at Donaghey.
Lower Carboniferous limestones with corals, algal reefs and shells are found in the Dungannon, Sligo and Ballyshannon areas.
Rhaetic and lias beds with ammonites, belemnites, bivalves, brachiopods are to be seen on the foreshore at Larne, at Island Magee, Portrush, and Collin Glen, near Belfast.
Upper Cretaceous chalk occurs also at Collin Glen and Portrush, and at Island Magee, Lisburn and Ballintoy.

Forests

Perhaps the most notable forests are Tollymore and Castlewellan, both in the Mourne Mountains. They are full of fine specimen trees including unusual Californian redwoods. Tollymore Forest has a wildlife museum. Much of the forestry in Northern Ireland is organised into forest for camping, fishing and recreational use. Among the best parks out of over 50 are: Lough Navar Forest Park, County Fermanagh; Slieve Gullion Forest Recreation Area, County Armagh; and Knocklayd Forest, Ballycastle, Co Antrim.

Castlewellan, Tollymore and Donard H9
Co Down. Three neighbouring forest parks in the Mourne Mountains with good collections of trees: silver firs and magnificent Wellingtonia (like Californian redwoods) that are now 120 feet high.

Lough Navar B7
Lower Lough Erne, Co Fermanagh. Good country park with spectacular views; the forest is mostly conifers. Small caravan site.

Seskanore D6
Nr Omagh, Co Tyrone. Beautiful mixed woodland in this small reserve. Look out for the game farm, but whatever you do keep your dog on a lead. Small caravan park.

Hills and mountains

Northern Ireland is shaped like a saucer with hills and mountains around the edge with Lough Neagh sitting in the middle, the largest lake in Britain.

Antrim H4
Co Antrim. A series of wooded valleys that run from the Antrim Mountains down to the sea. Dense foliage and rushing waterfalls and streams are your companions as you walk in these lush vales. At the foot of each glen is a village with a sandy beach – Glenarm, Carnlough, Glenariffe, Cushendall, Cushendun and Ballycastle.

The Drumlins

The landscape of County Down is dominated by many smooth, humpbacked hills called drumlins. They emerged from the melting glaciers of the ice age some 10,000 years ago when wolves, mammoths and the giant Irish deer were the only inhabitants.

Mountains of Fermanagh   B7
Co Fermanagh. A range that rises steeply from the shore of Lough Erne and is mainly limestone; there are plenty of unexplored caves. The Belmore Plateau is a Mecca for spelaeanologists. From the high point of Lough Navar Forest there are great views to the mountains of Donegal. Inside these great carboniferous limestone hills are the remains of animals over 320 million years old. Fine fossils can still be collected from the gorges.

Mourne Mountains, Co Down.

Mourne Mountains   H8
Co Down. A group of outstandingly beautiful mountains that lie just a little way from the sea. Most of the peaks are about 2,000 feet high, but one, Slieve Donard is almost 3,000 feet high. They are excellent for walking as no roads reach the higher regions. Look out for several secret lakes and the Mourne diamonds, semi-precious stones from quartz crystal which can be chipped from the rocks.

Slieve Gullion Mountains   G9
Co Armagh. On the border with the Irish Republic, their highest peak Slieve Gullion (1,894 feet) is mounted by a scenic drive that provides excellent views of northern and southern Ireland. This region is remote and quiet and the people seem to be occupying the last stronghold of a bygone rural life style.

Sperrin Mounthins   E5
Co Londonderry & Co Tyrone. An extensive range of sparsely inhabited peaks where the spirit of the stone age still walks. You can see the Beaghmore circles and alignments high up on the moors between Cookstown and Strabane.

Rivers and lakes

In this lush, green country of glens and loughs there are masses of rushing rivers and streams. There is not one major river that outclasses all the others but the capital of the province, Belfast, stands at the mouth of the River Lagan. The best reason for visiting the rivers of Northern Ireland is for the fishing which is best found in the following places:

Bann   G4
Co Antrim & Co Londonderry. Best river for grilse and sea trout, the centre for this river is Coleraine. Bann flows through County Londonderry where the fishing is even better; you can catch spring salmon, brown trout and a variety of coarse fish.

Dun   H3
Co Antrim. Good for spring salmon and brown trout, the best centre is at Cushendun. Fast flowing with attractive walks.

Erne   D8
Co Fermanagh. Like so many of the rivers of Ulster this one flows well into the neighbouring Republic counties particularly Donegal. It is a good source of trout (both the sea and brown varieties) and grilse. At Lisnaskea there is also coarse fishing.

Lough Catherine   D5
Co Tyrone. Good for brown trout and coarse fishing.

Lough Erne   C7
Co Fermanagh. An attractive, wild stretch of water with lots of splendid islands in both the lower and upper loughs. Of special interest is Devenish Island (round tower, ancient abbey, etc.) and White Island – a good boating centre.
Killadeas and Carrybridge are your centres to hire a boat, and then you can set off to explore one of the largest areas of navigable water in Europe with almost 200 islands. Good coarse fishing and a speciality is the massive Erne brown trout.

Lough Neagh, Co Fermanagh.

Lough Neagh   G6
153 square miles of water, this largest lake in the United Kingdom is fed by ten rivers but only one, the River Bann flows out of it to the sea. Beyond its shallow edges the lake drops sharply to a uniform depth of 40 to 50 feet. Vast numbers of wild fowl live on the lake; thousands of geese spend the winter here and in late autumn whooper swans rest after a direct 800-mile flight from Iceland. Salmon, eels and trout can be caught in the lake.

Canals

Northern Ireland is criss-crossed by canals but, sadly, not one of them is navigable for more than a couple of miles, and their appeal is limited to amateurs of industrial archaeology and canal history.
It is in a way surprising that so many artificial navigations were built in Ulster. Few of them, unlike those in England, withstood the wintry blast of railway competition in the 19thC. But canal promoters in Ulster were encouraged by two basic geographical considerations: the vast inland lake known as Lough Neagh, and the relative flatness of the landscape in the north. So the result was that there gradually sprouted a web of waterways radiating from Lough Neagh.
Newry Canal was thus the first purely artificial waterway in the British Isles. This ran as a barge canal from Portadown to the port of Newry, on the east coast, and thence by a ship canal for three miles down to the sea. But the barge canal has been closed for many years, and now even the port itself is to be closed down. There is however plenty of water still in the Newry Canal. Things to see include the flight of locks at Terryhoogan, and the old wharves in Newry town.
Other forgotten canals of Ulster include the Lagan Navigation, the Bann Navigation, the Coalisland Canal, the Tyrone Navigation, and the Ulster Canal. All these are disused, but all offer interest in the many bridges, locks and old machinery waiting to be unearthed. In this respect at least, the Ulster canals offer rich rewards to the walker

Archaeology

Aghanaglack B7
Between Belcoo and Boho, Co Fermanagh. A late Neolithic long-cairn containing two double-chambered galleries set back-to-back and separated by a common end-stone. Each gallery has a forecourt formed by the extended ends of the cairn.

Annaghmare F9
Nr Crossmaglen, Co Armagh. A well-preserved example of a single-court grave, a type of Neolithic burial cairn characteristic of the northern half of Ireland. The cairn is long, with one end extended into 'horns', forming a forecourt to the entrance; this court is lined with massive upright stones, alternating with drystone walling.
The gallery inside is divided by stone jambs into three chambers, and was originally corbel-roofed. Towards the back of the cairn are two later chambers, built back-to-back, with corbelled roofs and portals opening out at the sides.

Antrim Round Towers H5
Antrim. Co Antrim. Tall narrow round towers with conical stone roofs, such as this one at Antrim, were built at monastic sites of 10th-12thC date, and served as belfries and refuges.

Beaghmore F6
Nr Cookstown, Co Tyrone. This fine group of religious monuments, probably dating from the early bronze age, was discovered by peat-cutters earlier this century. There are seven stone circles, of which six are grouped in pairs, with alignments of stone uprights running from them, and several burial cairns, some of which are incorporated with the circles.

Boviel E4
Nr Dungiven, Co Londonderry. An example of a Neolithic wedge-grave, so-called from the sloping shape of the chamber, contained in an oval cairn. The chamber is divided by a stone doorway, forming an antechamber, and is lined with stone uprights. Only one of the roof-slabs survives, carried on a single row of corbels. A second row of stones follows the outline of the gallery, and the entrance is stone-faced.

Budore H6
Nr Crumlin, Co Antrim. A well-preserved pair of raths, typical of the many in south Antrim. The majority of these circular enclosures date from the first millenium, but they continued to be built during the middle ages.
The larger raths may have been forts, but they were more commonly the homesteads of farmers. The south rath at Budore has a single bank and ditch, and is probably the earlier as the ditch is more silted. The other has a double ditch and bank, of which the inner has been levelled off.

Drumena H8
Nr Lough Island Reavy, Co Down. The cashel at Drumena is a good example of these drystone enclosures, and probably held an iron age farmstead; the ruins of a more recent farm can be seen on the site today. There is also an iron age souterrain, an underground gallery now entered by modern steps, but with its original entrance and opposed chamber still preserved.

Giant's Ring D6
Ballynahatty, Co Tyrone. The large enclosure at Ballynahatty is probably a type of henge monument, dating from the later Neolithic period. The surrounding bank, standing twelve feet high, is built of stones, and has a slight depression around the interior; there are now five entrances, but these are probably not all original. Just off-centre is a grave with a single chamber, built of five uprights with a capstone seven feet across; there are also traces of an entrance passage.

Killadeas C7
Nr Lower Lough Erne, Co Fermanagh. The graveyard at Killadeas has three sculptured stones, including one with cup-marks and a second with a small Greek cross. The most interesting is the Bishop's Stone, which probably dates from the 8thC; this shows an ecclesiastic carrying a bell and crozier, and has a grotesque head carved on the narrow edge.

Knockmany E7
Nr Augher, Co Tyrone. A large round cairn containing an unroofed oval chamber; three of the massive uprights have incised decoration, including cup-marks, concentric circles, and twisting motifs. The chamber may have had a small entrance, but no passage; the radial slabs which project into the cairn from the chamber are an unusual feature.

Lough-na-Cranagh H3
Nr Ballycastle, Co Antrim. Lake-dwellings, or crannogs, were constructed on a foundation of brushwood and logs, or boulders and peat, from the Neolithic period until the early middle ages. The example at Lough-na-Cranagh is an oval island contained within drystone walling, which rises some six feet above the water.

Navan Fort F7
Nr Armagh, Co Armagh. Navan was the traditional palace of the kings of Ulster. An annual assembly place and the large circular hilltop enclosure, with its bank and internal ditch, suggests ritual rather than defensive use. The main earthworks are probably iron age in date, and they also contain an iron age rath and a possible iron age cairn.

Slieve Gullion G9
Nr Newry, Co Armagh. This massive cairn contains a fine example of an early type of Neolithic passage-grave, built almost completely of horizontal slabs without the more usual massive uprights. The polygonal chamber had a circular corbelled vault, and the walls survive to ten feet in height; at the end, opposite the passage, is a recess. The passage still has its flat slab roof, but the entrance end is destroyed. Also on the site is a large bronze age round cairn.

Tirnony F5
Nr Maghera, Co Londonderry. An impressive example of a 'dolmen', the massive stones left when most of a cairn has been robbed for use in building. The stones formed the entrance and chamber of a Neolithic portal-grave, a single-chambered cairn characterized by a tall built entrance. The grave at Tirnony also has a large pillar in front of one side, suggesting a built forecourt.

White Island C6
Lough Erne, Co Fermanagh. The ruined 12thC church on White Island contains several sculptured figures, including two bishops carved sometime after the 8thC. They were found built into the church, and were probably deliberately hidden because of their stylistic links with traditional pagan carvings.

Footpaths & ancient ways

Mourne Coastal Path H9
Co Down. On the Newcastle-Kilkeel road A2. The path follows the shores of Dundrum Bay with the highest peak in the Mourne Mountains, Slieve Donard, towering above. Don't miss the site of St Mary's, Ballaghanery – with its associations with St Donard.

North Antrim Cliff Path G2
Co Antrim. The eleven-mile-long footpath follows the wide arc of bays and stormy headlands from Runkerry to Ballintoy. It passes the cliff-like slopes of the Giant's Causeway, 'discovered' in 1692 by the Bishop of Derry, Dunseverick Castle, and White Park Bay.
This is a paradise for bird watchers. A wild romantic and forbidding stretch of the coast overlooking the North Channel.

Regional sports

Fishing
There are splendid facilities for coarse, game and sea fishing. Counties Fermanagh and Tyrone are noted for game and coarse fishing, and lakes and rivers there hold several coarse fishing records. Strangford Lough, County Down, is noted for gigantic skate of up to 180 lbs. The Giant's Causeway Coast, in County Antrim, attracts deep-sea shark fishermen.

Gaelic football and hurley
Gaelic football may be described as a combination of rugby and soccer, while hurley has been libellously called 'hockey without rules'. Hurley us an interesting game to watch, and a dangerous game to play as the sticks have broad, thin blades and can be whirled around the head. Both hurley and Gaelic football are generally played on Sundays. Big matches are held in Belfast, but other centres of the ancient Irish sport are Irvinestown, County Fermanagh and Kilkeel, County Down.

Horse racing
Particularly point-to-point steeplechasing is popular, the main meetings being at the Maze, Lisburn, County Antrim, and Downpatrick, County Down. International show jumping competitions are held at the Royal Ulster Agricultural Showgrounds, Balmoral, Belfast, at the end of August.

Motor-cycling
A passion with many in Northern Ireland. The Ulster Grand Prix on the Dundrod Circuit, County Antrim in August, and the North-West 200 on a circuit adjoining Coleraine, County Londonderry in May, are events that attract international riders. Motor-cycle grass track races are frequent events in many areas.

Festivals

Festivals
For information and tickets for festivals go to the local information centre of ticket agent.

The Queen's University Festival J6
Belfast, Co Antrim. Irish excess at its best. In a fortnight they get through about forty classical, eight folk song and seven jazz concerts, five operas, eight ballets, five plays, fifteen films and the very popular Guinness lectures. Many top British artists and the cream of Irish talent. *Mid Nov.*

Fun things

Boating
Upper and Lower Lough Erne constitute a continuous waterway over 50 miles long, in delightful scenery. The total area of water is many times that of the Broads in England. Motor cruisers equipped with depth sounders may be hired as may sailing boats.

Drum Manor Forest Park   F6
Nr Cookstown, Co Tyrone. This must be the only garden specially created to attract butterflies. It is full of wild plants and shrubs that are frequently covered with the most colourful species of butterflies.

Lammas Fair   H3
Ballycastle, Co Antrim. Held for two days every August, this popular fair is one of the best in Ireland. Dating back over 400 years, it is a mass of sideshows and showmen. Lots of stalls sell traditional 'fairings'.

Miniature railway   H5
Shane's Castle, Lough Neagh, Co Antrim. A steam engine pulls this train along the shores of Lough Neagh. A good diversion for the children visiting Shane's Castle Nature Reserve. *Open 14.00-19.00 Wed & Sun. 13.00-19.00 Sat & B. Hols.*

Riding and pony-trekking
There are advanced riding schools at Ashbrook, County Fermanagh; Comber, County Down; and Craigantlet, County Down. Pony-trekking stables are numerous, mainly surrounding the Mountains of Mourne and the Antrim Mountains.

Hotels

The following indicates the price of a single room per night:
£   inexpensive
££   medium priced
£££ expensive

Ballygally Co Antrim.   **J4**
Ballygally Castle Hotel, Nr Larne. Tel 212
A 17thC castle, overlooking Antrim, which offers many amenities. £.

Belfast Co Antrim.   **J6**
Royal Avenue Hotel, 23 Royal Avenue. Tel 26611. A busy hotel which has been modernised. Good service. ££.

Crawfordsburn Co Down.   **J6**
Old Inn, nr Helen's Bay. Tel 3255. This inn dates from the 17thC and many historic features have been preserved. £.

Dunadry Co Antrim.   **H6**
Dunadry Inn, Muckamore. Tel Templepatrick 32474. Conveniently situated for Aldergrove Airport, this cheerful, efficient inn is built from locally made bricks. Pleasant garden by the river and fishing. £££.

Dunmurry Co Antrim.   **H6**
Conway Hotel, nr Belfast. Tel Belfast 612101. A fine Georgian hotel with a landscaped garden and a swimming pool. Good food. ££.

Holywood Co Down.   **J6**
Culloden Hotel, Craigavad. Tel 5223. A confortable hotel which has an Adam fireplace in its drawing room. The restaurant offers good views of Belfast Lough. £££.

Kilkeel Co Down.   **H9**
Kilmorey Arms, Greencastle St. Tel 62220. A cheerful and cosy atmosphere pervades this hotel, with its stone-floored bar and interesting trimmings. £.

Larne Co Antrim.   **J6**
King's Arms Hotel, Broadway. Tel 3322. A new hotel which is convenient for Larne and Stranraer ferry passengers. £.

Newry Co Down.   **G8**
Ardmore Hotel, Belfast Rd. Tel 3161. Set in a landscaped garden, this Victorian-fronted hotel offers fishing to its guests. £.

Rostrevor Co Down   **H9**
Ballyedmond Castle Hotel, Kilowen. Tel 474. A splendid and elegant hotel set in woodland. Fishing is good and offered to guests. £.

Regional food and drink

Barm brack and colcannon
Two traditional Halloween foods. Colcannon is made of kale or cabbage, potatoes, leeks, and cream. Barm brack is a yeasted fruit loaf. Both have a gold ring added, and whoever gets it will be married within a year. A sixpence, a thimble and a button are also put into the colcannon and denote, wealth, spinsterhood and bachelordom respectively.

Boxty pancakes and boxty bread
The pancakes are made of potatoes flavoured with caraway seeds and cooked in bacon fat. The bread is traditionally served on Halloween and is referred to as boxty in the pan.

Guinness and stout
The Irishman's preference for dark stout is well known. This beer is brewed in the usual way but the malt is roasted. Guinness is the most popular. The quality varies from pub to pub but at its dark and creamy best it is almost as good as wine – especially accompanied by a dozen oysters.

Irish coffee
Most probably more popular with visitors

than the natives, but still an excellent end to a good dinner. Made by pouring a measure of Irish whiskey into a warm glass, then a spoonful of sugar, some hot black coffee, and after stirring whipped cream is floated on the top. Rich and warming.

Irish soda bread
One of the region's non-potato specialities, this is a bread raised with bicarbonate of soda and cream of tartar.

Irish stew
Very similar to the hot pots of Lancashire but simply made from potatoes, mutton and onions. It should be thick and creamy with not too much gravy.

Potato apple cake
Traditionally cooked on a griddle, now in the oven. A firm pastry is made with potatoes and filled with apples.

Potato bread
A bread-like thin pancake, eaten in the place of toast, or fried like fried bread. Made in many areas it can also be bought locally in some places.

Potatoes
The popularity of potatoes in Ireland dates from their arrival in the 17thC. The uses are numerous – either straight or in a variety of recipes similar to those given here. They were once the staple diet for a century or more.

Potato soup
This delicious creamy soup flavoured with chives, parsley and bacon is sometimes garnished with pieces of lobster or prawns.

Whiskey
Spelt with an 'e' to distinguish it from the Scottish variety – Irish whiskey is very pure and has an excellent flavour. The best whiskey comes from the Old Bushmills Distillery, County Antrim. No visit to Northern Ireland is complete without trying a glass of 'Old Bush'.

Restaurants

£   inexpensive
££   medium priced
£££   expensive

Belfast Co Antrim   **J6**
Thompsons (Grill Bar), 47 Athur St. Tel 23762. Good meat and fish grills. Crowded lunchtime. *LD. Closed Sun. ££.*

Dunadry Co Antrim   **H6**
Dunadry Inn. Tel Templepatrich 32474 Comfortable inn near Belfast. Rather 'expense-account', but handy for Aldergrove Airport. *LD. ££. Book.*

Holywood Co Down.   **J6**
Pepper Mill, 8 Church Rd. Tel 2120. Lively restaurant. French and British cooking. Imaginative. *D. Closed Sun. ££. Book.*

Killinchy Co Down   **J7**
Balloo House. Tel 210. Farmhouse/pub/restaurant. Plain cooking. *LD. Closed Sat L & Sun. ££. Book.*

Limavady Co Londonderry.   **E3**
Blades Restaurant, 17 Main St. Tel 3151. Small restaurant serving traditional British food. *D. Closed Sun & Mon. ££. Book.*

NICHOLSON GUIDES AND MAPS

LONDON GUIDES

NICHOLSON London Guide
The world famous pocket guide packed full of information covering every aspect of London. Lots of coloured maps and illustrations.

NICHOLSON Complete London
Deluxe edition of the famous Nicholson pocket guide produced in a larger format for the bookshelf, the office desk and the car. Full colour maps. *Also available in hardback.*

NICHOLSON Student's London
Pocket sized, directed specifically to the student's own needs. Shows where to get value for money in the capital. Coloured maps and index.

NICHOLSON Visitor's London
Lots of information specially for the tourist. Detailed shopping guide complete with shop by shop street maps. Full colour picture maps.

NICHOLSON London's Restaurants
Over six hundred selected restaurants. A complete gastronomic guide to the capital. Illustrations and full colour maps

NICHOLSON London Night Life
Not only the 'hot spots' but a practical guide to London after dark. Invaluable list of 24hr restaurants, shops and services. Coloured maps.

NICHOLSON American's London
Written by Americans for Americans in the famous Nicholson format. Coloured centre maps.

NICHOLSON Parents' Guide to Children's London
All a parent needs to know to keep the kids happy and informed. Coloured centre maps.

LONDON MAPS

NICHOLSON Central London Maps & Index
30 square miles of central London in two colours showing one-ways streets. Theatre, cinema, shopping and underground maps.

NICHOLSON London Street Finder
400 square miles of London with large scale centre section showing one-way streets. Theatre, cinema, shopping and underground maps. Two colours throughout.

NICHOLSON Large London Street Finder
Large scale and two colour maps throughout for extra legibility. One-ways in central London. Theatre, cinema, shopping and underground maps. *Also available in hardback.*

NICHOLSON Sightseer's London
An easy guide to localities wherever you are in London. Full colour.

NICHOLSON London Map
Large scale central London map in full colour. Comprehensive street index. Theatre, cinema, shopping and underground maps.

NICHOLSON 2 London Maps
Central London map in full colour with index plus Greater London route planning map. Also commuter and motoring maps.

NICHOLSON Visitor's Map of London
Colourful, easy to manage map of London showing all main tourist sights in 3D.

NICHOLSON Pocket Map of London
Compact, full colour map of London. Includes a street index, shopping, theatre, cinema and underground maps.

NICHOLSON London Route Finder Map
An easy guide to routes through the capital includes commuter and Great Britain Motorway maps.

GREAT BRITAIN GUIDES & MAPS

NICHOLSON Guide to Great Britain
An easy reference guide to all the family's interests and activities. Full colour maps and many photographs and illustrations. Fully revised.

NICHOLSON Illustrated Guide to Scotland
Useful introduction to Scotland followed by vivid descriptions of all places of interest. Many illustrations and full colour fold out map.

NICHOLSON Waterways Guides
A new, revised and fully up to date series of 5 guides to the canals of England and Wales with detailed maps.

NICHOLSON Real Ale Guide to the Waterways
Whether you are cruising, angling or walking this guide will tell you where to find beer brewed and served in the traditional manner, on or near the waterways.

NICHOLSON Great Britain Touring Map
Full colour motoring map of Great Britain, with motorways, A & B roads clearly marked. Includes a wealth of small villages. Also main ferry routes.